Earth in Flower
បុប្ផាលោកយ

Earth in Flower

The Divine Mystery of the Cambodian Dance Drama

បុប្ផាលោកយ

អាថ៌កំបាំងអាទិទេពនៃរបាំរាំកម្ពុជា

Paul Cravath
ប៉ុល ក្រវ៉ាត

Preface by Kent Davis
រៀបរៀងដោយ ខិន ដេវីស

DatASIA
MMXIV

About the Cover
Saèm, première danseuse en tenue de fête [*Saem in Her Festival Attire*] by Jean Despujols

In the 1930s, Saem performed as *première danseuse* with the troupe of Princess Wongat Say Sangvann, a former royal dancer married to King Sisowath's youngest son, Prince Yong Kath (see p. 141). Despujols painted Saem from Feb. 15-18, 1937, posing her on the Rainbow Bridge at Angkor Wat where special dance performances were held. Saem holds her right hand in the ritual *kbach* (gesture) symbolizing a flower (see p. 325).

Impressed by her skill, the princess adopted Saem; a true "Cinderella story" embodying the Cambodian dance tradition. In ancient times, girls from all levels of society pledged themselves to perform sacred dances in Khmer temples. Saem's devotion led to her royal adoption. Her story speaks to the modern spirit of Cambodia, empowering women and men from every level in society to participate in the Khmer Renaissance. Since 2007, the Nginn Karet Foundation for Cambodia has maintained this cultural legacy, training rural students at the Preah Ream Buppha Devi NKFC Conservatoire in the heart of the Angkor UNESCO World Heritage Park. To learn more visit www.NKFC.org.

The Artist - Jean Despujols

In 1936, the Société des Artistes Coloniaux in Paris selected Despujols to travel throughout French Indochina to record his impressions on canvas and paper. His evocative works were only exhibited a few times until 1969 when they became part of the permanent collection of the Meadows Museum of Art at Centenary College in Shreveport, Louisiana. Special thanks to the Meadows Museum of Art for their kind permission to feature this artwork: www.centenary.edu/meadows

DatASIA Press
www.DatASIA.US

© 2014 & 2007 DatASIA, Inc., Holmes Beach, Florida 34218.

All rights reserved. No part of this book may be reproduced, stored in a retrieval system, or transmitted, in any form without prior permission.

Second Edition

Printed simultaneously in the United States of America & Great Britain.

ISBN: 978-1-934431-29-0 (paperback: alk. paper)

Library of Congress Control Number: 2014915695

Cravath, Paul.
Earth in Flower: The Divine Mystery of the Cambodian Dance Drama
Includes bibliographical references and index.
1. Dance–Cambodia. 2. Dance–Cambodia–History. 3. Drama–Cambodia.
4. Drama–Cambodia–History. 5. Cambodia–Social life and customs.
6. Geographic: Cambodia–Social life and customs.

Production Credits

Cover: **Kent Davis, Becca Klein, Kristen Tuttle & Carol Yudofsky.**
Layout and graphic design: **Kristen Tuttle, Kent Davis, Daria Lacy.**
Index: **Timlynn Babitsky.**
Special thanks to **Colin Grafton, Tom Kramer, Chamroeun Yin & Sophaphan Davis**
for their important contributions to this second edition.

ការថ្វាយពុម្ពសៀវភៅប្រវត្តសាស្ត្រនេះដើម្បីឧទ្ទិសថ្វាយជូន
ព្រះអង្គម្ចាស់ក្សត្រីនរោត្តមបុប្ផាទេវ
ជាព្រះកត្តញ្ញុតាសនៃការចូលរួមដ៏ខ្ពង់ខ្ពស់របស់ព្រះអង្គ
ក្នុងការអភិវឌ្ឍន៍, ការអនុរក្ស និង ភាពគង់វង្សជាដ៏រាប
នៃរបាំប្រពៃណីបុរាណ
របស់ព្រះរាជាណាចក្រកម្ពុជា

Dedication

This historic edition is dedicated to
Her Royal Highness Norodom Buppha Devi
in honor of her vital contributions
in developing, preserving and perpetuating
the classical dance tradition
of the Kingdom of Cambodia.

Earth in Flower

TABLE OF CONTENTS

DEDICATION TO PRINCESS BUPPHA DEVI......................... V
LIST OF TABLES XI
ILLUSTRATION CREDITS XII
LIST OF ILLUSTRATIONS XIII
PUBLISHER'S PREFACE – 2007.. XX
PUBLISHER'S PREFACE – 2014.. XXII
NOTES ON CONTENT AND TRANSLITERATION XXIII
AUTHOR'S INTRODUCTION – 2007 XXIV
AUTHOR'S ACKNOWLEDGEMENTS – 1985.......................... XXVIII
AUTHOR'S PREFACE – 1985... XXVII

CHAPTER I
INTRODUCTION: SOURCES OF THE STUDY 1
Historical Perspective of the Present Thesis 2
Structure of the Present Dissertation... 7

CHAPTER II
THE CULTURAL CONTEXT OF PRE-ANGKOREAN DANCE 13
Earliest Evidence of Dance in Southeast Asia................................ 14
Cultural Similarities throughout Southeast Asia............................. 15
Dance in Funeral Rites and Megalithic Cultures 16
Royal Genealogy Derived from *Apsaras* 21
The *Devarāja*, Source of the King's Power 23
Pre-Angkorean Temple Dance 24
Sculptural Evidence 27
Jayavarman II and Javanese Influence 28

CHAPTER III
ANGKOREAN DANCE: 802-1431 37
Angkorean Cosmology 38
Religious Syncretism 41
The Myth of the Origin of Dance 46
Temple Dance 49
Court Dance 54
The *Devatā* 56
The *Apsaras* Prior to Angkor Wat 58
The *Apsaras* of Angkor Wat 64
Twelfth Century Dance 70
Dance in the Reign of Jayavarman VII 73
The Dancer in Late Angkorean Bronze 81
Post-Bayon Period Dance 87
The Fate of Angkorean Dance 91

CHAPTER IV
KHMER DANCE: 1431-1981 99
The Fifteenth Century 99
The Sixteenth Through Eighteenth Centuries 101
    The 1688 Account of La Loubère 104
Dance in the Early Nineteenth Century 106
Dance in the Reign of Ang Duong (1841-1859) 110
Dance in the Reign of Norodom (1860-1904) 114
    Thai Dancers at Norodom's Court 117
    Early European Accounts of Dance 119
Dance in the Reign of Sisowath (1904-1927) 124
    The Khmer Dancers in France 125
    Condition and Finances of the *Lakhon* 128
    Politics and Chanchhaya Pavilion 132
    Dance Personnel and Activities 135
    Non-Royal Dance 136
    French Attitudes Toward the Dance 137
Dance in the Reign of Monivong (1928-1941) 138
    The Contribution of Princess Say Sangvann 141
    The Contribution of Khun Meak 145
    The Water Festival 146
    Monivong's Dancers 148
    The Thai Perspective 152
Dance in the Sihanouk Era (1941-1970) 153
    Relations with the French Government 153
    The Contribution of Princess Kossamak 155
    Occasions of Performance 159
    Performance Locations 162

The "Friendship" Dance	163
Dance Personnel	165
Dance in the Republic (1970-1975) and After	168
The American Tour	170
Dance During the Siege	172
The Contribution of Chheng Phon	174
The End of the Republic	175
The Contribution of Mom Kamel	177
The Contribution of Phan Phuong	181
Classical Dance in Kampuchea	181
The School of Fine Arts	184

CHAPTER V
THE MYTHOLOGICAL FOUNDATION OF KHMER DANCE 193

The Myth of Liu Ye	194
The Myth of *Nāgī* Somā	195
The Myths of the Apsaras *Mera* and the *Nāgī* Earth Spirit	197
The Legend of Neang Neak and Preah Thong	198
The Primordial Maiden as Serpent	199
The Primordial Maiden as Tree Spirit	202
The Primordial Maiden and the Moon	203
The Primordial Maiden as Earth Spirit	204
The Unity of the Primordial Maiden	206
Complementary Dualism in the Dance Drama	207
The Dancer in Female Roles	208
The Dancer in Male Roles	212
The Dancer in Yakkha and Monkey Roles	213
The Archetype of the Androgyne	214

CHAPTER VI
THE MODERN REPERTOIRE OF THE DANCE DRAMA 221

The Dramatic Repertoire: *Roeung*	222
Dramatic Themes	265
The Dance Repertoire: *Robam*	267

CHAPTER VII
MUSIC, CHOREOGRAPHY & STAGING 293

Music History	293
The *Sralay*	297
The *Sampho*	299
The *Skor Thom*	301
The *Roneat*	301
The *Kong*	303
The *Chhing* and *Khrab*	304

Rehearsal Melodies	305
Musical Structure of Entrances and Exits	307
Dramatic Structure of Entrances and Exits	309
Pinpeat Melodies	311
The Chanters	315

CHOREOGRAPHY IN THE DANCE DRAMA 317

Khmer Choreography	317
The *Kbach*	318
The Hand Gestures	321
The Emotions	327
Floor Patterns	340
Style of Choreography	347

STAGING THE DANCE DRAMA 357

Staging Techniques	357
The *Kré*	358
Floor Plan	358
Representational Elements	358
Lighting and Curtains	361
Back Drops and Set Pieces	364
Scene Changes	366
Stage Attendants	366

CHAPTER VIII
THE ROYAL DANCER: TRAINING & COSTUMES 373

DANCER TRAINING 373

Entrance to Training	373
Group Training	375
Role Training	376
Teaching Method	378
Mental Qualities of the Dancer	378
The Annual Awards Ceremony	381
Life Style of the Palace Dancers	382

DANCER COSTUMES 385

The Costume Room	385
The Costumes: Some General Distinctions	386
Masculine Role Costumes	390
Feminine Role Costumes	397
Headgear and Flowers	403
Masks	407
Hand Props and Fingernails	409

CHAPTER IX
THE RITUAL FUNCTION OF KHMER DANCE 415
Dance as a Traditional Offering 415
The Ceremony of *Buong Suong* 417
The Dancer and Spirit Mediumship 419
The *Sampho* Drum and the Spirit World 422
Face Makeup and the Spirit World 423
The *Tway Kru* Ceremony and *Bai Sei* Offerings 425
The *Sampeah Kru* Ceremony 427
Lakhon Khol and the Spirit World... 433
Analogous Mask Empowerments 438
The Ritual's End 440

APPENDICES
I. The Royal Palace Theatre, ca.1910 445
II. Royal Palace Performance Programs 450
      Table 5: Selected Performance Sequence - King Monivong Reign................ 450
      Table 6: Selected Performance Sequence - 1941-1961 452
III. The Structure of Chorus, Orchestra and Dance Components 466
IV. Repertoire of the Pinpeat Orchestra 468

ABOUT THE AUTHOR 472

PUBLISHER'S NOTES:
The Story Behind *Earth In Flower* 474

ABBREVIATIONS USED IN THE BIBLIOGRAPHY 484

BIBLIOGRAPHY 485

INDEX.. 495

LIST OF TABLES

TABLE 1: Symbolic Values of Body Ornamentation in
Tantric Buddhist Iconography 80

TABLE 2: Cambodian Mythic Forms 200

TABLE 3: Symbols of Feminine-Masculine Dualism Associated
with Khmer Dance Drama 209

TABLE 4: Incidence of Recurrent Motifs in Selected *Roeung* 243

TABLE 5: Sequence of Program Pieces in Selected Performances –
King Monivong Reign 450

TABLE 6: Sequence of Program Pieces in Selected Performances –
1941-1961 452

ILLUSTRATION CREDITS

During his Cambodian research in 1975, the author received images from the Khmer Republic's Ministry of Culture, the Royal Cambodia Ballet, the National Museum of Phnom Penh, King Sihanouk's publication *Nokor Khmer* (with many un-credited photos the publisher attributes to the magazine's director, Charles Meyer), and named individuals. The publisher has made every effort to identify original photographers and secure permissions. Many photos were replaced with modern equivalents when that was not possible or when better images were available.

The publisher gives special thanks to four photographers who provided multiple high-quality images for this work:

John Gollings
www.gollingspidgeon.com

Michael Greenhalgh - Artserve
http://rubens.anu.edu.au/

Jaro Poncar
www.poncar.de

Vittorio Roveda
Author/photographer – *Images of the Gods*

LIST OF ILLUSTRATIONS

1-1	Three *Devatā* in Dynamic Positions at Angkor Wat	9
2-1	Dong-son Male Dancer and Musician	14
2-2	The Lady of Koh Krieng, 7th-8th Century	29
3-1	Temple as *Mandala*, Angkor Wat	40
3-2	Vishnu Reclining under *Nāga*	42
3-3	The Sleep of Vishnu, Preah Khan	42
3-4	Vishnu Reclining on Reachisey With *Nāga*	43
3-5	Spirit of the Earth Witnessing for the Buddha	44
3-6	Mahāyāna Buddhist Hevajra	44
3-7	The Nāga-Churning of the Sea at Angkor Wat	47
3-8	Details of *Apsaras* from the Churning of the Sea	49
3-9	*Devatā* with *Apsaras* from the Bayon	57
3-10	Ninth-Century Flying Figure	58
3-11	Ninth-Century Dancer	59
3-12	Flying Figure in the Bayon – 13th Century	59
3-13	Bayon Dancer	60
3-14	Banteay Srei Dancer and Musicians	60
3-15	The Apsaras Tilottama	61
3-16	Dancers in the Style of the Baphuon	62
3-17	Tenth-Century *Devatā* at Bantaey Srei	63
3-18	Details of Banteay Srei *Devatā*	63
3-19	Female Cham Dancer, Tenth Century	64

3-20	Creation of the *Apsaras*, Angkor Wat	65
3-21	Angkor Wat *Devatā*, West Gopura	65
3-22	Angkor Wat *Devatā*, Top Level	66
3-23	Two Angkor Wat *Devatā*, Cruciform Gallery North	66
3-24	Angkorean Dancers	67
3-25	Elements in the *Devatā* Headdress	68
3-26	Angkor Wat Bas Relief	70
3-27	Frieze of *Apsaras* from Preah Khan	71
3-28	Angkor Wat Dancers	71
3-29	Bayon Dancers on Lotus	74
3-30	New *Apsaras* Style from the Bayon	75
3-31	Angkor Wat Dancing *Apsara* on West Gopura	75
3-32	Bayon *Apsara* in Motion	75
3-33	Banteay Kdai *Apsaras* in Motion	76
3-34	Bayon *Apsaras* in Motion	76
3-35	Preah Khan Frieze with *Apsaras*	77
3-36	Bayon *Devatā*	78
3-37	Jayavarman VII	79
3-38	Bayon *Devatā* Smiling	80
3-39	Lokesvara with *Apsaras* from the Bayon	81
3-40	Bayon Style *Yoginī*	82
3-41	Bayon Style *Yoginī* (front)	82
3-42	Bayon Style *Yoginī* (back)	82
3-43	Angkor Wat Style *Yoginī* (front)	83
3-44	Angkor Wat Style *Yoginī* (back)	83
3-45	Twelfth-Century *Apsaras*	84
3-46	Angkorean Dancing Figures	85
3-47	Twelfth-Century Musicians and Dancers	89
3-48	Bayon Ensemble With Dancers	89

4-1	Royal Dancers with King Monivong Funerary Urn, 1941	107
4-2	King Norodom, 1860-1904	115
4-3	Dancers at Phnom Penh, ca. 1903	117
4-4	Dancing Girls, ca. 1875	119
4-5	King Norodom and Guests Viewing *Kennari* Dance, July 1866	121
4-6	Dance Drama Rehearsal at Battambang, ca. 1885	122
4-7	Dance Drama Rehearsal at Battambang, ca. 1885	122
4-8	Late Nineteenth-Century Traveling Dance Troupe	124
4-9	Pum, One of King Sisowath's Prima Ballerinas	127
4-10	Chanchhaya Pavilion of the Royal Palace, Phnom Penh	133
4-11	"Danseuse dorée (Rôle religieux)," G. Groslier, ca. 1911	137
4-12	King Monivong and the Resident-Superior M. Le Vol, 1928	138
4-13	Two *Premières Danseuses* of Royal Troupe, 1928	139
4-14	Say Sangvann with Her Dancers	142
4-15	Star of Say Sangvann's Troupe	143
4-16	Performance at Angkor Wat, J. Despujols, ca. 1937	144
4-17	Cambodian Dancer as *Devatā*, J. Despujols, ca. 1937	145
4-18	The Royal Palace Dancers, ca. 1932	149
4-19	Cambodian Royal Ballet, ca. 1929	149
4-20	Dance Rehearsal in Chanchhaya, ca. 1929	151
4-21	Student Dancers in the Palace, ca. 1931	151
4-22	The Royal Dancers at Angkor, 1964	157
4-23	Mehn Kosni, ca. 1967	160
4-24	Royal Ballet Group With Princess Buppha Devi and Menh Kosni	161
4-25	Richard Nixon in Chanchhaya Pavilion, 1953	163
4-26	Kem Bun Nak Teaching at the Palace Dance School, ca. 1969	167
4-27	Neang Bunnak at Angkor Wat, Age Fourteen, 1949	168
4-28	Menh Kosni as Sita in New York, 1970	169
4-29	Dancers During the Republic, ca. 1973	173

4-30	Khao I Dang Dancers after Five Months of Training	179
4-31	Saroeurm Tes in the Royal Palace, ca. 1968	182
4-32	Young Dancers in Siem Reap	185
5-1	*Mukhalinga* Revealing the God, 7-8th C Takeo	205
5-2	The Mythical *Kennari* Bird-Women	211
6-1	Hanumān and Sovann Maccha, ca. 1937	223
6-2	Manimekhala and Ream Eyso	230
6-3	*Robam* Tep Manorom, ca. 1962.	269
6-4	Dance of Gold and Silver Flowers With Voan Savay	273
7-1	Angkorean Musicians	296
7-2	Cambodian Female Ensemble, 1874	296
7-3	Theatrical Performance, 1880	296
7-4	Cambodian *Pinpeat* Orchestra	297
7-5	Pinpeat Orchestra Performing *Reamker* in Antique Tapestry	298
7-6	The *Sralay*	299
7-7	The *Sampho*	301
7-8	The *Skor Thom*	301
7-9	The *Roneat Ek*	302
7-10	The *Roneat Thom*	303
7-11	The *Kong* in Angkor Wat Bas-Relief	304
7-12	The *Kong*	304
7-13	The *Chhing*	305
7-14	The *Sampeah*	310
7-15	The General Entrance-Exit Structure of Dances	310
7-16	Chorus Placement in Chanchhaya	317
7-17	Transitional Movements and *Kbach*	322
7-18	The Basic Khmer Hand Gestures	325
7-19	Classification of Khmer Hand Gestures	326
7-20	Conventionalized Gesture of Flower Blooming	326

7-21	Unclouded Love	328
7-22	Love Shared	328
7-23	Love Sworn	329
7-24	Pursuit and Evasion	329
7-25	Seduction	330
7-26	A Love Duet	331
7-27	A Love Duet with Gentle Resistance	331
7-28	Rām and Laks Smiling	332
7-29	Modesty and Smiling	333
7-30	Rāb Laughing	333
7-31	The Emotions in Khmer Dance	334
7-32	The Meeting of Laks and Rāb	335
7-33	Battle Between Sugrib and Bali	335
7-34	Standing Pose to Indicate Flying	336
7-35	Princess and Prince in Flight, Kneeling	336
7-36	Solo Flying	337
7-37	Rāb and Laks in Gesture of Defiance	338
7-38	Rāb Expressing Anger	338
7-39	Posture of Rām Expressing Anger	339
7-40	Rām and Laks Expressing Grief	340
7-41	Grief	340
7-42	Separation - "We must part."	341
7-43	Separation - "Our hearts remain united."	341
7-44	Separation - "Dry your tears."	341
7-45	Separation - "Our sorrow is unbounded."	341
7-46	Separation - "Adieu my beloved."	341
7-47	Bronze Urn Found at Phnom Penh, ca. 4th Century	343
7-48	Bronze Dong-son Plaque	343
7-49	Exit and Spiral Patterns	344

7-50	Interweaving Dancers	344
7-51	Entrance Patterns	345
7-52	Spatial Relationships Between Female & Male Characters	346
7-53	Parallelism in the Flying Pose	350
7-54	Mom Dok Pei Teaching Young Dancers at UBA	351
7-55	Distinctive Circular Walk Pattern	352
7-56	Dancer of Male Roles at UBA	353
7-57	Circular Movement for Two Dancers	354
7-58	*Kbach* Identified with Vishnu	354
7-59	Position of Sitting in Attendance for Male Roles	354
7-60	*Yakkha* Roles at UBA	356
7-61	The Royal Wagon Stage Property	361
7-62	Sugar Palm and Fine Leaf Tree from the Bayon	365
7-63	Coconut Tree from the Bayon	365
7-64	Princess Buppha Devi Dancing in Garden of Forest Trees	367
7-65	Voan Savay in Royal Palace Courtyard with Coconut Palm	367
7-66	A Scene from the Legend of Keo Monnorea and Preah Sothun	368
8-1	Rehearsal for the Dance of Sovann Maccha and Hanuman	379
8-2	Costumes of the Four Basic Character Types	388
8-3	Masculine Role Costume of a Prince	391
8-4	Four Basic Bracelets, ca. 1932	392
8-5	Masculine Role Bracelets	393
8-6	Attendants in Foreground, ca. 1931	393
8-7	Hanumān Making *Sampeah*	395
8-8	The Costume of *Krut*, King of the Birds	395
8-9	The Kennara and Kennari Bird-People, ca. 1880	396
8-10	Rāb in Disguise as the Eysei Approaching Sitā	397
8-11	Youthful Princess Buppha Devi in Feminine Role Costume	399
8-12	Feminine Attendant-Servant Role, ca. 1931	400

8-13	The *Kennari-Kennara* Bird-People, ca. 1931	401
8-14	Sovann Machha, ca. 1931	402
8-15	*Apsaras* Costume and Jewelry	403
8-16	The *Mkot* for Masculine Roles	404
8-17	The *Mkot* for Feminine Roles	405
8-18	The *Panntiereth* Headdress	407
8-19	Mask of the *Krut* Role	409
8-20	Stage Weapons for Humans and *Yakkha*	410
8-21	Close-Contact Combat Weapons for Rāb and Hanumān	411
8-22	Male Role Dancer with Artificial Fingernails	411
8-23	Modern Makeup technique	412
9-1	*Buong Suong* Ceremony	416
9-2	Dancer Makeup Seen Offstage	424
9-3	*Bai Sei* Offered to *Kru* of the *Lakhon*	427
9-4	Headgear of Five Major Characters	431
A-I	The Royal Palace Theatre, ca. 1910	446
The Author Following His Escape From Phnom Penh, 1975		472
The Author as Iago in *Othello*, 1969		473
Kent Davis in his Study, 2007		474
Angkor Wat *Devatā*, Sappho Marchal, 1926		474
Angkor Wat *Devatā*, Sappho Marchal, 1926		481

Publisher's Preface – 2007

Like an elegant Khmer silk, *Earth in Flower* weaves the complex fields of dance, history, art, music, culture and religion into a captivating, coherent tapestry. Dr. Cravath's study reveals spiritual subtleties about the Khmer relationship between heaven and earth, illuminates Cambodian views of Masculine and Feminine balance in the universe, and shows how dance is essential to perpetuating Khmer cultural identity.

This book resulted from years of hard work and so many unlikely events that it is a miracle that it exists at all:

It is amazing that the new government of a country in the midst of a civil war, indeed *surrounded* by war, recognized the necessity of preserving ancient dance traditions.

It is amazing that their efforts attracted a competent scholar to collect and organize an esoteric body of research at such a troubled time and place.

It is amazing that one man spent more than a decade preparing this work; then, it essentially vanished for twenty years.

Finally, it is amazing that my life's circuitous path led me where it did, and blessed me with the opportunity to complete the process of sharing his research. At the end of this book, I've added a more detailed account of these events for interested readers.

Preparing this book for publication has been a labor of love for me, as it was for the author to create. It has been an exhilarating project that has rewarded me with many new friendships. True teachers are both mentors, who lead by example, and muses, who inspire students to seek knowledge. My gratitude goes to these special people who helped me make this book a reality:

Dr. Paul Cravath – www.EarthInFlower.com

> I approached Paul as a researcher seeking guidance on my own project. Soon, we were both irresistibly drawn into a mission to complete the work he began in 1974. Despite the twenty year delay, Paul participated wholeheartedly. He found time for my demands in his busy schedule as a college professor, even when this meant many long, pre-dawn telephone proofing sessions from his home in Hawaii. Thank you, Paul, for letting me help you give your gift of history back to the Khmer people.

Mr. Bernard Krisher – www.CambodiaSchools.com

Since "retiring," this remarkable man has secured donations to build more than 300 Cambodian schools. With his help, my wife Sophaphan and I built Srei Devatā Secondary School in Kampong Thom province, which opened in July 2006. His organization makes it easy for individuals to make a huge difference in many lives.

In Phnom Penh, Bernie's staff, particularly Mr. Meng Dy, helped me immensely with translations and in arranging my audiences with Princess Buppha Devi for the dedication. Thank you, Bernie, for giving expression to our love for the Cambodian people.

Dr. Helen Jessup - www.KhmerCulture.net

Helen is a dynamo, with pro-active educational projects supporting the Cambodian National Museum, Heritage Watch, Reyum Institute, Angkor Wat preservation, and many key causes. Her credentials as a scholar, curator and author result in a demanding schedule, but Helen was always generous with her time, helping me with countless contacts and details in arranging this publication. You are an inspiration Helen, and I am grateful to you for opening so many doors for me.

Dr. Jaro Poncar – www.Poncar.de

A professor at the University of Applied Sciences Cologne, Jaro acquired his PhD in theoretical physics before gaining renown as a photographer. Since 1993, his brilliant imaging work has defined Angkor Wat and the Bayon for the world. Jaro's logistical support helped me capture thousands of images in Siem Reap. His global network of friends provided key photos to complete this book. Thank you, Jaro, for all your kindness.

I am grateful to have been a small part of this book's story. I sincerely hope it inspires readers, writers, and heavenly dancers who live with us here on earth for many generations to come.

Kent Davis
Anna Maria Island, Florida
April 2007

*Of this absolute Beauty she is the sole pure expression,
with no tyranny, war, or blood behind it.*

She was born of the virginal sea.

*She is all the poetry, charm, and enchantment of this people,
their most distinctive work.*

*Her rhythmic steps have left behind
the most exquisite memories
wherever their delicate traces can be found.*

*Alone, she returns from the past to offer us her flower,
while all else about her crumbles....*

George Groslier
February 4, 1887 – June 18, 1945
Cambodian Dancers – Ancient & Modern

Publisher's Preface – 2014

My respect for Dr. Cravath's dedication in writing *Earth in Flower* has only continued to grow. Indeed, his research has directed and energized the core of my personal work and publishing mission over the past eight years.

His meticulous documentation established my understanding of the sacred Cambodian dance tradition as the essence of Khmer spirituality, culture and identity. It was he who introduced me to other visionary witnesses of Cambodian culture, including George Groslier, Roland Meyer, Henri Monod and Jean Despujols. Thanks to Dr. Cravath's mentorship and inspiration, these men will continue to teach in new editions of their original works.

My quest to understand the dance, the dancers, the women gracing the walls of Angkor Wat and the spiritual realization of the Khmer people continues. In my search, I gratefully find myself frequently referring to this pivotal work.

Kent Davis
Anna Maria Island
October 2014

Notes on Content and Transliteration

In publishing *Earth in Flower* our intent was to remain true to Dr. Cravath's doctoral thesis, without modifying, deleting or rewriting content where attitudes or conventions of use have changed in ensuing years. At the time of his original 1986 submission, the author had spent more than ten years immersed in his topic; his paper accurately reflects his insights and prevailing academic standards of that time.

Modern historians may question some cited research, for example the Javanese connections of Jayavarman II cited in Chapter 2. While newer theories may conflict with some items, we chose to maintain the paper's integrity by presenting it as researched between 1975 and 1985.

Completed before word processing gained popularity, his 659 page manuscript was manually typed. It contained eight languages and thousands of diacritical marks that the author painstakingly added by hand. All French, German, Dutch and selected Sanskrit diacritical marks remain intact in this published edition. Grammatically, the Sanskrit words *apsara*, *apsaras*, *devatā*, *nāga* and *yoginī* may indicate singular or plural.

As George Bernard Shaw observed, "England and America are two countries separated by a common language." Even thornier issues arise transliterating Asian tongues as many phonetic methods are used to write Khmer, Chinese, Sanskrit and Thai in English. For this reason, the publisher eliminated all marks for transliterated Asian languages, as well as Chinese characters and pinyin tonal marks. Transliterated Khmer spellings, when available, appear in parentheses following phonetic transcriptions. Non-English terms are italicized throughout the text (e.g., *robam*) unless appearing in proper names (e.g., the dance Robam Tewet). In some cases, the author includes alternate English renderings of Khmer and Thai words revealing hidden letters to help linguists locate the originals. Researchers should consult the original Asian alphabets and characters to reveal their true pronunciation and etymology.

Author's Introduction – 2007

My initial objective in undertaking this study was to document the history and performance style of the former Royal Ballet of Cambodia. My research in Phnom Penh convinced me that broadening the scope of my inquiry was essential to achieving the well-developed portrait that this dance tradition deserved. The resulting work necessarily went far beyond documenting the costuming, music, staging, training, choreography and history; by examining the inner dimensions of this tradition I discovered the dancer as not only an historical figure, but also as a ritual figure and an artistic figure portraying a mythic role in the Khmer court dance.

From January-August 1975, I conducted my field work in Phnom Penh and Bangkok, and over the next nine years I organized my primary documentation, interviewed refugee dancers in the United States, and conducted library research at the University of Hawaii and elsewhere. Personal observation of performances and scrutiny of earlier French studies expanded my view of the dance drama within a broad cultural framework. *Earth in Flower* reproduces, with only minor alterations, my complete text, originally submitted for a degree in Asian Theater in November 1984.

I chose to employ what was, in the late 1970s and early 1980s, a "new" interpretation of Southeast Asian history posited by Wilhelm Solheim and others towards understanding early Cambodian culture. This view rejected orthodox theories of an historical "Indianization" of Southeast Asia in favor of emphasizing a continuity of indigenous cultural forms and rituals from pre-Angkorean times. Indeed, while analyzing modern forms of the dance, any discernible Indian similarities became a "thin, easily flaking glaze" on the vast ritual-fulfilling body of Cambodia's indigenous dance; hand movements do not function as a "language" of gesture but as an ornament to narration; both melodies and the instruments that create them are clearly autochthonous; choreographic patterns and the presentation of emotions refute Cœdès-like claims that they are done "exactly as in Indian choreography." Cambodian dance was a tradition onto itself. My goal, therefore, was to define the truly "Cambodian" image, as opposed to "foreign," "exotic," or "derivative" alternatives.

In the protohistorical, early-Christian era, dance flourished in a culture dedicated to extensive navigation throughout the Indian Ocean and, at home, to the engineering of large stone works to control water and fertility. The Khmer dancer as a ritual performer in the court of that world is seen as early as the third century B.C. when dance appears to have been associated with large bronze drums, with funeral rites, with ancestor worship associated with stones, with a fertility cult likewise associated with stone structures, with a serpent/earth-spirit cult, and with a pattern of kingship incorporating communion with the ancestor/spirit realm in order to assure sufficient rains for the earth's fertility. Dance was primarily performed in temples dedicated to ancestral spirits residing in stones. With the adoption of Sanskrit and Brahmanic rites in the fifth century A.D., these deities, like the dancers themselves, often took on a Sanskrit name in addition to their original Khmer name. Dancers were highly respected "slaves" of the deity. It was a golden age for sculpture, and the quality of Sanskrit epigraphy was a match for the best India ever produced.

Earth in Flower presents a Jungian interpretation of the Feminine-centered mythology, the foundation of the dance drama itself. This is discernible in the performance repertoire and early Chinese accounts of the area, suggesting that the tension between Feminine and Masculine—cosmically, architecturally, and socially—was viewed as the source of continued fertility. Within this rich matrix of myth, the royal dancers traditionally acted as a ritual conduit to the nurturing energy of natural and ancestral spirits. Long associated with trance and spirit mediumship, their dances remained both an offering and an invitation to the spirits to assist in bringing rain, thereby perpetuating the fertility of the land through semi-mystical union with the king. Court dancers, as ritual artists, were members of the royal harem well into the twentieth century, and certain dances continue to function as sacred offerings even in modern times.

In the Angkorean period we see the elaboration of a Tantric symbology of the archetypal Feminine-Masculine contest and union: in architecture, in the bas-reliefs, in public celebrations, and in dance. Thousands of dancers served in the temples as an offering to the ancestral spirits, who could influence the cosmic interaction, particularly, of earth and water. Angkor Wat, for instance, gave form to the Myth of the Churning of the Ocean by placing the king in union with the *nāga* earth spirit; from their interaction the waters poured forth on the land and myriads of *apsaras* dancers emerged as the embodiment of the highest spiritual energy that can be created through the union of Feminine and Masculine.

At Angkor, the dancer clearly emerges as an historical figure; however, the evidence negates overly romantic claims that the modern dance preserves Angkorean movements. At Angkor, she and her male counterparts served the temples; her art was practiced even by the monarch; she performed Buddhist dramas as early as the twelfth century; and ultimately she was abducted by conquering Thais when they overran the Angkorean civilization in the fifteenth century. In the sixteenth and seventeenth centuries she performed indigenous, Khmer versions of the *Rāmker;* danced the *robam* in seventeenth-century funeral rites; and, by the nineteenth century, not only maintained an important ritual function within the court but also had become a powerful symbol of the monarchy and a pawn in French-Khmer political struggles. Her art reached its modern zenith during the reign of King Norodom (1860-1904), gaining European recognition in Paris starting in 1906. Finally, she achieved world acclaim during the Sihanouk era with numerous international tours during which the Cambodian dancers came to be recognized as one of the most refined performance troupes in Asia.

In its final form, *Earth in Flower* presents a comprehensive picture of the subtle nature of the dancers' mysterious elegance as well as their historical, ritual, political, and aesthetic power in traditional Cambodia. My sincere wish is that this knowledge will empower the Khmer people and their dance in the 21st century and beyond.

Paul Cravath
Honolulu, Hawai'i
April 2007

Author's Acknowledgments – 1985

Most grateful acknowledgment is hereby given to those responsible for making this study possible, beginning with Dr. James Brandon, chairman of my dissertation committee, as well as dissertation committee members W. Dennis Carroll, Edward A. Langhans, Roger A. Long and Alice G. Dewey.

Grants supporting my research included a National Defense Foreign Language grant, which allowed me to go to Cambodia in 1975; a JDR 3rd Fund grant to complete a period of research in Bangkok; and a Center for Asian and Pacific Studies (University of Hawaii) Research Fellowship during the period of writing the dissertation. To those invaluable sources of financial support, I am sincerely grateful.

This study was also made possible by a number of Khmers and others who took an interest. In Phnom Penh, everything achieved was due to the kindness and cooperation of Hang Thun Hak, Chheng Phon, Huot Kim Leang, Rene Pan Sothi, Kol Sa Im, Nuon Kan, Em Theay, and the teachers and students of classical dance at the University of Fine Arts.

In Bangkok I was greatly assisted by Chaturong Montrisart and Kun Kru Lamun Yamakupt in the Fine Arts Department, by Mattani Rutnin, by Colin Grafton and Terrence White, and by the staff of the Siam Society Library. In Washington, D.C., Sam and Vany Jackson, Phuong Phan, Tes Saroeurm, and James MacDonald were extremely helpful.

In New Orleans, Sean Ou and Betsy Martinez were unexpected treasures, and in Honolulu, members of the doctoral committee, Philip Jenner, Elizabeth Wichmann, the James Shigeta Fund, Demaris Kirchoffer, Freda Hellinger, Seang Seng, numerous friends, and my extraordinarily understanding parents all generously supported the completion of this thesis.

To those in the West, deepest thanks; to those in the East, sampeah; to all, Aloha.

Paul Cravath
Honolulu, Hawai'i
August 1985

Author's Preface – 1985

When Chief-of-State Norodom Sihanouk was deposed in 1970, the government of the new Republic of Cambodia continued to support a number of institutions previously of royal prerogative. One of these was the "Royal Ballet." As the civil war intensified, and a Khmer Rouge victory appeared increasingly probable, the Ministry of Culture perceived that it was the caretaker of an art form which stood little chance of survival intact, should a communist regime come into power. The Ministry wished to document this embodiment of Khmer culture which it was protecting, but there was little money available, and cooperation with foreign scholars or foundations was made difficult by the ever-tightening circle of war surrounding Phnom Penh.

In 1973 I wrote to the Ministry proposing to undertake as comprehensive a study as possible of the classical dance drama and in March of 1974 was invited to do so. That decision was made by Mr. Hang Thun Hak, the most respected authority on the dance drama in Cambodia and at the time a political adviser to President Lon Nol. The war pressure increased, but I was unable to reach Cambodia until January 1975, eleven days after the Khmer Rouge began the siege of Phnom Penh on New Year's Eve.

Rockets falling into the city almost hourly—one injuring a dancer within the palace grounds—had forced the "corps du ballet" into temporary inactivity, but the training classes at the Université des Beaux-Arts continued daily. I was able to watch rehearsals, conduct interviews with the aid of a trilingual translator provided by the Ministry, and gather written material—hampered only by the dancers' understandable distraction. Although advised in writing by the American Embassy on 14 February to depart, I remained in Phnom Penh until the forced military evacuation to Bangkok on 5 April 1975.

In addition to that twelve-week foundation of direct observation in Cambodia, and some five months of less intense, comparative research in Bangkok, this dissertation is a synthesis of all available previous documentation of the classical dance drama in French and English. Chinese sources referring to the early historical period have been re-examined. Relevant Sanskrit and Khmer epigraphy have been examined in French translation. Access to Dutch sources was limited to those in English translation.

The range of inquiry is limited to only a single form of theatre known during the Republic (1970-1975) as *lakhon kbach boran* (lkhona kpa'ca purana) or "ancient drama," but often called, as formerly, *lakhon lueng* (lkhona hlwna), "the king's drama." Historically, the dance drama was also referred to as *lakhon preah karuna* (lkhona brah karuna), "the drama of the king" or *lakhon preah riec traui* (lkhona brah raja drabya), "drama which is the fortune of the king."

Generically, the *lakhon* is a performance by non-speaking dancers to the accompaniment of an orchestra and a chorus of narrators. Almost all roles, including the masculine ones, are played by women. In 1975 it was performed only by the resident troupe of the "ex-palais royal" in Phnom Penh and by the student company of the Université des Beaux-Arts (UBA).

The purpose of this study is four-fold: to demonstrate that Khmer dance embodies indigenous cultural patterns dating from before the Christian era, to summarize the history of the dance drama in Cambodia, to describe the production elements in performance as of 1975, and to show the function of Cambodian dance within Khmer society. This study will not include either a musicological analysis or labanotation of movement.

Although the classical dance drama contains elements common to other performing art forms both in Cambodia and beyond, cross-cultural analogies will be of only secondary interest in the present study—the first written in English and the last examination of the dance drama as it existed in 1975. At that time it was one of the more refined theatre forms of Southeast Asia and, as one of the few remaining court traditions, one of the great performing arts of Asia.

The thesis of this study, stated in the most general terms, is that the royal dancers fulfilled a ritual function in the Khmer kingdom from pre-Angkorean times until the demise of the monarchy. In union with the king, the dancers— as his harem—continually provided a mystical regeneration of the fertility of the land, and their dances were offerings to the spirits of deceased kings to intercede with cosmic powers in providing rain.

The dancers' hand gestures are traditionally considered to be flowers and the dancers themselves the fairest flowers of the race. Embodying the energy of the fecund earth and in union with the king throughout his reign, they remained for hundreds of years the primordial Khmer symbol of the earth in flower.

Today Cambodia is a dry and barren land, ravaged by war and at the mercy of an ancient enemy (Vietnam). Classical dance selections are only a small item on proletarian entertainment programs. While we hope for rebirth, I have often heard in my mind the words of a French scholar writing of Khmer dance in an earlier bleak period: "I should have put all the verbs of this chronicle in the past."

CHAPTER 1

INTRODUCTION: SOURCES OF THE STUDY
ការបង្ហាញ: ប្រភពនៃការសិក្សា

 $\mathcal{T}$he rulers of Democratic Kampuchea, despite the barbarity of their 1975-79 control of Cambodia, attempted to re-educate the Khmer people in a number of areas including the knowledge of their past. Shortly before the demise of that regime at the hands of the Vietnam-led government of the People's Republic of Cambodia, an official in the Foreign Ministry of Democratic Kampuchea, Ok Sakun, told a *Washington Post* reporter who had been allowed into the country to visit Angkor, symbol of the nation, "When we were children, the French told us that the Brahmans of India were responsible for these monuments—that they were not ours." Another official, in speaking of the government's radical education policies, said, "Our civilization is 8800 years old, and we have a tradition of being independent, sovereign and self-reliant. I would like to stress to you that the civilization of Angkor is not a copy of any civilization, not in its architecture, nor its engineering, or its irrigation."[1]

Compare their attitude with the opening statement of a folk dance publication prepared by the faculty of the Université des Beaux-Arts in 1969 when Norodom Sihanouk was still Chief-of-State: "The Khmer civilization of which Cambodians of the present time are the trustees, was born about two thousand years ago,"[2] i.e., with the supposed beginning of Indian cultural influence in Southeast Asia.

The problem is that neither dating has much meaning. The royalists were trustfully repeating the theories of their former French colonial overlords, while the revolutionaries, in rejecting their definitions, resorted to a specificity that was compensatory and misleading. In broad scope, the conflicting views of Khmer "history" espoused by the revolutionary and by the colonially-educated bureaucrats illuminate the fundamental problem inherent in discussing any aspect of Cambodian cultural history: does one begin with an India-centric view or a Southeast Asia-centric view of cultural advancement? Or, if neither, how does one avoid the subtle prejudices which so often inform the past century's scholarly interpretations of inadequate data? This chapter will briefly survey the primary historians and their points of view regarding the early cultural history of Cambodia and the region. The point of view operating in the historical segment of the present study regarding the relationship between Southeast Asian and Indian culture will be clarified. The chapter will then conclude with brief comments on the methodology and content of each chapter's attempt to set forth the history and nature of Cambodian dance drama up to the present time.

Historical Perspectives of the Present Thesis

The historiography of Southeast Asia is a drama unto itself.[3] The early historians—for the most part, individuals in the colonial service of the Netherlands, Great Britain or France—tended to manifest what has been called a "Europe-centric"[4] bias from which we have only recently begun to free ourselves. Because the present thesis reflects a newer attitude, it is important to understand what is meant by that term. Wilhelm G. Solheim II has noted that a Europe-centric view is based upon the primary notion that

> ...Southeast Asian cultures lagged far behind those of the rest of the world and that all progressive culture change came into Southeast Asia from outside. Neolithic culture (horticulture and agriculture, polishing

of stone tools, pottery manufacture and other crafts) was presumably brought in by migrations from Japan and/or China. Metallurgy and the primary Southeast Asian art style, spread in Southeast Asia by the so-called Dongson (Bronze Age) Culture of northern Vietnam was said to have originated because of contacts with Chou China in the 3rd century B.C., or alternatively around the 8th century B.C. because of a migration from eastern Europe. Political organization leading to empires of one sort or another, monumental architecture, and writing (let's call it civilization) were brought in from India and China around 2000 years ago. The only culture truly of Southeast Asian origin was the Hoabinhian of northern Vietnam and farther afield, which was considered a late and very primitive Mesolithic culture....

This general conclusion that the Southeast Asian cultural region was backward was based not on an objective and independent analysis of the data, but on the prevailing philosophy of the late Victorian Age and the unconscious predisposition of the European and European-oriented archaeologists who were doing the research in and on Southeast Asian prehistory. The culture of western Europe was considered as the peak of civilization to that time, with the known cultural history which led to that peak—including the early historic Middle East to Greece to Rome—being the ideal path for culture to follow. The greater the difference and distance of a culture from that path, as expressed in the prehistoric artifacts and known history, the farther behind the ideal that culture was. What was known of Southeast Asian prehistoric artifacts and living ethnic groups indicated that they were very different from those of Europe, and thus were primitive. [5]

Southeast Asia has long been identified, on the basis of superficial similarities, with India. In the eighteenth century the area was known by such names as "India beyond the Ganges," "Ultra-Gangetic India," the "East Indian Islands," and even "East India."[6] In the nineteenth century, to English writers at least, "its mainland part was called either Further India or the Indo-Chinese peninsula, while its islands, save for the Philippines, were usually dubbed the Indian Archipelago."[7]

The Dutch called their empire Netherlands India, and when the area gained independence in 1949 it "perpetuated the erroneous concept of [its] Indian-ness"[8] by taking the name Indonesia, "The Indian Islands." Indian historians of the twentieth century, taking their cue from the Europeans, began to claim most of Southeast Asia as "Greater India," a term popularized by those historians who viewed "the early civilizations of Indochina and Indonesia as branches springing directly from the main trunk of Indian civilization."⁹ Foremost among these was George Cœdès.¹⁰

The Cœdès canon at the time of his death (in 1969 at the age of 83) was enormous. His contribution to a knowledge of early Southeast Asia by way of translations, particularly regarding Cambodia, remains without equal. The editors of the *Journal of Southeast Asian History* have called him "the father of Early South-East Asian History."¹¹

Cœdès' point of view has been clearly stated. "It is interesting to note that even in prehistoric times the autochthonous peoples of Indochina seem to have been lacking in creative genius and showed little aptitude for making progress without stimulus from outside."¹² In the introduction to his history of Southeast Asia in the early Christian era, the most comprehensive text on the subject to date, Cœdès stated that "my purpose is less to produce a history presenting all the details than to offer a synthesis showing how the various elements of the history are related."¹³ Given all the details, alternate syntheses are possible.¹⁴

The debate concerning the nature of so-called "Indianization" is fundamentally relevant to any inquiry into the historical roots of Southeast Asian performing arts—including the Cambodian dance drama—inasmuch as Cœdès' belief regarding them has been highly influential. In discussing the Indian epic literature, he wrote that

> in all of the Indianized mainland, in Malaysia, and on Java, this epic and legendary literature, to which was added the Buddhist folklore of the *Jātakas*, still makes up the substance of the classical theater, of the dances, and of the shadow-plays and puppet theater. From one end of Farther India to the other, spectators continue to weep over the misfortunes of Rāma and Sitā and to be moved by the virtues of the Bodhisattva, and the theatrical performances they attend have retained their original character of pantomime: the positions and the movements of the arms and legs and the gestures of the hands constitute a silent language capable of suggesting a subject, evoking an action, or expressing a sentiment, exactly as in Indian choreography.¹⁵

The present study will demonstrate that, aside from the versions of the Indian epics being used as the textual basis for performance, Cœdès' claim is largely inaccurate.

In fairness to Cœdès, we must acknowledge that his translations and editing of Khmer epigraphy and his discovery of other primary materials remains an invaluable service to many areas of Southeast Asian scholarship. The present study is indebted to his collation of a vast body of data; as will be seen, however, a very different interpretation of the data will be formulated.

By comparison, the Dutch historians appear more sensitive to the probable nature of cultural interaction between Indian Brahmans and Southeast Asian courts. F.D.K. Bosch, for instance, held that the

> awakened Indian spirit fecundated the living matter of [Southeast Asian] society, thus procreating a new life that was predestined to develop into an independent organism in which foreign and native elements were to merge into an indissoluble entity.[16]

While such an argument may appear persuasive, one also senses that it is inadequate when we consider the ruins of Cambodia's great Angkorean cities, to which there is nothing comparable in India.

A truly different interpretation of the prehistory of Southeast Asia, however, first appeared in the writings of the Dutch sociological historian J. C. van Leur, who called for a radical transformation in colonialist views. His untimely death in 1942 at the age of thirty-four limited his work to a doctoral dissertation and a handful of articles, and not until a collection of his work was translated into English in 1955 did he begin to have a broad influence. In a uniquely eclectic style, his writings "gave body to his heretical views by an astonishingly vivid evocation of an historically autonomous 'world of Southeast Asia.'" [17]

Van Leur wrote that

> all history, as a history of mankind, is of equal value. To allow a religious, a philosophical, or a biological attitude to prevail means to bring in a value judgment. To have a Christian concept of history, or a humanist one, or a progressive, or a racist, means to abandon the exact positivistic science of history.[18]

But few are free from "value judgment," and van Leur himself was perhaps premature in attributing to Southeast Asia what the historian

Harry Benda has called "a highly developed, well-integrated and virtually monolithic civilization."[19] Still, Benda himself stands in van Leur's debt when he writes that "Southeast Asia's history must be written 'from within', in other words, in terms of the area's internal developments, and not in terms—or periodizations—derived from the history of other parts of the world."[20] Van Leur's criticism of India-centric views is perhaps encapsulated in his oft-quoted dictum that in Southeast Asia both Hinduism and Islam were a "thin, easily flaking glaze on the massive body of indigenous civilization."[21] In the present study, Khmer cultural elements that are clearly borrowed from an Indian context will be viewed from that perspective.

Until recently, the available archaeological data were inadequate to accomplish the ascendancy of a Southeast Asia-centric interpretation. All of that has been changed dramatically by Professor Wilhelm G. Solheim of the University of Hawaii, together with a widespread network of colleagues. Acclaimed as "Mr. Southeast Asia" by some and "the van Leur of prehistory" by the more subtle, he has advanced a series of

> claims which uncompromisingly assert the primacy of Southeast Asians in all major Asian technical innovations and thus deny the region's dependence upon diffusion from China, India, the far West or anywhere else. On the contrary, many things are held to have been transmitted to parts of China, Japan, and the coasts of the Indian Ocean by Southeast Asian sailors and traders.[22]

In order to demonstrate the nature of Southeast Asian culture prior to the fourth century A.D., Chapter II of this study will briefly summarize the work of Solheim and his associates.

Acknowledging these influences, the present study assumes that historical scholarship must begin from the premise that the culture of Southeast Asia, like all cultures, regardless of age, material stature, or relationship with neighboring cultures, has an inherent unity, integrity, and unique identity. Sanskrit and Brahmanism provided a language for the transformation of the indigenous spiritual symbology of Southeast Asia. For Khmer dance drama, India may have provided a literary medium for mythological expression, and in a much later period the Thai influenced it as well. But in form, in structure, in spirit, and in the selective process operative in its evolution, the dance drama—like the culture in which it flowered—is exclusively a reflection of the Cambodian people. Beyond that, only the world as a whole may lay claim to it.

STRUCTURE OF THE PRESENT DISSERTATION

Accounts by envoys preserved in the Chinese dynastic annals and the increasing number of Sanskrit and Old Khmer inscriptions thereafter, provide the basis for reconstructions of pre-Angkorean history. From these, Chapter II will present an image of the function of Khmer dance from the fifth to the ninth centuries under a Brahmanic influence.

Dancers and musicians carved in bas relief on the temple walls during the Angkor period (Fig. 1-1), conventionally dated from 802 to 1431, furnish the primary data for Chapter III. The epigraphy further illuminates the status of singers, dancers and musicians involved in temple ritual.

Chapter IV will describe as completely as possible the fortunes of the royal dancers through the multi-demise of Angkor, kingdom, and republic, up to the present time. Late nineteenth-century accounts by a number of French explorers who passed through Cambodia, recent re-dating of texts, and Khmer oral traditions regarding the artistic evolution of the Khmer dancers into the performers we know today are examined in this section. Written descriptions of the dance drama by French colonial officers around the turn of the century have been invaluable to this study; the best is a twenty-five page article published in 1911 by Adhémard Leclère entitled *Le théâtre cambodgien*.

Further commentary was offered by a group of French scholars whose interest in the dance drama was tangential to their study of the sculpture and architecture of the Khmer Empire. Best known of these works is George Groslier's *Danseuses cambodgiennes anciennes et modernes*, published in 1913—a 175-page discourse on the dancers themselves as living embodiments of Angkorean sculpture. The romanticism inherent in this approach is common to numerous, brief re-countings of performances seen by other colonial bureaucrats and travelers who were guests of the Cambodian king in the late nineteenth and early twentieth centuries.

In the 1920s a more scholarly approach to the dance drama can be seen in the writings of Sappho Marchal and Jeanne Cuisinier. Each undertook to delineate the form by describing and cataloguing a number of production elements such as hand gestures and character roles. In 1930 Cuisinier assisted Samdach Chaufea Thiounn, a former Cambodian Prime Minister, in the preparation of *Danses cambodgiennes* which was re-published in 1956 by the Institut Bouddhique in Phnom Penh and remains the most complete study to date of the classical dance drama.

Danses cambodgiennes is also representative of a small body of scholarship produced by the Cambodians themselves who have, in general, been concerned with performance descriptions rather than with analysis. Since the dance drama lay under the king's patronage until 1970 and could be viewed only by royal invitation, scholarly criticism, whether Cambodian or foreign, was inappropriate. Consequently, from 1930 to the present, there are only brief photo-journalistic treatments of the dance drama, the most informative being a twenty-four page pamphlet entitled *The Royal Cambodian Ballet* published by the Ministry of Information in 1963, virtually the only publication of any significance on the subject written in English. Two photographic studies from different periods have provided visual documentation: Raymond Cogniat's *Danses d'Indochine* (1932) and Charles Meyer's "Cambodian Dances" in *Nokor Khmer* (1970).

Chapter V stands apart as a survey of the mythological foundation of the dance drama repertoire and, particularly, of the four major groupings of roles—female, male, monkey, and *yakkha* (giant or ogre). The chapter takes as its focus the five forms of a "Myth of the Primordial Maiden," the first having been recorded in the third century A.D. in the area that is today Cambodia. The story of this myth is still performed in the contemporary repertoire of the dance drama.

The dramas (*roeung*) and the dances (*robam*) performed today or in recent memory within the classical tradition will be summarized in Chapter VI.

Chapter I: Historical Sources of the Study 9

1-1. Three *Devatā* in Dynamic Positions at Angkor Wat, 12th Century.
Photo Kent Davis.

Plot résumés gleaned from performance programs in the Royal Palace Library were the primary source of data used in creating this survey of the repertoire.

Chapters VII and VIII describe production elements, divided somewhat arbitrarily between those which are teacher-focused (music, choreography, and staging) in Chapter VII and those which are dancer-focused (life style, training, and costumes) in Chapter VIII.

The final chapter will describe those elements of performance—such as ritual function within the court and the dancer's face makeup—which appear to be vestiges of ancient, indigenous rites for the purpose of renewing the society and assuring the fertility of the soil. Specifically the nature of communication between the royal dancers (as the King's harem) and the world of ancestral spirits (*neak ta*) will be examined.

Sources of information contained in the latter chapters include an array of eye-witness accounts, my own observations, and interviews with dance teachers. Foremost among these was Chheng Phon, a professor at the Université des Beaux-Arts (often called, after 1970, the University of Fine Arts, but usually just "UBA"). Surviving all disasters, he became Minister of Culture and Information in the early years of the Vietnamese regime in Phnom Penh. Hopefully the following chapters reflect his compassionate objectivity.

Endnotes

1. Elizabeth Becker, "A Firsthand Report from Angkor Wat," *San Francisco Chronicle*, 28 December, 1978, p. 15.
2. Hang Thun Hak, et al., *Folklore Khmer* (Phnom Penh: l'Université Royale des Beaux-Arts, 1969), p. 1.
3. An introduction to the more elder players, who until very recently continued to perform major roles, is available in D.G.E. Hall's *Historians of South East Asia* (London: Oxford University Press, 1961), hereinafter cited as *HSEA*.
4. A term coined in 1948 and given currency in D.G.E. Hall's *History of South-East Asia* (1955). See John R. W. Small, "On the Possibility of an Autonomous History of Modern Southeast Asia," *Journal of Southeast Asian History*, 2, No. 2 (1961), p. 72. This journal hereinafter cited as *JSAH*.
5. Wilhelm G. Solheim II, "Reflections on the New Data of Southeast Asian Prehistory: Austronesian Origin and Consequence," *AP*, 18, No. 2 (1975), pp. 146-47.
6. B. Harrison, "English Historians of 'The Indian Archipelago': Crawfurd and St. John" (Hall, *HSEA*), p. 245.
7. D.G.E. Hall, "The Integrity of Southeast Asian History," *Journal of Southeast Asian Studies*, 4, No. 2 (Sep. 1973), p. 159.
8. D.G.E. Hall, "The Integrity of Southeast Asian History," p. 159.
9. George Cœdès, *The Making of Southeast Asia* (Berkeley: University of California Press, 1972), p. 55. This text translated by H. M. Wright from *Les Peuples de la Péninsule Indochinoise* (Paris: Dunod, 1962) will be cited hereinafter as *MSA*.
10. Cœdès' view of Indian historiography is significant. "Curiously, India quickly forgot that her culture had spread over such vast domains to the east and southeast. Indian scholars have not been aware of this fact until very recently; it was not until a small group of them...studied with the professors of the Universities of Paris and Leyden that they discovered, in our works...the history of what they now call, with justifiable pride 'Greater India'" (*The Indianized States of Southeast Asia* [Honolulu: East-West Center Press, 1968], p. xvii). Translated by Susan Brown Cowing from *Les États hindouisées d'Indochine et d'Indonésie* (Paris: E. de Boccard, 1944; revised 1964), this text is hereinafter cited as *ISSA*.
11. *JSAH*, 4, No. 2 (1964), p. 1.
12. *MSA*, p. 13.
13. *ISSA*, p. xv.
14. The one which—for its well-reasoned and impartial scholarship—has most influenced the present study is Anthony Christie's "The Provenance and Chronology of Early Indian Cultural Influences in South East Asia," in *R. C. Majumdar Felicitation Volume*, ed. H. B. Sarker (Calcutta: Firma K. L. Mukhopadhyay), 1970, pp. 1-14. Christie acknowledges that his conclusions are "far removed from the presently accepted view."
15. *ISSA*, p. xvii.
16. "The Problem of the Hindu Colonisation of Indonesia," *Selected Studies in Indonesian Archaeology* (The Hague: M. Nijoff, 1961), pp. 20-21. This paper was initially delivered as an

inaugural address at the University of Leiden on 15 March 1946.
17 Smail, p. 72.
18 *Indonesian Trade and Society: Essays in Asian Social and Economic History*, trans. James S. Holmes and A. van Marle (The Hague: W. van Hoeve, 1955), p. 31.
19 Harry J. Benda, "The Structure of Southeast Asian History: Some Preliminary Observations," *JSAH*, 3, No. 1 (1962), p. 118.
20 Benda, p. 118.
21 van Leur, p. 169.
22 I. W. Mabbett, "The 'Indianization' of Southeast Asia: Reflections on the Prehistoric Sources," *Journal of Southeast Asian Studies*, 8, No. 1 (Mar. 1977), pp. 5-6. Part Two of this synthetic study is "The 'Indianization' of Southeast Asia: Reflections on the Historical Sources," *JSAS*, 8, No. 2 (Sep. 1977).

CHAPTER 2

THE CULTURAL CONTEXT OF PRE-ANGKOREAN DANCE

បរិបទវប្បធម៌នៃរបាំសម័យបុរេប្រវត្តិ

In the earliest stone inscriptions from the area of present-day Cambodia, dancers and musicians figure prominently in lists of slaves donated to religious temples. In classical Angkor, dozens of celestial dancers or *apsaras* were carved in bas-relief on the temple walls—Angkor Wat alone reputedly has 1,787. Dance has always been ritually associated with temple and monarch in Cambodia and in the modern period is considered to embody the essence of Khmer culture. In few societies can it be said that dance is so greatly respected as a rite of self-perpetuation. This chapter will examine the foundations of that rite as discerned in the pre-Angkorean period. The protohistorical data regarding dance will be examined together with ethnological accounts of historical practices thought to reveal ancient beliefs concerning the interrelationship of dance, the spirit world, and the king. This relationship was clarified and institutionalized in A.D. 820 when Jayavarman II ascended the throne and established the *devarāja* cult which will be the final consideration of this chapter.

Earliest Evidence of Dance in Southeast Asia

While it is assumed that dance has always been an integral part of Southeast Asian culture, the earliest material evidence of dance on the peninsula is a small figurine found in association with excavations of the so-called "Dong-son" culture in the area of present-day north-central Vietnam (Fig. 2-1). The image is of a dancer carrying a musician on his shoulders. The hair of both is highly stylized, the ears are pierced with enormous discs, and the wind instrument being played resembles the Dayak *keluri* or possibly the Laotian *khen*.[1] It is thought that the small bronze represents a mimetic dance related to "Dong-son" religious ritual.[2]

The "Dong-son Culture," distinguished particularly by bronze kettledrums dating from the fifth century B.C. onward,[3] is presently considered to be an indigenous "late manifestation" of the oldest bronze technology in the world. Recent excavation in northeastern Thailand has dated double-mold bronze casting at about 2700 B.C.[4] thereby indicating bronze manufacture up to a thousand years earlier than in either China or India and allowing speculation that "early in the fourth millennium B.C. bronze was invented somewhere in Southeast Asia."[5] The oldest types of Dong-son drums have been found from southern China to Indonesia including Cambodia, Thailand, and Malaya.[6]

2-1. **Dong-son Male Dancer and Musician**
Goloubew, L'âge du bronze, pl. xx.

Since many of the more highly-ornamental drums depict figures that appear to be dancing—although far more stylized than the "dancer with musician"—it is relevant to ask for what purpose drums and bronze implements in general were used by early Southeast Asians.

In excavations at Dong-son, the village for which the "culture" was named, the majority of bronze drums—together with ceremonial bronze axes, tools, vessels and ornaments— were found in association with burials.[7] Figures of boats manned by men wearing tall headdresses are incised in circles on some of the more elaborate drumheads, and it is believed that the boats were to escort the soul of the dead to its abode.[8] In the modern period Muongs hung such a drum over the head of the deceased and beat on it while food offerings were made. From such data, Cœdès has concluded that Dong-son-type drums were in wide usage for funerary rites;[9] in this century similar rites have been noted among the Dayak of Borneo.[10] Scholars have also observed affinities of Dong-son drum motifs with those of Melanesian art and Oceanic art in general.[11]

CULTURAL SIMILARITIES THROUGHOUT SOUTHEAST ASIA

On what basis do such geographically far-reaching similarities have validity in creating a composite view of early religious beliefs in Cambodia, especially regarding the function of dance? The available evidence appears to justify such a method. In the 1930s human remains excavated in Laos included a skull regarded as a

> prototype combining the characteristics of the earliest Europoids (such as Ainus, Polynesians, and later Indonesians), the Papuan negroids, and the Veddo-Australoids. His ancestors must have had their habitat somewhere in the south of China on the borders of Yunnan and Tibet, whence they must have spread towards the east and the south throughout the whole of South East Asia, in all parts of which remains of their culture have been found.[12]

This culture is now termed the Hoabinhian "technocomplex" or group of cultures sharing certain techniques,[13] spread through the vast circle of Southeast Asia.[14] Solheim believes that around 8000 B.C. or earlier, fully distinct cultures began to "crystallize" out of the Hoabinhian,[15] resulting ultimately in the cultural, social, linguistic and economic mosaic that we note today.

The broad dispersal over millennia of the Hoabinhian culture was made easier by the fact that much of the area was originally land-connected prior to a rise in the sea level sometime between the tenth and fifth millennia B.C.[16] Still, cultures with strong navigational skills developed, foremost of whom were peoples whose dialects lay within the Austronesian language family, especially the Malayo-Polynesian subclass of Island Southeast Asia.

Linguistic evidence suggests that from a homeland between Australia and the Asian continent,[17] Malayo-Polynesian civilization spread to the Asian mainland, west to Africa, and east as far as Easter Island. Traveling by outrigger canoe, they traded—particularly in cinnamon— with Egyptians, Phoenicians, and Hebrews near the mouth of the Red Sea by at least 1000 B.C.[18] Linguistic evidence suggests they reached East Africa shortly after 1000 B.C. and settled the previously uninhabited island of Madagascar around the time of Christ.[19] The arrival in West Africa of a "Malaysian complex," particularly including plants, is also dated around the beginning of the Christian era[20] and probably arrived by boat.[21] Finally, Malayo-Polynesian peoples in the East reached Easter Island by A.D. 450, having spread themselves half-way around the world by the fifth century.[22]

The prehistoric, cultural affinities between the Hoabinhian technocomplex and the Malayo-Polynesians have been demonstrated in order to compare with some validity the apparent similarities in cultural elements among geographically widespread, contemporary cultures. We will initially limit the discussion of similarities to the function of dance in ancient funeral rites and in megalithic cultures.

Dance in Funeral Rites and Megalithic Cultures

A seventh-century Chinese account in the *History of the Sui* makes the earliest written reference to dance in the area of Cambodia, in association with funeral rites:

> Whatever the status of the deceased, the body is wrapped, carried to the shore of the sea or of a river accompanied by the sound of drums and by dances, and then burned on a pyre set up by those present. When a

king's body is burned, the bones spared by the fire are put in a golden urn and thrown into the sea.[23]

Given the other evidence presented subsequently, it seems likely that the function of dance in this context was related to ancient rites of rebirth.

Burial sites near Thanh Hoa belonging to the Bacson culture dating from perhaps the fourth millennia B.C. reveal that the dead were buried in fetal position.[24] In some cases the body was not interred until all flesh had disappeared from the bones, a custom still practiced in pre-Hindu Bali and Java.[25] The bones were then tied into a fetal position and, together with accompanying artifacts, were painted red and buried.[26] A similar concern for rebirth marked the royal funeral rites in Cambodia as late as 1927 at the death of King Sisowath. His body was placed in fetal position in a silver urn filled with mercury for a lengthy period prior to cremation, the actual ceremony of which was largely a rite of rebirth into the ancestral world.[27] Significantly, attendants of this urn were dancers with ghost-white, painted faces (Fig. 4-1).

As another example of a cultural form appearing discontiguously over a broad geographical area and with relevance to Cambodia, we may look to the Megalithic culture appearing throughout Southeast Asia. A "fundamental homogeneity" among many forms of stone structures and beliefs held in association with them—observable throughout Southeast Asia, many islands of the Pacific, Madagascar, the east coast of India, and Assam—indicates that the essential elements of "megalithic ritual... must have already been developed before the beginning of the great Austronesian migration"[28] at least as early as 2500 B.C.[29]

Overall, megalithic forms are related to water and fertility or to burial and ancestors. Stone was used in "extensive series of complex irrigation works, consisting of ... terraces and tanks from which the water thus collected is fed as required to the rice fields below."[30] Such structures in Cambodia closely resemble counterparts in Assam and the Indonesian island of Nias, to the point of having similar waterspouts.[31] Sacred trees are associated with all of them, and one megalithic terrace in Java lies below a spring which is itself still considered sacred.[32] H.G.Q. Wales sees the monumental use of stone at Angkor as the later development of a fully megalithic Khmer culture—already manifesting causeways, stairways, ramparts and bridges —in which water tank, ritual terrace and sacred tree were frequently associated.[33]

Wales points out that in many areas in which megalithic culture is maintained, "upright menhirs now represent male ancestors, and recumbent ones (or dolmens) represent females, either as their 'memorials' or as seats on which they and the living may rest and commune."[34] Within circles of such stones ritual dancing is still performed, and it seems very likely that the single, indispensable stage prop used today in Cambodian dance drama—a low, wide bench that is not a bed—is a vestige, at least in function, of this megalithic, ancestral seat of communion.

Maintaining a relationship with the world of spirits—whether natural or ancestral—for purposes of assuring terrestrial fertility appears to have been the essence of Southeast Asian religious practices from the earliest period. In pre-Hindu Bali, for instance, the souls of ancestors were believed to dispense the vital "life power" which animates all men, animals and plants. They resided on a mountain at the hidden sources of rivers whose waters were necessary for all agriculture.[35]

In early Java and Bali, which Cœdès[36] and others[37] have taken as a model for understanding early Khmer practices, ancestral spirits were contacted in a sacred ceremony held at temples located in each village for that purpose.[38] In Cambodia, likewise, each community "had to maintain a shrine by which it could communicate with their [ancestral] spirits and receive 'life power' through certain rituals."[39] The Balinese believed that not everyone was capable of receiving the "life-power" unless their own was in equilibrium. Therefore, those with the greatest ability to receive the "life-power"—those with the greatest "equilibrium"—made the actual contact with the ancestors.[40]

Of relevance to the present inquiry is the question of how this communion and receiving of "life-power" was effected in Cambodia, and by whom. It appears that in Southeast Asia, overall, contact with the spirit world of the ancestors could be made most effectively by the king, his chief priest or by dancers. In the Cambodian context there were at least seven possible means: visitation, trance, dreams, sex, genealogy, the use of stone *linga* or statue-portraits, and dance. In light of the fact that the *raison d'être* of the royal dancer was to serve the king in his ritual function, let us briefly consider each of these in turn.

In ancient times the chief or king could commune with the ancestors by actually visiting a place identified with the ancestral homeland.[41] Early Khmers and others located the ancestral home on the top of a mountain or mountains.[42] Khmer kings from Jayavarman II onwards located a temple-mountain, symbolizing the abode of the ancestors, at the center of each of the royal cities. Thus, the king brought the mountain to himself, and whether his personal cult was Vaisnavite, Saivite, or Buddhist, "he could bring forth the protective force of the ancestors through a central cult based on the mountain-temple."[43]

Another means of ancestral communication was to invoke the ancestors' presence within an intermediary in a state of trance. In Bali the person conducting the ritual communication would induce a trance state during which the ancestral spirits flowed into him. Others knelt before this incarnation of the ancestors whose mere presence provided "life-power" necessary "to further the growth of rice, to calm the devastating overflowing streams, to subdue epidemics afflicting the population."[44] As we shall see in Chapter IX, this exact pattern took place in Cambodia even in this century on the village level where the king's dancers were considered to be a powerful magnet for the spirits to manifest themselves through trance. It is highly likely that this pattern was used in a royal context in earlier centuries.

A third means of communication, attributable to the king, was the ability to obtain knowledge from the ancestral spirits by means of dreams. For instance, in A.D. 850 the Khmer King Jayavarman III dreamed that he met a spirit who asked that he erect a statue in his honor and give a cult to that spirit, which the king did.[45] The inscription makes it clear that this power was the result of the king's asceticism.

A fourth means of communication with the spirit world was understood by the general population as sexual congress between fertility spirits and the king. Paul Mus has suggested that the two fundamental features of Southeast Asian religion prior to Brahmanic influence were ancestor worship and the fertility cult, and that the two were closely interconnected.[46] While the Khmers today believe in *neak ta*, or animistic spirits inhabiting all natural objects, veneration for three particular spirit forms—tree, stone and serpent—appears primary and is evident from the earliest times.

The spirits of trees were revered, possibly for their obvious manifestation of fertility and "life power." The old Khmer name for Cambodia itself was Kok Thlok which means "the land of the *thlok* tree."[47] Great power was attributed to the spirits of stones, and

> megalithic monuments became *linga*, especially of the kind that... had no *yonī* base and were thus able to impregnate the soil directly, at the same time that they represented the peaks of mountains, the source of 'life-power' and the abode of the ancestors.[48]

A third essential spirit in the pantheon of Khmer "deities" was the spirit of the earth itself, conceived in the form of a serpent. According to a thirteenth century account:

> There is a gold tower [the Phimeanakas] at the top of which the king sleeps. All the natives claim that there is a spirit in the tower, a serpent with nine heads, which is the master of the soil of the whole kingdom. It appears every night in the form of a woman. It is with this spirit that the king first sleeps and unites himself.... If one night the spirit of this serpent does not appear, then the moment of the king's death has come. If the king fails to come a single night, some misfortune is inevitable.[49]

The symbolism of the king in the golden tower that is at once *lingam* and mountain, in union with the spirit of the earth is obvious, and at Angkor Wat the great *nāga* balustrades radiating in four directions from the central *lingam* essentially give form to the concept of sexual union with the earth. The correlative on the material plane was the king in union with his harem of dancers.

A fifth means of maintaining contact with the ancestral spirit world—at least by the kings of Angkor—was through genealogy, a discussion of which provides an opportunity to briefly survey the protohistorical data regarding the area that is today Cambodia.

Royal Genealogy Derived from *Apsaras*

The kings of Angkor traced their lineage from one or both of the two kingdoms which previously held sovereignty in the region: Funan and Zhenla, the names for which are both known to us only through Chinese dynastic records. The Zhenla lineage was said to derive from the marriage of a celestial dancer, an *apsaras*, with a sage. Let us digress to consider the significance of the two kingdoms as matrices of Angkorean concepts.

Funan is the earliest kingdom in Southeast Asia of which we have historical accounts, primarily from the Chinese annals. One of these refers to an embassy sent from Funan[50] or "southern protectorate" to the emperor of China in 1110 B.C.[51] What the inhabitants called their country or themselves is unknown. Funan is believed to have included the area of present-day southern Cambodia and the Mekong delta, although a king ruling sometime prior to A.D. 200 was said to have built large ships, gone "sailing all over the immense sea," "attacked more than ten kingdoms," and extended his kingdom "over six thousand *li*" (3500 km.).[52]

We know nothing about dance in the Funan era, but clearly the kingdom was sufficiently sophisticated to maintain ritual dancers if that custom then prevailed, as seems likely. In A.D. 225 a mission from Funan to China offered glassware to the emperor.[53] An embassy in A.D. 243 included a present of musicians and products of the country.[54] Mid-third century accounts of Funan by a Chinese envoy, Kang Tai, mention books and libraries, silver eating utensils among the common people and taxes paid in gold.[55] The Funan city of Oc-eo on the Mekong delta "lay astride and eventually controlled much of the earliest international trade route through South East Asia"[56] and "may even have been the terminus of voyages from the Eastern Mediterranean."[57] Kang Tai described boats without sails in Funan that were a hundred feet long and carried a hundred oarsmen.[58] Another account, also attributed to the third century, tells of sailing ships up to fifty meters long which had four sails one behind the other, carried up to seven hundred men and transported a thousand metric tons of merchandise; their crews were chiefly *kun lun*, a term referring to Southeast Asians.[59] A Chinese text dated A.D. 817 speaks of *kun lun po* (or ship) of an earlier period that carried more than a thousand men plus merchandise.[60]

Interestingly, Funan's early commercial activity does not appear to have involved India greatly. About A.D. 245 the king of Funan—Fan Zhan in the Chinese sources—received a visitor from an area in western India. In response, he sent a relative to visit the Indian king. Kang Tai's account makes it clear that the two kings were learning of each other's country for the first time.[61] The evidence suggests, then, that "Indian influence" is not an issue in regard to protohistorical Funan, and, while efforts have been made to date so-called "Indianization" from the first century A.D. on the basis of mythology, there is no evidence of Indian influence in Funan prior to the second half of the fourth century A.D., with that influence clearly originating in Western India.[62]

At that time an Indian Brahman named Kaundinya arrived in Funan, was elected king, and "changed all the rules according to the methods of India."[63] Kaundinya was said to have married a daughter of the "king of the *nāga*" named Somā, who lived with him in a human dwelling.[64] The single, seventh-century inscription which recounts this marriage implies that they founded a lunar dynasty,[65] although the account reflects significant mythicization (see Chapter V).

During the second half of the sixth century, a kingdom to the north of Funan which had previously been a vassal state gained dominance. These people were the Khmers, known also from the ninth century as the Kambujas,[66] and their kingdom is commonly known by historians as Zhenla (or Chenla). The early Khmer kings traced their dynastic origin to a mythic event different from that of Funan. Mentioned in a tenth-century inscription, the reference has been interpreted to mean that "the origin of the kings of Cambodia goes back to the union of the hermit Kambu Svāyambhuva, eponymic ancestor of the Kambujas, with the celestial nymph Merā . . .";[67] Svayambhuva means "self-creating,"[68] and Merā was an *apsaras* or heavenly dancer given to him by Shiva.

A century and a half later, with very little centralization of manpower or territory remaining to Zhenla, Jayavarman II, founder of the kingdom of Angkor, effectively began his reign in 802—following the conquest of numerous regional chieftains—by the establishment of the *devarāja* on a mountain near present-day Angkor. Genealogically, it was said that like a "great lotus which has no stem, he rises as a new flower."[69] His successors, however, carefully traced their ancestry either to the Khmer, solar line of Kambu and Merā, or to the much more "authentic" and older, lunar line of Somā and Kaundinya, the progenitors of Funan. By 946 a stone inscription relating to King Rajendravarman II says that in him the solar and lunar races were conjoined.[70]

> The search for genealogy via both patrilineal and matrilineal succession was thus not merely an attempt by one king to link himself to his predecessors; rather it was the effort to channel the 'life-force' of these powerful individuals down through the ages into the Kambuja of his own day. By doing so through himself, the king demonstrated his personal capacity to receive this 'life force', thus legitimizing his claim to the throne.[71]

Two further means of maintaining contact with the ancestor/spirit world remain to be considered: the lingam and dance.

THE *DEVARĀJA*, SOURCE OF THE KING'S POWER

The essence of Angkorean kingship was contained within a dynamic "ambivalence" in which the Khmer tradition and the Sanskritic tradition were resolved.[72] This is no more clearly seen than in the *devarāja*, a term which properly refers to the stone lingam (or its attendant cult) named *Kamrateng jagat ta rajya*, or "Lord of the Universe, who is the king," which Jayavarman II first established with the ritual assistance of a Brahman priest in the capital of his expanding kingdom.

Recent scholarship suggests that the role played by megalithic monuments in embodying spirits, was transferred to the *lingam* when Brahmanic practices came to be adopted throughout Southeast Asia.[73] A *lingam*, in general, thus represented both a powerful local or ancestral spirit—one who had returned to the ancestral mountain abode—as well as a more universal deity in the form of Shiva. (Some local deities retained Khmer names throughout the Angkorean period; others were Sanskritized into a Saivite form.)

As the traditional abode of ancestor spirits, the mountain was already considered sacred by indigenous tradition. By incorporating the external god Shiva, who was known in Indian philosophy as the "Lord of the Mountain" and for his association with fertility, the king's position was reinforced. It remained for Khmer kings to associate themselves with this mountain and thereby symbolize their ability to guarantee the flow of life-power from the realm of the ancestors to their subjects.[74] Jayavarman II did this by instituting the *devarāja* on Mt. Mahendra and, later, by the erection of mountain-temples. When Jayavarman II declared that the most powerful of all the ancestral spirits—the "king of the gods"—was now embodied as the *devarāja*, resident in his capital, he gained a great asset to his campaign of centralizing loyalty to an ever-expanding political and economic core.

No Khmer king is ever referred to as god; there was no true deification of royalty at Angkor. Rather, the power of the king derived in large measure from the fact that he maintained the *devarāja*, known also—with marvelous ambiguity as "Lord of the Universe, who is the king." By maintaining the *devarāja*, Jayavarman demonstrated that he was the most powerful bearer and transmitter of ancestral power to the Angkorean people.[75] The Khmer king who, by definition, represented a medium to the spirit world by virtue of both genealogy and an ambiguous identification with the royal *lingam* or mountain-temple—as well as the other means we have discussed—would be concerned to demonstrate his "equilibrium" in a number of ways. One of these was dance.

Pre-Angkorean Temple Dance

At least two Khmer kings—Jayavarman I in the seventh century[76] and Yasovarman in the ninth century[77]—are mentioned in stone inscriptions as being accomplished dancers. By surrounding himself with dancers and by dancing himself, the king added one more element to a long-term process of "integrating indigenous folk traditions, symbols and religious beliefs into a cult which was visibly concentrated in the center."[78]

The reason that dance was such an effective symbol in the royal court was because in its own right—possibly due to an aesthetic involving an hypnotic sense of balance and suspension—Khmer dance has often been identified with spirit mediumship as well as with trance. As we shall see in Chapter IX there is a clear identification made between the dancer's headdress or mask and the very real spirit of that role. Well into the twentieth century the court dancers wore pure white face makeup, a color identified with the spirit world, and, in general, dancers were viewed as fundamentally "spiritual."

Dance in Southeast Asia appears to have always been a magico-religious activity. It undoubtedly took other forms as well, but the spiritual power of dance caused it to be associated with pre-Angkorean temples as well as the great monuments of Angkor. Our final consideration of this chapter will be an examination of the epigraphic evidence of dance in that context prior to the ascension of Jayavarman II.

Khmer stone inscriptions, in general, functioned as titles to lands and property belonging to a temple.[79] They included the names of slaves donated to the temple, usually by members of the royal family. Five inscriptions prior to 802 mention dancers specifically. The earliest is dated by George Cœdès as late sixth or early seventh century despite stylistic affinities with earlier fifth century inscriptions of Funan. The inscription (K.51) enumerates the gifts offered to the temple of a local deity by a certain Indradatta; heading the list are the names of the female dancers (*rapam*), though only four are legible: Kandin, Ata, Tittaru and Ngarngor.[80] Lancaster has pointed out that

> whereas the other slaves donated at that time are referred to by opprobrious Khmer names such as Chke (dog), Chmae (cat), or sauy (stinking), the ballerinas bear Sanskrit names such as "Adorable," "Gifted in the Art of Love," "Cousin of High Heaven," or "Spring Jasmine" (Vasantmallika)....[81]

The inscription clearly states that the dancers are to be assigned exclusively to the "Shrine of the Deity."

The oldest inscription in the Khmer language, dated A.D. 611 (K.600), is from a temple in which a god with the suffix -*isvara* (Shiva) has merged with another god whose name signifies a tree.[82] It lists the offerings of a certain Antār to the temple including seven female dancers (*jmah ge ram*) of whom six are named, eleven female singers (each named), and four female musicians (each named). Of the musicians, one plays *vina*, two *kanhjang*, and one *lahv*. Bernard Groslier identifies the first instrument with the Indian "guitar" and the latter two as "unidentifiable stringed instruments."[83] With two exceptions, the names of all musicians and dancers are Sanskrit while the names of others associated with the temple are almost exclusively Khmer.

A third inscription (K. 138), noting gifts made on the first day of the waning moon in an indeterminate month of A.D. 620, appears to indicate that two female and two male dancers (*ram*) were offered to a Shiva temple.[84] A seventh-century inscription (K.137) concerns a king's offering—his name is not known—of four hundred slaves to be divided between several temples. The names of five female dancers (*rapam*), ten female singers and two male singers are mentioned.[85]

Finally, a late seventh- or early eighth-century inscription (K. 155) details the gifts given by a dignitary holding the title "Chief of Granaries" to a Shiva temple erected by him. Included are nine male musicians (*gandharva*), nine female dancers (*rpam*), seven female singers (*camren*), three female dancers (*rpam*), and six female singers (*camren*); all are mentioned by name.[86] One scholar has suggested that the listing on this inscription of twelve dancers in two groups—as are the thirteen singers—is perhaps "a matter of different service or destination or even of dancers specialized in particular styles."[87]

The term for "dancer" in the five inscriptions discussed is always the old Khmer root *ram* which becomes by infixation *ramam/rmam* or *rapam/ rpam*, the same term used in modern Khmer. In the sixth- and seventh-century inscriptions the word seems always to imply feminine gender although later inscriptions, as we shall see, sometimes specify *rmam neak* or "male dancer."

Early inscriptions have other significant similarities. All the dancers are mentioned by name, which, with the exception of the earliest inscription and in a few other individual cases, is always Sanskrit while other names listed are usually Khmer. Seemingly, dancers used Sanskrit names to enhance the power of their ritual function "in the service of god" (K.600) or literally as "slaves of the god" (K.137). Interestingly the fact that slaves of the donor were dancers suggests, first, that they were previously trained or maintained as dancers in his residence or elsewhere, and, further, that accomplished, pre-Angkorean dancers fulfilled a function other than that of temple service exclusively.

In addition to music and dance, there is evidence that a literary basis for dramatic performance existed in Funan/Zhenla. A sixth-century inscription found near the Cambodian village of Veal Kantel just below the border of Laos listed gifts made by the brother-in-law of King Bhavavarman to a Shiva temple.[88] Included were copies of the *Mahābhārata* and the *Rāmāyana* from which daily recitations were instituted. That the highly dramatic *Rāmāyana*—chanted or otherwise—was revered in a period with significant amounts of music and dance in temples and elsewhere means that all the theatrical elements of dance drama were well developed arts, individually at least, prior to the Angkor period.

Sculptural Evidence

The pre-Angkorean art of sculpture may seem greatly removed from an analysis of Khmer dance, but this chapter will conclude with a brief commentary on statuary to complete the argument by inference for a complex and highly developed culture in the region which was not dependent on India as a source of inspiration for its creativity.

In sculpture, even Cœdès acknowledges "the very remarkable differences that clearly distinguish the oldest architectural and sculptural monuments of Champa, Cambodia and Java from those of India proper."[89]

This can be seen most clearly in the pre-Angkorean sculpture-portraits of ancestors. These were erected as a further means of maintaining contact with the ancestral world, and several are among the most exquisite works of art in the ancient world.

The earliest free-standing sculptures in Cambodia (A.D. 6th century) are female, and, since the royal dancers are ultimately representative of the Feminine principle—as this study will later demonstrate—it is important to note the nature of these early works. With the exception of certain figures in the bas-reliefs which appear to be in the pose that indicates an *apsaras* flying[90], there are no pre-Angkorean sculptural representations of women (or men) in dance poses. Rather, the image is a monolithic blend of human and divine. The finest of these works is known as the Lady of Koh Krieng (Fig. 2-2) and dates from the seventh century; she betrays no Indian elements whatsoever.

Of this sculpture, Madeleine Giteau has written:

> The realism of this image is startling. It owes almost nothing to India. The artist has used a living model ... a woman of Cambodia past her first youth and portrayed in the guise of a divinity. The mature body is modelled with rare verisimilitude.... The flat back and carriage of the head are typical of Cambodian women. The face, too, is intensely alive ... [with] an expression of dominance. She gives the impression of a great lady.... The artist was inspired by his observations of Cambodian women to produce one of the finest pieces of the pre-Angkor period, and the most moving female statue in Khmer art.[91]

The Lady of Koh Krieng is the prototypical female body in Khmer art and the precursor of the *devatā* images who figure prominently in the discussion of sculptured Angkorean dancers in the following chapter.

Jayavarman II and Javanese Influence

The advent of the Angkorean period is marked by the appearance of a ruler who gained a far greater regional authority than any previous known chieftain in mainland Southeast Asia. He integrated local customs of kingship with the authoritative voice of a Brahmanic priesthood. He created a centralization of power heretofore unknown in the region and laid the foundations politically—although not architecturally—for the civilization of Angkor. He was its first truly powerful ruler and one of the greatest to appear along the six-century trajectory of Angkor's rise and fall. Today he is known as Jayavarman II.

The family of Jayavarman II was distantly related to the ruling dynasty of Zhenla in the eighth century, but in that turbulent period, for whatever reasons, they lived in Java. The Srivijayan "Emperor of the South Seas" held virtual sway over much of Southeast Asia including their strife-torn homeland. Around A.D. 800 Jayavarman returned to Cambodia, unified the regional chieftains, took the Brahman priest Sivakaivalaya as his chaplain, and established the cult of the *devarāja* on a mountain near the future site of Angkor.[92]

It is generally assumed that he exerted strong Javanese influence on the newly-revived kingdom in a number of ways. In architecture, changes in the form of the *apsaras* and other decorative motifs, for instance, clearly bear this out.[93] In

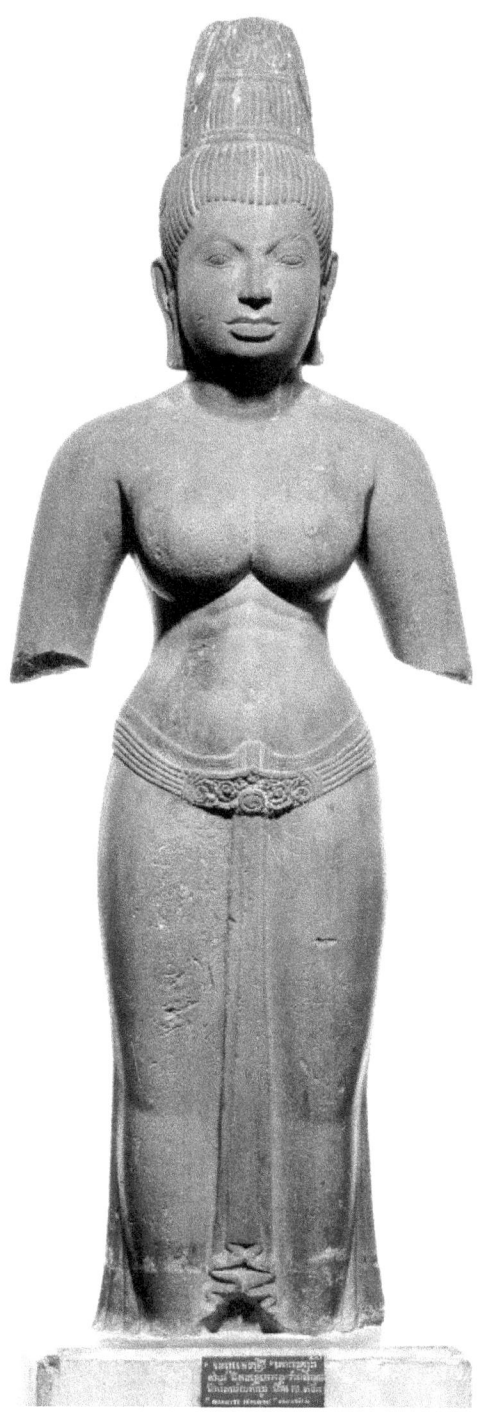

2-2. **The Lady of Koh Krieng, 7th - 8th Century.**
National Museum of Phnom Penh
Photo John Gollings.

dance, Cambodian scholars hold that there was a great Indonesian influence on Khmer dance in the ancient period,[94] but their claim is casually made and with no supporting evidence. We thus note this faint oral tradition, but in the present study, the ramifications are only very rarely considered.

Jayavarman II ruled the Kingdom of Angkor forty-eight years and died in A.D. 850, as one of the world's loveliest flowers of architectural magnificence was beginning to open. Virtually none of the available literature—nor any Khmer scholars—have attempted to demonstrate the specific nature of Indonesian influence on Khmer dance. If ever isolated, such influence may well date from Jayavarman's era and from the style of dancers in the entourage which accompanied him from Java. Half a century after his death, a poet wrote:

> He seated himself on the heads of lions that ornamented his throne, he imposed his will on the heads of kings, he established his residence on the head of Mount Mahendra, and still there was no pride in him.[95]

We turn now to an examination of his legacy and to the role of dance at Angkor.

Endnotes

1   Victor Goloubew, "L'age du bronze au Tonkin et dans le Nord-Annam," *BEFEO*, 29 (1929), p. 29.
2   Jean Przyluski, "Notes sur l'age du bronze en l'Indochine," *RAA*, 7, No. 2 (1931), p. 79.
3   George Cœdès, *MSA*, p. 17.
4   Donn Bayard, "Early Thai Bronze," *Science*, 30 June 1972, p. 1411.
5   Wilhelm G. Solheim II, "The 'New Look' of Southeast Asian Prehistory," *JSS*, 60, Pt. 1 (January 1972), p. 14.
6   B.A.V. Peacock, "A Preliminary Note on the Dong-so'n Bronze Drums from Kampong Sungai Langi," *Federation Museums Journal*, 9 (1964), pp. 1-3; Peacock, "Recent Archaeological Discoveries in Malaya 1964," *JMBRAS*, 38 (1965), pp. 248-255; Anonymous, "The Lampong Field Station in Thailand," *Newsletter of the Scandinavian Institute of Asian Studies*, 5 (1972), pp. 3-8.
7   Cœdès, *MSA*, p. 17.
8   Wilhelm G. Solheim II, "New Light on a Forgotten Past," *National Geographic*, March 1971, p. 337.
9   Cœdès, *MSA*, p. 18.
10 Goloubew, "L'âge du bronze," p. 36.
11 E. Patte, "L'Indochine prehistorique," *Revue anthropologique*, 46, Nos. 10-12 (1936), p. 303.
12 J. Fromaget and E. Saurin, eds., *Proceedings of the 3rd Congress on Prehistory of the Far East* (1938), p. 51.
13 Chester Gorman, "Excavations of Spirit Cave, North Thailand: some interim interpretations," *AP*, 13 (1970), p. 82.
14 The definition of Southeast Asia accepted by the Anthropology Division of the Pacific Science Congress in 1966 included the area from the Yangtze River in China to the tip of Malaya and from the South China Sea to the Irawaddy, together with Formosa and all the islands of the Philippines and Indonesia as far east as West Irian. See Wilhelm G. Solheim II, "Southeast Asia and the West," *Science*, 25 August 1967, p. 896.
15 Solheim, "Reflections on the New Data," p. 151.
16 Wilhelm G. Solheim II, "Reworking Southeast Asian Prehistory," *Paideuma*, 15 (1969), p. 133.
17 Isidore Dyen, *A Lexicostatistical Classification of the Austronesian Languages*, Memoir 19 of Indiana University Publications in Anthropology and Linguistics, Supplement to *International Journal of American Linguistics*, 31, No. 1 (1965), p. 83.
18 J. Innes Miller, *The Spice Trade of the Roman Empire* (Oxford: Oxford University Press, 1969), pp. 154-155, 171-172, 274-275. G. P. Murdock in *Africa: Its People and Their Culture History* (New York: McGraw-Hill, 1969) supports an even earlier date for contact: "Originally domesticated in Southeast Asia, the chicken was introduced into Egypt about 1450 B.C. and independently into East Africa about a thousand years later" (p. 104).

19   Andrew K. Pawley, "Austronesian Languages," *Encyclopedia Britannica: Macropaedia*, 15th ed. (1982), II, p. 488.
20   Murdock, p. 245.
21   J. D. Fage and R. A. Oliver, eds., *Papers in African Prehistory* (Cambridge: Cambridge University Press, 1970), p. 226.
22   Peter Bellwood, *The Polynesians: Prehistory of an Island People* (London: Thames and Hudson, 1978), p. 27.
23   Ma Duan-lin, *Ethographie des peuples étrangers a la Chine, ouvrage composé au XIII siècle de notre ère*, trans. Marquis d'Hervey de Saint-Denys (Geneva: Leroux, 1883), II, p. 424.
24   Cœdès, *MSA*, p. 15.
25   W. F. Sutterheim, *Indian Influence in Old Balinese Art* (London: The India Society, 1935), p. 2.
26   Cœdès, *MSA*, p. 15.
27   Guy Porée and E. Maspero, *Moeurs et coutumes des Khmers* (Paris: Payot, 1938), p. 147.
28   Christophe von Fürer-Haimendorf, "Megalithic Ritual among the Gadabas and Bondos of Orissa," *Journal of the Royal Asiatic Society of Bengal, Letters*, 9 (1943), p. 177.
29   Robert von Heine-Geldern, "Prehistoric Research in the Netherlands Indies," *Science and Scientists in the Netherlands Indies*, ed. Pieter Honig (New York: BNISC, 1945), p. 149.
30   H.G.Q. Wales, "The Pre-Indian Basis of Khmer Culture," *Journal of the Royal Asiatic Society*, Pts. 3-4 (1952), p. 118.
31   See M. Colani, "Emploi de la pierre en des temps reculés: Annam, Indonésie, Assam," *Bulletin des amis du vieux Hué* (1940). The entire volume focuses primarily on the Vietnamese structures.
32   H.G.Q. Wales, *The Making of Greater India* (London: Quaritch, 1961), p. 165.
33   "The Pre-Indian Basis of Khmer Culture," p. 120.
34   *Prehistory and Religion in South-East Asia* (London: Quaritch, 1957), p. 25. See also Claire Holt, "Dances of Sumatra and Nias: Notes by Claire Holt," *Indonesia*, 11 (April 1971), pp. 14-19.
35   See W. F. Stutterheim, "Some Remarks on Pre-Hinduistic Burial Customs on Java," in *Studies in Indonesian Archaeology* (The Hague: M. Nijhoff, 1956), pp. 74-90.
36   See "La destination funeraire des grands monuments Khmèrs," *BEFEO*, 40 (1940), pp. 315-344.
37   Nidhi Aeusrivongse, "*The Devarāja Cult and Khmer Kingship at Angkor*," *EESAH*, pp. 107-148.
38   Stutterheim, *Indian Influence*, p. 2.
39   Aeusrivongse, p. 122.
40   Aeusrivongse, p. 122.
41   In nineteenth-century Sumatra among the Batak, for instance, the presence of ancestral spirits was invoked with large "ancient" drums. The spirits were summoned by a shaman who was either second in importance to the tribal chief or was very often the chief himself. The ritual included the visit to a mountaintop by night to communicate with the ancestors, and gave to the chief control over the sun and rain (E. M. Loeb. *Sumatra: Its History and People* [Vienna: Institut fur völkerkunde der Universität Wien, 1935], pp. 82-83). See also S. A. Wilken (1893) as cited by Kenneth R. Hall, "State and Statecraft in Early Srivijaya,"*EESAH*, p. 84. It is thought that this practice derives from that of earlier Srivijayan monarchs whose ability to control agricultural prosperity was obtained by a boat journey over water (according to an inscription of A.D. 683) to gain *siddhayātra*, mythical supernatural power (K. R. Hall, pp. 64, 86, 89).
42   Aeusrivongse, p. 120. By contrast, in the Indian cosmology the "World of the Fathers" is never placed on a mountain top which "must therefore be a Khmer feature" of kingship (pp. 142-43, n. 46).
43   Aeusrivongse, p. 121.
44   Stutterheim, *Indian Influence*, p. 3.
45   Cœdès, *IC*, IV, pp. 167-69.
46   "L'Inde vu de l'est,"Cultes indiens et indigenes au Champa," *BEFEO*, 33, No. 1 (1933), pp. 367-410.

47 Lawrence Palmer Briggs, "The Ancient Khmer Empire," *Transactions of the American Philosophical Society*, 41, No. 1 (1951), p. 11. Sexual union with a tree spirit will be discussed in Chapter V.
48 Aeusrivongse, pp. 116-17.
49 Zhou Daguan, *Notes on the Customs of Cambodia*, trans. J. Gilman D'Arcy Paul (Bangkok: Social Science Association Press, 1967), p. 22 [translated from the French version by Paul Pelliot, "Memoires sur les coutumes du Cambodge de Tcheou Ta-kouan," *BEFEO*, 2 (1902), pp. 123-177]. This particular ritual was still performed in the twentieth century in Java. In 1920 Paul Mus visited in Solo a round tower in whose forbidden upper story a benevolent *nāgī* "goddess" had been visited periodically by the ruler's father "to guarantee the crops an abundant rainfall" ("Chronique," *BEFEO*, 28 [1928], p. 647).
50 Cœdès felt that Funan was also a transcription of the old Khmer word *bnam*, mountain, used in the king's title, *kurung bnam*, king of the mountain (*ISSA*, p. 36.).
51 James Legge, *Chinese Classics* (Oxford: Oxford University Press, 1893), III, Pt. 2, pp. 536-37.
52 Paul Pelliot, "Le Fou-nan," *BEFEO*, 3 (1903), p. 266; Cœdès, *ISSA*, pp. 40; 276, n.18.
53 O. W. Wolters, *Early Indonesian Commerce* (Ithaca: Cornell University Press, 1967), p. 4.
54 Pelliot, "Le Fou-nan," p. 303.
55 Pelliot, "Le Fou-nan," p. 254.
56 Wolters, *Early Indonesian Commerce*, p. 37.
57 Cœdès, *MSA*, p. 58. Of such voyages Kang Tai wrote that from the Southeast Asian island of Kanadvīpa, "boarding a great merchant junk joisting seven sails and with the favorable monsoon, in one month and some days one arrives in the [Eastern Mediterranean]." Cited by Paul Pelliot in "Quelque textes chinois concernant l'Indochine hindouisée," *Études asiatiques* (Paris, G. Van Oest, 1925), II, p. 252.
58 Pelliot. "Quelque textes." p. 253.
59 Pelliot. "Quelque textes," pp. 255-57. See also Wolters, *Early Indonesian Commerce*, p. 153 and Solheim, "Reflections," p. 157. That Southeast Asians manned large sailing vessels in this period is unsurprising. The spritsail, one of the two great classes of the world's sails originated in Southeast Asia as did the idea of two equal masts on a boat. The spritsail spread westward to Ceylon, Madagascar and Arabia through "Indonesian" migration, and the "ketch" rig became the "preferred mast arrangement" of the Arabs. See Richard Le Baron Bowen, "The Origin of Fore-and-Aft Rigs: Part I," *The American Neptune*, 19, 3 (July 1959), pp. 155-99 and "Part II," 19, 4 (October 1959), pp. 274-306.
60 Pelliot, "Quelque textes," pp. 257-60. Christie points out that *po* is not Chinese but rather the "transcription of a regional boat word." See A. H. Christie, "The Name K'un-lun as an Ethnic Term," *Proceedings of the Twenty-third International Congress of Orientalists* (Cambridge: Cambridge University Press, 1954), pp. 291-92.
61 Christie, "Provenance and Chronology," p. 4. This conclusion need not contradict the maritime evidence discussed earlier, since the Malayo-Polynesians seem to have skirted India, and in the early centuries A.D. most Indian trade with China was overland rather than through Southeast Asia. See Wolters, *Early Indonesian Commerce*, p. 33.
62 Christie, "Provenance and Chronology," pp. 2-3.
63 Pelliott, "Le Fou-nan," p. 269, citing the *Liang Shu*. Some feel Kaundinya was not the first Indian ruler of the area. An earlier king of Funan, Zhan Tan (or Chandan), who is known only by the recorded fact that in A.D. 357 he offered tame elephants to the Chinese emperor in tribute (they were refused), is considered by Pelliot ("Le Fou-nan," pp. 252-54, n. 4) and Sylvain Levi ("Kanishka et S'ātavahana." *JA* [January-March 1936], p. 82) as well as Cœdès (*ISSA*, pp. 46-

47) to have been Indian or Indo-Scythian. Their case rests solely on interpreting the Chinese transcription of Zhan Tan's antecedent title as the equivalent of a title used for Indian sovereigns. R. A. Stein thinks that Zhan Tan's origin in India is unlikely ("Le Lin-yi," *Hanhiue*, 2, pp. 257-58, n. 277), and Christie feels that "these speculations go further than any evidence at our disposal can possibly justify" ("Provenance and Chronology," p. 5). At any rate, Kaundinya was one of Zhan Tan's successors.

64 Louis Finot, "Les Inscriptions de Mi-son," *BEFEO*, 4 (1904), p. 923.
65 Cœdès, *IC*, IV, 95.
66 Briggs, *AKE*, p. 11. Legends of the Cambodian people themselves refer to the land as Kok *Thlok*, "land of the *thlok* tree," or Srok Khmer, "Country of the Khmers."
67 Cœdès, *ISSA*, p. 66. Briggs points out that "the term Kambu or any derivation of it does not occur in any inscription of the Chenla period" (*AKE*, p. 40). Not until after the ascension of Jayavarman II in 802 do the inscriptions use the term Kambuja or "descendants of Kambu" in reference to the earlier period (*AKE*, P. 11). In regard to the *apsaras* Merā, Cœdès suggests that "her name was perhaps invented to explain that of the Khmers" (*ISSA*, p. 66), but this seems unlikely; the Khmer kings appear to have observed matrilineal descent and Merā can be no less eponymous than Kambu.
68 Briggs, *AKE*, p. 39.
69 Cœdès, *ISSA*, p. 97.
70 Cœdès, "L'Inscription de Baksei Chamkron," *JA*, 23 (May-June, 1909), pp. 476-78 and *IC*, IV, 95. The basis for attributing either a lunar or a solar dynasty to Cambodia, however, is extremely problematic, as scrutiny of these two references will make clear.
71 Aeusrivongse, p. 130.
72 The nature of this ambivalence is examined by Aeusrivongse and by I. W. Mabbett, "Devarāja," *JSAH*, 10, No. 2 (1969), pp. 202-23.
73 Aeusrivongse, pp. 116-117.
74 Kenneth R. Hall, "An Introductory Essay on Southeast Asian Statecraft in the Classical Period," *EESAH*, p. 21, n. 21. Interestingly, the supreme deity of the "primitive" Samre people in Cambodia is Sdach Nung, "the king of the mountains," "whose realm is in the remote unexplored hinterland" (Wales, *Prehistory and Religion*, p. 45) which may express the indigenous belief in the fact that there was a "chief ancestor," with whom the king could also be identified ambiguously.
75 Aeusrivongse, pp. 132-34.
76 Auguste Barth, "Stele of Vat Phou," *BEFEO*, 2 (1902), pp. 234-40, st. 2.
77 "Temple de Loley," *IS*, pp. 319-31, st. 51.
78 Hall, "Introductory Essay," p. 8.
79 Aeusrivongse, p. 128.
80 *IC*, V, 14-16. K. refers to a standard number of all inscriptions found in Kampuchea. Sanskrit inscriptions appeared in Funan at a time "not much later" than those of India (D. G. E. Hall, *A History of South East Asia* [London: MacMillan, 1960]), p. 13. One of their eminent, early translators, Auguste Barth, praised the Zhenla period inscriptions as superior in finish, regularity and elegance to any found at any time in India (*IS*, p. 196).
81 J. Donald Lancaster, *Some Notes on the Classical Khmer Ballet* (Ithaca: Cornell University, 1971), *p. 9.*
82 Cœdès, *IC*, II, 23.
83 Bernard-Philippe Groslier, "Danse et musique sous les rois d'Angkor," in *Felicitation Volumes of Southeast Asian Studies*, (Bangkok: The Siam Society, 1965), II, p. 283.
84 Cœdès, *IC*, V, 18-19.
85 Cœdès, *IC*, V, 115-18.
86 Cœdès, *IC*, V, 64-68

87 Bernard Groslier, "Dance et musique," p. 284.
88 *IS*, p. 30.
89 *ISSA*, p. 255. He goes on to articulate the quintessential contradiction inherent in the India-centric view of Southeast Asian history: "We know of no monument in India resembling even remotely the Bayon of Angkor Thom or the Borobudur. And yet these monuments are pure productions of the Indian genius...."
90 See Henri Parmentier. *L'art khmer primitif* (Paris: G. Van Oest, 1927), Figs. 22 and 65, and Phillipe Stern, *L'Art du Champa et son évolution* (Paris: Musée Guimet, 1942), pl. 57-d.
91 *Khmer Sculpture and the Angkor Civilization*, trans. Diana Imber (New York: Harry N. Abrams, 1965), pp. 54-55.
92 See Cœdès' chapter on Jayavarman II in *Angkor: An Introduction*, trans. Emily Floyd Gardiner (Hong Kong: Oxford University Press, 1963), pp. 68-83.
93 Gilberte de Coral-Remusat, "Animaux fantastique de l'Indochine, de l'Insulinde et de la Chine," *BEFEO*, 36 (1936), pp. 427-35.
94 Samdach Chaufea Thiounn, *Danses cambodgiennes* (Phnom Penh: Institute Bouddhique, 1956), p. 26, and Chheng Phon, personal communication.
95 Cœdès, *Angkor: An Introduction*, p. 83.

Chapter III

ANGKOREAN DANCE: 802-1431
របាំសម័យអង្គរ: ៨០២-១៤៣១

The heart of Cambodia and the nucleus of its Angkor civilization, which flowered from the ninth to the fifteenth centuries, is one of the natural wonders of the planet: a river that changes direction twice a year. When the monsoon rains raise the level of the Mekong River to a sufficient height, the waters of its lesser tributary, the Tonle Sap River, are driven back upstream. Standing at the point where the two rivers meet, one can actually see the Tonle Sap hesitate and then reverse its flow upcountry, propelled by the Mekong flood. When the monsoon rains have ceased, the Mekong eventually recedes, and at a certain level, the Tonle Sap again turns and empties downstream. Today, at the point where the two rivers meet, stands the Royal Palace surrounded by the city of Phnom Penh as witness to this life-bringing "miracle."

Each year as the monsoon-flooded Tonle Sap pours northward, it empties into a vast natural reservoir known as the Great Lake—a food source so filled with fish that at lower water levels, the oars of boats are impeded. Like a channel of energy entering the womb, the river pours itself into the Great Lake, and near the northernmost shore, where the energy can expand no farther, the great city of Angkor was born.

The material remains of the Angkorean kingdom represent one of the greatest artistic achievements by a single culture in all history. At Angkor Thom "the Great Capital," according to one scholar, man

> wrought his dreams into magnificent stone temples and marvels of sculpture and decoration which nowhere else on earth has he ever been able to match—wonders which, for combined extent, magnitude and splendor, dwarf and reduce almost to commonplace, the much heralded wonders of Egypt and Greece and Rome.[1]

This art was the embodiment of spiritual symbols whose potency within the Cambodian mind was fundamental to political unity and to architectural construction, especially of the immense irrigation systems on which the kingdom's prosperity and expansion were based. Angkor was built as a *mandala*—a generative symbol in architectural form. Its purpose was to manifest—in harmony—the primary natural forces of earth and water and to be a point of contact with the spirit world which controlled their intercourse.

Whether the two great forces were expressed as female and male, earth and water, or dark and light, their interplay was conceived as a contest or battle expressible in dance, which was the embodiment of their rhythms. It is the thesis of the present work that Cambodian dance has always been a representation of the two natural forces or principles—the Feminine and the Masculine—in confrontation, and that, ritually, dance was a means of contacting the spirits who could influence the outcome of their interaction in any given situation. This chapter, investigating the nature and function of dance at Angkor, will examine, first, the cultural context of dance, the temple context, dance in the royal court, and finally, the appearance of the dance itself as pictured by Angkorean artists in bas-reliefs, free-standing sculpture, and in bronze.

ANGKOREAN COSMOLOGY

The distinguishing feature of Angkorean art—including dance—is its sense of balance, seen, first, in the harmonious correlation between the terrestrial and celestial planes of reality; second, in a generative balance between Feminine and Masculine; and third, in the syncretism of Indic forms with autochthonous content. Let us consider selected aspects of each in an interrelated manner.

Of the religious system indigenous to Southeast Asia generally, Geoffrey Benjamin has written that

> the animistic worldview posits the division of the cosmos into two dialectically conjoined planes of existence: the plane of things, matter, categories; and the plane of essence, spirit, soul. Entities on the two planes are readily conceivable as independent autonomous manifestations; but the normal 'resting' state of the cosmos is one in which for each entity on the plane of matter there is an equivalent entity on the plane of essence, and vice versa, in a one-to-one relationship.[2]

The implications of this belief or experience are seminal to all Khmer principles of creative and religious expression because in order to maintain a harmony between the two planes, Southeast Asians constructed temples, palaces, capitals, and even kingdoms as microcosms which duplicated the structure of the macrocosm.[3] In this way an intimate relationship also obtained between earthly dancers and their celestial counterparts. We do not know what the Khmers called those celestial dancers, but today we refer to their myriad images on the temple walls of Angkor by the Sanskrit term *apsaras*. It is therefore important to understand the general nature of the temples both as the context of dance and as an image of the cosmos whose rhythms the *apsaras* embodied.

Angkorean temples were built in harmony with the earth whose energies were therein concentrated. Bernard Groslier has expressed this point well:

> Like the embankment of the rice-field fitting closely to the contours of the land, or the village strung along the river bank, the temple outlined against the horizon crouches on the soil from which it derives its magic power.... Its sole *raison d'être* is to reproduce the sacred mountain, handiwork of the gods themselves. It is a magic diagram traced on the parchment of the plain, visible only from above, decipherable in fact only by the immortal gods, for whom indeed it was built.[4]

This principle (Fig. 3-1) was further empowered by a union of symbolic forces within architectural elements of the temples themselves. The causeway leading to the gates of Angkor Thom, for instance, has a balustrade of destructive *asura* (demons) on the right and one of protective *deva* (gods) on the left, permanently in balance. The most powerful symbols at Angkor, however, are those reflecting a harmony of earth and water.

Technologically speaking, Angkor is a vast system of hydraulics designed to break the seasonal cycle of eight months of drought followed by four months of monsoon. Angkor was designed to "create" water by the use of reservoirs and irrigation. At the center of the system was the temple mountain empowered by the *devarāja*, through which contact was made with the spirit world. What was required of the spirits—ancestral or otherwise—was assistance in obtaining water, and a primary element in the rites of communication was dance.

3-1. **Temple as *Mandala*, Angkor Wat.**
Photo adapted from satellite image.
Kent Davis.

Traditionally, our understanding of this phenomenon has been couched in Sanskritized terms: Indra's heaven included thousands of dancers and, consequently, the earthly king should be similarly attended.[5] This was the Khmer belief in part, but few have noted that dance at Angkor included male dancers in the temple context as well. The balance of male and female in ritual dance was consonant with the essential nature of the Angkorean cosmology, since even the temples themselves were considered to be either feminine or masculine. The names of temple mountains "representing the earth" often began with *ba* or "father," while names of temples "consecrated to the worship of the waters" began with *me* or "mother."[6]

In Chapter IX we will examine the ritual function of contemporary Khmer dance as a means of communication with the spirit world, especially to bring rain. Before surveying in this chapter the possible evidence of the same function at Angkor—whether performed by female or male dancers—let us briefly consider one further level on which Angkor maintained a dichotomous unity of balanced forces, namely in the syncretism informing its religious practices.

Religious Syncretism

Angkorean temples were built to house spirits whose ancestral and territorial nature combined with the Indic forms of Shiva, Vishnu, the Buddha, and others. The process whereby these anthropomorphic male forms came to be the embodiment of local Cambodian spirits parallels a simultaneous process in India in which Shivaism and Vishnuism were "born in the fourth to ninth centuries from the union of the vague aerial deities of Aryan Brahmanism and local Dravidian deities."[7] Several aspects of the Cambodian syncretism deserve attention in order to better understand the nature of the Angkorean *apsaras*.

In Khmer sculpture, which here means free-standing stone and bronze sculpture, the finest works are from the pre-Angkorean period. Statues of male divinities represent a unique synthesis. The prevailing anthropomorphic form worshipped during the Zhenla period was Harihara, represented by a male, four-armed figure divided exactly down the middle of the head and torso. The left half was Vishnu, the right was Shiva. This seventh- and eighth-century form is unique to Cambodia—it appears nowhere else in Southeast Asia or India—and starkly exemplifies Angkorean conventions regarding duality. The prototypical female form, seen at its most powerful in the seventh century (Fig. 2-2), owes nothing (as previously noted) to Indian influence[8] and represents a pure Khmer image of the Feminine principle. Four-armed "goddesses" were only later identified in part with Indic forms.[9]

In Khmer iconography there is also a syncretic union between the Khmer spirit of the earth—usually pictured as the *nāga* serpent—and the forms of Shiva, Vishnu, and Buddha alike. While Shiva was usually associated with the *lingam*, he can be seen dancing, accompanied by cymbal-playing musicians and with two *nāga* twined about his shoulders.[10] The four-armed Vishnu—far more closely associated with dance in Cambodia—was frequently pictured reclining on a seven-headed *nāga* accompanied by *apsaras* (Figs. 3-2, 3-3, 3-4). Among the Indic forms, however, the *nāga* was most clearly associated with the Buddha.

Left:
3-2. Vishnu Reclining Under *Nāga*.
Tuol Basset lintel. *Nokor Khmer*.
Photo attributed to Hans Hinz.

Below:
3-3. The Sleep of Vishnu, Preah Khan.
This Bayon *nāga* appears in a dragon-like form called a *reachisey*.
Photo Michael Greenhalgh.

3-4. **Vishnu Reclining on *Reachisey* With Nāga.** In this image, the *reachisey* and *nāga* appear together. Photo John Gollings.

There is a legend that after the Buddha attained enlightenment, the *nāga* king Mucilinda, who lived beneath the bodhi tree, spread his hood over the Buddha's head to shield him from the storms sent by Māra (Death) as a distraction. This image became the one most associated with the Angkor king in the twelfth century. Sculptors pictured the Buddha—ambiguously identified with the king—seated in deep meditation on the coils of a great *nāga* whose five heads (or seven or nine) arched behind his own. The *nāga* symbolized, among other things, the earth and water on which the kingdom rested.[11]

A related image, closer to that of the dancer—and relevant to our later discussion of hairstyles—is the spirit of the earth in the form of Neang Thorani (Fig. 3-5). When the Buddha had overcome the daughters of Māra he called upon the Earth herself to witness his steadfastness. Angkorean sculptors pictured her in bronze, kneeling and nude, wringing water from her snake-like plait of hair. In Cambodian iconography this water vanquished other Māra-sent demons,[12] who probably represented within the popular mind, the forces of drought or general destructiveness.

3-5. **Spirit of the Earth Witnessing for the Buddha.** National Museum of Phnom Penh. Photo Hanz Hinz.

3-6. **Mahāyāna Buddhist Hevajra.** Banteay Kdei, Siem Reap. Late 11th C. Hevajra is the most important deity in Tantric Buddhism. National Museum of Phnom Penh. Photo John Gollings.

In Buddhist iconography Avalokitesvara—often called Lokesvara, Lord of the World—was the most popular Buddhist form from pre-Angkorean times until the beginning of the thirteenth century.[13] Lokesvara had four or eight arms; another Mahāyanā figure, Hevajra—represented dancing on a demon (Fig. 3-6)—had eight heads and sixteen arms; and the female Prajñāpāramitā had eleven faces and twenty-two arms.

All of these multi-armed deities represent a synthesis of Indic forms with much older indigenous forms described in the third century by the Chinese emissary Kang Tai. About A.D. 250 he wrote that in Funan

> their custom is to worship the sky spirits. They make bronze images of these sky spirits; those that have two faces have four arms, and those that have four faces have eight arms. Each hand holds something—sometimes a child, sometimes a bird or a four-legged animal, or else the sun or the moon.[14]

None of these bronze images has been found. We have only their latter-day forms, which clearly exemplify—to the extent that Sanskrit names attributed to them actually reflect Angkorean usage—the Khmer pattern of religious syncretism.

The reasons for the Southeast

Asian adoption of Indic forms are not totally clear, but more than likely increasingly centralized governments needed increasingly powerful masculine religious forms with which to identify the king, thereby lending universal authority to his central role in the ancient fecundity cult and as chief contact with the ancestral spirit world. Simultaneously, local spirits, while still revered, were also identified with the Indic deities; "their names and, to a large extent their forms were transformed in the process of Sanskritization."[15] Significant examples of the original pattern, however, may be discerned.

A belief current in rural twentieth-century Cambodia was that certain female spirits inhabited large trees and that ten of these, known as *priay* guarded every statue of the Buddha. It was, in fact, to the *priay* that "Buddhist" offerings were made.[16] The identity between offerings to tree spirits and those made to the Buddha represents not only a syncretism of autochthonous and Indic religious beliefs, but also a union of the Feminine principle with the nature-controlling Masculine principle in the form of the ascetic. That union was fundamental to Angkorean notions of cosmology, architecture, agriculture, religion and art.

All evidence suggests that to the Angkorean mind it was the interaction of earth and sky, matter and spirit, female and male, rice and rain—in short, the union of the Feminine and Masculine—which engendered all fertility, spiritual fulfillment, and life itself. A Khmer myth, to be considered next, suggests that dance issues from the earth and is identified with the Feminine.

In Angkorean iconography the dancers are female and appear, in general, either in conjunction with large female figures, in long wavelike lines, or in association with scenes showing an interaction of the two primary principles. Like the energy of life itself, however, dance appears only through the interaction of the Feminine and the Masculine; thus in the actual temples, male dancers were required. Clearly, the most symbolically potent male dancer would have been the king, and we know that a number of Angkorean kings did dance, thus representing an informal enactment—if not a ritual act—central to the symbology of Angkorean religious belief.

THE MYTH OF THE ORIGIN OF DANCE

While there are several Indian myths attributed to Cambodia regarding the origin of dance,[17] the Khmer myth, at least at Angkor, has come to be known as "The Churning of the Sea of Milk." This Indian title is misleading, however, since in Cambodia the myth clearly focuses on the *nāga*, the embodiment of the spirit of the waters, which "haunts the whole of Khmer art, from the endlessly repeated theme of the churning of the Sea of Milk down to the most insignificant architectural element which will accommodate it."[18] The grandest treatment of the myth appears in reliefs on the southern half of Angkor Wat's east gallery (Fig. 3-7).[19]

At the bottom of the panel "the mythical ocean, symbol of the uncreated, is represented by the fish and marine creatures and, in particular, by the great body of the serpent . . . , god of the waters"[20] stretching the entire forty-nine yards of the bas-relief.

Above this, the *nāga* appears a second time—a convention suggesting a later action[21] —and is supported by two contending rows of figures. The third scene in the sequence appears above this contest in the form of hundreds of flying, dancing *apsaras*.

This scene is generally referred to as the "Churning of the Sea of Milk" because of similarities to an event related in the Indian *Bhagavata Purana*. That interpretation, however, ignores significant differences between the Khmer and the Indian myths. What follows is an original alternative analysis based on what is actually portrayed in the bas reliefs.

The sea depicted here is not one of milk containing the twelve precious objects of the Indian myth, but is very much a Khmer sea filled with the fish that represented Angkor's food and livelihood. In the Indian myth the serpent is wound around the upturned Mt. Mandara which is used as a churn, with demons pulling on the serpent's head and gods on the tail. In the Khmer myth the churning is certainly the main action—as seen by the turbulence among the fish, but in no way do the two contending forces show hostility. They are both moving to the left in unison and look more complementary than conflicting. The focus of this contest is not the two

3-7. **The *Nāga*-Churning of the Sea at Angkor Wat.** Photo Jaro Poncar.

groups doing the churning but, rather, the serpent and the central figure appearing in place of the churn.

Centrally seated—and very calmly—on a huge throne is a four-armed human figure facing left. While the throne rests on a tortoise as in the Indian myth, here there is no sign of the mountain; this central figure represents both the king and the mountain, which, by convention, he symbolized. In addition, the throne recalls the widespread use of large stone seats—probably representing the chief—which were associated with the ancient megalithic complex.[22]

The fundamental action of the myth, then, is the union of the king with the waters—activated by the two forces. Angkorean court poets compared this churning to "a great battle from which the king extracted good fortune and victory."[23] The conflict is not merely between *deva* and *asura* in the Indian sense,[24] but rather represents duality in general, as in the Harihara, or left and right, moon and sun, Feminine and Masculine. Clearly, both sides are necessary and equal. Their action is marked by symmetry and balance; they work together and symbolize the creative action of the central figure upon the waters.

In support of this Khmer-centric interpretation of the myth, we note that Bernard Groslier views the central action of the tableau as "the king, identified with Vishnu, in the act of churning the ocean of fortune in order to procure ambrosia, that is to say the welfare of his subjects."[25] That welfare is presented by a single image, the *apsaras* who issue forth on both sides of the king, dancing blithely sideways, facing front (Fig. 3-8). In clear contrast with the Indian myth, no further precious objects are forthcoming.

While the *nāga*—as the implement of this creation—represents the spirit of the waters, in universal mythology we experience "the serpent almost everywhere symbolizing what is latent, preformal, undifferentiated."[26] What the bas-relief appears to present then, is the manner in which this potential—the serpent power—is transformed by the dualistic forces which the king controls, into its highest realization. Keeping in mind that the land and waters of the kingdom were identified with a female serpent (see Chapter V), we should note that the king's function was expressed in a metaphor frequently appearing in Angkorean stone inscriptions: "The earth in intimate union with the passionate vital principle of this king brought forth untold riches."[27] Those riches, the highest achievement of the union of Feminine with Masculine, the rhythm of the dualistic churning of the universe at the king's left hand and right hand, the transformation of potential into its perfect fulfillment: all this is symbolized by the *apsaras*, the celestial dancer.[28]

George Cœdès has pointed out that bridges leading to the gates of several Khmer cities including Angkor Thom had *nāga* balustrades and that the city gates at each of the cardinal points reproduced the central temple in miniature. These gates "represent the extension and projection of the royal power emanating from the temple."[29] The entire design also recalls the churning of the great sea, since the moat of the city represents the ocean, the gate tower represents the mountain or king, and the *nāga* in the balustrade supported by "gods and giants" represents the cosmic serpent. The myth in question, then, was seminal to all Angkorean architecture and was the articulation of Khmer cosmology. It is no wonder that, as we shall see, there were thousands of dancers at Angkor. On the material plane,

3-8. **Details of *Apsaras* from the Churning of the Sea.** Photo Michael Greenhalgh.

they embodied all that the *apsaras* represented on the spiritual plane, and both revealed the form of the Feminine in its most perfect flowering.

Three brief excerpts from Sanskrit inscriptions associated with Angkor will suggest, finally, the reverence of the Khmers for the Feminine. Each is applicable to the dancer.

> Like the blessing of Spring on the garden, like the day of the fullness of the Moon, so has she risen, ravishing and splendid, in the loveliness of her fresh youth.
>
> Like the swarm of bees flying to the Pārijātā, like the souls of the Sages aspiring to the meditation of the *ātman*, so do the eyes of men lay aside all activity and direct themselves towards her alone.
>
> The thirst of the poor was quenched when they rejoiced to behold her like a great and peaceful lake covered with lotus flowers in full bloom.[30]

Temple Dance

For our purposes the distinction between "temple" and "court" at Angkor may amount to little more than the location of the king's residence. In terms of the king's function, the two were undoubtedly closely related, and activities in both were highly ritualized around the king. The importance of ceremony cannot be underestimated. As Hall has pointed out,

> royal ceremony generated the king's powers. The royal court, its activities and its style recreated a world of the gods—in theory, a heaven on earth. ...By successfully fulfilling his role as the hypothetical focus of all sanctity and power, the king maintained the orderliness of the world.[31]

Our inquiry turns now to a consideration of the evidence that dance was a significant aspect of royal ceremony. The evidence has been gleaned from the epigraphy in both Sanskrit and Khmer.[32]

When the Angkorean king or a high official founded a *lingam* to house the spirit of a deceased ancestor, dancers were installed in the conjoining temple. At Preah Ko, for instance, Yasovarman I (889-c.910) offered

> a great number of beautiful dancers, singers, reciters, musicians, players of *vina* and other instruments [all women], skillful at beating the clappers [and] a great number of handsome, mature men skillful in dance and the other arts, well dressed and adorned with ornament.[33]

As offerings, the dancers had to be physically perfect. When Yasovarman dedicated the temple of Loley (A.D. 893) to the worship of his ancestors, he also consecrated "men and beautiful women without blemish, skillful in song and dance."[34]

Yasovarman was more personally involved with dance, as we shall see, than any other king of whom we have knowledge. A prince, who was probably his son, Mahidharavarman, maintained the family custom, and in dedicating the temple of Prasat Kravan in 921, installed at least eleven female dancers, five male dancers, eighteen female singers, four female percussionists, and nine female players of stringed instruments, as well as male musicians, chanters, and a "singer of praise."[35]

Whether this was an average number for a temple in this period is not known. We do know that throughout Angkor's history, the numbers increased. The famous eleventh century inscription of Sdok Kak Thom lists at great length the gifts given to a temple by Sadāsiva, who was, for a time, the *purohita* or chief priest of the *devarāja* under Suryavarman I

(1011-1050). Sadāsiva was himself a skilled musician and donated to the temple "a hundred beautiful women beautifully adorned" accompanied by the "wonderful sound" of a hundred female musicians playing flute and stringed instruments, as well as fifty musicians with copper cymbals, drums and other percussion instruments.[36]

By the end of the twelfth century in the reign of Angkor's greatest king, Jayavarman VII (1181-c.1215), the numbers of temple dancers were at the zenith. In 1186 he dedicated the temple of Ta Prohm to the spirit of his deceased mother. This temple owned 3,140 villages and was served by 79,365 men and women, including 18 great priests, 2,740 officiants, and 2,232 temple assistants "among whom 615 women were dancers." We know that male dancers were also maintained because of a later reference in the same inscription to the fact that "all around here the men and women dancers dance."[37]

Five years later, in 1191, Jayavarman dedicated the Preah Khan temple to similarly honor his father. Furnishings were provided both by the king and by the 5,324 villages, including 97,840 taxpayers, who maintained the temple. At Preah Khan there were one thousand dancers. A total of 1,622 dancers were installed by Jayavarman in other temples throughout the kingdom in addition to those at Preah Khan and Ta Prohm.[38] Several aspects of the manner in which this vast number of dancers lived can be inferred from other inscriptions.

We have already pointed out that the dancers were both male and female; presumably they danced together or were at least associated. One inscription dated 1116 reports that Divākarapandita, the chief priest of Suryavarman II (1113-c.1150) who built Angkor Wat, installed in the temples at Wat Phu, Preah Vihear, and Phnom Sandak "male dancers, singers, clowns [and] musicians."[39] Female dancers are not mentioned, showing that both female and male dancers were not always presented to a temple at one time, which—like several other inscriptions—may even suggest that female dancers were not in residence. Nonetheless, the general picture of Angkorean temple dance is one in which both female and male dancers—with women in the majority—were accompanied by both female and male musicians and chanters.

Virtually all of the dancers, together with other temple servants, are referred to in the inscriptions as "slaves." Some mention that they were "bought" and give the price, which would indicate that they were bound to the temple.[40] One Buddhist inscription from Phnom Banteay Neang, dated 982, ends with this threat:

> Those who, having no other desire than to squander their own wealth, plunder the fields, the golden ornaments and precious stones and all that the founder has given to the farmers, to the dancers and the musicians, will see terrible punishment in hell.[41]

The fact that the dancers' possessions were thus protected, the fact that the inscriptions nearly always list the dancers by name, and the fact that their names are given in Sanskrit all lead us to believe that the status of "sacred slaves" was relatively high.

At the same time their maintenance and responsibilities were clearly set forth. A badly damaged inscription dated 1025 regarding the Preah Theat temple, which had a total of twenty-nine slaves, stipulated that

> two rice fields to the southeast of Travan Ulloka are reserved for...; to the west of this body of water, for the two cooks; to the north of this body of water, for the two paper makers; to the east of this body of water, for the... musicians; to the south... of this body of water and the *jranyan* tree, for the two [male] dancers and singers.[42]

From the much larger temple of Prasat Khna, an inscription dated 980 informs us that

> reciters, players of stringed and percussion instruments, male dancers and singers, cooks, makers of paper [and] carriers of water for the bath take service once a day; players of stringed instruments and players of drums take service three times a day. They do not have to be engaged in other transactions such as payment of castor oil plants, or outside of those things instituted for the offering of tax to the temple, so that they acquit themselves of their task with zeal during each half month.[43]

It appears that—as another inscription to be considered later (K.831) will verify—dancers and other temple personnel were in active service for half a month at a time, with music performed at least three times daily or even, as we shall see, "without cease."

It is important to note that Sanskrit terms in the inscriptions regarding dance are all forms of the root, *nrt*, "to dance" or "to mime." Derivative terms include *nartaka*, "dancer" as well as "singer" (K.713); *nritta*, "dance" or "mime" (K.283); *nrityagita*, "dance" or "pantomime" (K.872); *nritakārya*, "the one consecrated to the dance" (K.872); and *nartayitrī*, "master of the dance" (K.686). Significantly, there is no linguistic distinction made between temple and court dancer—a distinction asserted by those who would ascribe to the sacred dancers of Angkor a sexual function in the temples, akin to that of the ancient Indian *devādāsī*.[44] As Bernard Groslier concluded, "we cannot permit ourselves to infer that this . . . type of dancer existed in Angkorean Cambodia."[45]

There is some evidence to suggest that temple dance was a celebration—perhaps even the central rite—of the *nāga* cult. The inscription of Preah Khan mentions "the two Lords of the dance, made of gold, placed by the king before the Serpent."[46] As Jayavarman VII was a Buddhist, the golden statues were probably not of Shiva, although he was known in a dancing, five-headed, ten-armed form.[47] Even if they were of Lokesvara or Vishnu—or any pair among the three—the focus of the installation was clearly on the *nāga*. Cœdès suggests that this inscription refers to the nightly "rites of union of the king with the *nāgī* ancestors"[48] in the golden tower, as recounted by the Chinese envoy Zhou Daguan in 1297.[49]

If we are correct in assuming that temple dancers were associated with "the Lords of the Dance," then in Jayavarman's ancestral temple—and possibly as the common practice—the hundreds of dancers were integral to Angkorean rites honoring the *nāga* earth spirit. Our clearest evidence of this is the simple phrase occurring in the inscriptions: "slave for the sacred dance."[50] Thus, the earth and its energies were considered sacred at Angkor, and dance was a rite of worship.

Court Dance

Since they were of wood construction, the private quarters of the royal Angkorean household—as well as all trace of housing for an estimated twelfth-century population of seven to eight hundred thousand in the Angkor region[51]—have disappeared. To judge from the number of wives, concubines, dancers, and other women who surrounded the king (even the guards were female), the royal household must have been very large. Bernard Groslier felt that it would have included a huge dancing-hall where the dancers performed for the entertainment of the king, the five queens, and other court women.[52] Several more specific facets of court dance are documented by inscriptions.

The section of a badly damaged tenth-century inscription which traces the genealogy of Rajendravarman II (944-968), refers to a virtuous woman who "devoted herself to domestic cares regarding her husband." The next line says that she "had many charming female slaves dance."[53] While there is some ambiguity, it would appear that the dancers constituted a part of the woman's marital ministrations, and that dancers were maintained in the households of great families just as in the royal court.

Whether in the temple or court, we know that some dancers who were not slaves held high status and were very wealthy. An inscription dated 968 says that the priests of King Jayavarman V, while taking an inventory of temple goods in the village of Lingapura, issued a royal order to a dancer named Vap Anandana to report "the number of villages, rice fields, land revenues, slaves and all the goods which Vap Myan, dancer, and [another] Vap Myan, singer, had given to the temple" under the previous king. The inscription ends by stipulating that "the people of Vap Myan, dancer, [will serve] for the fifteen days of the waxing moon."[54] The inscription clearly shows not only that dancers and singers—in this case both male—could hold or amass sufficient wealth to make their own donations of slaves and other offerings to a temple, but also that those offerings, as Bernard Groslier has pointed out, were sumptuous enough for the King of Angkor himself to see to it that their wishes were carried out by appointing inspectors for that purpose.[55]

Public dance performance at Angkor was not limited only to those for whom it constituted a social role or livelihood. Training in all the arts including dance was part of a royal education, and skill was highly regarded. An interesting Buddhist inscription recovered at Beng Vieng temple near Siem Reap reflects a brief image of court life in the second half of the tenth century. The ancestors of the temple's founder included two beautiful women:

> ...the eldest was named Mādhavī, and her sister Kuntī. The daughter of Mādhavī became the wife of the fortunate [King] Rājendravarman; her elder brother the heavenly Vāsudeva was skilled in the art of dance. He who made the Law prosper built this tiered tower for the Muni.... Kuntī, named Kumāra, skillful in the art of dance, was made the head of the family. Here, to Jina [were presented] without cease, music, dances and songs.[56]

This mention of the two royal cousins' skill at dance, as the primary quality being memorialized, has the sound of a magical accolade—an authentication of superiority to be mentioned even before the founding of the temple. For reasons that have been suggested throughout this chapter, skill in dance was clearly one of the most prestigious qualities in the panegyrist's lexicon. Nowhere is this more obvious than in the inscriptions which concern King Yasovarman.

One splendid paean to Yasovarman states that

> the women of the Masters of the Earth danced in his presence taking from him the rhythm which he gave them by clapping his hands.... As for his glory, it danced without having learned, to the sound of the songs which were heard from the wives of warriors vanquished by him....[57]

Not only did he keep the time, he also danced himself: "he was learned in all the scriptures, in the use of all weapons, in all fine arts, languages and scripts and in dancing and singing as if he were the creator [of them]."[58] Even allowing for the hyperbole in that statement, at Angkor skill in dance was clearly commendable in kings.

The most important inscription yet found at Angkor regarding dance, however, does not concern the king, but rather dance drama in the court. Inherently, dance differs from dance drama in that for the latter, the dancer must assume a role in a narrative. While there is no graphic evidence in the iconography to show that dance drama existed at Angkor, one inscription clearly informs us that role playing did occur and that the performance, in this case, had a literary foundation in the *jātaka*.⁵⁹

In 1916 a large stele was found at the base of the Phimeanakas mountain-temple at Angkor Thom. The inscription, broken in seventy pieces but repaired, tells how, in the absence of Jayavarman VII on a campaign against Champa, his young wife Jayarājadevi wept like Sitā for her departed husband, offered prayers for his return, and finally found solace in Buddhist practices. As a vow,

> having realized the benefits of Buddhism, she charged her own dancers to perform and to give representations drawn from the Jātakas. . . . Having taken, as her own daughters, a miserable troupe of a hundred young women abandoned by their mothers, she increased the renown of a village named Dharmakirti for its virtue, happiness and prosperity.⁶⁰

While we do not know if the hundred orphans constituted the dance troupe which performed the *jātaka* stories, this single, highly reliable source clearly demonstrates the existence of dramatic performances by court dancers in twelfth-century Angkor.

THE *DEVATĀ*

We turn now to an examination of Angkorean iconography which yields a number of relevant details regarding dance, as well as offering a possible image of the dancers' appearance. As preface, a distinction must be noted between the two feminine forms appearing in the bas-reliefs: the *devatā* or large standing figures, and the more numerous but smaller *apsaras*—the dancers proper—always depicted in a dance position. Most writers use the terms indiscriminately or refer to all the figures as *apsaras*, but Philippe Stern, whose study of various architectural motifs including the *devatā* established the presently-accepted chronology of Angkor's monuments,⁶¹ always refers to the immobile forms as *devatā* and the dancing forms as *apsaras*.⁶² Visually, the distinction is easily made, and while the two forms are often associated (Fig. 3-9), their relationship is not altogether clear.

Use of the Sanskrit term *devatā* in reference to the large feminine iconographic forms—as Philippe Stern has pointed out—is "only a convenient designation masking our ignorance."⁶³ That the figures were known by the Angkoreans as *devatā*, or the derivative *tevoda*, is totally speculative.

Today the term *tevoda* is used over a fairly broad area of mainland Southeast Asia in reference to a "relatively undifferentiated category of divine benevolent agents."⁶⁴ In Cambodia they are understood to be very beautiful spirits dwelling in the heavens, who live millions of years, can transform themselves at will, and whose fundamental opposition to evil spirits makes them of great value in placating or exorcizing any malevolence on the part of the ancestral or earth spirits, the *neak ta*.⁶⁵ Offerings to the *tevoda* are particularly made to end droughts,⁶⁶ and dance is clearly associated with them.

3-9. ***Devatā*** with ***Apsaras*** from the Bayon.
Photo Michael Greenhalgh.

In the ceremony of initiation for young dancers, which we will examine in Chapter IX, offerings are made to the *tevoda* on small altars at the eight cardinal points,⁶⁷ and dancers performing the roles of *tevoda* in the *robam* dances fix their concentration on the nature of these celestial beings. Whether or not the large feminine figures in Angkorean bas-reliefs correspond to the contemporary belief in *tevoda* remains uncertain, but in both instances the *devatā* are clearly essential to the dancers' *raison d'être*.

THE *APSARAS* PRIOR TO ANGKOR WAT

Like twelfth-century Angkor Wat, the temples of the eighth and ninth centuries generally faced west,[68] the direction identified with death and the ancestral world. We also know that Jayavarman II in the early ninth century was considered master of the feminine earth.[69] That his temples included large *devatā* figures as a motif[70] may have been related to both of these ideas. Unfortunately, we have no corroborative iconographic evidence of celestial dancers in conjunction with the *devatā* at this early period. The iconography of the late ninth century and beyond, however, together with the epigraphical evidence already considered, suggests that the *apsaras*—as well as the earthly dancer—represents the transcendent energy of the *devatā* achieved through interaction with the Masculine in the form of the *lingam*, the king, or the temple itself.

3-10. **Ninth-Century Flying Figure.**
Many early flying figures, like this one from Bakheng, probably depict *gandharvas*, heavenly singers and musicians who lived in heaven, rather than *apsaras*. Photo Vittorio Roveda.

The earliest recognizable *apsaras*—a Sanskrit term which disguises the fact that we do not know the Angkorean name for the myriad dancing figures—date from the last half of the ninth century. For instance on bas-reliefs of the Bakheng (Fig. 3-10) wear a long waist-scarf accentuates the roundness of the figure which appears to be rising.

Wearing a similar if less exaggerated garment is another early representation of a dancer, possibly celestial in nature, from Preah Ko (Fig. 3-11). While this form of dancer appears masculine, its solidity and strength yield to delicacy in later periods. The dual images of apparently earthly dancers

3-11. **Ninth-Century Dancer.** This Preah Ko figure may also depict a *gandharva*. Photo Michael Greenhalgh.

3-12. **Flying Figure in the Bayon – 13th C.** Descending with flower garland. Photo Michael Greenhalgh.

as well as more stylized celestial forms (Fig. 3-12), occur throughout the Angkorean period. The emphasis is clearly on the latter form, and not until the thirteenth-century Bayon style are we presented unequivocally with an image of the human dancer in a mundane context (Fig. 3-13).

The age-old ancestor cult was well-maintained in the ninth and tenth centuries and with it the emphasis on the *devatā*. King Yasovarman built temples facing west on virtually every hill in the vicinity of his capital.[71] He built the great sanctuary of Lolei "consecrated to the memory of his parents deified in the forms of Siva and Uma."[72] Throughout the ninth century, the *nāga* was not used as a sculptural motif;[73] rather, it is the *devatā* that appears to represent the Feminine or earth energy. In the Bakheng temple, for instance, founded by Yasovarman in 893, large *devatā* with *apsaras* flying overhead are the primary image,[74] and the use of such figures increases throughout the ninth century.

In the wonderful tenth century bas-reliefs of the Banteay Srei temple (A.D. 967), we can see representations of both the flying *apsaras* as well as a fairly realistic standing dancer. The latter (Fig. 3-14) is not

3-13. **Bayon Dancer.** Photo Michael Greenhalgh.

3-14. **Banteay Srei Dancer and Musicians.** Photo Vittorio Roveda.

associated with *devatā* and appears to represent the temple or court dancer. Flanked by two players of cymbals—known today as *chhing* (jhina)—she nonetheless dances on a lotus which gives the image hieratic connotation. The treatment of the skirt, which is long and covers the deeply bent and wide-spread knees, does not appear in subsequent periods.

In the same temple, flying apsaras facing each other hover in one bas-relief over a scene from an Indian myth concerning an *apsaras* named Tilottama (Fig. 3-15). Generally, in Khmer iconography *apsaras* are seen in pairs or in rhythmic, wave-like

3-15. *The Apsaras* **Tilottama.** Photo John Gollings.

groupings, but here a single *apsaras* is the central figure in a drama staged by the gods. Wishing to destroy the two *asura* brothers Sunda and Upasunda, they sent the *apsaras* down to earth where the brothers killed each other fighting over her.[75] The *apsaras* who hover over the scene do not wear the long skirt usually seen on the female figures but rather a *sampot* with three long, stylized scarves trailing from the waist. Solidly built, they project a masculine quality.

The subject of male dancers in the iconography presents a problem. Some writers have asserted that in all the temples of Angkor, there are no male dancers depicted,[76] but certain figures are of ambiguous gender, as we have noted, and the epigraphy has made it clear that male dancers existed. While they were possibly not an appropriate subject for Angkorean temple walls, the same was not true in the sculptural art of Champa to the east. The bas-reliefs of the Baphuon style also include some dancers with more masculine features.

3-16. **Dancers in the Style of the Baphuon.** Boisselier, *La statuaire khmère*, pl. 61.

In his study of Khmer statuary, Jean Boisselier has noted that "previous to the style of the Baphuon, all the dancing figures wear the same long skirt as the other feminine images; the *sampot* appears only in this period."[77] This change can be clearly seen in an eleventh-century Baphuon bas-relief (Fig. 3-16) which includes both flying figures (detail upper right) as well as figures dancing on the earth. The resemblance of the standing dancers to the seated ascetic may suggest that the dancers are male; we cannot be sure. If Boisselier is correct, however, in saying that feminine dancing figures prior to the mid-eleventh century Baphuon style wore long skirts (Fig. 3-17), then the tenth-century flying figures in *sampot* at Banteay Srei above the *devatā* may very well be male as well (Fig. 3-18). The point is ultimately of small significance except to understand the sculptural convention. In regard to the Baphuon bas-relief, this matter is certainly subordinate to the fact that dancing and flying *apsaras* are associated with the meditation energy of the central figure, who has a tree or plant bursting forth immediately above his head—an identification that is rarely seen in the iconography. Overall, male dancers in the iconography are extremely rare, and their appearance seems limited to realistic scenes of Angkorean life.

The appearance of dancing figures in the bas reliefs prior to Angkor Wat, then, took basically two forms: first, the flying *apsaras*, usually in pairs hovering over a scene or *devatā* wearing *sampot*, and often masculine in appearance (Figs. 3-10, 3-12, 3-15, 3-18); and second, the earth-bound figures which ambiguously represent both celestial and earthly dancers (Figs. 3-11, 3-14, 3-16), to which we shall also refer as *apsaras*. None of the latter figures reveal the stylized grace of the female forms which appear with Angkor Wat, nor do any persuasively suggest what the actual court or temple dancers of the period looked like. Tangentially, we may note that a beautiful dancer from the iconography of Champa (Fig. 3-19) fills both of these gaps and represents a possible sphere of influence on the Angkorean sculptors if not choreographers.[78] Everything that preceded it, however—earlier styles or foreign influence—was a preface to Angkor Wat. There, with stupendous variety, the Feminine achieved a new level of expression unsurpassed at any time in Asian sculpture.

Right:
3-17. **Tenth-Century *Devatā* at Banteay Srei.**
Photo Michael Greenhalgh.

Below:
3-18. **Detail of Banteay Srei *Devatā*.**
Photo Michael Greenhalgh.

The *Apsaras* of Angkor Wat

3-19. **Female Cham Dancer, Tenth Century.** *From* the Tra-kieu pedestal, Quang-nam. Photo Henri Parmentier, 1922.

We turn now to the iconographic data presented by the vast variety of feminine forms at Angkor Wat. The temples of Angkor are of sandstone which was strong enough to build in great mass, yet soft enough to permit the development of superior carving technique. It is claimed that "just the approach to Angkor Wat is on a grander scale than anything in the living world. The piazza of St. Peter's at Rome, down the triple passages between Doric pillars... of Bernini's colonnades is as nothing in comparison to it."[79] It is the largest religious edifice ever built by man.

One striking stylistic element to be seen throughout the massive sculpture and bas-relief of Angkor Wat is a rhythm of repetition and elaboration which one art critic claims to be "derived from and related to the dance."[80] A quality of movement and flow infuses the majority of the bas-reliefs, and in none, appropriately, is rhythm more clearly expressed than in the "Churning of the Ocean" relief depicting the birth of the *apsaras* from the foam (Fig. 3-20). No two of the myriad *apsaras* are quite identical, yet with one knee leaping forward and the other heel facing heaven at hip level, their flying pose is rhythmically dance-like.

The distinction between *devatā* and *apsaras* is difficult to maintain at Angkor Wat because the non-flying *devatā* have taken on a refinement and delicacy suggestive of dancers, at least to the modern eye (Figs. 3-21, 3-22, 3-23), and, while the basis for distinction between apsaras and *devatā* made earlier still pertains, the *devatā* of Angkor Wat

Above:
3-20. **Creation of the *Apsaras*, Angkor Wat.**
Photo Jaro Poncar.

Right:
3-21. **Angkor Wat *Devatā*, West Gopura.**
Photo Kent Davis.

are today popularly, if inaccurately, considered to represent dancers. Angkorean dancers may indeed have had the appearance of these *devatā*, as modern re-creations have suggested (Fig. 3-24), but it must be stressed that none of the *devatā*—who, being at least twice the height of the *apsaras* and thus clearly distinguishable—can be seen in a dance pose. Each one stands formally or with preoccupied elegance but firmly on both feet.

The work of George Groslier, curator of the National Museum in Phnom Penh early in this century, lent authority to the popular notion of

66   *Earth in Flower*

Above:
3-22. Angkor Wat *Devatā*, Top Level. Photo Kent Davis.

Right:
3-23. Two Angkor Wat *Devatā*, Cruciform Gallery North. Photo Kent Davis.

Angkor Wat *devatā* as dancers. He argued that since *apsaras* and *devatā* were both divinities, either term used exclusively would do, and he called all the figures *apsaras*[81]. His drawings of "realistic" Angkorean dancers (Fig. 3-24) were the earliest in a vogue of juxtaposing the *devatā* with contemporary Khmer dancers to show the contrast between "past and present" (Fig. 8-2). It is important, therefore, that we examine the physical appearance of the *devatā* to understand both their symbolic nature and their influence on contemporary dance.

While there are numerous and highly dissimilar styles in the rendering of the Angkor Wat *devatā*, a consistent richness and delicacy can be seen throughout. The most sumptuous are found in the reliefs on the walls of the central sanctuary, the east entrance and, particularly, the west entrance, where they are also by far the most numerous.[82] For the first time, the *devatā* appear in groups, sometimes with an arm casually holding another's waist or shoulder, sometimes looking in a hand mirror or adjusting their hair, sometimes holding a long-handled fly whisk or a fan. Many hold a small pearl-like object or lotus between thumb and forefinger

3-24. **Angkorean Dancers.** G. Groslier, *Danseuses cambodgiennes,* 1913.

a few inches below the navel. Each figure stands on its own pedestal, feet usually angled sharply left or right despite the frontal orientation of the body. All are bare-breasted with elaborate but diaphanous skirts and splendidly ornamented coiffeurs, and almost all have flowers, either in the hair or held, long-stemmed, in the hand.

In her extensive study of ornamentation styles among the Angkor Wat *devatā*, Sappho Marchal concludes that the primary visual image in coiffeur, jewelry and clothing is that of flowers, especially those of the lotus, the coconut, and the areca-palm—the latter two being very similar.[83] The lotus is an infinitely repeated motif in the temple ornamentation, and the towers of Angkor are themselves said to be imitations of lotus-buds.[84] On the *devatā*, the lotus appears particularly in the headdresses, on bracelets, and in bud-form as earrings (Fig. 3-25H). A long-stemmed lotus—either in a realistic (Fig. 3-25B) or highly stylized form (Figs. 3-21, 3-22)—is held by most of the *devatā*.

The myriad carved coconut and areca flowers at Angkor Wat appear more symmetrical and stylized than in nature and are represented as long, flexible branches—sometimes mistaken for braids—used in headdresses and, in general, to frame the *devatā* faces (Figs. 3-25D and G). Today, coconut and areca flowers still play a significant role in numerous Cambodian

3-25. **Elements in the *Devatā* Headdress.** Drawing by Sappho Marchal, *Khmer Costumes and Ornaments of the Devatas of Angkor Wat*, 2005. Courtesy of Orchid Press, Hong Kong. Originally published as *Costumes et parures Khmèrs d'après les devatâ d'Angkor-Vat*, 1927.

ceremonies, especially the marriage.[85] For instance, the areca flowers offered by the groom to the bride are distributed to all the wedding guests, seemingly as a symbol of re-born fertility. To judge by their association with the *devatā*, the same flowers held symbolic value at Angkor as well.

In Chapter VII we shall consider the evidence supporting the argument that the choreography of Khmer dance is derived from plant imagery. For the moment, it is important to note that the ornamentation of the Angkor Wat *devatā* as a whole, clearly identifies them with the plant world and an earth energy. Among the variety of hair styles (Fig. 3-25A, C, D, F), for instance, many recall the long, serpentine, water-producing plait of the earth spirit Neang Thorani (Fig. 3-5). In some cases the hair projects straight up from the crown like a fountain or a serpent; in others, this image is modified by flowers and plant elements.

Insofar as such headdresses were actually worn by Angkorean women, it is surmised that they were constructed in part—like those of the modern dancer—of precious and semi-precious metal and stones.[86] Regardless of the degree of stylization, however, the coiffeurs of the *devatā* clearly identify them as images of the earth's fertility in blossom. Floral patterns on the skirts—especially on the left-hand panel—as well as flower, shell, and pearl motifs on all the belts and jewelry further enhance this image.

In contrast, the dancing *apsaras* in all periods of Angkorean art held a subordinate position to the *devatā*, and the development of the very striking *devatā* at Angkor Wat was not accompanied, unfortunately, by a similar blossoming of the *apsaras*. The symbolic function of the *apsaras* seems very clearly to have been the representation of an energy or force frequently associated with the earth. They usually appear in long flying rows, in identical or alternating reverse-image poses, and equidistant from each other, thereby creating a rhythm within the sculptural composition. They are frequently integrated into the overall floral composition of the bas-reliefs to the point of disappearance (Fig. 3-26).

There is some evidence to suggest that the *apsaras* were also pictured as though supporting some part of a building with their movement. At Angkor Wat, for instance, sandstone vaulting was used for the first time to

Above:
3-26. **Angkor Wat Bas Relief.** Female figures appearing in decorative vegetal scrolls (see top center) are called *neariphal*, literally meaning 'woman fruit.' Photo Kent Davis.

create pillared hallways; the walls are covered with *apsaras* and *devatā*. Later, during the reign of Jayavarman VII, friezes of *apsaras* with upraised arms appear to support structures at Preah Khan (Fig. 3-27), Banteay Chhmar, and elsewhere. On the Royal Terrace at Angkor rows of *apsaras* are thought to have upheld the great audience hall of the king mentioned by the Chinese envoy Zhou Daguan about 1296.[87] Despite this powerful function, however, it is easy to understand why, in the popular imagination, the *apsaras* are overlooked while the *devatā*—who never raise a foot—are viewed as the true "celestial dancers" of Angkor.

Twelfth-Century Dance

Amid the many styles of *devatā* and *apsaras* at Angkor Wat a small number of figures can be identified as earthly dancers. On the northwest pavilion, for instance, there is a bas-relief showing a group of women dancing joyously among the trees (Fig. 3-28). Like other court women depicted elsewhere, they are dressed in the elaborate manner of the *devatā*, but their frolicking clearly suggests the play of realistic mortals. Presumably these are court dancers then, but whether they danced in the court or the temple with similar abandon is unknowable.

It is possible to speculate knowledgeably regarding the content of more formal dance, however, since part of any ritual performance repertoire at Angkor in the twelfth century certainly included the story of Rām. We

Above:
3-27. **Frieze of *Apsaras* from Preah Khan.** Photo Michael Greenhalgh.

Below:
3-28. **Angkor Wat Dancers.** Photo Vittorio Roveda.

have already noted that as early as the sixth century, temple recitations of the Rām epic were performed daily. In the twelfth century this legend was the basis for the bas-reliefs of the entire west facade at Angkor Wat, half of the east facade, and elsewhere. It is closely related in mythological content to the "Churning of the Ocean" sculpture and to the myth of the *nāgī* ancestress as we shall see in Chapter V.

Scholars have shown that the version of the Rām legend depicted by Angkorean sculptors was indigenous to Southeast Asia and appreciably different from the written form known in India as the *Rāmāyana*.[88] Episodes from the *Rāmker*, as the legend is known in Cambodia, remain among the most popular in the dance drama repertoire in the twentieth century. Given the significance which the Khmers seem always to have attributed to this legend; given its inherently dramatic nature; given the Khmer concern to manifest a correlation between the spheres of spirit and matter; and given our knowledge of other twelfth-century dance drama performances such as those based on *jātaka* tales mentioned previously, we may conclude that the *Rām* legend is the most likely subject to have been performed as dance drama in the period of Angkor's greatest flowering.

That there was dance drama associated with Vishnu legends such as that of his avatar *Rām*—in the same way that dance drama was associated with *jātaka* stories of the Buddha's previous lives—seems likely in light of the fact that Vishnu has always been identified with dance. It was he who presided over the "Churning of the Great Sea" whose sole creation was the dancing *apsaras*.

Many of the Angkorean kings were identified with Vishnu, most notably Suryavarman II who built Angkor Wat. The twentieth-century king maintained the prerogative of Vishnu in surrounding himself with dancers who held a special position in the court. More than nearly anyone else, it was they who could "approach the king, speak to him, charm him and love him."[89] In 1970 when there was no longer a king, the dancers continued to honor the statue of his spiritual ancestor Vishnu,[90] present at all performances in both dancing pavilions of the palace.

Dance in the Reign of Jayavarman VII

In 1177 a fleet of ships from the kingdom of Champa sailed up the Tonle Sap River, sacked the Khmer capital, and retreated. The legitimate heir to the throne of Angkor who had watched usurpers bring the kingdom to such a point of vulnerability, finally acted. Within four years he was crowned king; within thirteen years he brought Champa under complete subjugation, and within the thirty-odd years that he reigned, the Khmer Empire achieved its farthest geo-political expansion and cultural zenith. Nearly half of Cambodia's great monuments are attributed to him, and he filled them with thousands of dancers. Jayavarman VII is considered the greatest ruler of Angkor.

Like his predecessors of the previous 150 years, Jayavaram VII was a Buddhist, but only with him did the Mahāyāna school of Buddhism —which had been known in Funan since the fifth century—become the state religion. So drastic were the changes that Jayavarman made—for instance, in substituting a *buddharāja* for the *devarāja* that some historians conclude that in 1177 the Chams had stolen away the royal *lingam* or the powerful priests of the *devarāja* who bestowed legitimacy, or both, "a typical practice in classical Southeast Asian warfare."[91] Along with the priests, court dancers were often removed to the conquering capital, as much, one suspects, for their beauty as for their ritual function.[92]

We noted earlier the epigraphic evidence for the numbers of dancers installed by Jayavarman in his temples. On temple walls, as well, both *apsaras* and *devatā* blossomed, particularly in the case of his greatest temple, the Bayon—distinguished by its more than fifty great towers on each of which is carved, in the cardinal directions, four huge faces of the Bodhisattva Avalokitesvara (Lokesvara) in the form of Jayavarman himself. Also carved on the walls of the Bayon we find the only instance in all Khmer architecture of non-religious, realistic scenes from daily life at Angkor, including scenes of dancers.

One large wall appears to depict the daily life of a dancer: "amid luxuriant vegetation in a closed garden, the dancers are bathing, arranging their hair, being massaged, exercising and playing."[93] In another scene we see a dancer—probably male—dancing in a military band of drums and trumpets (Fig. 3-13), where a similarity to the new form of the Bayon *apsaras* can be noted.

In his study of Khmer sculpture Jean Boisselier observed that after Angkor Wat, the attitude of dance was portrayed by a pose in which the knee was very highly raised, with the heel touching the thigh almost at the pubis, and with the two arms raised to the level of the face.[94] This can be seen in the Bayon *apsaras* (Figs. 3-29, 3-30) who reveal a grace first seen on Angkor Wat's West Gopura (Fig. 3-31). A solo dancer is serpentine, yet plant-like (Fig. 3-32); two together may retain those qualities within a rigid symmetry (Fig. 3-33) or within a slight asymmetry which lends movement to the lotus on which each stands (Fig. 3-34). The dancers in duo clearly reveal, in the alternate raising of the heels, that the heart of their dance is the energy of rhythmic interaction between left and right.

When two *apsaras* dance, their four elbows form an unmoving horizontal line from which all else seems suspended in undulation (Figs. 3-33, 3-34).

3-29. **Bayon Dancers on Lotus.** Photo Michael Greenhalgh.

Chapter III: Angkorean Dance: 802-1431 75

3-30. New *Apsaras* Style from the Bayon. Photo Kent Davis.

3-31. Angkor Wat Dancing *Apsara* on West Gopura. Photo Kent Davis.

3-32. Bayon *Apsara* in Motion. Photo Kent Davis.

76   *Earth in Flower*

Left:
3-33. **Banteay Kdai** *Apsaras* **in Motion.**
Photo Kent Davis.

Below:
3-34. **Bayon** *Apsaras* **in Motion.**
Photo Jaro Poncar.

3-35. **Preah Khan Frieze with** *Apsaras*. Photo Michael Greenhalgh.

When in rows, as on a frieze (Fig. 3-35), that line at finger level could hold the world—or any structural element the architects cared to choose.

The *devatā* appearing at the Bayon (Fig. 3-36) differ from those at Angkor Wat in calling to mind the calm solidity of the pre-Angkorean feminine forms. Others—now with longer, more opaque skirts, feet facing forward and body ornaments clearly serpentine—recall the elegance of the *devatā* at Angkor Wat (Fig. 3-21).

At their most delicate, however, the Bayon *devatā* manifest one of the most magical and oft-noted effects at Angkor. This is what Philippe Stern refers to as the "deep smile," a very rare motif in the history of art. The smile itself can be best seen in the portrait sculptures of Jayavarman VII (Fig. 3-37), which are less stylized than on the Bayon towers. The smile is a reflection of a fundamental principle of Khmer art, architecture and view of life. Stern asks,

> What does this smile really mean? For me it is a concrete example of the notion—basic to our aesthetic conceptions—which, when expressed in words, could be translated as a union of opposites, but which, in reality, are opposites that have not yet emerged as distinct entities. In other words a notion which transcends language and concepts.
>
> The closed eyes thus express an inwardness, set apart from everyday things, the search in one's innermost depths for a transcendental detachment

78 *Earth in Flower*

3-36. **Bayon** *Devatā.* Photo Jaro Poncar.

3-37. **Jayavarman VII.**
National Museum of
Cambodia, Phnom Penh.
Photo John Gollings.

and supra-human peace, the way to *nirvana*; whereas the smile, rising also from the innermost depths, represents the almost tender Buddhist charity of communication and communion with all creatures, imparted by the smiling expression to the face as a whole.[95]

As we shall note further in Chapter VIII, a similar smile remains one of the most striking features of the contemporary Khmer dancer's image. The smile, whether experienced by the viewer of dance or of sculpture, appears mysterious or half-present (Fig. 3-38). As an element of the Bayon period *devatā*, it seems to have been given form under a Buddhist influence.[96]

It is important to note that the components of body ornamentation on the Bayon *devatā*—the golden crowns and jewelry—reflect a very specific symbolism corresponding to that in Tantric Buddhist iconography. There are eight basic elements of ornamentation, each symbolizing one

3-38. **Bayon** *Devatā* **Smiling.**
Photo Kent Davis.

Table 1. **Symbolic Values of Body Ornamentation in Tantric Buddhist Iconography***

Ornament	Symbolic Value
Crown	Pure view
Earring	Pure understanding
Necklace	Pure speech
Long necklace	Pure action
Two longer necklaces across chest	Pure feeling
Bracelet	Pure effort
Ankle bracelet	Pure mindfulness
Belt	Pure Wisdom

* Source: His Eminence Tai Situ Rinpoche, public teaching (Honolulu, 25 April 1982).

kind of perfection obtainable through Buddhist practice, i.e., the purification of karmic obscurations (Table 1).

The five-pointed crowns, which are most frequently seen in this period, further symbolize—in the Buddhist view—the Five Buddha-Families and the transformation of the five poisons (anger, envy, pride, delusion and desire) into the five wisdoms. Body ornaments conforming to this model are found not only on the Bayon *devatā* (Figs. 3-36, 3-38), but also on the modern Khmer dancer (see Ch. VIII).

3-39. Lokesvara with *Apsaras* from the Bayon. Photo Jaro Poncar.

THE DANCER IN LATE ANGKOREAN BRONZE

The form in which we most clearly see the relationship between the Tantric branch of Mahāyanā Buddhism and dance is in the bronze sculpture recovered from Angkor. To a lesser extent we may note the relationship in the iconography, as in the numerous bas-reliefs of Lokesvara surrounded by dancing *apsaras* at the Bayon and elsewhere (Fig. 3-39). It is in the bronze works, however, that the dancer is best portrayed, and for the most part, the dancing figures are associated with the Tantric development of the Mahāyanā.

Tantric Buddhism had a great popularity in ancient Cambodia as seen in the many bronzes of Hevajra, Vajrasattva and Vajradhara.[97] It is with them, rather than with bronzes of the Brahmanic deities, that dance is associated. In fact, Cœdès believed that of all the ancient Khmer bronzes, only one could possibly be identified with the Shiva Natarāja, or dancing Shiva, and it has both feet firmly on the ground.[98]

82 *Earth in Flower*

3-40. **Bayon Style *Yoginī*.** Cœdès, Bronze Khmers, pl. XIX.

Associated with the tantric deity Hevajra, who—in a different form—we earlier noted in a dancing pose (Fig. 3-6), were a group of eight goddesses known as *yoginī*. Their function was "to destroy ignorance in the eight quarters of the universe, symbolized by the corpses on which the *yoginī* dance."⁹⁹ Just as often, however, the *yoginī* are seen dancing in the posture of the *apsaras* with one foot on a lotus (Fig. 3-40). In some instances the sculptural form became

3-41. **Bayon Style *Yoginī* (front).**
This 12th-13th century casting from Northeast Thailand represents Dombini, one of eight *yoginī* in the sacred *mandala* of Hevajra, the eight-faced god (See Fig. 3-6). Her left hand displays a distinctive *mudra*, or symbolic hand gesture, exhibited by hundreds of *apsaras* at Angkor Wat. Bunker and Latchford, *Adoration and Glory*, courtesy of Emma C. Bunker.

3-42. **Bayon Style *Yoginī* (back).**
The *vajra* in Dombini's right hand is her attribute as the *mandala*'s "keeper of the northwest portal." Originally, her left foot would have been resting on a supine figure. Bunker and Latchford, *Adoration and Glory*, courtesy of Emma C. Bunker.

truly dramatic, displaying a powerful sense of ecstatic movement captured at the moment of the dancer's (or *yoginī's*) greatest extension (Figs. 3-41, 3-42).

By the mid-thirteenth century, when the more austere Theravada Buddhism had superseded the Mahāyanā,[100] the *yoginī*, as an object of veneration, seems to have lost no popularity. Frequently, *yoginī* were cast in splendid detail, complete with the third eye and right foot positioned on left inner thigh (Figs. 3-43, 3-44). Some were cast holding a plowshare of a type still used today in preparing the rice fields.[101] While this clearly suggests her

3-43. **Angkor Wat Style *Yoginī* (front).** This late eleventh to early twelfth century Cambodian bronze casting captures the kinetic energy and power of this genre. Bunker and Latchford, *Adoration and Glory*, courtesy of Emma C. Bunker.

3-44. **Angkor Wat Style *Yoginī* (back).** She appears to hold a double-ended drum in her right hand, suggesting that she may be Cauri, "keeper of the south portal" in the Hevajra *mandala*. Bunker and Latchford, *Adoration and Glory*, courtesy of Emma C. Bunker.

3-45. **Twelfth-Century *Apsaras*.**
National Museum of Phnom Penh.
Photo Hans Hinz.

association with the ageless Khmer fertility cult and links her with other feminine predecessors in such a role, her actual pose, like that of Hevajra, is a dance of victory.[102]

In the Bayon period some of the bronze figures appear to be ambivalent forms of earthly/celestial dancers. Termed *apsaras* by Madeleine Giteau, the loveliest of these holds an almost realistic dance pose (Fig. 3-45). Another set of small bronzes has been recovered which also includes recognizable postures (Fig. 3-46). For these unusual pieces the dating is difficult; the long skirts recall the eleventh-century Baphuon style, or even tenth-century Banteay Srei (Fig. 3-14), but one scholar has placed them in the Bayon period on the basis of the poses.[103] Their quality is more that of folk art than the larger religious bronzes of the temples, but whatever their purpose, they confirm the popularity and importance of dance both within the Buddhist context and elsewhere.

Before completing this survey of the bronze works portraying dance, we should note a religious significance to the form itself: bronze was used particularly for Buddhist statuary as opposed to Brahmanic. Cambodian bronze probably reached its peak of excellence in the second half of the ninth century, and, almost without exception, the pre-Angkorean pieces represent Buddha or the Bodhisattvas.[104] In the thirteenth century, under the Buddhist influence of Jayavarman VII, the bronzes were encrusted with precious or semi-precious stones and adorned with filigree.[105] All of this was not only for the sake of beauty or the display of opulence; the material itself—that which gave the divinities form—was invested with symbolic significance.

The preferred alloy for casting the "lost-wax" process bronzes was called *samrit*. It was made of seven metals: gold, silver, copper, zinc, mercury, tin, bismuth, and lead, with the first three predominant and with the gold content of the better bronzes being extremely high.[106] What purpose did this hidden gold serve? The answer seems to lie in a realm of metaphor with which few today are conversant, namely the study of alchemy.

In many so-called "primitive" or "archaic" societies the preparation of ores, the making of coins, and the casting of gold and silver were a sacred procedure and the prerogative of a priestly caste. The sacerdotal origin of metallurgical procedures was due to the belief that gold and silver were like the purified forms of the self when freed from its baser elements. As a recent re-interpretation of Western alchemy—with its roots in ancient Egypt and the near-East—has pointed out,

> it is not quite right to say that gold represents the sun, and silver the moon; rather it is the case that the two noble metals and the two luminaries are both symbols of the same two cosmic or divine realities.[107]

The value of gold and silver, then, derived from their identification with the

3-46. **Angkorean Dancing Figures.** Bowie, *The Sculpture of Thailand*.

forms of the two ultimate cosmic principles, just as the obscured gold and silver "matter" of which Buddhist icons were made symbolized the precious goal toward which the "spirit" moved in the process of transmutation through Buddhist practice.

Interestingly, the Khmer dancer has always embodied the same goal, even to the point of being identified, whenever possible, with gold and silver. In the modern period the dancers' tiaras, jewelry and brocade were preferably of gold and silver, and one of their most important dances involved the presentation of gold and silver flowers—a symbol of homage said to have originally rained from heaven—which were often used in Cambodia's international affairs in the past as a sign of tribute. The *apsaras* dancer herself contains both gold and silver, sun and moon, Feminine and Masculine. She performs all roles of all genders (prior to very recent changes). She is like the androgynous mercury (or quicksilver)—"containing both sun and moon"—through whose action alone gold was believed to be extractable from metals.[108] In the simile which we are here considering, the Cambodian *apsaras*—created from the foam made by the churning of the ocean—embodies the energy of both the masculine king and the primordial sea of which he is the churn.

The simile between dancer and quicksilver is not totally theoretical. The Khmers have always placed a high value on mercury. In the thirteenth century, Zhou Daguan listed mercury among "Chinese goods that are sought after."[109] One of its important alchemical uses was in funerary rites. During his stay in Bangkok in 1855, Sir John Bowring noted that "after death ... the arms are raised as if in adoration, and a piece of gold or silver placed in the mouth. Quicksilver and honey are poured down the throat...."[110] The objective was to remove the dross and manifest the true golden purity of the deceased. In royal funerals this process was considered extremely important. When King Sisowath of Cambodia died in 1927, his body was "placed in a silver urn containing mercury, where it remained for a considerable time"[111] prior to cremation (Fig. 4-1). Like mercury, the dancer symbolizes the golden point of interfusion and transition between the mundane and the celestial.

On the more popular level of Khmer beliefs about creating the gold of earthly prosperity, the general view was that through the interaction of the Feminine with the Masculine, blessings will come dancing forth—like *apsaras* from the foam. This may still be seen during the celebration of the Cambodian New Year when "girls and boys take part in a tug-of-war which stems from the Churning legend and which is intended to produce heavy rainfall in coming months."[112] The dancers' embodiment of the energy of that interaction, as well as the resulting prosperity, is the fundamental, if veiled, action still discernible today at the heart of the dramatic structure and ritual function of Khmer dance drama.

Post-Bayon Period Dance

George Cœdès dates the death of Jayavarman VII around A.D. 1218 at an age of nearly one hundred. With his passing Angkor's greatness began a slow decline, although some have argued that his excesses in all fields bespoke desperation rather than a celebration. He built, for instance, at least 121 rest houses along the main roads of the kingdom, coupled with the construction of 102 hospitals,[113] for which later generations have tended to praise his vision. Others have cited him for "contributing more to [Angkor's] decline than any other Khmer monarch"[114] and would probably agree with Mahatma Gandhi's assessment that "a multiplicity of hospitals is no test of civilization; rather it is a symptom of decay."[115] For our purposes, however, and as we have seen, the inscriptions and iconography of Jayavarman's reign are among the most valuable sources of data concerning dance at Angkor, and they are nearly the last sources prior to the nineteenth century.

Before moving beyond the age of Jayavarman VII, however, let us note a final image from the temple of Banteay Samre, erected in the first half of the twelfth century. It shows kneeling musicians and possibly singers accompanying dancers (Fig. 3-47). The harp being played is no longer known in Southeast Asia, contemporary costumes are significantly different, and the dance pose is not recognizable in the modern period. Nonetheless, in the basic configuration, we are very probably seeing the earliest preserved image of Khmer dance with chant. Much later at the Bayon, a similar group of musicians and dancers is also depicted with the harp (Fig. 3-48).

In 1296-97 a commercial attaché accompanying an embassy from the Mongol emperor Timur Khan to the court of Angkor—the previously mentioned Zhou Daguan—included in his lengthy and now invaluable report only one reference to dance:

> The eighth month there is the *ngai-lan*, or dancing. They choose talented musicians who come to the palace each day to do the *ngai-lan*; there are also combats between elephants.... The festival lasts ten days.[116]

The palace in question was the one in which the king united nightly with the spirit of the nine-headed *nāgī* serpent who was "mistress of the earth of all the kingdom."

Cœdès has shown that *ngai-lan* was a transcription of the Khmer /thnai ram/,[117] and Eveline Porée-Maspero has persuasively argued, on the basis of similarities with the modern ritual of *lon neak ta* and other events involving elephant combats, that the *ngai-lan* was, in fact, a performance in which the dancers became possessed by the territorial spirits of the kingdom for the purpose of obtaining rain.[118] Significantly, Zhou does not say that dancers came to the palace, which may mean that it was the court or temple dancers who performed the ritual function. Since Zhou never personally made it inside the palace, he would not have recognized them as such. At any rate, he mentioned nothing about the actual dancing.

Whatever its form, we know that post-Bayon Period dance had a great influence on the court dances of contemporary neighboring kings, particularly in Thailand which emerged as an independent political entity in the first half of the thirteenth century. Cœdès has pointed out that, previous to that, "during their period of subjugation to Cambodia, they had been strongly influenced by the Khmer civilization of which...the theatre constituted a certain element."[119]

The oldest extant inscription in the Thai language, dated 1292, mentions a great annual festival involving music and singing, which

3-47. **Twelfth-Century Musicians and Dancers.** This female ensemble could be one of the earliest representations of "chanters" or "howlers" behind the musicians. Photo Michael Greenhalgh.

3-48. **Bayon Orchestra with Dancers.** As in Fig 3-47, we see the harp-like instrument that has since disappeared from Southeast Asian ensembles. Photo Michael Greenhalgh.

may well be a reference to the *len dukdamban* or "ancient tradition." This event is actually mentioned only once by name in Thai records, specifically in the later Luang Prasroeth version of the *History of Ayudhyā*: "In the year of the *nāga*, 858 [=A.D. 1496], the King [Rāmādhipati II] celebrated his twenty-fifth birthday and staged the ancient tradition (*len dukdamban*)."[120] Thai dance experts today feel that the *len dukdamban* was the equivalent of the *chhak nak dukdamban* or the actual acting out of the "Churning of the Sea" by dancers masked as gods and demons, and that that ritual was definitely of Cambodian origin. Probably last staged in the mid-eighteenth century, "certain features of it became incorporated in other ceremonies that were performed as late as the reign of King Chulalongkorn (1868-1911)."[121]

It is believed that the court dance tradition of Laos was also adopted directly from the Angkorean court by the first independent king of the Laotians, Fa Ngom, who had been raised there in exile. Fa Ngom and his Khmer princess wife returned to Laos from Angkor in 1353 with an army of 10,000 men and regained the throne.[122] There is an undocumented oral tradition that his retinue included Khmer musicians and dancers.

In the relationship between the Thai court and its neighbors in the nineteenth century, the royal dancers were considered almost part of the royal regalia. Rama III, for instance, refused to allow Thai dancers to train Lao dancers because it might mean that the Lao king—who had requested the instructors—"was trying to equal him." In similar manner, one Thai dance expert today claims that the Thai kings in some unspecified period refused to allow a royal troupe of dancers to be resident in Phnom Penh:

> To have a royal dance troupe in a court, you have to be a king or in the same position, so it's a status symbol. Since Cambodia was then a vassal state, Thailand did not permit it to have a royal dance troupe the same as the Thai king.[123]

The Cambodian point of view—like the historical evidence—contradicts this Thai point of view, as we shall see, but the guarded prestige of royal dancers in both countries is not in question.

The Fate of Angkorean Dance

Largely because of the mystery surrounding Angkor's seeming abandonment to the jungle and because of the confused state of the subsequent Cambodian chronicles or court histories, historians have tended to speak of "the fall of Angkor" as though it were a single, Troy-like event. Since the armies of Angkor battled the ever-increasing Thai power of Ayutthaya for much of the fourteenth and fifteenth centuries, however, the idea of a "fall" is simplistic, particularly when premised upon a single battle—usually held to be the assault of 1431-32.[124] A recent, meticulous study of the nineteenth-century Cambodian chronicles of the Khmer court concludes that "the fall of Angkor" was rather a gradual shift of economic and political power from Angkor to two new centers, Ayutthaya and the Phnom Penh-Lovek area, both more accessible to riverine commerce. The first sign of rivalry and conflict on such a basis can be seen in the chronicles with

> the occupation of Phnom Penh in 1409 by one branch of Ayutthayan royalty, who proceeded to set up their own state. The next step would have been the occupation of Angkor by the other branch of Ayutthayan royalty in 1430-31, and this was very likely due to rivalry between the two new states over their mutual old cultural capital.[125]

Within that rivalry, however, there can be no question that both contending spheres would maintain court dancers for any ritual function which assured prosperity, and Chapter IV will consider the data specifically demonstrating that dance drama was performed in Cambodia in the sixteenth and seventeenth centuries.

We must consider in conclusion to this chapter, however, the appeal of the belief that the dancers of Angkor were stolen away to Ayutthaya after "the fall." To some extent, this surely happened; Khmer dancers were taken to Ayutthaya. Dance, however, is an oral tradition, and, given the important symbolic value it appeared to hold for the Khmers as demonstrated in this chapter, there can be little doubt that young dancers were trained as soon as possible to replace those lost. Even today in the great *diaspora* of Khmer dance, this is the case.

There is appealing romance in the notion, however, that all the dancers of Angkor were stolen away as booty during the sack of Angkor. Cambodian government publications were not immune to such speculation:

> Although no specific mention is made of the fact in the annals of Cambodia and Siam, it seems fairly certain that dancers and musicians held a prominent place among those who were rounded up and taken away by the Siamese armies in the course of their invasions. It is most likely that this happened when Angkor was taken and pillaged by the T'ai king Ramadhipati, and probably thousands of Khmer artists from the royal court fell at that time into the hands of the Siamese and were sent to the newly-founded city of Ayuth'ya.[126]

Similarly, the contemporary raconteur I. G. Edmonds writes that "when Angkor was sacked by the Siamese in the fifteenth century, the 4,000 dancing girls were taken back to Ayuthia."[127] This extraordinarily large number—in light of Angkor's turbulent latter history and decrease in temple building—was more than likely engendered by Norodom Sihanouk's obsessive concern with previous Khmer glory. Sihanouk once told Malcolm MacDonald that when the Khmers abandoned Angkor, "the Royal Corps de Ballet were left behind by mistake."[128] Only the very essence of such tales is unarguable—that the dancers were of great cultural significance.

Angkor was not ultimately abandoned until the end of the sixteenth century, but by the nineteenth century its construction had come to be ascribed to a semi-divine craftsman, the son of an *apsaras* and a "Chinaman," who had been instructed in heaven by Indra's own architect. His name was Vishvakarman (Khmer: Pisnoukar), and he became a "master-builder, skilled in music and the decorative arts."[129] He returned to earth to construct Angkor on the model of Indra's stables as a palace for the Cambodian king. This king was named Ketumala, the son of a Cambodian queen and Indra himself. The legend corresponds to the primal Khmer myth of the powerful male from outside marrying the indigenous female ruler. In attributing to Angkor a divine origin, it further demonstrates the ancient belief that the temples were both a point of communion with the gods and a microcosmic copy of the spiritual plane of reality.

In a similar manner "it is also by the intervention of Indra that the *Apsaras*... delivered to the Khmers the secrets of choreography,"[130] contends one modern Khmer dance expert, without further elaboration. Again it is the essence of that statement which is significant. The Khmer dancer today maintains, in reduced form, the religious and cultural symbolism of her Angkorean predecessors, and at times the essence of her choreography does suggest divinity.

Endnotes

1. Briggs, *AKE*, p. 3.
2. *Indigenous Religious Systems of the Malay Peninsula*, Working Paper No. 28 (Singapore: Department of Sociology, University of Singapore, 1974), p. 2.
3. See Robert Heine-Geldern, *Conceptions of State and Kingship in Southeast Asia*, Data Paper No. 18 (Ithaca: Southeast Asia Program, Department of Far Eastern Studies, Cornell University, 1956).
4. B. Groslier, *Angkor Art and Civilization*, p. 13.
5. Bernard-Philippe Groslier, "The Angkor Kings," *RCB* (Preface), p. 4.
6. Bernard-Philippe Groslier, *Indochina: Art in the Melting-Pot of Races*, trans. George Lawrence (London: Methuen, 1962), p. 238. Rain is masculine in relation to the feminine earth but ground water is feminine vis-à-vis the masculine mountain.
7. L. P. Briggs, "The Syncretism of Religions in Southeast Asia, especially in the Khmer Empire," *Journal of the American Oriental Society*, 71 (1951), p. 230.
8. Giteau, *Khmer Sculpture*, p. 54.
9. Philip Rawson, *The Art of Southeast Asia* (London: Thames and Hudson, 1967), p. 60; Giteau, *Khmer Sculpture*, p. 52.
10. Giteau, *Khmer Sculpture*, pp. 49-50. The very rare Khmer images of Shiva dancing suggest none of the fearsome frenzy of his Indian counterpart. Khmer artists usually pictured him "in an idyllic pose, ...a gentle reassuring image" (p. 14).
11. Rawson, *The Art of Southeast Asia*, pp. 114-15.
12. Giteau, *Khmer Sculpture*, p. 156.
13. Giteau, *Khmer Sculpture*, p 15.
14. Pelliot, *Le Fou-nan*, p. 269.
15. Aeusrivongse, p. 115.
16. Eveline Porée-Maspero, "Notes sur les particularitiés du culte chez les cambodgiens," *BEFEO*, 44, No. 2 (1954), p. 628, n. 1.
17. G. Groslier, *Danseuses cambodgiennes*, pp. 130, 140.
18. B. Groslier, *Angkor Art and Civilization*, p. 218.
19. There are actually ninety-two figures on the left and eighty-eight on the right. All Khmer temples place slightly more emphasis on the left side if they are not symmetrical. See Briggs, *AKE*, p. 100.
20. Bernard-Philippe Groslier, "Reconstruction of Galleries at Angkor Wat," *Nokor Khmer*, No. 3 (Apr.-June 1970), p. 33.
21. B. Groslier, "Reconstruction," p. 33.
22. William J. Perry, *The Megalithic Culture of Indonesia* (Manchester: University Press, 1918), pp. 33-39.
23. Cœdés, *Angkor: An Introduction*, p. 48.
24. For an Indian version of the myth, see Veronica Ions, *Indian Mythology* (London: Paul Hamlyn, 1967), pp. 111-13.
25. *Angkor Art and Civilization*, p. 101.

26 Mircea Eliade, *The Myth of the Eternal Return* (Princeton: Princeton University Press, 1965), *p. 69*.
27 Groslier, *Angkor Art and Civilization, p. 30*.
28 This interpretation contrasts sharply with that of Cœdés who said only that their purpose at Angkor Wat, for instance, was "to transform this severe stone abode into a heavenly palace" (*Angkor: An Introduction*, p. 50). Similarly, Bernard Groslier attributes no inherent symbolic value to "dancing-girls [who] made of the temple an image of the paradise of Indra" (*Angkor Art and Civilization*, p. 163).
29 *Angkor Art and Civilization*, pp. 47-48.
30 B. Groslier, *Angkor Art and Civilization*, p. 104.
31 K. R. Hall, "An Introductory Essay," p. 7.
32 Sanskrit inscriptions were "addressed to the gods;" Khmer inscriptions to man. The former include a tribute to the deity, a eulogy of the founder of the temple, and a description of the deity being "installed." By contrast, the Khmer inscriptions, in general, detail the lands, art works, and servants belonging to a temple, and how they were acquired. They are "to some extent, a notary's deed placed under divine protection" and both types of inscriptions—often found in conjunction—close with imprecations condemning any who would destroy the "foundation" or its property. See Claude Jacques, "The Inscriptions of Cambodia," *Nokor Khmer*, No. 2 (Jan.-Mar. 1970), pp. 22, 24.
33 (K. 713), *IC*, I, 28.
34 (K. 323, A, 63), "Stèle de Loley," *IS*, p. 391.
35 (K. 270, 8-25), *IC*, IV, 69-70.
36 (K. 235, lxxii, cxii-cxiii), "l'Inscription de Sdok Kak Thom," ed. Louis Finot, *BEFEO*, 15, No. 2 (1915), pp. 83, 86.
37 (K. 273, LXIV-LXVII, LXXXVII), "La stèle de Ta-Prohm," ed. George Cœdès, *BEFEO*, 6 (1906), pp. 77-78.
38 (K. 908, cxliv), "La stèle du Prāh Khan d'Ankor," *BEFEO*, 41, No. 2 (1941), 297. None of the dancers in K. 273 or K. 908 are named.
39 (K. 194, II, 42-48; K. 383, 7-10), *BEFEO*, 43 (1943), pp. 134-54.
40 Jacques, "Inscriptions," p. 25.
41 (K. 214, X), *IC*, II, 204.
42 (K. 702, 9-12), *IC*, V, 225.
43 (K. 356, 17-22), "Le site de Janadvipa d'après une inscription de Prasat Khna," ed. George Cœdès, *BEFEO*, 43 (1943), p. 10.
44 B. Groslier, *Danseuses cambodgiennes*, p. 138 *et passim*.
45 B. Groslier, "*Danse et Musique*," p. 291.
46 (K. 908, XXX), p. 287.
47 Giteau, *Khmer Sculpture*, p. 77.
48 "La stèle du Prāh Khan d'Ankor," p. 287, n. 6.
49 See Ch. II, n. 49.
50 (K. 137), *IC*, II, 115.
51 Henri Stierlin, "Angkor: masterpiece of architecture and town planning," *The UNESCO Courier*, 24 (Dec. 1971), p. 9.
52 *Angkor Art and Civilization*, p. 165. The five wives represent a further manifestation of the Angkorean king's continual ritual fecundation of the earth, in that the first queen corresponded to the center of the kingdom and each of the other four to one of the cardinal points.
53 (K. 686, LII, XLIII), "Inscriptions de Prāsāt Hē Phkā," *IC*, IV, 86.
54 (K. 831, 7-14, 23-30), "Inscription de Tuol Kul," *IC*, V, 147-48. B. Groslier suggests that the remainder of the badly damaged text stipulated that the people "offered by Vap Myan the singer would serve during the fifteen days of the waning moon" ("Danse et Musique," p. 285). While

this seems a reasonable guess, the only legible elements of the text are a further indecipherable reference to Vap Myan, the dancer.
55 "The Angkor Kings," *RCB*, p. 5.
56 (K. 872, XVI-XX), *IC*, V, 100.
57 (K. 282, C. 27), "Stèles du Thnal Baray," *IS*, 59, p. 474.
58 "Temple of Loley," *IS*, p. 319.
59 The *jātaka* tales are comprised of 547 stories of the Buddha's incarnations. Ostensibly originating in India, Southeast Asian versions include many indigenous motifs and remain popular today.
60 (K. 485, LXXIII, LXXIX), *IC*, II, 178. The inscription says that Jayavarman VII, greatly upset by the death of Jayarājadevī who had been a great influence on him, subsequently married her older sister Indradevī, whom he had appointed previously to be head professor in a Buddhist monastery for women. At their marriage he gave her the title of first queen. It was she who wrote the highly informative account on the stèle of the Royal Palace, an inscription often cited as being composed in the purest Sanskrit.
61 *Le Bayon d'Angkor et l'évolution de l'art Khmer* (Paris: P. Geuthner, 1927).
62 *Les monuments khmers du style du Bayon et Jayavarman VII* (Paris: Presses universitaires de France, 1965), p. 15.
63 Stern, *Les monuments khmers*, p. 15.
64 S. J. Tambiah, *Buddhism and the Spirit Cults in North-East Thailand* (Cambridge: Cambridge University Press, 1979), p. 60
65 G. H. Monod, *Le cambodgien* (Paris: Larose, 1931), pp. 15-18; also Tambiah, pp. 59-60.
66 Porée-Maspero, "Notes," p. 624.
67 Solange Thierry, "Les danses sacrées au Cambodge," *Les danses sacrées* (Paris: Sources Orientales, 1963), p. 365.
68 Briggs, *AKE*, p. 92.
69 One inscription, for instance, says of him "...loaded with jewels of virtue he took the Earth to wife, and gave her his glory for a necklace." See B. Groslier, *Angkor Art and Civilization*, p. 153.
70 See Coral-Rémusat, "Animaux fantastiques," pp. 427-35.
71 Briggs, *AKE*, p. 110.
72 Cœdès, *ISSA*, p. 115.
73 Briggs, *AKE*, p. 112.
74 See B. Groslier, *Indochina*, p. 100.
75 Ions, *Indian Mythology*, p. 111. A second treatment of the same theme is pictured in Madeleine Giteau's *Guide du Musée National* (Phnom Penh: Office national du tourisme, 1960), II, p. 82. In both cases there is a strong identification of the *apsaras* with the central tree.
76 Xenia Zarina, *Classic Dances of the Orient* (New York: Crown, 1967). p. 60.
77 *La statuaire khmère et son évolution*, (Saigon: École Française d'Extrême-Orient, 1955), I, p. 77.
78 Stern dated the figure in the seventh century, but Groslier now dates it in the tenth (*Indochina*, p. 148). If Stern were correct, the dancing figure would precede by five hundred years anything of similar quality in Cambodia; Groslier's dating is far more reasonable.
79 Sacheverell Sitwell, *The Red Chapels of Banteai Srei* (London: Weidenfeld and Nicolson, 1962), p. 43.
80 Rawson, p. 89.
81 *Danseuses cambodgiennes*, p. 131.
82 Sappho Marchal, *Costumes et parures khmèrs d'après les devatā d'Angkor-Vat* (Paris: G. Van Oest, 1927), pp. 3-5, 20.
83 S. Marchal, *Costumes et parures*, pp. 3-5, 20.
84 Briggs, *AKE*, p. 196.
85 Mme. Pich-Sal, *Le mariage cambodgien, Culture et civilization Khmers*, No. 3 (Phnom Penh: Université Buddhique Preah Sihanouk Raj, n.d.), pp. 4-10.

86 Marchal, *Costumes et parures*, p. 13.
87 Briggs, *AKE*, pp. 227, 231.
88 See Francois Martini, "*En marge du Rāmāyana cambodgien*," *BEFEO*, 2 (1938), pp. 285-94; and "*Quelques notes sur le Rāmker*," *Artibus Asiae*, no. 3-4 (1961), pp. 351-62. See also Jean Przyluski, "La légende de Rāma dans les bas-reliefs d'Angkor-Vat," *Arts et Archéologies Khmers*, 1, No. 4 (1924), pp. 324-25.
89 G. Groslier, *Danseuses cambodgiennes*, p. 141.
90 The choice of Vishnu over Shiva reflects the Khmer perception of union in mind and body. The union of the Feminine with the body—as seen in the *nāgī* Soma's body pierced by Kaudinya's arrow—was the action of Shiva. The union of the Feminine with the mind—as seen in the wedding of Merā and the ascetic Kambu—was the action of Vishnu. The altar *lingam* was Shiva; the temple was Vishnu.

In Cambodia, Vishnu, not Shiva, is identified with dance. Only in trance is the union with the spirit of the body of the earth achieved. Non-trance dance as seen in its highest development—for instance, in performing the story of Vishnu's avatar Rām—embodies, by contrast, mind-shaped energy. Appropriate to the Khmer perception of the unity between seeming opposites, Khmer dance is often experienced, however, as being trance-like.
91 Hall, *An Introductory Essay*, p. 13.
92 Numerous instances of this practice are known, one being in 1044 when the Vietnamese captured the Cham Capital and took "nearly the entire court including musicians and dancers" back to Thang-long. See Keith Taylor, "The Rise of Dai Viet and the Establishment of Thang-long," *EESAH*, p. 178.
93 Zarina, p. 60. Photos are unable to verify that the court women in question are indeed dancers, as claimed by the author. One possible source for verification is *Le Bayon d'Angkor Thom* by Henri Dufour and Charles Carpeaux (Paris, 1910), containing a photographic record of the bas-reliefs.
94 *La statuarire khmère et son évolution*, p. 201.
95 "The Khmer Smile of the Bayon," *The UNESCO Courier*, 24 (Dec. 1971), p. 15.
96 There is absolutely no evidence to support one writer's claim that the voluptuous yet chaste attitude of the *apsaras* is "the result of opium" and that "opium ... is absolutely necessary for the comprehension of their art" (Geoffrey Gorer, *Bali and Angkor* [London: Michael Joseph, Ltd., 1936], pp. 178-80).
97 Georges Cœdès, "Bronzes khmers," *Ars Asiatica*, 5 (1923), p. 44. Cœdès' study comprises the entire volume of this journal.
98 Cœdès, "Bronzes khmers," p. 25 and pl. XIII. The case for identifying the figure with Shiva is unpersuasive.
99 Piriya Krairiksh, *The Sacred Image: Sculptures from Thailand* (Cologne: Museen der Stadt, 1979), p. 130. See also David L. Snellgrove, *The Hevajra-Tantra: A Critical Study*, 2 parts, London Oriental Series, vol. 6 (London, 1959).
100 Briggs, *AKE*, p.257.
101 Theodore Bowie, ed., *The Sculpture of Thailand* (New York: The Asia Society, 1972), p. 76.
102 Bowie, *The Sculpture of Thailand*, p. 73.
103 Bowie, *The Sculpture of Thailand*, p. 74.
104 Giteau, *Khmer Sculpture*, pp. 132, 119.
105 Giteau, *Khmer Sculpture*, p. 118.
106 Giteau, *Khmer Sculpture*, pp. 118-19. See also Cœdès, *Bronzes khmers*.
107 Titus Burckhardt, *Alchemy*, trans. William Stoddart (Baltimore: Penguin, 1971), p. 12.
108 Burckhardt, *Alchemy*, p. 139.

109 Zhou Daguan, *Notes on the Customs of Cambodia*, p. 34.
110 *The Kingdom and People of Siam* (London: J. W. Parker, 1857), I, p. 142.
111 J. A. Hammerton, *Manners and Customs of Mankind* (New York: Wm. H. Wise, n.d. [ca. 1928]), II, p. 487.
112 Christopher Pym, *The Ancient Civilization of Angkor* (New York: Mentor, 1968), p. 72.
113 Cœdès, "La stèle de Ta Prohm," *BEFEO*, 6 (1906), p. 80.
114 Briggs, *AKE*, p. 236.
115 "My Views on Medicine," *The Health Guide*, ed. Anand T. Hingorani (Bombay: Bharatiya Vidya Bhavan, 1965), p. 7.
116 Zhou Daguan, *Notes on the Customs of Cambodia*, p. 30.
117 "Notes sur Tcheou Ta-kouan," *BEFEO*, 9 (1909), p. 9.
118 Eveline Porée-Maspero, *Étude sur les rites agraires des cambodgiens* (Paris: Mouton, 1962), p. 236.
119 "Origine et évolution des diverses formes du théâtre traditionnel en Thailande," *BSEI*, 38 (1963), p. 493.
120 Cited by Prince Dhani Nivat in "The Gilt Lacquer Screen in the Audience Hall of Dusit," *Artibus Asiae*, 25 (1961), p. 275.
121 Dhani Nivat, "The Gilt Lacquer Screen," p. 282.
122 Briggs, *AKE*, p. 254.
123 Mattani Rutnin, personal communication, Bangkok, 7 May 1975.
124 Briggs, *AKE*, p. 257.
125 Michael T. Vickery, "Cambodia After Angkor, the Chronicular Evidence for the Fourteenth to Sixteenth Centuries," Diss. Yale 1977, p. 521. See pp. 511-521 for an excellent analysis of Angkor's demise.
126 *RCB*, p. 9.
127 *The Khmers of Cambodia* (Indianapolis: Bobbs-Merrill, 1970), p. 116.
128 *Angkor* (New York: Frederick A. Praeger, 1959), p. 32.
129 Pierre Fabricus and Donald Lancaster, trans., "Prasad Angkor Wat, Historic Tale," *Nokor Khmer*, No. 2 (Jan.-Mar. 1970), p. 54. The construction of Angkor was, according to the legend, initiated in A.D. 140.
130 Thiounn, *Danses cambodgiennes*, p. 29.

CHAPTER IV

KHMER DANCE: 1431-1981
របាំខ្មែរ: ១៤៣១-១៩៨១

This chapter will survey the historical data concerning Khmer dance during the past five hundred years with a major emphasis on the past century. The discussion will focus, first, on the fifteenth through eighteenth centuries, during which the evidence for court dance is clear though sparse. For convenience, Khmer dance in the nineteenth and twentieth centuries will be examined in correspondence with the reign of each Cambodian king separately since each had a considerable effect on the royal troupe. The final section will consider the position of the dance in the years between the demise of the monarchy in 1970 and the frail re-flowering of the dance at the present time.

The Fifteenth Century

To understand the fortunes of Khmer dance in the four hundred years when no historical account mentions it, we must first consider the relationship between Angkor and the Thai kingdoms to the west which adopted Khmer art forms as their own. Khmers of the eleventh and twelfth centuries considered the Thai, or Syam, to be "savages."¹ Recent Cambodian scholarship has cast the thirteenth and fourteenth-century Thai in the role of "barbarian invaders" eager to adopt the superior Khmer civilization. Cœdès writes that

> it followed quite naturally that the T'ai princes who were called upon to rule over ever larger and richer lands, should have been at pains to imitate as carefully as possible the court of Angkor whose splendour shone over the whole of southern Asia. Therefore music and dancing, which held such an important place in rituals and festivals, were probably among the first innovations to be introduced at the court of Sukhotai, and later at that of Ayuth'ya.²

This is not suggesting that the Thai did not have dance and music of their own—derived, like the Khmer, from village roots. Rather, what the Thai borrowed was the notion that dance, as an adjunct of royalty, could be a powerful symbol and an instrument of the king's force. More than likely, however, the Thai also borrowed much of the form of the dance along with this function.

The Thai city of Ayutthaya was founded in 1350, the year following the subjugation of the earlier, more northern Thai kingdom of Sukhothai. From the beginning, according to Cœdès, "they borrowed from Cambodia its political organization, material civilization, system of writing, and… the Siamese artists were beholden to the school of the Khmer artists…."³ There can be little doubt that the Thai borrowed from the Khmer dance tradition in this early period, just as it is generally accepted, in the oral tradition, that court dancers were taken to Ayutthaya in conjunction with the fifteenth century demise of Angkor.

The question to be considered in the early section of this chapter is—with all this "borrowing" by the Thai—to what extent was the court dance tradition in Cambodia maintained in the post-Angkor period? The answer to which all the evidence points, as we shall see, seems to be the one offered by contemporary teachers of Khmer dance, namely that "when Angkor was captured, some dancers went to Ayutthaya and some came to the new Cambodian capital with the king."⁴

The Sixteenth through Eighteenth Centuries

Those seeking written documentation of the Khmer dancers' court function in the fifteenth through eighteenth centuries have been largely disappointed. Cambodian scholars have pointed out that the Cambodian court chronicles

> give virtually no clue as to the form, content, or importance of music and dancing at the court of post-Angkorean Khmer kings. And an even more surprising fact is that the tales of Portuguese, Spanish and Dutch travelers of the sixteenth, seventeenth and eighteenth centuries seem to over-look the very existence of the palace dancers.[5]

Other sources of data, however, do exist.

The post-Angkor kings were continually involved in civil struggles for the throne or with the Thai, matters in which the court dancers would have little relevance. If the present interpretation of their function is correct, the dancers played a secondary role in certifying the legitimacy of the monarch to those beyond his borders, but they represented a primary means by which he carried out his responsibilities to the Khmer populace through the sponsorship of his dancers' communion with the spirit world. Such a concern would be of little relevance to the historical chronicles of the court or to the European community in the sixteenth century and later.

Before addressing the question of how it was that the early Europeans seem not to have even seen the dancers, let us consider the clear evidence of their existence as gleaned from a literary analysis of the Khmer epic story of Rām, the *Rāmker*.

In a grammatical, morphological and semantic study of the *Rāmker*, this "jewel of Khmer literature," Saverous Pou has isolated a version of the text evolved by a number of talented poets during the sixteenth and seventeenth centuries.[6] The five thousand stanzas in a carefully integrated style are in no way comparable to the Indian epic, particularly in their unelaborated "binary intellectual framework" of two fundamental forces in contention. Furthermore, Pou concludes, the materials included in the Sanskrit *Rāmāyana*, attributed to Valmiki, were here used by the Khmer poets to build a poem that is clearly Buddhist in its moral teachings.⁷ Thus, in the sixteenth century, ancient Austro-Asiatic themes and motifs were being re-worked in Southeast Asia just as they had been used by Valmiki in India and other poets elsewhere for millennia.⁸

The most important conclusion of Pou's study is the fact that the structure of "Rāmakerti I" reveals it to be unquestionably a work meant for recitation in theatrical performance. Essentially the text is "a long succession of tableaux in which the actions are announced by the chanter" with stock phrases clearly indicating scene changes and with textual indications of cadence or melody.⁹ If the text is of the very high quality and refinement attributed to it by this study, there is no question that it was performed both in the privacy of the court as well as in a more public arena. At any rate, the work "was conceived as a theatre script—this is undeniably its structure—to be recited and acted before an audience of faithful Buddhists."¹⁰

The thoroughness of this linguistic study of the *Rāmker* clearly indicates that in the sixteenth and seventeenth centuries, theatrical performances using newly reworked texts of very high quality took place in Cambodia. We cannot be far from the mark in concluding that these were offered at court and involved court dancers. Even in the twentieth century the best dancers in the country were those maintained by the king. For reasons of prestige alone, Khmer kings of an earlier century would likewise have maintained the best poets and chanters as well as dancers. Court chronicles or the accounts of foreign travelers may not have mentioned the king's dancers, but Pou's evidence of a high quality performance script in the sixteenth century strongly confirms the Khmer claim that the court-dance tradition in Cambodia remained unbroken from the pre-Angkorean period to the present.

In a later period further evidence regarding texts suggests that the Khmer dance tradition continued to flourish after Angkor with the help of manuscripts illustrating the classics of Cambodian literature. Such books are mentioned in one of the early accounts of Khmer dance by a European—the French Vice-Consul at Luang Prabang, August Pavie. In his travel observations from 1879 to 1895 he wrote that the principal episodes of Khmer epics "closely connected to dance" were reproduced in albums of drawings on mulberry-bark paper which "contribute above all to preserve the tradition of the costumes, the gestures and attitudes."[11]

One further account, written in 1937, clearly stated that "the dances are recorded in precious handwritten books, some of them very old, and kept wrapped in fine silks and brocades. These books are never opened without the ceremonial salute, the Anjali, being made before them."[12] In 1975 no reference to such books was ever made by an informant on behalf of this study, although one of the old teachers, Prum Sokhom (mother of the chanter Em Theay), did have a handwritten "old" notebook of songs and chants that she would not allow to be examined because it contained "the spirit of the *kru*."

To return to our main line of inquiry, then, if the court-dance tradition was always maintained in Cambodia, why did travelers prior to 1850 fail to mention the dancers? The answer may lie in the simple fact that unlike Pavie's "scientific expedition," earlier Europeans were either adventurers or priests—primarily Portuguese and Spanish Dominican and Franciscan friars[13]—who had no interest in recounting such things. In the late nineteenth century Pavie wrote that there were dancers to be seen throughout Cambodia in addition to the king's troupe, but no earlier European accounts mention these either.

It is also possible that the Khmer kings in question simply did not invite visiting Europeans to see the royal dancers perform prior to the nineteenth century. As precedent, we should note that Zhou Daguan in the thirteenth century never mentioned court or temple dancers either, although we know from other sources that there were hundreds. Even as an attaché with the embassy from the Mongol emperor, he never gained entrance to the palace.

The fact of the matter is that the dancers traditionally constituted a part of the royal harem and were not casually presented to guests for viewing. From Angkorean times the king's palace was primarily the precinct of women.[14] In mid-nineteenth-century Thailand, no male, save the king, could even enter that part of the palace inhabited by his six hundred wives and twenty-four female attendants[15]—protocol with which the Khmer King Ang Duong was reared in Bangkok, and which, to a somewhat lesser extent, he followed in Phnom Penh. While he was continually surrounded by young female attendants, no European accounts mention their dancing at any length. On the contrary, the subject of the king's harem was carefully avoided even by French Victorians, as we shall see.

We should note, parenthetically, that one account of Angkor by the official chronicler of Portuguese India, Diogo do Conto (1543-1616), does mention harvest dances observed in Cambodia between 1585 and 1588: "at this period numerous boats go about the lake gathering the rice with merry energy, dances and musical contests."[16] Groslier has pointed out that even in 1958 common village harvests of rice growing on the "great lake," the Tonle Sap, were accompanied by ritual games, especially using boats. Parties of men and women competed, but "the women always had to take back the victory which was held as a favorable sign of the group's prosperity... as a magic prefiguration of the soil's fertility."[17] The parallel to the ritual female-male tug-of-war discussed in Chapter III is obvious, and, as we shall see, the female-male "contest" by which fertility is engendered is the fundamental structural principle underlying virtually every plot in the classical dance drama repertoire.

The 1688 Account of La Loubère

Fortunately, one seventeenth-century account by a European who witnessed Thai court dancers has been preserved for us and is valuable in demonstrating continuity between Angkorean dance and that of the nineteenth century. In 1688 a French envoy of Louis XIV to the Thai court at Ayutthaya, Monsieur de la Loubère, reported that

> the *Rabam* is a double Dance of Men and Women, which is not Martial but Gallant.... These Dancers, both Men and Women, have all false Nails, and very long ones of Copper: they sing some words in their dancing, and they can perform it without much trying themselves, because their way of dancing is a simple march round, very slow, and without any high motion; but with a great many slow Contortions of the Body and Arms, so they

hold not one another. Meanwhile two Men entertain the Spectators with several Fooleries, which the one utters in the name of all the Men-dancers, and the other in the name of all the Women-dancers. All these Actors have nothing singular in their Habits.... The *Cone* and the *Rabam* are always call'd at Funerals, and sometimes on other occasions; and 'tis probable that these Shows contain nothing Religious, since the *Talapoins* [Buddhist priests] are prohibited to be present thereat.[18]

A number of points of significance are worth noting in this account—the earliest of Thai-Khmer dance written by a European.

When de la Loubère speaks of "Men-dancers" and "Women-dancers" he meant, according to Cœdès, "female dancers costumed as men" in the male roles.[19] In seventeenth and eighteenth century Thailand the term *robam* referred to a genre of dance derived from the ritual dances executed by the *rmam*, or dancers, of Angkor. Cœdès believed that the *robam*—performed in the palace exclusively by women playing the roles of both gods and goddesses—was originally "a spectacle of pure dance given on the occasion of royal ceremonies," particularly "those ceremonies designed to hasten the coming of the rainy season."[20]

Since the Khmer name of the *robam* dance "proves its Cambodian origin,"[21] and since the presumed function of the *robam* is identical with that of dances still performed in this century in Cambodia, we may conclude with reasonable accuracy that modern Khmer dance manifests a relationship with Angkorean dance which Thai dance no longer retains. The Ayutthaya kings "borrowed" the dancers of Angkor as well as the ritual function of their dance, but over the years the *robam* in Thailand melded with the dramatic form of the Thai *lakhon nai*, or "interior drama" of the palace, and the dance in Thailand lost its ritual function altogether. In Cambodia that function, like the dance itself, has always been maintained.

La Loubère's observations in 1688 suggest that at the time the *robam* in Thailand retained a ritualistic structure. He noted, for instance, that two male clowns were spokesmen for the dancers, one for the female roles and one for male roles. In this we see the serious nature of Angkorean dance as a female-male "contest" engendering prosperity, preserved in the *robam*. While the technique of using two spokesmen-clowns is no longer observable in modern Khmer court dance, a single clown and a pattern of frequently jocular interplay between female and male remains central to the structure of the dance dramas.

Cœdès, too, has noted the serious nature of the Thai *robam* in earlier years:

> The religious, ritual character of the *rabam* appeared moreover in the fact that it was especially presented on the occasion of ceremonies, and also at the beginning of theatrical performances as a curtain-raiser, and to put the spectator in some way under the invocation and the protection of the divinities incarnated by the dancers.[22]

This link with the "divinities" is significant, and La Loubère's account of the Thai *robam* in a period much closer to its Angkorean roots further clarifies the ritual function of the dance by noting that the *robam* was always performed at funerals, thus connecting the dancer, however obscurely, to spirit mediumship. At this point we may recall that in the twentieth century white-faced royal dancers still attended the corpse at Cambodian royal funerals (Fig. 4-1), thus perpetuating that ancient function.

Dance in the Early Nineteenth Century

When the Cambodian prince Ang Duong returned to Cambodia in 1841 after more than a twenty-year exile in Thailand, we are told that "he found classical dancing on the verge of total disappearance"[23]—a description nearly applicable to the kingdom as a whole. In the early seventeenth century Cambodia had become a vassal state of Siam; in the mid-seventeenth century the country was a vassal of the Nguyen of Hué (Vietnam); by the early eighteenth century the two neighbors were each struggling for control of Cambodia and the right to place a puppet-king on its greatly weakened throne. The Thai installed Khmer monarchs in 1794 and 1806; the Vietnamese chose a queen in 1835 and began a brutal campaign to "decambodgienniser"[24] the country, resulting eventually in a popular revolt. The Thai finally escorted Prince Ang Duong back to Cambodia in 1841 to the abandoned capital of Oudong. After more years of fighting, the Thai

4-1. **Royal Dancers with King Monivong Funerary Urn, 1941.** *France Illustration.* Attributed to Guy Porée.

and the Vietnamese rulers agreed that their deputies would simultaneously consecrate Ang Duong and invest him with the royal regalia including the sacred sword, palladium of the kingdom, then captive in Saigon. This was accomplished in 1848.

Since the countryside was controlled by provincial leaders from whom he was isolated by his own advisors, by protocol and by poor communications, and since all power was hedged about by the Thai king, who kept Ang

Duong's three eldest sons virtually hostage in Bangkok, the king's function was largely a ceremonial one. Ang Duong "busied himself with intrigue, pleasure and the performance of royal duties," namely "to bestow titles and ranks and to perform religious ceremonies that symbolized and defined the unity of the kingdom."[25] Clearly the royal dance was integral to this latter function and one of his dutiful pleasures, therefore, became the restoration of the royal dance troupe which he installed in a wooden palace newly constructed at Oudong.

Before proceeding with a survey of what is known about Ang Duong's effect on the royal dance troupe, it will be valuable to note other contexts in which dancers performed in mid-nineteenth-century Cambodia. We shall only briefly consider the village or folk tradition and focus primarily on troupes of dancers whose social role was limited, so far as we can tell, exclusively to dance.

The most comprehensive early study of Khmer geography and culture was that of August Pavie, mentioned previously. In one of the many volumes of his work he pointed out that there were three kinds of dance-theatre troupes in Cambodia in the 1880s: the royal troupe in Phnom Penh, secondary troupes maintained by provisional governors, and small traveling troupes including young girls as dancers but which occasionally used boys for certain roles.[26] Since many of the provincial governors were virtually independent even under Ang Duong's reign and maintained small courts free of major influence from the king, it seems more than likely that the situation which Pavie observed in the 1880s had obtained at least since the time of Ang Duong and probably for generations.

The foremost Khmer dance expert in the 1930s (and former Prime Minister), Samdach Chaufea Thiounn, also wrote of the fifteenth through eighteenth centuries that

> there always existed a more or less significant troupe of female and male dancers at the court of the various kings. Furthermore, the worshippers in certain monasteries where manuscripts of the *Rāmāyana* were preserved, formed troupes of male dancers from among the monks' students to amuse themselves and the children, and the choreographic tradition had been preserved in part by this method.[27]

A French observer's comment in 1910 provides corroboration of Thiounn's claim: "In the large monasteries...troupes not only of women but of young boys dressed as women, or men with the costumes that we see on female dancers today [*lakhon khol*], never ceased presenting the most easily performable plays and dancing the steps and mimes of the past."[28] Undoubtedly the dance was maintained in temples for reasons other than entertainment as well, and preservation in the temples is not surprising in light of the compatibility in the Khmer mind between Buddhist ritual and the ritual role of the dancer as communicant with the spiritual world—a function to be examined in Chapter X. By contrast, the 1688 performance witnessed by de la Loubère from which Buddhist priests were prohibited, suggests perhaps that the *robam* in Thailand had become separated from religious practices despite its ritualistic roots as perceived by Cœdès.

Informed scholars believe, then, that midway through the nineteenth century there was a vital, popular dance tradition in Cambodia which could renew the court tradition. It could also easily dilute what remained of it. The anonymous editors of *Royal Cambodian Ballet* acknowledged that prior to Ang Duong

> the closer contacts between the royal court and the people certainly facilitated the introduction of popular, profane elements into a form of classical choreography, which had already lost a great deal of its sacred character and even of its value as an essential religious rite. The dances ceased to be "regulated by the gods" and became open to every external human influence.[29]

In the same manner that various aspects of the popular theatre could have either regenerative or deleterious effects on a court dance tradition, the influence of a single, all-powerful individual involved in artistic housecleaning—in this case the king himself—was bound to eliminate as much in "tradition" as he gained in "modernity." Over-all, however, we may accept the Khmer claim that the dance "retained its hieratic character in spite of strong popular influence."[30]

At perhaps no period in Khmer history was the position of the royal dancer more precarious than in the years immediately prior to the ascension of Ang Duong, in that the throne was virtually empty following the death of King Ang Chan in 1835. The Vietnamese crowned his nineteen-year-old daughter queen in 1841 but kept her under guard or out of the country. Thus there was neither a resident monarch nor a palace for resident dancers between 1835 and 1841, and even with the uncrowned king-elect there was still no political stability until after 1848. Yet, as in the twentieth century, it was certainly the direct transmission from the old teachers to the young and ever-willing students which allowed the dance to be perpetuated, and it is that dynamic pattern which preserved the unbroken tradition of Khmer court dance from Angkor to the present day.

Dance in the Reign of Ang Duong (1841-1859)

Let us turn now to a consideration of Ang Duong and his influence on the royal dance troupe. Ang Duong's capital was at Oudong, some thirty miles northwest of Phnom Penh, with both cities in 1850 having less than 10,000 inhabitants.[31] The king's dancers were first mentioned by a European in 1850 by the missionary Bouillevaux whose travels antedated the more celebrated visit of Henri Mouhot by ten years. Bouillevaux clearly watched the dancers at some length to have gained an understanding of the story line, but his total, published observation—rather defensive in tone—was that "in the palace of His Majesty Duong, the first of that name, there is a great deal of music and theatre; I have caught a glimpse sometimes, much in spite of myself, of his concubines who simulate battles between the ancient heroes of India."[32]

A second account published by an anonymous "Madras officer" detailed his reception at the palace in May of 1854. He wrote that the audience hall was about forty feet square, "spacious and lofty," with a nearby "large paved court yard half roofed over. This was the place where the King retired of an evening to... amuse himself by seeing his women dance, and hearing other performances on various music instruments."[33] The Madras officer gave no account of dancing *per se* in the courtyard.

Ang Duong was enormously fat and naked to the waist, wearing only a "sarong" at the reception in question. He was continually attended by a host of young women of whom he had "about three hundred, besides four married wives." The Madras officer's comments on the king are most interesting, but of greater relevance is his description of the attendants.

> They all appeared to be very young, and were doubtless the best-looking girls we had seen in the country. Many of them had soft and regular features, and were it not for the disgusting habit of blackening the teeth and shaving the head, only leaving the short tuft of hair I have mentioned before, might really be called pretty, as all had most elegant features.... These odalisques were very thinly clad, wearing salendangs, and a long silk scarf thrown loosely over one shoulder and across the body: this piece of dress seemed to be used more as an ornament than as a necessary covering, for it was often allowed to slip off the shoulder, and had to be every now and then re-adjusted. We were told the greater proportion of the King's women were the daughters of his ministers, and other men of high rank, who all vie with one another for the honour of furnishing a fresh inmate for the royal harem. They not only consider it an honour to the family, but a possible source of future aggrandizement to the father and brothers of the girl should she captivate the affections of the King.[34]

In light of the casual court attire of both king and harem, it is surprising that one of Ang Duong's more fundamental alterations to the royal dancers was to clothe them in heavy brocade skirts with bodices so tight they had to be sewn in for each performance. Contemporary Khmer scholars suggest that the semi-nudity of the dancers was eliminated because it "was no longer suited to the morales and beliefs of the time, or more probably in imitation of the Siamese."[35]

Many of Ang Duong's choices regarding the dance should be viewed in light of the fact that he was generally more familiar with Thai custom than with Khmer. He was, for instance, fluent in the Thai language and clumsy in Khmer, though he actually preferred the latter.[36] Nonetheless, changes which the Thai monarch allowed his dancers in this period—such as authorizing them to perform outside the palace[37]—were not adopted by Ang Duong, who kept the court women cloistered in the palace—a custom that was carefully followed with few exceptions until the reign of King Monivong (1928-1941).

The changes which Ang Duong did effect, however, involved every aspect of the dance. For instance, before his reign, the dancer's costume was still Angkorean in style –"almost unchanged from that of the stone figures in the great temples. It consisted mainly of a light *sampot*, often draped round the waist and leaving leg movements completely free."[38] In contrast, the costumes which Ang Duong personally designed for each character, were of heavy gold and silver cloth that not only "completely changed the appearance of the dancers"[39] but also limited their freedom of movement and thus altered the basic choreography. Ang Duong also prescribed the smallest details of the costumes, jewelry, colors appropriate to rank, the heavy crowns, and all accessories. By fixing these technical elements he fabricated a "tradition" still closely followed in the 1970s.

Nonetheless, it is clear that, as reported, Ang Duong did rely on the old teachers' advice in purging the dances of "unsuitable" material that had been added over the years. Some of this may have included elements of Vietnamese origin.[40] One need only see a performance of *lakhon bassac*, the popular Cambodian theatre form greatly influenced by Vietnamese *cai luong*, to realize that today there are no discernible Vietnamese elements in the classical Khmer dance form—a separation which may not have always been so strict.

Cambodian dance scholars feel that two movement patterns in particular were excised by Ang Duong. One was a frequent stance particularly of male dancers, who also performed in the palace, in which the legs were "bent and very slightly apart and their elbows thrown back at shoulder height"—possibly a borrowing from the traditional Vietnamese opera. The second was a pattern of "quick shoulder and chest movements, and a way of shaking the body."[41]

One other specific change added by Ang Duong has been described—unfortunately with some ambiguity; Ang Duong ordered that "the arms should bend forward from the wrist, thus making a curve known as *bras en arc* and also that the body should lean on one bent leg, with the other also bent and raised towards the back."[42] It is thought that this and other specific postures were direct borrowings from the Thai court.

The only available account of Ang Duong's renovation of the royal "ballet"—as Europeans chose to call it—suggests that, in general, the dance was more "stiff and mechanical" and lacking in "elegance and suppleness" than Ang Duong was willing to allow.[43] In terms of the total aesthetic of the dance form, he seems to have reversed a fundamental balance of elements. Previously the dancers were semi-nude and had great freedom of movement but danced in a very controlled, often static, manner. The revised version insisted on heavy clothing and restricted movement but with a more lithesome choreography. In short, the evolution appears to have been a move from veiled solidity to encumbered softness.

One final element of the court dance which Ang Duong removed should be mentioned, namely, the men. For some indefinite period they had accompanied the women in popular dances and the alternating female-male songs known as *ayay*. The king "decided to divide his dancers into exclusively male and female groups, each capable of staging any of the classical dances of the repertoire."[44] He further enjoined the men to use the same training techniques as the women and to be more graceful. Again, as at Angkor, the role of male dancers is problematic. Had they, for instance, always been associated with the female dancers or only periodically when controls on the harem were perhaps less restrictive? What roles did they perform in the repertoire, since the women more than likely played the male roles as they do today? After Ang Duong's renovation a few men played the roles of "jesters or demons" we are told,[45] but of their position in the court or, indeed, the function of the new all-male troupe as a whole we know nothing.

Ang Duong established a school in the palace to train both girls and boys in the classical dance. Enrollment carried great prestige, and court dignitaries sought admission for their children. Rather inexplicably, we are told that very early in the reign of Ang Duong's successor, "several of the sons of high court officials, already married and with a family of their own, became stars of the royal ballet."[46] Unfortunately no further information is available on the subject of male "stars" in what is today—and has been for the last century, except for monkey roles—predominantly a performance by women.

The changes instituted by Ang Duong are considered in retrospect to be a conscious effort to restore to his court some of its "ancient splendour," and certainly he paved the way for the great flourishing of classical dance under the aegis of his successor. He is to be credited with giving Khmer classical dance a new shape and vitality. His greatest contribution, however, seems to have been the utilization of the court dance as a demonstration of the modern Cambodian throne's legitimacy in the Angkorean lineage, which the court at Bangkok had so persistently attempted to destroy. Ang Duong realized that, even if unseen, the royal dancers were as powerful a symbol of his own efficacy in the eyes of the peasant populace as the crown or sacred sword itself, and on that basis the "Royal Ballet" came to be increasingly cherished.

Dance in the Reign of Norodom (1860-1904)

In the second half of the nineteenth century, Khmer court dance experienced its greatest flowering of the modern period. Concurrently, however, Cambodia came under the colonial domination of France, leaving the monarchy virtually powerless. The king who presided over this circuit of fortune was Norodom (Fig. 4-2), eldest son of Ang Duong, who, like his father, was educated in Bangkok.

Ang Duong had been a man of wisdom—as well as luck—in protecting Cambodia's freedom from the grasp of both Thailand and Vietnam. Norodom was not so fortunate with the French. Shortly after Ang Duong's death, a younger brother of Norodom attempted to gain the throne, forcing Norodom to seek Thai protection in Bangkok. The Thai king returned him to Cambodia by steamer but with no military support, and into that relative vacuum stepped the French who controlled Vietnam and now forced on Norodom a "French Protectorate" against the Thai and innumerable rebels. The treaty was signed in April of 1864. In exchange for their assent and the return of the royal regalia, including the sacred sword, Thailand received the provinces of Angkor and Battambang from France. Norodom was crowned in June of 1864.

Khmers acknowledge that, in regard to the court dance, Norodom "always remained accessible to outside influence."⁴⁷ In the early years of his reign he was eclectic in support of numerous Southeast Asian musical traditions, allowing performers from Laos, Burma, China, Vietnam, Malaysia and, of course, Thailand to reside in the capital under royal favor.

In 1872 Norodom visited Manila and brought back musicians who formed "the beginning of the present royal orchestra."⁴⁸ In the same year he visited Singapore and invited a group of "Malayan coachmen" to reside in Phnom Penh under his protection;

4-2. **King Norodom, 1860-1904.**

the daughter of one of these eventually became a leading dancer in the royal troupe and subsequently one of the most respected teachers of princess roles.⁴⁹ All of these non-Khmer artists were allowed to learn classical dance while periodically performing their own arts for the king. It is said that in this exchange, the Burmese and the Lao, in particular, left their mark on the court dance.⁵⁰

According to Khmer scholars, Norodom's mélange of court entertainment eventually became the *yiké*, a kind of loosely structured variety show consisting of brief comic interludes, dances, songs, mime, monologue, and dialogue which parodied classical dances, legends and traditions. *Yiké* was very popular in the late nineteenth century, but when performed in the palace, it was always followed by the classical dance troupe.⁵¹

At the beginning of Norodom's reign this troupe included some five hundred dancers—both female and male—divided into three groups, one under the guidance of the king's first wife, Neak Preah Meneang Bopha Kessa, the other two under "lesser princesses."[52] At the king's death in 1904 there were approximately one hundred dancers in the troupe. Despite its decreasing size—probably due in large measure to the austerities imposed by the French who took control of the administration of the kingdom in 1884—Norodom's affection for the royal dancers appears eventually to have eclipsed his love of music. He was "increasingly devoted" to the classical dance troupe in his later years.[53]

Regardless of the contacts which the dancers must have made with outsiders, Norodom was relentless in maintaining the seclusion of the palace women. Unless she was driven out, a dancer might ask for permission only one day each year to leave, and then only to meet her parents in the city between dawn and sunset, accompanied by an "imposing" female guard.[54] In his old age Norodom watched the classical dance rehearsals daily—one early photo may even show him in attendance (Fig. 4-3)—which certainly bespeaks his personal affection for the dancers as well as their art.

We know little about the personnel in the dance troupe under Norodom, although their organization appears to have been similar to that in the mid-twentieth century. One 1883 account, for instance, mentions the official director of the palace theatre named Chomnitsophan, who received no salary but "only gifts and gratuities." The head of the orchestra was a high official but received only two hundred francs a year. He had to be present at all performances on festival days but was otherwise usually replaced by an assistant. There was also a solo singer who led the large chorus and sat with the text on a small music stand before her. Reports differ as to the actual supervisors of Norodom's three dance troupes. Moura wrote that Neak Preah Meneang Bopha Kessa, the king's first wife, took charge of all costumes as well as the instruction of young dancers within the palace, while two other princesses assisted her in this, conducted rehearsals, and dressed the dancers for performance.[55] Another reliable source reported that the first troupe—the most beautiful, the most skillful and the best

4-3. **Dancers at Phnom Penh, ca. 1903.** Louis Salaun, *Indochine*.

dressed—was under the "iron discipline" of the king's first wife, Princess Khun Tanh, while the second troupe was under his second wife Khun Preah Nieth, and the third troupe, comprised of students, was headed by Princess Man Soun.[56] Despite the discrepancy in names—due perhaps to the use of a stage name, the two accounts agree that the king's wives were responsible for the training and maintenance of the royal dancers.

THAI DANCERS AT NORODOM'S COURT

Let us digress momentarily to consider the matter of Thai dancers (Fig. 4-4) at the Khmer court during this period. In general, there were many more Thai functionaries at Norodom's court than had been at that of Ang Duong. In contrast to his father, Norodom spoke Khmer fluently but preferred Thai, particularly when entertaining. Yet, like his father, Norodom maintained "a great number of women, concubines or dancers, of Thai origin" in his court.[57]

One interesting anecdote regarding the arrival of a specific contingent of Thai dancers in Phnom Penh has been offered by Kukrit Pramoj, Prime Minister of Thailand during the 1970s. In a privately-published "gift-book" entitled *Skeletons in the Cupboard* prepared for distribution to friends on the occasion of his sixtieth birthday, Kukrit relates how one of his favorite old aunts, having been involved in some deviation from rectitude in her younger days, had chosen at that time to flee court and country. His account bears quoting at length:

> After these events, the next day Aunt Chawiwat hired a sailing boat, put in all her household treasures, took the *lakhon* troupe of Chao Chorm Manda Ampa [a high-ranking court lady], which subsequently became her own, together with all its accessories and the *piphat* orchestra, embarked at the nearby river in front of the palace at sundown and sailed all night. In the early morning, reaching the mouth of the river, she looked back and saw the royal steamboat in pursuit. Offering a prayer to a nearby wat for the success of her escape in the much slower boat, she saw the steamship break down and anchor immediately, permitting her to sail all the way to Cambodia.
>
> When Aunt Chawiwat reached Cambodia, Norodom was the ruling king. Norodom and Sisowath [his brother] had grown up in Thailand during the reigns of the third and fourth kings and were accustomed to the Thai court. When she arrived, therefore, she went directly to Norodom's palace, and, being of his station, he welcomed her.... But Aunt Chawiwat was clever enough to have brought the lakhon of Chao Chorm Manda Ampa—the famous *lakhon nai* teacher—with her, which was the key that opened Cambodia to her.
>
> In that time this *lakhon* was a significant thing because in that area *khon*, *lakhon* and the *nang* were considered as treasures which enhanced the owner, and every country wanted to have their own.[58]

At this point Kukrit explains that Cambodia was a vassal state of Thailand and, consequently, did not have the right to maintain "king's dancers." He cites the analogy of the Lao kingdom of Vientiane whose king, Chao Anou, came to Bangkok for the funeral of King Rama II in 1825 and took the opportunity, when bidding farewell afterwards to Rama III, of asking that "some dancers be given to Vientiane in order to have the *lakhon*."

Rama III, feeling that Chao-Anou "might presume to be his equal, having the *lakhon nai* for his own" refused to give it, and Chao-Anou departed in anger—a trigger in part to his subsequent rebellion and attack on Thailand.⁵⁹

Kukrit concludes: "When Aunt Chawiwat brought the *lakhon nai* troupe, Norodom considered this to be great fortune. He accepted her in the palace and gave her troupe the status of the Cambodian *lakhon nai*, and authorized her as the teacher of *lakhon thai* to the Cambodian court"⁶⁰ where she remained until returning to Bangkok during the reign of Rama VI (1910-1925).

4-4. **Dancing Girls, ca. 1875.** J. Thomson, *The Straits of Malacca, Indo-China, and China.*

There are no Khmer sources which corroborate this claim, although Chheng Phon, while a professor at the University of Fine Arts, offered the somewhat less chauvinistic counter-claim that

> in the reign of Ang Duong some Cambodian dancers went to Thailand and performed, and the Thai who liked the Cambodian dancing came afterwards to Cambodia to live. Thus two schools of thought concerning technique developed in Cambodia, and today there are still two groups of teachers: the Thai tradition technique and the Khmer technique.⁶¹

Unfortunately, little other information on the dual tradition in Cambodia is available.

Early European Accounts of Dance

Norodom ruled Cambodia forty-four years. Aside from general support of the royal troupe, one of his major contributions to the dance was his construction of a dance pavilion in the palace when he moved his capital to

Phnom Penh in 1866.⁶² A large, open-air, wooden building with a thatch roof and lit by torches, it remained a part of the palace complex until well after 1910 when Adhémard Leclère wrote a charming description of its physical elements and colonial protocol (Appendix I).

In July of 1866, shortly after the building's completion, a group of travelers including the French explorer Louis Delaporte were the guests of the King of Phnom Penh. Delaporte later wrote that King Norodom

> offered us a ballet performed by the entire corps of his [female] dancers.... What a pleasure to see the women evolving in accordance with prescriptions comparable to those of ancient choreography, in hieratic poses, their faces imprinted with a mysterious, distant thought, dressed in silk brocade of brilliant colors, the head crowned with a golden tiara of which the narrow point recalls the stupa in the pagodas.⁶³

Delaporte's accompanying sketch is the only graphic record available of the "old *rung ram*" and the earliest pictorialization of Khmer dancers recorded by a European (Fig. 4-5).

In 1883 Moura claimed that Norodom's *rung ram* or "dancing shed" was the only theatre in Cambodia.⁶⁴ In this he was possibly mistaken since photos of a theatre in Battambang were published by August Pavie in 1898—a theatre he had seen sometime between 1879 and 1895. Pavie's pictures of a rehearsal in the Battambang theatre are the oldest available photographs of Khmer classical dancers (Figs. 4-6 and 4-7).

One traveler to Cambodia between 1880 and 1884 attended a theatre in Battambang which may have been the same as that mentioned by Pavie. This account by Edgar Boulangier, published in 1888, contends that in the "ducal theatre" of the "vice-roi of Battambang," the choreographic traditions were the most faithfully preserved in Cambodia and that "the troupe of M. Catalone is considered superior to that of Norodom."⁶⁵

The point in question is not to determine how many theatres there were in Cambodia in the late nineteenth century but simply to demonstrate that there was a significant number of dancers and troupes. In reference to the Battambang theatre and to other troupes he had seen throughout the country, Pavie wrote that in the theatre the actors usually perform in a long, plain room which the spectators surround on three sides, the other being reserved for the entrance of characters, the orchestra and the chorus.

The artists in a single troupe are of the same sex, generally girls. However the traveling troupes are sometimes formed of children of both sexes. In the plays which require giants, ogres, animals, these roles are most often played by men....

The very beautiful costumes recall those in the ancient bas-reliefs. In the theatre of King Norodom at Phnom Penh, they are rich and truly remarkable. In troupes of the second rank or the traveling troupes, they leave much to be desired but remain for all that in the tradition.

The adaptation almost without change of literary works to the theatre results in endlessly long performances; rarely does one night suffice for the unfolding of a story.[66]

In a slightly earlier account Pavie mentions a specific performance which he saw at a marriage celebration on a country "plantation" (Fig. 4-8).

I watched for some hours...the performance of a small, traveling

4-5. **King Norodom and Guests Viewing *Kennari* Dance, July 1866.** Beauvais.

4-6. **Dance Drama Rehearsal at Battambang, ca. 1885.** Pavie.

Note: Probably dancers of Lok Muccha, who was Lord Governor of the province at that time.

4-7. **Dance Drama Rehearsal at Battambang, ca. 1885.** Pavie.

> Cambodian theatre troupe in front of the houses beside the river. The performers were young girls from twelve to fourteen years old; they interpreted with an extreme grace, on mats spread on the ground, the stories beloved in the country . . ..[67]

From such accounts it would appear that classically-oriented dancers were prevalent throughout Cambodia in this period.

The question of whether or not these dancers in the provinces may properly be termed "classical," can be answered at this late date only by pointing out that the performers in question—those observed and photographed by Pavie—are costumed more or less in the style of court dancers, their poses (Figs. 4-6 and 4-7) closely resemble the palace form, and they performed—at least in part—stories from the literary-based, classical repertoire rather than provincial folk forms. For these three reasons it seems fair to conclude that the court dancers represented a standard of form and quality against which secondary and traveling troupes (Fig. 4-8) measured their own repertoire and style.

In suggesting that classically-oriented dancers were numerous throughout the entire area and had been for some centuries, Adhémard Leclère drew analogies with Laos and Champa:

> In all of Laos, in Luang Prabang today, in Vientiane in the time when Géraerd Van Wustorf found himself there (1642), the dances that we study here were interpreted by the Laotian dancers, and it is probable that it was the same pieces that were played. In Champa, before the conversion of the Chams to Islam and perhaps after, there were numerous [female] dancers and dance troupes at the court of the kings and perhaps of the princes.[68]

Because of the prestige adhering to the court form, classical dance often appears to have been maintained outside the court *per se* throughout much of mainland Southeast Asia.

To conclude our discussion of dance during the reign of Norodom, we note that in 1903 the modern royal troupe achieved what was considered its greatest accomplishment to date when approximately one hundred dancers performed the "first-ever" full-length production of the *Rāmker* for the consecration of the Silver Pagoda (Wat Preah Keo Morokot) on the grounds of the royal palace in Phnom Penh.[69] A year later, in 1904, Norodom died.

A "well-established" Khmer court custom held that if they wished to do so, the court dancers could leave the palace following the death of a monarch. "Too distressed... to continue their dancing," two-thirds of the troupe chose this option following Norodom's death.[70] Only the younger dancers remained, and these numbered about a hundred in 1904.[71] Some of the former court dancers "formed private troupes which certain ministers

4-8. **Dance Drama Rehearsal at Battambang, ca. 1885.** Pavie.

considered their duty to maintain and present to the king on special occasions."[72]

There was great change in Cambodia during the reign of Norodom. The outside world and especially France was exerting great influence. Children of the princes and aristocracy were enrolling in the first Western-style schools. The court retained little real power, and the concept of a harem was coming to be viewed as anachronous. The new century brought great change, most fundamental perhaps being the fact that the Khmer court dance—which was soon to make its first international appearance—began to belong less and less to the Cambodian king and increasingly to the Khmer people and the world's acknowledged community of great dance traditions.

Dance in the Reign of Sisowath (1904-1927)

The fortunes of Khmer dance in the early twentieth century appear to have undergone great fluctuation. In 1906 a company pieced together from two private troupes and inmates of the debtors' prison was sent to Paris and Marseilles for the Colonial Exposition where they were hailed by August Rodin as the most perfect possible form of human nature. Six years later

Khmer dance was claimed by a French scholar to be "at the point of death," yet the next year a stunning new dance pavilion was erected in the Royal Palace. In 1920 there were 120 palace women associated with the dance, but at the death of King Sisowath in 1927, their situation was so precarious that the troupe was placed under the protection of the French colonial government. The details of such ironic contrasts, together with a survey of personnel, facilities, and the general position of dance within the court of Sisowath will be examined in this section of the present chapter.

THE KHMER DANCERS IN FRANCE

In December of 1904 George Bois, who was in charge of all Indochina exhibits for the Colonial Exposition to be held in Marseille two years hence, arrived in Phnom Penh seeking a troupe of Khmer dancers for performances at the Exhibition.[73] The Chief Minister of the palace, Okhna Veang Thiounn, refused to consider sending the few remaining royal dancers, but the Naval Minister Colonel de Monteiro offered his personal troupe on condition that he accompany them to France. His twenty dancers were insufficient, however, and Bois went in search of dancers who had previously been at court under Norodom.

We earlier noted that many of Norodom's dancers left the palace following his death for reasons of sorrow. Bois discovered, however, that many were also dismissed for reasons of financial necessity due to the much smaller annual pension of the new king, Sisowath Monivong, Norodom's brother. Regardless of the impetus to their departure, many of these dancers "were immediately seized for debts by the Cambodian prison"[74] and incarcerated. (There is no indication as to how the debts accrued while living within the confinement of the palace.) When Bois solicited prison director Rath for assistance, he was promised some additional dancers if Rath, too, were allowed to accompany the troupe to France.

Finally, following the intervention of M. Beau—the Governor-General of French Indochina then resident in Hanoi—King Sisowath himself graciously offered his royal dancers to the Exposition on the condition that he and a royal party accompany the troupe. Bois' happiness over the arrangement was more than matched by that of the French public when the King of Cambodia and his royal dancers eventually did arrive in Marseille.

The party included the king, Thiounn, Colonel de Monteiro, several of Sisowath's sons, Prince Sutharot (the son of Norodom), together with the dance company under the stern direction of the Princess Sounpady, and the King's secretary Son-Diep. (Rath seems to have been left behind.) There is some discrepancy in reports of the number in the company, but it included forty-two dancers, eight chanters, eight dressers, two jewelers, ten male musicians, and two clowns. The entire cost for more than eighty people was 145,000 francs, including stipends for each dancer.[75]

The "Royal Ballet" took France by storm. After three evenings of dance indoors, all remaining performances in Marseille were held on the grand terrace. Bois wrote that

> each night more than thirty thousand people crowded round the stage where the perfect forms of the lovely doll-like creatures glided to and fro in a dazzling display of gems and gold beneath the flood-lights. The effect was sensational. Everyone knew and talked about Cambodia, its king and its dancers.[76]

The gems were particularly stunning due to the fact that Sisowath had lent the dancers many of the most beautiful items from among the crown jewels so that the dancers' jewelry alone was valued at eight hundred thousand francs (Fig. 4-9).

Nothing intimidated the dancers. En route to Paris some of them slept on the luggage rack of the train. They pointed fingers in delight at the President of the Republic who greeted them, but swam with dignity in the garden fountain of their hotel. Finally, a single performance in Paris was arranged by the Minister of Colonies, M. Georges Leygues—who personally supervised the lighting—in a theatre seating only twelve hundred people but to which five thousand invitations were "somewhat imprudently" issued. In the ensuing riot the British ambassador was pushed about, society women lost their jewels and tore their clothes, and order was restored by the police

4-9. **Pum, One of King Sisowath's Prima Ballerinas.**
Prince William of Sweden, *In the Lands of the Sun*, 1915.

only when Princess Sounpady "resentfully" allowed a second performance at midnight for fifteen hundred pommeled and disheveled bitter-enders.[77]

The celebrated sculptor August Rodin, then aged seventy-three, spent many hours sketching the dancers and wrote that

> these Cambodian dancers have given us all that antiquity has to offer, their own antiquity, which is as valuable as ours.... It is impossible to see human nature taken to such a degree of perfection. There have been only these dancers and the Greeks.... These dances are religious. I have never distinguished between religious art and art. When religion is lost, art is lost also. All the Greek and Roman masterpieces, as well as ours, are religious. The Princess that looks so cross and the King must be great artists because, without them, all that would disappear.[78]

Rodin's observations, so much in contrast to the usual colonial sensibilities as we shall see, marked the advent of a new European point of view regarding Cambodian dance. The revolutionary notion that an exotic and totally unfamiliar art form could be understood and appreciated on its own terms was one of the more valuable and long-lasting results of the 1906 tour.

CONDITION AND FINANCES OF THE *LAKHON*

Despite the personal benefits and prestige which accrued to the king as a result of being the protector of the royal dancers, Sisowath appears to have made little effort to enhance their public image. To be sure, for two years following his ascension he provided those dancers remaining in the court with the best possible teacher, Khun Chom Bosseba—mother of Prince Sutharot and *première danseuse* of princess roles under Norodom.[79] When Sisowath returned to Cambodia from France, however, he made little effort to either increase the performance quality of the palace troupe or to make them more visible to the general public.

While the ritual function of court dance seems not to have changed significantly, financial limitations and the ever-growing appeal of French ways tended to erode the individual dancer's position in the court. In 1911 Sisowath allowed court dancers "to leave the company whenever they wished, and he even encouraged the younger ones to attend school,"[80] clear evidence of the irresistible social change being forced upon the monarchy by European culture.

Appropriately, then, it was a European who in 1912 wrote that the Khmer dancers were at the "point of death," and began an active campaign through his writings and personal influence to save them from extinction. This man was George Groslier, later curator of the national Albert Sarraut Museum in Phnom Penh. In his somewhat overstated presentation of the gravity of the dancers' situation lay the foundation for the eventual French takeover of their affairs.

In his 1912 text, *Danseuses cambodgiennes anciennes et modernes*, Groslier painted a grim picture: "the Khmer dancers are at the point of death. They are no longer anything but shadows. They are wearing out their last costumes. The princesses sell their jewels or take them to the pawn-shop… and the women… no longer weave the beautiful 'sampots' of years gone by."[81] Groslier blamed this on the decreasing interest of the general populace in the dance tradition and especially on the Khmers' new and consuming interest in "material things." His view of the degeneracy of the dance, however, should not unduly overshadow our understanding of the situation of the court dancers who seem to have carried on their function pretty much as always, although with lesser numbers than during the preceding reign. Certainly the general populace never had much opportunity to view the dancers anyway, and their decreasing numbers were more than likely due, as we shall see, to French "material" interests.

Groslier's text was written on the basis of very little actual contact with the palace dancers, and while Sisowath gave his approval to the work, he seems to have done very little in providing Groslier with a more rounded picture of the dancers' situation. Groslier wrote that the dancers only performed on five occasions: the king's coronation, his birthdays, royal marriage, the hair-cutting ceremony of a prince or princess, and at the visit to Cambodia of an honored guest. Only on the last of these—and one birthday—did Groslier ever see the dancers perform, and he wrote his book on the basis of only six viewings: three evening performances for the king's birthday, and three short scenes performed "in supplication" in the throne room. He was also able to speak with one Siamese teacher, some high palace officials and to view the store-houses for costumes and jewelry.

Thus we must balance Groslier's extremely dismal view with the fact that the dancers continued to fulfill their ritual function—the dances of "supplication" in the throne room were more than likely *buong suong*—which Groslier gave no evidence of understanding and did not include on his list of "occasions" for dance. Moreover, as Sappho Marchal pointed out in the final year of Sisowath's reign, the dancers were also the king's harem and closest companions, a role that had never been abandoned,[82] and a fact that tended to shield their true position from scholarly scrutiny.

Groslier's view of Khmer dance at its lowest ebb around 1912 has been widely accepted. For instance, the historical section of *Royal Cambodian Ballet*, the 1963 publication of the Cambodian Information Agency, was largely based on his interpretation. The data that are available, however—including some presented by Groslier himself—allows for an interpretation far less romantic than seeing Sisowath's dancers at death's door.

In 1908 Gaston Knopf observed that the palace dance troupe in Phnom Penh consisted of about six hundred members divided into three troupes: a primary troupe of women, a mixed troupe of women and men, and a troupe of men who played demons, servants and animals.[83] In 1912 the royal troupe was composed of eight *premières danseuses*, sixty-six to seventy other performers, and about forty little girl students.[84] In 1920 there were 150 palace women associated with the dance in some capacity.[85] A 1926 visitor to the royal palace wrote that dance performances sometimes included "several hundred performers,"[86] and a year later Sappho Marchal counted about a hundred royal dancers in the troupe.[87] In contrast to Knopf, both Groslier in 1912 and Marchal in 1927 were in agreement that the only males who performed with the palace dancers—besides the musicians—were two clowns who appeared infrequently. Groslier, updating himself, reported that in 1927 the royal troupe consisted of seventy-five "actresses" and eleven teachers.[88]

What we may conclude from these figures, regardless of the extent to which they reflect variations over the years (and Knopf's possible confusion with reported numbers of dancers in the reign of Norodom), is that rarely were there less than a hundred dancers resident in the court during the reign of Sisowath. Their position was one of high prestige as an indispensable part of his entourage, and he surrounded himself with dancers every minute of the day. Twenty of the most beautiful—together with a few musicians—attended Sisowath in shifts, each of the dancers being present for a quarter of the day. There were always two beside his bed night and day—one with a fan, the other with a fly-whisk—and the others were scattered about his chamber. Sometimes they sang in chorus, but we are told they never danced for him alone[89] as they had for his father Ang Duong eighty years earlier.

On these dancers, Sisowath spent a considerable amount of money. *Première* dancers received a stipend of thirty-five piastres per month; others, ten to twelve depending on their role; the little girls received three to six. When a dancer was accepted into the troupe, she received four piastres for food, with subsequent allowances on performance days of one piastre for the main dancers, ninety cents for difficult roles such as the mask-wearers, twenty-five cents for ordinary dancers, and twenty cents for the little girls. In 1912 fifteen instructors received stipends, and, although they appeared only for performances, salaries of three to five piastres per month were paid to four prompters, five singers, twenty-one time beaters and a large number of dressers all living outside the palace.[90] Seamstresses who made all the costumes, as well as the musicians were also paid.

In the early years of his reign, King Sisowath's total annual budget was 450,000 piastres.[91] Of that, he spent between thirty and thirty-five thousand (7-8 percent) on the various personnel and expenses—including jewelry and costumes (see Chapter VIII)—necessary to maintain the royal dance troupe.[92] All things considered, Sisowath appears to have supported his dancers—as well as French financial restraint allowed—to fulfill ritual functions, indulge his own pleasure, and guarantee transmission of the art.

Politics and Chanchhaya Pavilion

Further evidence that George Groslier's estimation of the royal dancers' position in 1912 was unduly bleak is the fact that in 1913 construction of the new Chanchhaya dance pavilion was begun.[93] This splendid edifice could only have been erected with French approval regarding the expenditure and would not have been constructed if the royal dance troupe was not of significant stature and importance.

Chanchhaya was erected on the same basic floor plan as the original *rung ram* built by Norodom in 1866, although consolidated under a single roof and with the dance theatre elevated to a second story (Fig. 4-10). There was one important change however. In the old *rung ram*, the dancers faced east and the king had his back to the north, i.e., the dancers had the most auspicious location. In Chanchhaya, the dancers entered from the north, and it was the king who faced east as he did when on the throne itself. It is perhaps for this reason that Chanchhaya is never referred to by Cambodians as the *rung ram* or *salle des danses*, a title reserved for Phochani Pavilion whose orientation exactly copied the original *rung ram*. Moreover, Chanchhaya also served as the "Royal Tribune" from whose upper gallery (facing east toward the river) subsequent monarchs publicly addressed their subjects, which points up the political nature not only of the building but of the dancers themselves.

Additional evidence that the financial situation could not have been unduly severe in this period is the fact that only six years after the completion of Chanchhaya a second dance pavilion was completed to replace the original *rung ram*. This appears to be the present-day Phochani Pavilion, but the sequence of construction is somewhat unclear. In 1920 Félix Cardi reported attending a performance in a large hall with blue columns open on three sides. He wrote that "they are finishing construction of the new 'salle des danses,' very showy, with fans and innumerable electric lamps pouring out torrents of light; we had the good fortune tonight of being in the old hall, very much more authentic and of a character less blemished by westernism."[94] He could not have been referring to Chanchhaya, which was completed in 1914, and since there is no other evidence dating

4-10. **Chanchhaya Pavilion of the Royal Palace, Phnom Penh**.
Royal Cambodia Ballet.

Phochani, we deduce that it was finished about 1920. The fate of the old *rung ram* is not known.

Writing some ten years after its completion, Thiounn claimed that the "Rong Ram"—he never uses the name Phochani—"is built on the model of ancient Cambodian halls; electric lighting adds a little modernism; the greatest concern for orientation ruled the placement of stage, entrance and so forth.... The entrance faces east; the dancers' foyer is on the west, ...the chorus is on the south."[95] The wall between the dancers' two doors as well as the ceiling are painted to depict episodes in the principal dances. Three sides of the hall consist of large doors that can be opened. While the pavilion appears to seat far fewer than Chanchhaya, the fact that it could be so open and that its floor is only perhaps five feet above ground made it the preferred setting for the large audiences on occasions such as the king's birthday when, presumably, people could stand or even sit throughout the surrounding courtyard and still see the dancers.

During the reign of Sisowath, the inevitable tensions between king and colonial overlord were intensified in Cambodia not only by the fact that the French had control of all finances including the size of Sisowath's privy purse, but also by French insistence on continual, high visibility of the Resident-Superior at the king's side. At performances of the royal ballet, for instance, which were formal to the extent that much of the regalia was present—including the small lance that was companion piece to the sacred sword—similar chairs for both the king and the French resident occupied the center of the royal box (see Appendix I). Not only was the Royal Ballet—in the words of one astute observer –"the principal emblem of royal power from which it was inseparable,"[96] it was the one realm of power into which the French could not easily penetrate. The women of the palace who surrounded the king symbolized the essential power of the monarch in the Khmer mind and as such the harem/ballet was inherently political.

Groslier's claim that the Cambodian dance tradition was at death's door was, in part, a political statement covertly supporting the notion that the French should have protective bureaucratic control over the dancers, which they did, in fact, assume upon Sisowath's death in 1927. As we shall see, the dancers had serious financial problems in this period, but we must look deeper than Groslier's superficial sketch of the dancer as employee to realize that the symbolic power and internal function of the court dancer was never really in jeopardy during the reign of Sisowath. We should also note, parenthetically, that for subsidies over which there was no political conflict, unlike the subsidy for the royal dancers, large sums were readily available, as witnessed by the construction of the huge new throne room—virtually the palace itself—for which Sisowath laid the cornerstone on 13 August 1920.[97]

Before concluding this discussion of the period between 1903 and 1927, a brief survey of three general areas of concern will provide a more complete picture of the state of court dance: royal troupe activities and personnel, non-royal troupes, and French attitudes toward the royal dance. Regarding the first, *Danseuses cambodgiennes anciennes et modernes* offers an excellent picture of the dancer's daily life and need not be duplicated here, although another court dancer's semi-fictionalized "autobiography" published in 1919 by Roland Meyer[98] is far closer to the Khmer perspective and is a valuable supplement.

Dance Personnel and Activities

All performance activities of the royal dance troupe during the reign of Sisowath were under the guidance of the Palace Minister Samdach Chaufea Thiounn, also known as Okhna Veang. A gracious and knowledgeable man, Thiounn had been general overseer during the 1906 tour, and much later, when dancers were sent to the Paris Colonial Exhibition of 1931, he wrote *Danses cambodgiennes* as a descriptive study and introduction. Actual supervision and training of the dancers were in the hands of a mistress of the ballet, a job which changed hands periodically. In 1922, for instance, it was held by Mme. Maleck who seems not to have been of the royal family.[99] Other large responsibilities were often handled by women of the court, as in the case of Princess Saunpady—ballet mistress for the 1906 tour—or Princess Rea Srey Yaolac, a former *première danseuse* who in 1911 was the directress of all costume construction.[100] Costumes were stored and maintained by a "responsible" man and woman.

Of the dancers themselves, only three are known to us now: in 1911 the star dancer and favorite of Sisowath was San Krinh,[101] and in 1922 the star dancer for the second European tour was Mlle. Ith.[102] A third *première danseuse* who was to have a great influence as teacher in the reign of Sisowath's successor was known as Khun Meak.

The tour of 1922 was a pallid affair compared to that of 1906. Only a "small group" of dancers and musicians attended the Colonial Exposition in Marseille. They did go on to Paris for just two matinee performances—31 May and 1 June 1922—although one of these was viewed by Antonin Artaud.[103] The program consisted of three pieces: The Dance of Welcome, the *Rāmker* episode of Hanuman and Sovann Machha, and the drama of Preah Somut.

Sisowath did not accompany the tour. Eighty-six years old and nearly blind, he found it increasingly difficult to support the royal dancers. One commentator shed light on their general situation in the 1920s when he wrote that Sisowath "no longer had the strength or the financial means necessary to struggle against the loss of traditions and the rising fashion for all the west had to offer of complete bad taste and inadaptability to Cambodian life."[104] The tour of 1922 was the last made by dancers of the court, prior to the reign of Sihanouk.

One important activity which occurred during this reign was the translation of a significant portion of the performance repertoire from Thai into Khmer—in some instances a return to its original language. According to Chheng Phon, many songs performed early in this century had always remained in their native Khmer,[105] a claim corroborated by Jeanne Cuisinier who reported in 1931 seeing singers with "old Khmer" performance texts.[106] The songs sung in Thai were especially associated with the relatively modern, dramatized literary tradition rather than with the more ancient dances of ritual significance.

Non-Royal Dance

Let us at this point note briefly the nature of non-royal dance troupes in Cambodia during Sisowath's reign, since later—in the 1930s—we will observe at least one of them vying for authority with the palace troupe. Provincial troupes such as the one that performed frequently at Angkor for tourists in the 1920s, were often trained by a former court dancer and maintained a fairly high standard of choreography in the palace style.[107] Groslier painted one such dancer in an outdoor setting for the frontispiece of his *Danseuses cambodgiennes* (Fig. 4-11). Other provincial troupes of lesser skill traveled throughout Cambodia, Thailand and Laos and were more eclectic in style, being greatly influenced by the *yiké* as well as by the Chinese, Malay, Vietnamese, and even European theatre.

Of greater relevance to the present discussion than either of these, however, were the private dance troupes maintained by high officials in Phnom Penh to perform on the occasion of traditional ceremonies, the most important being marriages and the "hair-cutting" ritual for infants.[108] In 1910, for instance, the Justice Minister had his own troupe of dancers and a theatre for performance, as had the Prime Minister some years earlier. Since the expense of their maintenance was considerable, Sisowath often furnished these troupes with singers and musicians as needed (see Appendix I). Performances were strictly private. The common view seems to have been that even this type of troupe was inferior to the king's dancers, however, in that the dancers were more "vulgar" and inadequately trained.¹⁰⁹

FRENCH ATTITUDES
TOWARDS THE DANCE

Despite their acknowledged superiority, a general lethargy seems to have settled over the royal dance troupe in the 1920s—to the point that shortly before Sisowath's death in 1928 the French authorities asked George Groslier, the Arts Director, to re-establish daily rehearsals and to determine the best way of restoring the troupe's former excellence. There was no precedent for such interference, and French objectives in the matter seem fairly clear since the new king, shortly after his coronation, agreed to sign an order placing the royal dancers under the authority of l'École des Beaux-Arts, making them, in effect, civil servants. He accepted this option as the only way of saving the *lakhon*.¹¹⁰

4-11. *"Danseuse dorée (Rôle religieux)"*
G. Groslier's painting of royal dancer Ratt Poss, *Danseuses cambodgiennes*, 1913.

The evidence concerning the French attitude toward the dancers suggests that the French wanted control of the royal troupe; otherwise it would have been far easier merely to increase the king's allowance for their maintenance. As we shall see, this struggle between the court and colonial authorities over the royal dancers continued for some years. What is important to note throughout, however, is that regardless of his ability to support them, the king never wavered in his insistence that the court dancers were his own prerogative. The explanation for this is that

4-12. **King Monivong and the Resident-Superior M. Le Vol at the 1928 Coronation.** Meynard, *Le couronnement.*

the dancers were not only a prize in the colonial game of pull-and-tug, they were also a ritually functioning symbol of the king's authority and spiritual power which he could not reasonably relinquish.

On the personal level, the French had mixed feelings about the Khmer dance. Their delight in exotica seems to have declined considerably between 1906 and the 1920s. One writer found the dancers unattractively "massive" and "heavily built."[111] Another noted the derisive laughter of "uncivilized" Parisians during the 1922 tour.[112] A third reported that while the French in Cambodia found the costumes beautiful, a quarter hour of the spectacle was enough for anyone, and "all the colonials believe that it would be self abasing to interest themselves in anything indigenous."[113]

Fortunately, not all the colonials were of this opinion and it was during the reign of Sisowath that the dance drama came to be appreciated by a broader, non-Khmer audience. Most importantly, it was Félix Cardi writing in 1920 who first described the dance as having a ritual nature, though he made little of the fact.[114] Others had superficially described it as "sacred" largely on the basis of the Khmer claim, one suspects, but only in this period did observers begin to note the ritual function within Khmer culture which the dance performed beneath its exotic glitter.

Dance in the Reign of Monivong (1928-1941)

During the thirteen-year reign of King Sisowath Monivong, Khmer classical dance became even more of a political pawn than in the preceding reign of his father. In this section of the present study we will examine the changes which, in that regard, affected the royal troupe by focusing on three women who—far more than Monivong himself—were major characters in the backstage drama of forces acting upon Khmer court dance. These three were Princess Say Sangvann, the wife of King Monivong's youngest brother; Khun Meak, a star dancer during the reign of Sisowath; and Princess Kossamak, Monivong's daughter.

The regnal transition in 1928 was of momentous significance to the classical dancers because the French used the opportunity to gain complete if short-lived control of the royal troupe. Tension between the new king and the

4-13. Two *Premières Danseuses* of the Royal Troupe, 1928.
Meynard, *Le couronnement.*

Resident-Superior was palpable from the time of his coronation (Fig. 4-12), on which occasion the French openly claimed that "today the religious dignitaries of Cambodia are no longer the only consecratory of royalty; the Governor-General of Indo-China and the Resident-Superior assume almost the role of chief priests during the five-day ritual of investiture."[115] As noted earlier, the French authorities had already prepared a document at the time of the coronation which transferred control of the dancers from the Royal Palace administration to the École des Beaux-Arts. The new king, apparently under great financial pressure, agreed to sign it. We know only that the terms were "accepted because it seemed a possible way of saving the ballet."[116]

That there was a need to save it is possibly suggested by the fact that only two dancers were left from the previous reign at the time that Monivong was crowned. These were the two star dancers, "supreme in grace and technical knowledge"[117] (Fig. 4-13). Presumably the other dancers took advantage of the time-honored option of departing the palace following a monarch's death, but, at any rate, Monivong inaugurated a new troupe together with new costumes for his coronation. Their first performance was offered on the evening of the fourth day of the ritual to an audience of European and Khmer guests. The number of dancers who performed is not known, but in the period immediately following—when the dancers were, in fact, French civil servants—there were forty.[118]

One account of the 1928 events—highly influenced by the French point of view—presented the intriguing claim that the Khmer court dancers "recently... became sufficiently modern to protest about their working conditions. They went on a strike and appealed to the French resident for a readjustment of their status. As a result they are no longer the dancers of the palace but a sort of state troupe whose performances are under the direction of the protectorate."[119] Such disloyalty to the sovereign seems unlikely, but no other sources clarify the events which were interpreted—or conjured—by the French to be a "strike."

French control of the royal dancers lasted less than a year. The period was marked by an unusually strict rehearsal schedule in preparation for the Saigon Exhibition late in 1928, but the traditional *raison d'être* of the dancers had been eliminated. Their overall function as attendants of the king and performers of ritual dances over which he presided had been replaced by a social role allowing them a personal freedom for which they were ill-prepared. Of the seventy-five royal dancers in 1927, for instance—the last year of Sisowath's reign—only four could read and of those, only two could write. Of the eleven teachers, one could read and write.[120] Rarely could the dancers speak French. Eschewing the protectiveness of the palace, however, thirty of the forty dancers under the French administration chose to marry.[121] The Khmer dance tradition on a more fundamental level than mere performance was rapidly deteriorating.

The low point of this process was reached at the Saigon Exhibition when the jewel-keeper, a man named Phen previously appointed by the king, took more than twenty-five kilograms of gold and silver ornaments and absconded to Thailand. The royal palace administration immediately resumed control of the troupe,[122] but the alteration of the relationship between king and dancer could not be reversed. The majority of the troupe having married, a return to the palace was inappropriate, with the result that by 1929 less than a dozen dancers and about as many singers and other assistants remained in the court. As this was too few even to meet the "strict minimum requirements" for the ritual offertory dances, older dancers from private companies had to be brought to the palace to fill the ranks and "allow the continued fulfillment of the ancient rites."[123]

THE CONTRIBUTION OF PRINCESS SAY SANGVANN

It is at this point in the history of Khmer classical dance that we have the data to allow a first glimpse of the machinations surrounding individual personalities associated with the fortunes of the dance. It is important to remember that in all periods the dancers themselves were one of the more impermanent elements of the dance. They ceased dancing upon pregnancy[124] or when youth's bloom had faded, and, given their intimate relationship with the monarch, it is understandable that most of them left the palace following the king's death. Thus, if the tradition were to be maintained, the continuity of teachers was far more important than that of the dancers themselves. It is for this reason that we next consider the contributions of two teachers in the 1930s whose loyalties—to the point of combativeness—were ultimately of great service to Khmer dance. The first of these was Princess Wongat Say Sangvann, a former royal dancer married to Prince Yong Kath, youngest son of the former King Sisowath and thus, by definition, a major character in the drama of the struggle for power and succession to the Khmer throne.

In 1931 the French government invited the Cambodian Royal Ballet to perform at the Colonial Exhibition being held at Vincennes. So depleted was the troupe, however, that the invitation was declined. This only compounded an already embarrassing situation for the French colonial government in that distinguished visitors to Cambodia, having heard of the royal dancers' reputation, were usually unable to view a performance. Sisowath had no desire to display a part of his private household to a flow of strangers, and the French could not openly force him to do so. All tension over the issue was resolved, however, when Princess Say Sangvann (Fig. 4-14) became embroiled in a domestic disagreement and left the court. The French government welcomed her gratefully.

Say Sangvann had her own troupe of dancers, hitherto a "pleasant amateur group," which she promptly offered to the French authorities as needed. They immediately arranged for her rapidly disciplined troupe to perform at the Colonial Exhibition, which it did with great success. Following their return to Cambodia, the troupe was granted a subsidy by the French government and declared to be the official "one and only true" Khmer dancers with exclusive rights of performance for distinguished guests both in the salon of the Resident-Superior and at Angkor Wat.[125] Definitely a coup. The greatly overshadowed palace troupe retained the prestigious title of "Corps de Ballet Royal" and continued to perform ritual ceremonies, but clearly to the French authorities they were extraneous.

4-14. **Say Sangvann with Her Dancers.**
Nokor Khmer.

Say Sangvann's headquarters were in Phnom Penh except during the tourist "season," when she moved to Angkor. Her dancers shared her home and were allowed great freedom; in 1936 they numbered nineteen;[126] in 1937 eighteen.[127] They sewed their own costumes, save for the crowns which were made at the Albert Sarraut Museum in Phnom Penh.[128] The group appears to have been very disciplined—with several hours of morning rehearsal daily—and to have maintained high performance quality, but its personnel underwent frequent change; four years after the 1931 tour only three of the original members including the star dancer (Fig. 4-15) remained in the troupe.[129]

A performance at Angkor by Say Sangvann's company was held whenever enough tourists were on hand to warrant it, and most of the local population not only attended but also provided the lighting, i.e., balsam torches which were made, sold, and carried by small boys at "four cents" apiece.[130] Up to a hundred torches preceded the dancers and audience as they moved together after sunset down the long moats to the Gopura or main entrance of Angkor Wat where the dancers performed. They began on the huge steps and then moved down to the main terrace. Provincial troupes at Angkor prior to this had accepted alms,[131] but Say Sangvann was subsidized by the government to the point that about 1937 performances began to be lit by electric floodlights.[132]

4-15. **Star of Say Sangvann's Troupe, ca. 1937.** *Nokor Khmer.*

The earlier torch-lit performances were said to be quite magical in effect. Certainly they made a deep impression on an imminent painter commissioned by the Grand Conseil Economique of French Indochina and the Société des Artistes Coloniaux in Paris, who traveled throughout the area recording a primarily rural way of life that was being drastically altered. His name was Jean Despujols, and he spent twenty months (December 1936-August 1938) in some of the remotest areas of Indochina. His splendid painting of a performance at Angkor in this period (Fig. 4-16) shows the illumination of fireworks within the galleries as well as of

4-16. **Performance at Angkor Wat, ca. 1937.** Painting Jean Despujols.
Photo courtesy Meadows Museum of Art.

torches, then used only for effect since flood-lights had already been installed.[133]

While numerous photos from this period reveal a French-created image of Angkor as exotic and bizarre—complete with elephants[134]—the dancers were, in general, identified with an ancient past and presented as elegant incarnations of Angkorean sculpture. Despujols painted a portrait of a dancer in this tradition (Fig. 4-17), identifying her with the standing *devatā* figures. Attractive though the dancer was, this tradition of literalism first discussed in Chapter III remains somehow grating.

Say Sangvann's troupe included no men except as musicians, and, in keeping with all previous tradition, the monkey roles were played by young girls of great gymnastic ability. Two ten-year-olds performed the monkey roles publicly, but, according to one 1936 visitor, two seven-year-olds of great skill played the monkeys in rehearsal.[135] We know little about other members of the troupe, although one of the most beautiful was Saem, the foster child of Say Sangvann, whose portrait Despujols painted in front of the causeway at Angkor (book cover illustration).

In its acquiescence to French requirements, Say Sangvann's troupe was very much a symbol of Khmer subservience to the French during the reign of Monivong. How many years the company performed at Angkor and in Phnom Penh is not known, but it is last mentioned in the literature as being active in 1941[136] when Sihanouk, the son of Princess Kossamak, succeeded to the throne, and the royal ballet again gained pre-eminence. It is easy to see how the pressure on Say Sangvann to accommodate the foreign and tourist desire for short-term entertainment was a great barrier to the maintenance of Khmer dance integrity in the traditional form. Certainly at the court her efforts were little appreciated. While she popularized the dance for personal—possibly even financial and political—reasons and made classical Khmer dance far more accessible to foreign journalists, European travelers and even the Khmers themselves, her company appears to have fulfilled no ritual function, as did the village troupes, nor been identified with the power of the king, as was the court troupe.

4-17. **Cambodian Dancer as Devatā, ca. 1937.**
Painting Jean Despujols.
Photo courtesy Meadows Museum of Art.

THE CONTRIBUTION OF KHUN MEAK

Khun Meak had been a *premiére danseuse* in the reign of Sisowath. In the 1930s, out of her despair over the deterioration of Khmer dance in the palace, within private dance groups that were adopting a "Western music-hall" style, and in commercialized companies such as that of Say Sangvann, she began to train a group of some twenty small girls in the most authentic style possible.[137] After four years of diligent work she offered the young but promising troupe to the king's daughter, Princess Kossamak, who in turn carefully guided its training and development although she herself was not a dancer. Khun Meak, then, is not as personally significant to our discussion as the traditional pattern which she followed at a critical point in the modern history of Khmer court dance: as a loyal subject she offered the best that she had to the king.

The substantive contribution of this great teacher provided Princess Kossamak with what she really needed for the elevation of Khmer dance to a far higher position than it ever attained during the reign of her father King Monivong, namely, an aggressive program of dance education within the palace itself. The value of this contribution, together with Say Sangvann's new identification between the classical dancers and a strongly projected, popular image of Cambodia's glorious past, were immediately recognized by Princess Kossamak and were adopted as the foundation of her methods in the 1940s to enhance the reign of her son Norodom Sihanouk.

THE WATER FESTIVAL

If we look momentarily at the provincial troupes' activities we will note that they too were ultimately focal points of support for the king. In the 1930s most sizable Cambodian villages still had troupes of female dancers who presented classical scenes from the *Rāmker* and other legends,[138] tutored in some instances by retired palace dancers. Certain regional governors also maintained private *lakhon*, and there were some traveling troupes as well.[139] The highlight of the year for the most accomplished of these troupes was the summer Water Festival known as Bonh Om Touk.

Xenia Zarina, one of the few westerners ever to take instruction in Khmer dance technique (which she received in 1937 from Say Sangvann), wrote a brief description of provincial dance troupes which had been invited to the capital that year.

> For the *Fête des Eaux* Cambodians come from far and near, from every province, to take part in or to witness the celebrations. Fireworks and street processions of amusing and clever paper figures, with lantern processions at night, make the town gay. Within the pink-red crenelated walls of the palace enclosure, in a spacious pavilion beside the famous Silver Pagoda, provincial ballets requested for the festivities dance all day. Anyone may come and watch. As the pavilion is open on three sides, the spectators sit where they wish, or where there is room to sit or stand. The ballets I saw there had excellent and well-costumed star dancers. They danced their very best, for if they pleased some palace talent scout they might be chosen for the King's ballet which would be a great honor, and their families would be well provided for ever after. There appeared to be quite a large membership in the ballets I saw, and in certain scenes representing processions or a trip to another locality, the whole troupe took part following the leading dancers, getting smaller and younger and less adept and less well costumed until the last tiny tots stumblingly brought up the rear, practically in rags, and doing their best not to forget the dance figures.[140]

Village *lakhon* in more or less the palace style appeared to be thriving.

The dominant presence at the Water Festival was the king who moved his residence to the royal houseboat, central to all the river-oriented rituals and contests. On the last day of Bonh Om Touk the king presided over a great regatta of huge canoes in the ancient style, followed, finally, by the climax of the week-long festival, the viewing of the royal dancers.

> In the evening after the regatta, there is a display of fireworks on the water; and then, out of the darkness over the river, appears a sight straight from the land of legends: the royal dancers, gleaming in their golden, jeweled costumes, dancing on a floating platform. They drift past the royal barge, past the pavilions on the riverbanks crowded with spectators, and disappear again into the darkness and distance. Only the tinkling, rippling music that accompanied them comes floating back to us. So brief, so lovely, so intangible, the passing of the Royal Ballet, apparently dancing on the water, seemed a mirage—an imagined vision.[141]

The only view of the king's dancers ever gained by the general public as a whole was that ethereal, glittering image from another world, identified with the monarch's aura of power which it enhanced.

Monivong's Dancers

We know little about the palace dancers themselves in this period. Monivong seems to have kept the few he had carefully sequestered, but Zarina, who saw them perform for thirty guests on the king's birthday, reported that they were unquestionably the best in Cambodia.[142] How many there were remains uncertain. As noted above, anything less than twelve was considered to be an insufficient number for the performance of offeratory rites. Monivong may have maintained the minimum number possible, as suggested by a photo of the palace dancers—presumably the entire troupe—published in 1932 (Figs. 4-18, 4-19). Thirteen mature dancers were included.

Some notion as to the social function of the palace dancers can be gleaned from a small number of performance programs preserved in the Royal Palace Library. In 1975 programs from 114 performances between 1931 and 1961 were still available, of which sixteen were from the reign of Monivong (see Appendix II, Table 5). Inclusion in the library files may have been haphazard since five of these sixteen were a portion of the king's sixty-third birthday celebration, dated 1-3 January 1939, and five were from his birthday celebration of 22-31 December 1933. Presumably, other performances occurred, for which no programs were preserved, but we cannot be certain.

This paucity of evidence, however, supports our earlier observation that the royal dancers performed only rarely for guests, and far less than the French would have preferred. Of the sixteen recorded performances, three honored the Resident-Superior, one honored the former Governor of Indochina Alexandre Varenne, one the French Minister of Colonies Paul Reynaud, and only one honored guests without high French government titles, the Duke and Duchess De Brabant. It is no wonder that Xenia Zarina felt herself fortunate in 1937 to be able to see the king's dancers on the occasion of his birthday; the available evidence does not suggest that they performed for guests on many other occasions.

That Monivong appears to have hosted, almost exclusively, the current top French official, has very much the feeling of political necessity. If so, he was in no way lacking in graciousness or skill at flattery. When the French Minister of Colonies, the highest ranking official known to have visited Cambodia during

4-18, **The Royal Palace Dancers, ca. 1932.** Photo Raymond Cogniat.

4-19. **Cambodian Royal Ballet, ca.1929.** Walter B. Harris, *East for Pleasure*, 1929.

Monivong's reign, was the honored guest at a 1931 performance, the program consisted of the "Apsara Dance with Gold and Silver Flowers" and "Preah Thong." While the former was a standard opening piece, gold and silver flowers had been a symbol of tribute between kingdoms in Southeast Asia for centuries, and Monivong himself wrote a poem which the chorus chanted during the dance:

> We lift our hands to salute His Excellency the Minister of Colonies to whom We dedicate this poem composed by Us in his honor. May his visit signify prosperity and peace for the country; we wreathe for him these flower blossoms on the earth of Cambodia. May our dancers show him the history of the powerful kings who first reigned in our kingdom. We raise these garlands in offering. May he receive them with our prayers for his family and for himself and may the protection of angels be on them all. His Excellency is like a didem [sic] on the head of the Kingdom, and the Kingdom venerates the Government like a father....[143]

According to the program, the main offering of the evening, "The Story of Preah Thong," was also "Taken from the History of Cambodia and Set in Verse by S. M. Sisowath-Monivong," which suggests that the king personally involved himself with the performance of his dancers both for enjoyment and for political practicality.

There is some indication that student dancers were also being trained in the palace during this period. In 1929 Georges Maspero published a photo of a dance rehearsal in Chanchhaya showing perhaps a dozen students (Fig. 4-20), and Sylvain Levi published a photo in 1931 of four very young dancers receiving instruction in the palace garden (Fig. 4-21). Thus, while the dance seems to have been taught in the palace during Monivong's reign, it may have been on a very small scale, which would have justified Khun Meak's donation of a separate troupe of young dancers to Princess Kossamak.

During the reign of Monivong the royal dancers were under the absolute control of his first wife. Whether she herself was a dancer we don't know, but one of his wives, Chea Sang, was a dance teacher who was still teaching female roles in 1975.[144] Monivong's dancers, like those in the private troupes of other officials, functioned as a harem, and it was

Chapter 4: Khmer Dance: 1431-1981   151

Above:
4-20. **Dance Rehearsal in Chanchhaya, ca. 1929.** Maspero, *L'Indochine*.

Left:
4-21. **Student Dancers in the Palace, ca. 1931.** Levi, *Indochine*

perhaps for that reason that Princess Kossamak's private troupe was not merged with the palace troupe until after the death of Monivong.

The Thai Perspective

Before considering the influence of Kossamak on the dance during the reign of her son Sihanouk, let us note the observations of a Thai informant who, during this period, stood apart from the royal palace troupe but eventually became the senior and most respected teacher of dance in the Department of Fine Arts in Bangkok. Seventy-one years old in 1975, Khun Kru Lamun Yamakupt spent one year in Battambang at age twenty-five as a dancer in a private theatre owned by Kao Pratatoowt, a Thai who had gone there to teach. In 1929 she joined her husband in Battambang where he too was teaching "wooden xylophone and oboe." Her troupe never danced in Phnom Penh, despite Monivong's appreciation of Thai *lakhon*, partly because the police considered all Thai to be political meddlers and called them by the pejorative term "Siam."

Khun Kru Lamun recalled that all Cambodian singers she saw then sang in Khmer, and that the dance in Phnom Penh was more stylized than in Battambang in the same sense that in Thailand, court *lakhon nai* was more stylized than provincial *lakhon chatri*. Two dancers from the Thai troupe eventually became teachers in Phnom Penh—Nieng and Pan—but both were dead by 1975.[145] Khun Kru Lamun represents the dance teacher who was familiar with variations on her own style but who, like Khun Meak in Cambodia, worked to perpetuate the form as she had received it.

Monivong's reign marked the end of a period in which the Khmer and Thai styles were able to co-exist in that manner. In March 1941 Japan forced Cambodia to cede three of its western provinces to Thailand, and in the same year King Monivong died. The new king was just nineteen, but one fact had become clear to him as well as to all other members of the court: Thailand's designs upon Cambodia were far from being a thing of the past. In the royal dance troupe, of which the new king's mother, Kossamak, now took charge, there was no longer room for the prestige formerly accorded Thai elements.

Artistic chauvinism for the purpose of strengthening the throne became the hallmark of the new court, and the royal dancers of Cambodia entered the most glittering chapter of their history since the demise of Angkor.

DANCE IN THE SIHANOUK ERA (1941-1970)

During the period that Cambodia was ruled by Norodom Sihanouk, first as king and then—after relinquishing the throne to his father, Norodom Suramarit, in 1955—as Chief of State, the royal dancers functioned as an adjunct to the pursuit of foreign policy at the highest level. This section of the present study will show the manner in which the Khmer classical dance was used initially by the Queen Mother to support Cambodia's bid for independence from the French and, then, to enhance the panoply of monarchy in the newly independent kingdom. It will survey both the changes she effected and the world reputation she engendered for the Royal Ballet as the symbol of Cambodia.

RELATIONS WITH THE FRENCH GOVERNMENT

Of the possible heirs to the Khmer throne following the death of Monivong, the French engineered the election of his nineteen-year-old, "playboy" grandson, Norodom Sihanouk, on the assumption that he could be manipulated to their ends. In this they failed to reckon with either his deep—if theatrical and self-serving—sense of patriotism, or the skill at intrigue of his mother Princess Kossamak. One of the earliest confrontations between the French and the new court was over the royal dancers, although the stakes were considerably higher.

The Emperor Bao Dai of Vietnam—like Cambodia, a French colonial protectorate, though far more rebellious—was invited to Phnom Penh in November 1942, about a year after Sihanouk's coronation. As a part of the ceremonies honoring this visit, Sihanouk planned to present the court dancers in their first public appearance since he had assumed personal financial responsibility for their maintenance—following a French attempt to dissolve the troupe (discussed below)—some months before. A flourishing troupe of royal dancers would clearly imply to Bao Dai a strong monarchy in Cambodia—at least to outward appearances. Consequently, the French protested. They objected to the program, they objected categorically to the appearance of the king's dancers, and they insisted until the last moment that Say Sangvann's troupe should perform for the state visit.

Kossamak, who had supervised intensive palace rehearsals for the preceding six months, gambled that her dancers were superior to those of Say Songvann despite the French money spent on costumes and production, and she forced the issue. At a dinner on 22 November 1942 in honor of Sihaunouk's twenty-first birthday, he presented his dancers in a program dedicated solely to the "Emperor and Empress of Annam" (Vietnam). The dancers' performance was stunning, and in that moment Kossamak gained a great victory on a small battlefield. For almost three subsequent decades the visible political activity of the Cambodian king would be identified with the art of his personal dancers, and, in that, Sihanouk gained an image of independence long before the political fact.

Let us look behind the scenes of Kossamak's triumph to see the manner in which the French had attempted to prevent such a situation. Just as in the early days of Monivong's reign—and taking advantage of the new sovereign's youth—the French in 1941 had transferred control of Royal Palace affairs to the Protectorate government which they controlled. Then, under the guise of economy, Resident-Superior Thibaudeau informed the Queen Mother that the troupe of palace dancers was to be eliminated. By so doing, the government would ostensibly save 600 riels per month— the maintenance expenditure for the dancers during the latter years of Monivong's reign—since, as Thibaudeau explained, the company of Say Sangvann "was quite able to maintain the tradition of classical dancing."[146]

Thibaudeau, accustomed to Monivong's silent accommodation to Say Sangvann's troupe, failed to realize the deep and emotional significance of the palace troupe, and his action polarized the situation. Kossamak determined that the Royal Ballet would be saved at all costs, and Sihanouk pledged his financial support from his own meagre stipend. For the six months of official mourning, they waited, and when rehearsals were resumed, popular support for Kossamak's commitment was manifest in the form of seven old teachers—each with the title of *kru* and two of whom were more than eighty years old—who appeared at the palace and assumed responsibility for the renovation of the troupe. Each of the seven had been *première danseuse* under a former king and together they were expert in all the roles. Kossamak demanded major changes in the structure of performance, to which the teachers agreed but in turn demanded the utmost rigor on the part of the students. For six months they worked with harmonious intensity in preparation for the "new" troupe's first appearance at the king's birthday party with the Emperor of Vietnam.

Conflict with the government was inevitable. The French refused to release any funds at all, for new costumes, and since the disrepair of the entire wardrobe "defied description," Kossamak collected silk from private sources and set the palace women, under the direction of Princess Nongleak, to the task of constructing the fourteen costumes that were required. The French further failed to realize the significance of the fact that Bao Dai's visit coincided with the annual Water Festival, when the king and his dancers traditionally appeared on the royal houseboat to be viewed by the entire population. Such petty obstructionism on the part of the French regarding the ancient ritual only unified the Khmers in opposition. Thus when November 22 arrived, it was Sihanouk—and his mother behind the throne—rather than the French, who appeared to all, including the neighboring Emperor, to be the sponsor and source of regality.

THE CONTRIBUTION OF PRINCESS KOSSAMAK

Few monarchs have been blessed with such an appealing stimulus to good public relations both domestically and abroad as Sihanouk with his dancers. Kossamak set about to exploit the advantage by perfecting the technical skill of the palace troupe while streamlining their performances to suit the king's need for easily appreciable theatrical entertainment. Her influence was all pervasive.

First, she set forth a model performance program lasting about two hours, consisting of an opening dance, a dramatic piece, and a closing dance. In general, either the introductory piece or the finale would be from the pure dance repertoire with the other being a short dance excerpt from one of the dramatic works chosen for its theatricality; one would be stately, the other martial or comic. Sometimes formal musical interludes by soloists or the palace *khen* orchestra (of Lao instruments) were included. A small selection of performance programs preserved in the Royal Palace Library (see Appendix II, Table 5) indicates that rarely was a program repeated exactly, since the repertoire was large enough to allow flexibility in choosing selections appropriate to the occasion or guest being honored.

Next, Kossamak shortened all the dramatic pieces as well as many of the pure dance pieces[147] to befit a royal entertainment which precluded an entire evening of dances in the traditional manner. At the same time she expanded a number of the pure dance pieces into large, theatrical, group-precision dances. The Tep Manorom, for instance, was originally the dance of a single prince and princess; Kossamak transformed it into a finale piece for twelve dancers moving in close synchronicity. The tradition of large dances of this sort was a stylistic convention of the ancient religious offertory dances to the spirits. Thus, while the Tep Manorom had no religious content it came to have a form comparable, for instance, to the large-group Mkaw or Makara Ballet, the sacred "Dance of the Sea Serpent."[148]

While the evidence is limited, it would appear that Kossamak not only eliminated certain pieces in the repertoire but eventually added others. A number of pieces popular in her father's reign do not appear at all in the programs preserved from the reigns of her son and, later, her husband (see Appendix II, Tables 5 and 6).

In addition to these adjustments to the repertoire, Kossamak added a new theatricality to the performances. For instance, she wanted a greater contrast between the monkey roles and the male or female roles, all of which were played with similar technique by the all-female palace troupe. Being much impressed with the monkey roles as performed by the all-male *lakhon khol* troupes, she invited male dancers of that role to join the

Chapter 4: Khmer Dance: 1431-1981   157

4-22. **The Royal Dancers at Angkor, 1964. Princess Buppha Devi in white at left**. *Nokor Khmer.*

royal company.[149] This convention has continued to the present day, and the highly acrobatic monkey roles played by males remain a great crowd pleaser.

By the 1960s at least, Kossamak had incorporated staging techniques from the European theatre into the dance drama performances. When the Royal Ballet performed for President and Mrs. Soeharto of Indonesia on the first day of their state visit to Cambodia, for instance, the set for the legend of "Preah Sothun and Keo Monnorea, the Kennari" included an elaborately painted drop and set pieces (see Chapter VII).

The theatrical effect of such settings, however, was minor compared to the great set on which Kossamak annually staged royal dances for the New Year's festival: namely, Angkor Wat itself. With elaborate lighting of both torches and a vast number of flood lights on the temple as backdrop, the dancers performed amid elaborate, hand-held pieces of artificial foliage and other images in the style of the Angkorean bas-reliefs.[150] The result was a danced ritual of delicate precision set in spectacular theatricality (Fig. 4-22).

In creating an international image for the Khmer royal dancers, Kossamak skillfully balanced their guarded palace life with carefully selected public appearances. Photo-journalists were permitted articles over the years, but these never involved interviews with the dancers themselves. While it is true that the dancers performed outside the palace during Sihanouk's reign with a far greater frequency than ever before, Kossamak managed to perpetuate an image of the troupe as a precious jewel—highly revered but distant.

In 1962 Kossamak allowed a three-reel documentary film on the Royal Ballet to be shot by Stanley Moss for the United States Information Service. Filmed in Phnom Penh and at Angkor, the film was granted royal sponsorship, and Kossamak herself appeared in it as patroness of the ballet. Only three known copies are extant in the United States,[151] and with the rapid deterioration of U.S.-Cambodian relations between 1962 and 1965, few people anywhere had the opportunity of viewing the film. Nonetheless, it is a clear example of Kossamak's high-toned style of publicity for the king's dancers and it remains the best film record of their world.

A further area in which Kossamak involved herself was that of teaching and rehearsal methods. In the period before Kossamak, there had always been disputes between two groups of teachers: those of the Thai style and those of the Khmer style. There were long-standing disagreements of a political nature as well, since each of the two dynastic families of Cambodia—Norodom and Sisowath—maintained troupes who "often disputed about the proper dance style."[152] Kossamak made strong efforts toward resolving their differences by forcibly joining the two schools of style. While she may have decreased conflict temporarily, there were still in 1975 two respected teachers of different styles at the University of Fine Arts. Bo, who taught "Thai style" and Mei who taught "Khmer style."[153] Nonetheless, as a Sisowath princess who had married a Norodom prince, she could appropriately attempt such a synthesis of the styles being taught.

In dance training, Kossamak greatly increased the number of students, and by 1962 there were 460 students at the palace.[154] An annual ceremony awarding prizes was instituted, and advanced students permitted to choreograph works for official performances. On the level of pedagogical method, Kossamak discouraged use of the stick for slow learners but in general took the traditional method and "joined it with more modern teaching methods."[155] The greatest change which Kossamak effected on the troupe, however, was returning members of the royal family to its ranks for training and ultimately for performance as stars. Best known of these was Princess Buppha Devi (Figs. 4-22 and 4-24), one of the two children born to Sihanouk's first wife, who was herself a royal dancer.

Princess Buppha Devi was King Sihanouk's favorite daughter. The fact that she was a most skillful and beautiful dancer—as one can see from her lengthy *buong suong* solo on the Stanley Moss film—made her a *première danseuse* and a star. That she was the former king's daughter made her a great political asset, and Kossamak used that fact to the greatest possible advantage from around 1958 until Sihanouk was deposed as Head of State in 1970.

OCCASIONS OF PERFORMANCE

All performances of the Royal Ballet during the Sihanouk era can be seen as fulfilling a political role, in addition to the more obvious purposes. Basically these were limited to five types of occasions: in honor of the monarchy, the Buddha, animistic spirits, foreign dignitaries, or Cambodia and her allies. Let us consider each briefly.

The royal dancers always performed on the king's birthday and, as noted earlier, at coronations and royal funerals. The king's memory was evoked on other occasions as well. For instance, a *soirée de gala* was held on 3 September 1941 both to honor Vice-Admiral J. Decoux, the Governor-General of Indochina, and to mark the end of the official period of mourning for King Monivong. The opening piece on the program was a "Dance of Offering to the Memory of His Majesty the late King." The following month the dancers again performed to jointly honor Governor-General Decoux and His Majesty Sisavang Yong, King of Luang Prabang; the opening dance

4-23. **Menh Kosni, ca. 1967.** Courtesy of Princess Buppha Devi.

4-24. **Royal Ballet Group With Princess Buppha Devi** (left center). **and Menh Kosni** (right center).

Courtesy Princess Buppha Devi.

of welcome, however, was listed in the program as a "dance to the glory of the new reign" of King Sihanouk. On these and virtually all other occasions the purpose of the dancers' performance was, in part, to honor and symbolize royal authority.

As protector of the Buddhist religion, the king frequently used the royal dancers to show his devotion. For instance, in 1952 relics of the Buddha and two of his disciples were brought to Cambodia for a brief visit. On October 5 they were received in Wat Preah Keo, at which time the king's dancers presented a drama entitled "Preah Pathamasampothi, a Story of the Life of Buddha." The drama, which seems to have been created solely for the occasion and never performed subsequently, concerned the confrontation of Mara and Gautama at the time of the latter's imminent realization (see Chapter VI). The dancers' more frequent association with animistic ritual—in addition to Buddhist—will be considered in detail in Chapter IX.

The distinction between performances for important guests

and those for political occasions is an arbitrary one; both were political in their goal of gaining good will. The former, however, were presented primarily as entertainment for distinguished individuals visiting Cambodia, while the latter may be seen as Sihanouk's effort to communicate an image of Cambodia to whole nations. The two clearly coalesced on occasions such as U.S. Vice-President Richard Nixon's visit to Cambodia in 1953 (Fig. 4-25).

For visiting dignitaries, Sihanouk created, according to one so honored, an "unearthly, imaginary, fairyland" scene. Following dinner, cigars, liqueurs and an inspection of the king's art works, Sihanouk and his guest strolled to the dance pavilion through the French-style formal gardens at the feet of palace spires made fantastical by a vast number of floodlights. Six torch-bearers preceded them, servants walked at their sides, and members of the royal family followed along the pathway lined with body guards at the salute. On entering Chanchhaya, lit by hundreds of candles in the chandeliers, all present rose and bowed to the king, thus giving the guest a vicarious experience of royalty.[156]

Performance Locations

All performance evenings in honor of individuals shared many of these same elements, with one significant variable—the venue. On the palace grounds there were four theatres suitable for dance performances. The most frequently used for state guests was Chanchhaya—the open-air, second story of one of the eastern gate-houses, visible to passers-by and seating about two hundred. Very special guests were entertained with more privacy and less pageantry in the Throne Room of the palace itself, the residence of Kossamak and King Norodom Suramarit, known as Khemarin Palace. When performance programs mention "The Royal Palace," it is usually to one of these two halls that they refer.

After 1956 dance performances for small audiences were also held in the Buppha Devi Palace which Sihanouk built near the west gate of the palace in honor of his daughter. Larger audiences of a less select nature—particularly for traditional festivals such as *Tang Tok*, the king's week-long birthday celebration, or large receptions such as the Christmas celebration for Europeans—were accommodated in and around the open-air Phochani Pavilion in the southeast corner of the palace grounds.

Outside the palace, the royal dancers occasionally performed for honored guests or very large audiences in the Chakdomukh Hall about a mile to the southeast of the palace on the banks of the Mekong. President Soeharto of Indonesia, for instance was entertained there in 1968. The hall seats about a thousand people. This was the location generally used for *lakhon* performances for those distinguished guests who were to be seen publicly.

THE "FRIENDSHIP" DANCE

During her years as overseer, Kossamak developed two ways in which Sihanouk could use the Royal Ballet to enhance the image of himself and Cambodia which he was attempting to project into the arena of world politics. Following the lead of Jawaharlal Nehru in India, he presented himself as the educated leader of a non-aligned but pivotal nation in which he fostered a blend of past royal splendor with modern democracy and technology. The methods Kossamak devised to support this effort were the "Friendship Dance" and the foreign tour on which the royal dancers

4-25. **Richard Nixon in Chanchhaya Pavilion, 1953.** *Nokor Khmer.*

accompanied Sihanouk abroad.

The idea of a "Friendship Dance" may have originated during the occupation of Cambodia by the Japanese, at which time Sihanouk first declared his independence of France on 13 March 1945. Shortly thereafter, on 1 April 1945, the royal dancers performed in honor of "His Excellency Lieutenant-General Manaki and His Excellency Consul-General Kubota." The program was of the model pattern discussed earlier. Two weeks later on 14 April when Sihanouk again hosted the Japanese commander, the closing dance was the "Mkaw Ballet," considered to be "one of the greatest sacred dances of the whole classical repertoire."[157] This time each dancer carried a Japanese flag.

While the evidence gives a limited record, only two other instances of using another nation's flag in the dances appear in the performance programs, and the custom seems to have been reserved for making a fairly straightforward political statement. On 8 December 1960, the royal dancers performed for a visiting theatre troupe from the People's Republic of China. The program included the "Dance of Khmer-Chinese Friendship" whose lyrics were similar in tone to those of the "Dance of Khmer-American Friendship" performed some months earlier on 22 July 1959, in honor of the visiting United States Secretary of the Interior Fred Seaton. An English translation printed in the program was as follows:

> Dance, dance ballerinas,
> Here opens the Road of Friendship
> All our lives our hearts will remember.
>
> All you Americans and Khmers
> United by destiny in a heartfelt friendship,
> Hand in hand, follow the road of peace.
>
> Friends, how priceless was your help.
> Thanks to you, now stronger and more prosperous,
> We have regained our place in the sun.
>
> Dance, dance, young girls,
> Entwine the colours of our two nations
> And may our fruitful friendship live for ever.

A photo in the program shows the dancers each carrying small flags of both the United States and Cambodia.

It is not known whether the dancers performed "Friendship Dances" on all their foreign tours or not; in fact, they would have been redundant. Kossamak knew that the dancers were Cambodia's best possible ambassadors. In allowing them to leave the palace and the kingdom, she understood that they lent authority to Sihanouk's presence. If he was willing to share his private dancers, including his own children, with another nation, and if those dancers were of rare quality, the likelihood of acceptance for the political friendship which he conjointly offered was increased.

Thus, in his wooing of both the Third World nations and the super-powers, Sihanouk took the royal dancers with him for much of his extensive travel. In 1956 the entire troupe toured the People's Republic of China. A smaller group including Princess Buppha Devi and the better dancers accompanied him to the United States in 1958, to the United Arab Republic and Yugoslavia in 1959, to Czechoslovakia, the Soviet Union, Mongolia and China in 1960, to Indonesia, Singapore and Malaysia in November-December 1962, to India and China in January 1963, and to France in 1964. The visibility of the troupe on these and subsequent foreign tours was largely responsible for the reputation soon gained by the Royal Ballet as being one of the great dance companies of the world, thus further enhancing the aura of political sway held by Sihanouk.

Dance Personnel

We shall conclude this section concerning the years between 1941 and 1970 with a look at what is known of the personnel associated with the troupe during that era. In 1941 there were forty-eight dancers in the Royal Ballet, including the troupe offered to Kossamak earlier by Khun Meak.[158] By 1962 the number of actual dancers was smaller but we know more about the support personnel for a troupe that was, overall, much larger and self-perpetuating. The company included:[159]

1	star dancer
5	*première danseuses*
25	dancers
4	clowns
160	dance students
17	dance mistresses
2	male dance teachers
10	singers and rhythm keepers (both male and female)
24	musicians
6	music students
14	dressers and make-up women
4	seamstresses
6	seamstress apprentices
6	jewelry keepers
284	

Among the total group it is unclear how the male monkey roles were categorized, but since they were usually played by young men, they may have been included under "students." The Royal Ballet School of Classical Dance offered "voluntary" classes each morning to 460 students, from whom the company dancers were eventually selected.[160]

Five years later the number of both dancers and musicians had hardly changed. According to Hang Thun Hak, Recteur of the Université Royale des Beaux-Arts, in 1967 the troupe included, in part:

1	star dancer
5	*premières danseuses*
18	female dances
5	male dancers
19	dance mistresses
24	musicians
10	singers
82	

The School offered classes, however, to three hundred students, aged four and above.¹⁶¹ This was a significant increase (Fig. 4-26).

The names of some of the dancers early in Sihanouk's reign are available and include, from a 22 November 1942 performance program, Neak Ly Onn, Neak Yat, Neak Saroeun, Neak Reun, Neang Chhoch and Neak Chantlou. A 10 November 1943 program listed the dancers for a performance of Preah Leak Sinnavongs as follows:

4-26. **Kem Bun Nak** (also known as Bunnak) Teaching at the Palace Dance School, ca. 1969. *Nokor Khmer.*

Leak Sinnavong	Neak Ly Onn
Leak Sinnavong as an infant	Neang Yitho
Neang Kessar	Neak Thach
Neang Kessar as an infant	Neang Bunnak
King Promateat	Neak Iem
Queen Sovann Ampea	Neak Samy
Second Queen	Neak Sunnary
Virulamat	Neak Reun
Princess Yisun	Neak Yath
The Eysei	Neak Rang
The Blackbird	Neak Nay
The Parrot	Neang Champei

This program is interesting in that the child's role was played by eight-year-old Neang Bunnak who was allowed—three years later, at age eleven—to dance the "Invocation to the Tevodas" accompanied by a *sralay* (oboe) solo in a performance honoring the French Vice-Admiral D'Argenlieu. At age fourteen (Fig. 4-27) she became a *première danseuse* and danced the leading

4-27. **Neang Bunnak at Angkor Wat, Age Fourteen, 1949.** Photo Guy Pourée.

roles until Princess Buppha Devi began to do so in the late 1950s.

In a 16 February 1951 performance of Preah Saing, Neang Bunnak played the adult Princess Recchana and Buppha Devi played the same role as a child earlier in the drama. The leading dancer of male roles in this and other performances in the 1950s was Neang Sokhan; Neak Denn played the demon roles. Other leading dancers were Neang Leas, Neak Samy, Neang Sangvar, Neang Lumchang, and Neay Cheng.

One visitor to Angkor in 1965 wrote that every Saturday evening the village folk would wend their way through the rice fields, pass among the flickering lamps of the food vendors on the great causeway, settle in to hear the small orchestra, and witness the dancers of the Royal Ballet emerge from the darkness of the building and dance on the broad steps of Angkor Wat.[162] While we cannot say with certainty that the elegant and extremely busy dancers of the Royal Palace did not spend their weekends at Angkor, it is more likely that what the villagers saw was another troupe in the classical style. Still, the illusion has substance in that during the Sihanouk era the Royal Cambodian Ballet reached its zenith, and the aura of the king's dancers was everywhere seen.

Dance in the Republic (1970-1975) and After

With the advent of the Republic on 18 March 1970 under the presidency of Lon Nol, the royal dancers lost their niche in the social structure of

Cambodia. The fundamental *raison d'être* of the Royal Ballet vanished with the kingdom, and while remaining prestigious employees of the state, the dancers' lives became—like the "ex-royal palace" in which they worked—increasingly empty. With the advent of the Pol Pot regime on 17 April 1975, classical dance disappeared with the nation into a four-year nightmare of cultural suicide from which it was awakened, ironically, by the invasion of Vietnam on 25 December 1978 and the subsequent establishment of the People's Republic of Kampuchea. This section will survey the situation of the lakhon during those three periods, focusing finally on a group of teachers who are working today to preserve the classical dance tradition both in Cambodia and among its refugees.

4-28. **Menh Kosni as Sitā in New York. 1970.** *Royal Cambodia Ballet.*

Following Lon Nol's successful coup, the government of the Khmer Republic found itself in possession of numerous valuable properties that were exclusively identified in the public's mind with the king. Foremost of these was the Royal Palace which Lon Nol chose, more or less, to ignore and which was commonly referred to as the "ex-royal palace." The Royal Ballet, by contrast, was necessarily embraced by the new government as a symbol of continuity; its name was changed to "The Classical Khmer Ballet" and its image as a symbol of Cambodia was perpetuated.

There were, however, significant changes. First of all, Princess Buppha Devi was gone, and the prestige of having a princess as star could not be replaced. In the course of the five-year Republic, numerous other dancers left as well. The court dancers, including many of the most beautiful women in the kingdom, were in many cases married to high officials, diplomats, and the wealthy elite, who increasingly chose to leave Cambodia as the inevitability of a communist take-over became obvious. By early 1975 the troupe retained no dancers possessing both outstanding beauty and lead dancer skill.

Dance training also underwent significant changes. Until 1970 training in the classical style had been the prerogative of the palace exclusively, even after the Cambodian Ministry of Education established the National School of Theatre at the University of Fine Arts (l'Université des Beaux-Arts, or UBA) in 1960. Under the Republic, all classical training was transferred to UBA, the recteur of which was Huot Kim Leang. In early 1970, prior to the coup, there were three hundred students at the palace;[163] by early 1975 maximum attendance at UBA was down to fifty.

This drastic decrease was due largely to the war, but, simultaneously, classical dance suffered a subtle loss of prestige as well, since at UBA the *lakhon* simply became one discipline among equals, the others being folk dance and music. Not only was the training program removed from the palace, it was administered separately from the performance troupe which was under the jurisdiction of the École Nationale des Arts et des Metiers.[164] Consequently the mature dancers and the student dancers came to have far less interchange during the Republic than in previous years, thus lowering the young dancers' commitment and their awareness of the traditional high position of their art in Khmer culture.

THE AMERICAN TOUR

During the five years of the Republic, the brightest time for the classical troupe was their international tour in 1971, particularly the reception given their first appearance in the United States. Highly praised in the American press for their art, the true purpose in placing the dancers on the world's stage was again political. Hard-pressed by the Khmer Rouge and by Sihanouk's alliance with the Chinese, the Lon Nol government took all possible measures to guarantee the continuing assistance of the United States. The dancers' visit was a means to that end and appeared to create much good will in this country.

In the *New York Times* Clive Barnes wrote of the company's six performances, which opened the Brooklyn Academy of Music's Afro-Asian Dance Festival (19-24 October 1971) that "they carry with them the values of a different time scale, and like so much of Oriental art suggest an inner harmony that can never be achieved by the deliberate stresses and strains of so much Western art."[165] While offering even higher praise, the *Village Voice* reviewer noted that the Khmer Ballet had come to Brooklyn as the result of a revolution and "either as an earnest of affection or to turn a fast buck. Never mind why."[166] Such crass considerations as the Cambodian government's motivation in sending the troupe paled in the presence of their art which was deemed by critics and presumably the audiences as "remarkable," "sensational" and "extraordinary."

The twenty-four female dancers in the 1971 touring company under the auspices in the United States of Mel Howard Productions and Madame Ninon Tallon Karlweis were Keo Yitho, Chum Hoeun, Mam Sovannano, Pen Sok Huon, Keo Davie, Men Saonna, Nhea Loren, Reath Moni, Khy Sophaneth, Chhoeun Angkeara, Lor Chindamony, Voan Savai, Menh Kosni (Figs. 4-23 and 4-28), Ung Pech, Roy Saroeurn, Sim Montha, Sok Yan, Chuon Nora, Hem Bunnarcth, Mac Savann, Sin Chantha, Sai Maly, Sam Sokhom, and Soth Sam On. There were six male dancers: Chap Seang, Pfang Ouch, Seng Chhieng, Khieu Kim Nhan, Lach Chien Serey, and Hul Cheng.

Others accompanying the dancers included three wardrobe mistresses, Chen Phi, Peou Khatna, and Chea Samy; two jewel keepers, Khem Nep and Kep Path; and just six musicians, Seng Sum, Sek Ouch, Bin Suon, Vong Chheng, Ek Sam Ath, and Long Khay. Four singers completed the troupe, Prom Sokhom, Em Nareth, Chea Khann, and Em Theay,[167] of whom the last was the primary singer in 1975 both at the palace and on special occasions at UBA.

As a part of the 1971 tour schedule, the Khmer dancers also

performed at the International *Rāmāyana* Festival in Indonesia. They presented a short version of the entire *Rāmāyana* lasting about one hour on 2 September (see Appendix II). One eminent Thai observer (who said the Thais would never do such a thing) believed the program had been prepared solely for the occasion and condescended that it was "a good, fast, modern, comprehensive adaptation which told the story and was good for foreigners."[168] As we shall see in Chapter VII, however, the flexibility allowable in Khmer dance choreography always permitted new pieces to be staged for specific occasions such as the Indonesian festival, and it is precisely that quality which contributes so strongly in the 1980s to the survival and revival of the dance.

Dance During the Siege

In 1972 the Khmer Rouge captured Angkor, dealing a serious blow to the integrity of the Lon Nol government if not the Cambodian people, since the guerillas now held a position in which they could not be attacked without destroying the symbol of the nation itself. It was a sober period, and the National Ballet subsequently performed primarily for purposes of morale building. Rehearsals still continued in the palace, while performances were most frequently held in the "Salle des Spectacles," a large auditorium, seating about a thousand on the bank of the Mekong. A commercial photo from this period somehow captures the uncertainty and fragility of the times (Fig. 4-29), as the high value placed exclusively on the classical dance was being undermined by a new egalitarianism.

In 1973 Sihanouk toured three northern provinces of the "liberated zone" including Angkor, where folk dances were performed in his honor at a large rally.[169] In the capital, too, folk dances were increasingly performed on the same program as classical dance and received at least an equal emphasis in the UBA curriculum. On both sides of the war front that was continually tightening around Phnom Penh, the dancers and culture of the "people" came to be a more acceptable symbol of the nation's art than the remote and refined dancers of the former king.

Nonetheless, the government continued to support the classical troupe. Realizing that if a communist government came to power, the classical dance would, as an aristocratic adjunct, be seriously endangered, the Republican government made efforts to document the dance tradition of which it was the caretaker. The man who approved all such projects and on whom responsibility rested for the arts in general during the Lon Nol regime was Hang Thun Hak, former rector of UBA during the Sihanouk era (then called the Université Royale des Beaux-Arts, or URBA) and in 1974 a political advisor to Lon Nol. Deferred to by all as the nation's *première* expert on classical dance, it was he who allowed the present study as well as other attempts at documentation.

4-29. **Dancers During the Republic, ca. 1973.** *Ministry of Culture.*

During the 1974 New Year's festival, for instance, a film was made of UBA students performing the legend of Preah Chan Korup at Wat Phnom, the temple on the small hill in Phnom Penh after which the city was named.

In December of 1974 the classical dance troupe made its last official state visit. With Phnom Penh waiting, as Sihanouk said in Peking, like a ripe apple about to fall, Lon Nol sent the national dancers to Bangkok. As part of an intense plea for Thai assistance, this final appearance of the dance drama in the diplomatic arena seems a feeble and outdated ploy. Four performances were given (21-24 December) in the National Theatre, and of the twelve items on the program, six were classical, six folk. In the final dance the two sets of dancers performed together. The company returned to Cambodia one week before the Khmer Rouge assault on Phnom Penh itself began, and the entire classical troupe never performed together again.

During the five years of the Republic, the palace dancers had undergone a great reversal in administration, purpose and prestige within Cambodia. Before considering their position in the latter days of the Republic—between 1 January 1975 when the first rockets, initially mistaken for fireworks, landed on Phnom Penh, and 17 April 1975 when the Khmer Rouge actually entered the city—let us take note of a man whose influence was soon to become the strongest force in the struggle to preserve any of the performing arts of Cambodia. His name was Chheng Phon.

The Contribution of Chheng Phon

To some extent the life of the University of Fine Arts proceeded as always in early 1975. Huot Kim Leang, the rector, soon to die, appeared in his office as usual. Nuon Kan, head of the classical dance division, received a scholarship to study Japanese theatre in Tokyo (where he stayed for several years before emigrating to the Los Angeles area). The teachers and rehearsal musicians maintained a fairly consistent class schedule except on the many days when the rockets were numerous and their commitment understandably waned. Even Mme. Chea Sany, who had been a wife of King Monivong, still taught female roles on better days. All of these people, if asked about the dance drama—past, present, or future—eventually referred all questions, as though by mutual agreement, to one man, Chheng Phon.

In his mid-forties, head of the National Conservatory, but with the mien of everyone's favorite village uncle, Chheng Phon was a visionary of formidable knowledge, dedication and energy. In the 1960s he had worked painstakingly to preserve the shadow theatre of Cambodia by collecting its musical scores and encouraging performers. In 1974 he started a performing arts farm as a branch of UBA on which 120 refugee, fine-arts students (together with three of his own sons) lived, studied, rehearsed, and worked growing vegetables and raising a thousand chickens and fifteen pigs. The farm, at Obek Khaom, was financed initially by the United States' Resettlement Development Fund and maintained by the daily sale of about seven hundred eggs. There were small open-air theatres, a large classroom, and living quarters. Twice a week free performances were offered to nearby villagers. Unfortunately, Obek Khaom was located between the airport and the radio station eight kilometers from the Conservatory in Phnom Penh and was vulnerable to attack at all times.

The farm was so inspiring, however, that urban students wanted to live there, and the twenty-five girls in residence who spent the nights in town for protection returned each day to work and study.

Primarily the students studied *yiké* as they had reconstructed it on the basis of three remaining Khmer *yiké* troupes in Takeo, Siem Riep, and Svay Rieng provinces. All students, however, studied classical movement for one year to learn the fundamental exercises for body suppleness and posture. Consequently, classical dance was performed periodically at Obek Khaom under the direction of the UBA teachers and musicians.

Aside from his expertise as a musician, dance researcher, and instructor, or his long-term projects for preservation of the performing arts, Chheng Phon was everyone's spokesman because he did it so well. On 11 February, for instance, at a military graduation in the "Salle des Spectacles," which included performances of folk dance, *lakhon bassac*, classical dance, *khol*, and an immense *yiké*, he afterwards harangued the audience—enjoyably but with mesmerizing intensity—on the value of preserving the culture. Following that, he spoke with great calmness in an interview, climbed behind the wheel of a dilapidated Red Cross truck loaded with waiting students and drove off to Obek Khaom.

The End of the Republic

Unfortunately, Chheng Phon's optimism and energy were lost in the stronger current of the war. By 28 March 1975 rehearsals had been cancelled indefinitely both at the palace and at UBA, due to the dancers' complaints about the rockets. A third classical dance troupe, formed during the Republic by General Chhim Chhuon—an action never possible in earlier times under Sihanouk—was comprised of dancers from both the UBA and palace companies. This military-supported troupe usually performed on television or for the public in a theatre just north of Wat Phnom. By early 1975, however, it too had ceased to function.

The palace dancers' refusal to attend rehearsals was only partly due to the rockets as stated. In thirteen weeks of shelling, only one small rocket (on 3 January) ever landed in the palace grounds. Throughout the Republic years, traditional palace lodgings remained available to the dancers, and the long row of open-air, though well-protected, rooms at ground level on the west side of the palace—away from the river and the rocket launchings—had occasionally been used. By 1975, however, all had been abandoned for reasons that reflect the true position of the former court dancers under the Republican government.

During the Shinanouk era court dancers were free to marry and could live either inside or outside the palace.[170] After 1970 the discipline which underlay such a lenient policy eroded to the point that by the end of the Republic, dancers avoided the palace with the same excuses used by innumerable others associated with the sinking bureaucracy.

The palace dancers almost never rehearsed in the first three months of 1975, and while it may be remarkable that they met at all, we must remember that the true origin of that pattern lay in the 1970 elimination of the dancers' bond with the monarch. With the departure of Sihanouk and Kossamak, the dancers lost artistic direction, strong external discipline, and the focus of their energy, purpose, and prestige. Subsequent performances rarely involved the entire company and were often items on a program of multiple genres. Increasingly the dancers rehearsed only prior to a performance. With Sihanouk at Angkor and elsewhere striving to return, commitment to the artistic policies of the Republican government was not high. Everyone was waiting, and until the conflict was resolved, all the dancers chose to live private lives in the city rather than in the relative security of the empty palace.

The resolution occurred in mid-April 1975, and the dancers who had become so casual about maintaining their art now found themselves deprived of it entirely. To best survey that dark chapter of the dancers' history we may recount the story of one dance instructor who endured the purges and eventually managed to reach the United States where she now teaches.

THE CONTRIBUTION OF MOM KAMEL

Mom Kamel, who began her classical dance training in 1941 at age eight, had been a lead dancer in the Royal Palace and toured with Sihanouk's company before becoming a teacher in 1970. When the Khmer Rouge captured Phnom Penh in 1975 she disguised her past and survived the subsequent class war against the educated elite as a farmer. Madame Kamel believes that half of the other palace dancers at that time were killed.[171] When the Khmer Rouge emptied the capital at gunpoint it is not known if they ransacked the palace—including the jewelry of the dancers which was kept in a room almost directly under the throne, but one of the initial demands of the soldiers was for all personal jewelry. This was the merest hint of the austerity and violence that was to follow.

For nearly four years Mom Kamel endured endless labor with little food—like virtually everyone in Cambodia—and with no education, religion, currency, newspapers, radio, postal service, hospitals or dancing. Even the *sampeah*, the gracious joining of the hands together at greeting, was forbidden because the subtleties of the gesture—who did it first, how high and for how long—indicated social status and had religious overtones.[172]

Under the leadership of Pol Pot and Ieng Sary, Democratic Kampuchea was almost totally sealed off from international contact. Only as the Vietnamese increased military pressure on the fragile regime were carefully selected outsiders allowed a limited view of the nation which President Carter had called "the number one violator of human rights" in the world. The first such Americans to be invited were conducted on an eight-day tour in April 1978 and subsequently published a naive but lengthy "photo-record" in praise of the new Cambodia.[173] In their scores of photographs there is not one dancer, an omission which in Cambodia can only mean that there was no dancing taking place—folk, classical or *yiké*—during the Pol Pot era, a national situation corroborated by Mom Kamel's personal experience.

Refugees from Democratic Kampuchea fled to camps in both Thailand and Vietnam, and although they staged masked dances for holidays in the Thai camps,[174] there is no evidence of classical dance performances among refugees in the area during this period.

Finally, on Christmas Day 1978, the Pol Pot regime was driven out and the nation occupied by Vietnamese troops who established Heng Samrin, a former Khmer Rouge commander, as the puppet president. With their country in the hands of the centuries-old enemy and on the verge of mass starvation, Khmers by the thousands now sought refuge in Thailand, and huge camps were opened to accommodate them.

In early 1979 Mom Kamel, with some dozen other palace dancers escaped to Thailand and eventually reached the Khao I Dang refugee camp (Fig. 4-30). Opened in November of 1979, Khao I Dang soon became the second-largest city in Thailand with 130,000 Cambodians. On 1 January 1980 the first theatre performance by adults took place, and by June 1980, two of the twenty-one sectors of the camp had Fine Arts Centers offering dance classes. Mom Kamel was the organizer and teacher of some one-hundred girls—two-thirds under age fourteen—selected to study classical dance. Two other teachers and some dozen of the students had studied dance previously.[175]

In a simple bamboo theatre, with musicians whose instruments had been buried for safekeeping during the Pol Pot regime, classical dances were rehearsed and performed alongside less formal dances similar to those of the camp's *yiké* troupe. Monkey and demon masks were used, and one American observer described the costumes as "elaborate" for a program of fifteen dances which she observed in June 1980.[176]

Other performers associated with the Khao I Dang dance group at that time included Mrs. Peou Khatna, who had been *première danseuse* in

1939 and later costume mistress for the 1971 U.S. tour; Mrs. Sin Ny, her daughter who became a featured dancer in 1968 and toured with Sihanouk; and Mr. Nuth Rachana who performed in the Royal Palace for twenty years. Musicians included Mr. Van Pok, a *pin peat* performer formerly with the Information Ministry in Phonm Penh; Mr. Phan Bin, Mr. Son Houen, Mr. Sao Sam and Mr. Pok Chuum, all *pin peat* performers from Battambang.

Two well-trained dancers were Mr. Chan Than and Mrs. Chey Saroeun, daughter of a former palace musician. Experienced dance students included Mrs. U. Vanna, Mr. May Someth, Miss May Sisopha, and Mrs. Poline, but students were so highly motivated that dancers having only five or six months of training performed with great sensitivity. The core group of performers including dancers, singers, musicians and a mask maker numbered about twenty-five.

In early 1981 the Khao I Dang performers were befriended by a Swiss film maker, Jean-Daniel Bloesch, and Barbara Byers, an American health educator, who presented their case to the U.S. Department of State. With

4-30. **Khao I Dang Dancers after Five Months of Training.** Photo Colin Grafton

assistance from the National Cambodia Crisis Committee, Buddhist Social Charities, and the National Council for the Traditional Arts, a number of dancers and their families emigrated to the United States, settling in Wheaton, Maryland, near Washington, D.C. More dancers arrived later until by late summer of 1981, most of the Khao I Dang troupe was in the Washington area. They gave their first "official performance" in August at the Wolf Trap National Park for the Performing Arts as part of the National Folk Festival.

Today the Khmer Classical Dance Troupe which Mom Kamel and others nurtured is under the Artistic Directorship of Peou Khatna. Chairman of the troupe is Lapresse Sieng. The president is U. Vanna; Sek Mau Raci is Vice President. Secretary and Treasurer are Sai Sara and Samreth An respectively; the two teachers are Nuth Rachana and Sin Ny. There are thirty other members of the troupe: Phan Bin, Yin Chamroeun, Sek Channy, Kong Chantith, Chum Chan Chhavy, Chheng Chhoeung, Sou Soern, Sou Howk, Sek Khalarath, Po Lin, Pao Neang, Srey Neang, Sam Oeun, Huon Phannary, Van Pok, Yin Pon, Sek Puthirith, Sar Saran, Huot Saroeuy, Heng Sary, Tim Savan, Tep Socum, Sek Sophal, Nou Sovannaro, Sarin Thom, Van Thuon, Phan Vanna, Les Vath, Heng Viphas, and Van Yan.

Unquestionably, this company has flourished. They have toured the East Coast, performed at the Library of Congress, the American Museum of Natural History in New York, and the Smithsonian. The company's publicity and brochures are elaborate and impressive. The official "Friends of the Khmer Classical Dance Troupe" include Rosalynn Carter, Joanne Woodward, and U.S. Senators Baucus, Danforth, Sarbanes and Tsongas among other notables.[177] Performance and tours were scheduled throughout 1984. Young dancers are being trained and the perpetuation of Khmer dance in the United States seems fairly well assured.

This conclusion is supported by the existence of smaller, less professional groups of performers in numerous centers of Khmer resettlement throughout the United States. Among the strongest and oldest of these is another troupe also based in Washington, headed by Phan Phuong who paved the way for the broad acceptance given the Khao I Dang troupe upon their arrival.

The Contribution of Phan Phuong

In the 1970s the largest number of former royal dancers resided in Paris where Princess Buppha Devi formed a classical troupe which still continues to perform and train dancers. In the United States a similar responsibility was assumed by a young, male dancer named Phan Phuong who had graduated from URBA in 1968 and received an Indian government scholarship to Santiniketan in West Bengal where he studied *kathakali* and *manipuri* dance and later *kuchipudi* and *bharat natyam*. In the late 1970s he formed a small troupe of dancers and musicians from the Khmer community in the Washington area which performs periodically as the Cambodian Dance Troupe. As artistic director, with great patience and energy, he has formed a highly versatile, if loosely structured, company capable of performing not only classical works but *yiké*, folk, and *nang sbek* shadow puppet theatre as well.

The Cambodian Dance troupe has given major performances annually for the April New Year's celebration; at the Indochinese Arts Festival in June 1980 in Washington, for the American Folklife Center (Library of Congress); and at the Jacob's Pillow Dance Festival in August 1981 in New York.[178] Mom Kamel and other recently arrived dancers periodically joined Phan Phuong's troupe for special performances, but a unified company of all classical dancers in the Washington area always seemed unlikely.

Major performers with the troupe included Sam-Ang Sam as chief musician, his wife Moly Sam, Vany Jackson, and the leading female dancer/teacher Mrs. Saroeurm Tes who was a featured dancer in the Royal Palace in the 1960s (Fig. 4-31). Young dancers are also being trained.

Classical Dance in Kampuchea

Finally, we turn to the dance situation in Cambodia itself since January 1979, a period marked initially by relief from the excesses of the Khmer Rouge and now, in 1984, marked by a new flowering of the classical dance. By mid-1979 former dancers had been organized into the Central Popular Culture and Art Troupe (CPCAT), which visited Vietnam and Laos in October, clearly a demonstration

4-31. **Saroeurm Tes in the Royal Palace, ca. 1968.** Courtesy of Mrs. Saroeurm Tes.

by the new regime to the Khmers and others of a more humane hand at the controls. Shortly after the troupe returned to Phnom Penh on 29 October 1979, Khmer leader Pen Sovan—soon to be Vice-President—congratulated the dancers and encouraged them "to work relentlessly to achieve the best interpretation of national art and to denounce through cultural means the crimes committed by the genocidal Pol Pot regime."[179]

Obviously, this latter injunction could not be met by the traditional content of the non-political, classical repertoire and, consequently, the "mass artistic activities" which sprang up did not include groups solely dedicated to *lakhon kbach*. In the new troupes, according to an illustrated pamphlet entitled "The Rebirth of Kampuchea," distributed to Hanoi officials at a press conference on 9 November 1979, by the Kampuchean ambassador Chea Soth, "their repertoires are built on the basis of restoring the ancient national culture while developing a new revolutionary culture. Many well-known actors and actresses who survived the persecution of the old regime thanks to the people's protection, have now come back to the stage."[180] It appears, however, that only a very small number of these were classical dancers, or at least only a small number were allowed to perform in certain circles.

On 5 April 1980, for instance, the CPCAT gave a performance in honor of the thirty-fifth anniversary of the "liberation of the Hungarian people" which featured, according to a government source, "songs applauding the militant solidarity and friendship between the Kampuchean people and the world's people including the Hungarian people."[181] A Western writer in attendance more candidly characterized the evening of "recently penned" revolutionary songs such as "Arise and Eliminate our Enemies," as a "potpourri of dreary socialist fare." There was one exception.

> Near the evening's end, hall lights dim and the sounds of classical Cambodian music rise from the orchestra pit. Madame Van Svay appears before the footlights. A wave of excitement passes through the Cambodian spectators because the woman on stage had formerly been one of a triad of stars in the Royal Ballet, her face well known from postcards and posters. Now in her early 40's, Madame Svay looks a shade thicker after five years of backbreaking labor in Pol Pot's rice fields. She is wearing the traditional, crown-like headdress and the tight-fitting, jewel-sprinkled costume....
>
> Elegant, refined, and still very beautiful, Madame Svay begins the dance of the *apsaras*,... and for a quarter-hour the stones of Angkor come alive.[182]

The powerful effect of the classical dance on the Khmer mind seems not to have diminished.

While the three-hour program in which Madame Svay appeared as the highlight was for bureaucrats only, classical dance performances—or at least excerpts—were apparently available to the general public by the same period. Workers for one humanitarian agency reported that "the national Khmer ballet and folk dances" were playing to full houses at the "National Theatre"[183] in early 1980, a probable reference to the Central Popular Culture and Art Troupe. What proportion of the programs was classical is not clear.

It is important to note, however, that within little more than a year from gaining power, a communist government could encourage (and present to foreign communists) an art form identified fundamentally in the mind of the proletariat with the former king—an art form that more than, perhaps, anything else had previously symbolized the now rejected social structure. Such a heresy was allowable not so much by the sheer beauty and power of the dance, as by the fact that two deplorable regimes intervened between the fall of Sihanouk and the advent of the People's Republic, and it was, ironically, those years of corruption and depravity which insulated the classical dance tradition from its royal past and rendered it acceptable within the "new revolutionary culture" as a symbol of the people's creativity, spirit, and endurance. The degree to which the content of the repertoire has been altered to contemporize that symbolic value remains to be seen.

In general, government-supported cultural revitalization proceeded briskly throughout 1979 and 1980. Each province established an "Arts' Troupe," and Phnom Penh had three: the CPCAT or national troupe; an army troupe, and a municipal troupe. In Kompong Thom province, Chheng Phon, who had survived the Pol Pot years, became the leader of a *yiké* troupe which toured the countryside performing its melange of dialogue, song, orchestral music and low comedy, conjoined with realistic portrayals of the violence recently experienced. Although carefully censored and laced with socialist jargon, the dramas had a powerful effect on audiences for whom they were a kind of psychodrama. In his travels Chheng Phon also sought out former artists to re-collect the words and music of the classical, folk, and *nang sbek* repertoires, collections of which in the National Conservatory had largely been burned.[184] Then, as though to re-affirm Kampuchea's commitment to continuity, Chheng Phon was named Minister of Information, Press and Culture on 27 June 1981.

THE SCHOOL OF FINE ARTS

The new government had been committed to dance education, however, from the beginning, and in late 1979, despite the critical food shortage and other difficulties, had opened a School of Fine Arts in Phnom Penh which selected a group of 10-13 year-olds as the first class. Two years later, in October 1981, a second class was chosen, and in attendance at that process was Peter T. White, Senior Editor of *National Geographic Magazine*. In the first class he saw 56 young girls (as well as young boys), and in the second, 24 girls who had been selected from 159 candidates. These latter had been sent to the capital from "provincial dance schools" and almost all were orphans, aged 12-17. White was told that there were 600 students in dance schools (Fig. 4-32) throughout the country.[185]

The head dance teacher was Mme. Chea Samy, 67, a former royal

4-32. **Young Dancers in Siem Reap.** Photo Jaro Poncar.

dancer and teacher, who was also serving in the National Assembly—on the occasion of its infrequent meeting—as an elected delegate (with 96.88 percent of the vote) from Kandal Province. She explained that all of the dances are new in terms of plot and songs, but that the "two thousand dance movements" are traditional; she herself had written a number of the new songs. White saw the following dances performed by the first class:

    1. "The Dance of Cultural Revival" in which the dancers carried shields, spears, hammers, and sickles, with five girls singing.

    2. "Production Dance."

3. "Dance of the Growing of Vegetables" in which the girls were the cabbages and the boys were digging them up, happy at their productivity.

4. "Dance to Welcome the Army" in which flower petals were thrown to welcome Kampuchea's defense forces.

5. "Dance of the Axe."

6. "Dance of the Doves of Peace" with the girls wearing papier-mâché bird sculptures on their heads.

7. "We Survive With Solidarity" in which two boys fighting over a girl are interrupted by three giants. The tallest boy present played "Reap, King of the Giants" against whom all united. Other defenders included Hanuman and a host of monkeys.

The dances included *apsaras* dancers and the traditional four roles of male, female, monkey, and giant, as well as the traditional portrayal of the four basic human qualities of being happy, sad, angry or shy. Yet, as Mme. Chea made clear, the dance—of which the classical style is only one component—is a form of political education for a socialist society.

Regardless of its new political content, the *lakhon kbach boran* appears to be flourishing in essence in its homeland as well as abroad. The clearest symbol included in White's account of his Cambodian visit[186] was that of an eight-year-old girl named Mom Kanika, who had been added to the first class five months previously because of her natural skill and charm. She, and countless Cambodian girls who have dedicated themselves to the dance tradition embody Cambodia's past… and its future.

Endnotes

1 Cœdès, *ISSA*, p. 191. Syam was another name for Sukhothai (see *ISSA*, p. 235).
2 *RCB*, p. 9.
3 *SSA*, p. 222.
4 Chheng Phon, personal communication.
5 *RCB*, p. 7.
6 *Rāmakerti* (XVIe-XVIIe siècles), Publications de l'École Française d'Extrême-Orient, 110 (Paris: l'École Française d'Extrême-Orient, 1977), p. 134.
7 Pou, *Rāmakerti*, p. 134.
8 The accuracy of this theory is generally acknowledged. In a standard text of Southeast Asian history, for example, D. G. E. Hall discussed the pattern in regard to Indonesia: "It seems certain also that Indonesia, before the coming of Hindu culture, possessed in its oral tradition stories of the same kind as the Sanskrit tales and it may be that when later on, after the introduction of written literature from India, we meet them in literary form with an Indonesian setting, they are not necessarily foreign importations which have been given an Indonesian twist, but represent folk myths and legends, springing from the same remote origin as the Indian stories.... Thus, it is argued, with the coming of Hindu culture Austric stories took on a Hindu garb, and the divergencies from the Hindu form in a Hindu-Javanese story are often re-creations of an old Austric theme" (*A History of South-East Asia* [London: Macmillan, 1960], pp. 9-10).
9 Pou, *Rāmakerti*, p. 52
10 Pou, *Rāmakerti*, p. 134.
11 *Recherches sur la littérature du Cambodge, du Laos et du Siam, Vol. I of Mission Pavie Indochine 1879-1895: Études diverses* (Paris: Ernest Leroux, 1898), pp. xii-xiii. Parenthetically, the art of making paper from mulberry-bark pulp is an ancient one, traceable to first-century China and cultivated in Japan (where it is known as *washi*) since the eighth century, and throughout Polynesia.
12 Xenia Zarina, "Royal Cambodian Dances," *Classic Dances of the Orient* (New York: Crown, 1967), p. 64.
13 Bernard P. Groslier, *Angkor et le Cambodge au XVIe siècle d'après les sources portugaises et espagnoles* (Paris: Presses Universitaires de France, 1958), pp. 27-34. This section is a study of the early missionary as historian.
14 See, for example, Zhou Daguan's account of the endless stream of women (p. 34) accompanying the king on his rare ritual outings – guards, palanquin bearers, etc. as well as his concubines and palace women numbering between three and five thousand (p. 16). Great numbers of women still surrounded the eighteenth-century kings Ang Ton and Chetta V as well. See "Chroniques Royales Khmer," trans. Martine Piat, *BSEI*, 49, No. 1 (1974), pp. 53, 81.
15 Bowring, *The Kingdom and People of Siam*, I, p. 90.
16 Diogo do Couto, *Cinco livros da Duodecima Decada da Asia*, Ch. VI, p. 42, Cited by Groslier, *Angkor et le Cambodge au XVIe siècle*, p. 73. The long-lost sixth chapter was published for the first time as a section of Groslier's text.
17 B. Groslier, *Angkor et le Cambodge au XVIe siècle*, p. 162.
18 Simon de la Loubère, *A New Historical Relation of the Kingdom of Siam* (London, 1693; rpt. Kuala Lampur: Oxford University Press, 1969), II, p. 49.
19 Cœdès, "Origine et évolution," p. 499.

20 Cœdès, "Origine et évolution," pp. 502, 498-99.
21 Cœdès, "Origine et évolution," p. 499.
22 Cœdès, "Origine et évolution," p. 499.
23 *RCB*, p. 10.
24 The term was coined by Adhémard Leclère, *Histoire du Cambodge* (Paris: Paul Guenthner, 1914), p. 422.
25 David P. Chandler, "Cambodia's Relations with Siam in the Early Bangkok Period: The Politics of a Tributary State," *JSS*, 60, No. 1 (Jan. 1972), pp. 155, 168.
26 Pavie, *Recherches*, I, p. xvii.
27 *Danses cambodgiennes*, p. 31.
28 Adhémard Leclère, *Le théâtre cambodgien* (Paris: Ernest Leroux, 1911), p. 31.
29 *RCB*, p. 8.
30 *RCB*, p. 10.
31 Chandler, p. 155.
32 C.-E. Bouillevaux, *L'Annam et le Cambodge; voyages et notices historiques* (Paris: Victor Palmé, 1874), p. 95.
33 *Three Months in Cambodia* (Singapore: Mission Press, n.d.), cited by Bowring, *The Kingdom and People of Siam*, II, p. 28.
34 *RCB*, pp. 30-31.
35 *RCB*, p. 11.
36 Leclère, *Le théâtre cambodgien*, p. 3.
37 Cœdès, "Origin et évolution," p. 503.
38 *RCB*, p. 11.
39 *RCB*, p. 11.
40 *RCB*, p. 10.
41 *RCB*, p. 10.
42 *RCB*, p. 10.
43 *RCB*, p. 10.
44 *RCB*, p. 11.
45 *RCB*, p. 11.
46 *RCB*, p. 12.
47 *RCB*, p. 12.
48 *RCB*, p. 12.
49 *RCB*, p. 12.
50 *RCB*, p. 12. Sir John Bowring in 1855 had noted the great reverence accorded Lao dance by the Thai, and, having witnessed several private performances, observed that "almost all of the opulent nobles have wives from Laos...." (*The Kingdom and People of Siam*, I, p. 90).
51 *RCB*, p. 12.
52 Harriet W. Ponder, *Cambodian Glory* (London: Thornton Butterworth, 1936), p. 248.
53 *RCB*, p. 12.
54 G. Groslier, *Danseuses cambodgiennes*, p. 29.
55 J. Moura, *Le royaume du Cambodge* (Paris: Ernest Leroux, 1883), II, pp. 415-16.
56 G. Groslier, *Danseuses cambodgiennes*, p. 95.
57 Leclère, *Le théâtre cambodgien*, p. 3.
58 M. R. Kukrit Pramoj, *Skeletons in the Cupboard* (Bangkok: n.p., 20 April 1971), pp. 69, 70-79.
59 Pramoj, p. 79. Kukrit does not mention the interesting fact that Chao-Anou was seeking a pretext for the attack and purposely made a number of other "unreasonable requests" of Rama III. (See D.G.E. Hall, *A History of South-East Asia*, p. 381.)
60 Pramoj, p. 80.
61 Chheng Phon, personal communication.
62 *RCB*, p. 14.

63 René de Beauvais, *La vie de Louis Delaporte Explorateur (1842-1925): les ruines d'Angkor* (Paris: Des Orphelins d'Auteuil, 1931), p. 66.
64 *Le royaume du Cambodge*, II, p. 414.
65 *Un hiver au Cambodge* (Tours: Alfred Mame et Fils, 1888), p. 261.
66 Pavie, *Recherches*, pp. xvi-xvii.
67 *Introduction, première et deuxième périodes 1879 à 1889*, Vol. I of *Mission Pavie Indochines 1879-1895: Geographie et Voyages* (Paris: Ernest Leroux, 1901), p. 27.
68 *Le théâtre cambodgien*, p. 5. As corollary to the earlier testimony of Pavie, Leclère, and Boulangier, we should note the observation of Etienne Aymonier, made in 1900, that the classical versified dramas "are hardly ever presented except at the Palace, where they are performed by members of the royal harem; nowadays popular theatrical troops are rare and unimportant" ("The Literature of Cambodia," *Le royaume actuel*, Vol. I of *Le Cambodge* [Paris: Ernest Leroux, 1900], p. 44). This is in no way a contradiction of the others' claims since, both in the palace and outside, dancers increasingly performed only short episodes of the classics. The same remained true in the 1970s.
69 *RCB*, p. 12.
70 *RCB*, p. 15.
71 *RCB*, p. 12.
72 *RCB*, p. 12.
73 George Bois, *Les danseuses cambodgiennes en France* (Hanoi: Imprimerie d'Extrême-Orient, 1913), p. 1. Unless otherwise indicated, all details of the 1906 tour are taken from this source which was also published under the same title in *Revue Indochinoise* in September 1913.
74 Bois, p. 3.
75 Bois, p. 11. Slightly contrasting figures are presented in *RCB*, p. 15.
76 Bois, p. 6.
77 During the performance of "Greek dances" which preceded the Cambodians, Princess Sounpady, oblivious to protocol and with all good intention, grasped the hand of the President of the Republic in greeting. Following this *faux pas* she left the théâtre in a snit and was subsequently indisposed to hear the requests of the Minister to allow a second performance. Since the music of the first performance was barely audible, however, over the sound of the melee and "animal cries" from outside the théâtre, the Minister persevered and ordered Picon bitters to be served – a new favorite of the princess – and she was eventually mollified, though never reconciled to French ways.
78 Bois, pp. 15-16.
79 *RCB*, p. 15. She took her name from the role of the legendary Princess Bosseba whom she "incarnated with matchless perfection." She had been trained at the court of Ang Duong, and eventually died living in a temple.
80 *RCB*, p. 16.
81 G. Groslier, *Danseuses cambodgiennes*, p. 120.
82 Sappho Marchal, "La danse au Cambodge," *RAA*, 4, No. 4 (Dec. 1927), p. 218.
83 "Le théâtre en Indochine," *Anthropos*, 3, No. 2 (1908), p. 292.
84 G. Groslier, *Danseuses cambodgiennes*, p. 96.
85 Félix Cardi, "Les danses sacrées au Cambodge," *Revue Musicale*, No. 1 (Nov. 1920), p. 38.
86 Lily Strickland-Anderson, "The Cambodian Ballet," *Musical Quarterly*, 12 (1926), p. 269.
87 Marchal, "La danse du Cambodge," p. 218.
88 George Groslier, "Le théâtre et la danse au Cambodge," *JA*, 214 (Jan.-Mar. 1929), p. 136.
89 G. Groslier, *Danseuses cambodgiennes*, p. 98.
90 G. Groslier, *Danseuses cambodgiennes*, pp. 37-38, 96.
91 Bois, *Les danseuses cambodgiennes en France*, p. 3.
92 G. Groslier, *Danseuses cambodgiennes*, p. 96. Some years later, in 1937, 35,000 piastres was the equivalent of U.S. $8,750 (see Zarina, p. 66); its value in dollars during the early years of Sisowath's reign is not known.
93 *RCB*, p. 14.

94 Cardi, p. 38.
95 Thiounn, pp. 53-54.
96 Cardi, p. 35.
97 Georges Maspero, "Littérature khmère et littérature laotienne," in *Un empire colonial français: l'Indochine*, ed. Georges Maspero (Paris and Bruxelles: G. Van Oest, 1929), I, p. 305.
98 *Saramani danseuse khmère* (Saigon: A. Portail, 1919).
99 Louis Laloy, "Les principes de la danse cambodgienne," *La Revue Musicale*, 3, No. 9 (July 1922), p. 2.
100 G. Groslier, *Danseuses cambodgiennes*, p. 69.
101 G. Groslier, *Danseuses cambodgiennes*, p. 41.
102 Laloy, "Les principes," p. 2.
103 Strickland-Anderson reported seeing the Khmer dancers perform at the 1921 Colonial Exposition in Marseille "before the splendid replica of the ancient Temple of Angkor-Vat" ("The Cambodian Ballet," p. 266). In seeming contrast, Cambodian records (*RCB*, p. 17) and the account of Louis Laloy ("Les principes," pp. 1-7) clearly place the visit in 1922 and do not mention a visit to Marseille. A 1936 account says that Khmer dancers performed at the 1931 Colonial Exhibition at Vincennes before "a reproduction of the central temple of Angkor Wat, approached by a Naga causeway" (Ponder, *Cambodian Glory*, pp. 239-40).
104 *RCB*, p. 16. For other accounts of the 1922 tour see Strickland-Anderson, pp. 266-67, and Louis Laloy, "Les principes," pp. 1-7.
105 Personal communication.
106 "L'Influence de L'Inde sur les danses en Extrême-Orient," *RAA*, 7, No. 1 (1931), pp. 8-14.
107 S. Marchal, "La danse au Cambodge," pp. 224-25. For accounts of performances by the Angkor troupe in this period, see Pierre Jeannerat De Beerski, *Angkor: Ruins in Cambodia* (London: G. Richards, 1923), pp. 291-94, who mentions five young female dancers alternating with two male clowns; Alfred Meynard, "The Stones of Angkor," *Asia and the Americas*, 28, 1 (Jan. 1928), pp. 68-69, who describes eight dancing girls; and Robert J. Casey, *Four Faces of Shiva* (Indianapolis: Bobbs-Merrill, 1929), pp. 146-52, who mentions fifteen dancers. None of these accounts name the teacher.
108 Marchal, "La danse au Cambodge," pp. 225, 228. See also Cardi, "Les danses sacree," p. 35.
109 Cardi, "Les danses sacrées," p. 35.
110 *RCB*, pp. 17-18.
111 Cardi, "Les dances sacrées," p. 36.
112 Laloy, "Les principes," pp. 1-2.
113 Marchal, "La danse au Cambodge," p. 224.
114 Cardi, p. 40.
115 Alfred Meynard, "A Cambodian Costume-Piece: The Coronation Rites in Which a People Cloaked in Symbols, Recovers Its Past," *Asia and the Americas*, 29, 6 (June 1929), p. 452. This article is a translation in abbreviated form of a gilt-edged, numbered commemorative publication entitled *Le courounement de Sa Majestè Monivong Roi du Cambodge à Phnom-Penh, 20-25 Juillet 1928* (Hanoi: Editions de la Revue Extrême-Asie, 1928).
116 *RCB*, p. 18.
117 Meynard, "A Cambodian Costume-Piece," p. 459.
118 *RCB*, p. 19.
119 Casey, p. 156.
120 G. Groslier, "Le théâtre et la danse au Cambodge," p. 136.
121 *RCB*, p. 19.
122 *RCB*, p. 18.
123 *RCB*, p. 19. By contrast, Thiounn wrote in *Danses cambodgiennes* (1930) that in the palace there were 106 female dancers, two clowns, eight female teachers of dance, two male teachers of chant, two lead chanters, two readers, twenty-five chorus members, twelve dressers, four jewelry and costume caretakers, nine musicians and two orchestra leaders (p. 53). The striking contrast between

these figures and those cited from other sources can only be explained by the assumption that, since the text was prepared for the 1931 visit of Khmer dancers – not the king's – to the Paris Colonial Exhibition, Thiounn chose to paint a flourishing picture far more descriptive of the earlier Sisowath court in which he had been Prime Minister than the 1930 court of Monivong, much beset by French penury.

124 G. Groslier, *Danseuses cambodgiennes*, p. 102.
125 *RCB*, p. 19.
126 Ponder, p. 235.
127 Zarina, p. 64. This account was based on a 1937 visit to Cambodia. See also Ponder, p. 235.
128 Ponder, p. 239.
129 Ponder, p. 240.
130 Ponder, p. 240. Casey (p. 146) says the torches were balsam; Ponder describes their construction but doesn't name the wood.
131 Meynard, "The Stones of Angkor," p. 69.
132 Zarina, p. 69.
133 Willard Cooper et al., *Meadows Museum of Art: For the Indochina Collection of Jean Despujols* (Shreveport, LA.: Centenary College), n.p. Despujols' work is preserved in the permanent collection of this museum.
134 See for instance J. A. Hammerton, *Manners and Customs of Mankind* (London: Wm. H. Wise, n.d.), II, pp. 362-68.
135 Ponder, p. 238.
136 *RCB*, p. 19.
137 *RCB*, p. 19.
138 Jeanne Cuisinier, *La danse sacrée en Indochine et en Indonésie* (Paris: Presses Universitaires de France, 1951), p. 26.
139 Raymond Cogniat, *Danses d'Indochine* (Paris: G. Di San Lazzaro, 1932), p. 12.
140 Zarina, pp. 68-69.
141 Zarina, p. 69.
142 Zarina, pp. 70-72.
143 Sisowath-Monivong, S. M. Preah Bat Samdach Prea, "Poeme votif," in *Danses exécutées par la troupe de S. M. Preah Bat Samdach Prea Sisowath-Monivong* (Saigon: n.p., 1931) pp. 6-7.
144 Chheng Phon, personal communication.
145 Khun Kru Lamun Yamakupt, personal communication, 18 August 1975.
146 *RCB*, p. 19.
147 Chheng Phon, personal communication.
148 *RCB*, p. 20.
149 Chheng Phon, personal communication.
150 For brief accounts of this annual pilgrimage see Ruth Tooze, *Cambodia: Land of Contrasts* (New York: Viking, 1962), p. 82; Keith Buchanan, "The Dancers in the Forest; Angkor Revisited," *Eastern Horizon*, 4, No. 5 (May 1965), pp. 24-32; and Thomas J. Abercrombie, "Cambodia: Indochina's 'Neutral' Corner," *National Geographic Magazine*, 126, No. 4 (Oct. 1964), pp. 527-31.
151 The three belong to the United States Information Agency, The Asia Society, and the Dance Library of the Performing Arts.
152 Chheng Phon, personal communication. This is the only source of reference to family troupes. They are more than likely the same as troupes belonging to "high officials."
153 Chheng Phon, personal communication.
154 *RCB*, p. 22.
155 Guy Porée, p. 579.
156 MacDonald, pp. 23-24.
157 *RCB*, p. 20.

158 *RCB*, p. 20.
159 *RCB*, p. 22.
160 *RCB*, p. 23
161 Hang Thun Hak, "Le Ballet Royal," *La Revue Française de l'élite Européene*, No. 206 (Jan. 1968), pp. 25, 27.
162 Buchanan, pp. 27-28.
163 Jacques Brunet, Jacket Notes, *Royal Music of Cambodia*, UNESCO Collection, Musical Sources: Art Music from South-East Asia IX-3, Philips, 6586-002, 1970.
164 Dean Barrett, "Agony of Khmer Dance," *The Asia Magazine*, 27 Jan. 1974, p. 16.
165 "Bas-Reliefs Come to Life," *New York Times*, 31 Oct. 1971, Sec. 2, p. 30, col. 8.
166 Deborah Jowitt, "Royal Treasure and Brown Climb Again," *Village Voice*, 28 Oct. 1971, p. 43, col. 1.
167 John Willis, *Dance World 1972*, 7 (New York: Crown, 1973), p. 71.
168 Matani Rutnin, personal communication, 7 May 1975.
169 "Samdech Sihanouk's Inspection Tour of the Cambodian Liberated Zone," *China Pictorial*, Special Supplement, No. 6 (1973), p. 33.
170 *RCB*, p. 23.
171 Seth Mydans, "Mme. Kamel wages an exotic war for an ancient culture," *Smithsonian*, Sept. 1980, p. 118.
172 John Burgess, "Cambodians Revive Lost Culture," *The Washington Post*, 27 Apr. 1980, p. A-24.
173 David Kline and Robert Brown, *The New Face of Kampuchea: A Photo-Record of the First American Visit to Cambodia Since April 1975* (Chicago: Liberator Press, 1979). The four journalists were associated with *The Call* newspaper in Chicago.
174 Henry Kamm, "The Agony of Cambodia," *New York Times Magazine*, 19 Nov. 1978, p. 42, col. 1; p. 152, cols. 3-4.
175 Gay Gibson Cima, "Cambodian Dance-Drama: A Chance for Survival in Asia?" *Asian Theatre Bulletin*, Winter 1981, published in *Theatre News*, Feb. 1981, p. 5.
176 Cima, p. 5.
177 *The Dance Lives: The Story of the Khmer Classical Dance Troupe* (Washington, D.C.: National Council for the Traditional Arts, 1982), n.p. This 12-page informational brochure was prepared by the NCTA, Suite 1118, 1346 Connecticut Ave., N.W., Washington, D.C. 20036.
178 The latter performance was intelligently reviewed by Deborah Jowitt in "Celestial Refugees," *Village Voice*, 2-8 Sept. 1981, p. 69, cols. 1-4.
179 *Daily Report: Asia and Pacific*, Foreign Broadcast Information Service, Vol. IV, no. 226, 21 Nov. 1979, p. H6.
180 *Daily Report*, 21 Nov. 1979, p. H14.
181 *Daily Report*, Vol. IV, no. 071, 10 April 1980, p. H2.
182 Denis D. Gray, "Cambodian Civilization at the Razor's Edge," *Asia*, Sept./Oct. 1980, pp. 6-7.
183 Joseph Short, "Alive Again . . . But on the Knife's Edge," *Oxfam America*, Spring 1980, p. 5.
184 Gray, pp. 11, 47.
185 Taped letter received from Peter T. White, 2 Feb. 1983.
186 Peter T. White, "Kampuchea Wakens from a Nightmare," *National Geographic Magazine*, 161 (May 1982), pp. 590-623.

CHAPTER V

THE MYTHOLOGICAL FOUNDATION OF KHMER DANCE

មូលដ្ឋានទេវកថានៃរបាំខ្មែរ

Anthropologist Mircea Eliade has written that "all dances were originally sacred; in other words...choreographic rhythms have their model outside of the profane life of man; ...a dance always imitates an archetypal gesture or commemorates a mythical moment."[1] In Cambodia, an origin myth first recorded in the third century A.D. is still to be found within the performance repertoire of the classical dance drama in this century. Four other, very similar mythologems recorded over a period of sixteen centuries present a total of five images of what we shall call the Primordial Maiden—the fundamental myth embodied in the *lakhon kbach boran*. This chapter is an examination of that mythic continuity.

Initially, the significance of the Primordial Maiden's association with serpent, tree, moon, and earth in the Khmer cosmogonic myth will be discussed. The chapter will conclude with a consideration of both the regenerative power of the myth and the totality of human experience symbolized in the classical dance through the dramatic roles of female, male, monkey, and ogre. Our purpose overall is to demonstrate why Cambodian dance has always been associated with the spirit of the earth and with the rites performed for her fertility.

A definition of myth in traditional, archaic or "primitive" societies will be of value before proceeding. Eliade's understanding, which we shall follow, is that

> myth narrates a sacred history; it relates an event that took place in primordial Time, the fabled time of the "beginnings." In other words, myth tells how, through the deeds of Supernatural beings, a reality came into existence, be it the whole of reality, the Cosmos, or only a fragment of reality —an island, a species of plant, a particular kind of human behavior, an institution. Myth, then, is always an account of a "creation"....[2]

THE MYTH OF LIU YE

The myth with which we are concerned was first recorded in the third century A.D. by Kang Tai, an envoy from the Chinese court of the emperor Wu (222-252) to Funan, a kingdom in Southeast Asia which occupied territory in the area of present-day Cambodia. Kang Tai's *Wu shi wai guo chuan* or *Account of Foreign Countries*—no longer extant—was the probable source for all subsequent Chinese historians' commentary on early Funan, though only one of these[3] credits Kang Tai's text[4] in which he wrote:

> At Funan's beginning, a woman served as ruler. Her name was Liu Ye. In the Country of Mo Fu was a man named Hun Tian who served the spirit with all his heart, unceasingly. He dreamed about a bow and was instructed to load a boat with merchants and set out to sea. The next morning Hun Tian went to the temple and found a divine bow under an old, sacred tree. He loaded a large boat. The spirits ordered the winds to turn and blow him to Funan. Liu Ye wanted to rob him so he picked up the bow and shot it, penetrating her boat. He had safe passage through and she fearfully submitted. Thereupon, he arrived at Funan.[5]

With some variation, the legend was included in Chinese dynastic histories, using Kang Tai's text as the common, primary source. In the *Xin shu* or *History of the Xin*, covering the period from 265-419 but compiled in the early seventh century, the ruler is Ye Liu and the "foreigner" Hun Kui—a change introduced perhaps by an inaccurate copyist. In this version "Hun Kui" only raised the bow without shooting it, and when Ye Liu became afraid and surrendered, "he took her as his wife and occupied the country. Later his descendants became weak and didn't continue and his general Fan Xin took over."[6]

In the *Nan Qi shu* or *History of the Southern Qi* (479-501), compiled in the sixth century, Hun Tian from the country of Ji—following his dream and departure—met Liu Ye who had collected her soldiers to resist him. Hun Tian shot an arrow through her boat, hitting one person. She surrendered in fear, and Hun Tian made her his wife. To cover her nudity, he folded cloth and passed it over her head. A number of descendants who ruled prior to Fan Xin are named.[7]

Finally, the *Liang shu* or *History of the Liang* (502-556) records that Liu Ye was young and strong, resembling a man. Hun Tian from the "bordering country" to the south came to Funan as in the other accounts, whereupon Liu Ye's people saw his boat and planned to rob him. "He picked up his bow, shot an arrow through the side of her boat striking one person, and fearfully she surrendered with all her soldiers. Hun Tian instructed her to cover herself. He ruled the country, married her and had posterity including seven sons."[8] Other descendants are mentioned prior to the rule of the great Fan Xin.

The Chinese sources which relate the Liu Ye legend were first translated into a Western language by the French Orientalist Paul Pelliot in 1903.[9] His concurrent interpretation of the story as an historical event whereby Funan came into existence has informed the work of all subsequent historians regarding the earliest history of Funan. This approach, however, has been seriously called into question by Christie and others.

THE MYTH OF THE *NĀGĪ* SOMĀ

The second available version of the Cambodian cosmogonic myth—which we shall consider before generalizing in regard to its content—concerns Kaundinya, mentioned in Chapter II. In the epigraphy of Cambodia, his name appears only briefly,[10] and it is in a single Sanskrit inscription from Champa dated A.D. 657 that the legend regarding him is recorded. At Bhavapura,

> Kaundinya, foremost of the brahmanas of this city, planted the javelin that he had received from the eminent brāhmana Asvattāman, son of Drona. There was a daughter of the king of the Nāgās of birth…who founded on the earth the race which carried the name of Soma: having adopted this state, remarkable thing, she lived in a human dwelling. The foremost of the Munis named Kaudinya married her for the accomplishment of the rites.[11]

The inscription does not say that Kaundinya became king.

A similar account of dynastic origin from a *nāgī* or serpent ancestress was recorded in the ninth century regarding the Pallava dynasty in southern India,[12] but, as Christie has stressed, that version is far removed in time from the third century events to which it purports to belong and appears two centuries after the legend is on record in Champa.[13] The crucial point, however, is that the legend of a *nāgī* ancestress is widespread.

Jean Przyluski has shown that similar legends are found in Champa, Funan, Pegu, Siam, Annam, Sumatra and in the *Sejarah Malayu*, as well as in India.[14] He believes that the *nāgī* origin legend is indigenous to the Austroasiatic peoples and in studying the motif concluded that "it is in the Austroasiatic world that it will be necessary to look for the source of diffusion from which certain stories have been sent towards China in the North and towards India in the West."[15] Przyluski's view appears to be gaining new adherents; Mabbett is simply expanding on his ideas when he suggests that the *nāgī* legend was used as a legitimization myth reflecting

> the indigenous complex of moon, water and serpent mythology that assumed Indian names (the name Soma is Indian) but has deep and strong autochthonous roots. The serpent princess, *nāgī*, is also Indian. Interestingly, however, *nāga* is not an Indo-European word (*srpa*. cognate with "serpent," is the Sanskrit term); it was incorporated from the pre-Aryan vocabulary of people for whom snakes, water and the earth had special sanctity, and these peoples were linked culturally with many of the inhabitants of Southeast Asia.[16]

The two stories considered thus far—that of Hun Tian and Liu Ye recorded in the third century, and the Somā-Kaundinya legend recorded in the seventh century—are fundamentally similar in expressing an important Khmer perception of the "beginning." Both embody the myth that the land belongs to a numinous woman until a man of spiritual power comes to her from abroad, and they form a union. In examining three additional versions of the myth, we will note that this vision remains nuclear.

THE MYTHS OF THE *APSARA* MERĀ AND THE *NĀGĪ* EARTH SPIRIT

As noted in Chapter II, the Merā-Kambu genealogical myth of Zhenla was ill-perpetuated, but even its brief inclusion in the epigraphy preserves the belief that a spiritually accomplished male married a woman identified by name with the indigenous people, to mark the beginning of the Khmer kingdom. As Louis Finot, who first studied this myth, wrote in regard to the genealogical tradition of the early Cambodian kings: "they descended from the *mahārsi* Kambu Svāyambhuva and from the *apsaras* Merā, two purely indigenous personages beneath their Indian disguise."[17]

A fourth, related myth—also mentioned in Chapter II—was the basis of a ritual practiced nightly at Angkor, a union between the king and the unnamed serpent spirit of the soil. In 1296, Zhou Daguan, an envoy to Kambuja from the Mongol emperor Timur Khan wrote that in the Royal Palace of the great city of Angkor

> there is a gold tower at the top of which the king sleeps. All the natives claim that there is a spirit in the tower, a serpent with nine heads, which is the master of the soil of the whole kingdom. It appears every night in the form of a woman. It is with this spirit that the king first sleeps and unites himself. ... If one night the spirit of this serpent does not appear, then the moment of the king's death has come. If the king fails to come a single night, some disaster is inevitable.[18]

The total welfare of the kingdom was dependent upon this ritual, whose power is understandable when one recognizes that legends regarding the *nāga* "seem to have been common to all Southeast Asia and to have been connected with agricultural rites assuring an abundant supply of rain."[19]

This particular ritual was still performed in the twentieth century in Java. In 1928 Paul Mus visited in Solo a round tower in whose forbidden upper story a benevolent *nāgī* "goddess" had been visited periodically by the ruler's father "to guarantee the crops an abundant rainfall."[20]

THE LEGEND OF NEANG NEAK AND PREAH THONG

The fifth appearance of the mythic pattern with which we are presently concerned—this time a semi-historical legend—is found in the "Chronicles" of Cambodia "which disappeared during the wars of the eighteenth century and were 'rewritten' early in the nineteenth...."[21] According to the oral tradition recorded by the Chronicles, Preah Thong was the son of a north Indian king who was banished and came to Kok Thlok where he drove out the Cham ruler prior to his courtship of the beautiful daughter of the King of the *Nāga*, called Neang Neak (nana naka) or "Lady Serpent." Following a grand marriage, the *nāga* king created a kingdom for his son-in-law by drinking the waters covering a vast area on which he then formed houses and a palace. This kingdom took the new name of Kambuja, and Preah Thong was the first Khmer king.[22] This legend is still included in the performance repertoire of the Cambodian classical dance drama in the twentieth century (see Chapter VI).

Another version of the Preah Thong-Neang Neak legend says that growing in the area where Preah Thong landed was a "wonderful Talok tree."

> He ascends, its branches to look about him, but the tree grows..., and he fears he shall never see his mother earth again. In descending, however, he finds himself in a wonderful grotto in the hollow of a tree, where he meets with the dragon king's daughter, and marries her.[23]

The more popular variation, and the one performed in the dance drama, is that one day on an excursion after conquering the Cham king, Preah Thong found himself on a sand dune of recent alluvion, surrounded by the rising tide on "a day of the full moon in the month of visākh."

> The daughter of the underworld king, with a suite of a hundred *nāgī*, slit open the earth and came into the world of men. Swimming from island

> to island, she arrived with her following at a larger island isolated in the sea which is the one where Preah Thong and his court found themselves. Then, because destiny wanted the *nāgī* to marry Preah Thong, they all fell asleep, except him.
>
> The *nāgī* and her followers transformed themselves into human beings, forming a royal procession. Preah Thong heard their rustling, saw the woman in the moonlight, approached them.... They made each other's acquaintance and Preah Thong asked for her hand. She replied that she must first ask the consent of her father.[24]

The *nāga* king consented and the elaborate marriage was celebrated.

After some time the new *nāgī* wife gave birth, surprisingly, to an egg. Furious, Preah Thong ordered that it be buried in the sand west of Angkor. The ambassador from Sukhotai of the kingdom of Bangkok, coming to offer the annual tribute for the Cambodian king's birthday, found the egg and took it back with him.[25] Having given birth to the egg, the queen desired to return to the kingdom of her father, but her husband begged her to stay.

> Ashamed and homesick, the queen went to bed. The King returned to her chamber and saw with horror a serpent on the bed. He retreated, ran into the door, and his blood spurted out on the ground. At the commotion, the queen woke up, hastened to take the king in her arms, ask him what happened and then to assure him that it was not to amuse herself that she took her serpent form again but rather that she was in a deep sleep.[26]

In the dance drama, the events subsequent to the marriage are not performed.

THE PRIMORDIAL MAIDEN AS SERPENT

The five accounts which we have so far examined—Liu Ye-Hun Tian, Somā-Kaundinya, Merā-Kambu, the *nāgī* earth spirit with the Angkor king, and Neang Neak-Preah Thong—represent a Southeast Asian mythology whose significance has been little appreciated. On the assumption that the five versions are facets of a single image, we turn now to an interpretation of this cosmogonic myth, seminal to Khmer culture and its former glory. The argument takes its structure from an examination of the symbolic values accruing to serpent, tree, moon, stone, and flower in Southeast Asia, and a comparison of the five mythic tales (see Table 2) will serve to illumine the integrity of Cambodian mythology within that context.

The myth on which we focus in this chapter may be called the myth of the Primordial Maiden. Its forms are the mythologems or tales concerning five female figures who display similar symbolic relationships and images, foremost of which is the serpent. Three of the five mythologems under consideration involve a serpent motif (Table 2: B, D, E) in which the serpent as master of the lower realm is male but appears in the upper world as feminine. A fourth and earlier version (A) is, in this regard, the most interesting since "in the beginning," the female ruler Liu Ye resembled a man. In light of her meeting with Hun Tian surrounded by water, she is at least an echo of the underworld despite the absence of a serpent form. In

Table 2. **Cambodian Mythic Forms**

CAMBODIAN MYTHIC FORMS OF THE PRIMORDIAL MAIDEN

Century Recorded	3rd (A)	7th (B)	10th (C)	13th (D)	19th (E) Oral Tradition
Name	Liu Ye	Somā	Merā	Anonymous	Neang Neak
ATTRIBUTES	ruled in "beginning"	daughter of the nāga king	born from ocean foam		daughter of the nāga king
	name = a tree	lived in a human dwelling		master of the soil resides in a tower	lives inside the earth found in a tree, grotto, or swimming
	masculine appearance	serpent form	celestial dancer	nine-headed serpent	human form
	meets male in a boat aggressive towards male	progenetrix	eponymic	assumes female form controls fertility and fortune	serpent form in sleep resents motherhood
	subdued by arrow or seeing bow	marries to fulfill the rites	given in marriage by Shiva		given in marriage by father
					gives birth to special son
	marries a man of the "spirit"	marries Brahman	marries mahārsi	nightly union with king	marries king
	clothed by a male	name = moon			appears at full moon
Theme	Creation	Succession	Transcendence	Fertility	Continuity

later legends (B, E), the land was ruled by a distinctly separate male and female—the *nāga* king and his *nāgī* daughter, although the ambiguity can still be seen in the thirteenth century legend (D).

The serpent is perhaps the commonest dream symbol of transcendence. Such figures inhabit both water and earth and, thus, "coming from the depths of the ancient Earth Mother, are symbolic denizens of the collective unconscious. They bring into the field of consciousness a special chthonic (underworld) message."[27] On the mythological plane this message appears to be that the primordial one-ness is manifest in union. Each of the five legends with which we are concerned is the story of a union between a woman identified with the earth and a man of some "spiritual" position; all five are concerned with progeny or the effect of the union, and one (E) explains how, as a result of this union, the dry land was created.

On one level, then, each of the five enacts what Eliade calls the transformation "from chaos into cosmos." In the "beginning" uninhabited and uncultivated regions still "participate in the undifferentiated, formless modality of pre-Creation."[28] Since the women in the legends are identified with the land and the men are not, we are certainly in the presence of the Cambodian myth of "cosmicization": the land, society, and culture are the product of a union between two forces, the unconscious represented by the female serpent, and consciousness represented by the Brahman (B), the *mahārsi* (C), a man of the "spirit" (A), or the king (D, E).

Only in the earliest version is there any suggestion that this union is achieved by a conquest. "A familiar paradigmatic myth recounts the combat between the hero and a gigantic serpent ...,"[29] but such is not the case here. Liu Ye, in one version, acquiesces merely upon seeing the bow, and in the seventh century legend (B) the thrown, phallic javelin is "planted" rather than hurled at the earth. The union of male and female is thus presented as one of comfortable accommodation despite differences.

The primary difference on the dramatic level, of course, is that the woman is a *nāgī*, although only in the most recent version (E) is this incongruity explored. The *nāgī* wife of the king enjoys neither motherhood nor life in the human palace and longs to return to her simpler serpent form.

The interpretation that this form represents the unconscious is substantiated by an early Buddhist text which says that while *nāga* appear to be human, "their serpent nature manifests itself on two occasions, namely, during sexual intercourse and in sleep."³⁰ Indeed, the thirteenth century legend (D) suggests that it is through nocturnal communion with the unconscious that man will flourish.

Parenthetically we note a correlation with Greek archetypal figures in that the serpent nature of the unconscious was personified in Greek myth as Hecate, the goddess of the underworld who corresponds to the dark side of both Artemis and Persephone as well as being one with Demeter, the goddess of agriculture.³¹ Before considering the correlative of Aphrodite, however, we turn to an examination of several other symbols associated with the Cambodian image of the Feminine.

THE PRIMORDIAL MAIDEN AS TREE SPIRIT

The old Khmer name for Cambodia is "land of the Thlok tree," and two of the goddesses are associated with a tree, Liu Ye by name and Neang Neak as a dwelling place. In addition, Hun Tian found his god-delivered bow under an "old, sacred tree." The Chinese transcription of the name Liu Ye means "willow leaf," which is troublesome in that the willow is unknown in Southeast Asia. Pelliot proposed a graphic emendation to *Ye Ye*, "coconut leaf,"³² and Christie now believes that "Liu-ye is a transcription of a word for coconut."³³

> The significance of a tree is universal.
>
> The Great Earth Mother who brings forth all life from herself is eminently the mother of all vegetation. The fertility rituals and myths of the whole world are based upon this archetypal context. The center of this vegetative symbolism is the tree. As fruit-bearing tree of life it is female: it bears, transforms, nourishes; its leaves, branches, twigs are 'contained' in it and dependent on it. The protective character is evident in the treetop that shelters nests and birds. But in addition the tree trunk is a container, 'in' which dwells its spirit, as the soul dwells in the body. The female nature of the tree is demonstrated in the fact that treetops and trunk can give birth, as in the case of Adonis and many others.

> But the tree is also the earth phallus, the male principle jutting out of the earth, in which the procreative character outweighs that of sheltering and containing. This applies particularly to such trees as the cypress, which, in contrast to the feminine forms of the fruit trees and leafy trees, are phallic in the accentuation of their trunks. The phallic nature of the tree... does not exclude the character of containing vessel....[34]

That the *nāgī* should be found inside the tree (E) suggests that the most recent legend develops logically out of the earliest (A). As the masculine quality became differentiated in the form either of husband or *nāgarāja* father, the androgynous coconut—both milk containing and phallic—was replaced by the more leafy feminine *thlok* tree in which the feminine serpent resides.

To bear the name of a tree—capable of self-reproduction, having both male and female organs—adds a further dimension to the image of Liu Ye as hermaphroditic progenitor akin to the androgynous Pallas Athene, goddess of wisdom. The difference, of course, is that Liu Ye forms a union with a personified form of wisdom, whereas Athene remains the "maiden goddess," born of no mother, embodying intellectual and spiritual power within her own person.[35]

THE PRIMORDIAL MAIDEN AND THE MOON

Lunar mythology has long been identified with Austronesian culture, particularly in the close relationship of moon, earth and stone.[36] In Cambodian mythology it is nuclear. We have seen how both Somā (B) and Merā (C) are associated with the moon, and noted that Neang Neak appeared to Preah Thong (E) in the light of a full moon.[37] This identification of the Primordial Maiden with the moon points to a similar association between her male partner and the sun. Taken as a whole, the five mythologems reflect the paradigmatic movement from lunar to solar and from the matriarchal to the patriarchal. Let us examine this claim in light of the oldest version of the myth, the Liu Ye story, which demonstrates it most clearly.

When Liu Ye surrendered to Hun Tian according to the *Nan Qi shu*, he folded cloth and passed it over her head. In the *Liang shu* account he instructed her to cover herself. European historians have interpreted this incident to mean that Hun Tian was "unhappy to see her naked."[38] That the incident should literally refer to clothing, however, is belied by the fact that when Kang Tai visited Funan in the third century A.D., men—including the king—went nude, while women wore only a brief covering below the waist.[39] It is equally possible that the gesture of passing cloth over the head of Liu Ye is a mythological motif corresponding to the marriage of sun and moon—found in other, later Khmer legends—as well as a figurative expression of eclipse or beheading. The motif of eclipse, in turn, appears frequently in cosmogonic myths and lunar mythology generally,[40] symbolizing the ascendance of patriarchy.[41]

For Cambodians, the natural function of the moon is to provide water and, hence, fertility. The moon "gives out the rain which fertilizes the rice fields; it stimulates the riches of the earth, the abundance of the monsoons, the prosperity of all beings."[42] The mythical union of sun and moon strongly suggests that the two have always been associated by the Cambodians with light and water, prerequisites for the earth to flower.

The Primordial Maiden as Earth Spirit

In his highly regarded study of indigenous and Indian cults in the early Christian-era kingdom of Champa to the east of Funan, Paul Mus wrote that

> the ancient occupants of India, Indochina and southern China believed in spirits, present in all things and in all places—disincarnated human spirits, spirits of water and forest and so forth—and that they attributed also to certain men the magic power to evoke them or to avert them.[43]

Pre-eminent among these spirits was the spirit of the earth itself. Never conceived anthropomorphically but rather in terms of events and as a localization, it was the place itself which was "god." Thus, Mus believed that the fundamental principle in this "religion of monsoon Asia" was the "deification of the energies of the soil."⁴⁴

The Khmer mythologems under consideration clearly show that the spirit of the earth was identified with serpent (B, D, E), tree (A, E) and moon (A, B, E) and was conceived as feminine. In the form she takes in the dance drama—that of the *nāgī* serpent—the Primordial Maiden is likewise associated with tree (A, E) and water (E).

In Chapter II we examined the Khmer belief in stone as a concentration of earth forces, and we noted that this belief was easily transposed into viewing the *devarāja* stone in the form of a *lingam* as the conjunction of earth's power with that of the ancestors. Significantly, the feminine earth spirit remained central to Angkorean religion and in some cases we see a human form revealed within the *lingam* itself (Fig. 5-1). This union of the Feminine and Masculine was the central focus of the thousands of dancers in Angkorean temples. In later centuries the female court dancers continued to represent the Feminine, and the king the Masculine. It is in this sense that we may say Cambodian dance has always played an important role in rites associated with the spirit of the earth.

5-1. *Mukhalinga* **Revealing the God, 7-8th C Takeo.**

Pre-Angkorian representations of Shiva often took the form of the *linga,* symbolizing fertility and life-force. The *lingam* bodies often represented the trimurti, or three main Hindu deities; the square base was four-headed Brahma, the octagonal section Vishnu and the circular section at the top, Shiva, including his face, which is expressed by the word *"mukha"* in the title. Photo John Gollings.

The Unity of the Primordial Maiden

While it is perhaps unwise to draw conclusions to any length, there does appear to be a development of theme in the five mythologems, corresponding, in part, to the perceived Khmer social evolution. We will consider each of the five in turn, noting first that the nucleus of each of the five stories is the union of the Maiden with a male; the nature of her subsequent motherhood is of little significance. While the earliest version is somewhat more concerned with what precedes the union and the latest version with what follows it, the revelation and essence of the overall myth lie in the regenerative union of Feminine and Masculine as the source of life. The tone, however, is expectant rather than celebratory, as though uncertain whether the *nāgī*—the Feminine form in three of the five versions—will remain in this world of men or return to the pre-existent sea. As Zhou Daguan wrote in the thirteenth century regarding the immensely long stone *nāga* which form the parapets of the causeways radiating in the four directions across the great moat surrounding Angkor Wat: "fifty-four divinities grasp the serpents with their hands, seemingly to prevent their escape."[45]

In the first version of the Primordial Maiden myth concerning Liu Ye, we see the creation of the way things are: a man and a woman will rule jointly, female aggression and dominion have been surpassed, power resides with the man of "spirit," and the land has been metamorphosed into a country. The salient feature of the second version is that the central feminine figure, the *nāgī* Somā, despite strong supranatural associations (moon, serpent body), agrees to dwell in human form and becomes the progenetrix of a race of men. Creation is being perpetuated, and legitimacy of succession for the later kings of Funan lay in tracing their lineage from this cosmogonic union.

Somā further represents the unity of nature. Like Artemis, the Greek goddess of the moon, she has a dark side—her serpent form. Thus, as both the daughter of the underworld king and the founder of a race on earth, she embodies—like Artemis—all the natural world. One seeming difference is that Artemis is identified with dancing,[46] but we should not overlook the demonstrated ambiguity which exists between *nāgī* and the *apsaras* dancer[47] and that both are universal symbols of transcendence.[48]

It is in the third mythologem of Merā, born like Aphrodite from the ocean's foam (Gr: aphros, foam), that we find the supreme symbol of transcendence in Cambodian mythology: the celestial maiden. Unlike the fourth and fifth mythologems, which return to a use of serpent imagery and a generalized concern for fertility and continuity, Merā leaves all chthonic forms behind. She is the only form of the Primordial Maiden who dances, and, as such, is the essence of a higher symbology which empowered Angkor.

Merā may be viewed as the secret of Angkor's greatness. Since both the king and the *devarāja* rested in the center of the enormous man-made reservoirs from which all water for a vast area was dispersed, and since the long *nāga* balustrades which bridged this "ocean" were symbolically "churning" the entire kingdom, it has been observed that the king "married the earth."[49] At the point of their union—where the hard rock of the Masculine most stimulated the primordial ocean of the Feminine—infinite hosts of apsaras dancers,[50] cosmic harmony, and Angkor itself emerged from the foam.

COMPLEMENTARY DUALISM IN THE DANCE DRAMA

While the Khmer *lakhon* are often described generically as *apsaras* dancers, we must carefully note the significance of other roles played by the human performers on the mundane stage. Thus, we turn to a consideration of the general role types performed by royal dancers. Complementary material will follow in Chapter VI concerning dramatic themes and in Chapter VIII regarding costume types.

The classical dance drama, as a reflection of Khmer belief in general, manifests a number of elements whose symbolic value can be best defined in terms of the relationship with a second, related complementary symbol. Elements of this dualistic pattern will be discussed at various points throughout this study, but for purposes of examining character roles generically, the general structure is presented in Table 3.

It should be noted that there is no element of "good versus evil" in the dance drama; the endless conflict between the *yakkha* giants and Rām in alliance with the monkey roles, for instance, are merely one form of the tension of opposites which is the fundamental dynamic of life. Sometimes, too, the duality as presented is unique to Cambodia. One instance of this is the Vishnu/Shiva dichotomy. As Chheng Phon has said, the popular view is that they are "something like good and evil,"[51] but even in the Harihara sculpture at Angkor we noted their unity. This particular opposition does not accord with the Indian view in which Vishnu transcends and contains all dualities.

A second example in which the Cambodian view is significantly different from the Indian is that of the *nāga*, which is always opposed by the *krut* or *garuda* bird in Indian mythology.[52] While the *krut* is a minor character on the Khmer stage, he shows no particular relationship to the *nāga* who, as we have seen earlier in this chapter, inhabit the sphere that is complementary to the human realm.

Finally, in several instances, our categorization places characters of both genders under the heading of Feminine but only characters of male gender under the Masculine heading. This is because the distinction between Feminine and Masculine, overall, does not concern gender exclusively. The division is rather one between the material, the intuitive, the earthly, and that which contains, in contrast to the spiritual, the rational, the heavenly, and that which inseminates. On that basis we turn to a discussion of the Feminine forms.

The Dancer in Female Roles

The term "female roles" generally refers to "princess" or "goddess" (*apsaras*), but there are other roles in the category as a whole which will be discussed in Chapter VIII according to their costume types. Here we will note the qualities of the primary female images on the Khmer stage: the *apsaras*, Sitā, Mekhala, and Sovann Machha.

The *apsaras* has been discussed at length as she appeared in Angkorean

Table 3. **Symbols of Feminine-Masculine Dualism Associated with Khmer Dance Drama**

FEMININE	MASCULINE
princess	prince
yakkha, yakkhinī	monkey
nāgā, nāgī	human
Shiva	Vishnu
Sitā	Rām
Reab	*eysei*
Sovann Machha	Hanumān
Mekhala	Ream Eyso
kennari	*kennara*
moon	sun
silver	gold
left	right
rice	fire
earth	rain
raw food on altar	cooked food on altar

sculpture; on the modern stage she embodies the same qualities—calm elegance, aloof mystery, and radiant beauty in trancelike motion. She is a spirit who appears, dances, and vanishes. She is celestial and, therefore, lacking in human traits.

Sitā, on the other hand, is the perfect woman—devoted, constant, and loyal—and yet these qualities are not the foundation of who she is on the symbolic level. One of the primary ways in which the various Rām stories are analyzed to demonstrate transmission between various cultures is by reference to Sitā's parentage, and she is, variously, the daughter of Janaka, the earth, Rāb or Dasaratha.[53] In the Cambodian *Rāmker*, Sitā "the white" is not born on this earth but is, rather, taken from the water of a river, where she reposed in an open lotus floating on a golden raft.⁵⁴

At the end of the *Rāmker*, in an accommodation to her past conflicts with Rām and unique to the Cambodian form of the epic, Sitā returns to the world of the *nāga* while Rām remains on the earth.⁵⁵ More than likely, then, Sitā is a Sanskritized form of the ancient mythologems of the *nāgī* Somā and Neang Neak. In the latter case, this possibility is further supported by a legend in neighboring Laos that Sitā—not unlike Neang Neak—was born from a tree.⁵⁶

What becomes apparent in this view of Sitā is that her story represents virtually another form of the Primordial Maiden myth. She is identified not only with the *nāga* and the land—and we may note Leclère's report that the Cambodian aboriginals were known as "nagas"⁵⁷—but she is also identified with another archetypally Feminine group of roles, the *yakkha*, and particularly with Rāb.

Numerous versions of the Rām story, including Tibetan, Khotanese, Indonesian, Malay, Thai and Lao versions, claim Sitā to be the daughter of Rāb⁵⁸ and, hence, a *yakkha* princess. The resulting incestuous implications in Sitā's abduction by Rāb do not appear at all in the Indian *Rāmāyana*; in the *Rāmker* they lie just beneath the surface. In Chapter VI we will discover that most princesses in the dramatic repertoire have a *yakkha* father. A handsome prince marrying a beautiful princess, who—it is casually mentioned—is the daughter of a *yakkha*, is a common motif within the dance drama. On the subconscious level, this theme lends great appeal to the story. In a less "dangerous" though parallel situation, Hanumān—a more child-like aspect of Rām— seduces another daughter of Rāb, Sovann Maccha. The two stories present both the comic and serious sides of the eternal father-daughter-hero triangle.

The Khmer heroine's association with the subterranean *nāga* realm is totally undisguised in the favorite and most frequently performed episode in the Khmer dance repertoire, the story of the fish-maiden, Sovann Machha. As we will note in greater detail in the following chapter, she struggles against Hanumān without benefit of her father's intervention and is eventually subdued, as was Liu Ye, the earliest Khmer progenetrix.

Another important aspect of the Khmer archetype of the Feminine is personified in Manimekhala, goddess of the clouds (often known, simply, as Mekhala). In her struggle with Ream Eyso, the Thunder-god, there is no suggestion of a higher patriarchal authority, and Mekhala fights her own battle to a draw. This has been interpreted by some, including one of the two *New York Times* reviewers for the 1971 United States tour, as a conflict between good and evil: "the feminine archetype...is a proud woman who humiliates her evil and male antagonist."[59] Such a view, however, obscures the main point. In the endless Masculine struggle to control the Feminine, we see a clear image of the archetypal essence of male and female—the action and resistance that create all waves of energy and eventually the pearl of life itself.

5-2 **The Mythical *Kennari* Bird-Women.**
Edger Boulangier, *Un Hiver au Cambodge*, 1885.

There is one sub-group of female roles whose true significance on the Khmer stage cannot at present be evaluated due to a lack of data regarding their relationship with other characters. These are the mythical *kennari* bird-women (Fig. 5-2) who live high in the mountains with their consorts, the *kennara*. The *kennari* movements and dances are livelier than those of other female roles and are said to be often purposefully provocative.

> The *kennari* are reputedly very amorous, lascivious, and unfaithful to their husbands—they pursue men and entice those who venture into the mountains, offering themselves and disputing among each other. They are lovers of all those who abandon themselves to them.... When they are together they play, dance, bathe, and amuse themselves by throwing round stones in the rivers to splash their comrades.[60]

Images of these roles are rarely mentioned in available descriptions. Photos from performers in 1880 and 1931 are included in Chapter VIII (Figs. 8-9 and 8-13).

THE DANCER IN MALE ROLES

In contrast to the essential image which unifies the many female roles, the male roles—limited largely to princes—appear monochromatic. The prince is a handsome, lovely person; adventuresome; dutiful to his master, the ascetic or *eysei*, and to his parents; totally enchanted by the princess but always restrained, elegant, and spiritually powerful.

Only four exceptions to this near-paragon are to be found among male roles. First is the virtuoso role of the *ngo*—Prince Preah Sang disguised as a trickster in a negrito mask to hide his true nature. Significantly, most male roles of the princely type bear powerful weapons, and Preah Sang, whose story is equally as popular as the *Rāmker* has a magic staff that is the most powerful of all.

He obtained this weapon from the king of the *nāga* who rescued him from drowning after one of his father's wives threw him in the ocean with a stone tied to his neck. He was then raised by "the widow of a king of the giants."[61] Thus, Preah Sang is the only male role who, like the *nāgī* Somā and Nang Neak, represents an integration of the Feminine and Masculine principles.

Another popular male image is the Thunder-god Ream Eyso. Discussed in the following chapter, we note here that he is solely the embodiment of a force of nature. He is the purest form of the Masculine, locked in eternal struggle with the more powerful Mekhala to gain the silver ball which knocks him to the earth each time she tosses it—the power she wields, which he can never attain.

There are two additional male roles which are polarized projections of the prince role—the *eysei*, who embodies all the wisdom and spiritual power of the Masculine, and the clown (*tluka*), who acts with un-selfconscious spontaneity. The *eysei* and the clown—the only two roles in the *lakhon* which were traditionally performed by men, as if they were furthest in tone from the archetypal Feminine—are closely related. In many appearances, the *eysei* is a comic figure,[62] while the clown's humor, in turn, points up the profound illusion of all phenomena.

THE DANCER IN *YAKKHA* AND MONKEY ROLES

The *yakkha*, or ogre, roles are categorized as Feminine because they are always in opposition to the Masculine roles of prince and monkey; because of their connection to the earth; and because they are associated with the princess. The *yakkha* represent a spiritually lower form of the Feminine in the same sense that the monkeys are a less-advanced form of the royal and semi-divine princes. Both the *yakkha* and the monkey possess very good qualities—helpfulness, loyalty, strength, and cunning, but in each case, some higher faculty is absent.

The *yakkha* king Rāb has great power. He can believably assume the guise of the *eysei* to trick Sitā, and in the theatre, his mask is considered to relay more power from the spirit world than any other (see Chapter IX). Rāb controls the earth as symbolized by his abduction of Sitā, who in some versions of the epic—including the Indian version of Valmiki—is born from a plow furrow and is the "daughter of the earth."[63] To retrieve her, Rām must align himself with his own instinctive self in the form of Hanumān. By so doing, he is successful in regaining Sitā—the source of fertility, the land, and its people. The three-way struggle of hero-heroine-*yakkha* or husband-daughter-father is eternally recurrent.

The role of the monkey in this struggle is ambivalent. Just as all dualities are relative, Hanumān represents the intuitive, Feminine aspect of Rām, while at the same time embodying the more rational Masculine principle vis-à-vis the *yakkha*.

There is a final aspect of the struggle, however, to be considered. Rāb may also be seen as representing a Tantric deity in competition with Hindu Rām for the Feminine as consort. In the *Rāmker*, Rāb initially appears before Sitā as an apparition in the form of a Tantric visualization: "first, the twenty arms, then the body, the legs and, last, the ten heads which come to rest—in the same moment as all the ornaments of jewelry and most beautiful stones—upon the torso."[64] Taking Sitā in his arms, he presses her against his chest and rises with her into the air in the image of Hevajra, Hayagriva, Cakrasamvara, or any other of the multi-armed and multi-faced Tantric deities in union with the consort.

While the Rām legend may be interpreted on the allegorical level as an historical Tantric Brahmanic religious struggle for the devotions of the Southeast Asian people—with Rām in the role of the proper, socialized Hindu god incarnate, it is on the more personal level of "What male will control the prized woman?" that the Khmer audience perceives the dramatic struggle, and it is that question which underlies the dramatic action of most pieces in the classical repertoire.

THE ARCHETYPE OF THE ANDROGYNE

On the psychic level of interpretation, the four roles of the Khmer *lakhon*—female, male, *yakkha*, and monkey—represent four aspects of a single integrated personality. They symbolize a process which takes place to greater or lesser degree in each individual. By encountering these elemental forms of meaning common to all human experience (i.e., the archetype) through the medium of an artistic performance, the Khmer dance drama is a profound revelation of the path to androgynous individuation. The following is an elaboration.

Each human being, if she or he is to develop their fullest potential of skill and wisdom needs to harmonize the forceful and jealous (Rām) with the passive and dependent (Sitā); integrate the baser elements of mind and body (Hanumān) with their imperfect nobility (Rām); bring to consciousness the love-hate attachment between parent (Rāb) and child (Sitā); transmute the libidinous forces of lust (Hanumān) and revulsion (Sovann Machha); and continually seek to resolve the conflicts between aggression (Ream Eyso) and pride (Manimekhala).

This relationship between the four roles is not some archaic or theoretical structure. The four archetypes appear to have informed the psychic world view of the Cambodians for over a millennium, and are capable of giving empowerment in modern life universally. The Center for Transpersonal and Expressive Arts Therapies near Los Angeles, for instance, sponsors a flourishing performing arts company which uses a method of psycho-dramatic improvisation both as therapy and in the creation of theatre pieces for audiences.

Under the direction of Dr. William Pennell Rock and his associates, all actors (or patients) explore

> the masculine, yang, or active principle (the hero); the feminine, yin, or receptive principle (the heroine); the ego-resistance by which the two are held in unconscious separation (the monster); and the nature spirit by which they are united in alchemical transformation (the magic helper).[65]

The correlation with Rām, Sitā, Rāb, and Hanumān as archetypes is unmistakable, and the true seer's experience of the roles in Khmer dance drama cannot be so distant from this modern theatre company's analogous exploration of the archetype of the androgyne: the internal union of Feminine and Masculine which is a timeless and gradually achievable goal.

Endnotes

1. Mircea Eliade, *The Myth of the Eternal Return* (Princeton: Princeton University Press, 1971), pp. 28-29. Translated from *Le Myth de l'éternal retour: archétypes et répétition* (Paris, 1949).
2. Mircea Eliade, *Myth and Reality* (London: Allen and Unwin, 1964), p. 5.
3. The *Tai ping yu lan*. See n. 5 below. For a discussion of sources see Pelliot, "Quelques textes," pp. 244-45.
4. Sections of various histories and encyclopedias attributed to Kang Tai have been compiled in an attempted reconstruction of his text: Xu Yungiao, ed. *Kang Tai wu shi wai guo chuan ji zhu* (Singapore: Southeast Asian Research Bureau, 1971).
5. Li Fang, ed., *Tai ping yu lan* (Beijing: China Book Store, 1963), III, j. 347, 1599. This is a facsimile reprint of a Song dynasty edition (Shanghai, n.d.), originally edited by Li Fang (925-996). The same reading is found in a Ming dynasty edition (n.p., preface 1574), j. 347, p. 17. (The "j." here and in subsequent citations refers to chapter or *juan*.) However, a third edition consulted—a reprint of a Song edition (n.p., 1812) j. 347, p. 14—says Hun Tian became "king" of Funan, rather than merely "entering" Funan. This presumably scribal error has had a significant influence: Pelliot failed to point out the two possible readings and cited a single 1818 Bao edition as the authority for his interpretation that a foreigner became king ("Quelque textes," p. 244).
6. Fang Xuanling, ed., *Xin shu* (Beijing: China Book Store, 1974), j. 97, p. 2547. Fang Xuanling lived from 576-648.
7. Xiao Zixian, ed., *Nan Qi shu* (Beijing: China Book Store, 1972), j. 58, p. 1014. Xiao Zixian lived from 489-537.
8. Yao Silian, ed. *Liang shu* (Shanghai: China Book Store, 1936), j. 54, p. 4. Yao Silian died in A.D. 643.
9. Le Fou-nan," pp. 248-303. In this study and one in the following year "...Pelliot, although he was only in his early twenties, produced two major works that set the study of Southeast Asian historical geography on a firm basis. Pelliot's presentation of his case was so lucid and his arguments were so convincing that most of his identifications for Chinese transcriptions of Indochinese and Insulindian place-names have attained magisterial status, and very few scholars have been audacious enough to question their authority" (Brian E. Colless, "The Ancient Bnam Empire: Fu-nan and Po-nan," *Journal of the Oriental Society of Australia*, IX, 1-2 [1972-73], p. 21). The interpretation he gave to the Liu Ye legend was adopted and expanded by Cœdès; no one challenged it.
10. Inscription K.5 speaks of the "moon of the family of Kaundinya"; K. 263 mentions "the moon of the race of Kaundinya"; K. 286 says that King Rudravarman traced his origin from "Kaundinya and the daughter of Soma." The latter two are from the tenth century. See Cœdès, "L'inscription de Baksei Chamkrong," pp. 476-78.
11. Louis Finot, "Les inscriptions de Mi-son," p. 923. Somā is "moon" as well as the daughter of

Soma (Cœdès, "L'inscription de Baksei Chamkrong," p. 477).
12 Not surprisingly, Cœdès considers the *nāgī* legend to be Pallava in origin ("La legende de la *nāgī*," *BEFEO*, 11, pp. 391-93) since the Pallavan dynastic progenitor Skandasisya was said to be the fruit of a marriage between Drona's son Asvattāman and a *nāgī*. He overlooks the fact, however, that the copper-plate inscriptions are not unanimous regarding the lineage. "In the Pallava inscriptions she is called an Apsaras, but a Nāgī in those of the Ganga-Pallavas" (Jean Phillippe Vogel, *Indian Serpent-lore* [1926; rpt. Varanasi: Prithivi Prakashan, 1972], p. 36). Other inscriptions say that Skandasisya was the son of a *nāgī*, but only mention Asvattāman as one of the ancestors (Sir Roland Braddell, "Ancient Times in the Malay Peninsula," *JMBRAS*, 17, No. 1 [Oct. 1939], p. 155). Cœdès further cites the *Manimegalai*, a Tamil poem thought to preserve a legend connecting the Pallavas, whose history extends from the third to the ninth century, with their predecessors, the Chola dynasty: Tondaiman, supposedly an early Pallava ruler, was the son of a Chola king and the daughter of the king nāga ("La légende de la nāgī." p. 392). There is serious doubt, however, as to whether this legend even concerns the Pallavas (see R. Gopalan, *History of the Pallavas of Kānchī* [Madras: University of Madras, 1928], pp. 21-22). Since the *Manimegalai* cannot be dated earlier than the fifth century (see K. A. Nilakanta Sastri, *The Colas* [Madras: University of Madras, 1975], p. 15, n.3), and since the Pallavas were "foreign to the locality over which they ruled" (Braddell, p. 153) from A.D. 200 onwards, the legend was undoubtedly evolved from other traditions—including Southeast Asian—for the purpose of dynastic legitimization. This is suggested not only by the fact that the *Manimegalai* mentions two kings of Java who claimed to be descended from Indra (J. P. Vogel, "The Yupa Inscriptions of King Mulavarman from Koetei," *BTLV*, 74 [1918], p. 171), but also by the Pallava's tracing of their lineage to Drona and Asvattāman, heroes of the epic *Mahābhārata*.
13 "Provenance and Chronology," p. 8.
14 "La princesse à l'odeur de poisson et la *Nāgī* dans les traditions de l'Asie orientale," in *Études asiatiques* (Paris: G. Van Oest, 1925), II, pp. 265-84. Vogel also cites examples of this regarding the dynasties of Udayana in northwest India, Kashmir, the Rājas of Chhota Nāgpur, Manipur, and among the Bastars and the Gonda of central India—all claim a *nāga* progenitor, usually male, however (*Indian Serpent-lore*, p. 36).
15 "La princesse," p. 284. Przyluski feels that the original form of the motif—that of the fish-born princess—underwent significant change as it "diffused" to India and to China where, for instance, it became a male dragon ("La princesse," pp. 280, 282).
16 Mabbett, "The 'Indianization' of Southeast Asia," Sept. 1977, p. 146. Numerous scholars have pointed out that in India serpent worship is not associated with Aryan people or with the Vedas. James Fergusson, *Tree and Serpent Worship* (1868; rpt. Delhi: Oriental, 1971), p. 58. J. Ph. Vogel points out that in contrast to reverence for serpents, the *Rig-veda* frequently mentions a mythical, white "solar" horse which tramples serpents under its feet (*Indian Serpent-lore*, pp. 6, 11). Przyluski is of the opinion that the prefix *ku-*, found in the *nāga* names *Kuthara*, *Kuhara* and so on, points to a possible connection with non-Aryan languages, and he specifically assigns an Austroasiatic origin to the name *Karkota*, "the Created One" (cited by Vogel, *Indian Serpent-lore*, p. 6, n. 5).
17 "Sur quelques traditions indochinoises," in *Mélanges d'Indianisme offerts par ses élèves à M. Sylvain Levi* (Paris: Leroux, 1911), p. 208.
18 See Zhou Daguan, p. 22. This important excerpt is here translated by the present author from Paul Pelliot's French version: "Memoires sur les coutumes du cambodge de Tcheou Ta-kouan," *BEFEO*, 2 (1902), p. 12.
19 Briggs, *AKE*, p. 14.
20 Paul Mus, "Chronique," *BEFEO*, 28 (1928), p. 647.
21 Briggs, *AKE*, p. 40. The chronicles use the old Khmer name for Cambodia, Kok Thlok, "the land of the *thlok* tree" and include legends and other data whose value regarding the early history of the Khmers has been underestimated. Such is the initial claim of an article whose significance and broad

application to the study of Cambodia's early history seems to have been generally overlooked: Eveline Porée-Maspero, "Nouvelle étude sur la Nāgī Soma," *JA*, 233, No. 2 (1950), p. 238.

22 J. Moura, *Le royaume du Cambodge* (Paris: Leroux, 1883), II, pp. 9-10. Moura obtained this legend in a manuscript of the royal annals prepared for him by King Norodom. Eveline Porée-Maspero cites other versions of the legend recorded in the twentieth century and argues that they reflect historical fact in regard to driving out the Chams and the establishment of the Khmers in the area ("Nouvelle étude," pp. 263-64). Briggs (*AKE*, p. 15) and Cœdès (*ISSA*, pp. 65-66) are basically in agreement.

23 Fergusson, pp. 50-51.

24 Document 40008 in collections of the Commission des Moeurs et Coutumes au Cambodge quoted by Porée-Maspero ("Nouvelle étude," pp. 242-43). Part of the ceremony included the giving of new names by the *nāga* king. Preah Thong became Preah Bat Atitvongsa, designating the solar race; the *nāgī* became Neang Tavottei and the island of Kok Thlok became Kampuchea Thipdei.

25 This egg eventually became Phra Ruang, the legendary king of the Siamese (Porée-Maspero, "Nouvelle étude," p. 243) and represents a wonderful use of symbolic language to encapsulate historic events.

26 Porée-Maspero, "Nouvelle étude," pp. 243-44.

27 Joseph L. Henderson, "Ancient Myths and Modern Man," in *Man and His Symbols*, ed. Carl G. Jung (Garden City, N.Y.: Doubleday, 1964), p. 154.

28 Eliade, *The Myth of the Eternal Return*, pp. 9-10.

29 Eliade, *The Myth of the Eternal Return*, p. 37.

30 Cited by Vogel, *Indian Serpent-lore*, p. 3.

31 The basis for a Cambodian-Greek comparison—or for any two Feminine mythologies—is suggested by C. Kerenyi in his study of the *kore* or "maiden" goddess in Greece and Indonesia in *Essays on a Science of Mythology: The myths of the divine child and the mysteries of Eleusis* (New York: Harper and Row, 1963), pp. 101-55.

32 "Quelque texts," p. 245, n. 2. This is suggested by the "clan du cocotier" in ancient Champa.

33 "Provenance and Chronology," p. 8: "...the Chinese characters in their reconstructed form being an equivalent of Cam *lu-o* (cf. Semang: *lo-urr*)."

34 Erich Neumann, *The Great Mother: An analysis of the archetype* (New York: Pantheon, 1954), pp. 48-49.

35 Kerenyi, *Essays*, p. 106. Parenthetically, a further difference concerns Athene's origin—springing "full blown from the head of Zeus," clearly reflecting a patriarchal consciousness. Neumann points out that "the male proceeds to deny the genetic principle, which is precisely the basic principle of the matriarchal world.... [He] makes himself the source from which the Feminine—like Eve arising from Adam's rib—originated in a spiritual and antinatural way" (p. 58). The Greeks made Athene wise but un-fecund. The Khmers transformed Liu Ye into the moon, allowing for no more than occasional eclipse.

36 See Wilhelm Schmidt, "Grundlinien einer Vergleichung der Religionen und Mythologien der austronesischen Volker," *Denkschriften der kaiserlichen Akademie der Wissenschaften in Wien, phil.-hist. Klasse*, LIII (1910), pp. 1-142.

37 A moon reference perhaps can be read also in the mythologem of the nightly tryst between the Angkor king and the *nāgī* earth spirit in that the tower in which they met was the Phimeanakas or "dwelling place of the sky."

38 Cœdès, *ISSA*, p. 37.

39 Pelliot, "Quelque texts," p. 293.

40 Porée-Maspero and Bernard-Thierry, "La lune, croyances et rites au Cambodge," *La lune, myths et rites* (Paris: Editions du Seuil, 1962), p. 270.

41 In his study of the Archetypal Feminine, Erich Neumann, a student of Carl Jung, suggests that "throughout the world, lunar mythology seems to have preceded solar mythology," and that "the Feminine is preponderant over the Masculine" in early mankind. Mythologically, this is expressed by reference to the sun and moon: "by way of simplification we correlate the sun with the patriarchal consciousness and the moon with the matriarchal consciousness" (*The Great Mother*, pp. 56-57). Neumann warns that "...it should not be forgotten that 'early mankind' and 'matriarchal' stage are not archeological or historical entities, but psychological realities whose fateful power is still alive in the psychic depths of present-day man" (p. 43). The present analysis accepts the validity of these views.
42 Porée-Maspero and Bernard-Thierry, "La lune," p. 263.
43 "L'Inde vue de l'Est," p. 373. I.W. Mabbett has acknowledged his indebtedness to Mus ("Devarāja," p. 209) and Cœdès has acknowledged the article's significance (*ISSA*, p. 8).
44 Mus, "L'Inde vue de l'Est," p. 374.
45 *Notes on the Customs of Cambodia*, p. 21.
46 Kerenyi, p. 107.
47 Vogel, *Indian Serpent-lore*, p. 36.
48 Henderson, pp. 150-53.
49 In exactly the same manner (as noted earlier), the royal *lingam* had no *yoni* base and thus was able to impregnate the earth directly (Aeusrivongse, p. 117).
50 It is said that there are 1,737 *apsaras* on the walls of Angkor Wat alone (B. P. Groslier, "Preface," *RCB*, p. 3).
51 Personal communication.
52 Heinrich Zimmer, *Myths and Symbols in Indian Art and Civilization* (New York: Bollingen Foundation, 1946), pp. 85-86.
53 C. Bulcke, "La naissance de Sitā," *BEFEO*, 46, No. 1, pp. 107-17.
54 François Martini, "Quelque notes sur le *Rāmker*," *Artibus Asiae*, 24, Nos. 3-4 (1961), p. 355.
55 Hang Thun Kak, *Rāmker (Rāmāyana khmer)* (Phnom Penh: L'Université Royale des Beaux-Arts, 1969), p. 59.
56 Sahai Sachchidanand, "Study of the Sources of the Lao Rāmāyana Tradition," *Bulletin des amis du royaume lao*," No. 6 (1971), p. 221.
57 Leclère, *Le théâtre cambodgien*, p. 7.
58 Sachchidanand, p. 221.
59 Anna Kisselgoff, "Ballet, from Cambodia, the Khmer," *New York Times*, 21 October 1971, p. 55.
60 Leclère, *Le théâtre cambodgien*, pp. 20-21.
61 Sappho Marchal, *La danse au Cambodge*, p. 222.
62 "Other Khmer performing arts include clown figures, but none are based on the *eysei*" (Chheng Phon, personal communication).
63 Martini, "Quelque notes," p. 354.
64 Hang Thun Hak, *Rāmker*, p. 69, n. 3.
65 *Boddhisattva Arts*, a brochure published by the Center for Transpersonal and Expressive Arts Therapies, 3537 Old Conejo Road, Newbury Park, CA 91320.

Chapter VI

THE MODERN REPERTOIRE OF THE DANCE DRAMA

បញ្ជីរឿងសម័យទំនើបនៃរបាំ

  Even within the memory of the dance teachers living today, a very large number of different dance drama episodes have been performed in the twentieth century. This fact, together with the possibility of new pieces being choreographed at any time, allows the claim that the Khmer Classical Dance is not based on a static or limited repertoire. It is true, however—both performance records and informant testimony agree—that most of the dramatic episodes performed originate from about forty stories. From some, single episodes have remained popular; in other cases the entire story telescoped into a flexible series of episodes is presented. This chapter will first survey the stories, or *roeung* (riana), performed, noting in the synopses whenever possible which episodes have most often been dramatized. Themes common to the repertoire as a whole will be discussed. The second half of the chapter will examine the repertoire of the dances, or *robam* (rapama), many of which were originally excerpts from the dramas.

  It would not be completely accurate to say that this chapter concerns the literary basis of the dance drama because, although virtually all of the stories have been written down, most recount legends and mythic tales transmitted orally for generations prior to transcription. Rather, this chapter distinguishes those performances which are dramatic—with plot, character and dialogue—from those which are single, non-dramatic dances. Understandably the distinction is not always a clear one.

We noted in Chapter IV that public performances in the 1960s were given a general structure of opening and closing with dance pieces framing one or two dramatic pieces, the entire combination being dependent on the sophistication of the audience or other considerations of the moment. Many of the dance pieces, however, originated in the dramatic works and were increasingly presented as isolated jewels removed from context as demands for short duration, high interest-level performances developed.

THE DRAMATIC REPERTOIRE: *ROEUNG*

The following listing of dramatic works, which are the matrix of either episodes or dances, is based, in part, on records in the library of the Buddhist Institute, the Khmer Cultural Library, and the Royal Palace Library. From these sources, a list of thirty items was prepared in 1975 by Chet Chheng, a sort of records-keeper of the dance, particularly of texts.

Corroboration of Chet Chheng's list, as well as ten additional items, was found in 114 performance programs dating from 1931 to 1961 preserved in the Royal Palace Library (Appendix II). A discussion of these forty items follows. To indicate the relative congruence of data from the two sources, all titles will be followed by either an "X" indicating the existence of that work in the Palace performance records, or an "0" indicating an entry on Chet Chheng's list of the dramatic repertoire, or both.

The entries which follow are made in the order of frequency of performance as noted in the available sampling of Palace programs. Thus, the number which follows the "X"—indicating the incidence of that piece in the programs—in no way suggests the total performances of that work over the thirty-year period. Rather, it reflects the popularity of a given episode relative to others.

SOVANN MACHHA (X-24, 0)

The seduction of Sovann Machha, Queen of the Fish and daughter of Rāb (corresponding to the Sanskrit Rāvana), by Rām's white monkey general Hanumān is the single most popular dramatic piece in the entire dance drama repertoire. Eighteen of the twenty-one times it appeared in the random sample of palace programs, it opened the performance. Categorized here as a drama because of its place in the *Rāmker*, the piece is fundamentally a dance duet. Significantly, it is not found in the Sanskrit *Rāmāyana*.

The episode concerns Sovann Machha's obstruction of Hanumān's plan to build a causeway to Lanka in order to rescue Sitā. As fast as his monkeys lay the stones, her fish remove them to the shore. The performance may include Hanumān's chase of the small fish, a popular subject of study for younger dancers, but the scene usually consists of the King of the Monkeys catching sight of their queen and his attempt to seduce her (Fig. 6-1).

6-1. **Hanumān and Sovann Maccha, ca. 1937.**
Nokor Khmer.

It is also possible to stage the subsequent story of her son, who was at birth attended by *apsaras* descending to earth to rejoice at the strength of the new baby. In fear of her father, Sovann Machha left the child on the ocean shore in the care of a white dove and the *apsaras*, where he was eventually taken to the underworld.[1] In 1913 George Groslier also mentioned a drama entitled Chantalivong in which Sovann Machha was a main character, but he gave no details.[2]

Rāmker (X-19, 0)

Not including the episodes of Sovann Machha or the Battle of the Black Monkey and the White Monkey, the Rām and Sitā sections of the *Rāmker* taken as a unit are the second most popular story in the repertoire. (If Sovann Machha and the Black-White Monkey battle are included, the *Rāmker* comprises about 27 percent of all performance content recorded in the programs.)

In a lengthy and excellent publication concerning all aspects of the *Rāmker*, professors at the Université Royale des Beaux-Arts in 1969 listed the eleven scenes from the epic that were performed by the classical dance troupe:

1. Rāb sees Rām and Sitā
2. Rām follows the golden deer.
3. The abduction of Sitā.
4. The battle between Sugrib and Bali, and Rām's killing of Bali.
5. Hanumān and Sovann Machha, and the monkeys.
6. The battles of Lanka: Kumbhakar, Indrajit, and Rāb.
7. Sitā and the test of fire.
8. Condemnation of Sitā and the test of the sword.
9. Rāmlaks and the test of the horse, reconciling Rām with his sons.
10. The attempted reconciliation of Rām and Sitā.
11. Rām and the test of the funeral urn.[3]

Performance records from earlier years confirm that, after Scene 5, Scenes 1, 2, and 3—performed consecutively—were the most popular, followed by Scene 6, Scene 8, and Scene 9 in that order.

Some clarification of this scene division, however, along with synopses, will be valuable in understanding the possibilities for selecting a program. The plots of Scenes 1 and 2 are well known. In Scene 3 Rāb, disguised initially as a comic hermit, tells Sitā not to worry because she is destined for Rāb instead of Rām anyway. When Sitā insults and strikes him, he becomes angry, appears in his true form, and flies away with her. This scene may be followed immediately by Scene 6, Rām leading his army to victory over the forces of Lanka. The scene may have several lesser battles prior to the climactic encounter between Rām and Rāb. The most popular of these is the semi-comic confrontation between Hanumān and Indrajit, Rāb's son, which is often staged as a discrete performance.

One UBA publication clearly indicates that an earlier scene in the palace of Rāb was often played in which Sitā's body, protected by the gods, radiates such an intense heat that Rāb's physical assault is repulsed. Becoming angry, he orders two of his female servants to punish her, but they are interrupted by Hanumān's arrival.[4] This scene was not included on the list above but, like most of the subsequent scenes, was optional to the performance. In this and all other patterns of piecing together various elements of the total scenario, the primary concern was to create a coherent and unified story.

This principle resulted in flexible performances of various scenes or parts of scenes in conjunction. For example, Scene 8 may be divided into Part A—Sitā's painting of Rāb's portrait after her rescue—and Part B—Lak's attempt to execute her on Rām's orders. Likewise, Scene 9 may be divided into Part A—the birth of Rāmlaks and his duplication by the kind hermit—and Part B—the two grown sons' conflict with Hanumān and their reconciliation with Rām. Records show performances consisting of 8A-B and 9A-B; 8B and 9A-B; 8B and 9A; or only 9B. As some elements of these scenes are uniquely Khmer, synopses, as found in performance programs, follow.

In Scene 8A, Rāb revenges himself on Sitā by rendering her life with Rām impossible. The method is somewhat ambiguous. In the *Rāmker*, the supposed death of Rāb is the most vague and least developed section, with the oldest literary version actually ending before his death. In the oral tradition, Rāb's female cousin takes human form and becomes a servant in Rām's palace in order to avenge her uncle,[5] but one performance program clearly states that "the King of the Giants, Krung Reap, frustrated in his desires, continues to nourish his distress and returns disguised as a female servant."

Regardless of her true nature, the female servant begs Sitā to draw a portrait of Rāb because she desires to know what he looks like. Sitā, believing the woman to be a palace attendant, draws the portrait, whereupon the servant disappears. Stricken with fear, Sitā tries to tear up the portrait but in vain. She tries to erase it, but to no avail. When Preah Rām arrives he becomes angry and accuses the queen of having been the lover of Rāb and of being unfaithful. He orders his brother Laks to put the queen to death in the forest and return with her liver.

In a more detailed version of the scene, Sitā hides the portrait under Rām's bed where, unable to sleep, he discovers it and denounces the artist as a black magician. Sitā confesses that she'd drawn the portrait in innocence, but from that moment Rām's suspicions begin to grow.[6] This variation does not appear, however, in any of the performance programs.

Scene 8B consists of Laks' attempt to kill Sitā in the forest as Rām has ordered. Initially, he believes she has remained true to the king and wants her to remain peacefully in the forest. Sitā, however, refuses to live under Rām's unjust condemnation and tells Laks, "I am guilty. I did love Rāb, and Rām has reason to be offended." In great anger, Laks looses his bow, but the arrow is transformed into a garland of flowers around Sitā's neck as proof of her purity. In great amazement Laks begs Sitā's forgiveness and departs.

Variant versions of the Khmer *Rāmker* may have contributed elements to the dance drama performance that cannot be documented by palace program notes. For example, while Sitā's virtue transformed the arrow into a garland, one version says that the god Indra took the form of a deer whose heart Laks offers to Rām as proof of the killing. (Its dark color confirmed to Rām his wife's "black designs.") It was also Indra who transformed himself into a buffalo on which the pregnant Sitā could ride to the dwelling of the hermit Vijjaprit, who subsequently protected her.[7]

In no program did the performance actually end with Scene 8B, Sitā alone in the forest after Laks' departure. As a unit, the story of Scene 8—the painting of Rāb's portrait as a projection of Sitā's guilty conscience and unconscious attraction to him—is always conjoined with at least the first part of Scene 9, Sitā protected by the hermit.

Scene 9 is the story of Sitā's children. Shortly after arriving at the hermitage, she bears a son in the exact image of Rām, and to this child Vijjaprit is very devoted, often caring for the infant when his mother goes gathering the wild fruits which they eat from the forest.

Once, upon returning and finding her son awake beside the old hermit deep in a profound meditation, Sitā takes him in her arms for a walk. The hermit, on opening his eyes and discovering the disappearance of the child, believes that he has been carried off by a wild beast and to prevent greater sorrow for Sitā, sets about creating—thanks to his magic powers—another boy similar to the one who has disappeared. When Sitā returns, both she and the hermit are amazed, and Vijjaprit offers to destroy the new child. Sitā begs him to keep the infant as a companion for her son and to name him. The eldest he calls Rāmlaks and the youngest Jupalaks.

Scene 9B makes a great leap in time to the point when the hermit's training of the two boys has been completed. As symbol of the powers he has given them, he confers on each a large bow and sends them to the jungle to test their skill. Choosing an ancient tree (named Rangkalpa), they exultantly reduce it to powder with their arrows. The noise of this conflagration reaches the ears of their father, named, variously, "Harira-Rāma" or "Preah Nareay" (Vishnu)—presumably a device to recall their own divine nature. At any rate, Rām calls his *yakkha* astrologer Bibhek (by shooting an arrow into the air where he is flying), who predicts the arrival of extremely powerful princes, and Rām sends Hanumān to investigate.

The scene may be shortened at this point by the arrival of Hanumān and Laks with the two boys, who are recognized by their father, and conclude with preparations for the return of Sitā. Programs from both 1949 and 1959, however, describe a much lengthier scene in which Bibhek sends Hanumān to the jungle with a horse bearing a kind of written passport which states that whoever steals the animal will be put to death. (Another variant has Hanumān writing the message himself after reaching the forest.)

Rāmlaks and Jupalaks find the horse and joyously ride him all around until Hanumān tries to arrest them. They beat Hanumān, whom they conclude is a domestic rather than a wild monkey, and tattoo him with an un-removable message which reads "None but his own master will be able to free him from his ties." Hanumān returns in disgrace to Rām, who is enraged and calls forth his troops to capture the two troublemakers. None of the available program notes indicates performance of the actual reconciliation of Rām and his sons, but the Khmer version of the story, which may have been staged in non-documented performances, indicates that Rāmlaks was first captured, freed by Jupalaks with the assistance of Sitā's ring, and, in the subsequent battle that ends Scene 9, both boys are finally recognized by their father.[8]

Of the eleven *Rāmker* scenes said by the URBA professors to be performed by the Royal Ballet, there is no evidence in the program notes of Scenes 7, 10, or 11 ever being staged. Those scenes are Sitā and the test of fire, the reconciliation of Rām and Sitā, and Rām's futile attempt to use his supposed funeral urn to lure Sitā back. If these were performed, they were certainly the least popular episodes. Clearly then, the relationship between Rām and Sitā is of far less interest to the Khmers than Sitā's actual location, her safety, and ultimate loyalties; and the story, overall, is not complete until her husband and sons are reconciled, even though Sitā herself chooses to return to the forest and the *nāga* kingdom.

Preah Sang (X-19, 0)

Of equal popularity with the *Rāmker* is the story of Preah Sang (often written "Saing"). The term *preah* is a Mon-Khmer word meaning "god" or "saint," and in some languages of that family means "sky"—in some cases it is the only word for sky. It is in no way Sanskrit-derived. Like virtually all of the dramatic repertoire of the *lakhon kbach boran*, Preah Sang is about a hero who bears the title *preah*—in the sense of "divine object or being"—in apposition to his personal name. Of all the divine-being/hero figures, Preah Rām and Preah Sang are the equal favorites.

Preah Sang, as performed by the Royal Ballet, is one version of the *jātaka* tale of Sang Thong, the Prince of the Golden Conch (*sang* or *saing* is conch; *thong*, gold).[9] Also known as "Kehang Saing," after the shell in which he was born, the story tells of a golden-skinned youth originally born in a conch, who subsequently disguises himself in the form of a *ngo*, or negrito, and who has magic powers gained from his *yakkhinī* (demon) stepmother. This ancient folk tale came, in time, to be considered a depiction of one of the Buddha's anterior lives, with Sang Thong as the Bodhisattva. Three episodes were popular on the stage: his youth with the *yakkhinī*, his marriage, and the subsequent testing by his father-in-law.

In the palace performance programs, Preah Sang (also known as Preah Bat Saing) is most often portrayed gaining the Princess Rachana as his wife. A lengthy summary of the plot may be found in Thiounn's *Danses cambodgiennes*,[10] but, in brief, the princess chooses Preah Sang as her husband because she sees his golden form, whereas everyone else, including her father, sees only his ugly disguise. Preah Sang's youth and marriage (separated by twenty years) were often staged in a series of short scenes performed by four main dancers playing the roles of the *yakkhinī*, King Bat Samal, Preah Sang, and Princess Rachana. In a more elaborate staging, one set of dancers sometimes played the youthful roles of the child Rachana, Preah Sang as the *ngo*, and Sopantharos (also Sapannaros) the *yakkhinī*, while another set played the Prince and Princess as young adults and the yakkhinī in old age.

There is no evidence of the trials through which King Samal put Preah Sang ever being staged in conjunction with the first two sections. Preah Sang's success in the trials placed on him—at the expense of the other six malevolent sons-in-law—was performed separately. Despite strong comic elements, it was this episode which was selected to be performed at the laying of the cornerstone of the Royal Palace on 13 August 1920.[11]

Manimekhala and Ream Eyso (X-12, 0)

The story of Mekhala (*mekhalā*), "Goddess of the Waters," and Ream Eyso (rāma 'isū), the Storm-Spirit, is basically a dance duet. It is categorized here as a drama because it can be placed anywhere within the structure of a program, including the central "dramatic" position, and because it is the first of a two-part episode attributed to the *Mahābhārata*.[12] The story, however, is the purest archetypal contest between the Feminine and the Masculine principles in the entire repertoire and is acknowledged by Khmers as one of their own most popular legends.

Manimekhala, holding in her hand a glittering, crystal ball, emerges from her Kingdom of the Sea to go and pay her respects to Vorachhun, "King of the Divinities." (One program merely says she is playing on the waves.) On her way she is detained by Ream Eyso (sometimes written Rāmasoan), "the Storm Spirit, who has been trying from the beginning of time to wrest her magic attribute from the Goddess."[13] Ream Eyso—also referred to as "King of the Ogres"—attempts to persuade Mekhala to part with her magic crystal ball by resorting to honeyed words, but when she mocks him, he becomes enraged and rushes at her, brandishing his magic axe (Fig. 6-2). Mekhala merely shows him the crystal ball by tossing it from her right to left hand, and, blinded by the dazzling light which emanates from it, Ream Eyso collapses on the ground. Time and again he picks himself up for a new assault but finally must retreat with threats of future vengeance.

A standard program note states that this conflict represents a thunderstorm with Mekhala's ball the lightning source and the falling axe of Ream Eyso the thunder. The earliest account of a Mekhala performance, by Adhémard Leclère in 1911, reported that "Preah Eso" was vanquished by Mekhala, "The Lady of the Clouds," using a wooden ball ornamented with blue and green foil.[14] It is also interesting to note that Zhou Daguan, visiting Angkor in the late thirteenth century, mentioned a festive "throwing of the ball" which Cœdès identifies with a modern-day equivalent which is accompanied by "alternate chants of boys and girls" at New Year's celebrations.[15]

6-2. **Mekhala (Kem Bun Nak) and Ream Eyso (Soth Leas).** Photo Colin Grafton.

Thus Manimekhala appears to embody not only the dominant force of the Feminine, but expresses it in a manner used by the Khmers for centuries to symbolize the dynamic tension between female and male.

PREAH SOMUT (X-12, 0)

Palace performance programs and other published accounts make it clear that two different versions of the Preah Somut story were popular with the classical dancers. Both episodes end with the marriage of the hero and his beloved, but since it is not the same woman, we may assume there are numerous legends about Preah Somut or that the common textual source is of a length and complexity sufficient to recount the winning of several wives.

In 1911 Adhémard Leclère described a performance in which Prince Preah Somut runs away from the kingdom of his adoptive father Kanureach, i.e., King of Kanu, to travel to the country of the Princess Vimana Chanta (Vimean Chin in a later version), at the same time that the princess dreams of a lover whom she doesn't know at all giving her a ring surmounted by three precious stones. When she awakens, she is so sad at not finding the ring that she eventually becomes ill. Her father, King Krongcrut-Sorikan, knowing the cause of her affliction, begins a search for a ring similar to the one in his daughter's dream.

Preah Somut, who possesses a magic wand, happily informs the king's messengers that he can provide the ring and is escorted before His Majesty, where he refuses to sell the conjured ring but offers it as a gift. When the princess sees the ring she is overjoyed, falls in love with the prince, and that night welcomes him to her chamber. When the king learns of this from his servants the next day, he sends his officers to arrest Preah Somut, who is to be punished. The princess intervenes and obtains from her father permission for their marriage.[16] This version was also produced during the reign of Monivong (on his sixty-third birthday, for example) and later.

In the second Preah Somut story a princess named But Somali (sometimes Bout Sumali) dreams that she is embraced "body and spirit" by a dragon, a sign of approaching marriage. Soon after, she obtains permission from her father King Kulachak (one program says Rulachak) to go for a walk in the garden. Pream Somut sees her, is captivated, and carries her off in the air to his kingdom. The frightened servants bring news of the kidnapping to King Kulachak, who immediately calls forth his army. Meanwhile, a young *yakkha* (demon) named Veyakan sees the pair, as they stop to sleep on a mountainside en route, and throws a spell over Preah Somut. The princess is unable to awaken him as Veyakan—wearing a blue mask—attempts to hustle her off, but as a last favor the demon grants her wish to leave behind Preah Somut's "stave" and boots.

Once in the jungle, But Somali escapes, returns to Preah Somut, and, finding his magic wand, conjures a number of other *yakkha* who kill Veyakan. Preah Somut awakens and, happy over the downfall of Veyakan as well as But Somali's newly realized love for him, flies with her through the air "admiring the stars and planets and tasting of celestial beauty." In a final scene, the army of Preah Somut's father, King Kanurat, confronts the attacking army of King Kulachak, routs them, and Preah Somut returns victorious to his capital with his new bride.

One writer in 1929 reported seeing this version performed at Angkor with eight young girls in each army,[17] and Sappho Marchal reported only this story in her 1926 summary of the Preah Somut plot.[18] An excerpt from this scenario was often performed as a dance duet—with But Somali and Preah Somut in the garden. A three-character scene of the prince, princess and Veyakan was also frequently performed, for instance in honor of the commanding officer of the Japanese occupation forces on 1 April 1945.

Manimekhala and Vorachhun (X-9, 0)

The drama of Vorachhun (warajana) is categorized as distinct from that of Ream Eyso because the two were usually performed separately, even though—as in Bangkok in 1974—they appeared on the same program. The sequence of events, however, is ambiguous. The Bangkok program says that Mekhala, en route to pay her respects to Vorachhun, is waylaid by Ream

Eyso. A subsequent program item says simply that "Vorachhun, while flying down to the beach, met the Goddess Mekhala who was playing in the surf. He then joined her in the Dragon dance."[19]

The Manimekhala-Vorachhun episode is basically a dance duet and was in fact categorized by Chet Chheng as a *robam* or dance. Still, their meeting is part of a larger drama. In an early program performed for King Sisowath Monivong's birthday (22 December 1933), the evening's performance was broken into four scenes:

1. A dance performed by sixteen dancers representing *apsaras*.
2. Preah Vorachun joins the group and dances with them.
3. The "Goddess of the Seas," provided with a dazzling jewel, enters and also dances with the others. Preah Vorachhun entreats her in vain to give him the jewel.
4. The giant Ream Eyso, dazzled by the glow of the magnificent jewel which Mekhala juggles, enters furiously and pursues the troupe of *apsaras*. He also beseeches the "Goddess of the Seas" to give him the jewel, but in vain; he follows her and engages Preah Vorachhun, whom he encounters en route, in combat.

Clearly the essence of the drama is that Manimekhala, embodiment of the Feminine principle, has a powerful attribute which cannot be relinquished to a masculine force of either fearsome or benign nature.

There is at least one pure dance from the preceding scenario which is often staged separately—the Robam Mkaw or Makara, referred to above as the Dragon Dance. Taken as a whole—Mekhala with Ream Eyso, with Vorachhun, and in the Robam Mkaw, the story of Manimekhala appeared thirty-four times (17 percent) in the programs of palace performances, making it, after the *Rāmker*, the second most popular drama in the repertoire.

Preah Soriyavong (X-8, 0)

There are so many elements common to the stories of Preah Soriyavong and Preah Chinavong (see below) as performed by the palace dancers, that one cannot fail to see the similarities in overall structure as well. The plot of the former is as follows: After completing his studies, Prince Soriyavong takes leave of his master the *eysei* (hermit) to return to his homeland by flying through the air. Resting in a forest, he is seen by the *yakkha* Asoreiphat, who owns the area and who descends from the sky to attack him. Soriyavong kills him with a single blow, but then, realizing the weakness of his adversary and remembering the teachings of his master, he brings the *yakkha* back to life with a few drops of sacred oil. Asoreiphat, recognizing the power of the prince, offers to serve him, and they travel until they reach a river where they see the daughter of the *yakkha* king.

In three of the four available program notes, the princess is named Botum, but in the fourth she is called Tepsokonth. In an apparently optional scene, having had a happy dream, she asks her father King Tossavong (also named Essorah) for permission to bathe with her ladies along the river until evening. The king agrees, and when Soriyavong sees her there, he falls in love. Changing his form, Soriyavong becomes a beautiful girl child accompanying Asoreiphat in the guise of an old woman selling cakes from her boat. The princess takes the child home, and, feeling deep sympathy for the child, calls her to sleep in her own chamber. Soriyavong assumes his true form once the princess is asleep, but she soon awakens and, appreciating the beauty of the young prince, takes him as her husband.

Preah Chinavong (X-7, 0)

Two synopses of the Chinavong legend as performed by the Royal Ballet are available—one from the palace program notes and one written by a guest of King Sihanouk in 1959.[20] They agree in virtually all details.

Having completed his studies, Prince Preah Chinavong takes leave of his teacher, the great *eysei*, who gives him a magic sword for the return trip home. Later, while resting under a tree, this sword is stolen by a white monkey. At the same time, Preah Bat Chetra, king of the *yakkha*, meets the monkey, fights to the death, and returns to his palace with the sword. Preah Chinavong comes upon the monkey whom he restores to life and together they go off to regain the sword.

They arrive at Preah Bat Chetra's palace just as the king's daughter Anchean Pichet is walking in the garden. Preah Chinavong transforms the monkey into a baby monkey who runs toward the princess causing her to send her ladies in pursuit of it. All the attendants lose the trail except for the chief among them named Mearadey (one version says Nearadey), who follows the monkey to the waiting Preah Chinavong. The two fall in love and the prince asks her to give the sword to the monkeys who will return it. Mearadey proposes that the monkey return with her to the princess. Chinavong agrees. Mearadey presents the baby monkey to the princess, who argues tearfully with her father for permission to keep him.

Alone in the forest, Preah Chinavong waits anxiously, and, finally, the monkey returns with the sword, and they both return to his home. The actual filching of the sword is not part of the dramatic action, and Mearadey is apparently left behind.

PREAH LEAK SINNAVONG (X-9, 0)

In 1911 Adhémard Leclère wrote briefly about a number of forms of Cambodian theatre of which we have no other records. One of these was the description of a lengthy performance of the story of Leak Sinnavong which must have lasted several hours, judging by the extensive dialogue which Leclère recorded from Scene Six (the departure from the *eysei*).[21] In more recent times the playing time of the story has been condensed and appears to have been performed without benefit of a final plot resolution of any sort. Program notes from 10 November 1943 and 14 April 1945 present the following story.

King Preah Bat Promateat, on the advice of his second wife, drives Queen Sovann Ampea, together with her young son Leak Sinnavong, into exile in the forest. There the *yakkha* Virulamat sees them and, seduced by the Queen's beauty, kidnaps her. Leak Sinnavong, alone, is adopted by the great *eysei*, who raises him along with a young girl named Neang Kessar in an idyllic situation with a black bird and a parrot as companions.

When Leak Sinnavong has grown and completed his study with the *eysei*, he receives permission to go in search of his mother and leaves Neang Kessar behind. In his travels Leak Sinnavong sees the daughter of King Thao Sourikane, Neang Yisun, walking in her garden, and they fall in love. Sometime later, Neang Kessar, disguised as a Brahman, comes to offer her services to the king, Preah Leak Sinnavong, which she does through the intermediary of a hunter. In the role of a young page, Neang Kessar is invited to sit beside the king who is taken with her beauty. Forgetting the queen at his side, he caresses her until Neang Yisun becomes jealous, jumps from the dais, and berates Neang Kessar. The synopsis concludes with the statement that "the incident was happily resolved by the intervention of the charming Prince."

There is no record of events in the story beyond that point ever being performed, and under the artistic hand of Queen Kossamak the scene appears to have been limited even further. The fragment in which Leak Sinnavong and Neang Kessar, as children, gambol in the garden with the black bird and the parrot (see below)—often played by four young dancers—came to be the primary part of the Leak Sinnavong story that was performed during the Sihanouk years.

Preah Vong Sovann (X-6, 0)

The story of Vong Sovann has many familiar motifs: having completed his studies with the *eysei*, Prince Vong Sovann takes his leave to return to his own country. En route he encounters a *yakkha* named Asoreiphat (cf. Preah Soriyavong), who is conquered in battle and then joins the prince as an attendant. While traveling, he spies Tip Sokhonn—daughter of Virulphak, king of the *yakkha* walking in her garden and falls in love. That night, taking the form of a black bird, he enters the princess' window as she sleeps. Vong Sovann resumes his normal shape and, upon awakening, Tip Sokhonn takes him for her husband.

A second series of scenes may also be performed in which Virulphak, the princess' father, is informed of Vong Sovann's presence and sends his niece, Neang Kakna, to seize him. Although she takes the form of Tip Sokhonn, Vong Sovann perceives the subterfuge and captures her. Neang Kakna eventually succeeds in escaping, however, and goes to alert the king. As in the case of other dramatic works, the performance of further episodes seems probable, but the plot as described appears to have been considered complete.

Preah Chey Sain (X-4, 0)

As the *eysei* in the story points out, the plot of Chey Sain presents a reversal of the usual pattern of love motifs seen so far in the dramatic repertoire. Initially, Princess Sovanna falls in love with Prince Chey Sain from a neighboring, enemy kingdom and sends one of her maids in search of an *eysei* capable of making a love potion to charm him. The maid brings a famous and capable *eysei* who agrees to help, and the princess asks what the payment will be. He replies, "Until now I have been in the habit of making a woman love a man, and in such cases my recompense is unimportant. But in his case the situation is reversed and promises to be difficult." The princess heaps gold and silver on him, and, eventually satisfied, the *eysei* thanks the princess and departs.

At home, the *eysei* conjures several beautiful roosters with variously colored plumage whom he trains to dance so exquisitely that all who see them are captivated, and he sends them off toward the neighboring kingdom. Preah Chey Sain, bored and walking through the forest, has stopped to rest under a tree when a white cock appears before him ("in a cage") and begins to dance. Fascinated, he begins to chase the cock, which eludes him until he has gone far beyond the frontier of his own kingdom. When the cock suddenly disappears, Chey Sain is confronted by the beautiful princess with whom he immediately falls in love, and they finally marry. Parental concerns do not appear to be a consideration, nor is there intervention by any *yakkha*.

The role of the cock is considered a beautiful one and was danced in 1956, for instance, by the young Princess Norodom Sorya Roeungsi. There is some evidence to suggest that the Cock Dance (see below) is an excerpt from the story of Preah Chey Sain.

Kray Thong (X-4)

During the reign of King Monivong, a number of pieces were performed by the royal dancers—presumably in classical style—which were folk tales with a high level of realism and without most of the recurrent themes noted thus far. The story of the crocodile charmer Kray Thong is one of these, and the synopses of two episodes have been recorded.

In the first, two daughters of a wealthy man—Sampeou Meas and Sampeou Keo—receive permission from their father to bathe in the river, accompanied by both male and female servants. The men, who remain in boats, warn the girls in vain not to stray too far from the bank, but Neang Sampeou Meas is soon carried off by a huge crocodile known as Chealavann (or Chharava). The remainder of the group reports her loss to the father who is distraught, and news of her demise spreads. Kray Thong, a man of great courage, lives in the neighborhood. According to the older recounting of the tale, he could walk on the surface of water as well as dive to its depths. He offers to assist the old man, who in turn offers the girl in marriage and a substantial reward if Kray Thong can kill the crocodile and rescue Sampeou Meas. Kray Thong promises to return in three days.

Taking the girl to his cave, meanwhile, Chealavann assumes human form before Sampeou Meas regains consciousness and then speaks in a kindly manner to her. When Kray Thong appears, however, he hides the girl, reverts to his true form, but is soon slain by Kray Thong's sword. Finding Sampeou Meas unharmed, Kray Thong informs her of her father's promise and asks if she agrees. She does, they leave the cave, return to her father, and are soon married.

The second and older recounting of the tale attributes to Kray Thong much greater powers. After slaying the crocodile, he marries both Sampeou Meas and Sampeou Keo as well as the wife of the deceased crocodile, the beautiful Vimalea, whom he "seduces with the aid of a magic candle" once she assumes human form. The pair are seen by the gardener and his wife, who tell Kray Thong's first two wives of his infidelity. When Vimalea responds in anger to the wives' jealousy, the spell placed on her is broken and, reverting to her original form, she returns to her underwater home.

PREAH SOVANNAHANG (X-4, 0)

Despite its complexity, the story of Preah Sovannahang was performed by only six dancers, together with attendants as needed. As with the Chey Sain story, it is the woman on whom the dramatic action is focused.

Princess Ketsoriyong—daughter of King Yutsorivong known also as Preah Chetra (cf. *yakkha* king in Preah Chinavong story)—is in love with Preah Sovannahang, son of King Sophannarith of a neighboring kingdom. The guards of King Yutsorivong's palace learn of Sovannahang's nocturnal visits to the princess' chamber, and, fearful of the king's wrath should he hear of it, they catch him one night and wound him so badly that his pages have to return him to his kingdom where he dies. Princess Ketsoriyong meanwhile, tired of waiting for the prince, goes to the garden, discovers blood and, realizing the source, loses consciousness from weeping.

The god Indra takes pity on the princess, descends to earth to give her a magic, male disguise; medicine to restore life; a magic bow and arrows that will enable her to find the prince; and then disappears. On awakening, the princess disguises herself as a Brahman, tries the crossbow and departs from her kingdom.

Later, while resting at a *sala*, or roadside shelter, she is seen by the *yakkha* Kompol who falls in love with her. On approaching, however, he discovers that his love is a young man, and so ashamed of this feeling is he, that he kicks the princess. She, on waking up, engages in a great combat with Kompol, who is beaten and becomes her servant after obeying her order to disguise himself also as a Brahman to avoid frightening the people along the route they intend to travel. During their travels, the *yakkha* entertains the princess with comic gestures and mockeries of Preah Sovannahang.

Meanwhile King Sophannarith, bereaved over his son's death, has sent messengers to the four corners of his realm, offering half his kingdom to any magician who can restore his life. Brought before the king, Neang Ketsoriyong sprinkles the medicine given her by Indra on Sovannahang's remains, and the prince is revived. The scene ends with the king's offer of half the kingdom as promised. There is no suggestion that the removal of the disguise is staged.

Logically, the story should be called "Princess Ketsoriyong," but it is not. Today only a small fragment is performed, and it is called "Chau Pream." Pream is another name for Ketsoriyong, and the scene in question is the princess' solo dance when, dressed as a man and testing her bow, she sets off in search of her husband. It was performed on the 1971 United States tour.[22]

Preah Anurudh (X-3, 0)

Unlike the legends in which Indra resolves the action, the story of Preah Anurudh (often written Unaruth) is initiated by a divine being who simply puts the lovers together, thus dispensing with many conventional plot complications. The story begins when an *apsaras* carries off Prince Anurudh and deposits him in the chamber of the sleeping Princess Osa in a neighboring kingdom because "fate has decreed" that they are to be wed. (In one version, earlier scenes depict the princess' father Krong Pean, king of the *yakkha*, receiving the respects of Princess Osa and her brother Prince Tossamok; the princess in her garden in the moonlight before going to bed; the actual abduction of Anurudh; and the wrathful departure of his grandfather Prince Borom Chakrith on his winged steed "Krut" in search of him.)

Once Anurudh is in the bedroom of Princess Osa, there are two possible story patterns. The simplest is that Prince Tossamok learns of his sister's dalliance and informs their father, who has Anurudh brought before him and then suspended from the palace tower. Osa begs her father's pardon but in vain and, returning to her chamber, faints with weeping. At this point Anurudh's grandfather arrives, learns of the situation from the princess, frees his grandson, and returns home with the new royal couple.

In a more complex version of the tale, the *apsaras* brings Anurudh to the princess, they fall in love immediately, are permitted to yield to their passion, but are forbidden to utter a single word. When they fall asleep, the *apsaras* carries off Anurudh and deposits him beneath a *chrey* tree, from which, upon awakening and not finding the princess, he sadly departs for his own kingdom. Princess Osa, meanwhile, becomes so mournful that her confidante Soppalak takes pity on her and leaves in search of the prince. She returns with portraits of all the princes she has found, but the princess recognizes none of them.

Osa then gives Soppalak a letter and a scarf and sends her on a further search. This time she does meet Anurudh, who recognizes the perfume on the scarf and is conducted back to his love. This version ends with Tossamok's attack on Anurudh directly, but it is in vain and the young couple are soon happily married.

There is other evidence in the early palace programs of a third, very different scene in which Anurudh performs a dance of seduction with the *kennari* or bird-women. No details are offered, however, and there is no evidence of this performance during the reign of Sihanouk.

Preah Chan Korup (X-3, 0)

The story as performed by the palace dancers is as follows. Having completed his studies with the *eysei*, Prince Preah Chan Korup prepares to return to his own country. The *eysei* gives him a sword and a box made of *mora* stone, warning him not to open the box until he reaches his own palace. Meanwhile, in the forest a band of robbers realize that their provisions are nearly depleted and are enjoined by their chief to pursue a new victim. Chan Korup, traveling through the area, is unable to control his curiosity; he opens the box, and a beautiful young girl appears who becomes his wife. She is called Neang Mora after the stone.

Soon they meet the brigands, whose chief asks for Neang Mora, and when Chan Korup refuses, they prepare to fight. The prince gives his sword to Neang Mora for her own defense. The brigand is bested, and Chan

Korup asks for the sword back to kill him, but at the same moment the chief also requests that she give *him* the sword. Having pity for him and wishing to save him from dying in a battle fought over her, she holds the sword toward both combatants but with the handle toward the highwayman, who immediately wounds the prince mortally. Consoling Neang Mora, the robber chief takes her away.

Assailed by bad feelings, the god Indra looks around to find the cause and, seeing the dead Chan Korup, descends to earth to revive him. After doing so, he warns the prince not to regret the disappearance of Neang Mora who is not a virtuous woman. Having thanked Indra, the prince continues on to his own kingdom.

In the final scene, the brigand chief and Neang Mora are sleeping in the forest when Indra comes and transforms her into a gibbon who starts waking up the thieves. One of them, believing that she woke him up for love, follows her off saying, "If you love me, begin by embracing me," and the gibbon jumps on his back. Satisfied, the robber suggests she embrace his neck, and she does. Happier still, he seizes her hand to kiss it, but when he turns to face her and sees the gibbon, his cries bring all the others who see the animal and flee in panic.

PREAH SOTINNACHAK-CHAKARITH (X-3, 0)

The story of Sotinnachak very nearly conforms in all motifs to the structural model on which the majority of the dramatic repertoire appears to be based (Table 4). The opening scene, however, portrays not the orphan or lost child but the dutiful prince seeking permission of his parents, King Darachak and Queen Phay Noleak of the Kingdom of Kharintareac, to go and study magic and to find a wife, and they agree.

Traveling through the air, Prince Sotinnachak arrives at the retreat of the *eysei* Preah Monichak Oudom, who instructs him in his art and at the end of his studies presents him with an enchanted bow and a magic sword. The *eysei* also predicts that he will soon have as a wife a princess of great virtue, Anong Reacsmey, daughter of the *yakkha* King Anorchak and

Table 4. **Incidence of Recurrent Motifs in Selected *Roeung***

	Ramker	Preah Saing	Preah Somut	Preah Soriyavong	Preah Chinavong	Preah Leak Sinnavong	Preah Vong Sovann	Preah Chey Sain	Preah Sovannahang	Preah Sotinnachak	Preah Bat Chey Chet	Chakravong	Chey Toat	Sovannapong
Hero (heroine) in Exile	X	X	X	X	X	X	X	?		X		X	X	X
Hero (heroine) Helped by Eysei	X			X	X	X	X	X		X		X	X	X
Hero Meets Heroine		X	X	X	X	X	X	X		X	X	X	X	X
Heroine is Yakkha Daughter				X	X		X		?	X	X	X	?	X
Marriage Opposed by Heroine's Father		X	X				X			X	X	X		
Hero (heroine) in Conflict with Yakkha	X		X	X			X	X		X	X	X	X	
Hero Assisted by Magic Weapon		X	X		X				X	X		?		X
Hero Uses Disguise to Meet Heroine		X		X	X		X	X	X					
Heroine (Hero) First Seen in Garden			X	X	X	X	X	X	X			X	X	X
Yakkha Attempts Seduction of Heroine	X		X						X					
Hero Helps Exiled Mother	X	X				X								
Hero Assisted by Animal	X				X						X			
Hero (heroine) Assisted by Yakkha				X			X		X					

Source: Compiled from Royal Palace Library records.

Queen Kathin Kessar of the Kingdom of Khemavantheani. With obeisance to his master, Prince Sotinnachak departs in search of the princess, eventually spending the night at a *sala* in the middle of a forest in the *yakkha* kingdom.

Meanwhile the princess dreams that an *eysei* gives her a beautiful *nāga* serpent as a gift, which her father immediately seizes. When the prince actually arrives, he seduces Anong Reacsmey, and they "conceal their love" in a mountain cave. Anorchak, furious at his daughter's kidnapping, calls forth his army to pursue the culprit. Prince Sotinnachak battles him, slays him, and resuscitates him, after which the king agrees to relinquish the hand of his daughter. Then the king, prince, and princess return to the Kingdom of Khemavantheani and the queen, and live thereafter in happiness and in peace.

Preah Thong (X-3, 0)

Preah Thong is clearly one of the oldest stories in the dramatic repertoire. Professors at URBA claim that Preah Thong is another name for Hun Tian,[23] the mythical progenitor of the Kingdom of Tok Thlok or Cambodia (see Chapter V). While the similarities are actually greater between Preah Thong and Kaundinya—the fourth-century Indian Brahman who married the indigenous *nāgī* Princess Somā—the general pattern of all the stories is similar.

Probably the most elaborate staging of Preah Thong in recent times occurred on 21 October 1931 to honor visiting French Minister of Colonies Paul Reynaud. It was performed by twelve leading dancers and numerous soldier and servant characters. A gilt-edged and very elaborate program announced that the story had been adapted by King Monivong himself "from the history of Cambodia" and rendered by him into verse. The dramatization focused on basically two episodes from the full-length tale (see Chapter V): Preah Thong's usurpation of the throne of Kok Thlok (the land of the *thlok* tree), and his marriage to the *nāgī* princess.

Initially, the powerful King Atichavong is told that his eldest son Preah Thong is planning to seize the throne and immediately orders his youngest son to place his brother on a raft to be set adrift. The younger brother is told by Preah Thong that, for the sake of peace, he will go willingly, and tearfully the two obey the father's order. Accompanied by numerous retainers, Preah Thong sets off on a turbulent sea. His raft is surrounded by sea creatures, but eventually the winds carry him to a new shore where he lands with great joy, and his servitors set about building a sumptuous new palace called the Preah Banlea.

The king of this land, whose name is Assachay, hearing of the new prince's arrival in his land, sends his four Malay ministers to investigate. When they ask Preah Thong his purpose in being there, he replies, "My father has driven me from his kingdom, but have no fear. I wish to make no conquest and ask only your hospitality to live in peace." On receiving this message, Assachay is touched but says nothing.

Soon, because of his integrity, intelligence and courage, the inhabitants of the kingdom become eager to make Preah Thong's exile agreeable—to the point that Assachay grows jealous and calls forth his army to drive him out. Preah Thong, sad at the thought of breaking their pact of friendship, nonetheless prepares his own army. Each led by a prince mounted in great splendor, the two armies converge, and eventually Assachay is forced to seek refuge abroad. Thereafter Preah Thong rules the land, Cambodia, in peace.

The second episode begins with Preah Thong traveling through the countryside of his new realm. Arriving at a beach and feeling tired, he stops to rest in the shade of an ancient *thlok* tree which happens to be the spot where the beautiful Princess Theara Vaddey (known popularly as Neang Neak), daughter of the king of the *nāga*, comes each day from her underwater realm to play on the beach with her attendants. When the prince sees her, he falls instantly in love and says, "Here at our first meeting I already feel the truest love and I adore you more than my life. Won't you have pity on a lonely prince and help me in the governing of my kingdom?"

The princess accepts his love, sets a rendezvous for the marriage —at the same spot seven years hence—and returns to her parents. Seven years later Preah Thong arrives in time to meet the *nāga* king and queen who come accompanied by servants bearing him casks of diamonds. The king agrees to the marriage as a union of their destinies and utters the words "Such is my power: behold." Suddenly there arises from the sea a vast and sumptuous palace of seven concentric walls of gold, and the waters all around retreat, leaving a network of roads.

Preah Thong and Theara Vaddey are married and receive the new names Komereach and Pheakavaddey. The *nāga* king gives his new son-in-law a golden crown and a sacred sword and declares him "the first King of the great new Kingdom of Cambodia," and the drama ends with the departure of the *nāga* king and queen back to their underwater domain.

In one version, an embellishment on the actual first meeting of Preah Thong and the princess explains the origin of the well-known "Preah Thong" melody. When Neang Neak realizes at her first meeting with Preah Thong that she has stayed past the time allotted by her father, she suggests that he accompany her to beg the *nāga* king's pardon. Preah Thong thus travels to her home by holding on to the end of his love's scarf. Upon returning, he orders his musicians to transcribe a song, which he had heard in the *nāga* kingdom, as a commemoration of his forthcoming marriage. Some accounts do not mention the subterranean origin of the song and merely report that Preah Thong commissioned the melody to symbolize his safe and happy journey through the ocean's depths.[24] Palace programs show that this melody accompanied a dance, the Robam Preah Thong, which on occasion was performed as an opening number and was one of the most sacred dances in the repertoire.

The "Preah Thong" melody is considered to have great ritual significance. It is one of the seven sacred songs associated with the *buong suong* ritual (see below) and is traditionally performed today at Khmer weddings to mark the entrance into the sleeping chamber for the final rite of union itself. The melody is believed to bestow good fortune on the newlyweds' future conjugal life.

In Thailand, the "Preah Thong" melody is one of the four tunes that must be played when the gods and goddesses are dancing in the *lakhon nai*. The Thai, who also consider it one of their oldest songs, perform it on numerous auspicious occasions and strictly require it as prelude to any performance of Manimekhala and Vorachhun.[25]

In the present context let us consider a tale with striking similarities to the Preah Thong story but with significantly different elements as well. No proper names are associated with this story but it is far more closely related to Preah Thong than to any other work in the repertoire. In 1911 Adhémard Leclère published the following account:

> Two or three yeas ago a troupe of the king's dancers gave a performance under a temporary awning constructed at the base of the small knoll or *phnom* [for which the city is named]. The subject of the dance was one of the most interesting imaginable.
>
> A Hindu prince, dressed in his most beautiful finery...coming from Benares, disembarks with his wife, sister and servants on the Indochinese coast, in a period when the country was still inhabited by negritos with frizzy hair but who were somewhat civilized and were ruled by a king. The Hindu prince, his wife, sister and servants walk through the forest admiring the country, and the prince decides to establish himself there. The indigenous king sees them, approaches, and watches them—worried at first but with enthusiasm over the beauty of the young girl. When the prince and his family retrace their steps, he follows at a distance, observes their movements, and when they stop, tries his best to see the sister of the prince who is seated between two other women. He mimes words to her which the singers repeat after the prompter. The indigenous king falls in love with the princess, desires her and wants to carry her away.
>
> He calls his troops, shows them the distant object of his passion and begins an attack. The tumultuous battle is represented by four warriors (women) who, from one side to the other, struggle with bows, short lances and sabers. Six times the vanquished king returns to the charge, finally provoking the prince himself who descends from the low bed where he is seated, and then follows the singular fight of a foreign prince against an aboriginal king.
>
> Finally, they make peace; the king declares his love, the princess rejects him with indignation because the king is a negrito between whose race and her own there can never be such an alliance. The prince who wants to obtain a corner of territory on which to settle, consents to give his sister to the king, and the sister despondently descends from the bed where she is seated and tearfully puts her hand in that of the negrito king who, very agitated by the fire of love which consumes him and animated with joy, rapidly removes her. This is the first act.
>
> In the second, the princess runs away from her husband's house and seeks refuge with her brother. The king searches, finds her and demands her

return. The prince refuses and war is re-ignited between the foreigners and the locals. The king is again defeated but this time his country is taken from him and he submits. He is not given his wife back but is given a wife of less elevated station from among the conqueror's ranks and he bows in the manner of all vanquished kings—very low and very humbly.

This is the story of the conquest of territory belonging to semi-primitives by a more civilized prince, the story of the creation of a Hindu colony on the Indochina coast and what formerly occurred between the Hindu adventurers and the Cambodian aboriginals whom they named nagas.[26]

While this interpretation of the story reflects Leclère's belief in the supposed "Indianization" of Southeast Asia, the story's greatest significance lies in its contrast with the Preah Thong legend. Here the love of a Cambodian king for a Hindu princess stands in contrast to the love between Preah Thong and the *nāgī*. Here the feminine force comes from outside to attract the masculine force controlling the land. This is a complete reversal of the Preah Thong story. In this drama, the foreign prince is already provided with a wife, thus precluding his involvement with an indigenous female figure, which is the primary theme of the earliest Khmer legends discussed in Chapter V.

Whether this story recounted by Leclère is an authentic segment of the ancient Preah Thong legend we cannot say—although certainly the baggage of a wife and sister suggests otherwise. We would do well to remember, however, that in the Khmer dance tradition new works and variations can be choreographed at any time. The "Indianization" theory was very fashionable around the turn of the century, thanks to the works of Finot, Cœdès, Pelliot and other French historians discussed in Chapters I and II, and the performance in question took place shortly before 1910. Thus, whether the drama was actually prepared to conform to the "new view" of Indo-Khmer history, whether Leclère simply interpreted it as such, or whether this tale is, in fact, a variant of the Preah Thong story, we are probably safest to conclude that since the ancient archetypal confrontation between female Khmer ruler and foreign male intruder has been replaced by a male-male battle, the untitled fragment recounted by Leclère is of a later vintage than the Preah Thong story.

Preah Botum Sorya (X-2, 0)

While there is no textual evidence, a number of informants have claimed that this story is part of the Preah Chinavong legend. It appears in the program notes twice with no attribution to a larger drama and is, at any rate, not to be confused with the story of Princess Botum and Preah Soriyavong.

The plot is that Salikan, king of the *yakkha*, has kidnapped Queen Botum Sorya and made her his slave after having no success with an attempted seduction. He gives her to a servant named Mea who mistreats her, and then for humiliation, sends her to the market to buy fish. Prince Chetarovong, who, in the guise of a young girl has followed his mother Botum Sorya, is so shocked at the treatment inflicted on her that he resumes his true form and kills the servant Mea. Presumably this episode is only one part of a complex plot.

Preah Bat Chey Chet (X-2)

In its shortest form, recorded in 1944, this story is a brief, cautionary tale of motherhood, as follows. King Chey Chet returns from a hunting party to find that in his absence Queen Sorincha has given birth. What he doesn't learn is that seven women of the court, out of jealousy, exchange the newborn son for a wooden doll, so that when they come and tell him the false news, he interprets it as an omen of disaster and orders the queen's death.

The court ministers intervene on behalf of the queen and point out the simplicity of the deception, and Chey Chet changes the order from death to exile. The queen herself wishes to petition the king's good graces but is opposed in this by one Neang Vila who conducts the queen to her own country.

A somewhat longer version performed, for example, in 1936, has the second wife of Chey Chet as the sole villain of the piece. She charges outright that Sorincha has given birth to a monster. As the executioners are walking her into the jungle, they meet two officers of her father, the king of the *yakkha*, who return the queen to Chey Chet and request a lighter sentence, at which point he merely banishes her.

The queen, however, has a cat who, having seen everything, leads her mistress to the place where the newborn child was buried. As the child has been taken to paradise by the gods, the cat begs them to return the baby, and it is delivered by a god who joins the *yakkha* king in hearing his daughter's tale. In great anger this king gathers his army and defeats Chey Chet, after which Chey Chet and Sorincha are reconciled.[27]

A third much longer version of the tale as performed in the 1920s includes most of the motifs noted in the structural model of the dramas (see Table 4). The princess, now called Souvinichar, raises from infancy a cat named Mela. Leaving her father's palace one day carrying this animal, she is adopted by Seng Houm, king of the *yakkha*. One day while bathing in a pool in the garden she is seen by Prince Chey Chet. They fall in love and despite the king's wish to kill him, the wedding proceeds. Souvinichar becomes the first wife over the jealous second wife Surya.

The episode presented earlier begins one day when Chey Chet is off trying to capture a white elephant seen in the jungle. Surya orders the newborn baby to be buried, and the cat watches as the servants inter the infant under a banyan. The god Indra, having seen all of this, sends a *tevoda* (or angel) to save the infant and give him three gifts: a bow, a sword and a horse. This *tevoda* is a clown role.

Following the scene in which Surya presents the wooden doll to Chey Chet, he calls forth the wise-woman for advice. This worthy appears on stage alone initially: a male clown dressed in a long, white wig and the usual Khmer woman's scarf, who regales the audience and finally announces that she has received five hundred piastres from Surya to confirm her words. The wise-woman goes in to advise the king, and the scenes proceed as noted previously (except that the two executioners are also clowns). Presently the cat reminds Chey Chet of his love for the queen, and it is that which lightens her sentence to exile. Mela the cat also persuades Souvinichar not to humiliate herself before the king, and together they go in search of the child.

Finding nothing beneath the banyan, they pray to the *tevoda*, who brings the child to its mother, along with the bow, sword and horse. The horse is also played by a clown wearing a horse head, and a comic scene ensues between him and the queen's two servants—also clowns who amuse and imitate the baby with laughing, crying, singing and so forth. Then, guided by the *tevoda*, Souvinichar returns to her adoptive father's home where she loses consciousness.

Seng Houm, the *yakkha* king, sends for a doctor, played by another clown as a white-clad, iodine-dabbing European. Upon reviving, Souvinichak refuses to tell her tale, so the cat reveals all to the king, who becomes furious, battles Chey Chet, spares his life, and oversees the reconciliation of the prince, princess and their new son.[28]

In these three versions of the Chey Chet tale, as performed in three successive decades, we clearly see the process of reduction by which a story, originally of Shakespearean scope, is today unknown to most Khmer dancers and even teachers. The story is also of great value as the best available example of how the clown was integrated into a classical performance.

Inao (X-2, 0)

George Cœdès has suggested that the tale of Inao as performed in Cambodia "is nothing but the Javanese story of *Raden* Panji adapted by Siamese court poets in the early nineteenth century"[29] from whence it was imported by the Khmers. Interestingly, however, the Javanese legend has in no way had the popularity in Cambodia that it enjoyed in Thailand. In all the preserved palace performance programs, it appears only twice. In part, this may be due to the fact that as a mildly adventurous and fairly realistic story based on false identities—to judge from the only available performance resume which follows—it lacked many of the motifs that repeatedly occur in the more popular dramas.

One day in the forest Prince Siyakra, son of King Daha, sees a peacock-like creature sent by the *tevoda* as a sign that he will meet members of his family from whom he has long been separated. The prince and his party pursue the bird until it disappears on the border of the Kingdom of Kalaing. In disguise as Yarann, the prince meets General Pannyi (Panji) and his adopted brother Sangkhamorta and asks to be introduced to the king as a servant. They arrange the audience and eventually Yarann gains favor and high military rank. General Pannyi continues to be his friend, as does Sangkhamorta.

One moonlit night Pannyi's sister, Kenlong, goes picking flowers in the garden and is seen by Yarann, who falls in love with her, declares his feelings, and initiates an immediate abduction. Kenlong screams for her maid Orsa who is nearby, but Yarann will not let her go. Sangkhamorta arrives and is told by Orsa that she can handle the situation, but in that moment Yarann flees with the girl. Sangkhamorta understands the reasons behind Yarann's impetuosity but goes to report to the king; Orsa goes to tell Pannyi of his sister's fate.

Elsewhere, Kenlong refuses to yield to Yarann's love, but he insists so strongly that when Pannyi arrives he does not even let her out of his arms. Momentarily struck by the appropriateness of the couple, Pannyi is chided by his sister, and the two men begin a fight that is interrupted by the king, who immediately suggests that Pannyi offer his sister to Yarann in marriage. Despite Pannyi's feeling that it would indeed be a good match, he draws his sword to protest. Upon seeing the name Inao inscribed on the blade, the king recognizes Pannyi as the son of his brother Korepann.

Embracing his new-found nephew, the king tells Yarann that Pannyi, now known to be of royal rank, cannot have a mere adventurer for a brother-in-law, thus precluding any marriage with Kenlong. At this, Yarann draws his own sword which reveals that he is actually Prince Siyakra, son of King Daha, a second brother to the monarch. The king therefore agrees to the marriage of the two cousins, and all ends happily.

More than likely other episodes from the lengthy Javanese romance were performed in Cambodia, but the only clear evidence is another item on the repertoire list prepared by Chet Chheng, entitled Preah Bantum, or "the Royal Bedchamber," and a dance entitled Chhom Kala Bosseba. No other information regarding the former piece is available, save for the fact that several informants have attributed it to the Inao cycle; the latter appears to concern Pannyi's beloved Bosseba.

Bunloy (X-1)

The only recorded performance of Bunloy took place on 31 December 1938. Even then, the story appears either to have lost much of its once original depth or else to be one of the more non-traditional, realistic dramas that King Monivong was known to enjoy.

Bunloy is a young man whose old mother, named Lam, dies in an early scene, at which point he goes to live with Sophandy, his wife Sangiem and their daughter Maly, who is Bunloy's friend. Bunloy also has a brother named Marika who has been away studying *selapak*, or magic, with an *eysei*.

One day two thieves, who want to have wives, kidnap Maly but soon encounter Marika returning from his studies. Marika rescues Maly and then learns that his brother is now, living with her family. The brothers meet, Marika is told of his mother's death, and the two depart to offer their services to the king named Tevea.

When an Indian king comes to seek the hand of Tevea's daughter, Princess Chhayya, he refuses and war breaks out. Bunloy and Marika lead Tevea's troops to victory and are rewarded by being made the personal, right and left bodyguards of the king. Marika then falls in love with Princess Chhayya and after stealing her away asks Bunloy to care for her. The king arrests and imprisons Bunloy, Marika frees him, and the story—so far as it is known—ends with the two brothers going to seek the king's forgiveness.

Preah Chakravong (X-1, 0)

Nothing is known of the performance history of the Chakravong story, save that it was performed for the fifty-eighth birthday celebration of King Monivong in December 1933. Many of the motifs, however, conform to the classical model.

Prince Chakravong requests and obtains permission from his parents King Promarith and Queen Amporbopha of the Kingdom of Khemovong to leave on a voyage in search of a wife. Traveling through the air, he meets an *eysei* who tells him that his future wife will be the incomparably beautiful and virtuous Princess Mealikessar, daughter of Tosschak, king of the *yakkha* in the Kingdom of Vibolrith. Meanwhile King Tosschak sees in a dream a splendid jewel fall on his daughter and so informs his wife; they conclude that the princess will soon gain a powerful husband.

Chakravong arrives at Vibolrith where he receives both the hospitality of an old gardener and confirmation of the princess' high reputation. To this garden Princess Mealikessar and her younger brother Tossmit come for a walk. When she sees Preah Chakravong, they fall madly in love. She returns to the palace, offers flowers to her parents, and then retires to her chamber, where Chakravong joins her after putting everyone to sleep with a magic spell.

Soon Tossmit awakens all the court women and surprises his sister with the prince. He informs the king who furiously calls forth his army, surrounds the chamber and finds Chakravong, whom he attacks in vain thanks to the arrival of the prince's four officers. The king shoots an arrow at the prince, but it returns to him, and at this proof of Chakravong's power, Tosschak gives him the hand of his daughter. Following the celebration of their union, their kingdoms remain prosperous and continually at peace.

CHAU YEUNG DATTDA (X-1)

The story of the Princess Chau Yeung, performed in 1939 with no mention thereafter, is distinguished primarily by its use of the spirit motif and the fact that it is one of the few pieces in the repertoire named for a woman. Presumably the version which follows, to judge by its ending at least, is the fragment of a once richer tale.

One day Princess Chau Yeung, together with her servant Tanyong, go to the market where a man named Bunchhouy sees her and professes his love. The princess' bodyguard of the right observes this and confronts the man. Another man named Bunchhou, who also witnesses the event, assists the guard, and Princess Chau Yeung falls in love with him. (Later, however, Bunchou and Bunchhouy become friends.) Bunchhou requests that the princess allow him to live in the palace, and she agrees.

The bodyguard, who loves the princess to no avail and who cannot stand the fact that she now loves Bunchhou, disguises himself, takes her into the jungle, and abandons her. There the princess meets a spirit who shows her the way out of the jungle, where she meets an old man and woman gathering fuel wood, and they take her home and feed her.

Bunchhou and Bunchhouy, in search of Princess Chau Yeung, become tired and lie down under a large tree. When a beautiful girl comes and lies down with them, they ask for news of the princess and only then realize the girl is a spirit. Eventually they find the princess and return her to the palace. Later Bunchhou marries a rich man's daughter, and the last event of the scenario recorded in the palace library synopsis is that Chau Yeung goes to comfort him.

CHAU DAMREI SAR (X-1, 0)

During the reign of King Norodom (1860-1904) we are told that he liked to close palace performances of *yiké* with a classical piece, and that he usually preferred a simple, comic dance called "the story of the King with the white elephant,"[30] also known, according to Chet Chheng, as Punyianoi, probably the main character. The only other record of a piece even similar to this is from early in the reign of Sihanouk in a performance program dated 24 September 1947 which mentions "Preah Chau Damrei Sar, Roi Elephant Blanc" or "White Elephant King" (*damrei* is elephant). The "comic episode" described seems to be only one segment of a longer work, since there is no mention of Punyianoi, no allusion to an elephant, and since the king is only a secondary character. The story is as follows.

A poor man named Mak Theung accompanies his wife every morning to the market where she sells perfumed oils and powders. He sets up her merchandise, goes home, and returns for her each evening. One day Prince Phya Nay, the son of Preah Chau Damrei Sar, goes walking in the market accompanied by his servant Daut, and he sees the make-up seller, whose name is Meuy Manik and falls in love with her. He makes her an amorous proposition and although the lady is confused, she is also flattered that a prince is interested in her. Prince Phya Nay tells Daut that he wants him to conduct the beautiful woman to the palace, and although he protests that she is married—and in his own heart pities her husband—he has no choice but to obey the prince and escorts Meuy Manik to the prince's quarters.

That evening Mak Theung returns to the market to take his wife home and, not seeing her, questions the neighboring stall keepers who tell him what happened. Feeling sad and mortified, he decides to present his case to King Preah Chau Damrei Sar, the father of Prince Phya Nay.

The next day before giving audiences, the king is informed by Daut that one Mak Theung wishes to make a "request." The sovereign, who is hard of hearing, at first thinks he said a "show" and then a "cat" (because these three words have the same ending in Khmer) and becomes angry. Finally, after hearing the complaint, he sends for his son whom he scolds. Then he calls for the lady in question, and, immediately struck by her beauty, he smiles and chortles his pleasure. He enumerates her charms, asks her name—which he hears wrongly as *kapik* or "shrimp-paste"—and says, "This pretty woman deserves to be loved by the prince, but I want to hear her voice. If it's good, she is the best of all the palace women."

Meuy Manik begins to sing and the king, joining in, is ecstatic. Becoming calmer, he then asks if she wants to return to her husband, and when she says no, he orders a large gift of gold, silver, and cloth to be prepared. This he gives to Mak Theung, tells him to go find a new wife, and conducts the prince and new daughter-in-law into the palace. Mak Theung refuses the gift and sorrowfully returns home. The servant Daut takes the abandoned gift, goes to a woman he had seen previously in the town, and promises her all his fortune if she will become his wife. The episode closes with her acceptance as the two dance together.

Pheah Chey Toat (X-1, 0)

Only the briefest outline of the Chey Toat story is known, but it is distinguished by the motif noted in the Preah Chinavong story of the prince falling in love with the servant either before or instead of the princess herself. In the available fragment, Princess Vorchan, daughter of King Preah Bat Santrea, goes walking in the royal gardens accompanied by her ladies-in-waiting among whom is Neang Cheata. The ladies dance and amuse themselves and then retire, except for Neang Cheata who goes looking for flowers to make bracelets. Suddenly she meets Prince Chey Toat who is returning by that route to his own kingdom after completing his study with an *eysei*. Seduced by the prince's beauty, Cheata falls in love with him. The program cryptically concludes, however, with the statement that the prince eventually marries Princess Vorchan.

Preah Pathamasampothi (Buddha) (X-1)

This drama is included on the present list not because it was a standard repertoire item—it does not appear on Chet Chheng's list, for instance—but because it is a prime example of the way any story can be dramatized. In this case, a very special event on 5 October 1952 was the occasion for presenting a dramatization of the old legend of Preah Pathamasampothi subtitled "the story of an episode in the life of Buddha."[31]

The occasion was the reception of relics of the Buddha and two of his disciples in the "Silver Pagoda," Wat Preah Keo, immediately south of the Royal Palace. The program specifically states that the dances were "organized for the reception." The theme of the Earth Goddess protecting Buddha Sakyamuni, however, is very ancient and was discussed in Chapter III. The story is not a *jātaka*; it concerns the life of Sakyamuni immediately prior to his enlightenment, and the powerful forces symbolized in that event are here given very literal and concrete form.

Having learned of the imminent enlightenment of Siddhartha Gautama, Marathiraj angrily calls forth his army to oppose it. Knowing his hostile plan, and as a witness to the legitimate aspirations of the Sakya prince, the Goddess of the Earth, Thorani, suddenly appears to protect him. On the arrival of Marathiraj, she wrings the water out of her hair in such a quantity that a flood drowns the entire army which is then "eaten by crocodiles, sharks and ray-fishes." Marathiraj, riding his elephant Gari Mekhala, recognizes defeat, offers flowers to the Buddha in homage, and departs.

When news of the Buddha's enlightenment reaches paradise, Indra, Devaputta, Devatā, and Devakanna descend from the celestial world, blow conch shells, offer gold and silver flowers to honor him, and again ascend. Following this scene an intermission is indicated, the only time in all the programs where this occurs, from which we may conclude that the drama was lengthier than most.

In the next scene the three daughters of Marathiraj—Tanha, Arati, and Raga—come to their father's palace to pay respects. Not finding him, they search him out sitting alone at a crossroads meditating on the reasons for Buddha's power, plunged in sorrow, and planning his revenge while doing a "calculation with pebbles." The daughters offer to help seek vengeance and Marathiraj happily accepts their aid.

The three beautiful girls then appear in front of the Buddha, offer to serve him according to his desires, and silently hope he will fall into their trap. Knowing their plan in advance, however, the Buddha is without fear, and because of their wish to harm him, they are instantly transformed into three old women who, bewailing the loss of their beauty, return to their father. Marathiraj does not recognize his daughters till they tell their tale, and he becomes angrier than ever. The drama ends abruptly at this point with a regretful kiss for each daughter and a retreat into the palace.

Preah Sovannapong (X-1)

The story of Sovannapong—not to be confused with Sovannahang—contains one unusual variation among other familiar motifs in that there is no conflict between the hero and his *yakkha* father-in-law; in fact, quite the opposite is true.

King Sumalarith of the Kingdom of Entarak-Sema, in audience with his ministers, decides to send his son Sovannapong to an *eysei* for instruction, prior to giving him the throne. In the next scene of farewell the prince is told of his parent's decision and dutifully departs. In the forest Sovannapong meets the *eysei* Oudam Muni who accepts him as a disciple and gives him (presumably when the training is complete) a magic wand having the supernatural power of resuscitating the dead with its pointed end and, with the wide end, of transforming the body of its possessor according to his desire.

In the following scene Tuassapong, king of the *yakkha*, leaves his queen to go walking in the forest where he meets Prince Sovannapong, whom he loves as his own son and whom he brings back to the palace to meet the queen. The king and queen inform the prince of the death of their eldest son and then send for their daughter Savandara to greet Sovannapong whom they propose to give her as a husband. The beautiful princess appears before her parents, who invite her to salute the prince; the two fall deeply in love with each other immediately.

In the final scene Sovannapong is told the circumstances of his brother-in-law's death, is conducted to the room containing the corpse, and by the power of his magic wand, restores him to life. The wand's second attribute never comes into play which seems to suggest other un-dramatized adventures.

TIP SANGVAR (X-1, 0)

The story of the Princess Tip Sangvar was still popular in the *lakhon bassac* theatre in 1975, but the only record of its performance at the palace was during the seven days and nights of performances in honor of King Monivong's sixty-third birthday in 1939. The story as performed at that time was as follows.

Prince Preah Phirun, having completed his study of magic with the *eysei*, leaves his teacher to return to his father's country. Meanwhile Preah Pinurat, king of the *yakkha*, sends his messengers to Queen Preah Phaysomaly requesting Princess Tip Sangvar as a wife for his son Veyrat. Following the queen's rejection, Preah Pinurat angrily summons his son, calls forth his army, and declares war on Preah Phaysomaly.

She and her daughter Tip Sangvar, upset at the news, inform the "King of the Dragons" (perhaps *nāga*) who hastens to reassure her and transforms Princess Tip Sangvar into a valorous warrior. The battle rages as Prince Preah

Phirun, passing through the air en route to his father's country, appears unexpectedly, assists Tip Sangvar in routing the *yakkha*, and then seduces her. The final scene consists of a promenade of nymphs in a garden.

Preah Vesandar (X-1,0)

Preah Vesandar—the story of Sakyamuni Buddha's penultimate incarnation—is a dramatization of the Vessantara *jātaka*,[32] well known to all classes of Khmers. In brief, the story tells how Prince Vesandar upset his father by his extreme generosity, even giving away the white elephant, palladium of the kingdom. Banished from the court, he gave away his children and, finally, his wife. A *Washington Post* reporter who saw this story performed in the Khao I Dang refugee camp in 1980 found it a striking metaphor for the Khmer people themselves.[33]

The version performed by the palace dancers consisted of seven scenes. In the first, Preah Vesandar tells his wife Neang Metri of his plan to become a monk because of popular dissatisfaction with his donation of the royal treasury to the poor. She joins him in exile, together with their children Prince Chaly and Princess Krihsna. In Scene Two an ambitious beggar named Chou Chuk agrees to send his unhappy young wife back to her parents and promises to send her servants and maids to attend her. In Scene Three Chou Chuk meets a hunter named Chettabot who has been sent by the king of that area to guard Vesandar's refuge. Chou Chuk lies and says he brings a message from Vesandar's father King Sanchchey calling him home. The hunter shows him the way to Preah Vesandar.

Scene Four begins with Vesandar hearing his wife's dream of being split in two to remove her liver; despite his prescience, he reassures her, and she departs to gather fruit. Chou Chuk arrives and requests servants for his wife. Vesandar says he will give the beggar his children as alms. Hearing this, his children hide in a lotus pond (by walking backward to disguise their whereabouts) until Vesandar, berated as a liar by the beggar, explains to them that they are the only boat that will allow him to reach the farther shore, i.e., to attain Buddhahood. Sadly they concur with their father's method of gaining merit and go with the beggar who is told to ransom them from their grandfather for a hundred pieces of gold, a hundred man-servants and a hundred maid-servants each.

The beggar ties the children's hands, but when he also beats them, Preah Vesandar grows momentarily angry and threatens him with his bow. Due to that moment of anger, he failed to obtain enlightenment in that lifetime. Meanwhile three *tevoda* or gods, incarnated as two tigers and a lion, cause Queen Metri to faint in order to delay her return. When she recovers in Scene Five she tells Vesandar what occurred. He, feigning jealousy, accuses his wife of being late due to dallying with hunters. The queen faints in grief and upon being revived by water asks for her children. Vesandar says that he gave them to a beggar, and his wife replies that if he had told her at once she would have understood his meritorious action.

In Scene Six King Preah Bat Srey Sanh Chey, Vesandar's father, calls for an astrologer to interpret his dream of a person offering him two lotus flowers; the astrologer says he will unexpectedly meet two members of his family, and shortly afterwards the "Brahmin" beggar passes by with the two children. The king does not recognize them but, charmed, asks them to sit beside him. They decline, modestly pleading their low station. The king eventually pays the ransom and offers food to Chou Chuk who eats so much he bursts.

In the final scene the king, queen, and grandchildren go to persuade Vesandar to return. On seeing him, they all weep and faint until they are revived by Indra, whereupon the "six princes" return joyfully to their home.

Lesser Dramatic Works

The following stories appear on the repertoire list compiled by Chet Chheng but are included in none of the palace performance programs. Only in that sense of not being frequently performed are they "lesser" works; Ket Mealea, for example, is a popular legend known to all Khmers. In general, however, little is known about these eleven tales as performed by the palace dancers.

Neang Champa Thaong (0)

Chey Sorysak (0)

Eysei Dach Chhean (0)

The title means the "*eysei* who transgresses" or "the fallen *eysei*." The title role is played by a clown character, the *tlok*, and a segment of this story appears in the 1963 USIS film on the Royal Ballet.

Preah Ket Mealea (0)

This legend concerning the divine architect, who supposedly constructed Angkor, was also included in the 1963 film made during a performance in the Angkor ruins. More than likely the dramatic plot follows the general outline of that tale as published in 1970.[34]

King of the Dragons and Prince Khobut

This drama is not mentioned by any of the Khmer sources considered heretofore. Jeanne Cuisinier, however, published a photo from this dance in 1927, captioned "the King of the Dragons challenges Prince Khobut who expresses his contempt."[35] The photo shows the dragon king holding a distinctive, thin lance approximately a meter in length.

Preah Lin Thaong (0)

Informants feel, though with no great certainty, that this story is different from Preah Thong and Neang Neak discussed earlier, but its content is unknown.

Neang Kakei (0)

This lengthy story is well known in Cambodia, and its authorship is attributed to King Ang Duong. What parts were performed as dance drama is not known.

PECHAIGN MEAR (0)

PREAH NOREAY BAIMPEAT

This work, whose title means "The Transformation of Vishnu," was included in the dances staged for the 1981 Khmer New Year in Washington, D.C. (See Robam Preah Noreay Baimpeat below.)

PREAH SAING HUN (0)

This story is said to be distinct from that of Preah Saing.

PREAH SOTHAVONG (0)

PREAH SOTHUN (0)

While there is no record of this story in the available palace programs, a photo in *Kambuja* magazine (reprinted in Chapter VII) shows a performance of "the legend of Keo Monnorea, the Kennari or female bird, and of Preah Sothun the Prince Charming."[36]

PREAH SUTHINARITH (0)

FRAGMENTS

A number of plot fragments gleaned from various non-Khmer sources are here mentioned for the benefit of future researchers. Zarina mentions the story of a princess who goes to seek help from a *yakkha* king, and she includes a lengthy description of the movement.

> The Princess enters the court of the Yeak King, and salutes him with Anjali [*sampeah*]. The King greets her with anjali, and tells her it is

a pleasant surprise to see her in his court; what news does she bring?

The Princess replies that she has…news of a grave nature. Her realm is menaced by a powerful enemy. Her father, the King, is greatly worried, for he cannot resist. There will be war, and many will die. She wishes to avert this, so she has come to entreat the Yeak to lead his army to their aid. The Yeak listens attentively, then considers his forces, the military strategy, counts his troops; he gives his consent to the Princess. The Princess, who has been waiting tearfully and anxiously for the Yeak's decision, now thanks him with deep gratitude, and leaves his court, returning home joyfully.[37]

The title of this work is not known, as is the case with two other fragments which incorporate distinctive staging techniques and will be discussed in Chapter VII. One concerns a princess whose husband is in love with her servant and who eventually hangs herself; the other is about a statue which comes to life under the influence of a flower.

Dramatic Themes

Earlier scholars have attempted to dismiss the complexity of dramatic theme within the Khmer dance drama by oversimplification. In 1900, for example, Aymonier set forth a skeletal plot to which he claimed the entire repertoire could be reduced:

> A king and his queens occupy the throne in glory and prosperity. Intrigues soon arise which lead to violent scenes of jealousy. These compel the young princes or princesses to leave the court under a cloud of disgrace, condemned to exile or even death but saved miraculously.
>
> The exiles wander in the forest, meet with other princes or princesses with whom they readily unite. Or they have equally agreeable adventures with *kinnari* (beautiful women with the feet of birds). They join battle with *yaksa* and *yaksi* (ogres and ogresses), who are fond of human flesh. They meet with *rsi* (anchorites) with the power of flight. They become lost, while out hunting, by the futile pursuit of a golden hind.
>
> After an adventure of like kind, the heroes or heroines are reconciled with their now disabused parents, and they live happily ever after with the various women they have married during their wanderings. As religious as it is erotic, the tale ends with the assimilation of the main character and his parents to the bodhisattva and members of his family.[38]

This model informs the view held by most of the early twentieth century observers.

In 1929 George Groslier allowed that there were no more than thirty dramas in the repertoire through which one would "search in vain for more than ten different themes."[39] Had he enumerated them, as we shall presently do, he might have observed that they all illumine a single, pervasive theme of the struggle between Feminine and Masculine, presented in endless variation.

The works discussed thus far in the chapter may be seen to fall into three categories: those which have a great many plot similarities, those which have a number of distinguishing realistic or "modern" features, and those which are unique in form. The first group may be analyzed in reference to a number of plot motifs partly discernible in Aymonier's more general description. These motifs in fourteen of the dramatic works suggest a plot model in which the hero—in exile or after studying with the *eysei*—sees the heroine in a garden, uses a disguise to meet her, and eventually weds her despite her *yakkha* father's opposition. Table 4 shows other variations of the model.

While Aymonier's model purports to describe the Khmer literary romance in general, Table 4 is an analysis only of the segments presented in the theatre. It is important to note that only the most striking scenes "as far as their dramatic interest and their significance for the whole of the epic poem are concerned" are staged as dance drama.[40] This is the case whether the story being dramatized reflects the "romantic" model seen in Table 4; the more realistic and modern stories such as Chan Korup, Bunloy, Chau Damrei Sar, and Chau Yeung Dattda; or the singular dramas such as Vesandar, Mekhala, Preah Tong, and Pathamasampothi.

In his commentary on the use of the *Rāmker* in Khmer theatre, Jacques Brunet has suggested that at first glance dramatizations seem limited to "abductions, epic combats, deaths and resurrections, and general reunions," but that "as soon as one goes into details one discovers Khmer rituals. The main Cambodian royal ceremonies are portrayed, and folk rituals also abound."[41] This conclusion holds true for the repertoire as a whole.

A second view regarding the repertoire, as one scholar noted in 1932, is that its sole subject is love and war, which are the primary themes of dance not only in Cambodia but throughout mainland Southeast Asia.[42] While some of the dramatic works may concern events in the lives of proto-historical kings such as Preah Thong, Preah Sorivong and Chey Chet,[43] many Cambodians also claim—as did Chheng Phon—that in general the repertoire presents the conflict between the forces of good and evil.[44] These various interpretations of the repertoire as the embodiment of Khmer ritual, as the objectification of war and love, or as the conflict between good and evil are not mutually exclusive if viewed from a broader perspective.

The present study holds that the eternal struggle dramatized in the Khmer dance drama is one for control of the Feminine, and the struggle exists on two levels: the realistic and the archetypal. On the realistic level the struggle concerns the timeless, painful passing of the female from father to husband. The hero-husband requires magic power and even help from animal energies to wrest his beloved from her father, who is in most instances a *yakkha*, or ogre. The *yakkha* does not represent evil but rather the older order with an incestuous aspect. This can be clearly seen in the prototypical struggle between Rām and Rāb in the *Rāmker* (see Chapter V). With regard to the Khmer repertoire as a whole—save for the *jātaka*-based dramas— the question of who controls the Feminine force is fundamental.

As noted in Chapter V the oldest Khmer myths concern the union of a female-male pair of progenitors. The contemporary repertoire of the dance drama adds pair after pair of characters to this list. It is by the action of the Male upon the Female that fertility is achieved and must be achieved in the face of all opposition. Opposition may come from the father, as we have noted, or from the female herself. It is this latter form of the struggle that is presented in two of the most powerful and popular pieces in the repertoire, Sovann Machha and Manimekhala.

THE DANCE REPERTOIRE: *ROBAM*

The distinction between those stories which are dramatized through dance and those dances which are non-dramatic is one clearly recognized by Khmer dance scholars. The dramas, or *roeung*, are considered to be, in general, of much newer vintage than the *robam*, or dances. This distinction is also the basis of program selection as established by Kossamak, who developed a standard program pattern of *robam/roeung/robam*. In this second half of the chapter we will first note the ritual nature of the *robam* and then examine a list of about sixty known dances, including several newly-created ones which demonstrate the fact that the Khmer dance repertoire is both sizable in its number of standard works and also capable of expansion. We shall then consider the nine most popular individual *robam* in the repertoire, together with some ten related dances or variants. Following that, dances less frequently performed by the royal troupe will be considered, although in many cases little is known about the dance except the name. Mention will be made of newly choreographed works, and the chapter will close with an examination of the *tep robam* and *buong suong*, which are ceremonies at which *robam* are performed for purely ritual or religious reasons. As mentioned previously, an "X" following a dance name indicates a performance recorded in palace programs (Appendix II); "0" indicates inclusion in the repertoire as delineated by Chet Chheng.

The relationship between *robam* and the *roeung* highlights the fundamental distinction between Cambodian and Thai classical dance. All the evidence available to this study both in Phnom Penh and in Bangkok indicates that the following statement by Chheng Phon is accurate:

> Previously in Cambodia there was not drama, only dance for the gods, and when they came to play the *lakhon* for the king as well as the god, drama was born. The Thai only have the drama and not the sacred dance. Because they wanted to have something distinctly Thai, they adopted the drama and abandoned sacred dance.
>
> Thus the *robam* are older than the *roeung*. Some pure *robam* such as Manimekhala and Vorachhun, which are not a mélange, are still

performed, but many others are mixed in with stories. Some of these stories came from Thailand, but the most sacred *robam*, which are very slow, are not known to the Thais.[45]

This view is supported by Cœdès, who points out that the oldest *robam* were originally ritual dances to hasten the coming of the rains, performed—according to the earliest descriptions—as a "double dance of men and women."[46]

The original religious significance of the *robam* can be inferred to some extent by the fact that in the seventeenth century they were customarily performed "on the occasion of ceremonies and also at the beginning of theatre presentations by way of a curtain-raiser and to put the spectator in some way under the invocation and the protection of the divinities incarnated by the dancers."[47] Thus Kossamak's choice of beginning a program with a dance piece reflects ancient ritual practice as well as a good sense of theatricality, since the *robam* tend to be more visually spectacular, more compact, and of greater intensity than the dramatic repertoire.

ROBAM TEP MONOROM (X-27, 0)

The Tep Monorom is the most popular dance in the classical repertoire, appearing in palace performance records twenty-seven times—a primacy which it maintained during the years of the Republic as the favorite large-group classical dance. Basically the dance is the dancers' supplication to the gods to be transformed into *apsaras* or celestial dancers. The prayer is heard and answered; the dancers become *apsaras* and offer thanks to the gods (Fig. 6-3).

The partial song lyrics which are available suggest two specific interactions, the first being the erotic pursuit of the *apsaras* by the male celestials:

> When gods and goddesses
> Descend on earth
> With joy to dance all day
> A goddess chaste must often flee
> An ardent god's embrace.[48]

Chapter VI: The Modern Repertoire of the Dance Drama 269

6-3. *Robam* **Tep Monorom, ca. 1962.** *Nokor Khmer.*

Second is the harmonious union of the gods and goddesses expressed through dance:

> The heavenly maiden is beautiful.
> She dances with harmonious grace.
> In near embrace with the beloved
> But held back by a graceful hand,
> Now circling and coiling,
> The prince and princess dance joyously.[49]

Originally a dance for a single prince and princess, it was adapted by Kossamak for twelve dancers.[50] This may explain, in part, why it was not acceptable as an offertory dance in the *buong suong* ritual (see below) even though it is a large group dance of paired male and female roles.[51]

ROBAM PLET (X-18, 0)

Robam Plet or "Fan Dance" is also a large group dance; Leclère saw it performed prior to 1911 by twenty female dancers "representing the blessings of Indra's paradise."[52] While a 1946 program described one performance as "modern," a 1971 UBA publication says that the *robam* was traditionally offered as a "mark of respect and expression of good wishes to Khmer sovereigns."[53] Nowadays the same sentiments are directed to the audience. Lyrics are not available, but a notation of the music was published in 1906 by Louis Laloy.[54]

DANCE OF WELCOME (X-15)

The title "Dance of Welcome," or "Overture," is probably a generic one but also represents something of a problem since there is another, clearly separate dance called Chap Robam which translates as "Dance of Overture."[55] Palace records report a performance of the Chap Robam only twice but on both occasions mid-way through the program. To further complicate the matter, on one of those occasions (28 October 1941) the program also opened with a "Dance of Welcome or Overture." Nothing else is known about the Chap Robam, and whether the "Dance of Welcome" is a discrete dance remains uncertain.

What is clear is that a number of other dance pieces were also labeled "by way of overture" or "as a dance of welcome." These included "Battle Between White Monkey and Black Monkey" (6 February 1950), "Battle Between Two Princes and Two Monkeys" (25 November 1950), "Battle Between Two Princes and One Monkey" (25 May 1947), "Dance for Two Dancers" (16 February 1951 and 7 September 1949), "Dance to the Glory of the New Reign" (28 October 1941), "Dance of the Tevoda" (22 November 1942), and "Preah Thong" (1 April 1945), from which one concludes that a great many different pieces could be performed as overture in the opening position of a program. Nonetheless, fifteen different programs open with "Dance of Welcome" or "Overture" and provide no further identification of that *robam*. Neither Chap Robam nor Dance of Welcome is included on the repertoire list of Chet Chheng.

ROBAM MKAW (X-13, 0)

The Robam Mkaw (mkawa), or "Dance of the Sea Serpent," is "one of the greatest sacred dances of the whole classical repertoire."[56] Often transcribed as "Mokar" or "Makara," the *robam* is probably the actual dance performed by Mekhala and Voracchun—or at least by their retinue, since one program says that:

> ...the Queen of the waters is now seen in the company of Vorachhun along with many gods and goddesses. Arrayed in her finest apparel Moni Mekhala moves gracefully and swiftly in the midst of her suite who watch her admiringly evolving in a heavenly dance. The other gods and goddesses start dancing in turn, imitating the movement of a Makara (a mythical creature, half-fish, half-snake).[57]

Robam Mkaw may also be related to "Dance of the Naga" (see below), but is clearly similar to the female earth or water spirit genre of myth and dance, of which both Mekhala and Sovann Machha are examples.

The sacred nature of this *robam*, however, does not preclude adaptations, and for the 14 April 1945 performance in honor of the occupation forces, the royal dancers carried Japanese flags during the Robam Mkaw. To the Khmer mind, this seemingly unusual choice may have lent greater sincerity to the expression of good will.

ROBAM PHKAR MEAS PHKAR PRAK (X-12, 0) AND OTHER FLOWER DANCES

The "Dance of Gold and Silver Flowers" is one of the most beautiful in the entire repertoire (Fig. 6-4) and was a standard opening piece during the Sihanouk era.[58] The dance was traditionally performed by eight dancers—all female roles—and seems always to have been offertory in nature.

The offering of gold and silver flowers has been a standard form of political tribute for centuries in mainland Southeast Asia. In 1768, for instance, the Thai king Taksin demanded gold and silver flowers from the King of Cambodia, who refused.[59] Thus it is interesting that when the French Minister of Colonies visited Cambodia in 1931, King Monivong wrote a poem, chanted by the chorus accompanying Robam Phkar Meas Phkar Prak (quoted in Chapter IV), which swore fidelity to France "to the end of the world."

The "Dance of Gold and Silver Flowers" is not to be confused with Robam Kanh Phkar (0), meaning the dance of holding or picking flowers, and Robam Champa Meas Tes (0), a dance honoring a particular white flower. Both titles appear on Chet Chheng's list of *robam* but neither is found in any palace programs, with the possible synonymous exception of a single mention of Dance of the Flowers (X-1) on 22 May 1951.

Robam Bach Phkar Chuon Par

This *robam*, whose title means "tossing flowers to wish good luck," is usually called simply "Bai Pka." It also appears in palace performance programs as both "The Dance of Good Wishes" and "Sinuon" (X-1), which is the name of the tune that accompanies it. The distinguishing feature of the dance is that the nine dancers—one leader and eight others, all female roles—each carry a golden cup of flowers (sometimes made of paper) which they toss towards the audience as the dance comes to a close.

There have undoubtedly been numerous lyrics to the song accompaniment performed over the years. In 1975 the chanters in Phnom Penh sang:

> Let us unite together
> To give benefit to the nation
> Great progress to society
> And Enlightenment to all.
> The Dance of Tossing Flowers
> Is to wish you the very best.
> May comfort and good fortune
> Be always with you.

Robam Tewet (X-8, 0)

This *robam* was traditionally performed within the context of the Leak Sinnavong story and was known as "Tewetiasai" (devadāsi), a Sanskrit-derived title meaning "maidservants of the god." Like the Tep Monorom or Robam Apsaras, it is another dance in which these beings are incarnate in the dancers. Prior to 1947, there are instances of a performance entitled Invocation to the Tevoda (X-3) for a solo dancer and *sralay* (oboe), used to open the program. After 1946 this piece is not mentioned, but Robam Tewet (or "Tevet") appears as one of the most popular group dances. Seemingly Tewet is another example of Kossamak's adaptation and expansion of an already popular *robam* into a much larger piece which is now rarely identified with the Leak Sinnavong story at all. It should be remembered, however, that if Chheng Phon is correct in claiming that the *robam* are older than the *roeung*, the essence of the Tewet dance may well pre-date the Leak Sinnavong context from which it has today been isolated.

A portion of the song lyrics are as follows:

> The heavenly maidens are pleasing.
> Hands flow with the body to the left and to the right.
> As celestial youths begin to dance
> The maidens pretend to be unaware.
> Each man dances closely and the woman flies away.
> Gliding together beautifully, he halts and teases her.

The dance was interpreted by Kossamak to show respect and express welcome to the audience.[60]

6-4. **Dance of Gold and Silver Flowers With Voan Savay** (center). Photo Colin Grafton.

Battle of the Black and White Monkeys (X-8)

This *robam* may originate in the *Rāmker* from the battle between the two monkey brothers named Sugrib and Bāli, although there is no known reference to that dramatic context, and the *Rāmker* clearly states that Sugrib and Bāli were so identical that Rām could not tell them apart. Thus the origin of the "black vs. white" motif is uncertain. In 1911 Leclère noted a danced battle between black monkeys and white monkeys over the fruit that they gathered from trees in the jungle;[61] presumably they performed as today with a single powerful leader of each group, but all that can be said with certainty is that the white monkey is not Rām's general, Hanumān.

Parrot Dance (8-8)

The popular Parrot Dance may correspond to Robam Sek Sarika (0), or "Dance of the Parrot and Mynah Bird." Robam Sek Sarika may be, in turn, an excerpt from the story of Preah Leak Sinnavong who, at one point, accompanied by Neang Kessar, amuses himself in a garden with a black bird and a parrot.

The song that accompanies part of the *robam* may be translated as follows:

> The wind blows with flowers' scent and enters the heart.
>
> The maidens sing and dance as the hero plays the *sralay* with the musicians.
>
> The beautiful melody spreads throughout the forest.
> Listen to the song.
>
> The sound is soft and sweet
>   mixing with the scent of the flowers.
>
> It captures the mind and makes the body feel like music.
> The dancer's body is like the celestial maiden,
> And all is beauty.

By contrast, Chheng Phon has said that the "words are not about a mynah or parrot because the title is older. The words are to admire the king, and the melody is also old." Thus the words have changed but the melody and title have remained as before.⁶²

The lyrics cited above, taken from a dance student's notebook in Phnom Penh, do not speak of admiration for the king or of birds. The dance is, thus, a clear example of the many transformations that lyrics to a traditional melody may undergo. In this *robam*, however, as popularly performed, the roles were of a mynah and a parrot and were often taken by the youngest dancers in their first performances.

ROBAM APSARAS (X-7, 0)

The *apsaras* are the celestial dancers who entertain the gods in Indra's paradise. In this *robam* they descend to earth with their queen to gather flowers. The chanters sing:

> We come into this garden
> Where bright enameled flowers lie.
> These we will gather and carry
> Up the staircase of the sky.
> O flowers bound for Heaven
> To ravish all hearts.
> O flowers of *phkol*
> Lovely beyond compare.
> Man's stony heart will be captured
> By the garland our Queen will wear.⁶³

The dance is considered to be "divinely pure" and, on the technical level, among the most difficult.

Turning now to the list of less frequently performed dances, many of which do not appear on Chet Chheng's list, we shall proceed alphabetically except in the case of related dances. As with the second example, nothing may be known of the dance except its title. In most cases, translations of the original Khmer titles are unavailable due to the fact that they were Romanized in the programs or because the titles are simply too esoteric to be recognized. Some of the dances are also of recent creation and can be termed as *robam* only in the most general sense.

Robam Bopha Lokhai

This dance is in the performance repertoire of the dancers directed by Phuong Phan in Washington, D.C. It is either a new dance or was referred to by Chet Chheng, if at all, under a completely different name.

Brahmane and the *Apsaras* (X-1)

Dance of Brahme (X-3)

Presumably this dance and the preceding one are similar in some respects to *Robam Apsaras*, most probably in the female roles. However, a program note from Sihanouk's twenty-fifth birthday celebration says the dance portrays a young Brahman trying the bow he received from Indra (9 November 1946). It is possible that the *apsaras* deliver the bow, and that the two dances coincide.

Dance of the Butterflies (X-1)

This dance was performed about 1956 for Ambassador Donald Heath, and was reported by Malcolm MacDonald in 1959 to be "enchanting."[64] Its relation to *Robam* Puo Me Ambao (0), "The Dance of Snake and Butterfly," is unknown. Lyrics to the latter are in the form of a dialogue; in the text obtained from a student dancer's notebook, the butterfly appears to be the female.

>
> Male: Where are you coming from, my love?
> Female: I come from drinking water.
> Male: Where is the pool that you drank at? Please tell me.
> Female: I'll tell you.
> Male: All right. Don't wait so long.
> Female: I went to drink. I go back and forth.

Male:	I feel a great love for you. May I ask you more?
Female:	Then ask what you really want to know.
Male:	When you went there, did you only drink water?
Female:	I only drank my fill of water.
	(They both go to drink water at the rock well.)
Male:	I love very much the way you fly up and down.

The earthy content of the lyrics seems inharmonious with the general tone of the classical dance, and perhaps there are other more chaste versions presently unavailable.

ROBAM CHHOM KALA BOSSEBA (0)

The title cannot be translated from the transcription but presumably concerns Bosseba, the consort of Inao.

ROBAM CHHOU CHHAY (X-1, 0)

The title of the dance cannot be translated from the Romanized form. It was accompanied on 10 May 1949 by a *sralay* solo.

CHINESE DUO (X-1)

A single appearance in a 30 November 1948 program describes the piece as a "comic scene executed by two clowns of the Royal Troupe" who were probably male.

Robam Chmar (0)

The "Dance of the Cat" does not appear in any palace program but is perhaps associated with the cat role in the story of Preah Bat Chey Chet. A student dancer's notebook in Phnom Penh included the following lyrics:

> We kneel before the great power,
> The exalted king.
> You govern all the people
> Like the king of the gods.
>
> Your throne is famous
> Throughout all the world, from which
> Envoys come to pay respect.
> It equals your moon-like radiance.

Thus, the song was popular in recent times, especially with young dancers for whom it would be appropriate to perform these lyrics entitled "Dance of the Cat Singing for the King."

Robam Chuon Por Tiahian Chah (0)

The title translates as "Dance of Good Wishes to All the Soldiers." A 1981 performance program by Phuong Phan's dancers in Washington, D.C., included a dance called "Chun Pao" or "giving blessings." If this is the same dance, it probably has several lyrics—at least one for soldiers and one for more peaceful times.

Robam Chwia (0)

One informant suggested that *chwia* is an old place name, possibly Java. A student dancer's notebook included these lyrics:

Step forth.
She reveals herself exquisitely, then halts.
She begins to dance, swaying gracefully with the wind.
All applaud and shout with excitement.

Nothing more is known of the dance.

Cock Dance (X-4)

The Cock Dance appears four times in palace performance programs and is perhaps an excerpt from the story of Preah Chey Sain. It may correspond to *Robam* Moen (0), "Dance of the Chicken," cited by Chet Chheng. A song from one of the UBA dance student's notebooks in 1975 entitled "Chrbot Moen" or "Heavenly Chicken" may also be related to the Cock Dance. The following lyrics from that source are loosely translated; a prince is speaking ambiguously of a maiden.

> This chicken is like gold; the beauty of her
> Body is unmatched in the world.
> Her feathers charm all viewers by their light
> Which the gods have given only to her.

> This divine chicken with bright eye and neck of gold:
> All eyes are attracted to her flight.
> Her cry turns people's thoughts to love and beauty.
> Rarely is such beauty found.

> She stands near him without noticing
> And then flies away unaware.
> He hides behind the flowers,
> And she passes by.

> He takes her hand.
> Surprised, she attempts to flee.
> He speaks of love and offers her his life.
> And together they depart.

The problem of gender—in that the cocks in the story of Chey Sain, as well as in the Cock Dance itself, preclude identification with a female—

may mean that these lyrics are of a song not included by title in the present listing.

A 1911 description of an interesting piece from the repertoire may have some relation to the contemporary Cock Dance or *Robam* Moen. Leclère writes,

> in another piece two princes who cannot conquer each other agree to abide by the results of a cock fight: the owner of whichever cock wins will gain the territory of the other prince. Two women crouch, jump, beat their arms as cocks beat their wings, and cry "kokoriko." They are put in place by the two princes who stroke their hands and release them. The fight begins with small leaps, includes tosses of the head ... and ends with the fall of one combatant on her side as the winner shakes her head in triumph.[65]

It is difficult to imagine this folksy fare in the classical repertoire, and, indeed, the only two elements that support such a notion are the presence of princes and the cock roles being played by female dancers.

ROBAM DEVKANNIA (X-1)

In the story of Preah Pathamasampothi, "Devakanna" refers to a celestial being in Indra's heaven. One informant has suggested that a more accurate transcription would have been *tepkhanha*. Nothing further is known about the *robam*.

ROBAM HANGSAS

Nothing is known about this dance either, although one informant thought perhaps it was a dance of the "golden bird."

Robam Hokkrasat (X-1)

The program for 16 April 1947 says only that the dance was "executed by six small dancers."

Robam Kanichha (X-1)

Robam Ken Saing (X-3, 0)

This is the "small scarf dance" (kansena), as opposed to *Robam* Krom (krama), the "large scarf dance"—with the distinction being between numbers of dancers rather than dimensions of the scarf. The program from 10 November 1943 reports that on that evening the dancers carried scarves which were blue and yellow, the colors of His Majesty the King. It is not known whether the dance is still performed today.

Robam Kenvilara (X-3)

The undated program (c.1950) in honor of General George Revers says only that "the gracious Princess Kenvilara dances with the charming Prince Unaken," which refers to no other known story.

Robam Krom (X-1)

This is the "large scarf dance."

Robam Krut

This "Dance of the Garuda" was witnessed in Cambodia in 1975 but does not appear on Chet Chheng's list or in any of the palace performance programs. It is perhaps included in one of the dramas but is certainly not new; prior to 1911 Leclère witnessed a dance portraying "the flight of a garuda which a king rides."[66]

Robam Ksat (X-1)

Robam Lao (X-4)

Usually referred to in the programs as the "Laotian Ballet," the dance is accompanied by a piece of music entitled Lomphat Phay.

Robam Lia (0)

Lia means farewell, and the dance may correspond to the Farewell Dance (X-1) mentioned in palace programs. *Lia* is also the name of a specific piece of music used at the end of numerous pieces to indicate the final exit.

Robam Mithapheap (X-1,0)

This is the "Friendship Dance" discussed earlier.

Nāga Dance (X-1)

No description of this dance is available, but it was performed for Zhou Enlai on 22 November 1956 and must correspond—because of the significance of that occasion—to a major *robam*, possibly Robam Mkaw, the "dragon dance," as performed by Mekhala and Vorachhun.

Robam Neari Chea Chuor (0)

The title (nārījājwra) seems to translate as "Girls in a Line" and probably corresponds to Phuong Neari. Witnessed in Phnom Penh, the dance was performed by eight girls in two lines of four facing the audience. The floor pattern of movement was far simpler than most.

Robam Phuong Neari (X-5)

The popularity of this dance both in the palace programs and with contemporary dancers—it is one of the staples of Phuong Phan's troupe, for instance—makes it very odd that the title does not appear on Chet Chheng's list; yet that is the case. *Phuong* or "garland" of girls seems close to "girls in a line," and this title is far better known than Neari Chea Chuor. The piece does not appear in program records prior to 1950.

Robam Preah Noreay Baimpeat

Often known as the "Candle Dance," this *robam* does not appear in any of the records of performance in Cambodia. Nonetheless, it is a popular and important dance in the repertoire and has been staged several times in the United States since 1980. It was performed on 11 April 1981 in Washington, D.C., by Phuong Phan's troupe for the Cambodian New Year (under the title "Preah Norei Bain Baipia"). It was also performed for the International Music Festival at the Twenty-seventh Annual Meeting of the Society for Ethnomusicology held in July 1982 at College Park, Maryland, with Nuth Rachana in the leading role, accompanied by ten boys as the manifestations of Vishnu. The number and gender of these manifestations is optional—since it can also be done with female-male couples—and this may account in part for its popularity in recent, dancer-short days.

In the dance, the god Noreay, a manifestation of Vishnu, "multiplies his soul infinitely throughout the universe, represented by the worshippers' candles. The brightness of the fire symbolizes the power and wisdom which the god imparts to the world."[67]

Parade of Dancers (X-3)

"Parade of Dancers" closed the three programs in which it appears in palace records and, hence, may be another name for "Final Dance" or *Robam* Lia.

Peacock Dance

There is a peacock dance in the section of Inao discussed earlier, to which this may correspond.

Robam Pou Thao (0)

The "Axe Dance" includes these lyrics as translated from an UBA student's dance notebook:

> We dance and we dance with the rhythm of Cambodia.
> Never change.
> The axe dancing comes from age-old times.
> Its fame spread over the world without end,
> And everyone admires our skillful dancing.

The axe is the hallmark of the *yakkha* or giant role and this may be a standard entrance dance for those roles.

Robam Salama (X-1)

Robam Sramoch

The "Ant Dance" (sramocha) is a popular dance for very young dancers, which may explain why it never appears on palace performance programs nor was included on Chet Chheng's list of the repertoire. As performed in Phnom Penh in 1975, five very little girls presented the five-minute dance using very simple floor patterns of movement: entrance, dancing in a line, followed by a simple exit without the usual circuitous processions.

Robam Srang Trong Kruong (0)

The title means "dressing after the bath." Nothing else is known of it.

Sword Dance (X-1)

A dance described as the "Sabre Dance," witnessed in Phnom Penh in 1975, is probably the same dance as the "Sword Dance" listed in a palace performance program for 9 September 1957. The "Sabre Dance" was performed by five dancers each carrying two swords and a round shield on which was painted a *yakkha* face. At the end of the dance, all weapons were hurled to the ground.

Robam Takheng (X-3)

Robam Tep Nikaw (0)

Robam Truetpol

The "Dance of Inspection" (trwtabala) is performed by *yakkha* roles or by strong martial characters. It is accompanied by *kraw nak* music and can be inserted into any of the dramatized *roeung* calling for a grand entrance and inspection of the troops.

Dance of Vilanda (X-2)

Robam Yeaks (X-2)

There are so many appearances of *yeaks*, or *yakkha*, in the stories that the title could refer to almost any appearance of them—all of which, of course, would be similar.

Original Dances

At this point it is important to note that the dances in the repertoire cannot accurately be limited to a specific number because new works can be choreographed at any time. Sometimes these may remain popular—as with the *Robam* Chuon Por Tiahian Chah, "wishing good luck to all the soldiers," in the years of the Republic—but others simply commemorate a single occasion. The melody remains in the musicians' repertoire, and the choreographic movements remain accessible. Their union into a specific dance as well as the words which accompany it, however, will pass. We noted this pattern in the dramatic repertoire, for example, with Preah Pathamasamphoti; with the *robam*, one example can be seen in the 14 August 1943 performance of a "Votive Poem" in honor of the French Vice-Admiral Jean Decoux. The piece falls within the general category of "friendship dances" as demonstrated by the following accompanying chant:

> The gracious anjali salutation that Sitā gives to Rām
> We dedicate on this auspicious day to the Great Commander, friend of peace.
>
> He has descended from his northern home to visit our beloved King,
> This one whom we respectfully call the wise protector of the empire.
>
> In the old Kingdom of Kambuja shining with a glorious heritage,
> Choirs of angels and gods sing for Admiral Jean Decoux
>
> And will repeat for future ages the radiant remembrance of this festivity
> When France and Cambodia once again celebrate their great friendship.

The dance and song were both composed "originally" for the occasion; the *premières danseuses* of the palace performed, and the melody was Chin Lomphat.

Using the traditional choreographic elements, new dances are today being added to the repertoire of those groups performing outside Cambodia. Moly Sam in the company headed by Phuong Phan in Washington, D.C., for example, has created a *Robam* Priapsar, or "Dance of the White Dove," which she performs as a solo piece. The same company performs a "Candlelight Dance" for four or eight female-male couples that is also newly choreographed. This flexibility is one of the major sustaining factors of the dance and will be considered further in Chapter VII.

There is one final group of dances to examine in this chapter, regarding which the evidence is not totally consistent, namely those dances considered sacred and those included in the *buong suong* ceremony.

Chheng Phon has said that there are seven dances more sacred than any of the other *robam*. They are *Robam* Voracchun, *Robam* Mekhala, *Robam* Ream Eyso (these three form a unit), *Robam* Preah Thong, *Robam* Baolut (paula'ta), *Robam* Sarahbarom (sarahparama), and *Robam* Baramit (paramitra). An eighth, *Robam* Tiyae (tay"e), is sometimes included among this group.[68] Even allowing for discrepancies in transcription, four of these eight dances never appear in either palace performance programs or on Chet Chheng's list of the repertoire. As we shall see in Chapter IX, the most important occasion for the performance of these dances was in the *buong suong* ceremony to invoke the aid of the *tevoda* in protecting the kingdom, a ceremony over which the king himself presided. In the available data documenting such performances, only the Voracchun-Mekhala-Ream Eyso *robam* are mentioned,[69] but the significant point is that four of the eight sacred dances were never performed for public audiences so far as we can tell.

The term *buong suong* is a general one referring to the ritual of making a promise of future offerings in exchange for divine assistance in the present. On the individual level one may promise such things as offering music, money, or all one's hair if one is granted a particular wish such as passing an exam, giving birth to a son and so forth. In the present context, *buong suong* refers to the same ritual on the national level and was used to end drought or other plagues on the country, such as rockets falling on the palace as discussed in Chapter IV. Chheng Phon also noted that *buong suong* sometimes accompanies the *tway kru* ceremony honoring the dance teachers and their spiritual counterparts.

According to Jacques Brunet, "*buong suong* is the oldest dance which is still executed at the present time. Its use is confined to the cult of the manes of deceased kings and to certain ceremonies for protecting the Kingdom."[70] Parenthetically, the ceremony was performed during Sihanouk's reign both in the Silver Pagoda and in front of the statue of King Norodom. Brunet claims that the *buong suong* can be comprised of any selected series of dance-melody elements from among more than three hundred titles. A dance and its corresponding melody often have the same name, but the latter are far more numerous.

In a *buong suong* performance described by Brunet, there were eighteen melodies—probably in correlation with the eighteen major kru of the dance—but only two correspond by name to *robam*. The eighteen are Sathukar, Krao Nay, Kom Vean, Rour, Preah Thong, Phleng Chhar, Banchos, Phleng Lea, Phleng Smeu, Yani, Phleng Klom, Choeut, Long Song Mon, Reay, Chhoeut Chhoeung, Reu Reay, Khop Khat, and Choeut Chhing.[71] What we cannot discern from this list is which of the eight sacred dances—besides Preah Thong—might have been danced with this accompaniment. One final sacred dance of which little is known is the Tep Robam, a dance of offering to the gods. It included the musical pieces Preah Thong and Baolut and, presumably, the corresponding dances. It was privately performed within the palace.

In this chapter we have examined the repertoire of both the dramas and the *robam*, noting their original ritual function and their pervasive theme of struggle for control of the Feminine. In closing, what should be emphasized is that many of these dances are not performed now in 1984, but if the story is known, most can be re-created; if the accompanying melodies are remembered, new words can easily be written. Chheng Phon has said that Khmers like to make variations of old melodies rather than invent new ones. As this chapter has demonstrated, words are more easily forgotten than a melody, and new words are often written for old tunes. The spectrum of longevity for performance elements, according to Chheng Phon, begins with the costumes—the tradition most easily preserved. Then follows melody, title of melody, words to the melody, and, finally, most impermanent of all, the dance movements. In the following chapter we turn our attention to that most fragile element of performance—the dance itself and the music which accompanies it.

Endnotes

1. A palace performance program states that "Sovann Machha, Queen of the Tides and daughter of Totsakan, has a fish tail and body, and a human face and arms. Hanumān seduces her as she's dismantling the causeway his monkeys are building. She had a son Matchanu, named by the *apsaras* who cared for him when, out of fear of Toksakan, the mother left him on the ocean shore in their care. A white dove also cared for him, as did the *apsaras* who had come down to rejoice at the strength of the baby. Maiyarap eventually took the child to the underworld of Badan which he inherited from his father and ruled."
2. "Le théâtre et la danse au Cambodge," p. 137.
3. Hang Thun Hak, *Rāmker*, pp. 137.
4. *Khmer Classical Dance* (Phnom Penh: Université des Beaux-Arts, 1971), p. 12.
5. Hang Thun Hak, *Rāmker*, p. 50.
6. Hang Thun Hak, *Rāmker*, p. 50.
7. Hang Thun Hak, *Rāmker*, p. 51.
8. Hang Thun Hak, *Rāmker*, pp. 53-54.
9. See Jean Drans, "Histoire de Sang Thong (Conque d'Or)," *Histoire de Nang Manora et histoire de Sang Thong* (Tokyo: Presses Salésiennes, 1947), pp. 41-64.
10. Pp. 92-95. Another is available in Sappho Marchal's *Danses cambodgiennes* (Saigon: Extrême-Asie, 1925), pp. 38-46.
11. Maspero, "Littérature khmère," p. 39.
12. Phuong Phan, personal communication, 27 May 1981. Also mentioned in the program notes of the 1971 U.S. tour.
13. *Khmer Dances* (Bangkok: n.p., 1974), p. 15. This program for the 21-24 December performances includes notes in both Thai and English. Cœdès identifies Ream Eyso as the demon Paracurāma—Rāmāsura, grandson of Braham ("Origine et évolution," p. 499).
14. Le théâtre cambodgien, p. 7.
15. *ISSA*, p. 215.
16. Program note for 7 January 1936.
17. Casey, pp. 150-52.
18. *Danses cambodgiennes*, pp. 46-48.
19. *Khmer Dances* (Bangkok: n.p., 1974). This program from the December 1974 Bangkok performances is in both English and Thai and is 20 pages in length. Vorachhun is identified by Cœdès as Arjuna, the god of war who "comes to the aid of Mekhala and after a great battle is vanquished by Ramasura who seizes him by the feet and knocks him against the sides of Mount Meru" ("Origine et évolution," p. 499). This tradition, however, is not known in Cambodia.
20. MacDonald, pp. 27-30.
21. *Le théâtre cambodgien*, pp. 8-12.
22. Kisselgoff, p. 55.
23. Hang Thun Hak, *Musique khmère* (Phnom Penh: L'Université Royale des Beaux-Arts, 1969), p. 113. The musical notation is included.
24. Hang Thun Hak, *Musique khmère*, p. 113.
25. The tune has been recorded by Alain Daniélou, *Music of Cambodia*, in "Musical Anthology of the Orient" (UNESCO), Bärenreiter-Musicaphon, BM 30L2002, n.d.
26. *Le théâtre cambodgien*, pp. 6-7.
27. Ponder, p. 246.
28. Sappho Marchalt, *Danses cambodgiennes*, pp. 32-38.
29. "Littérature cambodgienne," in *Indochine*, ed. Sylvain Levi (Paris: Société d'Editions Geographiques, Maritimes et Coloniales, 1931), I, p. 188.
30. *RCB*, p. 12.

Notes for Chapter VI: The Modern Repertoire of the Dance Drama 291

31 The story of *Pathamasambodhi* has been transcribed in Pali "under the direction of Phra Parahuchit Chinarot in Bangkok after the destruction of Ayutthaya" according to Maspero ("Littérature khmère," p. 299) and has been translated by Leclère (*Les livres sacrés du Cambodge* [Paris: Ernest Leroux]).
32 See Leclère, "Le livre de Véandar, le roi charitable," in *Contes et légends du Cambodge* (Paris: Ernest Leroux, 1895).
33 Burgess, p. A-24.
34 Fabricius, pp. 46-61.
35 "The Gestures in the Cambodian Ballet: Their Traditional and Symbolic Significance," *Indian Arts and Letters*, 1, No. 2 (1927), figs. 6, 13.
36 *Kambuja*, 4, No. 37 (15 April 1968), p. 89.
37 Zarina, pp. 77-79.
38 Etienne Aymonier, *Le royaume actuel*, Vol. I of *Le Cambodge* (Paris: Ernest Leroux, 1900), p. 44. It may be noted that Aymonier is somewhat of a hostile witness, having claimed a page earlier that the Khmer theatre dating from "very early times" may have been the source of the romantic literature of Cambodia which "is dull, repetitious, devoid of originality, inseparable from Siamese literature and wholly subordinated to Indian literature."
39 George Groslier, "Le théâtre et la danse au Cambodge," p. 126.
40 Hang Thun Hak, *Rāmker*, p. 69.
41 "Themes and Motifs of the Cambodian Ramayana in the Shadow Theatre," *TDMSA*, p. 4.
42 Cogniat, *Danses d'Indochine*, p. 87.
43 Moura, *Le royaume du Cambodge*, II, pp. 7-15.
44 Chheng Phon, personal communication.
45 Chheng Phon, personal communication.
46 "Origine et évolution," pp. 498-99. Cœdès sees the origin of the *roeung* within masked dances traditionally performed by men and later adopted by female palace dancers who had performed *robam* from time immemorial and wanted something more "realistic" and dramatic in addition (p. 499).
47 "Origine et évolution." p. 499.
48 *Khmer Dances*, p. 17.
49 From the song notebook of an UBA student in February 1975.
50 *RCB*, p. 20.
51 Chheng Phon, personal communication.
52 *Le théâtre cambodgien*, p. 8.
53 *Khmer Classical Dance*, p. 13.
54 "Musique et danses cambodgiennes," *La Revue Musicale*, 15 August 1906, p. 104. The dance is described on pp. 106-107. See also Pich Sal, pp. 17-18.
55 G. Groslier, "Le théâtre et la danse au Cambodge," p. 140.
56 *RCB*, p. 20.
57 *Khmer Classical Dance*, p. 17.
58 *RCB*, p. 20.
59 Piat, p. 69. See also Chandler, p. 154.
60 *Khmer Classical Dance*, p. 13.
61 *Le théâtre cambodgien*, p. 7.
62 Chheng Phon, personal communication.
63 *Khmer Classical Dance*, p. 8.
64 *Angkor*, p. 32.
65 *Le théâtre cambodgien*, p. 21.
66 *Le théâtre cambodgien*, p. 8.
67 Chinary Ung, Jacket Notes, *Cambodian Traditional Music*, Vol. II, Folkways Records, FE-4082, 1979.
68 Personal communication. See also Chapter IX.
69 "Sacred Dances at the Palace to Bring Rain," *Kambuja*, 15 August 1967, pp. 20-23; *Kambuja*, 15 September 1965, p. 19.
70 *Royal Music of Cambodia* (jacket notes).
71 Jacques Brunet, *Royal Music of Cambodia*. See Chapter VII for the available transliterations of these titles which have here been left in the transcriptions rendered by Brunet.

CHAPTER VII

MUSIC, CHOREOGRAPHY AND STAGING

ភ្លេងខ្មែរ, នាដសាស្ត្រ និង សម័យកាល

An audience experiences the Khmer dancer within an immediate context of production elements; she is on some sort of stage or delineated performance area, she moves in patterns which soon become at least superficially familiar, and she is continually accompanied by musicians as well as, periodically, by chanters. This chapter will examine those elements beginning with the music; we will look briefly at its history, the components of the *pinpeat* orchestra, the most frequently heard melodies, and the relationship between the dancer and musicians. Turning to the actual choreography, we will examine the structural elements known as *kbach* as well as the hand gestures, floor patterns, the portrayal of emotions, and the general style of the movement. The chapter will conclude with descriptions of various staging techniques used in this century.

Music History

The literature on Khmer music is extremely limited and, regarding its history, largely conjectural. Only Jacques Brunet has offered an historical overview in which he posits (1) an autochthonous, polyphonic music produced by a variety of gongs, drums, mouth-organs, and horns still discernible in certain mountain-dwelling tribes, as well as a five- or seven-stringed zither mentioned in a sixth-century Chinese text, (2) the introduction from India of the harp, vina, certain drums, and cymbals as seen in the bas-reliefs of Angkor, many of which are no longer to be found in Cambodia, (3) an Indonesian influence presumed to originate with Jayavarman II in the early ninth century, (4) a fifteenth to nineteenth century Malay influence for which he acknowledges there is no solid evidence, and (5) Chinese influence seen only in the Khmer choice of particular instruments.[1] Brunet's conclusion, in harmony with the general re-interpretation of Southeast Asian history described in Chapters I and II, is that

> contrary to the generally accepted notion, Cambodian music owes very little to Indian influence. It gradually evolved on the basis of the autochthonous stratum, systems that originated in the local culture, and instruments which for the most part are indigenous to the Indo-Chinese peninsula where they have reached their present development.[2]

While much of the past remains obscure, Brunet's main contention regarding Khmer music today is that it is uniquely Khmer.

> Despite the inevitable set-backs of history, despite the many additions from outside and the continual contacts with neighboring civilizations, no hybridization has taken place. The contribution made by Indian culture has in no way made Cambodian music a modal music; in the same way the contacts with Chinese culture and the adjacency to Vietnam have not imparted any Sinesian features to the music.[3]

While no previous scholars have stated the case quite so pointedly, none of the early twentieth-century French scholars mentioned below disagree with Brunet's point of view.

There is such a variety of music in mainland Southeast Asia that about the only two generalities one may draw are that "all the major genres rely on oral learning rather than notation, and most musics are related to or inspired by some form of theatre."[4] In Cambodia, where music is nearly inseparable from dance and dance drama, both certainly hold true, but there is a third generality which is also valid: to the Khmers, music—unless it is a mere demonstration—is always considered to be an offering to the deities or spirits.

In the temples, for instance, small *pinpeat* orchestras perform music on holidays in exchange for monetary offerings as a means of intercession with the invisible powers. These and all musical performances in Cambodia are expected to maintain the highest possible traditional standard of performance in order to clarify music's deeper meaning and fulfill its offertory function: "a musical performance should be beautiful because, as an ancestral heritage, it is sacred."[5] This appears to be the belief from earliest times.

One indication of the age of Khmer music is suggested by the fact that it is based on a scale of seven equidistant tones, considered by some musicologists to be the lost *gandhara-grama*, or "celestial" scale, mentioned in Sanskrit texts and said to have "returned to Paradise."[6] Although the *gandhara-grama* disappeared in India over a thousand years ago, it remains the basis for much of the music throughout Southeast Asia. Legend attributes it to the *gandharva*, or celestial musicians, who accompany the dances of the *apsaras* in paradise;[7] in Cambodia that is still the case. In the historical period the bas-reliefs of Angkor display a great variety of instruments. Generally speaking, they are grouped into percussion orchestras and string orchestras, with the former accompanying religious or military processions and the latter used for sacred dance and court festivals.[8] Notable among the string instruments is a harp (played by women), which no longer exists in Cambodia today but is the chief accompaniment to the dance as pictured on the walls of Angkor (Fig. 7-1). Nineteenth and early twentieth century illustrations show both female (Fig. 7-2) and male orchestras (7-3, 7-4 and 7-5) accompanied by percussion. Significantly, classical dance performances today use an all-male orchestra. How this reversal came about is not clear.

As for Khmer music today, a musicological analysis would be of great value both to scholars and to the musicians who are now attempting to rebuild the repertoire. Such a study might begin with the preliminary work of Knosp,[9] Danielou,[10] Laloy,[11] and other Europeans, as well as of Khmer[12] and Thai scholars.[13] The best sources for such a study, however, are what remains of the orally transmitted tradition among contemporary Cambodian musicians or recordings made in this century and preserved in French

7-1. **Angkorean Musicians.** Photo Michael Greenhalgh.

7-2. **Cambodian Female Ensemble.** Frank Vincent, *Land of the White Elephant*, 1874.

7-3. **Theatrical performance.** Thomas W. Knox, *The Boy Travellers: Two Youths in a Journey to Siam and Java*, 1880.

7-4. **Cambodian *Pinpeat* Orchestra.**
Photo Paul Cravath.

archives, since virtually all such holdings in the National Conservatory in Phnom Penh were destroyed during the Pol Pot regime.[14] For purposes of the present study we turn initially to a description of the *pinpeat* orchestra and its relationship to the classical dance.

As introduction to his description of Khmer musical instruments, the French musicologist Alain Danielou asserts that

> Cambodian music is polyphonic and it developed complex musical formulas long before the Occident. One finds in it the free use of massive sound effects to create atmosphere and suggest dramatic intensity, while Occidental counterpoint has scarcely freed itself from melodic compulsion. To succeed in obtaining greater freedom in the relations of volumes of sound, the Cambodians used instruments which were admirably adapted to the demands of their polyphony.[15]

These include melodic percussion instruments—particularly xylophones, metallophones and sets of gongs; wind instruments—particularly flutes, reed instruments; drums, tambourines and cymbals. From these, the *pinpeat* orchestra has evolved a standard ensemble of nine instruments (Figs. 7-4, 7-5).

THE *SRALAY*

All instruments in the *pinpeat* ensemble are percussive, save for the *sralay*—a kind of oboe—from which some claim the orchestra takes its name, since in Thai the *sralay* is called *pi nai* and the classical Thai

7-5. *Pinpeat* Orchestra Performing *Rāmker* in Antique Tapestry. *National Museum of Cambodia.* Photo Kent Davis.

orchestra is *pi phat*.[16] Khmer scholars, however, claim that *pin* refers to the ancient harp (*pin*) which formerly led the other instruments (*peat*) but is no longer included in the ensemble. They hold that

> the absence of the *pin* and other string instruments in the makeup of the current orchestra is probably due to the necessity of creating a more powerful musical ambiance than in the past and to accompany the classical dances which required a rhythm that only percussion could provide—aided by the sonorous power of the *sralay*.[17]

This is unpersuasive in light of the fact that harps and other string instruments are seen accompanying the dancers in the bas-reliefs of Angkor with sufficiently "powerful" force, we may presume, to be heard in performance areas that were certainly as large as any used in modern times.

It is more likely that with the demise of the harp tradition in Cambodia, the ensemble accompanying dance simply did without strings but kept the name *pinpeat*, retaining the *sralay*—which appears in numerous Angkorean bas-reliefs[18]—as the featured instrument. Even without the string instruments, any ritual function of the *pinpeat* would have been preserved by the *sralay* which today remains an important ritual instrument: accompanied only by drums, it forms the funeral orchestra (*skor yaul*) and—in a simple bamboo form—is the only wind instrument in both the marriage orchestra and the ensemble used in spirit-mediumship (*phleng arak*).[19]

The *sralay*, which is often called *pey*, is generally made of hard wood—infrequently of ivory—and is about 35 cm. in length (Fig. 7-6). There are two sizes—*touch* (small) and *thom* (large)—but each has six holes; the *sralay thom* is included in the *pinpeat*, although sometimes one of each may be used. The mouthpiece is unique to Cambodia, Laos, and Thailand in that it is comprised of not two, but four rounded reeds of palm leaf or leather in the mouthpiece. This allows the player several octaves using only six finger holes.[20] The *sralay* is played by maintaining a constant wind stream through the instrument during both inhalation and exhalation, in the manner of bagpipes. Like a nineteenth-century *prima donna*, the *sralay* rarely attends rehearsals, appearing only for a performance.

Today the *sralay* remains without question the distinguishing instrument of the *pinpeat* ensemble. Its shrill, piercing sound is strikingly similar to the equally haunting, high-pitched voice of the solo chanter. Together they dance in sound above the soft-toned foundation of the percussive ensemble, with only the metal-keyed *roneat dek* as periodic intermediary. Even the drums defer to the *sralay* and singer in duet, for it is said that in the hands of a master the *sralay* can give the impression of everything in nature.[21] Danielou

7-6. **The Sralay.** *Musique du Cambodge.*

claims that the *sralay* comes from India, from which it can be traced back to Sumer by way of the Persians.[22] Regardless of its lineage, the Khmer form of the instrument is unique to the peninsula where it has accompanied the royal dance and other rituals for at least a thousand years.

THE *SAMPHO*

The instrument which leads the *pinpeat* ensemble is the two-headed drum, the *sampho*, which is itself the object of a cult. Throughout mainland Southeast Asia most musical instruments and particularly those of the royal orchestras are considered to each embody a powerful spirit. As sacred receptacles, they are kept in distant rooms to avoid troubling people.[23] In

Cambodia the most powerful of these spirits resides in the *sampho*, and before each performance—and in brief form before each rehearsal—obeisance is made to the spirits by the offering of candles, food, or flowers, but always incense.

Very strict conventions guide the life of craftsmen constructing musical instruments and particularly the drum-maker. He may not speak, for example, during working hours, and traditionally no one, including his wife or children, may touch him at all until the drum has been completed. Once the drum is placed in an orchestra, each musician begins every performance by placing an offering to its spirit in a prescribed manner on a small tray beside the *sampho* player, who is the master of the ensemble. The purpose of this ritual is to gratify the spirits, to prevent technical errors, and to infuse the musicians with great skill.[24] At the beginning of each rehearsal, dancers also kneel and pay respect to the drum in the same manner as to their masks.

The *sampho* is made from a single hollowed-out block of wood—usually teak—about 48 cm. long, with the right hand end about 24 cm. in diameter and the smaller left end about 22 cm. The right drum head is of ox or goat skin; the left of calf, and both are tightened by leather thongs joining them. Each end has a lacquered circle about 9 cm. in diameter in the center of the drum head on which a "tuning paste" is applied for each performance. Traditionally this paste was of thick, mashed, cooked rice mixed with the ashes of burnt palm fronds. Today the crust-free part of freshly baked, white bread is easier to obtain and easily made into a paste. The thicker the paste, the deeper the drum tone, and a precisely chosen sound is thus obtainable.

The *sampho* is played with both hands as it rests on a special stand (Fig. 7-7), and the player is master of at least eleven different varieties of sound[25] by which the other instruments as well as the dancers are directed. It is the *sampho*, for instance, which, like the *kendang* in the Indonesian *gamelan*, provides all the accents by which the dancers time their movement. Hence, for technical as well as ritualistic reasons, no rehearsal is possible without the *sampho*. Both dancers and orchestra have followed its lead since Angkorean times, and in the hands of a great master it is said to "speak" with an expressiveness which unifies all other performance elements.[26]

THE *SKOR THOM*

In the *pinpeat* orchestra, rhythm and major accents are provided by a pair of large barrel drums with tacked heads of buffalo hide known as *skor thom* (*skor*, drum; *thom*, large). Said to resemble both Arab and Persian drums, the form is unknown in India.[27] They are used both in popular music and to accompany the classical dance. By use of the tuning paste described previously, one drum is given a higher pitch than the other; unlike the *sampho*, they are sounded by use of two bamboo sticks. The *skor* are played only on one surface while supported by a wooden stand (Fig. 7-8). They are usually included in rehearsals because of their basic support of dance movement.

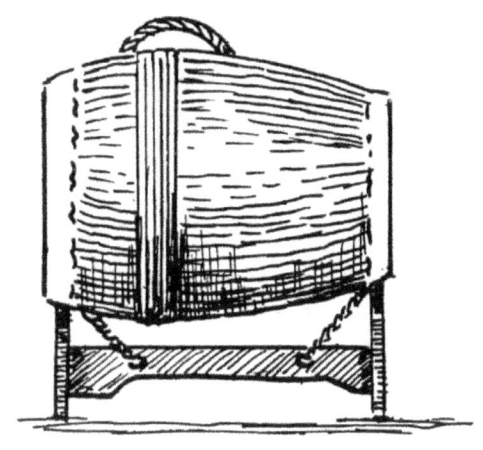

7-7. The *Sampho*. *Musique du Cambodge*.

THE *RONEAT*

There are three forms of *roneat*, or xylophone, included in the *pinpeat*. The first, *roneat ek*, provides an elaborate form of the melody of all songs; it is indispensable to both rehearsal and performance. Thus, the *sampho* drum, the *skor thom* and the *roneak ek* accompany rehearsals, while the other instruments provide depth, embellishment or variety in full performance.

7-8. The *Skor Thom*. *Musique du Cambodge*.

The *roneat ek* is, relatively, a tenor instrument, as distinct from the bass *roneat thom*—also included in the *pinpeat*. It is said to correspond to the *kinnari* xylophone of Bengal,[28] from whence it was imported to Thailand around 1790 and later to Cambodia,[29] but there are Burmese, Chinese and Javanese forms as well.

The *roneat ek* is made of hardwood—usually teak—with twenty-one keys of hardwood (or a special form of bamboo) that are struck with two mallets. The round, flat-ended mallets about 40 cm. long may be either soft or hard depending on the desired tone. A one-octave interval is always maintained between the two keys struck simultaneously by the mallets.[30] The instrument itself is about 120 cm. long, while the keys on each instrument vary from 30 to 40 cms. in length depending on the pitch. Exact tuning is achieved by adding a paste of scraped lead and bees' wax in varying quantities to the underside of the keys. The keys are suspended on cord over a sounding box shaped like a boat, which is often richly carved and inlaid with mother-of-pearl or ivory (Fig. 7-9).

The *roneat ek* is sometimes called *roneat roth* meaning "the *roneat* that runs." Its sound is best when "dizzyingly wild" in the hands of a master, and, regardless of its origins, its graceful, liquid, elaborate precision is identified by most savants as quintessentially Cambodian.

In performance the *roneat ek* is counterbalanced by the second *roneat*, the *roneat thom* or "bass" *roneat*. This instrument is somewhat broader and of a slightly different shape and has only sixteen keys made of hard wood (Fig. 7-10). It is played in the same manner as the *roneat ek*, with the exception of the fact that only soft-ended mallets are used. The keys are thicker and longer than those of the *roneat ek*—ranging from 42 cm. for notes of deepest pitch to 34 cm. for the highest. Also known as the *roneat thoung*, it plays the basic melody in simpler form than the *roneat ek*, variously braking or stimulating the pace of that lead instrument. The *roneat thom* "plays broadly and leisurely by duplicating, anticipating, retarding, hesitating, or syncopating the principal melody in a hide-and-seek fashion, using sometimes broad skips of large intervals and sometimes moving in conjunct degrees."[31] Two

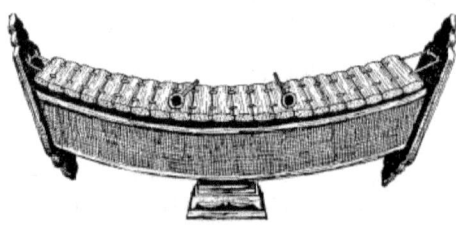

7-9. **The Roneat Ek.** *Musique du Cambodge.*

sizes of *roneat thom* are distinguished in Cambodia, the *roneat thom thom* (large) and the *roneat thom tauch* (small); both are used in the *pinpeat* simultaneously on occasion.

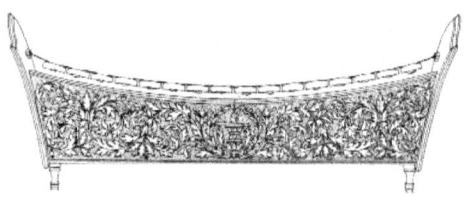

7-10. The Roneat Thom. *Musique du Cambodge.*

The third *roneat* in the *pinpeat* ensemble has twenty-one steel keys and produces the same scale as the *roneat ek*. It is called *roneat dek*. Because of its construction, the metallic sound is thinner and more piercing than the *roneat ek*. Similarly, however, two sets of buffalo-hide mallets are used to produce either a hard or soft tone. The *roneat dek*, unlike the other *roneat*, is not shaped like a boat, but is more or less a tapered rectangle 104 cm. long. The keys vary from 30 to 35 cm. in length and overhang the sounding box on both sides. The manner of playing the instrument is identical to that of the *roneat ek*, but its musical part is more sedate and "neutral" than the other *roneat*. It proceeds in a regular and precise manner to carefully mark each beat and requires a very steady player.[32]

THE *KONG*

An essential element of most Southeast Asian percussion ensembles is a circle of knobbed gongs known in Cambodia as *kong*, of which there are two forms—*kong thom* (large) and *kong tauch* (small); one of each is included in the *pinpeat* orchestra. This instrument is unknown in India and appears to belong to the earliest strata of Southeast Asian music. The *kong* is pictured in the bas-reliefs of Angkor Wat in a portable and upright form (Fig. 7-11).

The contemporary *kong* are each made of sixteen inverted, bowl-shaped gongs decreasing in size from left to right and suspended 30 cm. off the ground in a circular rattan frame about 120 cm. across (Fig. 7-12). The gongs, made of a brass alloy, are played by a player seated in the center—one mallet, with either a hard or soft leather end, in each hand. The musician must be very agile in his rotation and is often required to strike the exact

7-11. The *Kong in Angkor Wat Bas-Relief.*
Photo Michael Greenhalgh.

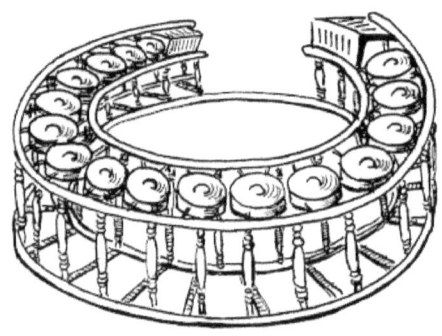

7-12. The *Kong. Musique du Cambodge.*

raised center of numerous gongs in a very rapid, gliding sequence. The effect is one of continuous sound interrupted by tremolo.

The gongs of the *kong thom* range in size from 16 cm. to 12 cm. (for the highest tone) and are tuned with the same wax substance as the *roneat.* The smaller gongs of the *kong tauch*, ranging in size from 13 cm. to 9 cm., are one octave higher in pitch than the *kong thom,* and its third gong duplicates the eighth gong of the *kong thom.*

The *kong thom* plays the principal melody in all musical accompaniment, which is elaborated upon by the *roneat ek* and by the *sralay* and supported by the *kong tauch.* In general, the *kong* are instruments that support and steady the ensemble, while their "trembling, metallic tone strengthens the more hollow sonority of the *roneat*"[33] and blends the *sralay* into the orchestral unity.

The *Chhing* and *Khrab*

The actions of the dancers which require special emphasis, such as martial walking, battles, or when miming choral chants, are accented by the *chhing*, a pair of small cymbals 6 cm. in diameter, made of thick iron or brass (Fig. 7-13). Their sound is considered to be "dry." Short, crisp clicks alternate with long, vibrating rings to mark the down and up beat of the music and set the rhythm for both singers and orchestra. One pair is included in the *pinpeat* ensemble.

Fulfilling basically the same function as the *chhing* are the sets of short, flat bamboo "clackers" used by the chorus to keep the rhythm during rehearsals when the *chhing* is not present. These are the *khrab* and provide such splendid cracks of emphasis that the chorus often uses several pair of them in performance.

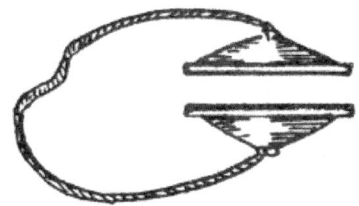

7-13. **The *Chhing*.** *Musique du Cambodge.*

This concludes the description of the nine basic instruments comprising the *pinpeat* orchestra. Variations on these nine occur from time to time; for example, both sizes of the *roneat thom* can be included and even other instruments can be used. A 1911 account, for example, described the *pinpeat* as including two *sangna* drums—a part of the Thai *pi phat*—and a *khloy*, or flute.[34] Parenthetically, bowed string instruments (the *tro*) are never included because they cannot blend with the roneat. Basically, then, the *pinpeat* is a stable ensemble in the form described.

REHEARSAL MELODIES

Enumerating the *phleng pinpeat*, or tunes performed by the *pinpeat* orchestra, is a confusing affair since many pieces mentioned by earlier writers are not remembered by current performers and there is often uncertainty as to whether various pieces belong to the *pinpeat*, to other musical ensembles, or to neither. In 1911 Moura was told by one of the chief musicians in Norodom's court that the "modern" orchestra knew two hundred ancient tunes.[35] A list of 271 song titles prepared in the 1960s by the Université des Beaux-Arts and supposedly performable by the *pinpeat* (Appendix IV), is of little value in clarifying the repertoire, since each title is in French and none correspond to the brief description of the thirty-eight Khmer titles which follow and are known to have been included in dance drama performances of recent years.

To begin a catalogue of the *pinpeat* repertoire, we shall first consider five well-known melodies which are a part of all rehearsal exercises for the roles of prince and princess. All dancers and musicians know these tunes which give form to a fairly standardized rehearsal routine (see Chapter VIII). Simultaneously we will note the ways in which these five function in performance. Next we will consider the general musical structure of entrance and exit music which is largely dependent on these five, in conjunction with several others. Finally in this section, the remaining known melodies—with descriptions whenever possible of their function in the main body of the dance—will be enumerated in alphabetical order. In most cases the term "*phleng*" ("melody" or "music") which precedes each name has been omitted for convenience. Examples of usage are drawn primarily from the traditional performance of *Rāmker* scenes as a kind of standard;[36] variations on these patterns are numerous.

The following discussion is premised on a formal distinction between "pure dance" and "expressive dance." (This distinction is simply taken for granted by Cambodians, who appear to have no Khmer terms denoting the difference.) According to Chheng Phon, pure dance is that which has no sung accompaniment; by contrast, if words are chanted, then the dancer is involved in performing those words and, hence, performing expressive dance. When any section of expressive dance is finished, it is always followed by a section of pure dance to show that the former is completed and well done. For example, when the central dance and choral chant in the Robam Tewet have been completed, there is a short pure dance section which is either *cha* or *banchok*.

The five musical sections accompanying all male-female role rehearsals—monkeys and *yakkha* use others—are *cha*, *banchok*, *chut*, *smeu* and *lia*. *Cha* (*cha*) is a melody used in rehearsal of the *roeung* for "expressing sentiments," according to Chheng Phon, but in performance it is also one of the primary entrance accompaniments as well as an accompaniment for pure dance segments. It can be fast or slow throughout, or change from fast to slow or vice versa; there may be a number of sections, each of a different speed, but together they comprise *cha*. *Banchok* (*panchuh*) is a more rapid melody also used for pure dance segments. In rehearsals the *banchok* may be very long, whereas in performance it is a short segment for aesthetic display only.

A third piece of rehearsal music which plays a double role in performance is the *chut* (joeta), a confusing term in that there are several forms of *chut* all known by the same name. In rehearsals *chut* accompanies the postures of flying. In performance it is one of the possible melodies accompanying both entrances and exits. *Phleng chut* (known sometimes as *phleng doeur*) may also accompany travel or pursuit to or from a distant locale—including, logically, an exit or entrance. *Chut* is used, for instance, when Rām approaches Sitā (from afar) in disguise, when the armies of Rām and Rāb separately depart, or even when the armies approach each other for battle.

The *smeu* (smi), meaning "equal" or "united," is a melody which accompanies walking but only in relatively familiar circumstances such as the palace, garden, or village. As Sitā, Rām, and Laks pass through the forest in exile, for instance, the *smeu* melody initially indicates that they are peacefully "at home." Smeu is used for the entrances and progressions of principal characters, whether prince, princess, monkey, or, *yakkha*, and there is only one *smeu* for all. *Smeu* is also identified with the locale changes of groups of characters either by exit or re-entrance or by a simple walk round the stage. It is definitely used for locale changes of the king (because he is always surrounded by a group) and may be used—among a variety of options—for the movement of other groups. There are no words to *smeu*.

The fifth piece of music known by all dancers as a standard rehearsal element is *phleng lia* (la) used for exits of both solo characters and groups. It is a slow and consistent melody, as opposed to the two other, more rapid tunes which may accompany exits, *rua* (see below) and *chut*.

MUSICAL STRUCTURE OF ENTRANCES AND EXITS

In the Khmer *lakhon*, the musical structure accompanying any dance is flexible, in that various introductions and exit pieces may be used. The number of "paragraphs" of that music may also vary, thus affecting overall length. (Decisions regarding such selections are made by the manager of the troupe prior to each performance.) The five melodies we have so far considered are known by all dancers familiar with the standardized rehearsal sequences. Before examining how these five are used within a performance structure, we must add several other names to the list of entrance and exit melodies.

Nowhere are the problems of transcription more critical than in the titles of Khmer melodies, and, among them, none are so confusing as the four apparently separate melodies of *ro* (rowa), *reo* (re'wa), *rua* (rwa), and *riey* (raya), together with their variant forms. *Ro* literally means "unrolling." It accompanies the appearance of a new and important person, fact, or action in a scene, and it is used to indicate a character's magical transformation. There are three forms of *ro* whose use is dependent upon the importance of the character or action being accompanied. The three are *ro samealea* used to indicate those of greatest importance, *ro phat* for those of secondary importance, and *ro tauch* used to mark changes in the choreography or to underline the development of a new though ordinary action.

The subtlety in usage of *ro* can be very revealing. For instance, only *ro tauch* is used in the *Rāmker*. When Rāb enters—clearly an important character—*ro samealea* would theoretically be used. However, Rāb's shady intentions, combined with the mood of peaceful repose surrounding Rām, Sitā, and Laks, cause the less tumultuous *ro tauch* to be preferred. Another instance in which we see the same pattern is when Rām brandishes his great bow to shoot the golden deer. The hero's arrows are not able to even wound the magical animal, and to underline Rām's impotence, the ordinary *ro tauch* accompanies the scene. In brief, then, *ro tauch* underscores heightened momentary actions of transformation, anger or recollection.[37] Chheng Phon has also said, however, that *ro* is used as an exit tune which builds to a relatively high pitch at the moment of departure and is used especially for the *kennari* bird roles. As an exit tune, it is to be clearly distinguished from the exit music known as *phleng reo*.

The *reo* melody used to accompany exits is of a faster tempo than the cha with which it is often conjoined. If both cha and reo are used together at an exit, *reo* must follow *cha*. There is another melody of specific function which may be related to the reo. This is known as *chongka reo* (cankahriawa) and is the music which accompanies the Tep Manorom.[38] One source says that *chongka reo* (which may have the meaning of "slender hips") can accompany with stylistic variations—a dispute, a recollection, or a walk in the forest or garden.[39] It is used, for example, when Rām and Laks are collecting fruit and flowers for Sitā. As noted earlier, the *chongka reo* can also be included in the *buong suong* ritual dance.

The melodies of *rua* and *riey* are two common pieces of introductory music in general usage. If four pieces of dance are to be performed, four different introductions will be used, for example, *rua*, *riey*, *smeu*, and *chut*. No single introduction is prescribed for a given dance, and the manager will decide what pieces should be used in each situation. *Rua* is used to indicate a change of locale and to "change the choreography," according to Chheng Phon. *Riey* is used to accompany descriptive narrative sung by the chanters.

Dramatic Structure of Entrances and Exits

The reason for extended concern over entrance or introductory music, and exit music is because such sequences are of comparatively long duration and flashiness and fulfill a specific ritual function. Furthermore, they are clearly separated from the main body of the dance by the kneeling gesture of respect known as *sampeah*, thus creating an overall dance structure of entrance sequence / main dance / exit sequence. The divisions are made in all the dances by all the dancers forming ranks, kneeling, and with fluid grace, placing their palms together in front of forehead, throat, and heart. This gesture, the *sampeah*, is directed toward the god or gods, the spirits, the *kru*, the king, the *sampho*, the audience, or all together, depending on the occasion and one's interpretation (Fig. 7-14).

In this way a classical dance is framed by both the *sampeah* and by a general pattern of the melodies we have examined thus far (Fig. 7-15).

7-14. The *Sampeah*. Royal Cambodia Ballet

It must be emphasized that other melodies may be substituted and variations of this pattern do occur, but this is the general contour of the *robam* and of many segments of the dramatic works as well.

Instances of entrance/exit structure given by Chheng Phon do not all conform to the above model, and to quote at length from his comments will be the easiest method of discerning the conventions.

For one dance, different introductions and endings can be used. For example, in Tewet they can choose *rua* for the introduction and then, after the main dance, play *smeu* or chut for the ending. But if the main piece is slow, the production will be fast and the ending will be at least faster than the main section.

> After the final *sampeah*, then, they play *cha* or *reo* or both, and then *lia*, *chut* or *ro*—only one; these are the three possible exit musics. At the end of a section of music, the dancer may give a signal to indicate which piece is to follow; for example, after *cha* they may do *reo* or choose *chut*, *lia* or *ro*. Both dancer and musician know when the *cha* is finished—for example, because they completed one hundred beats or a given number of 'paragraphs' even though they may also have improvised within them— and the signal is only to indicate what is to follow.[40]

ENTRANCE		BODY OF DANCE		EXIT		
(One only) rua chut riéy smeu	S A M P E A H		S A M P E A H	(One or both) cha réo	(One only) lia chut

7-15. The General Entrance-Exit Structure of Dances.

The subtleties of the signals mentioned above cannot be described within the scope of the present study except to say that, in general, there is a three-way system of signals between dancer, musician and singer, with major signals passed verbally from the chorus leader to the *sampho* master, whose drum indicates to all others the next sequence. For dancers' movements within a section—for example, when they begin to walk around in the long entrance and exit patterns described below—there is no signal at all; the dancers simply must know when to do this, and it is not an easy thing. As Chheng Phon said about the inexperienced student dancers at UBA, "They don't know when to begin, and they exit before the music is done. They don't know the rhythms so they just go out."

Pinpeat Melodies

1. *Phleng aut* is a tune of sadness and anguish used, for example, to express Sitā's sorrow and despair while imprisoned at Lanka. It is often transcribed as *ott*.
2. *Baloem* is the name of a sung melody, mentioned by Chheng Phon, corresponding to a tune of the same name.
3. *Baolut* (pauluta) is a very slow, sacred tune associated with goddesses. Together with the *Preah Thong* melody, it is included in the *tep robam* ritual, a dance to the *deva*. (See also "*Sarabarom*" below.) In general, music for the sacred dances is said by Chheng Phon to be different from other classical dance music, but it is not clear in what manner it differs.
4. *Preah bathum* (padhama) is the tune offered to the *kru* of the monkey roles.
5. *Chet choeng* (jet jhina) is a tune for inviting the spirit of the *tevoda* to be present and, according to Chheng Phon, includes *kraw nak* and *khlom*. It is also used to suggest pastoral settings, especially underwater scenes or frolics in water. *Chet choeng* comprises the whole of the aquatic Sovann Machha-Hanumān dance, which may be long or short depending on the choreography selected. Like

virtually all pieces of music, the length of *chet choeng* in performance is determined by repetition of sections or of the entire piece but must retain its various segments in a fixed order.

Chet choeng may also be used for Manimekhala in the sequence *smeu*, chant, *chet choeng*, and *chut*. For both Manimekhala and Sovann Machha the music is virtually the same, but because the first takes place in the sky and the second in water, the music is given a different emphasis in each, particularly by the drums. At the same time the dance movement in the two pieces reflects the different media as well.

The problem of transcriptions without reference to Khmer spelling allows no indication as to whether another tune of similar name is related to *chet choeng*. That melody is the *chet chean*, or *damnoeur yut* said to accompany slow, cautious movements such as Rām's pursuit of the golden deer.[41]

6. *Chhakry*, or *damnoeur en an*, is a melody used for alluring, swaying coquetry. The song describes the movement, words, and advances made by Rāb to seduce Sitā.

7. *Phleng chhung* is a piece of music used to create an ambiance of stealth or to indicate a ruse. It may be used, for instance, when Rāb is disguised as the *eysei*.

8. *Chin lomphat* is a tune known to have accompanied an "original dance" (see Chapter VI) with lyrics written for the occasion (14 August 1943).

9. *Chos touk*, "embarkation," describes the feeling of sadness at departure, as when Sitā waits in the jungle for the return of Rām.

10. The music known as *éopang* (qewapā"na) was said by Chheng Phon to be included in the *cha* of Robam Tewet, the central section of the dance.

11. One Khmer scholar lists *kbak* as a melody showing joy, irony, or light, hasty movement, as when Rām happily goes to find Sitā after his victory over Rāb.[42] More than likely *kbak* is a specific usage of *kbach* (kpa'ca) or "movement" as discussed below.

12. *Khlom* (khluma), together with *kraw nai*, may be included in *chat choeng*, at least when that music is invoking spirits.
13. The title of the melody, *khmer thbanh*, or "Khmer weaver," is used in the *Rāmker* and other contexts to accompany grief—for example, when Rām experiences Sitā's loss. The melody has no words.
14. All that is presently known of *konsai* is that there are two forms—one short and one long—and the dances for each are different.
15. *Kraw nai* (kraunai) is the music traditionally offered to the *kru* of the *yakkha* roles for ritual purposes, and in performance the identification with giants continues. It is used, for instance, during the tumultuous preparations and subsequent procession of Rāb's army.
16. *Kraw nak* (kraunaka) is part of *chat choeng* and is used to accompany Rām's review of his troops.
17. The Robam Lao or "Laotian Ballet" is accompanied by *lomphat phay*, at least as performed on 24 September 1974, according to the palace programs.
18. The melody known as *o pileap* is a song of sadness and despair that accompanies Sitā's captivity.
19. *Phoumea doeur yut* is a slow, elegant Burmese melody of graceful tempo used to show Sitā's admiration for the beautiful golden deer and her desire to have it.
20. *Phleng phleh* (phlia) is the music offered to the *eysei* in *sampeah kru* (see Chapter IX).
21. *Ponhea dour* is a gay melody that marks, for example, the happy ending of the *Rāmker*.
22. *Preah thong* (brah thona) is the melody described in Chapter VI under the drama of the same name and is reputedly of other-worldly origin. It is part of the *tep robam* ritual as an offering to the *kru*.
23. *Prathom*—probably a variant of *preah bathom* (brah padhama)—can be used for the assemblage and procession of Rām's army of monkeys.

24. The melody of *sarabarom* (sārahpārama) is included in the *robam* of the same name, one of the seven more sacred dances of the repertoire. Chheng Phon cited this music and that of *baolut* as two examples of melodies that the Thai previously sang. They are "transcribed in books" but have not been danced in Thailand "for twenty-five years" (as of 1975) and are unknown by contemporary Thai dancers. His point is that some segments of the classical dance repertoire have actually been better preserved in Cambodia than in Thailand where the ritual significance of the *robam* was nowhere as great.
25. *Salamar* is "considered to be an example of old military music and is used in accompanying battle scenes,"[43] particularly in the *Rāmker*. The piece is comprised of two parts—the first for saluting the guardian deities and personal preparation for battle; the second is a quicker rhythm accompanying the battle itself. The instrumentation is very simple, consisting of the *skor* drums and solo *sralay*. The music is often called *sarama* (sārama"), or *prayuth*, or *preah yuth* (brah yūtha). Chheng Phon described it (together with *ĕopang*) as being part of the *cha* segment of Robam Tewet. Whether it is often used in non-martial situations is not clear.
26. *Simun* (simiana) is a Thai name used for a piece of music included, for instance, in the Vong Sovann story (along with *reo*, *banchok* and *lia*). Its general function is not clear.
27. *Sinuon* is the melody used in the Robam Bach Phkar Chuon Par, "The Dance of Tossing Flowers," and is also the tune used to accompany the *kennara* and *kennari*, male and female bird-human creatures appearing in the Anurudh story and elsewhere.
28. *Phleng svaa* is the music which accompanies the monkey roles. Phuong Phan says that there are twelve kinds of this music but they are unnamed.[44]
29. *Phleng trak* (traka') is the primary music for *yakkha* roles and belongs to a general group of tunes called *phleng cham* (bhlena

cham), suggesting an identification with and possible origin in Champa, the ancient kingdom to the east of Cambodia. During *phleng trak*, other characters who may be onstage—even, for example, during the *sampeah kru* ceremony—display fear at the power of the *yakkha*.

In addition to the melodies described above, we should note that the components of the choreography known as *kbach* are often called by the same name as the music which accompanies them. Thus a number of *kbach* whose names are known, more than likely indicate melodies that should be added to the present list. Thiounn, for instance, mentions *pathum* in the "Dance of the Nagas"; *krut* in the "dance of the Garudas"; *pream chol* and *pream chenh* (royal entrance and exit); *preah reach damnoeur* (royal march); *kreas ram* (joyous dance); *sen sra* (wine offering); the *kbach trak*, which, in addition to what we have already mentioned, accompanies magical incantations; and *kbach mul*, a general movement cadence for gods and princes.[45]

THE CHANTERS

The chorus of chanters comprise—together with the musicians and dancers—one of the three primary performance elements of Khmer dance drama. With rare exceptions, they sing all "dialogue" transpiring between the characters, who, in turn, mime the choral chant. In general, the chant is a slow, high-pitched song interfused with the *sralay* and presented by a female chorus of elder, former dancers among whom the voice of a soloist is prominent.

The chorus sings either descriptive narrative or the words being expressed by a dancer through movement. The chants range in length from fifteen seconds to two minutes in contemporary *Rāmker* productions for instance (see Appendix III). In the case of characters' sung "speeches," the chorus usually sings for only one character per scene. (Scenes are differentiated by the entrance or exit of a major character.) Only in a climactic or highly confrontational scene does the chorus sing the words of one character followed immediately by the words of a second, and then—as in the case of Rāb's attempted seduction of Sitā at Lanka—each character "speaks" only once per scene.

Thus, there is no real dialogue in the sense of back-and-forth in any scene. As for the dancers themselves, they never utter a word in the *robam* and only infrequently speak briefly in the dramas. The *aria*-like choral chants are virtually the only form of verbal expression in Khmer dance drama.

Cœdès contends that originally the *robam* were accompanied solely by choral chants and that the introduction of an orchestra can be dated only from the nineteenth century."[46] While he cites no evidence for the claim, it may be noted that the chorus and orchestra do not perform together. Only the *chhing*, the *sralay*, and the *sampho* (or the *sralay* with a single, soft *roneat*) accompany the chorus. The complete orchestra gives the chorus an introduction and briskly takes over when they finish, but there is little integration of the two. This tends to support Cœdès' claim and to explain the close relationship between the chorus and the ancient *sralay* and *sampho*—a relationship that is not shared with the other, seemingly newer percussion instruments.

Traditionally, the soloist of the chorus reads the scenario from a text, phrase by phrase, with the chorus following her lead. The text is in verse, seven syllables to the line, and the hand-copied book itself is considered to hold the spirit of the *kru*, thus precluding examination by the uninitiated. An 1883 observer wrote that the chorus leader, or "*neak boc bat*," sat in front of the chours at a small lectern.[47] This does not seem to be the case today, since the soloist is nearly undifferentiated except by her earlier entrance into each opening musical phrase.

Customarily the chorus is seated at a right angle to the musicians. In Chanchhaya Pavilion the chorus members were seated at floor level on the east side facing the king (Fig. 7-16). The soloist, also known as *srey ambat*, sat among them on the central mat.

The soloist is not necessarily the oldest or most experienced chanter; rather, the best voice leads the others. In the 1970s that was clearly Em Theay, who had been given the title "Lady with Flower-sweet Voice" by the king. She used the text of her mother, Prom Sokhom, who also sat in the chorus.

In 1970 Brunet wrote that "a doubtful modernism has now led to a reduction in the number of singers and the replacement of half of them by men."[48] In attempting to restore the traditional chorus for recordings which he made for UNESCO, the royal troupe used three soloists: Neak Neang Samneang Dantrey, Prom Sokhom and Em Kunthear Theay. As of 1975 no male singers were in evidence in the national troupe, and at UBA, as well, an exclusively female chorus was the standard.

CHOREOGRAPHY IN THE DANCE DRAMA

Khmer Choreography

There are five main areas of choreography that may be fruitfully examined in describing the style of classical Cambodian dance, without recourse to dance notation or entering into the realm of ethnochoreology. These are *kbach* (kpā'ca) or standard mime "poses," the hand gestures, the portrayal of emotions, floor patterns, and the general style of body movement. A brief prelude regarding origins begins the discussion.

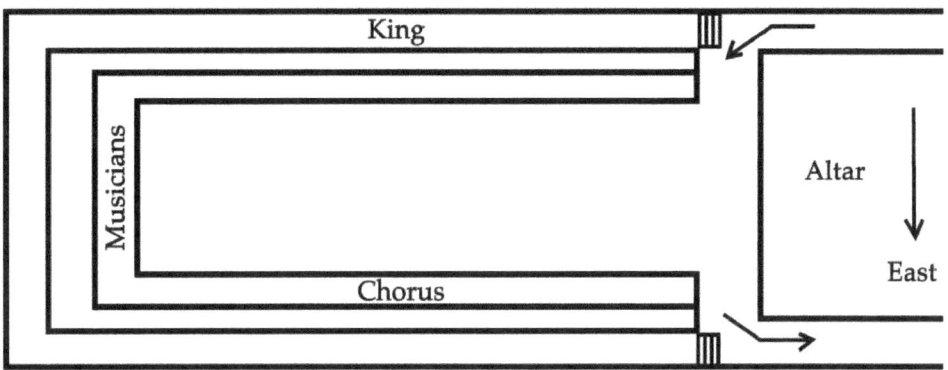

7-16. Chorus Placement in Chanchhaya. *Illustration Kristen Tuttle.*

Cambodian scholars seem somewhat ambivalent on the relationship between Khmer dance and any possible Indian ancestor. On the one hand, Phuong Phan has claimed that, while the Indian *Natyasastra* does not mention it by name, there used to be an Indian *apsaras* dance. It is known only from unspecified legends concerning Shiva, and from this form, some believe, Khmer dance is derived.[49]

Far more persuasive are Phan's contrasting claims on the basis of his training in both Khmer and Indian dance, that

> the main characteristics, the movement, the aesthetic, the beauty of the *apsaras* dance does not exist in India, nor does the form of the Cambodian *apsaras* appear in Indian art or architecture. The *Natyasatra*'s description of a woman's movement is not relevant to Cambodia where the levels of foot-work, the postures, walk, gestures and behavior are expressed differently and according to the feeling of Southeast Asian people.[50]

Unless actual similarities in the dances of Cambodia and India can be demonstrated, we must conclude that Khmer dance evolved from indigenous roots to fulfill local functions. At the present time, assignation of an Indian origin cannot be shown for any aspect of Khmer dance, particularly the choreographic elements. The following discussion of *kbach* and *mudrā* will further develop this thesis.

The *Kbach*

Throughout this chapter, a distinction is made between "pure dance" and "expressive dance." The latter refers to those segments of the performance accompanied by the chorus, when the dancers are basically illustrating the song through movement. "Pure dance" segments, i.e., without choral accompaniment, are the context for the *kbach*, or the frequent, static poses— briefly held—which form the structure of the "pure dance" segments of Khmer *lakhon*. The word *kbach* refers to the whole body posture and should never be translated as "mime," since the images rarely hold denotative value. There are a great many *kbach* of standard composition but whether the number is finite has been much debated. Phan, for instance, says that there are "more than a hundred—or a thousand." George Groslier claimed in 1929 that there were 1,165 principal attitudes.[51] Teachers at UBA in 1975 said they had "heard" that there were sixty-eight body positions but seemed to have no real interest in the matter.

The confusion as to the number of *kbach* derives from varying views on their origin. Those who believe the *kbach* constitute a virtual language or mimed, denotative gesture—as in Indian *kathakali* dance, for instance—have attempted to enumerate a vast number of specific poses, together with their "meanings." Groslier's claim that these number 1,165, however, simply cannot be verified. Nuon Kan, the head of the Classical Dance faculty at UBA, has pointed out—with a pleasing sense of accommodation—that this number may have "historic value," but that today the number is greatly reduced.[52]

The suggestion that there are sixty-eight body poses comes from the modern Thai tradition which recognizes sixty-eight specific, named poses constituting the "alphabet of Thai dancing."[53] Many are similar to the Khmer. The Thai, however, say that there are a "great many" other movements, and that the names given by teachers to specific figures were "merely to help the students in inventing the appropriate movements and gestures by themselves, according to the injunction 'Dance with your head'."[54]

The notion that *kbach* can be enumerated is simply inaccurate. Selected poses may be frequently used and even named, but each teacher and choreographer will prefer certain *kbach* and use them within an innumerable flow of other unnamed gestures according to their own memory and interpretation of the tradition. That is why today few photographs of Khmer *kbach* are even recognized—much less approved—by Thai teachers. Names which have been appended to *kbach* are for the purpose of stimulating the students' feeling in the preparatory moments. According to Dhanit Yupho, the dean of Thai classical dance, to teach dancers only poses or the names of poses is "training their memory more than their imagination."[55]

Nonetheless, there are a number of *kbach* which maintain a standardized form despite a great flexibility at the hands of a choreographer. One, for instance, is called "looking at Preah Chan" (the moon). Of this,

Phuong Phan says "I know elements of movement in order to compose, but the *kbach* I have to guess at a bit. Maybe it starts this way, maybe this other way, but it will still end up to be 'looking at the moon'."[56]

The *kbach* are only the major poses or positions which comprise the dance; transitional movements between them are the prerogative of the choreographer. The *kbach* are the vehicle for expressing beauty and are considered in most cases to have no inherent meaning. Different teachers call the same *kbach* by different names, and the names are poetically descriptive rather than analytical. The "snake playing with its tail," for instance, is used to indicate flying. Others include "the peacock spreads its tail" and "fish gliding by the riverbank."[57] These sensuous images are as much guides to the dancer's inner feeling as they are specific choreographic movements.

The term *kbach* refers to an entire body position. Expressive dance, performed during choral narration, as well as the standardized patterns of portraying emotions, generally do not include *kbach*.

The manner in which pure dance is structured by the *kbach* can be seen in the hypothetical sequence shown in Figure 7-17. In the first six pictures a dancer of female roles demonstrates a variety of postures which could occur while walking, depending on the type of character, the plot, and so forth. These are only transitional movements with no "meaning" or name. In the seventh picture (bottom left), the dancer is pointing, or exclaiming, or challenging, as the case may be; in the eighth she takes flight; and in the ninth she is poised in mid-air in the culmination of the *kbach* which is recognizable as the hallmark of the character Mekhala. The earlier transitional poses flow into one another, but in the last, more dramatic pose, the *kbach* is completed and momentarily held.

The word *kbach* also means "cadence" and, as in English, implies both a rhythmic sequence as well as the actual beat or tempo. Thus the word *kbach* refers to various poses, to specific sequences of movement, and to the music which accompanies or compels them. In this latter sense there are said to be basically two *kbach*, the slow and delicate *kbach cha* and the faster *kbach banchok*. These are general classifications of music, and there are many examples of each. *Kbach roenvull* refers to an additional group of music selections, all of which are comparatively slow and are considered to be the best for dancer training.[58]

We conclude this section by noting that Phuong Phan has said each of the dance *kbach* has a name. By contrast Chheng Phon says that in Cambodian dance "there is no name for each gesture although such an intellectualization did take place in Thailand."[59] The two statements are contradictory only at the semantic level because the dance, which, in the words of one analyst, is characterized by "the contrast of the dynamic and static elements,"[60] has a vast vocabulary of momentarily static poses—the *kbach*—as well as innumerable other gestures of mime and movement bearing no name. Thus, Khmer dance can be likened to a wave-like sequence of expanding and contracting energy in which only a select number of the expansive, static moments are given descriptive names. These are the *kbach*, and they are the structural elements of the pure dance sequences.

THE HAND GESTURES

Heretofore, scholars have used the Sanskrit term *mudrā* in reference to perhaps the most distinguishing feature of Khmer dance movement, the hand gestures. This is extremely misleading, because it implies a link to Indian dance *mudrā* which in many cases form an actual language of denotative gesture. Nothing could be farther from the truth in Khmer dance, in which the often-elaborate mime, including standardized forms of portraying the emotions, are largely accomplished with only four basic hand positions. To illustrate a particular sentiment in expressive dance, these four are used in conventionalized ways, but in pure dance sequences, the same gestures are simply the way the hands are held during a particular temporal unit. One of the four basic hand gestures, for example, almost always signals the end of the dance, as we shall see. Consequently, the word *mudrā* will not be used in the subsequent discussion except to note immediately the probable origin of the four basic Khmer dance hand gestures.

Mudrā, which is today identified with Indian and Buddhist iconography as well as with Indian dance, actually dates from pre-historic

322 *Earth in Flower*

7-17. Transitional Movements and *Kbach*. Photo Paul Cravath.

times in Southeast Asia and certainly from the pre-Vedic in India. Dale Saunders describes *mudrā* as the "primitive gesture of the exorcist" which even today remains "the sign of a pact, of a solemn contract which binds the officiant to the world of the divinity and which permits him to become integrated into this world."[61] The *mudrā* is a seal which fixes the magic of a rite, and in Tantric practice is identified particularly with divine, feminine energy. One feels quite clearly that Khmer hand gestures in pure dance sequences retain this original function of being a bond held firmly between the forces of the physical universe and the dancer's inner world.

In Khmer dance, hand gestures are very limited in number, whereas in Indian dance they have become a virtual sign language, due in part, no doubt, to the Indian propensity for elaboration. The two traditions should not be unfairly associated, and all effort should be made to avoid, for instance, calling a particular Khmer hand gesture a *brahmara mudrā* simply because it somewhat resembles a gesture of that name used in north Indian *kathak* dance.

On close examination, not a single hand gesture in Khmer dance is identical with those of Indian dance, a point which is acknowledged but thereafter ignored in Jeanne Cuisinier's major study of Khmer hand gestures—a study which insists upon an Indian origin and assigns Indian names to Khmer gestures.[62] This compulsion to interpret Southeast Asian phenomena through an Indian vocabulary is a colonial vestige discussed in Chapter I; by contrast, the subsequent discussion will describe Khmer dance hand gestures and other movements solely from the Cambodians' view of their meaning and function.

The basic Khmer hand gestures derive from nature images, according to one male teacher at UBA, whose discourse on the matter brought all the chorus and dancers present to close attention. He spoke with calm, strong, and persuasive authority, but, unfortunately, due to the chaotic period and the fact that this man was not known to the translator, his name is unknown. No Khmer scholar consulted since has denied his interpretation, however; nor, in fairness, has anyone declared it exclusively correct. The essence of his lecture is included herein as the interpretation which best conforms to other data regarding the form and function of Khmer dance.

According to the UBA instructor, Khmer choreography originated as an imitation of natural forces. The positions of standing are from the undulation of water, music comes from the sounds of nature and animals, dance movements come from the trees which are represented by the dancer's body. The four gestures in which her hands continually appear during "pure dance" sections are the leaf, flower, tendril, and fruit of a plant (Fig. 7-18), and there is no moment of the dance—save for on-stage "relaxation"—when the hands are not held in one of the four signs. These are not to be viewed too strictly as images connoting nature, however, since they are felt to add beauty rather than meaning to the dance. They are, in a sense, a dance unto themselves.

In addition to that function, hand gestures are used in three other ways on the Khmer stage in the expressive dance segments of performance (Fig. 7-19). In expressive dance, which comprises about 50 percent of a performance, the dancer illustrates the feeling—and, to a lesser extent, the meaning—of the choral chants. First, her four primary gestures may take on specific denotative value when used in a particular configuration or context. The leaf held above the eye, for instance, indicates weeping; held low on the chest, it indicates sadness; near the heart shows anger; near the ear is extreme anger; and resting on the chest indicates shyness or modesty. To put the flower low on the chest implies "me" or "I," while holding it under the mouth indicates a smile, even though the face remains neutral and nearly empty of expression. When both hands appear in the fruit gesture, it will be only moments before the second finger snaps off the thumb—as though the fruit had fallen or the dance reached fruition—and the final *sampeah* and end of the dance will follow shortly.

Second, the four primary hand gestures are integrated into full body positions and movements having standardized forms and meaning. All such gestures will be described in subsequent discussion by the term "conventionalized movements," among which Khmer teachers specifically delineate "the emotions" (Fr.: *les sentiments*), which will be discussed below. A further example of the conventionalization, however, is that the change

7-18. The Basic Khmer Hand Gestures. *Nokor Khmer.*

from one gesture to another has significance. When telling someone to go, for instance, the hand gesture changes from flower to leaf; when calling someone, the gesture changes from leaf to flower. Often in expressive dance, then, the four primary hand gestures are simply exquisite ornaments to conventionalized patterns of mimed expression.

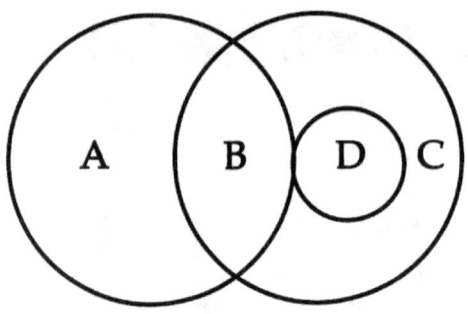

7-19. Classification of Khmer Hand Gestures.

Circle A: The Four Primary Hand Gestures with Connotative Meaning (Pure Dance);
Area B: Primary Hand Gestures with Denotative Meaning (Expressive Dance);
Circle C: Conventionalized Movements (Expressive Dance);
Circle D: Other Hand Gestures with Denotative Meaning (Expressive Dance); Illustration Kristen Tuttle.

7-20. Conventionalized Gesture of Flower Blooming. Photo Paul Cravath.

A third use of hand gestures in expressive dance is in conventionalized movements which are clearly mimetic and in no way resemble the four primary gestures. Let us consider a simple example. If the chorus makes reference to a flower blooming, and the choreographer wishes to illustrate the image literally, a standard mime is to hold the hand in such a way that the fingers imitate flower petals (Fig. 7-20). This gesture is used in both Cambodia and Thailand but is rare. A more common method—and the one used throughout the "pure dance"—is simply to leave the hands in the primary "flower" gesture and allow the dancer herself to represent the flower blooming.

In terms of conventionalized movement, it is neither possible nor of great value to attempt a catalogue of the many ways in which the Khmer dancer expresses a story with her mime. Each gesture's meaning is modified by those that precede and follow, by the dramatic context, the choreographers' choices, and the movement style of the character being portrayed. As the most authoritative article yet written on Khmer choreography points out—an article prepared under the sponsorship of the Queen Mother in 1969—

> a movement of the hand never evokes the clouds, the sun, the night, a mountain or a forest as it does in Indian dancing. When it depicts an action, for instance the plucking of a flower or a challenge hurled at the enemy, its meaning is universal and immediately recognizable.[63]

To be sure, the conventionalized expression of feeling that is clearly meaningful to a Khmer may not be as universally understood as this statement assumes; thus we turn now to an examination of the most important of the conventionalized movements in the Khmer dance aesthetic, those which express the emotions.

THE EMOTIONS

The following series of illustrations can no more than suggest the graceful and restrained movement that precedes and follows each of the conventionalized expressions of emotion or feeling in the classical dance. Each image should be considered as a still photo from a film, since in the flow of performance it is in no way isolated as the camera has done here. The illustration merely represents the essence of the emotion, which may occur many times in a single scene. In addition to the feelings of reverence and supplication (already mentioned in regard to the *sampeah* salutation), the primary emotions mimed by the dancers are love and combat and will be discussed in that order.

Technically, of course, "combat" is not an emotion, but the word is used to suggest the feelings of hostility and aggression which accompany physical battle and are the essence of the conflict. In the same manner, the term "emotion" will often be used in the following discussion in reference to the physicalized presentation of a feeling as well as the feeling itself.

Love is presented on the Khmer stage either as a blissful *fait accompli*, as in the case of Rām and Sitā, or takes the form of a seduction—often with combative overtones—resulting in either an off-stage consummation or an on-stage rejection. Rarely does the female acquiesce to male advances in the same scene that they are first made, unless the princess is discovered

7-22.**Love Shared.** *Nokor Khmer.*

7-21.**Unclouded Love.**
Menh Kosni as Sita (left). *Nokor Khmer.*

sleeping, in which case the prince often meets with only token resistance when she awakens.

The low bed-table, known as *kré*, is usually the setting for the expression of that love whose tranquility is made more delicate by the audience's awareness of its imminent disruption. As the lovers languish (Fig. 7-21), the male character sits stage left of the female or slightly upstage of her; the female always has her legs stage right. Devotion to each other is mutually expressed (Figs. 7-22 and 7-23) and the lovers declare that they will never abandon each other. Arms crossed on the chest with fingers touching opposite shoulders is the basic gesture expressing love.

Before love has reached this point, numerous other dances present the patterns of pursuit and seduction. The two principals on stage alone proceed through elaborate floor patterns of restrained chase and evasion (Fig. 7-24), as the female keeps the male character at a distance. When he touches her, he is rebuffed (Fig. 7-25); he returns immediately, only to be rejected with a delicate pinch (Fig. 7-25). Eventually she accepts his open-armed invitation and they begin to move as one—(Fig. 7-25), always with

7-23. **Love Sworn.** *Nokor Khmer.*

7-24. **Pursuit and Evasion.** *Nokor Khmer.*

the female on his right. All these sequences of emotions or "sentiments"—as the Khmers term them—are rehearsed as standard love duets and can be used with variation in any number of dramas. In some of the large group dances, a number of couples perform the seduction ritual simultaneously.

The primary visual focus—as the chorus chants verbal accompaniment—is on the hands, particularly when the dancers are seated. The lovers' feelings are expressed by the intertwining touch (Fig. 7-26), by resistance (Fig. 7-27), or by the general position of their hands, which, for the most part, display variations on the "leaf" gesture. In short, the hands are the nucleus of the visual expression of all sentiments.

One important gesture that is not immediately recognizable is smiling. Much has been written concerning the Khmer dancers' smile. Unlike the Thai grin, the Khmer smile is veiled and mysteriously half present; the impassivity of the face betokens the dancer's harmony with her movement. When the role specifically requires a smile, however, it is indicated by holding the left hand in "flower" gesture just below the chin (Fig. 7-28). When a lover smiles at his beloved she does not smile

7-25. Seduction. (Top Left - Rebuffed. Top Right - Delicate Pinch. Bottom Left and Right - Dancers Move as One). Photo Paul Cravath.

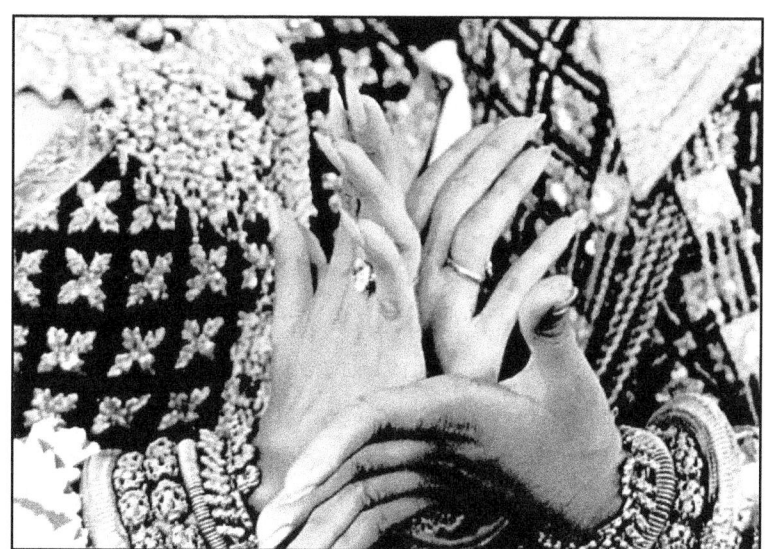

7-26. **A Love Duet.**
Nokor Khmer.

back but, rather, expresses modesty or shyness by laying her hand beside her cheek (Fig. 7-29), even though it is often her modesty which causes him to smile. With some characters the smile or laugh is considered to be very large or boisterous and is shown by using both hands (Fig. 7-30). In general, the smile symbolizes happiness and peace.

Having noted the constellation of feelings which comprise the basic positive emotions or love sentiments, we turn now to the negative ones. Together the two form a wheel

7-27. **A Love Duet with Gentle Resistance.**
Menh Kosni as Sita (left). *Nokor Khmer.*

with Love-Combat and Flight-Pursuit as the primary axes (Fig. 7-31), as shown in the schema below. While such a spectrum is universal—with the seed of every emotion being present in its opposite form—the twelve emotions illustrated form the thematic core of Khmer dance and are presented in more or less conventionalized patterns in whatever story they occur.

Combat is a significant element of Khmer dance drama, whether in actual battle scenes from the *Rāmker* and other *roeung*, or more symbolically, as in the eternal contest between Manimekhala and Ream Eyso. The music which accompanies combat is comparatively loud, but it is the tension of restrained movement which gives the battles their excitement and power. In a stylized manner and with frequent static moments, the dancers allow the imagination of the audience to transform the smooth, spare strokes of their duels into mythic battles. The monkeys are the most nervous and active characters in combat; the *yakkha* are forceful and aggressive; the princes and heroes are calm and deliberate.

Regardless of plot, all battles follow certain conventions: "the adversaries sight each other, exchange defiant gestures, gracefully cross and knock their bows together. Then, after a few skirmishes, they briefly hold a stance clearly marking the superiority of one or other of them—or the certainty of the outcome of the struggle."[64] It is these stances which end up

7-28. **Rām and Laks Smiling.** *Nokor Khmer.*

Chapter VII: Music, Choreography and Staging 333

Right:
7-29. **Modesty and Smiling.** Menh Kosni as Sita (left) *Nokor Khmer.*

Below
7-30. **Rāb Laughing.** Portrayed by Soth Leas. *Nokor Khmer.*

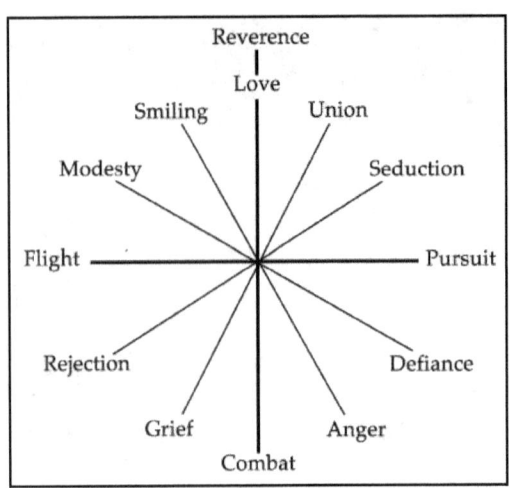

7-31. **The Emotions in Khmer Dance.**
Illustration Kristen Tuttle.

on post cards and in travel magazines and, because of their theatricality amid such general restraint, lead one to believe they could be counted or catalogued as, say, the *mié* in Japanese Kabuki. This is not the case, however, since dance teachers seem to have a small but expandable repertoire of such tableaux. In the meeting of Laks and Rāb, for instance (Figs. 7-32), the important thing is to show Laks' dominance; depending on the length of the version being performed, a number of different poses may be used. No one can say how many there are, and both variation and innovation seem possible.

Much has been made of supposed similarities between dance poses of this sort and poses seen in the bas-reliefs of Angkor. While rare similarities may be observed (Fig. 7-33), there is no assurance that the contemporary choreography is not a recent imitation. Angkorean sculpture reveals only a tiny number of dance poses, and most of these do not appear in the modern repertoire. Furthermore, when a sculpture does portray a battle, there is also no justification for assuming that actual dancers at Angkor mimed combat with similar poses. In general, the argument that the age of Khmer dance can be discerned from the appearance of its choreographic figures in Angkorean sculpture is insupportable.

Combat on the Khmer stage rarely involves physical contact except in the poses. The battle is choreographed to the accents of the *sampho* drum, and its sound represents the blows from which the struck dancer recoils. A variety of bows (without arrows), knives, swords, and axes is used as weapons by various characters and, like the fists of Ream Eyso and others, have a magical rather than a physical power in proportion to the mental force of their wielders. The end of combat is indicated, first, by the exit of the vanquished and then some moments later—depending on whether or not he is in hot pursuit—by the exit of the winner. There are no conventions regarding on-stage deaths; characters in combat, as in love, reap their karma off-stage.

To include the action of flight under the heading of "emotions" seems, initially, inappropriate, but any familiarity with the dances confirms that virtually every piece involves characters flying in a display of freedom and power. Thus the word "flight" is used here ambiguously in the sense of "flying above it all" as well as "escape from pursuit." The Khmer characters who fly include princesses, princes, ogres, monkeys and *kennari*, i.e., virtually everyone

Above: 7-32. **The Meeting of Laks and Rāb** (portrayed by Soth Leas). *Nokor Khmer.*

Below: 7-33. **Battle Between Sugrib and Bali.** Shown in tenth century sculpture and classical dance. *Nokor Khmer.*

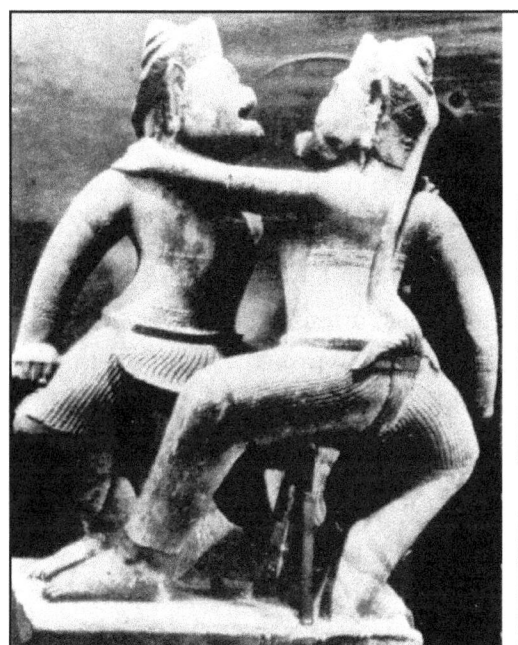

7-34. **Standing Pose to Indicate Flying.** In this scene, Mani Mekhala (Bunnak), holding her magic crystal ball, flies to the celestial palace of Vorachhun. *Nokor Khmer.*

7-35. **Princess and Prince in Flight, Kneeling.** Menh Kosni as Sita (left). *Nokor Khmer.*

possessing those supernatural powers that exist just beyond the limits of this mundane world.

In Khmer flying, what is important is not the act itself but, rather, what the character does during flight. Flight is presented as a state of mind physicalized at length in a nearly static posture, during which the audience experiences the rapture of the lovers, the transcendent nature of the *apsaras*, the powerful presence of the *yakkha* and so on. Technically this is achieved either with the dancers standing (Fig. 7-34) or kneeling (Fig. 7-35).

The distinguishing characteristics of flying are the back foot raised so that the sole faces upward and, when performed solo, the resting of the wrist or elbow on this upturned foot (Fig. 7-36). One of the most difficult and impressive movements in all of Khmer choreography is a slow-motion descent from standing-flying to kneeling-flying while this posture is maintained.

When hostile characters meet, the emotions of defiance or challenge are expressed. The general form of this gesture is a pointed finger meaning "You!" In the case of refined, human characters such as Rām and Laks, there is no quality of anger in the gesture—only confrontation (Fig. 7-37). When defiance is expressed, combat is inevitable.

The emotion of anger is considered by Buddhists to be the most destructive of all emotions

7-36. **Solo Flying.** Photo Paul Cravath.

and by the Khmers to be the most ridiculous of all feelings. On the Khmer stage no character who displays it can ultimately triumph. The antidotes for anger are calmness and laughter, which is why angry characters are always presented in a partially humorous manner. Anger is shown by holding the hand—in "flower" gesture—behind the ear, the fingers are spread to suggest a flaring up of energy which is undercut by a laughable quiver of the hand (Fig. 7-38). The opposite arm as well as the body itself are held with a rigidity that foreshadows toppling.

Anger may be expressed by characters possessing a higher consciousness, but it is done in a more restrained and intellectual manner than when expressed by gross characters such as Rāb. The main indication of anger in a refined character such as Rām, for instance, is a straight-armed, gentle tap on the lower thigh. The other hand briefly indicates the heart (Fig. 7-39), considered to be the site of the mind, now momentarily ruffled.

A further emotion which may include some sense of anger is rejection. In playful form it is found in all the seduction scenes when the princess pushes away the hand or arm of the beloved or uses a variety of small gestures which, on the surface at least, suggest "go away!" When

7-37. **Rāb and Laks in Gesture of Defiance.** *Nokor Khmer.*

7-38. **Rāb Expressing Anger.** *Nokor Khmer.*

the situation involves pursuit by an inappropriate and even dangerous partner, the rejection becomes more serious, taking the ultimate form of a slap. When Sitā is resisting seduction by Rāb, she resorts to slapping, even when he is in the form of the *eysei*. When Ream Eyso pursues Mekhala she rejects him with the power of her magic ball so intensely that he is slapped to the ground repeatedly. Thus, the gestures that express rejection are only one remove from those of combat.

There are very few instances in the dance drama repertoire of a lover being permanently rejected, but lovers who are separated are innumerable—giving rise to the sentiment of grief due to separation. The standard indication of grief is a lowering of the head, with the hand at the brow. This gesture indicates

7-39. **Posture of Rām Expressing Anger.**
Photo Paul Cravath.

general suffering, but the cause is usually separation from the beloved, as when Sitā is captured, and Rām and Laks grieve (Fig. 7-40). Another expression of grief is to place hands on opposite hips and shift the weight to the back foot (Fig. 7-41). When male characters are seated in grief, they remain with the left hand to head and rest the right hand on the left thigh. Separation, like the majority of dramatic events, is indicated by recognizable mime in stylized sequences (Figs. 7-42 to 7-46, page 341).

7-40. **Rām and Laks Expressing Grief.** *Nokor Khmer.*

7-41. **Grief.** Photo Paul Cravath.

Floor Patterns

One of the most interesting aspects of Khmer choreography to those seeing it for the first time is the use of elaborate promenades of dancers moving swiftly in curves and circles around the stage especially upon entry and prior to exit. When questioned as to their significance, Khmer dance teachers say, if anything, "That's just the way we do it. It has no meaning." The following observations will suggest, however, that the movements have a very specific function as salutations to the earth spirits of the four directions.

There is a very ancient belief in Cambodia, still prevalent among mountain tribes and such people as the Samré near Siemreap, that in all dealings with the earth itself, respect must be shown to the huge *nāga* serpents who dwell just beneath the surface. In plowing a field, for instance, one must take care to follow the contours of the *nāga* body, particularly

Chapter VII: Music, Choreography and Staging   341

7-42. **Separation "We must part."**
This series shows Kem Bun Nak as Sita with Sam Sokhan as Rama. *Nokor Khmer.*

7-43. **Separation "Our hearts remain united."** *Nokor Khmer.*

7-44. **Separation "Dry your tears."** *Nokor Khmer.*

7-45. **Separation "Our sorrow is unbounded."** *Nokor Khmer.*

7-46. **Separation "Adieu my beloved."** *Nokor Khmer.*

in the first ritual soil-breaking of the season. A French ethnologist has observed that

> on the edge of the rice field the plow inscribes a furrow that goes from west to south. On its second crossing to the east, after a round and a half, the plow share traces a short furrow stopping perpendicular to the first. The laying out must not strike but must follow the body of the subterranean Nāga whose head is in the west and tail in the east. This first labor [of the season] is symbolic; one resumes it later ... when the rains have moistened the soil.[65]

This ritual was performed annually in Phnom Penh—as it still is in Bangkok—on an empty field north of the palace with the king himself at the plow. The contemporary pattern of the symbolic furrow is not known.

For Cambodians, dance is considered to be an effective and requisite element of rituals designed to achieve harmony with nature spirits. The dancers' movements over the ground must necessarily be respectful of those spirits, especially the *nāga*. In an earlier age, such considerations undoubtedly played a major role in determining the pattern followed by the long line of dancers in single file, which today still coils rapidly around the stage during all mass entrances and exits.

The idea that particular curves and spirals hold symbolic value is not merely conjectural. One of the distinguishing features of early Southeast Asian cultures such as the Dong-son was the distinctive use of spiral designs on the ceremonial bronze drums and on their elaborate vases symbolizing the all-containing earth itself (Fig. 7-47). Protective bronze plaques—reminiscent of Hmong embroidery patterns—are adorned with similar spirals (Fig. 7-48). Such designs represent an ever-widening circle at whose infinitely small, theoretical center is found nothing—a nothingness which, paradoxically, gives rise to all things including the cycle of life itself. As such, the spiral symbolizes the Feminine principle.

On the Khmer stage, spatial orientation is based on a center and four distinct corners or directions. Upon entering the stage, the dancers proceed in a single file to each of the four corners and immediately prior to exit, pass through the center. The exit from Robam Apsaras demonstrates this clearly. Figure 7-49A indicates the floor pattern followed by all dancers in single file behind the exit leader (0). During such promenades, each dancer changes her hand gestures and arm positions as she passes at least three of the four corners (Fig. 7-49B). The style of walk also changes at the first corner and significantly accelerates when nearing the actual departure from the stage.

In performance, dancers in vertical lines, i.e., parallel to the audience's line of vision in proscenium staging, often perform a spiral or braided pattern with each dancer following the one in front (Fig. 7-49C). This, like most of the large group movement, creates very busy patterns of inter-weaving curves and circles (Fig. 7-50). That these lines and spirals are also offertory in nature is suggested by the fact that dancers may face upstage a considerable length of time with their backs to the audience while the movements are performed.

For entrances, the simplest pattern is an upstage curve (Fig. 7-51A), but in most cases they are far more elaborate. Morning rehearsals at UBA in 1974, for instance, included over forty-

7-47. **Bronze Urn Found at Phnom Penh, ca. 4th Century.** *National Museum of Phnom Penh.* Photo John Gollings.

7-48. **Bronze Dong-son Plaque.**
Adapted from B.P. Groslier, *The Art of Indochina.*

344 Earth in Flower

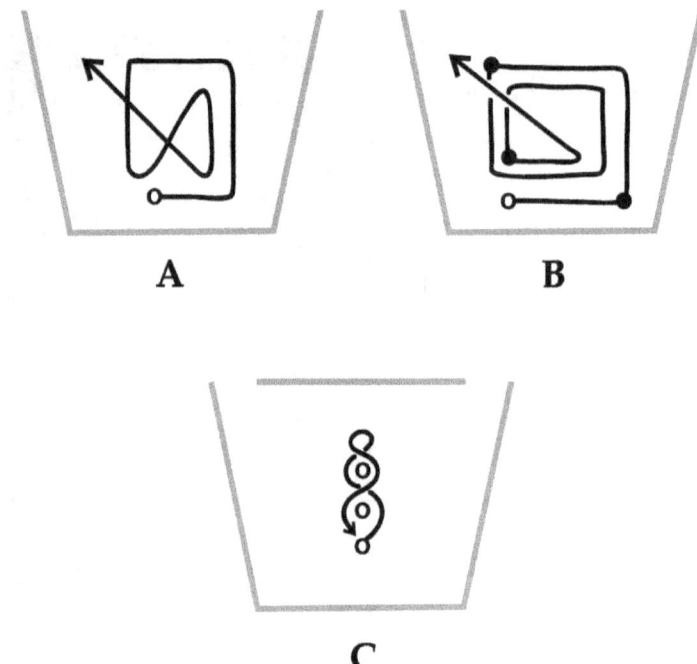

7-49. Exit and Spiral Patterns. NOTE: Audience is at the bottom of each sketch; "o" represents the lead dancer; "•" indicates a change of hand gesture. Illustration Kristen Tuttle.

7-50. Interweaving Dancers.
Princess Buppha Devi (left center) with Menh Kosni (center). *Nokor Khmer.*

five dancers following each other through a circuitous homage to the four directions—simplified in Figure 7-51B—before forming vertical lines upstage for the first exercises.

During the *buong suong* and several *robam* noted in Chapter VI, the choreography includes symbolic offerings in silver cups made in a stately manner to the four directions in turn. Careful observation of the group entrance and exit patterns used throughout the repertoire appears to indicate that the circular floor movements are a shorthand,

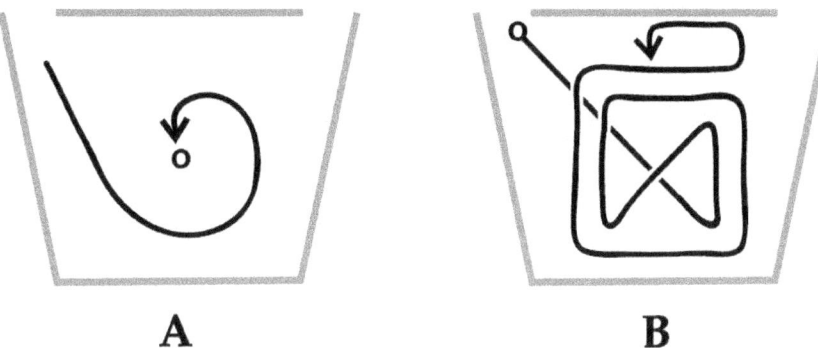

7-51. **Entrance Patterns.** Illustration Kristen Tuttle.

mobile version of the same ritual.

A second conclusion that can be drawn from studying the floor patterns in the main segments of each dance is that Khmer dance is the artistic representation of the tension between the Feminine and Masculine principles as well as their ultimate harmony on the social level. In the *robam*, and to a lesser extent in the *roeung*, this balancing takes the form of ritualized interaction between female and male. Dancers perform in couples, in fairly static floor positions and in rows that are either horizontal that is to say perpendicular to the audience's vision (Fig. 7-52A), or vertical (Fig. 7-52C). Thus a row of female characters dancing at length beside or in front of a row of male characters is the most frequent spatial configuration found in Khmer dance.

The elaborate patterns of switching these rows from horizontal to vertical and back again—as well as to other groupings and similar configurations comprise the greater part of floor movement patterns in the *robam*. The large circular movements by which this is effected resemble entrance and exit patterns but are generally of shorter duration.

Dancers are often in vertical lines at the beginning of a dance and in one or more horizontal lines at the end of a dance prior to exit (Fig. 7-52F). When the rows are vertical, the male characters always form the row on stage left; female characters form the stage right row. Vertical rows may at times join together, but the female's partner is always either on her left or

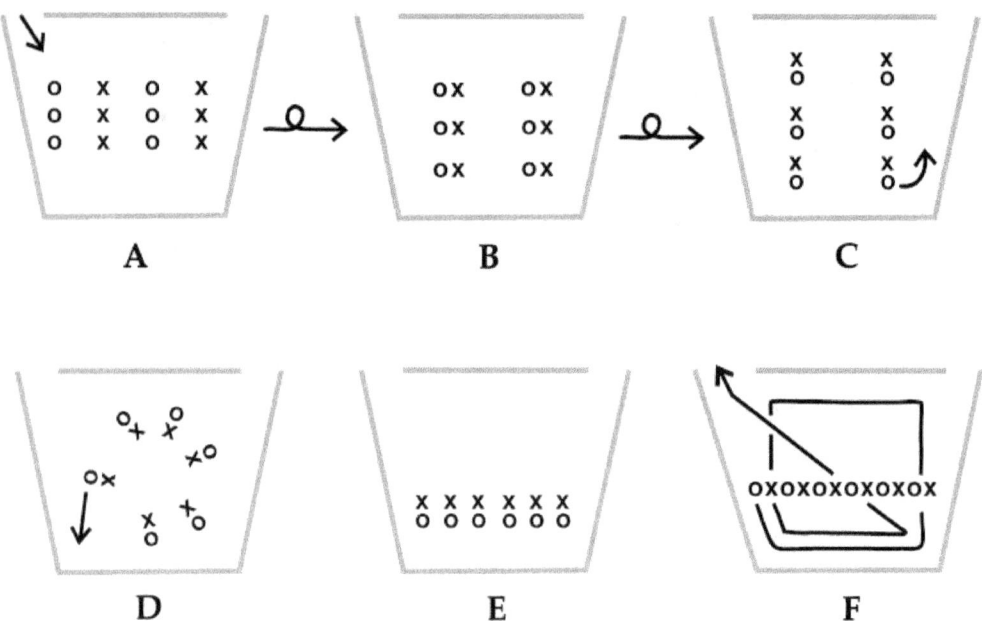

7-52. **Spatial Relationships Between Female & Male Characters.** Illustration Kristen Tuttle.

behind her. In horizontal rows, male characters stand behind their partners unless the dance is nearly completed at which time they may simply move downstage to form a single line of alternating male and female characters for the final *sampeah* prior to exit. In general, however, there is always some sort of circular promenade marking the transformation of rows from vertical to horizontal or to any other of the innumerable variations.

Never are the female characters all on one side of the stage and all the male characters on the other; the rows which they form will always alternate. When two of those rows move closer together—following a promenade—to form couples, all couples simultaneously perform in place the stylized movements of pursuit, seduction, or other themes of the narration.

Often there is a pair of lead dancers who are each the leader of a vertical row and who lead the promenades. They may be placed in the center of a circle of couples and are often the last to exit from the stage at the conclusion of a group dance. If the dance is part of a *roeung*, they are the prince and princess, for example, who are the main characters of the story.

Thus, what the floor patterns suggest is that in the Khmer view, individual partners in the dance of life are always part of a society of equals. Within this society there may be a prince or superior person, but everyone is pursuing the same pattern of action. Never is the entire society severed by group-to-group confrontation since the conflict or tension of any single couple disappears within the objectively viewed balance of the society at large. Never does one structure simply change into another, but through the circular pattern of dissolution and rebirth, a new image emerges. Still the female-male polarity—both individually and socially—remains, and in the final, closely-formed lines and circular exit, we see that social balance and harmony as well as rebirth are both represented and invoked.

STYLE OF CHOREOGRAPHY

In Chapter VI we pointed out that new works in the style of Khmer classical dance can be choreographed at any time. What must be emphasized here is that despite the idiosyncrasies of choreographers, teachers, and dancers, the classical dance style is so distinct and precise that all will strive to reflect it perfectly in their work. As a result, Khmer dance remains clearly distinguishable from Thai and Lao dance, its nearest stylistic cousins. The following discussion will examine the distinctive features of Khmer choreographic style regarding energy, space, and body movement, in answer to the general question, "How do the dancers move?"

The essential energy quality experienced in the *lakhon* is the opposition between static and dynamic. Neophytes invariably describe the dance as slow because of its many attitudes of near immobility. The more experienced are aware that the periodic rapid movement creates great energy which is then contained and amplified in the long moments of seemingly suspended movement. Overall, this gives the dance a sustained, undulating energy. Comparatively large movements of arms or legs, together with various forms of turning, walking, and kneeling alternate with long periods of standing in a single spot performing very small movements of hands, feet and head, often in delicate interaction with a partner. Nonetheless, the elbows are continually away from the body, one or both arms are usually extended at shoulder height, the fingers are always taut with energy, the knees are bent, and one foot is often raised for long periods—all of which contribute to a hypnotic balance of movement and stillness.

Actually, of course, the dancer is never still. She radiates a continual vibration of energy and is always involved in some movement, however small, which focuses the tension. She dances with the rhythm of the music, most notably when the *sampho* drum and her extensions coincide, but also when her large gestures follow the beat of the *skor thom* drum and the bamboo *khrab*. Moreover, the continual flutterings of the *roneat* set the tempo of her overall movement. The dancer does not stop for these or in any way acknowledge them; the restrained, undulating flow of her energy simply proceeds with subtle shifts in speed and size of gesture. Throughout the dance, there is a unique smoothness to all movement, a continuity which gives the entire scene exceptional grace and lightness.

In terms of space, there is a very strong feeling that the dancers, who are considered in many dances to embody divine spirits, come from a sacred place into a space which is, in turn, sanctified by their presence. For the *robam*, that space is empty of props, furniture or set pieces. In the dramas this sense of appearing without reference to time or space is altered by plots and staging techniques, which, as we shall see, localize the dancers in palaces, forests, skies, and, in general, the human realm.

In both of the major performance pavilions in the royal palace, dancers entered and exited from upstage right. This custom is still followed today wherever the dance is performed. The dancers' slow, stately entrance in lines that circle the stage before and after their deeply respectful *sampeah* salutation to those assembled; their restrained energy while dancing; their dazzling beauty and warmly distant, unchanging smiles; and their return through the same portal from which they first appeared—all this gives the dancers a quality of mystery. We are willing to believe that they inhabit all space but have appeared on the present stage as spirits who need nothing and who leave behind only flower petals and a vision.

Regarding the more visible reality of the dancer's space, we note that she moves always in synchronicity with others. In the *robam* all the female characters on stage make identical moves simultaneously; the male characters do the same. Often the two groups dance the same movements with slight variations of degree appropriate to their gender—the male's gestures are broader, his stance is wider and so forth. Thus, in the *robam* the dancer is rarely a solo performer; she is a member of a group that moves as one. Often, however, she has a partner of opposite character-gender and, like neighboring couples, shares certain cues for timing and movement which are unique to them. Frequently—in scenes of seduction, for instance—with many couples on stage simultaneously, all the princes' gestures are synchronized, as are the princesses' responses.

The dancer moves with her many "partners" through a choreography primarily comprised of lines and circles. The lines are generally stationary; that is, she dances in a fixed floor location. The circles are usually transitional movements. A few *robam* do include sequences of fixed and rotating circles which focus on a dancer or a couple in the center, but far more frequently the dancers, in rank and file or in couples, are focused outward toward the audience and space.

Never does the dancer—even the lead dancer—attract the focus of audience attention away from the group through distinctive movements, and never does the group deflect focus from itself. At the same time there is absolutely no eye contact between audience and dancer, further contributing to the other-worldliness of Khmer dance.

While the dancer's use of stage space is comparatively simple, her body movement within those patterns is complex and difficult. It is said, for instance, that there are fifteen different ways of walking.[66] What can be examined in the present context is not that variety of movement but the basic stance or posture that is the basis for all movement. The male characters involve great physicality at times, as do the *yakkha* roles, and the monkeys are fully gymnastic; our focus, however, will remain on the typical female and male characters in the *robam* and in the dance segments of the *roeung* because they embody the essential image of the classical dancer.

The slow, graceful, and almost gliding movements of the female and male characters are performed, upon closer examination, by dancers who maintain an extreme angularity within the body. This is best observed in the *kbach* poses when various parts of the body must be parallel with other specified planes of the body (Fig. 7-53). In flying, for instance, the sole of one foot—usually the right—is raised behind the body as high as possible, but ideally so that the foreleg is parallel with the left thigh when viewed in profile. Similarly, the right thigh and the left foreleg should be parallel.

By observing the teacher's attention to the various angles of the body during rehearsals, one learns some of the subtleties that ultimately define the style. Let us examine a selection of these.

Without question the most distinguishing feature of the body's general posture in Khmer dance is the deep inward curve of the lower spine, an angle so extreme that to the uninitiated it may appear grotesque (Fig. 7-54). Teachers are relentless in requiring this curve, especially in the case of younger dancers who are continually reminded of it—by a sound slap if the pressure of a gentle hand is not heeded.

Many of the young dancers who are receiving instruction in the United States today, like those who were taught outside the palace or UBA traditions prior to 1975, do not have this fundamental posture. Nor do the Thai dancers have it, and when teachers at the Department of Fine Arts in Bangkok were questioned about this point, they said the posture was wrong according to their standards. Yet without it, both Thai and Lao dancers seem, by comparison, very light and ungrounded.

The Khmer dancer, for all her delicate grace and elegance, paradoxically presents an appearance of extreme solidity and bent-kneed stability upon the earth. The source of this strength is the arching of the back, possibly because it stretches and accentuates the area below the navel from which fully developed

7-53. **Parallelism in the Flying Pose.**
Photo Paul Cravath.

7-54. **Mom Dok Pei** (center left) **Teaching Young Dancers at UBA.** Photo Paul Cravath.

movement originates and body energy is said to flow. It is this curve which is the subtle hallmark of Khmer dance style. It is seen in all roles and held throughout all movement. Parenthetically, it can also be seen in Angkorean bronze sculpture.

Among other important body angles is that of the head. Teachers continually make almost imperceptible adjustments to the dancer's head so that the chin is parallel with the ground and more importantly that, like the torso itself, the head is never on a perfect vertical axis. Rather, the head follows and completes the curve of the spine in all movements and subtly balances each shift of weight. As the dancer performs a stylized walk, for instance, the crown of the head tilts to the left as the weight shifts to the right leg and vice versa. Since, in many standing positions, the weight can shift back and forth with some frequency, a subtle wave of energy is experienced passing through the dancer's body much of the time.

This concern with the mindful flow of such movement's energy to the farthest extremity of the body lends an often pendulous quality to the dancers,

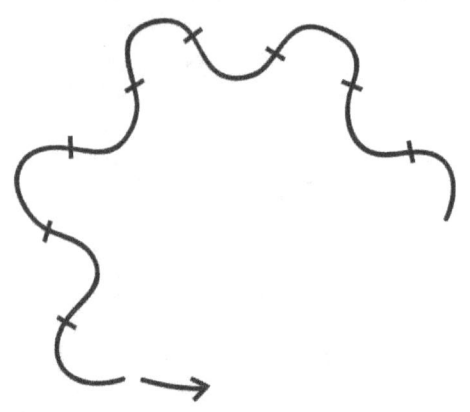

7-55. **Distinctive Circular Walk Pattern.**
Illustration Kristen Tuttle.

giving rise to the comparison—a highly complimentary one in Southeast Asia—with an elephant's precise walk and swaying grace. One particularly beautiful instance of this is a circular walk consisting of many small curves of alternating direction (Fig. 7-55). On successive curves the body faces and leans slightly into and then away from the circle's center, and by a pattern of small steps for each curve—together with the wing-like extension of each arm alternately on the outer side of the curve—creates a very powerful sensuality.

Aside from the beauty of the face and costumes, what one notices first about the Khmer dancer is her hands. Here too the principle of energy extended to the extremities is applied. Even with mature dancers, the choreographer or elder teacher frequently raises the dancer's arms further from the body, strengthens the curve of the fingers, focuses the eyes on the hand gesture to lend it still more energy, and in every possible way forces the dancer's consciousness into her fingertips. Figure 7-56 shows the best dancer of male characters at UBA in 1975; her elevation, her awareness of the pose, and her full body energy were acknowledged even by the Thai teachers, who saw this photo in Bangkok, as "beautiful." The sharp curves of the wrist, the hyperflexion of the fingers, and the balance between the two hands are considered exquisite.

One clarification regarding choreographic choice is worth noting: certain distinctive hand gestures and other poses are identified with particular dances, outside of which they are rarely if ever used. For example, in the Robam Sramoch or Ant Dance, often performed by the very youngest dancers, there are two distinct hand gestures. In one, the thumb and forefinger of one hand are grasped onto the opposite wrist, and in the other, both arms are extended equally while the hands flutter. Another example is associated exclusively with the golden deer in the *Rāmker*; the dancer indicates the deer's horns by holding both hands near the head (or with movement thereabouts) in the position of the western "peace sign." A third example involving two dancers is used in circular movements of partners (Fig. 7-57). As with many elements of Khmer choreography, these hand gestures have limited usage in specific contexts. Figure 7-58, as a further example, shows a *kbach* pose for two dancers which was identified at UBA as being exclusively associated with Vishnu. It is used in Tep Manorom and also, presumably, in the Robam Preah Noreay Baimpeat.

7-56. **Dancer of Male Roles at UBA.**
Photo Paul Cravath.

The arms in Khmer dance are almost never both in the same posture or held at the same height. One in the air balances one on the thigh, one held high balances one with the hand at navel level, and so forth. But never do the arms relax or hang loosely from the shoulders. The most extreme instances of this are the positions involving hyperflexion of the elbow, an ornamentation admired in many genres of Southeast Asian dance. In 1857 Sir John Bowring, one of the first Europeans to view the classical dance in Thailand, wrote that such hyperflexion in the arm "is deemed an aristocratic accomplishment among the Siamese ladies."[67] Today it is simply "the way it's done" and appears to have no symbolic significance.

In the group dances, perhaps 70 percent of all movements are done in a standing position. Many dances, however, include lengthy periods of kneeling in the style used for *sampeah* (Fig. 7-14), "walking" on the knees (Fig. 7-50), attending the prince or princess, waiting and watching used

Top Left:
7-57. **Circular Movement for Two Dancers.** Photo Paul Cravath.

Top Right:
7-58. **Kbach Identified with Vishnu.** Photo Paul Cravath.

Left:
7-59. **Position of Sitting in Attendance for Male Roles.** Photo Paul Cravath.

particularly in martial scenes in the dramas (Fig. 7-59), and in other less frequent forms of seated dance movement. During the major portion of most group dances, when the dancers are performing in basically standing positions, there is very little movement of the torso. The chest is held high, the shoulders and arms are very active, and the hips are involved in large movements—balancing on one foot with the other knee raised waist high, for example—but the torso itself remains relatively still.

One is reminded of the bas-reliefs at Angkor with *devatā* holding a hand in the flower position just below the navel (Figs. 3-21, 3-22, 3-23). Often the thumb and first finger hold a pearl or jewel-like object corresponding, one imagines, to an internal pearl which the modern Khmer dancer seems to be delicately balancing within her lower abdomen. There is flexibility and some lateral movement within the torso, but even during the *sampeah*, the torso remains upright with only the head and hands performing the salutation.

There is one tiny but interesting move in Khmer choreography that is very distinctive. When dancers are kneeling, particularly in the *sampeah*, there is a kind of upward bounce that is made by tightening the hip muscles, after which the body is held elevated for a beat and then relaxed. The movement is also found in Thai dance and, with a different feeling, in Javanese dances. In Cambodia it is said to be only an accent but one not clearly indicated by a beat of the music. The bounce appears unexpectedly within long, languid phrases of movement but rarely as a burst of accent as in Thai dance. It occurs, for instance, during the *sampeah* when the hands are at both head and heart level.

Because the Khmer dancer moves slowly in performing floor patterns, we experience large or fast movements only in her use of arms and legs. The largest moves—with the exception of the monkeys' gymnastics—are performed by the giant or *yakkha* roles. *Yakkha* leg movements are the largest gestures on the Khmer stage outside of combat scenes. Giants stand with knees bent and much further apart than the male roles. For a display of power, they rise to the balls of the feet and, with knees still bent, alternately stand on the left and right foot while remaining in place.

The tempo of *yakkha* movement and music is faster than for female and male roles. When walking, giants lift the front of the foot, tap it back down, lift a bent knee high and to the outside, and straighten the leg before lowering it. Either the heel or toes forcefully touch the ground first (Fig. 7-60). This often results in showing the sole of the foot directly to the audience, a gross action appropriate to *yakkha* characters. Parenthetically, the right hand is usually in a fist with thumb extended to indicate the weapon being carried.

For female and male roles, all walking movements are far more sedate and slower than for the *yakkha*. Often, while the arms of a dancer are

7-60. *Yakkha* **Roles at UBA.** Paul Cravath.

extended, the only visible movement may be a delicate swaying of the head and torso and small movements of the feet. In a common pattern, the weight is on the right foot, which is flat on the floor; slightly behind it is the left, with weight only on the ball of the foot. The left foot is then brought forward to tap the floor first with the heel and then the ball of the foot (with toes arched upward), after which it returns to the original position. There is a slight coordinated sway to the body, and this slow graceful move is repeated by the dancer while the arms are either stationary or performing a sequence of large gestures to an even slower beat. In many cases the choreography of the legs includes very tiny gestures, such as the toes on a weight-bearing foot being raised on a particular beat of the music. The angles of the body in all of these moves, as well as the proper elevation of each limb, are all of great importance to the visual balance demanded by the teachers.

As far as can be determined, the many choreographic choices known to the teacher—the traditional style itself—exist today only in her or his head. The only evidence to the contrary is a 1936 account which mentions that the "ancient, emaciated dame" who instructed a troupe of children at Angkor had before her "a little book in which the gestures are illustrated and numbered,"[68] although she seldom looked at it or turned a page. No such little books exist today, or if so, they are complete secrets.

When all is said and done, probably the most memorable element of Khmer classical choreography is one over which the teacher has little control: the smile. The dancer's face, unlike that of the Thai dancers, is immobile. A mysterious half smile, whose cause is never shared with the audience, hovers on the face, which used to be, until well into this century, painted pure, mask-like white. More will be said of the significance of this attitude in the following chapter.

STAGING THE DANCE DRAMA

STAGING TECHNIQUES

Commentators who viewed Khmer *lakhon* during the four decades prior to Sihanouk's ascendancy usually noted that no stage settings were used. While this has always been accurate to some extent, there are important exceptions. First, western theatre techniques for staging appear to have had strong appeal early in this century as well as during Sihanouk's reign. Second, when the dancers performed in the palace or at Angkor, additional set pieces would only have gilded the lily, but outside that context—and especially on tour—the *lakhon* used stage sets. The following discussion will illustrate these two points.

THE *KRÉ*

For the most part, Khmer dancers and musicians can perform any work in the repertoire in any location whatsoever using only a single, multi-purpose stage prop, the low bench known variously as *kré*, *tiang*, or *balang*.[69] Usually red with gold and sometimes green ornamentation, it is approximately six feet long, three feet wide and fifteen inches tall (Fig. 7-40). The *kré* is variously a bed, a throne, a hill, a reviewing stand, or can represent virtually any locale. In proscenium staging it is placed upstage center where it remains even during scenes in which it is not utilized.

The *kré* is used far more in the *roeung* than in the *robam*, which do not have strong story lines requiring locales. In the dramas it is indispensable. During performances in Chanchhaya, two *kré* were often used—one at either end of the rectangular performance area—so that two courts or armies or sets of lovers could be viewed alternately, as the plot required. When the *kré* represents the bed of a princess, it can be covered with a rich cloth and a pillow at the stage left end, but usually it is bare.

Floor Plan

The only stage requirement besides the *kré* is a curtained entrance—or preferably two—since the dancers remain apart from the audience except during the performance. In the three major performance halls in Phnom Penh—Chanchhaya, Phochani pavilion within the palace and Chakdomukh Hall beside the Mekong—as well as in all sets that went on tour, two entrances are provided. As noted earlier, the entrance upstage right, i.e., to the audience's left, is primary; all entrances and exits during the *robam* are made there.

In the dramas, the upstage right doorway is also preferred for entrances, but often due to the appearance of characters in the following scene, exits are of necessity made upstage left as well. Both portals can be used for entrances, however, when characters from two different locales are to meet, for example, prior to a scene of battle. The more noble combatants will enter upstage right. While it is unprovable, one feels strongly that the second entrance is inherent to the dramas and was not used originally for the much older *robam* in which the dancer-spirits always returned from whence they came. Having pointed out the simplicity of the floor plan and the highly presentational style of production, which a prop such as the *kré* implies, we turn now to evidence suggesting that, by contrast, relatively realistic stage effects were once popular in the Khmer court.

Representational Elements

According to a Royal Palace program of auspicious performances in honor of King Sisowath's sixty-third birthday, those on the afternoon of 3 January 1939 included a French comedy/drama done in Khmer style and entitled *Paspatou*. It was performed by the Keaknak Lakhon Watthana Pirum dance troupe, and its plot was a *mélange* of elements from East and West.[70] The performance included guns and other "modern" elements on stage. Presumably, the popularity of such works had been responsible for certain theatrical innovations in palace performances at least as early as the turn of the century.

In 1911 Adhémard Leclère reported that in the old dance pavilion that occupied the site of present-day Chanchhaya from 1866 until 1913, there was

> a catwalk beneath the roof almost as long as the room, suspended by iron triangles. It is with the aid of this catwalk that the women suspended on cables can represent the goddesses of the air or the princesses and princes traveling through the clouds.[71]

George Groslier, Leclère's contemporary, corroborated this unexpected stage practice.

> When they wish to thicken the plot they suspend some sorry young dancers by cords which hang from the ceiling. Thus they are taken for an airing, held under the arms, jostling through the chandeliers, as they shrivel into some nearly impossible poses with no support at all.[72]

Leclère seems to have been fully aware of the distinction between representational, or "realistic," and presentational stage techniques. Consider his comments on the following two scenes which he viewed some time around 1910. They correspond to no known works in the repertoire and are included here as long forgotten examples of staging. They are most unlikely dramatic offerings, at least by recent palace standards.

> A small piece which was played the day after the last act [of the *Rāmker*] presented a prince in love with one of his wife's servants, the despair of the princess, her watchfulness of the lovers, her supplications, and, finally, her flight to the forest where she hangs herself from a tree branch with the aid of her scarf attached to a cord, which her servants—sensibly in the wings, where, conventionally, they are not to be seen—pulled before the audience. One realistic trait attracted my attention; from the open mouth of the victim protruded her tongue which flowed with the juice of chewed betel nut which resembled blood.[73]

A second untitled fragment is fully presentational, but nothing like it is known today:

> In one piece there is an attempt to pull down a statue represented by a dancer who, dressed as a man, is masked with a head of fleecy hair. The rope used is represented by a half width of red cotton of which one end rests on the side of the *balang* or throne on which she is seated. This cloth, at least two meters long, is held by four men without costumes and extends to two princesses who tie the four men... and while singing a lively tune everyone makes the movements of pulling together. In fact the female dancers who play the princes are holding nothing and when, with a slight pressure, the ends slide from the throne signifying that the cord has broken under the strain, everyone falls to the ground.
>
> ...Next sixteen small girls...enter on their knees in two lines. These are the populace, the indigenous country people who come to salute the noble foreigners and who beg them not to overturn the statue. After discussions they finally reveal not only that the statue is heavy and difficult to move from the *balang* but that it is impossible to move unless one knows the secret of making it move itself. The princes request the secret and the locals tell them. Then a new accessory appears: a flower tied to the end of the lash of a small whip. The principal dancer takes this object from a bush and advances toward the statue which quivers, descends from the *balang*, and follows the flower around the stage. She escapes, remounts the *balang*, is again seduced, brought back by the flower, escapes again, is re-conquered by the flower, tries to grasp it and, finally, follows it faster and faster three times around the stage and disappears into the left door which is always used for exits, proceeded by the prince holding the flower and followed by several other characters. This scene is charming.[74]

There is one further realistic element to be considered which was used within the memory span of current teachers and is still used in Thai dance drama regularly. This is the cart or wagon on which royal characters may be brought on stage (Fig. 7-61). Leclère says it was called *bossabok*, was made of gilded wood, and was pulled by two men wearing on their heads tall *papier-mâché* horse heads, hat-like.

The cart, as Leclère saw it in 1910, was decorated with "ritual ornaments" and consisted of two levels, the highest being for the principal character, usually the princess role. The prince could also ride on the wagon, and there was room on the lower level for two servants—one in front and one behind.[75] Leclère's sketch also includes a footman wearing a bird head;

he gives no explanation. In a second sketch, Leclère shows "Dame Bossaba dancing" while seated on the wagon. Whether the cart was named in her honor is uncertain. In 1975 Chheng Phon and others said that the cart had been used in Cambodia in the story of Preah Vesandar exclusively.

A similar cart is used on the Thai stage in both *lakhon nai* and *lakhon nok*. The bearers do not wear horse heads, and the female attendant walks. The Thai model is at least ten feet long. While it is easily maneuvered, a cart of this size may have discouraged extensive usage in Chanchhaya or the Khmer Royal Palace in general. When it was last used in Cambodia is unclear.

7-61. **The Royal Wagon Stage Property.** *Le théâtre cambodgien*

LIGHTING AND CURTAINS

Norodom Sihanouk was considered by many to be a master of theatrical gesture and always for a political purpose. Significantly, he paid great attention to lighting—to the image the world saw of him. To understand the great care taken in lighting his dancers most effectively, one should know how he lit their environment, the palace itself. Malcolm MacDonald wrote of the courtyard in 1959.

> The night was velvety black, and myriads of stars jewelled the heavens. Nearer the earth another mysterious illumination lit the darkness. It was a vivid brightness which seemed to float in mid-air about a hundred feet above our heads, and to concentrate in the region of the palace buildings. It gleamed on the roofs of the Throne Hall, the Royal Treasury, the Silver Pagoda and neighbouring edifices, leaving everything above and below in shadow whilst the details of the roofs ... were fantastically accentuated; their up-curling eaves, steep decorated gables, stag's-horn finials and successions of over-lapping, receding tiers of rooflets climbing as if by steps to the supreme, soaring spires, all appeared suspended in air.... The illusion was so dramatic that at first one attributed it to some strange miracle, and only on further examination realized that it was due to a skillful manipulation of flood-lights inserted amongst crevices in the buildings. The scene had an unearthly, imaginary, fairyland quality.[76]

During the reign of the previous monarch, the roofs and spires of the palace were "outlined in small electric lights...like so many Christmas trees,"[77] but Sihanouk's method appears to have been more subtle—the unseen source of light being, by implication, the king himself.

In this context, the royal dancers traditionally entered into a performance area in which general illumination—for post-daylight events—was provided by candles or torches. They were not revealed by a drawn curtain, nor was special heightened lighting used for their appearance, unless it was from torch-bearers who preceded them, which was the custom at Angkor in this century. The royal dance pavilion formerly occupying the site of Chanchhaya was initially lit with palm oil torches, then torches of kerosene and oil, and, by 1910, with electric bulbs and a few gas lamps (see Appendix I). Chanchhaya was well-equipped with recessed, general illumination but used no differentiated area lighting. MacDonald's description of the lighting and general atmosphere of Chanchhaya can perhaps best portray the dancers' environment in 1959.

> The King invited me to walk with him across the lawn to the Pavilion of Dancers, and we took our place at the head of a procession. Before us strolled six torch-bearers holding tall candles with naked flames, beside us marched other servants carrying bamboo staves like wands of office,

> and behind came the company of princes, courtiers and ladies. Along either edge of our path soldiers of the King's Bodyguard stood at the salute....
>
> One building ahead of us was even more brightly illuminated than the rest. It was the Pavilion of Dancers. A two-storeyed structure, its lower floor was shrouded in darkness, but the upper was lit by hundreds of candles in sparkling chandeliers. That was the theatre. The great room had no walls, being open to the elements, with only tall, widely spaced pillars supporting the customary series of roofs mounting steeply to a central spire. So the whole glittering chamber was exposed to our gaze, and ... we entered the building and climbed a staircase to the theatre.
>
> The place was a mixture of spaciousness and intimacy. A stage filled its centre, sunk slightly below the level of the auditorium, like the arena in a circus. Round three sides of it rows of chairs were set for spectators, whilst the fourth side was open for the entry of actors. An audience of about two hundred persons already filled the seats—as many as the chamber could hold. They rose and bowed to the King as we entered. He and I sat in grand armchairs opposite the centre of the stage, and a hush of expectancy fell on the crowd as servants crawled on their knees to His Majesty offering him programmes for our instruction and drinks for our refreshment.[78]

For performances at Angkor Wat, electric lighting on the entrance causeway was first installed around 1937. By the time Sihanouk used that setting to entertain special guests such as President Tito of Yugoslavia and Jacqueline Kennedy, the entire frontal vista could be illuminated with red and gold light to highlight the dancers as they appeared from within the temple—gliding along the great causeway of giant stone serpents.

Obviously in such a situation, no thought is given to entrance curtains, but there is some evidence to suggest that when a front curtain is available in less grandiose proscenium stagings, it is used in the dramas to good effect. The University of Fine Arts (UBA) has a small, perhaps 200-seat proscenium auditorium used especially for choreographic and performance examinations. During one final project on 6 February 1975, the following staging was used: at the climax of a concluding battle scene, the white monkey Hanumān decapitated a fallen foe by jerking off his mask and fleeing with it under his arm as the curtain closed on the still, on-stage "corpse."

It is possible that this gesture was used in traditional staging—but with the vanquished corpse making a quick, "headless" exit, staggeringly, as characters usually do prior to expiration. However, the specificity and brutality of this action were not conventionally shown on stage, and the "beheading" seems to have been a choice based directly on the availability of the curtain and its function. At any rate, front curtains were available both at UBA and in Chakdomukh Hall where, at least periodically, they were theatrically integrated.

Back Drops and Set Pieces

An audience seated in Chanchhaya was already inside a palace. At the north end of the pavilion, great columns flanked the many-tiered altar surrounding a small statue of Vishnu in front of an enormous painting of the Bayon bodhisattvas (Fig. 7-35). Other buildings of the red and gilt palace could be seen from the south and west sides of the second-story hall, both open to the air. The east wall, also open, was the direction the king faced upon taking his place, and his view was of the outer world, with the Mekong River in the distance. An audience needed no further theatrical heightening of palatial illusion.

When the royal dancers performed outside this context, however, and especially when, after 1970, they did so without the presence of a monarch as their *raison d'être*, the matter of stage sets took on great importance. In Chapter IV we noted Queen Kossamak's contribution in heightening the theatricality of dance performances in the 1950s and 1960s. Let us consider now a few of the innovations in staging as well, which evolved during those years.

The first element which Queen Kossamak chose to put on stage with the dancers was trees. Not only did the dancers' movements symbolize these natural forms—on one level of interpretation—but also the free-standing trees were designed as copies of the distinctive shapes of trees in the bas-reliefs at Angkor, thus further identifying the dancers (and the monarch) with ancient splendor. Three trees are primarily pictured in the bas-reliefs, and each was carefully re-created: the coconut palm, the sugar palm, and an unnamed forest tree (Figs. 7-62, 7-63). Their modern forms were as stylized

7-62. **Sugar Palm and Fine Leaf Tree from the Bayon.** Photo Michael Greenhalgh.

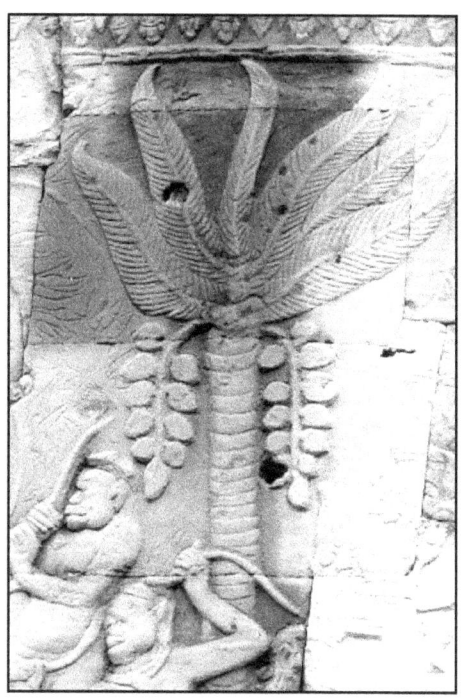

7-63. **Coconut Tree from the Bayon.** Photo Michael Greenhalgh.

as the originals (Figs. 7-64, 7-65).

These trees were used selectively and were accompanied in many cases by no other set pieces. In performances at Angkor, for instance, six trees—two of each type—remained upstage of the dancers after being carried into view by young men, who moved down the causeway with them. A few other trees were already in fixed position on the sides of the actual performance area. On the 1971 world tour six single, free-standing trees were used, with the central two placed upstage of the *kré*.

In addition to this use of very

366 *Earth in Flower*

7-64. **Princess Buppha Devi Dancing in Garden of Forest Trees.** *Royal Cambodia Ballet.*

accompany the dancers on foreign tours. From films in the Dance Collection of the New York Public Library, we know that on the 1971 world tour, even Mekhala danced in front of a painted backdrop. Finally, in the last appearance of the Khmer classical dancers outside Cambodia, their dances in Bangkok in December of 1974 were performed in front of an elaborate facade depicting an Angkorean temple through whose ornate arches—four on each side of a larger central arch—the dancers appeared.[79]

Scene Changes

There is no evidence of how or if set pieces were changed during a performance, but their multi-purpose image suggests fixed positions until the end of the *roeung*. It is very important, however, to note that the traditional method of changing locations when the Khmer stage is totally bare is inherent in the structure of the drama and accomplished through the use of music. In Khmer dance the music flows almost continually and without discernible shift—save for the breaks in which the chorus chants what the dancers mime. Changes of melody are usually very subtle. What should be noted is that the music from a previous scene overlaps the entrance of the dancers in a subsequent scene, as sound is edited in film. Thus the performance is given a cinematic continuity by a musical shift occurring only when a dancer, whom we have had a moment to study, begins to dance or the chanter begins to "speak" for her. By this technique our focus is continually guided through the story without interruption as we move from locale to locale.

Stage Attendants

A final element of staging that was definitely not in use after 1970 and, in fact, is not mentioned by any observers during Sihanouk's reign, is the supposedly "ancient tradition" of having two old women as stage attendants. "They represent 'guardians'," wrote Zarina in 1937, "and pick up fallen jewels, straighten costumes, and make themselves useful in other ways during the dance."[80] One special function was to approach the king whenever he beckoned, in order to deliver small purses of money to the lead dancers or his favorite. The old woman took the gift on a silver tray and, crouching inconspicuously among the dancers who did not stop for a moment, knelt before the honored dancer, who gave only the slightest sign of recognition. She then took the purse to the doorway where the dancer could claim it upon her exit. This often happened more than ten times in a performance, with many repetitions to the favorite.

7-65. **Voan Savay in Royal Palace Courtyard with Coconut Palm.** *Khmer Dances.*

7-66. A Scene from the Legend of Keo Monnorea and Preah Sothun.
Featuring Princess Buppha Devi (center). *Kambuja*, 15 April, 1968.

We close this chapter by noting that the Khmer custom, at least through the reign of Monivong, was never to applaud the dances.[81] In recent times, with the transformation of the dancers' life style and ritual function, that is no longer the case.

ENDNOTES

1. The Origins of Cambodian Music," in *TDMSA*, pp. 210-11.
2. Jacket Notes, *Royal Music of Cambodia*.
3. Brunet, "The Origins of Cambodian Music," p. 212.
4. William P. Malm, *Music Cultures of the Pacific, the Near East, and Asia* (Englewood Cliffs, N.J.: Prentice-Hall, 1967), p. 88.
5. Jacques Brunet, "Music and Rituals in Traditional Cambodia," in *TDMSA*, pp. 219-20.
6. Alain Daniélou, *La musique du Cambodge et du Laos* (Pondichéry: Institute Français d'Indologie," 1957), pp. 2-4.
7. Daniélou, *La musique du Cambodge et du Laos*, p. 4.
8. Brunet, "The Origins of Cambodian Music," p. 213.
9. Gaston Knosp, "La musique indo-chinoise: la musique cambodgienne," *Mercure Musical*, 3 (1907), pp. 889-928.
10. *La musique du Cambodge et du Laos*.
11. "Musique et danses cambodgiennes," pp. 98-112.
12. Hang Thun Hak, *Musique khmère*; "Musique d'accompagnement de 'Reamker'," *Annals de L'Université des Beaux-Arts* (Phnom Penh), 1, No. 2 (1972), pp. 71-96; *Musique du Cambodge* (Phnom Penh: La Direction du Tourisme Khmer, n.d.).
13. Phra Chen Duriyanga, *Siamese Music in Theory and Practice as Compared with that of the West and a Description of the Piphat Band* (Bangkok: The Department of Fine Arts, 1948).
14. Chheng Phon quoted by Gray, p. 11.
15. Jacket Notes, "The Music of Cambodia," p. 2.
16. Daniélou, *La musique du Cambodge et du Laos*, p. 12.
17. Hang Thun Hak, *Musique khmère*, p.121. See also Brunet, "The Origins of Cambodian Music," p. 213.
18. There are other string instruments played in Cambodia today, but these—and particularly the bowed ones—appear to be of comparatively recent vintage; at any rate, they are not pictured on the walls of Angkor.
19. Hang Thun Hak, *Musique khmère*, pp. 68, 70, 98, 105, 119.
20. Malm, p. 93. See also Chen Duriyanga, pp. 7-8.
21. *Musique du Cambodge*, p. 16. This anonymous, 35-page publication contains considerable valuable information. Interestingly, it claims that "the classical orchestra is today called *pey-phat* because the pey [*sralay*] is the instrument which directs it" (p.1). While the statement is partly correct in that the "oboe" is the chief instrument, it does not "direct" the ensemble – the function of the *sampho* drum – nor has it been demonstrated that *pin* (harp) is linguistically related to *pey*.
22. *La musique du Cambodge et du Laos*, p. 28.
23. Daniélou, *La musique du Cambodge et du Laos*, p. 17.
24. Brunet, "Music and Rituals," pp. 220-21.
25. Chen Duriyanga, pp. 14-15.
26. Hang Thun Hak, *Musique khmère*, p. 138.
27. Daniélou, *La musique du Cambodge et du Laos*, p. 32.
28. Daniélou, *La musique du Cambodge et du Laos*, p. 27.

29. *Musique du Cambodge*, p. 24.
30. Hang Thun Hak, *Musique khmère*, p. 137.
31. Chen Duriyanga, p. 12. Parenthetically, the Thai forms of both the *roneat ek* and the *roneat thom* are distinguished by each having an extra key for the highest notes.
32. Hang Thun Hak, *Musique khmère*, p. 137.
33. Hang Thun Hak, *Musique khmère*, p. *138*. See also Daniélou, *La musique du Cambodge et du Laos*, p. *17*.
34. Leclère, *Le théâtre cambodgien*, p.22.
35. *Le royaume du Cambodge*, p. 410.
36. "Musique d'accompagnement de 'Reamker'," pp. 81-85. Various data regarding melodies were also obtained in interviews with Chheng Phon.
37. "Musique d'accompagnement de 'Reamker'," pp. 82-83.
38. Chheng Phon, personal communication.
39. "Musique d'accompagnement de 'Reamker'," p. 83.
40. Chheng Phon, personal communication.
41. "Musique d'accompagnement de 'Reamker'," p. 84.
42. "Musique d'accompagnement de 'Reamker'," p. 85.
43. Brunet, Jacket Notes, *Royal Music of Cambodia*.
44. Personal communication, 29 May 1981.
45. *Danses cambodgiennes*, pp. 76-77.
46. "Origin et évolution," p. 499.
47. Moura, *Le royaume du Cambodge*, p. 415.
48. Jacket Notes, *Royal Music of Cambodia*.
49. Phuong Phan, personal communication, 29 May 1981.
50. Phuong Phan, personal communication.
51. "Le théâtre at la danse au Cambodge," p. 134.
52. Letter received from Nuon Kan, 29 August 1977.
53. Dhanit Yupho, *The Preliminary Course of Training in Thai Theatrical Art* (Bangkok: The Fine Arts Department, 1972), pp. 26-28. Each pose is pictured on subsequent pages.
54. Dhanit, p. 25.
55. Dhanit, p. 25.
56. Personal communication, 29 May 1981.
57. George Groslier, *"Le théâtre et la danse au Cambodge,"* p. *134*
58. Chheng Phon, personal communication.
59. Chheng Phon, personal communication.
60. Jeanne Cuisinier, "The Gestures in the Cambodian Ballet: Their Traditional Symbolic Significance," *Indian Arts and Letters*, 1, No. 2 (1927), p. 95.
61. Dale Saunders, *Mudrā: a study of symbolic gestures in Japanese Buddhism* (New York: Pantheon, 1960), pp. 7-8, 25.
62. "The Gestures in the Cambodian Ballet."
63. Charles Meyer, "Cambodian Dances," *Nokor Khmer*, 1, No. 3 (Apr.-Jun. 1970), p. 11.
64. Charles Meyer, "Cambodian Dances," p. 27.
65. R. Baradat, "Les Sâmrê ou Peâr: population primitive de l'ouest du Cambodge, *BEFEO*, 40, No. 1 (1941), p. 675.
66. "Shadow Plays in Cambodia," *TDMSA*, p. 49.
67. *The Kingdom and People of Siam*, I, p. 90.
68. Ponder, p. 238. Zarina corroborates that "the dances are recorded in precious handwritten books, some of them very old, and kept wrapped in fine silks and brocades. These books are never opened without the ceremonial salute, the Anjali, being made before them" (p. 64). Zarina does not mention illustrations.

69 At UBA this piece of furniture was known as *kre* (gre) but was also referred to by the Sanskrit word *asaneah / qesanah*. Early in this century Leclère called it the *balang* (*Le théâtre cambodgien*, p. 19), and in 1937 Zarina knew it as *tiang* ("Royal Cambodian Dances," p. 70).

70 A detective named Valentin takes his friend to drink at a shop. When they see the shopkeeper's daughter named Davi, who is selling wine, they wish to love her. The father, perceiving this, sends a letter to his nephew named Paspatou who is living abroad to ask him to come and take over the shop. When Valentin is unable to make love with Davi, he takes her by force. Paspatou comes to help her. Davi's father marries her to Paspatou. Later Valentin goes to steal the fortune of the daughter of King Robert. The king orders the detective Valentin to find the thief. Valentin goes to arrest Paspatou, and declares that he is the thief, and the king imprisons Paspatou.

Another detective sends a letter in secret, saying that Valentin is the thief. Lily (the princess) takes pity on Paspatou and brings him food. Valentin sees this and also sees her find the letter, which she takes to the king. Valentin tells the king that the princess loves Paspatou. The king, becomes angry and imprisons his daughter.

Later, when the detectives under the supervision of Valentin go to tell Davi that Valentin is the thief, Davi goes to tell the king, and (finally) the king imprisons Valentin. The king forgives his daughter and marries her to Paspatou. As for Valentin, he attempted an uprising in prison and was executed.

71 See Appendix I.
72 *Danseuses cambodgiennes*, p. 68.
73 *Le théâtre cambodgien*, p. 8.
74 *Le théâtre cambodgien*, p. 20.
75 *Le théâtre cambodgien*, p. 18.
76 MacDonald, p. 23.
77 Zarina, p. 70.
78 MacDonald, pp. 23-25.
79 Chaturong Montrisart, personal communication, 20 June 1975. Chaturong is a teacher in the Department of Fine Arts, Bangkok.
80 Zarina, p. 71. The author notes that "in Java, also, the tradition of two guardians for the court dancers is conserved."
81 Sappho Marchal, "La danse au Cambodge," p. 224.

Chapter VIII

THE ROYAL DANCER: TRAINING AND COSTUMES

អ្នករបាំព្រះរាជទ្រព្យ: ការបង្រៀន និង របៀបស្លៀកពាក់

𝓘n 1926 one of the earliest English-speaking observers of the Cambodian Royal Palace dancers wrote that they comprised the largest dance ensemble known in the East.[1] To achieve the stability implied by that relative size within the four score years following King Ang Duong's inheritance of the fragile tradition, demonstrates the monarchy's deep concern for the perpetuation of the *lakhon*. The traditional training method on which this strengthening was based is still essentially practiced today. In this chapter we will examine the training in its original palace context and then survey the costumes which were worn by the various groups of dancers once they had officially "graduated."

DANCER TRAINING

ENTRANCE TO TRAINING

To become a royal dancer traditionally meant a life-long and nearly irrevocable commitment to the cloistered entourage of the monarch. Most dancers entered the palace at a very young age, as offerings made by their parents to the king. Gaining royal favor was not the parents' sole motive, since it was believed that "their daughters, if given to the King, would call down upon themselves and their families the good will of the spirits and divine protection."[2] This association between the royal harem, the spirit world, and the continuity of family lies at the heart of the dancers' ritual function and will be considered in some detail in the final chapter of this study.

On the mundane level, however, parents whose daughters were received by the king were given a gift, the size of which was determined by the child's beauty. In general, only the most beautiful child in a village could be offered to the king and her selection needed to be approved in advance by the local temple astrologer. Around the turn of the century parents offering a child received between 20 and 500 piasters as well as a special *sampot* and a length of silk cloth, the latter gifts being left with the child.[3]

Children presented to the king were usually about six years old and in many cases would never see their parents again. As part of the harem, they never left the palace, although complete cloistering was gradually altered in the twentieth century. King Norodom allowed his dancers only one day—from sunrise to sunset—each year to meet their families in the city. King Sisowath allowed several days, and outside women could visit the dancers' quarters inside the palace. Still, if the child came from a distant village, family contacts could be almost negligible. By the reign of King Sihanouk, dancers could choose to live either in the city or the palace.

Children could "offer themselves" to the king, but most were accompanied by parents. The child's face was powdered white, and, wearing the common *sampot* of a dancer in rehearsal, she knelt at the king's feet to offer either a simple bouquet or a woven structure of flowers. Once accepted, the child received a minimum "advance" of 100 piasters (in 1930) in the form of between two and four bars of silver (*nen*), the amount again dependent upon the beauty of the child.[4] Thereafter, as a member of the royal household, she received a monthly allowance and, upon reaching the age of seven, began her training as a dancer.

Group Training

The importance of the fact that the dancers constituted a major part of the king's harem must not be overlooked. Ultimately, the years of training isolated from society were dedicated to pleasing the king and attracting his notice. The possibility of a leading position in the dance as well as the enhancement of natural beauty through developing skillful technique were both highly motivating even to those dancers whose childhood enthusiasm for the splendor of palace life may have waned. As a result, training—in the time of Norodom at least—was rigorous.

In order to realize the aesthetic ideal, extreme demands were made on the dancer's body, and, as George Groslier pointed out, "she must exercise stubbornly if she wishes that one evening the enchanted King will desire her and the people will applaud."[5] To these ends, the earliest phase of training was the same for all dancers, and the basic exercises were practiced for years, daily preceding any individual or small group training. The same group exercises are still used today and their purpose is to locate and perfect the superior dancers while developing a strong ensemble.

These first exercises of the palace dancers are basically a warm-up sequence designed to develop and maintain the body's suppleness. They were traditionally done by young dancers every morning at an early hour—when the dew was still on the grass—and lasted 30 minutes if done quickly. The warm-up was unaccompanied by music. Mature dancers did not do the exercises together as when they were children, but even when the lead dancers of the national troupe rehearsed in 1975, they individually loosened their bodies with movements selected from the warm-up sequence.

There are roughly twenty segments in the warm-up exercises and most are done seated on the floor. Every possible joint is stretched. The student lies alternately on her back and stomach while a partner stretches her legs and feet. Fingers are bent back until each knuckle cracks. Arms are bent over horizontal forelegs (resting on a knee) to stretch the elbow, and partners bend each other's arms backward over their knees as though breaking a branch. A certain speed and rhythm are maintained and a full sweat is achieved.

On the one hand the purpose is to achieve the hyper-flexion, strength, and ability to isolate a movement that are required of the dancer, but the exercises also allow the teachers an opportunity to note the personality, endurance, body type, and gracefulness of each student. This culminates in the division of students into three role groups: female, male, and giant or ogre (*yakkha*). Traditionally, girls also played the monkey roles, but as noted earlier, this group of roles came to be assigned to boys in this century.

The boys' training is completely separate from the girls, including their earliest practice of these warm-up exercises. As noted in Chapter IV, boys from the *lakhon khol* troupes were first invited by Kossamak to join the royal troupe, and a number of male dancers came from the ranks of the royal family itself. There is no evidence of boys being offered by the general populace. With the creation of the National School of Theatre at the Université des Beaux-Arts in 1960, the training of monkey roles seems to have been centered there, and the male dancers joined the palace women only for performances.

Role Training

Today as always, beginning students are grouped into roles largely on the basis of body type: those who give promise of being taller are the princes, the most delicate and beautiful are the princesses, and the more thick-bodied are the giants. In the latter case, beauty is of less consequence since, in the *roeung* at least, they will always be masked. Once cast, a dancer never changes categories and learns the dances only in the style of her role group. Following the warm-up sequence—and the daily offering ritual described in Chapter IX—all the roles together dance two series of movements and poses from which all others are more or less derived: a slow cadence, *kbach rongvoel*, and a fast cadence, *kbach banchok*. Each lasts about twenty minutes. While there are slight variations in body posture and movement style for the various roles, the two *kbach* form the basic training in balance, timing, and the correct body positions for all dancers.

This training previously began in the palace when the dancers were about eight years old. In 1911 George Groslier reported that dancers of that age practiced daily from eight o'clock to eleven o'clock in the morning and from two to five in the afternoon for at least a year before knowing the basics.[6] In 1931 Thiounn wrote that it took three months to learn the slow *kbach* and two months for the fast *kbach*.[7]

At the beginning level each of the role groups—gods or princes, goddesses or princesses, and *yakkha* or giants—was traditionally instructed by two teachers and two assistants. When young girls still played the monkey roles, however, that group had only one teacher, who was, like the others, a woman.[8] In 1975 at UBA each group still had that number of teachers, but the boys playing monkey roles were taught by one man whose assistants were also male. In all periods, group rehearsals for each character-type were held completely separate from each other.

Included in the beginners' training was instruction in the *kbach* specifically associated with each role. This was given daily, following the all-school practice in the slow and fast *kbach*. This rehearsal included specific instruction in a group *robam* or an episode from one of the *roeung* dramas. Solo performances were also prepared.

Certain *kbach* were common to several roles but needed to be learned in accordance with stylistic variations of each role. Foremost among these were the *kbach lia*, or farewell, which, according to Thiounn, could be learned in three days; the *kbach choet* for fast movement and flight, which could be learned in ten days; *kbach smeu* for entrances and exits, which required eight days to learn; and the *kbach chet choeng* for princes' combats and princesses' aerial flights, which took three months to learn. One final important cadence was *kbach mul*, the general movement pattern of princes and gods, which required a month of training. Derived from it, however, was the movement of the *ngo* prince in the Preah Saing drama, which involved complicated moves with the magic staff and required six months to learn.[9]

The traditional method of rehearsal did not include accompanying music or song; "the mistress strikes the floor with a rod to give the rhythm, and with the rod corrects the pupils' positions or points out mistakes," reported Zarina in 1937.[10] In 1975 at UBA, however, the *sampho*, one *roneat*, and usually the *skor thom* accompanied all rehearsals; the older teachers used *khrab* to keep rhythm and often sang if the dance was going smoothly.

Teaching Method

In the Khmer method of rehearsal, the students at first follow the example of one of the assistant teachers, who demonstrates each segment, often at great length without a pause. The music or rhythm beaters stop only if the teacher so indicates. Never, for any reason whatsoever, does the student speak. Questions are never asked. Complaints are unheard of. A formality and a silent respect for the teacher inform the entire rehearsal. In each segment, the student does not stop dancing, regardless of her errors or the teachers' corrections.

Teachers give instruction to students by moving their bodies into the correct position while the student is dancing. The teacher rarely speaks. Rather, she holds the student or pushes and pulls her into each correct posture or movement. Never does she stop and re-work a movement unless she brings the entire class to a halt and begins the whole segment again. Thus, it is the student's body which learns the dance—a kinesthetic, non-intellectual method used in much of Southeast Asia.

Mental Qualities of the Dancer

In addition to creating skillful dancers, the Khmer training method inculcates two important qualities: a fierce pride and a supremely trained memory. Regarding the latter, palace dancers at age twelve were formerly skilled in all the important *kbach* appropriate to their role group. For a role such as Sovann Machha, however, only one dancer among the princess-role dancers would learn it and often with very little rehearsal (Fig. 8-1). George Groslier insisted, for instance, that at age eighteen a dancer could be abruptly chosen to play Sovann Machha and could learn the role—consisting of hundreds of combinations of elements already individually known to her, and "lasting several hours"—in four or five long rehearsals without asking questions or taking written notes, and that two years later she could re-perform it after a single rehearsal.[11]

8-1. **Rehearsal for the Dance of Sovann Maccha** (right) **and Hanuman** (left).
Photo Paul Cravath.

The important factor in Groslier's example is that the dancer in question was eighteen; with younger dancers it may very well take six months, as Thiounn claimed, because many years were required to learn all the variations of the *kbach*. Quite simply, what dancers traditionally did with their time—aside from eating and gossip—was to memorize with the body. The cumulative effect of this can be seen in the statement of Em Theay— the best chanter throughout the 1960s and the early 1970s and a former dancer—who said, "If I know the words, I never forget how to dance."[12]

As for the pride of the palace dancers, it was monumental and came easily to them. They were the most beautiful women in the kingdom, they were indulged and revered, and they were members of the royal entourage, more visible than aristocracy. During the Sihanouk era, they were widely traveled and married the top generals and the elite of Phnom Penh. Their self-image is perhaps best articulated in the words of Saramani, the hero of Roland Meyer's highly regarded account of a palace dancer's life early in the century.

> . . . We are not made like the women of the people; in the palace, far from the world, the existence that we lead has transformed our mind and made our body a precious thing, fragile and delicate through the power of compliance; our energy feeds a fire which is not a physical force as much

> as an excitement, a flight of joy, an opportunity for extravagance, beauty, art, music, all blended with a mystic awe of the spirits, the *kru lakhon*, the invisible protectors of all those involved in their worship.[13]

Beneath its French intellectual form, this statement captures the aura of pride and privilege surrounding even the ex-royal dancers in 1975.

The dancer's pride in her position and her art was traditionally accompanied by a moral code which further set her apart from society. In the annual *sampeah kru* ceremony—the ritual significance of which will be considered in Chapter IX—all dancers took the five Buddhist vows to avoid killing, stealing, causing infidelity, lying, and alcohol.[14] This suggests the mental strength of character that dancers were expected to develop.

As for what transpires in the mind during performance, Chheng Phon has said that while the dancer knows the technique, understands the movements, and may even be aware of theory or "meaning," she still remains a "natural person." During the dance, however, she must concentrate on her role, "not like a real person but as a person in another space."[15] Always facial expressions are restrained; when Rām discovers Sitā's abduction, for instance, his face remains nearly impassive. Thus, despite the distractions of audience, costume, and the unexpected, the dancer must practice, above all, a calmness of mind.

How this was taught is not known, but the evidence suggests that it was primarily by silent example. If the dancer never experienced verbal interchange in any aspect of training—which was certainly the case—and only rarely was spoken to by the teacher, the dancer's mental questions, doubt, and commentary were probably much restricted as a result. Zarina recounts that when she studied Khmer dance with Say Sangvann, the princess told her, "Don't smile with your mouth. Smile with your eyes."[16] What this means in broader application is that the Khmer dancer's performance is largely non-cerebral and that she does not communicate to the audience with either words or thoughts; she herself is the communication. Thus, according to Chheng Phon, "what remains uniquely in Khmer dance is interior serenity, concentration and meditation of the dancer."[17]

The Annual Awards Ceremony

Distinct from the annual *sampeah kru* ceremony in which all dancers were presented to the *eysei* as the symbolic leader of the ensemble, a modern awards ceremony in which certificates and prizes were awarded to selected dance students was organized by Princess Kossamak, Sihanouk's mother, after she became Queen. The ceremony never gained the popularity or held the significance of the *sampeah kru* and was not held after Sihanouk's demise in 1970.

The program describing the "distribution of certificates to student dancers" on Saturday, 21 December 1957, at 8:30 p.m. (in contrast to traditional dance ceremonies always held on auspicious Thursdays during the day), does not name recipients of the certificates. It does list nine prize-winners, however. Beginning with star dancer Neang Bunnak, followed by others whose names frequently appear in Royal Palace performance programs of the 1950s, the list concludes with Princess Buppha Devi who received the highest award, the White Lotus.

The event is interesting in that the *première* dancers performed only a single, brief dance after watching a program of young student dancers—including the princess, who then received a higher prize than any of them. The program consisted of ten dances: four by young dancers in the classical style, three comic scenes by the National Theatre (UBA), a "Mongolian Dance" by the National Theatre, and two dances which had been taught to the classical dancers by members of the Cultural Mission by the People's Republic of China.

The first of the Chinese dances, listed as a "ballet," was entitled "Picking the Tea," but was seemingly performed in the Khmer style. The story was simple; eight sisters on a mountain picking tea pursue a butterfly in vain. Curiously, the program lists seven different schools in which the nine performers were enrolled. Two were from École de Danse Royale, two from École Botum Reachea, and one each from École Malika, Lycée Descartes, and Chrui Changwar. "Her Royal Highness Princess Norodom Buppha Devi" from College Preah Norodom played the youngest sister, and

"His Royal Highness Prince Chakrapongs" of École Norodom carried the butterfly. The significance of these schools in classical dance education is unknown.

The second Chinese dance, entitled the "Lotus Dance," was performed by the "Royal Ballet," after which the nine prizes were awarded and tea was served. One feels that an important purpose of this modern ceremony was to distinguish members of the royal family who had recently revived the ancient custom of receiving dance training.

Life Style of Palace Dancers

As with harems in other cultures, the Cambodian palace dancers were traditionally under the direction of the king's principal wife. In the reign of Sisowath, for instance, the first wife was "absolute mistress" of the *lakhon* in giving punishment, regulating discipline, supervising rehearsals, and assuring the regularity of their attendance upon His Majesty.[18] The same was true during the reign of Monivong.[19] Under Sihanouk, these functions were fulfilled by his mother—who later did become queen.

The society in which Khmer dancers traditionally lived was almost totally one of women in a strict hierarchy of servants, students, administrators, dancers, lead dancers, teachers, members of the court, and the royal family. With the exception of the king and a small number of his household, the only men seen with any frequency by the dancers were the musicians. (There seems always to have been a great social chasm, however, between the dancers and the musicians; even in 1975 the dancers rarely spoke to the musicians, except for the old lady teachers who yelled orders at them or occasionally chided *en masse*.) Maintenance of the dancers' ignorance—beyond the realm of hearsay—regarding city boys, palace guests, and the king's relatives, engendered, according to the earliest female scholar of the dance, a "small feminine world" perpetually agitated by intrigue and jealousy.[20]

The chief reward in the traditional dancer's world, apart from the prestige of being a lead dancer or the financial gain accorded the king's favorite, was the possibility of bearing the monarch a child. The ritual function of Khmer dancers was not based upon virginity; quite the opposite. "When they attained the age of puberty, they were destined first for the pleasure of the king, but once deflowered they did not cease to dance," observed Jeanne Cuisinier. "Maternity alone brought an end to their career."[21] As Groslier pointed out, this could happen at age fifteen or earlier.[22]

A dancer could be "driven out" of the palace for other reasons,[23] but in the case of pregnancy, she was automatically set up in a small house near the palace and provided by the king with both money and respectful attendants. Occasionally, as with Sihanouk's first wife, the dancer was married by the king, but, remaining within the palace, she no longer danced.

Regarding the accommodations provided for dancers within the palace, Groslier wrote in 1911 that

> while the favorites and *premières danseuses* have isolated houses where they live surrounded by servants whom their pay permits them to keep, the other dancers must be content, each with a compartment in a long, yellow and smoky house. This compartment is divided into two rooms. In one, the actress eats and makes her toilet. The other room is the bedroom.[24]

Surprisingly these quarters in 1975 remained very much as Groslier had described. They contained a few pieces of furniture—a wooden bed, some mats, a chest, a small cupboard—and a few personal possessions. No dancers, teachers, dressers, or servants lived there anymore, but a few former dancers maintained their compartments and occasionally spent the night. While they were run-down and felt abandoned, these dancers' quarters (to the west of the throne room) retained the peaceful charm of some very special village.

Dancers did not do their own cooking. For four piasters a month (in 1911), meals were provided at 10:00 a.m. and 6:00 p.m., either by women from outside the palace or by the dancer's own family. Women vendors also wandered through the area from morning to night selling such inexpensive delicacies as "rice cooked in coconut-milk or cakes made from ducks' eggs, …mangoes, bananas dried in the sun and flavored with vanilla; watermelon seeds and grilled lotus; and guava confections served in sugar flowers."[25]

The only demands on the dancers' time were rehearsals—which, after the age of eighteen, were not lengthy—and attending the king for a quarter of the day. In later years, very young dancers sometimes spent their evenings learning to read and write. Beyond that, they were totally free. They bathed, ate, sewed, enjoyed friends, listened to the stories of current marvels, slandered and criticized their companions, discussed the gossip from town and country brought in by the cooks and servants, and, like virtually all the young and old of Phnom Penh who strolled along the Mekong each evening, they dressed in their finest clothes and walked at dusk through the palace gardens with arms entwined, singing softly.[26]

Before this life style was radically altered by the permission given dancers to live outside the palace, the *lakhon* continued in this pattern until she ceased dancing. According to Em Theay, this usually occurred around age thirty "if they are not as beautiful as before, because the dance requires beauty."[27] Upon retiring, dancers could leave the palace, but most had nowhere to go and so remained in the society they knew, selling off their few treasures and working as chorus members or as teachers, seamstresses, dressers, and, at the lowest point, as servants and dealers in second-hand clothing. In 1911 Groslier noted that the palace was peopled with "frightful old women" always at the center of every intrigue.[28]

In an important sense, however, the retired dancer took on a new role in perpetuating the method and knowledge of the dance. She taught the next generation the movements and the secrets, such as how to rub the early-morning dew on muscles and joints daily to aid suppleness,[29] or the formula for the foolproof unguent that could heal the most seriously sprained ankle in twenty-four hours.[30] She knew how to make the ritual offerings and perform the ceremonies required by the king. She understood the spirits. She knew the lyrics to all the songs from which other elements of performance could be re-created. Unless she came to be favored by the king, she lived her life in what amounted to a sensuous nunnery, dedicated solely to the dance. When she became sick with old age, her body was carried outside—since no one could die within the palace enclosure—and at death, her body was burned without ceremony.[31]

DANCER COSTUMES

THE COSTUME ROOM

As in many theatre companies, the palace costume shop tended to be a nucleus of energy second only to the stage itself. With the almost total cancellation of performances in the early months of 1975, the costume shop was the one spot in the dancers' world that remained largely unchanged. Located, in part, beneath the audience hall of the throne room, the costume shop was a large space with thirteen-foot ceilings that rambled around four huge central pillars. On three sides were large alcoves with eight-foot ceilings containing enormous glass-fronted armoires stuffed with piles of fabric, embroidered costume pieces, and boxes of necessities. In various corners of the room were large trunks of wood or metal for costume shipment on tour. To one side was a sewing machine under a skylight. Ladies at work with hand-sewing sat on woven mats in the center of the room.

One of the pillars supporting the throne room was provided with hooks on which hung about forty masks, ten to a side, belonging to the monkey and demon roles. Shelves were everywhere. The jeweled *mkot* and other head ornaments for the prince and princess roles were in safekeeping at some other location, but the room betrayed glimpses of gold, brocade, and silk throughout. Only one door was visible, with entry from the south; there were no windows in the thick stone walls.

Against the wall that faced the door was the altar. Flower and incense offerings were made each morning by the seamstresses and others who stopped by. When Em Theay went to teach Chheng Phon's students on the farm at Obek Khaom, she carried incense from this altar. Each Thursday the dance teachers made offerings here in a simple ceremony known as *twaj kru* (further discussed in Chapter IX), so that the altar was beautifully filled with flowers, fruit, and the small *bai sei* structures made from banana trunk decorated with flowers and surmounted by an egg.

The Costumes: Some General Distinctions

In the course of a dancer's training, the *sampeah kru* ceremony marked the point at which she first received the teacher's permission to perform the role she had been studying and to wear the costume and ornaments of that role—particularly the numinous mask or headpiece. This annual ceremony will be discussed at length in Chapter IX. At this point we should only note that the *sampeah kru* was a dedication, an empowerment, and a graduation, and that all of these were symbolized by the costume which the young dancer who had performed the ceremony was permitted to wear. Thus, we turn to an examination of the costumes worn by each of the distinct role types, in accordance with Thiounn's delineation of eight masculine and five feminine categories. As prelude, we will note a number of qualities that distinguish the costume types, as well as other general qualities which all of them share.

Basic Khmer dress traditionally consisted of a single piece of cloth, the *sampot*, wrapped around the lower body and gathered at the waist to form a skirt. Both men and women then drew the front pleats between the legs and tucked them into the belt at the back, creating loose pants. Women, who in Angkorean times were bare-breasted, in later centuries wore a second piece of cloth tucked into the waist at the right side and loosely draped over the left shoulder. Khmer dance costumes are, with one exception, an elaboration of this model.

As significant as the close relationship between the dancers' costumes and those in popular usage, is the fact that costumes used in the context of other rituals in Cambodia are very similar to the royal dancers'. The dress of the king at his coronation, for instance, is identical to that worn by a dancer-prince. In the same way, the costume of a dancer-princess is "similar to those worn in everyday life by little girls at the ceremony of the cutting of the hair and by brides."[32] Given the nature of these rituals, in which all elements must scrupulously re-create the traditional pattern, it is unlikely that these costumes have changed significantly in hundreds of years.

On the Khmer stage, however, the fabrics have become heavier and more ornate than those in traditional popular usage. Added front and side panels have duplicated the image of the central vertical pleats. For the female roles, a barely visible bodice, which leaves the right shoulder bare and has a single shoulder strap on the left, now adds modesty beneath the scarf. This originally diaphanous shawl is today made of stiff, gold-embroidered brocade which hangs down the back to mid-thigh level. Feet have remained bare.

Only in the masculine roles has a completely new element appeared—the tight fitting, long-sleeved jacket with small wings, or *entam*, on the shoulders. While the four basic character types in Khmer dance are male, female, monkey and ogre, all character costumes may be loosely divided into masculine and feminine and all are based—with the addition of jewelry, masks and headgear—on this general model (Fig. 8-2).

Popular belief holds that the tight fitting, heavy dance costumes reflect a Thai influence, since the Thai originated in the "cold north" and were "used to wearing a lot of clothes." During the years when Khmer court dance was being adopted by the Thai court at Ayuthaya, the semi-nudity of the dancers was considered inappropriately pastoral or savage, so it is said, and as a result the dancers came to be dressed more in the style of elaborate Thai court uniforms.[33] The argument seems reasonable, in part, especially regarding the addition of the male roles' jacket—on which shoulder wings appear for kings, princes, soldiers, gods, and giants (but not for monkeys).

While the shoulder wings are common to the Khmer, Thai, and Lao dance traditions, they are also known in Indonesia. In the ancient martial dances of Sumatra and Nias, performed by men, "the main feature of the warriors' costume [is] a metal armor jacket with upturned shoulder wings...."[34] These represent a tradition much older than the Thai and one from which Khmer tradition holds that many elements of their dance originated. Such elements notwithstanding, the fundamental Khmer dance costume, and certainly the accompanying jewelry, is derived from popular dress and from Angkorean styles and their antecedents.

A word may be said about the undergarments common to all roles and probably derived as well from the Thai court. Just as the feminine bodice

8-2. **Costumes of the Four Basic Character Types.** (l-r: male, female, monkey, ogre) Cogniat, *Danses D'Indochine*, ca. 1932.

maintained the lines of the breast scarf by having no right sleeve or shoulder, all roles now wear fitted pants under the *sampot*, which do little more than add layers of fabric to the same silhouette, presumably for modesty. On the masculine roles, the embroidered bottoms of the trouser legs, which reach to the upper calf, accentuate the border decorations on the *sampot* more than they actually change the manner in which the *sampot* covers the leg. Similarly, feminine roles wear somewhat smaller pants as well as an underskirt, but neither is ever seen beneath the ankle-length *sampot*.

Each group of roles in the classical dance has a costume whose details and number of ornaments are scrupulously fixed according to a strict hierarchy. Attendants, for example, wear similar but less elaborate forms of the costumes worn by those whom they serve. This principle also applies to the masks worn by many of the masculine roles, in that the monkey or ogre general, for instance, will be more elaborately dressed and wear a more distinctive mask than his soldiers. One method of distinguishing levels of hierarchy is with the use of color.

Colors used in masks and colors used in costumes are not dictated by the same conventions on the Khmer stage. While it is certain that the color of a mask is fixed for each character and serves as a badge of identification, the same is not always true for costume colors, which may vary. In the *roeung* dramas, costume colors tend to follow certain patterns but with no great significance. Rām, Sitā, and Laks, for instance, all wear dark green or blue outer garments and Sitā wears a distinctive bodice, usually red—though it can also be yellow or blue—beneath her gold-embroidered shawl. These colors, however, are almost totally obscured by the heavy gold and silver embroidery, and it is that level of ornamentation rather than the color of the basic fabric which identifies a character's stature.

In the *robam* the costumes are lighter in weight, generally less ornate, and are designed with greater variety of color. Well into this century, the choice of color was based on the calendar, as George Groslier noted in 1913.

> In the court, the *sampot*, the costumes, are subject to a daily color change: Sunday, red; Monday, light yellow; Tuesday, green; Wednesday, violet; Thursday, dark blue; Friday, light blue; Saturday, black. According to the ballet taking place on these days, the *sampot* of the actresses, have a corresponding color.[35]

The close link between the dancer and the cycle of nature revealed by this practice suggests that her appearance, like the seasons, may change. By contrast, her mask or headdress represents the form of a timeless principle.

Masculine Role Costumes

The following discussion follows Thiounn's delineation of eight types of masculine roles: gods and royalty, governors or generals, *yakkha* (ogres), monkeys, birds, the *ngo*, the *eysei* (hermit), and the clowns. Distinctive costume elements, jewelry, and props will be noted: crowns, masks, and headgear will be discussed separately. The transcriptions of Khmer terms are Thiounn's.

Gods and kings, known collectively as *neay rong ek*, together with princes (*neay rong raong*) comprise the first category of male roles. Costumes for all are the same and consist of pants (*choeng khor*), a jacket (*ao-pak*) of silk brocade with a silk embroidered collar (*srang kar*), two small shoulder ornaments (*entam* or *intanou*) shaped like wings, a gold or silver *sampot* called *sarabap* secured with a silk belt, a panel of cloth (*robaing muk*) hanging in front like a narrow apron flanked by side panels (*cheay kreng*), and a silver filigree belt with a gold buckle (Fig. 8-3). This belt, formerly set with diamonds, covers the first belt. At one side of the belt was often placed a gold stiletto (*sang ver*), made in latter times of gilded wood.

In 1931 Thiounn wrote that wrist jewelry for the *neay rong ek* included four pairs of bracelets—one of each pair on each arm—consisting of two sets of rings (*kangkan* and *kangrak*), a set made of filigree (*kravel day*), and a fourth set (*patrum*) made of forty small beads of gold. He reported that feminine roles of high stature wore only three sets of bracelets—*kang day*, *kravel day*, and *patrum*.[36] Photographs from the period, however, show the bracelets to be different from Thiounn's description (Fig. 8-4).

Interestingly, Groslier's description of the jewelry in 1913 conforms more closely with current usage.[37] Five pair of bracelets, in an unchangeable order, are worn on each wrist, in addition to which the masculine roles wear a wide cuff simulating five more ring bracelets on the upper wrists (Fig. 8-5). Parenthetically, the fifth bracelet from the hand represents a strand of tightly strung flower buds.

On the ankles are worn a pair of rings (*kang choeng*) and a pair of filigree anklets (*kravel choeng*). Other jewelry includes a band of five chains (*khsé khluon*) worn crosswise over the chest and back and often known by the French term *sautoir*; a pendant (*slek por*) in the shape of a banyan leaf; a pair of earrings (*tumhou*) ornamented with diamonds; and the crown (*mkot*).

The second category of male costumes is that of generals or governors (*phi lieng ek*) and their attending officers. In the *roeung* requiring these roles, there are four governors and twelve officers. Governors' costumes are similar to those of kings and princes with these differences: the *sampot* (*lboeuk*) is made of plain silk rather than brocade; a satin sheath replaces

8-3. **Masculine Role Costume of a Prince, ca. 1932.** Cogniat, *Danses D'Indochine*.

the actual stiletto; and the headpiece is a diadem (*pannthiereth*) made of gilded cardboard set with glittering fragments and supporting false hair pieces which cover the back of the neck. Costumes for the twelve attending officers (*sena ek*) are of the same style but less elegant than those for the generals. Their wide outer belt is of satin with a gilded leather buckle; only one pair of ankle bracelets is worn (*kang choeng*); their *patrum* wrist bracelets consist of twenty silver beads; and only three chains are worn crosswise over the chest.

Attendants to the officers do not usually wear the false hair either. However, a photo from about 1932 shows what is either the governors with false hair—albeit very short (and missing one ankle bracelet)—or the attendants with their own hair unusually visible (Fig. 8-6). The foreground

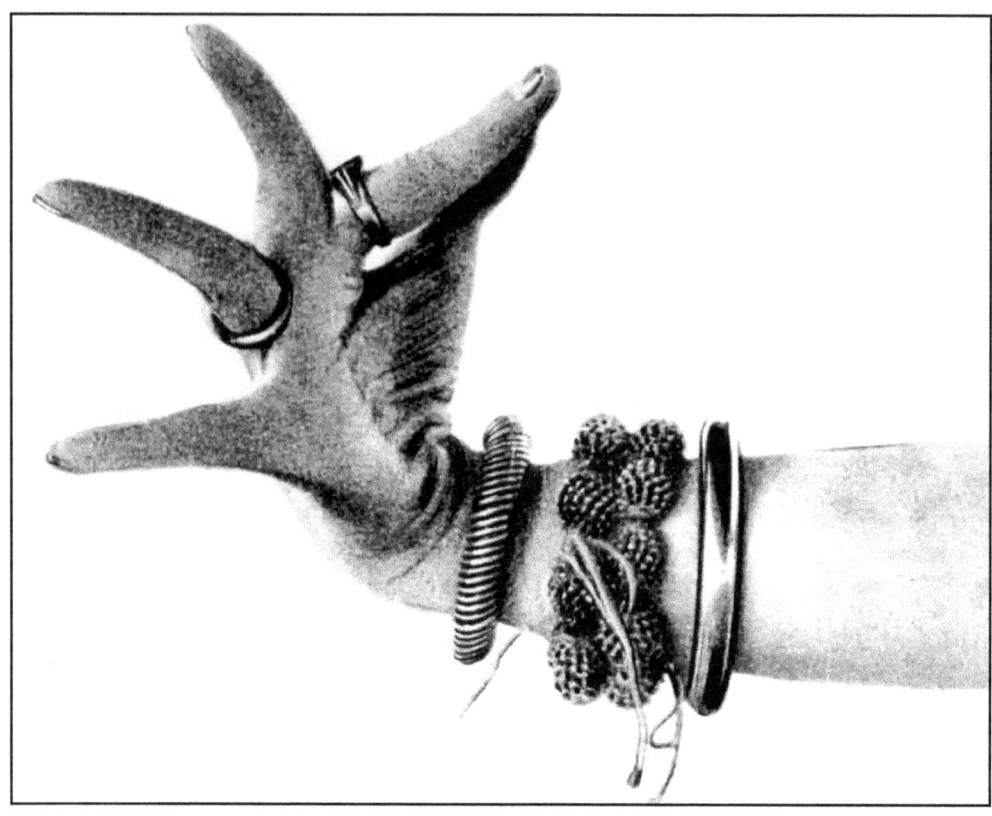

8-4. **Four Basic Bracelets, ca. 1932.** Cogniat, *Danses D'Indochine.*

characters are probably the latter, since their *panntiereth* crown is of a simpler form than that worn by governors (Fig. 8-18). The photo notes that it was taken at a rehearsal, which may explain the casual costume procedure.

A third group of characters identifiable by costume are always masked; these are the *yakkha*, the giants or ogres. Like the monkeys, their ranks form a hierarchy of officers, chiefs of soldiers, and soldiers. Above them all stand Rāb, the King of the Giants (*yak ek*), and his aide-de-camp the Prince (*yak raong*), whose personal name is Muk Kantuy Man, a reference to the rooster tail which adorns the crown of his mask.

Rāb's costume is exactly that of a king. Together with the mask and other jewelry, his costume is the most costly in the entire ensemble; in 1930, for instance, the gold and jewels for Rāb alone were worth U.S. $1,000.[38] Rāb's costume differs slightly from that of a human king or divinity in that the panels on each leg are not rectangular but, rather, cut to a point and slightly turned up toward the back where there is a fourth hanging panel. In addition to the stiletto, Rāb carries three daggers (*kroeus*) in his belt.

The Prince of the Giants wears a similar costume and the same jewelry, except that silver gilt replaces the gold. He does not have the three daggers, however. The point of his mask is nearly as tall as Rāb's but takes the form of a stylized rooster tail; it has no extra faces carved into it. There are four *yakkha* officers dressed like the human officers, but their large-fanged masks give them the image of having enormous heads covered with short, curly hair. Two soldier chiefs (*neay khen yak*) wear no jewelry and almost no accessories; their jackets and silk *sampot* are red. Their pants (*attalat saron*)—also red—are longer than those of the others. The soldier chiefs wear a red silk scarf (*tuon*) with a lace border as a kind of baldric in place of chains across the chest, and their hair is in a red silk turban with gold flowers. A complete *yakkha* army includes twenty soldiers (*puok khen yak*), who do not wear the shoulder scarf and, instead of silk, wear a cotton *sampot* (*khien*).

8-5. **Masculine Role Bracelets.** *Nokor Khmer.*

8-6. **Attendants in Foreground, ca. 1932.** Cogniat, *Danses D'Indochine.*

The fourth group of masculine roles is the monkey army consisting of officers, chief of soldiers (*neay khen sva*), and soldiers (*puok khen sva*). Their costumes and jewelry have the same components, correspondingly, as the human and *yakkha* armies, except that all costumes have a tightly twisted length of silk tied at the back to represent a tail. There is also a distinctive spiral pattern on the fabric which represents hair.

Monkey masks are the same color as the costume, which in the case of the officers are also badges of identification. Hanumān, also known as Sva Sar, is in white (Fig. 8-7); the black monkey (*Nillaphat*) is known as Sva Khmao; Sugrib (Sugriva), the red monkey is called Nilla Ek, Maha Chumpou, or Chum Pou Pean; and Bāli, or Angkot, is the green monkey. Even the monkey generals, however, do not wear the pointed crown or shoulder wings. The standard number of soldiers in the monkey army number at least as many as the *yakkha* army.

The fifth group of masculine costumes belong to the birds, of whom the main character is *krut*, or *garuda*, the King of the Birds (Fig. 8-8). His jacket is of silk *lamé*. The panels in front and on the side are replaced by a pair of shin guards (*snap choeng*) and knee pads (*snap chung kong*), both of red embroidered silk. He also wears on either hip a gold *lamé* wing which is supported on a brass frame, as is his silk tail rising in the air behind. A panel of unique design hangs at his front, and he wears winged wrist guards (*snap day*) on both forearms. His small collar and the small wings on the shoulder are slightly different in shape from those of the princes' costumes; the jewelry, however, is similar. The *krut* mask holds a large pearl between the two points of its beak and has the pointed crown common to other royalty.

Others in the bird group are the *kennara* and the *sarika*, or talking blackbird. The costumes of the four dancers playing the *kennara*, a group of mythical bird-men (and partners to four *kennari* bird-women whose mythological prototype is shown in Fig. 5-2), are a mixture of those of the princes and the *krut*. The pants, the velvet jacket and gold leather collar encrusted with small pieces of mirror, the *mkot* crown, and the jewelry are all similar in design if not material to those of the *krut*. The *kennara* are further distinguished by a pair of armbands of embossed and gilded leather,

Chapter VIII: The Royal Dancer: Training and Costumes   395

8-7. **Hanumān, Making** *Sampeah*. *Nokor Khmer.*

a leather plate (*phchet*) similarly decorated covering the stomach, a silk flap (*tat*) which narrows as it descends to the knees, and a breast cover made of two small cups of gilded brass joined together by small thin chains (Fig. 8-9).

The *sarika* role, or blackbird, although belonging to the same group, has a completely different costume and is entirely dressed in black. The jacket, pants, wings and tail are of thick satin; the gloves, socks and garters are of thinner silk. All jewelry and accessories are eliminated except for a blackbird mask.

Thiounn places the role of the *ngo*, the disguised form of Preah Sang, in a category unto itself, despite the fact that his costume is basically that of a prince. The belt on his black brocade costume, however, is that of the officers, and he wears

8-8. **The Costume of** *Krut*, **King of the Birds, ca. 1932.** Cogniat, *Danses D'Indochine.*

8-9. The *Kennara* and *Kennari* Bird-People, ca. 1880. Pavie, *Géographie et voyages*.

a red silk scarf (*pha hum*) unique to the role. The *ngo* is set apart by Thiounn not only because it is the most popular character outside the *Rāmker* and the most difficult of all roles to perform, but also because the *ngo* wears a black, grimacing mask which is removed when others in the play come to realize his true beauty—seen initially only by the princess. The black mask has no head ornament whatsoever but at the play's end Preah Sang appears wearing the *mkot* crown symbolizing his true royalty. The main accessory of the role is a large, glittering cane, the proper manipulation of which is extremely difficult.

The *eysei*, one of the two roles always played by a male, forms a separate category of masculine costumes and consists basically of a long hermit's robe and a special, very sacred mask. For comic versions of the *eysei*, the mask is often replaced by a simple helmet (Fig. 8-10).

The final, masculine roles, the two clowns, wear a pants and jacket of gold-flowered silk and a cotton *sampot* (*pha lay tath*). As clowns, however, they are given license to modify the costume in imaginative ways and to add the most surprising and incongruous accessories, often from modern, everyday life.

Feminine Role Costumes

Of the five categories of feminine roles, the most noble is that of goddesses, queens and princesses (*neang ek*). They wear, in addition to a lace underskirt (*ao sbay*) embroidered with silver gilt thread, a silk bodice—with no right sleeve or shoulder piece—called, like the male role's jacket, *ao pak*; a silk collar (*srang kar*); a *lamé sampot* spangled with gold or silver (*sarabap*); and a heavy velvet scarf, or *sbay* (*spai*), crossing the bodice to the left shoulder and hanging down the back in a band to mid-thigh level. This scarf matches the *sampot*—although it is lined with silk in a contrasting color—and together they can be any color deemed appropriate for the role. Early in this century Groslier

8-10. **Rāb in Disguise as the Eysei Approaching Sitā.** *Nokor Khmer.*

held that this *sbay* was usually light green, light yellow, crimson, or white.[39] In the early 1970s Sitā wore dark green—almost black—but with a bright crimson *ao pak* underneath.

The *sampot* for feminine roles is about 3 ½ yards long and 1 ½ yards wide. The front is pleated and tucked securely into a cord worn under the belt in such a manner as to form a fan of pleats hanging over the belt (Fig. 8-11).

Jewelry includes a gilded silver belt and a gold buckle set with diamonds; five chains worn crosswise from the left shoulder to the right hip; a neck pendant in the stylized shape of a banyan leaf (*slek por*), which is far more ornate than the masculine role pendant; a pair of diamond roseate earrings (*tumhou*); and an arm bracelet (*baing phap*)—not used by masculine characters—made of precious stones and worn on the bare right bicep, reproducing a similar armlet worn by feminine figures in Angkorean sculpture. Two ankle bracelets and the gold *mkot* crown complete the jewelry. For princesses (*neang raong*), the crown is not as tall as for male roles, and is often made of simpler materials—gold-lacquered leather or cardboard encrusted with tiny mirror pieces. Until at least early in this century, leading dancers wore large rings on each of the four fingers of both hands; by the 1960s, dancers usually wore just one ring on the third finger of each hand.

The second category of feminine roles includes the four consorts of the governors (*phi lieng ek*) and their twenty attendants (*kom nan*). These female governors are dressed like the queens except that the *sampot* is of silk rather than the heavily spangled *lamé*; they wear only three chains over the shoulder and these are of gilded silver; one ankle bracelet and the precious stones in the armband are eliminated; wrist bracelets are smaller; and they wear a low diadem in place of the *mkot* crown (Fig. 7-64).

The diadem (*kbaing na*) of the attendants is even less elaborate than that of the female governors, and, in general, they are dressed less elaborately; they wear only three bracelets, for instance. These attendants, however, often appear on stage singly as servants and are distinguished by one significant difference in costume: their shawl is much larger than all other feminine roles and is of a different design, gathered in front and hanging down the back of both shoulders like a cape (Fig. 8-12).

The female ogres, the *yakkhini*, are the third category of feminine roles. Unlike their male counterparts, they are never masked and are recognized by their style of movement, by the music and *kbach* associated with them, and by the choral recitation and song regarding them. Their costumes are also hierarchical, corresponding in elegance to princesses, female governors, and attendants.

While there are no female roles corresponding to the male monkeys, four female *kennari* bird-women are the consorts of the male *kennara*. Their costumes are identical; the wings and tail are worn with a yellow jacket and purple pants. The fact that they wear the *mkot* crown shows their stature and nobility to exceed that of even princes and princesses. Interestingly, both the *kennara* and *kennari* wear the brass *brassière* (Fig. 8-13).

The fifth and final feminine category belongs to the single most popular character (and episode) in the entire Khmer dance drama repertoire: the Queen of the Water, Sovann Machha. Her costume somewhat resembles masculine roles in that she wears a long-sleeved, red silk jacket—the only feminine character to wear sleeves. In the 1930s Sovann Machha wore a silk *sampot* in the style of a relatively

8-11. **Youthful Princess Buppha Devi in Feminine Role Costume.**
Courtesy of Princess Buppha Devi.

8-12. **Feminine Attendant-Servant Role, ca. 1932.** Cogniat, *Danses D'Indochine.*

full skirt (Fig. 8-14), but by the 1960s it was much tighter fitting, in the style of all other feminine roles. The costume includes a large fish tail, a strong belt and an ornate front panel. Her diadem and jewelry are similar to the female governors'. In the modern hierarchy of characters Sovann Machha's costume places her below the divinity of gods and princes, symbolized by those who wear the *mkot*. Given her mythological significance and the great age of this legend, however, the Sovann Machha crown may very well represent a style much older than the *mkot*.

All of the preceding descriptions of costumes are of those used primarily in the *roeung* dramas. In the *robam*, however, and particularly in the large group dances such as the Robam Apsaras, the female costumes are significantly different. With the exception of the lead dancer—if there is one—who may wear a different color, members of the ensemble are dressed identically. Their costumes are designed

8-13. The *Kennari-Kennara* Bird-People, ca. 1932. Cogniat, *Danses D'Indochine*.

specifically for each *robam*, but since, in many cases, the dancers are representing celestial beings, a basic costume can be noted.

The costumes of these *apsaras* differ in three ways from those of the *roeung* characters. First, there is no *sbay*, the heavy shawl hanging from the left shoulder. This makes the costume significantly less expensive than other feminine costumes and much easier to re-design in different colors. Second, the dancer wears a skin-colored, closefitting, sleeveless bodice which gives the appearance of nudity beneath her jewelry. Third, the crown, shoulder necklace, belt, and style of *sampot* are duplicates of those seen on the *devatā* in Angkorean sculpture (Figs. 7-65 and 8-15).

The significance of the first difference needs further explanation. One of the primary reasons for not changing color schemes in *roeung* costumes—both feminine and masculine—is not so much symbolic as financial. To make one *sbay* requires two or three seamstresses working for a full month at the low frame on which it is stretched. Throughout the 1970s the gold cloth of which it was made was imported from France, and the gold thread for the heavy embroidery came from India. In 1975 this thread alone cost 600,000 riels (U.S. $220) for a single *sbay*. Masculine role jackets, out of deference, have to contain even more gold.

Expense is further increased by the fact that a single costume cannot be worn indefinitely. Because the heavy, upper-body costume pieces have no fastenings but are sewn onto the dancer prior to each performance, they are easily sweat-soaked. Groslier has reported that

8-14. **Sovann Machha, ca. 1932.** Cogniat, *Danses D'Indochine.*

> a *première danseuse* wears her costume only about ten times. After that it is worn by ordinary dancers for thirty appearances.... Then it is cut to the figure of a little girl and finally,... soaked with sweat and soiled with paint, it is burned.[40]

A costume in a color identified exclusively with Sitā or Rām could not have been passed on to other dancers, and the alternate system of simply giving the main characters the richest, newest and freshest-colored costumes, regardless of color, prevailed. If the costume colors had symbolic value, a different system would undoubtedly have evolved.

We complete this discus-sion of costumes by noting that traditionally they were stored in the costume room and were checked out during the day to the dancers who would be performing that evening. After the performance, each dancer returned her own costume "in good condition and neatly folded, under penalty of a fine or of some strokes with the rattan."[41] All jewelry, by contrast, was taken from the dancer immediately following the performance and locked away by the jewel-keeper.

HEADGEAR AND FLOWERS

8-15. *Apsaras* Costume and Jewelry. *Nokor Khmer.*

There are five kinds of crowns worn by the classical dancers: the *mkot* in two forms, the *panntiereth*, the "circle of wings," the simple diadem (*kbaing na*) worn by the young dancers, and the *apsaras* headdress. Correctly speaking, the *mkot* is the crown of the Khmer king, and only the crown of the leading male-role dancer, which is an exact replica of the king's crown, should be called *mkot*. In popular usage, however, the shorter crowns of the princes as well as the different style of pointed crown belonging to the princesses are all referred to as *mkot*.

Basically, the *mkot* is a slender, multi-tiered spire which calls to mind the top of a Buddhist *stupa*, or shrine. The form worn by male roles is supported on a base larger in circumference than the head (Fig. 8-16); the feminine form has a much smaller base and is precariously perched on the top of the head (Fig. 8-17). The *mkot* of feminine roles is further distinguished by a crescent-shaped diadem framing the upper face.

The weight of the *mkot* and the difficulty in balancing it on the head may have influenced the erect manner in which dancers hold the head. The *mkot* was formerly supported by a cord under the chin, but the light weight versions in general use today dispense with this device.

The height of the feminine *mkot* is always less than that of the corresponding masculine role. It is also less ornate. In both the feminine and masculine *mkot*, side wings rise above the ears and up the back of the head. Traditionally, the male crown was decorated with diamond roseates suspended on tiny springs; the feminine *mkot* had only mirrored glass, but both sparkled with the smallest head movement. At the center of the crown, the most "favored dancer" wore a small bird made of diamonds (Figs. 7-21 and 7-35).

The *mkot* was formerly made of gold leaf and gems on a leather or cardboard base and weighed nearly two pounds; parenthetically, other jewelry worn by a lead dancer weighed about six pounds.[42] In 1930 Thiounn estimated the value of the *mkot* at U.S. $200 (800 piastres), the value of the jewelry for a king or deity costume at more than $500, and the total cost of costume and jewelry together at $950.[43] Only seven years later the estimated cost for a complete princess' costume, jewelry and *mkot* was $1,250 and for a king's regalia $2,000.[44] Since the 1930s these costs have skyrocketed, with the result that for roughly 5 percent of the cost of the lead dancer's *mkot*, a gilded cardboard facsimile, which is also much lighter in weight, has come to be used by all dancers wearing this style of headdress.

8-16. The Mkot for Masculine Roles.
Nokor Khmer.

Before the *mkot* is placed on the dancer's head prior to performance, she always salutes it with *sampeah*, perhaps in part because the headdress is said to symbolize Mt. Meru,[45] the mountain believed to stand at the center of the universe in the Buddhist cosmology. While the present form of the *mkot* is often attributed to a Thai origin because it does not appear in precisely the single-spired form in the bas-reliefs at Angkor,[46] the present-

8-17. **The Mkot for Feminine Roles** (featuring Menh Kosni). *Nokor Khmer.*

day feminine *mkot* is, in fact, very similar to headdresses in the general Angkorean style;[47] only the height of the spire has increased.

Whether the dancer venerates the *mkot* for its Buddhist symbology, for its link with Angkorean dance, for its identification with the king and divinities, or because, like the mask of her associates, it embodies the spirit of the role, we cannot say. Certainly, however, the crown is believed to have great power. If the smallest gem or piece of the crown falls off during performance, it is considered a sign of grave misfortune, and the dancer must subsequently make prayers and offerings at the altar in order to avoid negative effects.

The crown worn by the second rank of roles—specifically, the male and female governors (generals) and their attendants—is known as *panntiereth*. (Thiounn's transcription is *pancharet*. Figure 8-18 shows a purported general wearing the *panntiereth*, but the 1913 sketch omits both the false hair worn at the back and the ankle bracelets required of a general.) This crown is very light in weight and is usually hung with small flower garlands. In the past, if the favorite dancer of the king played the role of a general, her *panntiereth* could also be ornamented with the diamond bird.

The third style of headdress is the low "truncated cone" surrounded by small flame-like wings pointing upward (Fig. 8-14). It is worn by servant/soldier roles and by Sovann Machha.

The fourth style of head ornament is worn only by very young dancers. It is a simple crescent-shaped diadem which holds the hair in a chignon and is worn on the very top of the head.

The fifth crown, that of the *apsaras*, attempts to faithfully copy the headdresses seen in Angkorean sculpture and is an innovation of the Sihanouk era. These crowns are exquisitely constructed of delicate materials representing gold (Fig. 8-15). Presumably they were made by the royal jewelers, long reputed to be smokers of opium;[48] if so, these intricate crowns are truly worthy of their finest dreams.

Traditionally, dancers' hair was clipped to a very short length; such was the Khmer custom for young women, but it was also an advantage in wearing the masks and crowns. In the 1880s, however, Pavie reported that most of the dancers playing feminine roles wore wigs.[49] At approximately the time that modern, beauty-enhancing makeup came to be worn by the dancers—certainly by the Sihanouk era—dancers no longer cut their hair short and began to maintain fashionable hair styles often partly visible beneath their headgear.

The final element of ornamentation worn in the manner of jewelry is the dancers' flowers. These are traditionally prepared in the afternoon (following a morning rehearsal) on those days when there is to be an evening performance and are kept in water until shortly before performance. For the most part, only jasmine and champa flowers are worn, and they are used in two ways. A pendant of champa flowers hanging from small strings of jasmine is attached to the *mkot* of all masculine and feminine roles of noble stature. Feminine roles wear the pendant in front of the left ear and place a single large flower of any variety above the right ear; masculine roles reverse the sides, but the flowers are identical (Figs. 8-16 and 8-17).

Finally a wrist bracelet of tightly compacted jasmine buds is built on a base of banana leaf and worn above the other bracelets. It is made with colored material in a

8-18. The *Panntiereth Headdress*.
G. Groslier, *Danseuses cambodgiennes*, 1913.

spiral design. Monkey roles wear none of these flowers; *yakkha* roles may wear a single flower above the right ear of their mask.

Masks

On the Khmer stage masks, which cover the entire head, are worn by *yakkha* and monkey roles; by the *krut* (*garuda*), the King of the Birds; by Preah Sang in disguise as the *ngo*; by the *eysei*; and by a few animal characters who appear infrequently. Despite some misunderstanding on this point,[50] masks are never worn by gods, kings, princes, human generals and soldiers, or by any of the feminine roles.

Like the *mkot*, character masks are the object of extreme veneration by the dancers and are the main objects on the altar during all ritual ceremonies (see Chapter IX). When a dancer is ill, she requests permission to borrow the *mkot* or mask of the role she plays, places it beside her bed, offers candles to its spirit, and explains to it her illness and her wish to be restored to health.[51] If the dancer has well served the spirit embodied by her mask, that spirit will in turn take care of her.

The masks are made of a cardboard-like material and are held on by a cord that is grasped by the teeth. They rest on a twisted handkerchief placed on the crown of the head. The only openings are the two eye holes, which makes it not only very difficult to see but also extremely hot and hard to breathe, particularly in the strenuous battle scenes. Monkey role masks have extended simian jaws (Figs. 8-7 and 8-21). *Yakkha* role masks have wide painted mouths with the large fangs of the wild boar on the upper jaw; they are also much heavier than the monkey masks due to the tall *mkot* built on the top. Masks for both *yakkha* and monkey roles are larger than the human head, and both have the small wings attached on the side just as with the *mkot*.

The largest, heaviest, and most expensive of all the masks is that of Rāb. With the exception of the *eysei* mask, it is also the most revered. Like all of the *yakkha* masks, it is surmounted by the *mkot* spire, the height of which—like the length of the tusks—bespeaks the character's position in the hierarchy of power. In Rāb's case, the *mkot* is as tall as Rām's and has nine small faces carved into it, from which the mask takes its colloquial name *muk dap* or "ten faces"—the mask's own being the tenth, presumably. The topmost head is three-dimensional and wears a *mkot* (Fig. 8-21). The mask is basically gold and white with red eyebrows and lips.

There is one other mask whose distinctive qualities should be noted in this context; that is the mask of the *krut*, King of the Birds (Figs. 8-8 and 8-19). Interestingly, he seems to have no relationship with the *kennari-kennara* bird-people, who are not masked. Groslier describes him as "the ravisher," and the mount of Vishnu; he carries a magic wand, and the bead in his beak is said to render him invisible.⁵² Like each of the *yakkha* masks, the style of the *mkot* which crowns the *krut* mask is unique to his character.

HAND PROPS AND FINGERNAILS

The hand props used by court dancers are generally considered to hold great power and during ceremonies are placed on the altar near the masks. There are three props considered to be the most important. The first is Mekhala's magic ball, which represents lightning. In 1911 it was said to be made of wood and ornamented with green and blue foil,⁵³ but today it is bright silver in color. Second is Ream Eyso's small hatchet with which he creates the thunder, and third is the eighteen-inch long, silver sword which is the talisman of Vorachhun.

There is an array of other less powerful weapons for both the human characters (Fig. 8-20A) and *yakkha* roles (Fig. 8-20B). These include the pliable gold colored bow with flames—or perhaps foliage—at either end; the arrow, which doesn't fly but after being aimed and the string released is simply returned to the belt where it is carried; and a light wooden sabre called *khant* (Skt.: khanda) about seventy centimeters long with which the *yakkha* often replace a larger club known as *dambang*.⁵⁴

8-19. **Mask of the *Krut* Role.** *Nokor Khmer* – Attributed to Guy Porée.

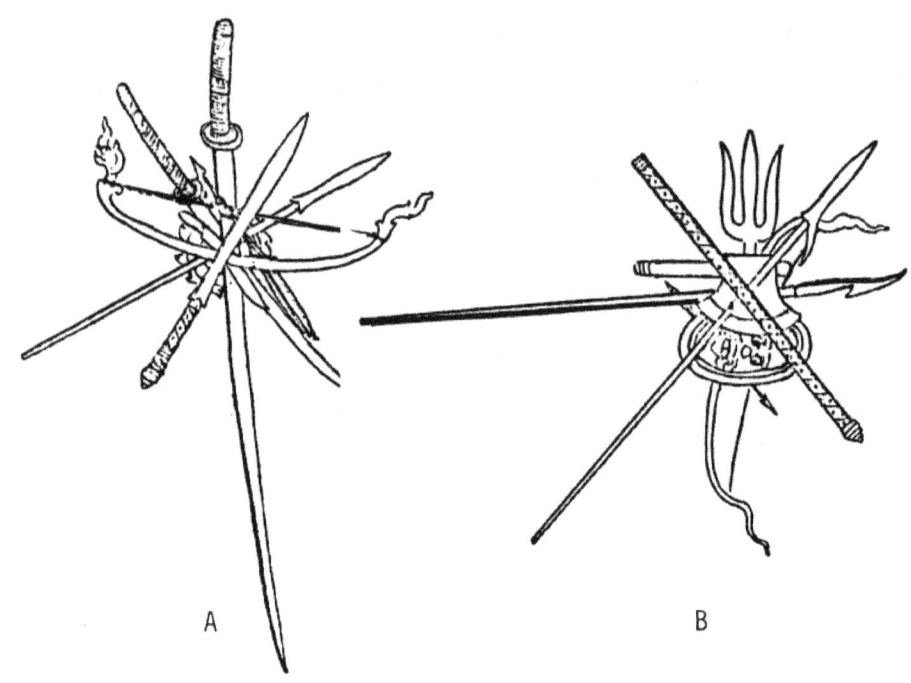

8-20. **Stage Weapons for Humans and *Yakkha*.** Leclère, *Le théâtre cambodgien*, 1911.

The *yakkha* may also carry a shield with a *yakkha* face painted on it. In the Sword Dance, five military dancers—Rāb and four generals, for instance—each carry two swords and a shield. During the first half of the dance, the shield and one sword are placed on the ground while the second sword is kept in the belt; in the second half, both swords are twirled and manipulated to simulate combat. At the end of the dance both swords are tossed to the ground.

Other hand props include a dagger for Hanumān, a short hatchet used by Rāb (Fig. 8-21), the large staff of the hermit, and the long, mirror-encrusted cane of the *ngo*. Other props considered to be less worthy of reverence, which are not usually placed on the altar, include fans for the Fan Dance as well as for the hands of princesses, servants or *yakkhini*; scarves for the Scarf Dance; gold and silver flowers or real flower petals in silver offering goblets for the flower dances; and a few other objects required by the dramatic action, such as the red cloth that symbolizes binding someone's hands.

Among the more interesting objects formerly used to focus attention on the hands were long, golden, crescent-shaped, artificial fingernails, which by the Sihanouk era were worn only rarely. While they are not pictured in carvings at Angkor, the French envoy of King Louis XIV to the Thai court, Simon de La Loubère, noted in 1688 that in the *robam* "both men and women have all false nails, and very long ones, of copper."[55]

A French traveler in Cambodia in the late 1870s has left a sketch of a male role dancer wearing the nails (Fig. 8-22), but by 1913 when George Groslier mentioned the nails, he added that they were no longer in use.[56] Today, long nails remain popular in Thailand but in Cambodia since World War II, dancers' nails, like their makeup, are most often Revlon's best (Fig. 8-23).

This chapter has focused on the more personal aspects of the court dancer's life style—elements not seen by an audience—as well as the appearance she presents to the world. In that the position of the royal Khmer dancer was somewhat of a barometer of the strength of the Cambodian court, what has been

8-21. **Close-Contact Combat Weapons for Rāb and Hanumān.** *Nokor Khmer.*

8-22. **Male Role Dancer with Artificial Fingernails.** Delaport., *Voyage au Cambodge: L'architecture Khmer, 1880.*

412 *Earth in Flower*

8-23. **Modern Makeup technique.** Photo Jaro Poncar.

said of her training refers to a time now past. To preserve the dance at all, new methods based on a freer cooperation between all those with any knowledge to share appear to be evolving. It is to be hoped that when dancers are trained, they will reappear in the beautiful images described in this chapter, and that their skill and artistry will justify their continuing existence, even without benefit of their ancient ritual function—the subject of the final chapter in this study.

Endnotes

1. Strickland-Anderson, p. 270.
2. George Groslier, *Danseuses cambodgiennes*, p. 27.
3. George Groslier, *Danseuses cambodgiennes*, p. 28.
4. Thiounn, p. 36.
5. *Danseuses cambodgiennes*, p. 33.
6. *Danseuses cambodgiennes*, p. 31.
7. *Danseuses cambodgiennes*, pp. 40-41.
8. Porée, p. 580.
9. Thiounn, p. 41.
10. P. 62.
11. "The théâtre et la danse au Cambodge," p. 137.
12. Personal communication.
13. *Saramani, danseuse khmère*, p. 59.
14. Thiounn, p. 42.
15. Personal communication.
16. "Royal Cambodian Dances," p. 71.
17. Personal communication.
18. George Groslier, *Danseuses cambodgiennes*, p. 95.
19. Zarina, p. 60.
20. Marchal, "La danse au Cambodge," p. 219.
21. *La danse sacrée en Indochine et en Indonésie*, p. 51.
22. *Danseuses cambodgiennes*, p. 101.
23. *Danseuses cambodgiennes*, p. 29. The specific reasons for dismissal are not known. Also, for some infractions, the penalty in earlier days was not merely banishment but death. The French explorer Louis Delaporte wrote the following in regard to King Norodom in 1866: "One day in conversation he requested some details on the European method of execution. Without attaching any importance to it, we satisfied the monarch's curiosity. Two hours later we were astonished to learn that four young women of the harem had been killed by European weapons and were horrified to then see their bloody heads hung up near the Palace" (Beauvais, p. 66).
24. *Danseuses cambodgiennes*, p. 105.
25. *Danseuses cambodgiennes*, p. 108.
26. The elements of food, friends, leisure, and gossip herein described are still combined by Khmer women—as well as Thai and Lao—into an idyllic ambiance unique to Southeast Asia. In his portrayal of this mood seventy years ago, George Groslier is especially perceptive (see *Danseuses cambodgiennes*, pp. 97-113).
27. Personal communication.
28. *Danseuses cambodgiennes*, p. 118.
29. Zarina, p. 62.
30. Ponder, p. 251.
31. George Groslier, *Danseuses cambodgiennes*, p. 118.
32. *Danseuses cambodgiennes*, p. 63.

33 Norodom Sihanouk as quoted by MacDonald, p. 33.
34 Claire Holt, "Dances of Sumatra and Nias," p. 4.
35 *Danseuses cambodgiennes*, p. 97, n. 18.
36 Thiounn, p. 67.
37 *Danseuses cambodgiennes*, p. 81.
38 Thiounn, p. 59. Thiounn sets the value at four thousand piastres. The calculation in U.S. dollars is based on Zarina's statement that in 1937, four piastres equaled one dollar (p. 66).
39 *Danseuses cambodgiennes*, p. 70.
40 *Danseuses cambodgiennes*, pp. 69-70.
41 *Danseuses cambodgiennes*, p. 69.
42 *Danseuses cambodgiennes*, p. 82.
43 *Danseuses cambodgiennes*, p. 59.
44 Zarina, p. 66.
45 George Groslier, *Danseuses cambodgiennes*, p. 89. Mt. Meru in turn is widely believed to symbolize the "central channel" that runs parallel with the spine and through which the enlightening energy of *kundalini* is thought to rise.
46 *Danseuses cambodgiennes*, p. 155.
47 J. Donald Lancaster, *Some Notes on the Classical Khmer Ballet* (Ithaca, N.Y.: Cornell University, 1971), p. 11. This excellent pamphlet was "prepared on the occasion of a performance by the Classical Khmer Ballet of Cambodia in celebration of twenty years of Southeast Asian studies at Cornell University."
48 Laloy, "Musique et danses cambodgiennes," p. 99.
49 Pavie, Études diverses, p. xvi.
50 Confusion has arisen over the green mask worn by Ream Eyso, which some observers have in the past attributed to Rām (e.g., Porée, p. 582). Rām is never masked.
51 George Groslier, *Danseuses cambodgiennes*, p. 78.
52 *Danseuses cambodgiennes*, pp. 48, 64.
53 Leclère, *Le théâtre cambodgien*, p. 19.
54 Leclère, *Le théâtre cambodgien*, p. 18.
55 La Loubère, p. 49.
56 *Danseuses cambodgiennes*. p. 81. Pavie noted as a matter of course that "actresses" in the 1880s wore "artificial fingernails" (*Études diverses*, p. xvi).

CHAPTER IX

THE RITUAL FUNCTION OF KHMER DANCE

មុខងារនៃក្បាច់រាំខ្មែរ

Traditionally, certain performances of the classical dance drama in Cambodia were viewed as a means of communication with the world of spirits, particularly those spirits believed to control the water and thereby the fertility of the land and the prosperity of the populace. Such public performances, as well as ceremonies performed privately, were seen either as propitiatory gifts to the spirits or as media whereby the spirits could manifest themselves to men. This chapter will examine a number of performance elements and periodic ceremonies associated with the royal dance—as well as analogies in other performing art forms—in order to clarify the nature of the Cambodian dancer's relationship with the spirit world and her ritual function in Khmer society.

DANCE AS A TRADITIONAL OFFERING

Despite an overlay of Brahmanic and Buddhist influence, Cambodian society, like many others in Southeast Asia, maintains a belief in countless animistic spirits of varying power and domain. One of the fundamental methods of retaining harmony with these spirits has always been the giving

9-1. **Buong Suong Ceremony.** At Wat Preah Kanlong near the Royal Palace.
Royal Cambodia Ballet.

of gifts: rice, water, candies, incense, prepared food, roast meat including pigs' heads, eggs, areca nut and betel leaf, as well as a major form of offering—of which there are many elaborate types—made from a decorated section of banana trunk. A Cambodian scholar has suggested that such gift giving is probably an "autochthonous" custom growing out of "magic rites" that preceded both Brahmanism and Buddhism.[1]

One other powerful offering that can be made to the spirits is dance. In her study of the "sacred dances" of Cambodia, French ethnologist Solange Thierry pointed out that many folk dances were traditionally considered to represent a point of contact between the celestial and terrestrial worlds.[2] One folk dance, for instance—the *leng trott*, in which a deer hunt is enacted—is considered to be an ancient rite for obtaining rain.[3] "Peasants of the present day affirm that the *trott* assures a good harvest and sometimes dance it in the course of the year if drought threatens."[4] The same is true for the classical dance. It is believed not only that the rains can be affected by the performance of particular dances, but also that the most powerful dances will have the greatest effect. Thus, performances in the Royal Palace by the king's dancers were thought to be an offering capable of eliciting assistance from supernatural powers in creating a climate favorable to good crops throughout the entire nation. Our initial concern is with this ritual known as *buong suong*, considered to be the most powerful form of Khmer dance as offering.

The Ceremony of *Buong Suong*

The royal ceremony to bring rain was known as *buong suong tevoda* or simply *buong suong* (*pwanga swanga*); loosely translated it means "paying respects to the heavenly (feminine) spirits." Implicit in the ceremony is making an offering and requesting that a wish be granted. Any ordinary person could do the *buong suong* ritual in very simplified form at any temple.[5] The royal version was performed as a general blessing for the nation, as well as to alleviate specific conditions. It was usually performed in the throne room, at Wat Preah Keo, or in some other important *wat* (Fig. 9-1).

Buong suong without dance was also performed in the palace. One such *buong suong* was performed in mid-March 1975 to protect the palace itself from Khmer Rouge rockets. The Minister of Culture, as curator of the palace, presided. From then until the Khmer Rouge victory in mid-April, no rockets hit the palace. Significantly, this was a non-elemental problem and the dancer's aid was not invoked.

Due to the essentially private nature of performances by the king's dancers prior to 1970, little has been written about this ritual. Notable exceptions are brief announcements published in *Kambuja* magazine in 1965 and 1967. In both years, with continuing serious drought in a number of provinces, Head of State Samdech Sihanouk received delegations of peasants requesting that he perform the *buong suong tevoda* ceremony to bring rain. The ceremony, which Sihanouk on both occasions ordered performed and over which he presided, consisted mainly of "sacred dances."[6] In the presence of ritual offerings and following the invocation of supernatural forces (*neak ta*) and the spirits of dead kings by the palace astrologer, the *hora*, the *buong suong tevoda* was performed first in the throne room of the palace and then at the Royal Monastery of the Emerald Buddha (Wat Preah Keo) in front of the statue of King Norodom.

The dances performed as the offering in *buong suong* must be among those considered sacred, of which, according to Chheng Phon, there are seven: Robam Vorachhun, Robam Mekhala, Robam Ream Eyso, Robam Preah Thong, Robam Baolut (paula'ta), Robam Sarahbarom (sārahpārama), Robam Baramit (paramitra). An eighth, Robam Tiyae (tay"ē), is sometimes considered of equal rank.[7] The first four of these have been discussed in Chapter VI (as *roeung*); the remaining four names appeared in no palace performance programs nor on any informants' listing of repertoire. Either they have secondary names or are never performed for the public or even for royal guests. Both instances of the *buong suong* mentioned above consisted of an unnamed group dance followed by performances of the three-part Mekhala-Ream Eyso-Vorachhun *robam*.

The *buong suong* began with the entrance of the dancers each holding a silver tray of offerings. They performed a dance in which these trays were raised to each of the four cardinal points. Then they performed the three dances, culminating in a battle. First Ream Eyso entered in the midst of his followers and danced, wielding his magic axe. He exited and Mekhala appeared playing with her magic crystal ball surrounded by her followers, the *tepthida*. Then Vorachhun all in gold, armed with a sword and surrounded by his followers, the *tevoda*, joined the goddess and, together with their followers, executed a dance expressing peace, joy, goodwill and serenity.

Into this harmony burst Ream Eyso, jostling both *tevoda* and *tepthida* in trying to reach Mekhala. Three times she threw her magic ball into the air and caught it, representing three flashes of lightning that knocked Ream Eyso to the ground, blinded. In the fracas, *tevoda* and *tepthida*, as well as Vorachhun, departed, leaving the two principals to their eternal contest which symbolizes the tension of lightning and thunder, earth and sky, refinement and coarseness, passion and aggression, female and male. The dance concluded when Mekhala flung her lightning bolt one final time and ran away smiling, leaving Ream Eyso temporarily vanquished. "From their invisible confrontation in the skies there results, so it is said, the rainfall which fertilizes the earth"[8] and causes the rice to grow.

Significantly, the dances included in the *buong suong tevoda* were not esoteric in nature. In fact, some were among the most popular in the repertoire and would have been known by most classically trained dancers, including dance students at the University of Fine Arts. Within the ritual context of the *buong suong tevoda*, however, and following the preparatory rites, the dances assumed a unique power, due to the fact that the celestial deities, or *tevoda*, actually appeared in the dances as the main characters. The dancer performed the role of *tevoda* or other supernatural force, and the giver, the gift and the recipient became one. In a limited sense, the spirit entered the dancer.

THE DANCER AND SPIRIT MEDIUMSHIP

The Cambodian dancer was not a spirit medium in the sense that she became possessed by a spirit manifesting itself in ecstatic behavior and trance state as a matter of course. That role was traditionally fulfilled by a medium known as the *rup* (rupa)—a word literally meaning "image" or "form"—"with whom dance was often associated.

In a study of religious practices in Cambodia, Eveline Porée-Maspero described the *rup* as an intermediary,

> one in whom the spirits incarnate themselves and who gives form (*rup*) to the territorial spirits (*neak ta*) from whom one requests the rain and good health, and to the dangerous spirits (*arak*) that one wishes to exorcise.[9]

On those occasions when a spirit became incarnate in the *rup*, he might dance in ecstasy[10] or more calmly answer questions, especially regarding illness-causing spirits inhabiting the body. The *rup* had the power to cure, either by sprinkling jasmine water or daubing the sick party with bee's wax, and was in attendance at many traditional ceremonies and important events, including childbirth.

Until recent times, one function of the Khmer dancer was to attract the *neak ta* spirits into the medium. The king's dancers were considered to have great power in this regard. In his 1919 fictionalized autobiography of a court *lakhon*, Roland Meyer described the following event which occurred during the dancer's annual visit to her family.

> My father had found a medium, a fat old man skilled at evoking spirits. The people of the village of Sra Lao, happy to attend the dances that my father proposed I perform in honor of the local spirit, offered to prepare the makeshift shed necessary for the ceremony. I therefore put on my jewelry and my rehearsal costume and, accompanied by a crowd of people, I embarked in a large boat for the sanctuary of *neak ta*.
>
> ...They had set up a shed of branches in front of the niche...; the medium, a fat old man, seated himself in the middle of the audience on mats spread out on the grass; some young volunteers had brought their musical instruments and formed an improvised orchestra.
>
> They made me enter into the circle of spectators where I was all white with powder as for a dance rehearsal....
>
> Plates of food and incense were placed before the niche of the *neak ta* and, in the interior, one saw only a large, grey stone: the incarnation of the spirit of Sra Lao!
>
> The medium joined his hands and lowered his eyelids; his lips murmured some magic incantation, all his body was taken by nervous shaking. The silent audience had their eyes fixed on him and suddenly, the orchestra began after a fashion the tune of *chabanchok*. Mother urged me to dance, but the discordant music played wrong and irregularly and I resigned myself to dance the same, more attentive to the attitude of the old medium than to the correction of my movements.
>
> A fearful cry made the audience shudder; fear made me stop the dance a moment. The invisible spirit had left its stone and become incarnate in the body of the old man! The possessed one, his arms extended in front, had been jolted by a cold fit and had uttered his frightful noise; nevertheless, the orchestra did not weaken and I redoubled my ardor from fear of the spell of the medium who watched me fixedly with bloodshot eyes and laughed mockingly like a madman. Little by little, the music, my gestures and the invocations of the audience entreating the spirit to grant our family happiness and prosperity, calmed this acute fit; the voice of the old man, sweeter now, responded to the unanimous prayers: 'it is nothing, do not worry, I grant you my protection.'
>
> After a period of prostration, the possessed one shuddered and seemed to awaken: 'it is gone,' he declared and, in fact, the Spirit of Sra Lao had left his body and re-entered the large inanimate stone in the bamboo niche.[11]

There is some evidence to suggest that not only did dancers attract spirits, they occasionally embodied them in trance as well. This phenomenon is particularly associated with the masks and will be discussed shortly, but we may note an event occurring in Bangkok in 1975 which is strongly reflective of the Khmer attitude regarding the potential for the dancer to fall into trance.

During the annual *wai kru* ceremony presented by the School of Fine Arts in Bangkok, all proceedings were brought to a halt when a young dancer went into trance. She spoke with a loud, bass voice and moved with the extremely contorted walk of a very old body. After some time she led most of the students and several hundred of the audience across the grounds of the National Theatre to retrieve a mask which by mistake had not been placed on the altar—a mask "belonging" to the spirit then inhabiting her body. In Cambodia (and presumably in Thailand as well), one of the reasons for such great concern and care with the masks was to avoid or at least control the possibility of this type of occurrence.

Other evidence from neighboring cultures further suggests a regional tradition of priestesses associated with dance and/or trance. As late as the nineteenth century the people of Champa, the ancient kingdom in the present area of southern Vietnam, presented offerings to Po Ino Nogar, "the great mother goddess of the kingdom," their most powerful divinity. She was born from the clouds or the sea foam and was also called "mother of the dragons." She created rice, was responsible for prosperity, and protected agriculture. If drought or heavy rains threatened the harvest, the Cham people had recourse to the *paja*, a priestess and prophetess who communicated with the spirits in a state of "sacred trance." The *paja* were supposed to be celibate but often in modern times were not. In the courts of the ancient Cham kings, the *paja* (which signifies princess) were of royal blood and were invested with certain religious functions.[12]

To the west, on the Malay Peninsula, the *ma'yong* dance drama is of indeterminate age. All roles are played by young women, preferably teenage girls. One scholar of this nearly extinct form, after analyzing the performance and the preparatory rituals performed by a *bomor*, has concluded that

> it is possible that the Ma'yong was at one time performed as a ceremonial propitiation of powerful spirits.... The word 'Ma'yong' may be related to 'Ma'Hiang'—the mother spirit—which was believed to protect the rice crop, and may indicate that she was once required to assume a wider responsibility, with the 'Bomor' as a shaman.[13]

The Cham and Malay models, while not identical to the Khmer, demonstrate regional correlatives of the popular Khmer belief that dance in association with trance is both an offering and an invitation to the spirits to assist in obtaining sufficient rain from cosmic forces. To further support this claim we turn now to a consideration of two performance elements, the *sampho* drum and the dancers' makeup, in which we may still discern—beneath refined court-dance conventions—vestigial patterns of the dancer's communication with the spirit world.

THE *SAMPHO* DRUM AND THE SPIRIT WORLD

Like all musical instruments in Cambodia, drums are made with ritual care.

> The drum, once it is in an orchestra, continues to be the object of a ceremony that is repeated before each concert: facing the drum which is the dwelling of the spirits of music, each instrumentalist brings an offering which is placed, in accordance with established rules, on a small tray by the master. The purpose of these offerings is on the one hand to gratify the spirits, and on the other to enable the musicians to play well and to avoid any technical mishap during the concert. Among many instrumentalists the drum still remains the object of a particular cult.[14]

This is especially true with the dance drama. The *sampho* drum, which leads the orchestra and the dancer, is highly venerated, and prior to the *sampeas kru* ceremony, considered below, dancers traditionally placed the head of a pig before it.[15]

Drums are closely identified with the spirit world in Cambodia.[16] As Mircea Eliade has pointed out in his study of shamanism, the belief that the drum summons or imprisons spirits is extremely widespread,[17] as is the symbol of a tree situated at the center of the world from which the drum is made. When the drum is beaten, the shaman is transported in ecstasy toward the Cosmic Tree.[18] While the Cambodian dancer is not a shaman, she is definitely guided by the spirit of the drum. We noted in Chapter V that the *apsara*, which the dancer so often portrays and which she symbolizes, is a symbol of transcendence. For the dancer, the vehicle of that psychological ascension is largely the drum.

Face Makeup and the Spirit World

A second element which traditionally identified the dancer with the spirit world was her makeup, the technique of which is unexpected and highly symbolic. On evenings when performances were scheduled—for the usual nine o'clock curtain—the makeup process began at two in the afternoon. An old lady and a number of assistants worked on each of the dancers. First, a pinch of saffron was mixed with coconut oil and rubbed slowly and carefully over the face, neck, and arms until, initially, all the dancers became "the color of gold."[19]

Second, this layer of gold was completely covered over with a thick white paste made—around the turn of the century at least—by kneading lead carbonate in water. This substance was very bad for the skin and required careful washing with soapy water and citrus juice immediately following the performance.[20] In later years white rice powder seems to have replaced the lead.[21] With this powder a distinction was made between feminine roles and masculine roles; the former were left "dead-white" while a bit of saffron was added to "warm" the latter.

Third, the eyebrows and eyelashes were blackened by lampblack taken from a plate held over a candle and applied with an oiled bamboo stick.[22] Finally the lips were tinted with red Chinese paper. Any number of commentators experienced the starkness of this makeup as creating "the white faces of phantoms,"[23] or the "inexplicable impression of seeing a spirit."[24] The makeup "changes her physiognomy completely [and] immobilizes her features,"[25] wrote Groslier. This effect would have been heightened by the harem's traditional custom—both on and off stage —of blackening the teeth, as noted in Chapter IV.

The function of the dancer is clearly symbolized by this makeup. Like the Angkorean bronze sculptures in which gold and other precious metals were, in a sense, hidden in the alloy, the modern dancer was similarly a golden treasure beneath her impersonal, non-egoistic, white exterior (Fig. 9-2).

In this context George Groslier has perceptively noted the significance of white.

> According to tradition, the actress is covered with white so that she will become more unhuman, more inscrutable, a little virginal wave on that Sea of Milk from which, legend has it, she was born. She is white because white is the symbol of the invisible, the divine, the spotless, the immaterial, the serene. It is the color of the royal parasol, of the robes of the Brahmans, of the sacred lotus, of the sampot of the astrologers, of the moon and of the guardian elephant of the realm. She is white because, having become an ideal Princess, she must no longer have any personality, any trace of that which she was before the dance.[26]

Moreover, the color white is identified with death throughout much of Southeast Asia. For instance, at funerals in the ancient culture of the Indonesian island of Nias, "death is dramatized by placing rice powder on the faces of the participants and attendants."[27] White is also associated with funerals in Cambodia,[28] as well as with the offerings made to the spirits of dead ancestors.

The female spirit mediums of southern Thailand rub their faces with white rice powder in preparation for going into trance.[29] Whether the Khmer dancer's makeup is the vestige of any similar function is unprovable, but unquestionably, the thick white

9-2. **Dancer Makeup Seen Offstage.**
Cogniat, *Danses D'Indochine*.

powder gave her the appearance of a dissociated, other-worldly spirit. Of possible significance in this regard is the fact that in Khmer the word for entering the stage is *chaen* (cenya), "to go out," while leaving the stage is *chol* (cūla), "to enter," as though suggesting that the dancer goes somewhere in performance and upon her exit from the stage re-enters this world.

Finally, it is worth noting that white face makeup was not limited to dancers in Cambodia; it was also an important element at points of feminine change. On the day of the celebration of puberty, the faces of young girls were painted white, and on their marriage day, brides were also white-faced[30]—just as the faces of small girls were painted white by their parents when they were symbolically wedded to the king as future dancers and members of the harem. These events share the common motif of cosmogonic re-creation through fulfillment of the Feminine principle and union with the Masculine.

Today, and since the 1940s, Khmer dancers wear western makeup and retain a personal physiognomy. Simultaneously, they no longer ritually engender—with the Lord of the Land—the fertility of Cambodia. As late as 1975, however, they were still believed to be able to call for assistance in that regard from the spirit world of the nation's ancestors. This bond between spirits and dancers was maintained through several important ceremonies to which we now turn our attention.

Tway Kru Ceremony and *Bai Sei*

In essence, the *tway kru* ceremony is a very simple acknowledgment of the spirits, or *kru* (grū). It was performed in 1975 in three ways—privately, as a troupe, and for the nation. The first, primarily performed by individual teachers, took place at the altar in the costume room. Presumably, dancers and teachers who did not come to the palace could do the ritual at any altar. This homage was offered daily. The entire troupe did *tway kru* every Thursday. For the nation, it was performed at the request of the leader.

On the personal level, the purpose of *tway kru* was to assure good health for the dancers and proper rhythm for the musicians. If the ceremony was not performed, a spectrum of bad results was believed possible. The dancers could get headaches. They would not be able to remove the masks or tiaras. When dancers were to perform at nine o'clock in the evening, they began to dress at two or three, and from that time could not use the bathroom; it was felt that the *tway kru* invoked the aid of the *kru* in complying with this need and that to omit the ceremony was to invite disaster.

In addition to very brief silent prayers, seated on the ground with both legs to the right, the ritual consists chiefly in placing *bai sei* on the altar. This was always done for the Thursday *tway kru*—but separately from the troupe ceremony—and could be done at other times as well.

While there are many forms of *bai sei* (pāya si) and each for a specific purpose,[31] all consist of natural plant materials. For one *tway kru* in March 1975, three pair were offered to the *kru* of the dance. Each consisted of a piece of peeled banana trunk about four inches in diameter with three wide bands to hold folded banana leaf decorations and the stems of flowers (Fig. 9-3). On the top of each was a cone of banana leaf out of which protruded a bamboo pick surmounted by an egg (boiled earlier on a nearby hot plate). On the top of the egg, a thin candle was inserted so that the egg was above the level of the flowers and appeared to be suspended midway on a long spindle crowned with a flame. The *bai sei* were about eighteen inches tall. Incense sticks had been placed among the flowers, and after they and the candles went out, the eggs were removed and anyone could eat them. Only women made *bai sei*, and no men—not even musicians—participated in the women teachers' casual, intimate ceremony of homage to the *kru*.

The Thursday *tway kru* was held in a large rehearsal space on the ground floor of the palace. There were no altars, candles, incense, or *bai sei* present. Instead, the musicians were in attendance, and those dancers who showed up performed a dance for each of the four basic character types. Five pieces of music were absolutely required for the Thursday *tway kru*: *sathukar*; *chabanchok* (chāpancuh), to which all the performers of prince and princess roles danced; *preah thom* (brah dhama), to which all those performing *yakkha* roles danced; *kraw nai* for all the monkey roles; and *smeu*. Each piece was played by the musicians even if there were no performers of that role present to dance. For instance, on 6 March 1975 there was only one monkey present and no *yakkha* at all, but all five were played, in addition to other pieces.

The king (or president) could ask that the *tway kru* be performed to "create security" for the country or to realize some need—as if the women were in contact with the causative spirits even in their private ritual. This *tway kru* was held in the palace rehearsal hall or elsewhere, but, unlike the *buong suong*, there was no audience. On such occasions the troupe expanded the *tway kru* by adding up to thirty pieces of music lasting up to two hours. If a performance of the dance drama was held on Thursday, it did not affect either the Thursday morning *tway kru* of the individual teachers or their brief daily homage at the altar.

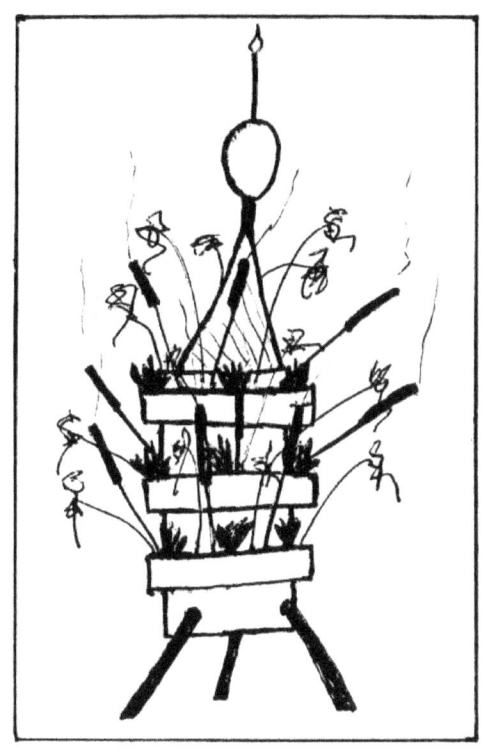

9-3. *Bai Sei* Offered to *Kru* of the *Lakhon*. Sketch Paul Cravath.

SAMPEAH KRU CEREMONY

There are two forms of *sampeah kru*—a term basically similar in meaning to *tway kru*, or "salutation to the spirits." The first is performed daily by students in homage to the teacher; the second is held annually to gain permission from the spirits to perform the dance. Only after a student had completed the annual *sampeah kru* could she dance in public or wear the mask and costume of the role she had studied.

Each morning prior to the rehearsal, all royal dancers formerly performed the *sampeah kru*; in later years during the Republic, students at UBA enacted a much abbreviated form. In its traditional form, the main teacher sat beside the altar that was a part of every rehearsal venue, and the students brought offerings which were placed before her. Each student saluted with the *sampeah* gesture while kneeling, and the teacher sprinkled perfumed water—one of the offerings—on her head and wished her success.

Thiounn has written that the daily offerings were elaborate and included five rolled betel leaves, five candles, five sticks of incense, five cigarettes, and a bottle of water perfumed by the smoke of beeswax to which three herbs, or *anchien*, had been added "to quickly attain success and to preserve freshness and beauty." In addition, each dancer offered from one to five flowers from the eggplant (*trap kha*), which the dance spirits preferred above all others, and, finally, a needle whose sharp point symbolized the "perseverance with which the student would apply herself in pursuing the secrets of her art."[32]

Students designated to study the leading roles also offered two bouquets of artificial flowers arranged in small pieces of banana trunk to form a small three-tiered *bai sei pakchham* (pāya si pā'kchama). Students performing major supporting roles offered two similar bouquets, also using banana trunk but in a much flatter design known as *sla thor* (slā dharma). All these offerings were presented on a tray before the teacher.

When the teacher had poured a bit of the scented water on the student's head, the dancer then drank a few sips and briefly rinsed her face. After the rehearsal she took the bottle home with her because, by convention, it contained enough water for three days of this very specific daily ritual of homage to the spirits, or *kru*, of the dance and to their earthly form, the teachers.

The second form of *sampeah kru* is more significant as a ritual and far more elaborate. In full, it is called *pithi sampeah kru lokhon krop muk*, or "ceremony of homage to the spirits and teachers for wearing the masks." The ceremony traditionally took place on a Thursday in one of the two lucky, female months, corresponding roughly to March or May.[33] In this century, however, it has usually been held in the month of *asath* or July-August. The ceremony was last performed in Chanchhaya in November 1974 prior to the departure of the classical troupe for the performances in Bangkok.

The purpose of the annual *sampeah kru* (the form to which all subsequent allusion shall refer unless otherwise stated) is to make offerings to the *kru* of the dance in order "to gain their power."[34] There is evidence to suggest, however, that the ceremony was once used to gain power in realms other than the dance. Specifically, the data suggest an association with the process of gaining spiritual assistance in the king's annual expedition to capture elephants—especially a spiritually symbolic white one.

Even in the 1970s the offerings placed on the altar by the dancers included a thong of buffalo hide, a goad, and a shackle, all used in capturing elephants. Thiounn says these were "to control misfortune," but the dancers are in no need of such literal protection. Formerly, when *sampeah kru* was performed twice a year, the elephant elements were omitted on one of these occasions.[35] This suggests that the dancers could enact the ritual without benefit of the elephant hunting objects, but that the elephant capture could not take place without the dancers' participation, as well as that of the spirits whom they invoked.

The power which the dancers gained from the *kru* was embodied in the mask or headdress, which the completion of *sampeah kru* allowed them to wear. Although the ceremony began with an invocation to Vishnu, the structure of the event was a process of conjoining the dancer with the spirit of her role. All members of the dance troupe, all students of the dance, and all the teachers were present; there was no other audience except for the king or queen.

Offerings for the ceremony were first made the day prior to the actual *sampeah kru*. Eight small altars about a meter high were erected at the cardinal and ordinal points of the hall to be used, with the altar on the east being slightly more elaborate with three levels. On each altar were placed two *bai sei*, two *sla thor*, two vases of lustral water, five candles, eight sticks of incense, five small bowls of popped rice, five bowls of flowers, one pack of cigarettes, and some betel nut. In the evening ten monks were invited to recite the *sot monn* prayers and hear all the students and teachers repeat the five Buddhist precepts (*sel pram*) discussed in the previous chapter.[36]

Early the next morning the main altar was prepared. It was covered with a white cloth, and the major masks and headdresses were placed on the highest level. Thiounn reports that the placement of the masks was as follows: in the center was the *eysei*, to his left was Rāb, to his left were the *mkot* of the female roles, and to their left the *yakkha* masks. To the *eysei's* right were the *mkot* of the male roles and then other male role masks.[37] This placement sequence—of significance to the arguments presented in Chapter V regarding female-male dualism—is corroborated in more detail by Guy Porée.[38] The only available photo, however, shows a sequence of Rām (or the leading masculine role), the *eysei*, Rāb, Ream Eyso, and Sitā (or the leading feminine role), which suggests that the order may not be inviolate. Parenthetically, Figure 9-4 also shows the relative heights of the headwear and suggests why today the mask maker's art is one of the most difficult to restore to pre-1970 standards.

On the second level of the altar was placed the *krut* mask (in the center) flanked by lesser headdresses, and on the third level were all the major weapons and props. In front of these were the offerings. In addition to the elephant implements on a wooden plate, offerings included four pair of *bai sei* (one pair of each style having nine, seven, five and three tiers), one pair of *bai sei pakchham*, one pair of *sla thor*, two vases of perfumed water, a huge bowl for lustral water (*tik sambuor*), and a number of food offerings for the spirits. Primarily these consisted of two raw pigs' heads, two cooked pigs' heads, two cooked chickens, two cooked ducks, two cooked fish (*ras*), two coconuts, two packs of ground sesame seed, two plates of cakes, two plates of sweets, plus cups of banana in sugar cane juice.

A second series of offerings was made to the musicians seated on the east side of the hall (the main altar was on the north). These included *bai sei pakchham*, *sla thor*, a third kind of flower structure known as *chram* (crama), a bowl of popped rice, five candles, five sticks of incense, five units of money, five lengths of white cloth, a covered plate of food and one of sweets, a pair each of cooked chickens, cooked ducks, and cooked pigs' heads, and, finally, five additional lengths of white cloth which were placed specifically on the *sampho* drum in which the spirits of the music were believed to dwell.[39]

A third group of offerings was made to the dignitary who officiated over the entire ceremony, the *tep robam*.⁴⁰ He was offered five lengths of white cloth, four *chram*, four plates of fruit, five candles, five sticks of incense, a bowl of popped rice, five units of money, and twelve other lengths of white cloth.

The principal female teacher began the actual ceremony before all the offerings were in place by lighting the incense on the altar, after which

9-4. **Headgear of Five Major Characters.**
Photo Colin Grafton.

she and the other teachers invoked Vishnu and the spirits of the *sampho*. The students then entered in a simple dance-walk, circled, and knelt facing the masks. Finally the *tep robam* appeared wearing a yellow robe and the golden mask of the *eysei*. Bent to suggest age and carrying a gnarled staff, he approached the altar and turned to face the audience of dancers, who all sang. Then he placed the *eysei* mask on the center of the altar and draped himself in white,⁴¹ for it was he who actually invoked the spirits.

The *tep robam* was not a dancer. Traditionally he had three functions. The first was to perform the role of *eysei* in *sampeah kru*; as such, he was considered to represent the chief *kru* and the spirit of the dance. The second was to play a comic and often libidinous *eysei* role which appears in a number of *roeung*. The third function of the *tep robam* was to play the rarely performed role of Preah An (Indra). Technically, the title of *tep robam* could only be granted by the king to a man who knew the dance well. He was often the company manager, who assisted the queen. In 1974 a Mr. Chen acted as the *tep robam* although the title had never been conferred upon him officially.

The invocations to the *neak ta* spirits as performed by the *tep robam* were comprised of about thirty elements punctuated by corresponding pieces of music. They lasted about an hour and included a group dance in which the student dancers, each carrying a tray of offerings on her head, presented it to the cardinal points in the sequence east, south, north and west, after which the offerings were placed on the altar. One dancer poured coconut milk at the altar, another poured alcohol, and then all threw popped rice to the four directions in turn.[42] Although eighteen pieces of music were traditionally played to salute the eighteen main *kru* of the dance drama, only four are documented: *sathukar* as an introduction, *kraw nai* for the *kru* of the *yakkha* roles, *preah bathom* (brah padham) for the *kru* of monkey roles, and *phleh* (phlia) for the *eysei*.[43]

Next occurred an ancient rite called the "turning of the *popil*" which was performed in Cambodia on occasions of entering into a new phase of life—puberty, ordination, marriage, coronation, naming a baby, or, in this case, consecrating young dancers. It was fundamentally a magic circle; the persons being honored were surrounded by the audience who passed the *popil*—a metal plate often in the shape of a heart, with a lit candle affixed—in a circle around the honorees. Usually three *popil* were passed for nineteen rounds, the number of "essential spirits" in man as well as in rice. Special candles were often used with nineteen threads in the wick.[44] During the turning of the *popil*, the entire audience was also encircled by a single cotton thread.[45]

Finally, the central core of the *sampeah kru* ceremony was performed. Placing the mask of the *eysei* over his head, the *tep robam* took each of the masks and *mkot* in turn, beginning with Rāb. He placed each one briefly on the head of the dancer who had learned that role, and then removed it. At that point and, according to Jacques Brunet, whenever they are put on subsequently,

> the masks are in fact regarded as living spirits as soon as they are worn by the dancers. The purpose of all the invocations before the dance is to ensure that the masks are "possessed" so that the dancers may become one and the same person with the mask.[46]

In the same manner all headdresses are viewed as the embodied spirit of the role.

The *tep robam* next attached to each dancer's wrist a thread of untwisted cotton dipped in lustral water, sprinkled each one with the same water and then anointed the foreheads of each teacher with perfume and rice powder. The teachers then did likewise to each of their students.⁴⁷ The *tep robam* wished each student success and good luck, after which there was a group dance in which each performer wore her headdress for the first time. The *sampeah kru* concluded with a dance by each of the role groups—*yakkha*, masculine roles, feminine roles, and monkeys in that order.

The bond established between spirit and dancer in the ritual act of placing the mask on her head in the *sampeas kru* was highly respected by all performers. The dancer always saluted the mask with *sampeah* before wearing it and never put the mask on by herself. Even for simple dances, she took the mask and had it placed on her head by the teacher of that role, thus receiving the spirit (*kru*) of the mask from the *kru* of the role. When a young dancer feared performance or had difficulty remembering her role, the *tep robam* placed the mask of the *eysei* momentarily on her head to infuse her directly with the spirit of the dance, the chief *kru*.⁴⁸

To gain a clearer understanding of the relationship between the *kru* and the royal *lakhon kbach boran*, we now turn to a brief consideration of another, closely related theatre form in Cambodia in which the additional element of spirit mediums in trance is integral to the dance drama. In that form, the *lakhon khol*, the process of empowering the masks is analogous and more detailed.

Lakhon Khol and the Spirit World

Lakhon khol refers to performances, more or less in the palace style, by all-male troupes of dancers performing outside Phnom Penh. The best known of the few troupes remaining in the 1960s performed near Phnom Penh in the village of Vat Svay Andet. While the early history of *lakhon khol* is uncertain,⁴⁹ in the late nineteenth century it was performed annually for seven days to celebrate the king's birthday.

In recent years the *lakhon khol* was not performed in the palace at all, but episodes from its repertoire—essentially derived from the *Rāmker*—were staged in the village during the first seven nights following the Khmer New Year in April.⁵⁰ In 1967 there were sixty dancers. Associated with the all-male troupe were a number of *rup*, or spirit mediums, of whom two were women. The style of dance was very similar to that of the female court dancers, although it was less formal, precise, and well-executed, due to the infrequency of rehearsal and performance. Costumes, masks, and jewelry for the performances were often borrowed from the palace.

The *lakhon khol* was performed as an offering to the *neak ta* (anaka tā), or local spirits, that control the waters, prosperity, and good health. The dance was considered to have a direct effect in preventing drought. Significantly, villagers believed that the most important episode performed was the story of how Komphakar, the brother of Rāb, was tricked into releasing the waters after he had imprisoned them. Numerous accounts document the disasters that befell the village on those occasions when the *lakhon khol* was not performed properly or on seven consecutive nights.[51] The dances were offerings to the *neak ta*—also known as *kru* or *as lok* (a's lok)—to demonstrate the allegiance of the villagers; in return, the *kru* granted their protection and thus assured prosperity.

The villagers of Vat Svay Andet acknowledged fifteen *kru*. Neak Ta Kai (anaka tā kē) was the spirit of the village itself, the spirit of the troupe, king of the *neak ta*, and the most powerful spirit in the strict hierarchy. Thirteen were male, two were female, and each could be incarnate in a *rup* of corresponding gender. The *rup*—literally meaning "image" or "form"—was the spirit medium used by the *kru* to communicate with men. The hierarchy of power among the spirits was reflected in a hierarchy of privilege among the *rup* in the community, so that the world of the *kru* was a "double" for that of the *rup* on the social plane. The *kru* retained the same *rup* for life and when the *rup* died would usually take possession of one of his relatives.

The *rup* were not performers in *lakhon khol* in the sense of being trained in the dance movements. Nonetheless, if a *kru* was unhappy with any aspect of the performance, he could possess the *rup*, who—following a general pattern—would speak, dance, enter into a trance state, and then collapse, always in the same manner. The performance could be totally disrupted if the wishes of the *kru* were not fulfilled. Consequently the role of *rup* was central to the *lakhon khol* performance and its ritual effectiveness.

Cambodians use the word *kru* not only for the *neak ta* but also for the teachers of dance. Thus, at Vat Svay Andet one *kru* taught the movements for giant roles, another for monkey roles, and a third the prince and princess roles. Simultaneously, one of the *neak ta* was the spiritual *kru* for those roles.

Second in the hierarchy of *neak ta* was Tos Muk (Rāb), who was also the spirit of the *lakhon khol* troupe and the *kru* of the demon roles. Kamheng (kamhēna) was the *kru* of monkey roles. Socheat Bopha (sujātī pupphā) was the *kru* of male and female roles. These two *kru* are of particular interest to us because, incarnate in their respective *rup*, they initiated the *lakhon khol* on the first of the seven nights with an important ceremony. Because of the striking similarity of this ritual to the *sampeas kru* ceremony performed by the palace dancers, we shall examine it in some detail to illumine the context of spirit mediumship in which Cambodian dancers of both palace and village perform.

One observer of *lakhon khol* wrote, fittingly, that

> the ceremony which takes place the first day following the Khmer New Year, prior to the cycle of dances, is at once overture, invocation, and propitiation. Brought face to face with spirits, the community experiences the opening into another world.[52]

The opening ceremony lasted from two to three hours beginning at seven in the evening with all the dancers present. The musicians played the twelve pieces of music that were salutations to the *kru*;[53] then came the verbal salutation. The orchestra was seated at the east end of the rectangular stage facing the altar of offerings at the opposite end. Behind the orchestra on a separate raised platform were the *rup*; behind the offering altar was a separate altar holding the masks. Several of the offerings appeared in sets of five signifying one for each of the four cardinal points and one for the center. Many of the objects were white—eggs, sticky rice, face powder, candles, jasmine water, and lengths of white cloth—a color having special identification with the *rup*. Five lengths of white cloth were placed on the *sampho* drum which led the orchestra and was considered to be inhabited by the spirit of the music. Other offerings included cooked chicken, a pig's head, coconut, cakes, uncooked rice, bananas, wine, money, areca nuts, cigarettes, as well as numerous *bai sei*.

Behind the offerings were the masks in two rows; in the first was the mask of the *eysei* with Rāb on the left and the *mkot* of the male and female roles on the right. In the back row were the masks of the secondary characters. One of the three singers seated amidst the offerings, faced the masks. He spoke to the *kru*, his salutations alternating with pieces of music. Several times he threw popped rice and sprinkled jasmine flowers on the principal masks and to the four cardinal points. Then followed perhaps the oldest element of the preliminaries, the rite of *chem much kru* (caima mukha kru)—the "awakening" of the masks.

In this rite, the masks were carefully washed, and the eyes "opened." A brush soaked in a mixture of water, perfume, and coconut oil was passed over the brows of the masks and the edges of the tiaras. Then a mirror was held facing each mask, and the lacquered surface of each mask was "combed" using a real comb to mime the gestures. This rite of washing and awakening the masks was accompanied by the music *long song* (lun sun), after which the candles and incense were lit.

At that point the music changed to *trak*, and the *rup* of Kamheng, the spirit of the monkey roles, rushed forward to the center of the stage, began to mime the movement of the dance of the monkeys, and, shortly after, fell backwards and remained inert. Members of the troupe raised him up, sprinkled him with jasmine water, and when the spirit left his body, he revived.

Then the music changed to *kraw nai*, and the *rup* of Tos Muk (Rāb) appeared and stood immobile, supported by a long staff, with eyes closed. He invoked the spirit, moved forward, leapt about, whirled the staff, mimed the movements of the dance of the *yakkha* (demon) roles, and collapsed backwards. The music stopped, candles and incense were lit, and the ceremony was over.

Various *rup* appeared at points throughout the seven subsequent nights of performance, and on the final night all appeared together. Each one, possessed by its spirit, "danced" to a particular piece of music, after which the *rup* of Neak Ta Kai and the *rup* of Kamheng seated themselves on the altar. Each *rup* in turn saluted them, and all the spirits departed, the last being Neak Ta Kai who promised the villagers happiness, prosperity, and longevity.[54]

Seen overall, the activities of the *rup* constitute a framework in which the *lakhon khol* performances were set. The purpose of the performance was to "liberate the waters" by pleasing the spirits with dances and other offerings. The *rup* not only enforced proper execution of the dances but also acknowledged the offerings overtly and, possessed by the spirits, responded favorably.

The ritual function of *lakhon kbach boran* is nearly congruent with that of *lakhon khol*, but it differs from the *lakhon khol* in retaining only vestigial traces of the spirit mediumship framework, and these are easily overlooked. The few writers who have described the palace dancers as being sacred—especially within the context of *buong suong tevoda*—experienced the performances merely as an offering to the supernatural powers. Few perceived the power of the masks given by the *kru* in return.

Before moving on to the final considerations of this chapter, we should note specifically the significance of the *chem mukh kru* rite of empowering the masks in *lakhon khol*. Brunet, cited earlier, has suggested that the headgear in *lakhon kbach boran* are similarly empowered. Only two faint vestiges of the rite, however, can still be discerned in the royal *lakhon*. In the daily *sampeah kru*, as noted, teachers sprinkled lustral water on the head of each student prior to the beginning of rehearsal. Second, during the annual *sampeah kru*, one of the trays on the altar contained "*accessoires de toilette.*"[55] These may very well be the mirror, comb and other implements used for awakening the masks in the rite of *chem mukh kru*. The paucity of evidence concerning this rite in the classical dance context is fortunately mitigated somewhat by evidence from both the annual *wai khru* ceremony performed by the classical Thai dancers in Bangkok, and the Khmer shadow puppet theatre, the *nang sbek*.

Analogous mask Empowerments

As noted in Chapter IV, the Thai *lakhon* is primarily a derivation from Khmer *lakhon*, but as the Cambodian teachers point out, the Thai have abandoned all sacred or ritual value inherent in the specific dances, and the *tep robam* function is fulfilled by a trained dancer. Only in the annual *wai khru* "custom" of paying homage to the teachers of *lakhon* do we see any vestige of the dance as an offering to the spirits. Three points of similarity with the Khmer are relevant. First, "spirits of the departed teachers of the dance" are invited to attend the ceremony. The invitation takes the form of a dance performed by the senior male teacher wearing the mask of the old hermit *eysei* and carrying a gnarled staff. Second, the music *longsong* is played when he bathes the "deva-images" just as in the "awakening" of *chem mukh kru* in *lakhon khol*.

The third way in which the Thai *wai khru* reveals its roots in animistic ritual reflective of the Khmer correlate, is in the two dances which follow the awakening of the masks. As in the Cambodian ceremony, all the students dance and present an offering. Then, according to the foremost expert on Thai *lakhon*, the presiding teacher performs a dance of slicing pieces from the pig's head and other offerings.[56] Immediately thereafter, all the students dance, simultaneously holding up an offering. A change in music then indicates a time for the spirits of teachers to feast on food offerings,[57] after which popped rice is scattered. The ritual pattern, then, of periodically invoking the presence of spirits

As late as the ninteenth century, human sacrifices to the neak ta were documented at Ba Phnom, the hill adjacent to the earliest known capital of Funan. There is a Khmer belief that "...people gave up killing men and sacrificed buffaloes instead [until] the sacrifice of buffaloes was abandoned, and live ones were offered symbolically instead. About twenty years ago (c. 1924) people began to sacrifice a pig instead of a buffalo, but afterwards even this stopped and now (1944) the sacrifice takes the form of an offering of cooked pork, purchased at the market...."[57]

by washing or sprinkling with holy water the images or masks of the *kru* to awaken them, by presenting a group dance to offer them food, and by scattering rice, is fundamental to the Khmer *lakhon kbach boran* as well as its homologous forms, the *lakhon khol* and the Thai *lakon*.

There is another theatre form, popular throughout Southeast Asia, in which the same ritual pattern of communication with the spirits is to be found. This is the shadow puppet theatre, of which we will briefly consider two forms, the Javanese *wayang kulit* and the Cambodian *nang sbek*.

The age and origin of the shadow theatre has been much debated,[58] but the most persuasive arguments view performances as evocative of an ancient rite to assure the fertility of rice.[59] One Indonesian scholar holds that *wayang* was performed as animistic worship of ancestral spirits.

> A performance of wayang purwa (shadow play) was at its earliest stage a ceremony to worship the spirits of the ancestors . . . residing in big trees, big stones and in mountains; they could help anybody who knew how to worship them with offerings, magic formulae and music. To call up those spirits a ceremony was held by a medium. Those ancestral spirits made their appearance in the form of shadows.[60]

Invocations preceding performances of *nang sbek* in Cambodia suggest that this view accurately describes the ritual function of Khmer shadow theatre as well.

Jacques Brunet has pointed out, that "in the *nang sbek* the leather hides may be compared with the masks" of the dance drama, and that the purpose of the preparatory ritual is similarly to cause the puppets to be possessed by the spirits.[61] Prior to a *nang shek* performance, in which the puppets are actually carried and manipulated by dancers, the master of the troupe first invites the spirits to attend the rites, after which three puppets are placed against the screen: the ascetic, or *eysei*, in the center, Vishnu on the right, and Shiva on the left represented with a bow drawn and facing Vishnu. The troupe master next affixes small candles and incense sticks to the skin of the puppets, describes the usage of the figures that will enable the spirits to enter them, and then "awakens" the figures by sprinkling them with water. He passes a comb over their "hair," rubs their eyelashes "to open their eyes" and finally holds a mirror in front of them so they can see themselves.⁶² From that moment the puppets are considered to be alive, just as the masks in *lakhon khol* are awakened in the *chem mukh kru* ritual.

Once the spirit has taken possession of either the puppet in *nang sbek* or the mask in *lakhon khol*, there is a bond between it and the dancer, who becomes the "vehicle" of the spirit, a kind of medium without trance. In *nang sbek*

> an *identification* is... established between the dancers and the hides, since it is forbidden for anyone to pass between the leather figures and the dancers during the salutations so as not to break the link between them.⁶³

Each dancer sprinkles himself with holy water, and from that point the dancer and the puppet are one. This rite was maintained in the palace dances only in abbreviated form, as though it were assumed that the masks already contained the spirits. Certainly the veneration always accorded them would suggest this.

The Ritual's End

All that has been discussed in this chapter is explication of the manner in which the *lakhon kbach boran* is a "sacred dance" by women traditionally set apart for service to the spirit world. In 1968 Hang Thun Hak, then Recteur of the Université Royale des Beaux-Arts, wrote that

> the Ballet is secluded from external influences by the fact that it preserves within the royal palace the ritual role of making offerings to the spirits of the deceased kings. ... If the dances have lost in part their sacred character, they retain no less of an important ritual function.⁶⁴

This can be seen most clearly in the *buong suong* ceremony of propitiation and in the *sampeah kru* ceremony of consecration.

Khmer royal dancers were not spirit mediums in the sense of entering trance, but they appear to have ancient associations with such phenomena. Their function is best seen as holy in its own right—holy in the sense that they were dedicated by their culture to the preservation of a wholeness, a harmony in the complex unity of spiritual and mortal existence. The cosmic and terrestrial forces which were united within their dramas and by their ritual intercessions are the essential forces of the cosmological dualism lying at the heart of the Southeast Asian world view from the earliest times: the conflict and unity between light and dark, female and male, earth and sky.

In these modern days, however, when the soil of Cambodia no longer blossoms, and beliefs fade, the specific relationship of the few remaining Khmer dancers to the spirit world can be of little significance. Far more important is the fact that—as virtually all written accounts of the dance have observed—the dancers themselves give every appearance of being spirits in their own right. The trance-like slowness; the mysterious smile; the frequent gestures of flight; the hypnotic, moving stillness of the hands; and the silent, gliding, glittering appearance as of a precious jewel in a dream—all these need no higher referent to be called spiritual. As Chheng Phon has said, "when they are dancing they seem not to be like other men." As both generative maiden and transcendent *apsara*, the Khmer dancer is, herself, the spirit of the earth in flower. We pray for her longevity.

Endnotes

1. Lim Siv Choan, "Les offrandes au Cambodge," Annales de l'Université Royale des Beaux-Arts (Phnom Penh), No. 1 (1967), p. 7
2. "Les danses sacrées," p. 350.
3. Thierry, "Les danses sacrées," p. 6. See also Porée-Maspero, *Études sur les rites agraires de Cambodigiens*, I, pp. 207-32.
4. Thierry, "Les danses sacrées," p. 351.
5. Any Cambodian individually could offer *buong suong* to request something from the spirits or to fulfill a promise made if a wish came true. Offerings of coconuts, flowers, incense, candles, all one's hair, or a piece of music provided by a singer and small orchestra stationed in particular temples, were customary.
6. "Sacred Dances at the Palace to Bring Rain" *Kambuja*, 15 Aug. 1967, p. 23. See also "Sacred Dances," *Kambuja*, 15 Sep. 1965, p. 19.
7. Personal communication.
8. "Sacred Dances" (1967), p. 23.
9. "Notes," p. 620.
10. Thierry, "Les danses sacrées," p. 355.
11. *Saramani danseuse khmère*, p. 158.
12. Antoine Cabaton, *Nouvelles Recherches sur les Chams* (Paris: Ernest Leroux, 1901), pp. 16-17, 28-31.
13. Mubin Sheppard, "Ma'yong—The Malay Dance Drama," *TDMSA*, p. 141. See also Ghulam-Sarwar Yousof, "The Kelantan Mak Yong Dance Theatre: A Study of Performance Structure," Diss. University of Hawaii, 1976. Yousof, too, sees *ma'yong* as developing out of shamanistic ritual.
14. Jacques Brunet, "Music and Rituals in Traditional Cambodia," *TDMSA*, p. 221.
15. Guy Porée, p. 581.
16. The *skor arak* (sgara ārakkha), for instance, was a standing drum made of terra cotta with a head of snake skin, used in rites of exorcism. See Porée-Maspero, "Notes," p. 637.
17. *Shamanism: Archaic Techniques of Ecstasy*, trans. Willard R. Trask, Bollingen Series, 76 (Princeton: Princeton University Press, 1964), p. 168.
18. Mircea Eliade, *Images and Symbols*, trans. Philip Mairet (New York: Sheed & Ward, 1969), pp. 42, 46.
19. George Groslier, *Danseuses cambodgiennes*, p. 85. Sappho Marchal says the makeup was also used on the lower legs ("La danse au Cambodge," p. 221). Pavie wrote that the yellow was created by using turmeric (Études diverses, p. xvi); in light of turmeric's irremoveability, this seems unlikely.
20. George Groslier, *Danseuses cambodgiennes*, p. 86. The lead carbonate, says Groslier, was sold by Chinese merchants.
21. Thiounn (p. 69) says the powder was made of rice. Writing in 1936, however, Ponder calls the substance "Chinese white" which was "anything but soothing to the complexion" (p. 249).
22. One observer in the 1920s wrote that the eyelids were "tinged with antimony" (Strickland-Anderson, p. 269). There is no corroboration of this in other accounts.

23 Laloy, "Les principes de la danse cambodgienne," p. 6.
24 Cardi, p. 37.
25 George Groslier, *Danseuses cambodgiennes*, p. 86. See also p. 55 for reference to blackening of teeth.
26 George Groslier, *Danseuses cambodgiennes*, p. 55.
27 Peter Suzuki, "The Religious System and Culture of Nias, Indonesia," Diss. University of Leiden, 1959, p. 94.
28 Porée-Maspero, "Notes," pp. 625, 636.
29 Mary Jane Gandour and Jackson T. Gandour, "A Glance at Shamanism in Southern Thailand," *JSS*, 64, Pt. 1 (Jan. 1976), p.100.
30 Ponder, p. 249 and G. Groslier, *Danseuses cambodgiennes*, p. 86.
31 Lim Siv Choan, pp. 7-21.
32 Thiounn, pp. 38-39.
33 Thiounn, p. 33. The Cambodian calendar had 30-day, female months and 29-day, male months.
34 Chheng Phon, personal communication.
35 Thiounn, pp. 41, 43.
36 Thiounn, p. 42. Unless otherwise noted, the description of the *sampeah kru* is drawn from Thiounn's account, from Chheng Phon's remarks, or from the USIS film which includes a section of the ceremony.
37 Thiounn, p. 43.
38 P. 582. Porée says the second level of the altar included, in the center, the *krut* mask and to the left the "horse head, lion, golden deer headdress, blackbird headdress, and parrot headdress." To the right were the masks of the monkeys. On the third level were the weapons and major hand props.
39 Brunet, "Music and Rituals." p. 221.
40 Thiounn, p. 44. Thiounn also called him *chumit sophan*; Chheng Phon used the term *moa tao*.
41 Guy Porée, p. 582.
42 Chhuk Meng Chhansan, "Le ballet classique khmer" (Phnom Penh: n.p., 1973), p. 11. This unpublished, mimeographed film script was approved by the Ministry of Culture but was never shot.
43 Chheng Phon, personal communication.
44 Porée-Maspero, "Notes." pp. 624-25, 640.
45 Guy Porée, p. 582.
46 "Music and Rituals," p. 221.
47 Guy Porée, p. 582.
48 Chheng Phon, personal communication.
49 Chheng Phon, personal communication, 19 March 1975. According to Chheng Phon, the form developed when the male teachers in the palace departed and began teaching boys, because villages wanted their own dance troupes but couldn't copy the king by using girls: "They used men to make it different even though the dance was the same." Only in Battambang city do men and women play together in *lakhon khol*.
50 Sem Sara, "Lokhon khol au village de Vat-Svay-Andet, son rôle dans les rites agraires," *Annales de Université Royale des Beaux-Arts* (Phnom Penh), No. 1 (1967), p. 158. They performed from 11:00 a.m. to 5:00 p.m. and from 8:00 p.m. to midnight. Since 1964 with the accord of all the *rup* of the village, the dance took place at night only.
51 Sem Sara, p. 162.
52 Sem Sara, p. 164.
53 They were *sathukar* (sādhukāra), *trak* (trāka), *kaman* (kamā'na), *thom lek* (dhama loeka), *chet ching* (coeta jhîna), *chet muy choen* (coeta mwaja cā'na), *prathum* (prathum), *khlom* (khlum), *kraw na* (krawa nai), *smeu* (smī), *lia* (la), and *rua* (rwa)

54 Sem Sara, pp. 167-70.
55 Thiounn, p. 43.
56 Dhanit Yupho, *The Custom and Rite of Paying Homage to Teachers of Khon, Lakon and Piphat*, trans. L. Lauhabandhu (Bangkok: The Fine Arts Department, 1961), p. 12.
57 Any consideration of the offering as sacrifice lies beyond the scope of the present inquiry but the fact that spirits feast on the pig's head suggests that the ritual is ancient and certainly indigenous. An interesting article documenting human sacrifices is David P. Chandler's, "Royally Sponsored Human Sacrifices in Nineteenth Century Cambodia: the cult of *nak ta* Me Sa at Ba Phnom," *JSS*, 62, Pt. 1 (July 1974), pp. 221-22.
58 Scholarship regarding a Southeast Asian versus Indian origin has been summarized by Cœdès (*ISSA*, p. 265. n. 54).
59 See Anker Rentse, "The Origin of the Wayang Theatre (Shadow Play)," *JMBRAS*, 20, No. 1 (1947), pp. 12-15.
60 Sri Muljono, "Performance of Wayang Purwa Kulit (Shadow Play)," *TDMSA*, p. 58.
61 Brunet, "Music and Rituals," p. 221.
62 Brunet, "Music and Rituals," p. 222.
63 Brunet, "Music and Rituals," p. 222.
64 "Le Ballet Royal," p. 25.

APPENDICES
បន្ថែម

APPENDIX 1

THE ROYAL PALACE THEATRE, ca. 1910
(A translation of Leclère's *Le théâtre cambodgien*, pp. 23-25)

There are in Phnom-Penh, and in all Cambodia, only three theatres, two of which are within the royal palace.

One is in the second courtyard, accessible to all, and the Europeans call it therefore "the public dance hall"; the locals call it the *ruang lokhon luong*, "hall of the king's dancers."

The second theatre is located inside the palace and is only accessible to the people of the palace and to those Europeans especially invited by the king.

The third theatre is that of the Justice Minister (*oknha youmreach*). There was another previously, that of the Prime Minister (*akkamohasena*), who died seven or eight years ago. The Justice Minister has a troupe of dancers who cost him dearly. The singers, the

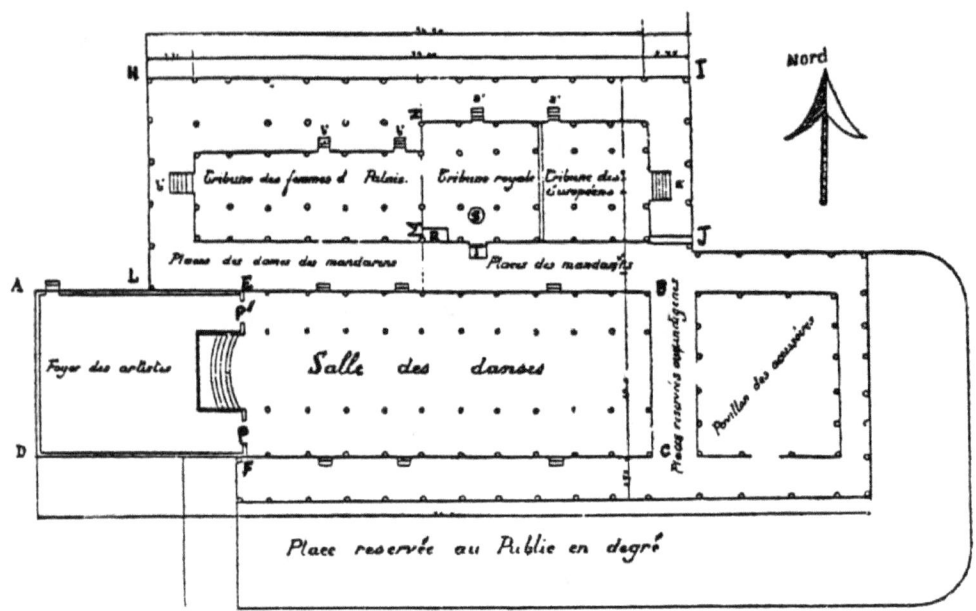

Figure 162. **The Royal Palace Theatre Floorplan, ca. 1910.**
Source: Leclère, *Le théâtre cambodgien*, p. 24.

prompter when one is needed (*neak boek krang*), and the musicians are graciously furnished by the king.

Sometimes on the occasion of a festival, the king sends one or two groups of dancers to dance in a makeshift shed, constructed of straw at the foot of the *phnom* or hill that is at the center of the capital.

I do not speak here of the private dance theatres of the king and of the Justice Minister. I am concerned only with the public theatres....

The present theatre consists of three buildings joined together (Fig. 162), first the dancing room (ABCD) which measures 53.6 meters long by 10 meters wide. It is a vast shed open to all breezes of which the roof of the section reserved for the dances (EBCF) is supported by 44 wood columns placed in four lines. The western extremity of this building is reserved as a green-room for the artists. This green-room (AEDF) is separated from the theatre by a wall having two doors; that on the southwest (P) is the door for the dancers' entrance, that on the northwest (P') is the exit-door. Between the two doors is a large (*apparat*) stairway leading from the theatre, to a catwalk beneath the roof almost as long as the room, suspended by iron triangles. It is with the aid of this catwalk that the women suspended on cables can represent the goddesses of the air or the princesses and princes traveling through the clouds.

The dances take place in the space EBCF. The stage of this room is elevated about 60 centimeters above the ground.

Separated from the dancing room, on the north side, is another building (HIJL) the roof of which joins the roof of the first building above a large gutter. This building equally open-air and containing 76 columns is comprised of two parts: one part at ground level where the ministers and the other high officials take their place—some years ago they were seated on mats, but now they are on chairs—and another part raised as a grandstand.

This seating area raised about one meter off the ground is divided in two equal parts by a wooden partition (MN) containing a mirrored door permitting passage from one part to the other. The west seating area is reserved for women of the palace, the east area for the king, his European guests and for dignitaries—princes who remain at his disposal.

The last area is in two parts, one for the king and his invited guests, the other a step lower where the European public sits. A sort of royal bed (R) or *balank* surmounts a white dais fringed in gold about 60 centimeters high against the partition. On it is a mattress of brocade and a white silk pillow. This bed serves no purpose; the king never employs it, but it attests to the usage earlier kings of Cambodia made of it in stretching out to watch the dances.

The present king, like Norodom, prefers a simple gilt wood chair placed a little distance and to the east of the bed in front of a small table (S) and facing a small box (T) a meter and a half square which is detached from the seating area and projects toward the stage. It is in this box that the king sat previously when he did not want to lie on the bed. But since the Europeans attend the dances, he never takes his place there and remains seated on his small and thin chair of gilt wood beside another similar chair that the *résident supérieur* occupies to his left. Next to these seats are four Louis XIV sofas, then some Thonnet chairs and behind the sofas and chairs, six rows of other chairs. Behind the king and the *résident supérieur* is the round table (S) covered with a rich gold brocade cloth on which are placed all the objects which constitute the royal insignia: the box of finely worked gold for betel nut the cover of which bears a cluster of diamonds embedded in a flower, and resting on a gold embossed goblet; the royal sword which is placed on another cup of embossed gold…; a gold embossed goblet in which is placed a wick in the form of a cord which allows the king and his guests to have a flame within hand's reach to light their cigars or their cigarettes; a plate containing the various utensils necessary for making a leaf of betel or areca even though the king does not chew, nor does anyone around him.

Two stairways (a, a') on the north side and another (a") on the last side permit access to this seating area.

Three others (b, b', b") permit access to that of the palace women, but a wall with a door (Q) always closed and protected by a male palace guard (*kromoveang*) prevents the public from entering behind this seating area and communing with the women.

The prompter or reader (*srey-ambat*) who in fact is really the "howler" and the singers who also beat time, place themselves opposite the seating area reserved for the king and the Europeans, in a single line sometimes in two when there are many.

Above the stage, suspended from iron bars is a catwalk and many apparatus with whose aid "goddesses of the air" or princes in possession of a talisman permitting them to travel through the clouds can pass above the stage.

This entire room, whose roof is held up by thin columns encircled with red cotton cloth and sometimes decorated with branches when the scene presented is either a park or a forest, was previously lit by torches soaked in bowls of palm oil. Later they replaced this oil by a mixture of gasoline and oil which gave a brighter light. Men moving in a squat position exactly like a monkey whose arm holds a large fruit and who uses the other hand placed on the ground to move faster, ran from one lamp to another, constantly occupied with trimming the wick.... Today the theatre is lit with large gas lamps hung from the ceiling but chiefly by electric bulbs.

Finally to be complete, although this building is not part of the theatre, I will mention a pavilion located to the east which hides the theatre a bit and obstructs the sun from entering there in the morning. This pavilion, which is in the Khmer style and which can be locked, serves to hold the chairs, sofas, the end table and all the theatre furniture that is moveable.

Appendix II
Royal Palace Performance Programs

This appendix consists of primary data regarding dance drama performance within the Royal Palace between 1931 and 1961. These data are presented in Tables 5 and 6.

Table 5: Sequence of Program Pieces in Selected Performances During theReign of King Monivong

Date	In honor of	Program 1	Program 2
1931-Oct. 21	Minister of Colonies Paul Reynaud	The Dance of Gold and Silver Flowers	Preah Thong
1932-Mar. 20	The Duke & Duchess De Brabant	Gold & Silver Flowers	Sovann Machha
1933-Dec. 22, 9 PM	King Monivong's 58th birthday	Manimekhala & Vorachhun	Ream Eyso
1933-Dec. 23, 9 PM	King Monivong's 58th birthday	Gold & Silver Flowers	Suthinchak
1933-Dec. 24, 9 PM	King Monivong's 58th birthday	Sovann Machha	Chakravong *
1933-Dec. 26, 7:30 PM	King Monivong's 58th birthday & Resident-Superior M. A. Silvestre	Sovann Machha	Suvannapong *
1933-Dec. 31, 2-5 PM	Birthday (program in Khmer only)	Kraythong	-
1936-Jan. 7, 7:30 PM	Resident-Superior	Gold & Silver Flowers	Preah Somut
1937-Apr. 9, 7:30 PM	Former Governor of Indochina Alexandre Varenne	Gold & Silver Flowers	Suthinchak
1938-Dec. 31, 2-5 PM	King Monivong's 63rd birthday	Dance of the Fans	Kraythong

Date	In honor of	Program 1	Program 2
1938-Dec. 31	King Monivong's 63rd birthday (program in Khmer only)	Bunloy	-
1939-Jan. 1, 2-5 PM	King Monivong's 63rd birthday	Anurudh	Preah Somut
1939-Jan. 1, Evening	King Monivong's 63rd birthday (program in Khmer only)	Chaoyingdada *	-
1939-Jan. 1, 9-12 PM	Birthday	Dance of the Fans	Sovannahangs
1939-Jan. 2, 9-12 PM	Birthday	Battle of the Black & White Monkeys	Tip Sangvar **
1939-Jan. 3, 7:30 PM	Birthday and Resident Superior Thibaudeau	Gold & Silver Flowers	Suthinchak *

Not mentioned in records during the Sihanouk era
** Not mentioned in records during the Sihanouk era.
This single performance also added
Dance of the Fans as Program 3.
Source: Royal Palace Library Records

Appendix II
Table 6
Page 1

Date:	In honor of:	Location	Overture/Dance of Welcome	Dance of Gold & Silver Flowers	Tep Manorom	Fan Dance	Robam Mkaw	Robam Tewet
1941, Sep. 3	Vice-Admiral J. Decoux, and to mark the end of official mourning	X						
1941, Oct. 28	Gov. General of Indochina J. Decoux & Sisavang Vong, King of Luang Prabang	X	A					
1942, Jan. 3	Resident-Superior Thibaudeau	Palais Khemarin						
1942, Jan. 8	Resident-Superior M. de Lens	X						
1942, Nov. 22	The Emperor and Empress of Annam	Royal Palace	A					
1943, Mar. 22	Resident-Superior M. de Lens	Chanchhaya						
1943, Apr. 9	Resident-Superior Georges Gautier	Chanchhaya	A				D	
1943, Aug. 14	Vice-Admiral Jean Decoux	X						
1943, Nov. 10	King Sihanouk's 22nd Birthday	Royal Palace						
1944, Oct. 25	King Sihanouk's 23rd Birthday	Royal Palace						
1944, Dec.	Resident-Superior Berjean	X	A					
1945, Apr. 1	Lieut. General Manaki Consul General Kubota	X						
1945, Apr. 14	Japanese Guests	X					C	

Appendix II: Royal Palace Performance Programs 453

Major Dramatic Pieces													Other Pieces
Black & White Monkeys	Parrot Dance	Robam Apsara	Sovann Machha	Rāmker	Preah Saing	Preah Somut	Manimekhala & Ream Eyso	Vorachhun	Vong Savann	Soriyavongs	Chinavongs	Leak-Sinnavong	
									B				See Note 1 below
								D	B				C-Chap Robam E-Dance of Princess Botum F-Parade of Dancers
					E								See Note 2 below
								D	B				A-Laotian Ballet C-Cambodian Ballet
									C	B			See Note 3 below
												B	A-Scarf Dance C-Dance of Brahmans and the Apsaras
								C					B-Dance of Yeaks
												B	A-Original "Poème Votif" and dance C-Laotian Ballet
							A					B	C-Scarf Dance
								A					B-Preah Bat Chey Chet
									C			B	-
								C				B	A-Preah Thong
												B	A-Dance of Yeaks

Appendix II
Table 6
Page 2

Date:	In honor of:	Location	Overture/Dance of Welcome	Dance of Gold & Silver Flowers	Tep Manorom	Fan Dance	Robam Mkaw	Robam Tewet
1945, May 27	X	X				A		
1945, Nov. 14	King Sihanouk's 24th Birthday	Royal Palace					C	
1945, Dec 27	General Alessandri	X				C		
1946, Jan. 29	Vice-Admiral Thierry D'Argenlieu	Chakdomukh Hall	A				D	
1946, Jul. 30	General Alessandri & Comm. Penavaire	Khemarin Palace						
1946, Sep. 21	X	Khemarin Palace				D		
1946, Sep. 28	X	Khemarin Palace						
1946, Nov. 9	King Sihanouk's 25th Birthday	Royal Palace						
1946, Dec. 29	French Foreign Minister Marius Moutet	Khemarin Palace	A					
1947, Apr. 16	High Commissioner of France to Cambodia M. Ballaert	Royal Palace		A				
1947, May 25	Commissioner of France to Cambodia M. Pignon	Khemarin Palace	A			C		
1947, Sep. 24	Commissioner Pignon	Khemarin Palace						
1947, Nov. 28	Commissioner Bollaert	Royal Palace			A		C	
1948, Feb. 7	Commissioner Bollaert	Royal Palace						C

Appendix II: Royal Palace Performance Programs

Major Dramatic Pieces

Black & White Monkeys	Parrot Dance	Robam Apsara	Sovann Machha	Ramker	Preah Saing	Preah Somut	Manimekhala & Ream Eyso	Vorachhun	Vong Savann	Soriyavongs	Chinavongs	Leak-Sinnavong	Other Pieces
						B							C-Preah Chan-Korup and Neang Mora
			A		B								–
						B							A-Dance of Brahme
								C					B-Invocation to the Tevodas (1 dancer and sralay)
							C	A					B-Souvannahongs
							C						A-Invocation to the Tevodas B-Dance of Salama
							D	A				B	C-Preah Thong
		A							D		C		B-Dance of Brahme
							D		C				B-Invocation to the Tevodas
				B			C						D-Dance of Hokkrasat
										D			B-Dance of Vilanda
													A-Scarf Dance B-Preah Chau Damrei Sar C-Laotian Ballet
											B		–
				B									A-Kenvilara

APPENDIX II
Table 6
Page 3

Major Robam-dances

Date:	In honor of:	Location	Overture/Dance of Welcome	Dance of Gold & Silver Flowers	Tep Manorom	Fan Dance	Robam Mkaw	Robam Tewet
1948, Aug. 5	Gen. Blaizot	Khemarin Palace						
1948, Nov. 17	X	Royal Palace						
1948, Nov. 30	Commissioner Pignon	Khemarin Palace		C				
1948, Dec. 18	The Queen of Laos	Royal Palace			C			
1949, Mar. 29	Commissioner of France to Cambodia M. de Raymond	Royal Palace			C			
1949, Apr. 20	The French Delegation	Royal Palace						
1949, Apr. 25	The Laotian Government	Royal Palace				C		
1949, May 10	High Commissioner of France for Indochina M. Pignon	Royal Palace			C			
1949, Sep. 7	The King & Queen of Laos	Royal Palace	A				C	
1950, Feb. 6	International Horse Show of Phnom Penh	Royal Palace			E			
1950, Mar. 19	United State' Economic Mission	Royal Palace			E			
1950, Mar. 20	7th American Fleet Comm. Admiral Russell S. Berkey	Royal Palace				D		B
1950, Apr. 19	X	Royal Palace						
1950, Sep. 10	X	Royal Palace			C			
1950, Oct. 27	Letourneau	Royal Palace			C			
1950, Nov. 25	King Sihahouk's 29th Birthday	X	A		C			
1951, Feb. 16	Commander-in-Chief Gen. Delattre de Tassigny	X	A		C			

Black & White Monkeys	Parrot Dance	Robam Apsara	Sovann Machha	Ramker	Preah Saing	Preah Somut	Manimekhala & Ream Eyso	Vorachhun	Vong Savann	Soriyavongs	Chinavongs	Leak-Sinnavong	Other Pieces
			A		C								B-Kenvilara D-Dance of Kanichha
		C	A		B								D-Parade of Dancers
			A										B-Chinese Duo
							A				B		-
			A			B							-
		C					A	B					-
				B									A-Dance of Brahma
				B									A-Ch'uych'ay with sralay solo
				B									-
A	D							B					C-Cheyteat
	C					D		B					A-Phuong Neari
			A								C		-
						C	A						B-Phuong Neari D-Dance Kset
A													A-Phuong Neari
													B-Anurudh
													B-Souvannahongs
				B									-

Appendix II
Table 6
Page 4

Major Robam-dances

Date:	In honor of:	Location	Overture/Dance of Welcome	Dance of Gold & Silver Flowers	Tep Manorom	Fan Dance	Robam Mkaw	Robam Tewet
1951, May 21	Mme. DeRaymond	Royal Palace						
1951, May 22	X	X						
1951, Aug 15	Governor-General of Indochina Georges Gauthier	Royal Palace						
1951, Dec. 17	Christmas	Phochani				D		
1952, Apr. 30	Letourneau	Royal Palace				D		
1952, May 28	Commissioner of France to Cambodia Jean Ristenucci	Royal Palace					C	
1952, Aug 19	Minister of State Letourneau	Royal Palace			B			
1952, Oct. 5	Visit of Buddha's Relics to Cambodia	Wat Preah Keo						
1952, Oct. 10	Visit of Buddha's Relics to Cambodia	Royal Palace	A				C	
1952, Nov. 2	Ass't US Secretary of State John M. Allisen	Royal Palace						
1953, Aug. 17	President of France Paul Reynaud	Royal Palace				C		
1953, Nov. 1	Marc Jaquet & Marice Dejean	X	A					
1955, Feb 15	Governor Adlai Stevenson	Royal Palace				C		
1955, Mar. 14	Visit of British Ship Opossum	Khemarin Palace						C
1955, Oct. 5	X	Khemarin Palace						
1956, Apr. 11	Secretary of State Henry La Forest	Royal Palace	A			C		

Major Dramatic Pieces													Other Pieces
Black & White Monkeys	Parrot Dance	Robam Apsara	Sovann Machha	Ramker	Preah Saing	Preah Somut	Manimekhala & Ream Eyso	Vorachhun	Vong Savann	Soriyavongs	Chinavongs	Leak-Sinnavong	
			C				A						B-Preah Chan Korup and Neong Mora
A									B				C-Dance of the Flowers
A		B	C										D- Phuong Neari
		A											B-Laotian Dance C-Kraythong
	A	B			C								-
A										B			-
				A									-
													A-Preah Pathamasanpathi
											B		-
													A-Peacock Dance B-Souvannahongs C-Final Dance
A					B								-
		C		B									-
			A										-
	A												-
				B									A-Phuong Neari
				B									-

Appendix II
Table 6
Page 5

Date:	In honor of:	Location	Overture/Dance of Welcome	Dance of Gold & Silver Flowers	Tep Manorom	Fan Dance	Robam Mkaw	Robam Tewet
1956, Jun. 29	Nationalist Chinese Foreign Minister George Yeh	Khemarin Palace						
1956, Oct. 6	Czech & Chinese Economic Mission	Khemarin Palace			C			
1956, Oct. 10	US Ambassador Robert MacClintock	X			C			
1956, Oct. 28	Price Axel of Denmark	Khemarin Palace			C			
1956, Oct. 29	X	Kantha Bopha Palace			C			
1956, Nov. 22	Chou En-lai	X						
1956, Dec. 14	Prince & Princess of Denmark	Kantha Bopha Palace			C			
1957, Jan 22	Soviet Ambassador Alexandre S, Anikine	Kantha Bopha Palace			B			
1957, Feb. 6	John D. Rockefeller III	Royal Palace						C
1957, Mar. 6	Birthday of King Norodom Suramarit	Phochani		A			C	
1957, Mar. 21	Polish Prime Minister Jozefa Cyranikiewicza	X		A	C			
1957, Apr.	Crew of the Thai Ship Mai Klong	Government Hotel			C			
1957, May 16	Foreign Delegation to Buddha's Jayanti in Cambodia	X		A			C	
1957, Aug. 28	Yugoslav Vice-President Svetozar Vukmanovic	X			C			
1957, Sep. 9	Indian Vice-President Dr. Radhakrishnan	X						C
1957, Nov.	British Commander-General Sir Robert Scott	Royal Palace			C			

Major Dramatic Pieces													Other Pieces
Black & White Monkeys	Parrot Dance	Robam Apsara	Sovann Machha	Rāmker	Preah Saing	Preah Somut	Manimekhala & Ream Eyso	Vorachhun	Vong Savann	Soriyavongs	Chinavongs	Leak-Sinnavong	
		C		A									B-Dance of Hangsas
	A		B										-
			A										B-Preah Cheysen
			A										B-Preah Cheysen
			A										B-Preah Cheysen
			A										C-Cock Dance D-Dance of the Nagā
			A										B-Preah Cheysen
				A									-
			A							B			-
											B		-
				B									-
A					B								-
													B-Preah Vesandar
			A		B								-
			B										A-Sword Dance
											B		A-Cock Dance

APPENDIX II
Table 6
Page 6

Date:	In honor of:	Location	Overture/Dance of Welcome	Dance of Gold & Silver Flowers	Tep Manorom	Fan Dance	Robam Mkaw	Robam Tewet
1957, Nov. 21	Japanese Prime Minister Nobusuke Kishi	X					C	
1958, Jan. 16	Czech President Viliam Siroky	X			C			
1958, Feb. 9	X	Government				C		
1958, Feb. 22	Lao Prince Souvanna Phouma	X						C
1958, Mar. 6	Birthday of King Norodom Suramarit	X						
1958, Mar. 8	French Foreign Minister Christian Pineau	X					C	
1958, Aug. 5	Political Advisor to Vietnam President Ngo Dinh Nhu	Phochani			D			
1959, Mar. 11	United Nations Secretary General Dag Hammarskjold	X			B			
1959, Jun. 20	Indonesian President Sukarno	X					C	
1959, Jul. 22	US Secretary of the Interior Fred A Seaton	X						
1959, Aug. 18	Ministry of Finance Leram Rajasombat	X				B		
1959, Oct. 19	Mekong Development Survey Committee	X				B		
1959, Nov. 15	Admiral Gerald Gladstone	X			B			
1960, Mar. 17	Count Beaumont	X			C			
1960, Dec. 8	People's Republic Triiew Coow Theater Troupe	X						

Appendix II: Royal Palace Performance Programs

Black & White Monkeys	Parrot Dance	Robam Apsara	Sovann Machha	Rāmker	Preah Saing	Preah Somut	Manimekhala & Ream Eyso	Vorachhun	Vong Savann	Soriyavongs	Chinavongs	Leak-Sinnavong	Other Pieces
				B									A-Cock Dance
													B-Anurudh
	A								B				-
					B								A-Takhoeung
A													B-Eynao C-Devkannia
					B								A-Takhoeung
			A		B								C-Cock Dance
													A-Kraythong
A													B-Eynao
													A-Dance of Khmer-American Friendship
				A									-
				A									-
					A								-
					B								-
					A								B-Dance of Khmer-Chinese Friendship

Major Dramatic Pieces

Appendix II
Table 6
Page 7

Date:	In honor of:	Location	Overture/Dance of Welcome	Dance of Gold & Silver Flowers	Tep Manorom	Fan Dance	Robam Mkaw	Robam Tewet
1961, Feb. 25	King Leopold of Belgium	X	A					
n.d. (c. 1948)	M. & Mme. Pignon	Royal Palace						
n.d. (c. 1950)	Gen. Georges Revers	X						C
n.d. (c. 1951)	Minister of State Hubert A. Graves	Khemarin Palace					C	
n.d. (c. 1956)	Ambassador Donald R. Heath	Khemarin Palace	A					
n.d.	Prime Minister of India Jawaharlal Nehru	Khemarin Palace			A	C		
97 Total Performances		Total per piece	15	6	27	15	13	8

Major Robam-dances

Major Dramatic Pieces													Other Pieces
Black & White Monkeys	Parrot Dance	Robam Apsara	Sovann Machha	Rāmker	Preah Saing	Preah Somut	Manimekhala & Ream Eyso	Vorachhun	Vong Savann	Soriyavongs	Chinavongs	Leak-Sinnavong	
			C		B		D						-
											B		A-Dance of Vilanda B-Preah Chan Korup
											B		A-Kenvilara
		A			B								-
							B						-
			B										C-Dance of the Butterflies
7	8	7	21	18	19	10	11	8	6	8	7	7	

Note 1.   A-Dance of Offering to the Memory of King Monivong; C-Princess Botum; D-Chap Robam; E-Chey Chet excerpt; F-Sai Klen with sralay solo; G-Parade of Dancers
Note 2.   A-Original Dance; B-Sinuon; C-Takheng; D-Krom
Note 3.   This was the first performance after Kossamak's renovation of the troupe. Source: Royal Palace Library Records

APPENDIX III
The structure of chorus, orchestra and dance components in the Cambodian Dance Drama.

The following chart is based on a performance of the *Rāmker* as performed at the *Rāmāyana* Festival in Indonesia on 2 September 1971. The total performance time of the segments performed was about seventy minutes, but this included the favorite scenes most frequently staged from the epic. The chart indicates approximate temporal units of performance, the action, and whether it was accompanied by the chorus or orchestra. The final battle and conclusion are not included in the chart.

TIME	MUSIC	ACTION
1 minute	Full orchestra	Introduction
15 seconds	Orchestra--especially *roneat* and *sralay*	Rām, Sitā and Laks enter.
2 ½ minutes	Full orchestra	Procession, *sampeah* kneeling.
1 minute	Chorus; rare *chhing* and *sampho*	Rām mimes words to Sita; they embrace.
1 ½ minutes	Full orchestra only	Rām and Sitā kneel on bench and embrace.
1 minute	Orchestra continues	Rām enters with other *yakkha* and watches.
30 seconds	Chorus only	Rāb mimes instructions to *yakkha*.
1 ¼ minutes	Full orchestra only	Yakkha exits; golden deer enters (transformation); Rāb exits.
1 minute	Chorus only	Sitā asks Rām to catch prancing deer.
15 seconds	Orchestra only	Rām prepares to leave.
1 minute	Chorus only	Rām bids Sitā farewell and exits.
1 minute	*Sralay* and one *roneat*	Laks scouts the area, joins Sitā.
45 seconds	Chorus only	Sitā tells Laks to follow Rām.
1 ½ minutes	Orchestra only	Laks kneels, departs. Rāb enters.
30 seconds	*Sralay* and *roneat*	Rāb exits, *eysei* enters, Sitā sees him and rises on bench.
2 minutes	Orchestra-no chorus	Comic *eysei* and Sitā meet and mime.
2 minutes	Chorus only	*Eysei* mimes. Sitā mimes. She repulses his advances with slaps.

Appendix III: The Structure of Chorus, Orchestra and Dance Components

30 seconds	Full orchestra	Angry *eysei* exits. Rāb returns.
1 ¼ minutes	Melodic orchestra	Rāb joins Sitā on bench. She is afraid, runs, slaps him and Rām exits with her in tow.
4 ½ minutes	Full orchestra with subtle changes in the melodies	Rāb pursues deer, shoots with arrow, Deer falls, rises and exits. Laks enters and circles stage with Rām.
45 seconds	Chorus, one *roneat*	Rām and Laks see empty bench.
½ minute	Orchestra: strong *sralay*	Rām and Laks simultaneously on bench.
1 minute	Chorus only	Laks mimes explanation. Rām upset.
½ minute	Orchestra	Rām rises. Hanumān enters and bows.
1 minute	Chorus only	Rām mimes request to Hanumān and gives ring. Hanumān dances.
1 ¼ minute	Full orchestra	Hanumān exits. Laks and Rām exit.
½ minute	-continuing	Rāb enters with Sitā, resisting.
½ minute	Chorus [then brief pause); Chorus	Rāb mimes his love. Sitā mimes her rejection.
1 minute	Orchestra, especially *sralay*	Sitā runs, pleads: Rāb tries force but is repulsed by force of her virtue.
15 seconds	Chorus	Rāb strikes her with his bow.
45 seconds	Orchestra	Rāb exits in fury.
45 seconds	Chorus (wailing)	Sitā mimes her sorrow.
45 seconds	*Roneat tauch*: playful After pause: chorus	Hanumān enters. Sitā sleeps. Hanumān mimes.
½ minute	Lively orchestra	Hanumān looks her over sadly.
45 seconds	Chorus	Sitā awakens; Hanumān bows, gives her the ring from Rām.
1 minute	Orchestra	Hanumān bows, she gestures, he rises, does cartwheels, etc. He exits. Sitā rises and exits.
14 minutes	-Continuing	Hanumān enters. Three monkeys join him carrying rocks to build causeway. Sovann Machha enters after their exit. Three other fish join her and dance to the four directions. They remove the rocks. Hanumān re-enters; other monkeys chase fish; Hanumān leaves. Sovann Machha dances solo and is seen by Hanumān. Energetic seduction and both exit.
7 minutes	-Continuing Lots of drums for emphasis	Four *yakkha* enter. Rāb enters and they salute him. He poses, gestures to go, stands in the center of them, embraces each, stands on bench, they salute, all five exit.
3 minutes	-Continuing	Hanumān and four monkeys enter and perform standard monkey gymnastics. Laks enters.

APPENDIX IV
Repertoire of the Pinpeat Orchestra

The following list of alleged *pinpeat* song titles in French was available at the Université des Beaux-Arts in Phnom Penh in the late 1960s in mimeographed form. No author is cited and the list is undated. A large number of the titles include Chinese, Malay, Mon or Lao allusions. Certain numbers on the list are followed by a question mark in the original, which suggests a finite number or a distinct sequence of tunes. In those cases where the original spelling is illegible, a second question mark in parentheses has been added. There appears to be correspondence between only four of these titles (nos. 1, 180, 181, 184) with those Khmer titles discussed in Chapter VI known to be associated with classical dance; thus the list is included in this study solely for purposes of historical preservation.

1 —Khmer Preah bantum
   —Pour le sommeil d'un Roi Khmer
   —Version khmère du sommeil d'un Roi
   —Thème khmer pour le sommeil d'un Roi
2 —Thème cambodgien de la moisson
   —La moisson cambodgienne
   —Les cambodgiens en train de moissonner
3 —Comment les cambodgiens tisseur les fils d'or
   —Pour des tissus lamés d'or
4 —Berçeuse cambodgienne
5 —Marche khmère
6 —Les cimes des pins dans le vent
7 —Guirlande cambodgienne
8 —Les cambodgiens de la province de Pursat
9 —Thème cambodgien d'une musique jouée avec des feuilles d'arbre
   —Musicien cambodgien jouant en soufflant dans la feuille d'un arbre
10 —Khmère krourn
11 —Le chinois
12 —Le voisin chinois
13 —Le vieux chinois
14 —Les chinois de Canton
15 —Le potier chinois
16 —Le chinois ouvre ses rideaux
17 —Le chinois s'embarque dans un bateau
18 —Chin soa pak kuoy ? (?)
19 —Chinois tanant une tasse de the
20 —Chinois se tenant a la proue d'un bateau
21 —Chinois dansant avec un eventail
22 —Le chinois lent
23 —Le chinois vif
24 —Chinois cueillant des fleurs
25 —Un chinois poltron
26 —Un chinois des basses-terres
27 —Chinois cueillant des feuilles d'arbre
28 —Marche chinoise
29 — ?
30 — ?
31 —La danse Môn
32 —Le Môn en bateau
33 —Variation sur l'air Môn
34 —Un Môn jetant son épée
35 —Un Indien en pays Môn
36 —Le malais conducteur d'éléphant
37 —La tristesse malaise
38 —Malais dansant avec un éventail

39 —Le malais aux yeux de tigre "de braise"
40 —Un malais faisant l'invocation aux génies sous l'au vent
41 —Le malais lève l'ancre "tirant la chaine d'une ancre"
42 —Le malais errant
43 —Le malais qui s'est installe dans la lère moitié du village
44 —Le malais dans la Zème moitié du village
45 —Le malais de Rajaburi
46 —Le malais de Lopburi
47 —Le malais de Chan Sen
48 —Les sanglots du malais
49 —?
50 —La danse malaise
51 —La musique malaise
52 —Prélude musical joue par une divinité
53 —Trouble marveilleux—émotion
54 —Le sommeil du Dieu
55 —Les rêves du Dieu
56 —Fille de la Cour
57 —?
58 —Contemplation des étoiles
59 — L'étoile d'or
60 —L'étoile scintillante
61 —L'étoile flottante
62 —Un rayon de lumière auréole de gloire
63 —Parodie de théâtre chinois
64 —Une forêt nouvelle
65 —Préciosité—morceau de musique précieux
66 —Un couple bien accordé
67 —Harmonie
68 —Couleurs fondues
69 —La couleur des guirlandes
   —Guirlandes de toutes les couleurs
70 —La poupée
71 —l'éclat du diamant
72 —Croissant de lune
73 —La lune ronde
74 —La lune d'argent
75 —Invocation à la lune
   —Jeune fille appelant la lune

76 —Contemplation de la lune
77 —Louange à la lune
78 —La pleine lune
79 —La belle
80 —L'aigle royal
81 —Variation sur l'air de l'aigle royal
82 —Le lion "a trots rythmes"
83 —Le lion (variation)
84 —L'allégresse (joie de singe)
85 —L'harmonie
86 —Voix d'or
87 —Pollen d'or
88 —Tout prés de soi
89 —Les 4 amis
90 —Princesse laissant tomber son anneau (?)
91 —Jeune Seigneur (Le Brahman) renassant l'anneau
92 —Le jeune noble (Le Petit Brahman)
93 —Ballade du Jeune Seigneur (Le Brahman errant)
94 —Le Brahman jounant du Sadeav
95 —L'émotion de la Dame
96 —L'émotion du mandarin
97 —Tristesse du mandarin
98 —Plainte du gibon
99 —Complainte du mandarin
100 —?
101 —Les 3 filles
102 —?
103 —Danse des épées
104 —?
105 —Tendresse japonaise
106 —Guirlande de Takol (?)
107 —Guirlande de fleurs
108 —Guirlande de Melis (Jasmin) (?)
109 —La crocodile a tongue queue
110 —La brise
111 —Le vent des montagnes
112 —Le vent souffle sur l'étang (?)
113 —La brise de la montagne
114 —L'odeur du Melis (Le senteur du jasmin)
115 —Fleurs odorantes (?)

116—La bien-aimée
117—L'averse (?)
118—Le tonnerre
119—F—utons le tonnerre (?)
120—Le coup du tonnerre
121—Le chérie
122—Les filles pliant le riz
123—? Krâssing Teap (?)
124—L'étang Peay (?)
125—Fleurs en guirlande
126—A la mer (en mer)
127—La mer démarche (?)
128—Compassion (?)
129—Emotion
130—Paroles douces (?)
131—Comme de d'or pur (?)
132—Lion d'or
133—Palais d'or
134—Moineau d'or (?)
135—Fleur de Champa d'or
136—Le pas du cheval (?)
137—Cris de joie des Birmans (Allégresse)
138—Civière de diamant
139—Tresse de cheveux
140—Guirlande d'or
141—Puissance
142—Maharik ? (?) -Gloire-Noblesse
143—Grande victoire
144—Le Môn nouveau
    (Les Môns de maintenant)
145—Comprends-moi
   —Confiance
   —Accorde moi ta confiance
146—Ouverture de l'Urne royale
147—Pour le recueil des mânes du Roi
148—Midi d'aplomb
149—Vissakan ?
150—Le Hangsa en or
151—La tortue mange les liserons (?)
152—Le poisson d'or
153—Les lapins au clair de lune
154—Jeune laotienne aux douces paroles
155—Complaints de la jeune fille Lao
    —La petite fille lao navré
156—Guirlande de fleurs d'or
157—Laotions hautains poitrine de poulet
158—La jeune fille Lao sur le chemin
    de la riviére
159—Le laotien attrapant des tourterelles
160—Le laotien dans la forêt
161—Laotien adressant louange à la lune
162—Lao adressant des voeux avec des
    bougies
163—L'eau court sous le sable
164—Poursuite d'un derf d'or
165—? Sipha Kandal
166—Quatre mélodies (quadruor)
167—Six mélodies
168—Huit mélodies
169—Audience du Roi
170—Petit Khim
171—Au bout du Khim
172—Grand Khim
173—Cercle musical
174—En quittant la citadelle
175—Au Coeur du Nagara
176—?
177—?
178—?
179—?
180—Preah Thong
181—Néang Neak
182—Quatro voix
183—Bouquet à quatre couleurs
184—Sinuon
185—En contemplant ta silhouette
186—Séduction
187—La grenouille sautillant
188—Yani
189—?
190—?
191—?
192—Jeunes lao pleurnichant
193—Separation

194—Allure trainante
195—Merceau final
196—Marche silencieuse
197—Marche du Roi des Hansa
198—Marche épanouie
199—Solitude
200—Forme modelée
201—Marche de Phnom-Penh
202—L'éléphant qui s'amuse avec ses défenses
203—Pleurs des Echassiers
204—Prince Lao
205—Jeune fille svelte
206—Promenade dans le jardin céleste
207—Cocher et son char
208—Fleur transformée
209—Mon amour
210—Temps moderne
211—Paon d'or
212—Grand regret
213—A la mode
214— ?
215— ?
216—Sariyaing
217—Longévité
218—Songe
219—Feuille de chaume
220—L'hirondelle
221—L'oiseau "Kalavék"
222— ?
223—Mélodie birmane á 5 registres
224—Démarche ondulante

MUSIQUE LAO

225—La solidarité laotienne
226—Nation lao
227—Extase lao
228—L'enfant lao
229—Charmante laotienne
230—Guerrier lao
231—Tempérament lao
232— L'éléphant nettoyant la cour

233—Rose fanée
234—Fleur de "Champa"
235—En cueillant la fleur
236—Fleur de Romduol fanée
237—Rose de Paksé
238—Fleur de Makry (?)
239—Romduol sauvage
240— ?
241—Pleine lune
242—Clair de lune
243—Fricheur de la brise
244—Lueur de la lune
245—Feuilies de Java ?
246—Pour vivre longtemps
247—Danse lao
248—Venez-vous refraichir
249— ?
250— ?
251—Grande douleur
252—Le vieux Cham
253—Jeune fille s'ébattant dans l'eau
254—Rénuphar (?) aux feuilles vertes
255—Paix intérieure
256—Birman
257—Nostalgie
258—Fleur d'Arabic
259—En écoutant la voix d'un Arabe
260—Danse malaise
261—Flots se brisant contre le rivage (?)
262—Danse de Bombay
263—Aribaba
264—Flamme satisfaite
265—Amour sans espoir
265—Amour et séparation
267—Amour de Kangri
268—Rahu de Surin
269—Fleur profane
270—Jeune fille à la fille indienne
271—Bandalinga

About The Author

Paul Cravath is a scholar, teacher, actor and theatre director. He began teaching at the University of Hawaii in 1986, and is currently Professor of Theatre at the University of Hawaii-LCC.

During his career, he has directed more than sixty productions, many based on Hawaiian mythology, history, contemporary social problems, and dance. Despite the effects of full paralysis from infantile polio, Cravath pursued a full life in the theater and has performed fifty roles in professional and university productions, including three summers with the Utah Shakespearean Festival (Iago, Richard III, Prospero).

Cravath received his Bachelor's degree from Luther College (Decorah, IA) in 1966 when he was 21 and immediately accepted a Fulbright Tutor Grant to teach in India. This initial immersion in South Asian culture, a process he has likened to "being born," gave him the opportunity to study the Indian film industry and aesthetics.

In 1967, he traveled to Sophia University (Tokyo) to study ancient Japanese literature. He then enrolled at Tulane University, completing his M.F.A. in directing in 1970. That same year, an historic event occurred in Southeast Asia that would soon change Cravath's life: a right-wing coup in Cambodia deposed the monarchy that had ruled that kingdom since ancient times.

In 1971, Cravath enrolled at the University of Hawaii at Mānoa to begin his doctoral program under the guidance of renowned Asian Theatre scholar James R. Brandon. Initially, Cravath focused on Chinese theatre, the Beijing Opera and Mandarin language (Taipei 1972).

Meanwhile, the Southeast Asian conflict worsened. Surrounded by war, and in the midst of a civil war, the newly

The author following his escape from **Phnom Penh,** Bangkok, April 1975.
Photo Terrance White

formed Cambodian Republic's Ministry of Culture realized they were saddled with an unusual responsibility: preserving the history of the Cambodian classical dance drama, a cultural treasure lying at the heart of Khmer self-identity.

The Ministry approached a number of universities worldwide seeking research assistance; Dr. Brandon accepted their project, offering one of his doctoral students the opportunity to document the Royal Cambodian Ballet. Cravath ended his Chinese studies and prepared to travel to Phnom Penh, Cambodia.

With the Ministry's support, Cravath gained full access to the "formerly royal" palace theatres and archives, as well as the dancers and teachers who perpetuated this ancient court tradition. From January to April 1975 he worked diligently, even as rockets, up to 100 each day, fell on the city. Days before Phnom Penh fell to the Khmer Rouge he was forced to evacuate on a military transport with a single suitcase. He abandoned his personal possessions to retain his notes and photos and continued his Asian research in Bangkok until returning to the United States in late 1975.

The author as Iago in *Othello*, Utah Shakespearean Festival, August 1969.

At the University of Hawaii he devoted 10 years to refining his thesis, conducting archival research, scrutinizing earlier French studies, and interviewing refugee dancers in the United States. Cravath submitted his 680 page doctoral thesis in 1985 but the world had changed: the Cambodian government so keen for his research had disappeared. Cambodia had plunged into a dark age, first at the hands of the genocidal Khmer Rouge and then under the control of an occupying Vietnamese government. His paper and its intent were virtually forgotten, but it was inevitable that a body of knowledge this significant could not stay hidden forever.

Earth in Flower now appears as a legacy for the new Cambodia.

Publisher's Notes: The story behind *Earth in Flower*

The book you are holding resulted from such a diverse series of coincidences and unlikely events that I elected to share its story in these end notes. This is my personal account; it is not part of Dr. Paul Cravath's original research or thesis; however, parts of it are based on conversations I have been privileged to have with the author over the past two years.

For more than a decade, I've been expanding my library to satisfy my interest in Southeast Asia. My collection, including many obscure and antique volumes, has grown to over fifteen hundred books, with more than two hundred relating to Cambodia.

One of my frustrations with older editions is that the authors, their motivation, their personal relationships with their topics and the events leading to the subsequent publication of their work are usually shrouded in mystery. Many authors are now little more than names whose lives have vanished. This sad reality motivated me to include this section. But it had never occurred to me to publish a book, until I read the thesis, *Earth in Flower*.

My connection to this story began shortly after 10:35 AM on November 2, 2005. That's the time stamp on my first photo of Angkor Wat as I walked across the Rainbow Bridge on my first visit. My life was about to change forever. It's easy to look back and see life's pivotal moments but we never see them coming. And only rarely do we have an inkling how significant they are at the time.

I was no stranger to Southeast Asia. In the early '90s I worked in Thailand for five years and traveled the region studying language, culture, history, and religion. I met my wife Sophaphan in 1992 and we've shared our adventures together since. But it took fifteen years for my Cambodian odyssey to begin.

Kent Davis in his study, 2007.
Photo Sophaphan Davis.

Despite my growing familiarity, every Asian visit revealed new wonders. I knew, and still know, that a lifetime of secrets and surprises awaits there. As I soon discovered, a genuine epiphany was only a few steps ahead. But it was more than thirty-five years earlier that the stage was set for *Earth in Flower*.

CAMBODIA'S SECRET NATIONAL TREASURE

By the late 1960s, Southeast Asia was immersed in violence. The Vietnam and Laos wars raged, frequently spilling over onto Cambodian soil. For years, Cambodia's monarch, King Sihanouk, had steered his country through perilous political waters, trying to keep his small kingdom neutral in the face of aggression on all fronts.

In March 1970, a military coup deposed the monarchy that had ruled Cambodia since ancient times. The coup that gave birth to the Khmer Republic was the final spark igniting civil war in Cambodia. Americans old enough to remember the war protests will never forget May 4th, 1970 when National Guard troops killed 4 students at Kent State University. What most don't remember is that the students were protesting the American invasion of Cambodia, initiated by President Nixon only days before on April 25th.

Unofficially, American incursions and extensive bombing on Cambodian soil began in 1965 under the direction of the CIA and US Special Forces. By the time Congress stopped American bombing in August 1973, American planes had dropped more than 2,700,000 tons of bombs on Cambodia, a country the size of the US state of Missouri. This quantity of bombs exceeded those dropped by the combined Allied forces during World War II, including the atomic bombs dropped on Japan.

War has little respect for human life and, apart from looting, almost none for culture, art and history. The knowledge mankind has lost in the heat of battle is unimaginable. Yet, in the midst of this chaos, a small door opened.

Even in this turbulent period, the new Cambodian Ministry of Culture realized that they were now charged with the formerly royal responsibility of preserving their country's dance drama, a cultural treasure that had defined the Khmer race for more than a thousand years. Having a dramatic tradition so vital to cultural identity seems unusual to Westerners; we prefer tangible, inanimate objects like the Crown Jewels, the Magna Carta, the Declaration of Independence or the Eiffel Tower. Cambodia, as Paul Cravath discovered in the course of his research, enshrined its spirit in a *living* tradition of dance, passed on through countless generations.

In 1973, the Ministry of Culture began reaching out to a number of universities seeking help documenting their heritage. Dr. James Brandon at the University of Hawaii responded to their request. Brandon, renowned for his Asian theater studies, was unable to participate but he thought one of his doctoral students possibly could; Paul Cravath was quickly drawn into the adventure of a lifetime. Brandon couldn't have found a better candidate.

The Ideal Archivist

The Greek word drama means "action"; Paul's active life to that point had been devoted to learning and teaching theater. But that was an unlikely path.

In 1946, when Paul was an infant in Minnesota just learning to walk, he was struck by polio. His only luck was living near the Mayo Clinic, a pioneering center for muscular rehabilitation. With the help of multiple surgeries, and leg braces that he wore throughout his adult life, Paul would walk. The real miracle is that his mind danced. Physical challenges never dampened his spiritual quests. By 1973, Paul's studies had already drawn him to Asia to work in India, Japan and Taipei.

As a graduate student with extensive Asian travel experience and a keen eye for detail, he was an exceptional candidate for the Cambodian project. But it was his passion to understand the spirituality underlying humankind's desire to perform and observe performances that made Paul the ideal scholar to pursue the mysteries of *Earth in Flower*.

The concept of studying the Cambodian Ballet intrigued him because it was a court form of dance, nurtured under royal patronage for more than a thousand years. Many considered it one of the great performing arts forms in Asia, yet there was only one troupe in the world. Finally, almost nothing was written about it in English. Paul was hooked from the minute he began his research.

With the Ministry's endorsement and approval, Paul traveled to Cambodia. By the time he arrived in January 1975 the Khmer Rouge had effectively cut all roads leading to and from the capital city; Phnom Penh had become a shrinking island of peace surrounded by war. Flights to the isolated city were a favorite target of enemy rockets, requiring planes to ascend and descend abruptly, in a dangerous cork-screw pattern.

The Ministry granted Paul extraordinary first-hand access to the formerly royal palace, to its theaters, archives and, most important, to the dancers and teachers who preserved this ancient living tradition. For hundreds of years the latter privilege would have been unthinkable for a man outside of the royal family. In the past, dancers were the personal property of the king and were kept sequestered; contact by anyone outside his household was forbidden, formerly under penalty of death. (See Chapter VIII, Endnote 23 for a particularly graphic account of one incident.)

From his arrival, Paul diligently used his privileged access, but conditions were difficult. Khmer Rouge rockets fell on the city almost daily, even on the palace grounds, disrupting transportation, rehearsals and interviews. By February most foreign nationals had already left and the US Embassy gave Paul written notice to evacuate. Paul respectfully declined. He was then required to do a weekly check-in with an embassy evaluation officer, who encouraged him to leave the country on each visit. On April 1, 1975 Prime Minister Lon Nol himself fled Cambodia for exile in Hawaii. Four days later, on his next embassy check-in, Paul's liaison directed that he was scheduled to leave on a military transport…immediately.

Paul rushed to his room to gather his materials, distraught because he would miss another photo session he had scheduled for the next day. He was only allowed one suitcase so he gave away his personal effects to make room for his research documents, cramming them into one heavy bag. Back at the embassy he joined a small group of foreigners and boarded a bus for Pochentong International Airport.

When they arrived, the airport was under attack; they were hastily ushered into a bunker made from sandbags and plate steel built directly on the runway. When the shelling stopped, they were told to run to a newly arrived C-130 transport. It lacked seats; everyone scrambled to find a place in the webbing that lined the plane's two sides and held on. The pilot set the four turbo-prop engines on maximum thrust and did his best to climb steeply to avoid groundfire, passing the wreckage of other planes that weren't so fortunate.

On April 17th, Pol Pot's Khmer Rouge troops entered the city to begin their destructive reign, emptying Phnom Penh at gunpoint, claiming that an American attack was imminent. With the exception of about four hundred people who took refuge in the French embassy, Paul was one of the last foreigners to leave; he escaped with his research, notes, film and photos intact. Two weeks later, Paul saw news images of helicopters on the roof of the American Embassy in Saigon, only 130 miles from Phnom Penh. America's war in Southeast Asia was over.

What no one knew, or perhaps what many people chose to ignore, was that Cambodia was about to suffer one of the worst genocides in human history.

Paul returned to Hawaii to assemble his materials, but now he knew too much about his topic to write a limited study. He worked for ten years, conducting archival research, refining his data and exploring the implications of myriad related topics that manifested like branches on a huge tree.

In 1985 he finally submitted his thesis titled *Earth in Flower*, earning Paul his Ph.D. Soon he began the job that he holds today, Professor of Theater at the University of Hawaii, filling his life with the energizing responsibilities of students, assignments, play productions and performances. [Note: Paul retired from his professorship in 2011.]

Eleven years of painstaking work devoted to Cambodia's dance tradition faded, but remained a milestone in his life. The Cambodian government and most of the people who facilitated Paul's work had vanished. Cambodia itself, devastated by years of war, became virtually invisible to the world.

After the doctoral committee completed their evaluation Paul carefully boxed his original materials and put them away. Apart from two published articles, *Earth in Flower* also disappeared. Nearly twenty years later I began walking across the Rainbow Bridge.

KHMER PORTRAITS OF THE FEMININE DIVINE

I had no strong preconceptions or clear expectations of Angkor Wat; however within minutes of entering I was overwhelmed, but not by the impersonal magnitude of its soaring structures in the cleared, hot jungle setting. I had expected "architectural grandeur" from one of the Wonders of the World, but I wasn't prepared for the temple's human side as realistic carvings of women greeted my wife and I in our exploration.

The maidens, now called *apsara* or *devatā* (no one knows what the ancient Khmers called them), encountered me at every entrance, in every sanctuary and on every level of the structure. Friendly, frozen faces peacefully gazed at me from another era, yet their features were quite familiar. Clearly, their daughters are still selling water outside the temple. I just passed one of their sisters, walking across the Rainbow Bridge with her wedding party, and even my own wife, born just two hundred miles to the north, echoed their beauty and strength.

In the back of my mind questions began taking shape; I was perplexed by what I saw. Quite obviously the images of these women were a major part of the monument's design and purpose. Quite obviously they have dominated this Khmer monument, and many others, since it was built. Nothing I had read mentioned that very clearly. Tourist books dismissed the *apsara* with a clichéd sentence or two, "… and beautiful carvings of heavenly dancers are used to decorate the temple's bare limestone walls."

Angkor Wat *Devatā*. Drawing by Sappho Marchal, 1926. Courtesy Orchid Press, Hong Kong, *Khmer Costumes and Ornaments*, 2005.

In my soul I knew these women were much more than "decorations." These were portrait carvings, not random faces dreamt up by simple stone carvers. Behind each visage was a story about a woman as real as you and me; they laughed and loved and dreamed in this world, not in heaven.

Who were they? Where did they come from? How much power did they wield? Why were they glorified so prominently at such a fantastic cost to the empire? What sort of hierarchy do they represent? What happened to them? How could anyone write *anything* about Angkor Wat without speaking of them immediately and at length? Has anyone else seen what is so clear to me: that this temple is here *because* of the women?

That night I fell into my bed exhausted but sleepless, my mind ablaze under the *apsaras'* spell: nearly 900 years ago, one of the most powerful Khmer rulers controlled a vast empire…King Suryavarman II built the largest stone religious monument on Earth…yet his will was for *women* to dominate his temple…he gave them precedence over his own image or that of any male…even his god Vishnu is portrayed in a minor role compared to the multitude of 1,800 females realistically immortalized in stone….Slowly, the Khmer empire declined…Angkor Wat and other magnificent structures were devoured by jungles as power shifted…time dispersed and diluted their traditions throughout the region…others laid claim to their ancient genius… the Khmers all but disappeared to the West.

In my mind's eye, in that world between wakefulness and sleep, I saw their stone portraits precisely coded with myriad variations of crowns, jewelry, poses, ethnic features and attributes. A quantitative analysis could unlock the secrets these complex women have guarded for so long. I began designing my scientific study. Spiritually, it is more accurate for me to say that the *devatā* enlisted me to do so.

As I drifted to sleep, I pledged myself to serve the *devatā* as they pledged themselves to serve the Khmer empire so long ago. I expected to return to a Western world filled with historical research about these fantastic women. With 140 years of intense Cambodian study surely there must be volumes of books written about them. Instead I found that, perhaps blinded by their beauty, historians, scholars and archeologists had written almost nothing.

In 1916 l'École Française d'Extrême Orient (EFEO) appointed Henri Marchal as the second curator of the Angkor Wat conservation project. His daughter Sappho literally grew up among the ruins and spent years drawing *devatā* and their accoutrements. In 1927, Sappho published *Costumes et parures khmèrs d'après les devatâ d'Angkor-Vat*, the first and only quantitative analysis of these women ever done. She was 23 years old.

Sixty-seven years would pass before Dr. K. M. Srivastava, a renowned archaeologist with the Archeological Survey of India, wrote the second and *only* other book about the *devatā* of Angkor Wat. Starved for more information I began scouring online archives for papers. I soon found a 36-page booklet called *Apsara: The Feminine in Cambodian Art*, published in 1987 for a Los Angeles exhibition.

Angkor Wat *Devatā*. Drawing by Sappho Marchal, 1926. Courtesy Orchid Press, Hong Kong, *Khmer Costumes and Ornaments*, 2005.

Inside, a four page essay by Robert L. Brown, "Female Imagery in Ancient Khmer Sculpture," gave me a new clue. Brown quoted two profound sentences from Paul Cravath's unpublished Ph.D. dissertation *Earth in Flower*. These brief passages convinced me that their author would have additional insights on the *devatā* and their relationship between heaven and earth.

Google quickly located Paul's university email address. I typed up an explanation of my study and asked how I could see his paper. Within hours, I was thrilled to get his reply; University Microfilms could make me a copy and he would be happy to consult with me about my research. I ordered Paul's thesis for $60. One week later, UPS brought a box heavier than I expected; it contained a copy of his 680-page dissertation.

The document's depth and Paul's fastidious attention to complex details were immediately apparent. The photocopy showed a hand-typed paper with English, French, German and Vietnamese as well as transliterated Thai, Sanskrit, pinyin Chinese and Khmer. Chinese characters and diacritical marks beyond the typist's ability were added by hand.

Paul later explained that he prepared the paper just before computers became ubiquitous in our lives. He paid his typist $2 per page for her daunting work and told me that she never worked for this low rate again. I spent nearly two years preparing his manuscript for publication… my heart truly goes out to her!

As I read Paul's paper, my sense of wonderment grew. He spoke directly to many of my questions, and inspired new insights in my own research. The more I read the more I realized that he accomplished a mission of immense significance, for human spirituality and especially for the history of the Cambodian people. Yet, his amazing work remained unpublished and virtually unknown. I emailed Paul to request a telephone appointment.

Earth in Flower

Imagine someone charging into your life, passionate about a thing you were passionate about…twenty years earlier. Our first conversation lasted for hours. Even after two decades Paul's command of his research was impressive. His emotional commitment to the topic and his dedication to refining his data so long ago came though clearly.

He told me that I was only the second person to call him about his paper in 20 years, the first being a student from Minnesota years before. I thought of the *devatā* at Angkor Wat, so obviously important and yet somehow doomed to intellectual obscurity.

"Where's your paper now, Paul?" I asked.

"Where it's been for 20 years...under my bed." We were both laughing when he went on to say, "You know, it's funny. A couple of weeks ago I was thinking about cleaning house and getting rid of all my old papers...."

This inspired a quiet moment for both of us.

My position—my epiphany, if you will—did more than give me the conviction that the "Daughters of Angkor Wat" hold unrealized significance. After fifteen years on the Thai side of the border I now realized that the Khmer civilization was very much alive, even though I hadn't seen it when it was right before my eyes.

Political borders don't define the essence of a people. My brief visit to the heart of Cambodia showed me that the ideas, the religion, the accomplishments and the magic of the ancient Khmer civilization still lived within the inhabitants of the entire region.

Soon after reading *Earth in Flower* I began to learn more about the dark era Cambodia entered as Paul fled Phnom Penh. His paper helped me realize that the Khmer culture wasn't just held in libraries or artifacts or buildings that Khmer Rouge, American, Vietnamese or Cambodian violence may have destroyed. The Khmer connection to the universe is, and always was, its people. Paul Cravath documented the most formalized and extraordinary expression of that Khmer relationship: their dance drama tradition.

Towards the end of our first talk I shared my newest conviction with Paul: *Earth in Flower* was too significant to remain unpublished. We both knew that many people who helped Paul and many of the archives he accessed were lost forever. We clearly saw that the academic importance of this book paled when compared to adding this knowledge to the cultural record of the Khmer people.

With Paul's encouragement, I promised to find a way to issue his work and disseminate the knowledge he risked his life to compile. If you are reading this we succeeded. It is our hope that this record helps to preserve the Khmer legacy, that still thrives in its children throughout Southeast Asia and the world.

Kent Davis — kentdavis@gmail.com
Anna Maria Island, Florida
April 2007

ABBREVIATIONS USED IN THE BIBLIOGRAPHY

Journals

AP	Asian Perspectives
BEFEO	Bulletin de l'École Française d'Extrême-Orient
BSEI	Bulletin de la Société des Études Indochinoises
JA	Journal Asiatique
JMBRAS	Journal of the Malayan Branch of the Royal Asiatic Society
JSS	Journal of the Siam Society
RAA	Revue des Arts Asiatiques

Collections of Articles

EESAH   Hall, Kenneth R. and John K. Whitmore, eds. *Explorations in Early Southeast Asian History: The Origins of Southeast Asian Statecraft.* Michigan Papers on South and Southeast Asia, 11, Ann Arbor: University of Michigan, 1976.

TDMSA   Osman, Mohd. Tabid, ed. *Traditional Drama and Music of Southeast Asia. Proc. of the International Conference on Traditional Drama and Music of Southeast Asia,* 27-30 Aug. 1969. Kuala Lumpur: Dewan Bahasa dan Pustaka, Kementerian Peljaran Malaysia, 1974.

BIBLIOGRAPHY

Books, Pamphlets, and Collections of Articles

Aeusrivongse, Nidhi. "The Devarāja Cult and Khmer Kingship at Angkor." *EESAH*, pp. 107-48.

Aymonier, Etienne. *Le royaume actuel*. Vol. I of *Le Cambodge*. Paris: Ernest Leroux, 1900.

Barth, Auguste, and Abel Bergaigne, eds. and trans. "Inscriptions sanscrites du Cambodge." In *Notices et extraits des manuscrits*. Paris: Académie des Inscriptions et Belles-Lettres, 1885, pp. 1-180, 293-588.

Bellwood. Peter. *The Polynesians: Prehistory of an Island People*. London: Thames and Hudson, 1978.

Benjamin, Geoffrey. *Indigenous Religious Systems of the Malay Peninsula*. Department of Sociology Working Paper, 28. Singapore: University of Singapore, 1974.

Boddhisattva Arts. Newbury Park, CA: Center for Transpersonal and Expressive Arts Therapies, n.d.

Bois, George. *Les danseuses cambodgiennes en France*. Hanoi: Extrême-Orient, 1913.

Boisselier, Jean. *La statuaire khmère et son évolution*. 2 vols. Saigon: École Française d'Extrême-Orient, 1955.

Bosch, F.D.K. "The Problem of the Hindu Colonisation of Indonesia." In *Selected Studies in Indonesian Archaeology*. The Hague: M. Nijhoff, 1961, pp. 3-22.

Bouillevaux, C. E. *L'Annam et le Cambodge; voyages et notices historiques*. Paris: Victor Palmé, 1874.

Boulanger, Edgar. *Un hiver au Cambodge*. Tours: Alfred Mame et Fils, 1888.

Bowie, Theodore. *The Arts of Thailand*. Bloomington: Indiana University Press, 1960.
——*The Sculpture of Thailand*. New York: The Asia Society, 1972.

Bowring, Sir John. *The Kingdom and People of Siam: with a Narrative of the mission to that country in 1855*. 2 vols. London: J. W. Parker, 1857.

Brandon, James R. *Theatre in Southeast Asia*. Cambridge: Harvard University Press, 1967.

Brunet, Jacques. "Music and Rituals in Traditional Cambodia." In *TDMSA*, pp. 219-22.
——"The Origin of Cambodian Music." In *TDMSA*, pp. 208-15.
——"Themes and Motifs of the Cambodian Ramayana in the Shadow Theatre." In *TDMSA*, pp. 3-4.

Burckhardt, Titus. *Alchemy*. Trans. William Stoddart. Baltimore: Penguin, 1971.

Cabaton, Antoine. *Nouvelles recherches sur les les chams*. Paris: Ernest Leroux, 1901.

Casey, Robert J. *Four Faces of Shiva*. Indianapolis: Bobbs-Merrill, 1929.

Chen Duriyanga Phra. *Siamese Music in Theory and Practice as Compared with that of the West and a Description of the Piphat Band*. Bangkok: The Department of Fine Arts, 1948.

Chhuk Meng Chhansan. *Le ballet classique khmer*. Phnom Penh: n.p., 1973.

Christie, A. H. "The Name k'un-lun as an Ethnic Term." In *Proceedings of the Twenty-third International Congress of Orientalists*. Cambridge: Cambridge University Press, 1954, pp. 291-92.

Christie, Anthony. "The Provenance and Chronology of Early Indian Cultural Influences in South East Asia." In *R. C. Majumdar Felicitation Volume*. Ed. H. B. Sarkar. Calcutta: Firma K. K. Mukhopadhyay, 1970, pp. 1-14.

Cœdès, George. *Angkor: An Introduction*. Trans. Emily Floyd Gardiner. Hong Kong: Oxford University Press, 1963.
——*The Indianized States of Southeast Asia*. Trans. Susan Brown Cowing. Ed. Walter F. Vella.

Honolulu: East-West Center Press, 1968.

—ed. and trans. *Inscriptions du Cambodge*. 5 vols. Paris/ Hanoi: E. de Boccard, 1937-1966.

—"Littérature cambodgienne." In *Indochine*. Ed. Sylvain Levi. Paris: Société d'Editions Geographiques, Martitimes et Coloniales, 1931. Vol. I. pp. 180-192.

—*The Making of Southeast Asia*. Trans. H. M. Wright. Berkeley: University of California Press, 1972.

Cogniat, Raymond. *Danses d'Indochine*. Paris: G. Di San Lazzaro, 1932.

Cooper, Willard et al. *Meadows Museum of Art: For the Indochina Collection of Jean Despujols*. Shreveport, LA: Centenary College, n.d.

Cuisinier, Jeanne. *La danse sacrée en Indochine et en Indonésie*. Paris: Presses Universitaires de France, 1951.

The Dance Lives: The Story of the Khmer Classical Dance Troupe. Washington, D.C.: National Council for the Traditional Arts, 1982.

Daniélou, Alain. *La musique du Cambodge et du Laos*. Pondichery: Institute Français d'Indologie. 1957.

de Beauvais, René. *La vie de Louis Delaporte Explorateur (1842-1925): les ruines d'Angkor*. Paris: Des Orphelins d'Auteil, 1931.

Delaporte, Louis. *Voyage au Cambodge: L'architecture Khmer*. Paris: C. Delagrave, 1880.

Dhanit Yupho. *The Custom and Rite of Paying Homage to Teachers of Khon, Lakon and Piphat*. Trans. L. Lauhabandhu. Bangkok: The Fine Arts Department, 1961.

—*The Khon and Lakon*. Bangkok: The Fine Arts Department, 1963.

—*The Preliminary Course of Training in Thai Theatrical Art*. Bangkok: The Fine Arts Department, 1972.

Dyen, Isidore. *A Lexicostatistical Classification of the Austronesian Languages*. Indiana University Publications in Anthropology and Linguistics, 19. Bloomington: Indiana University Department of Anthropology, 1965.

Edmonds, I. G. *The Khmers of Cambodia*. Indianapolis: Bobbs-Merrill, 1970.

Eliade, Mircea. *Images and Symbols; Studies in Religious Symbolism*. Trans. Philip Mairet. New York: Sheed and Ward, 1969.

—*The Myth of the Eternal Return*. Princeton: Princeton University Press, 1971.

—*Myth and Reality*. London: Allen and Unwin, 1964.

—*Shamanism; Archaic Techniques of Ecstasy*. Trans. Willard R. Trask. Bollingen Series, 76. Princeton: University Press, 1964.

Fage, J. D. and R. A. Oliver, eds. *Papers in African Prehistory*. Cambridge: Cambridge University Press, 1970.

Fang Xuanling, ed. *Xin shu*. Rpt. Beijing: China Book Store, 1974.

Fergusson, James. *Tree and Serpent Worship*. 1868; rpt. Delhi: Oriental, 1971.

Finot, Louis. "Sur quelques traditions indochinoises." In *Melanges d'Indianisme offerts par ses élèves a M. Sylvain Levi*. Paris: Ernest Leroux, 1911, pp. 193-212.

Fromaget. J. and E. Saurin, eds. *Proceedings of the 3rd Congress on Prehistory of the Far East*. n.p., 1938.

Gandhi, Mohandas. *The Health Guide*. Ed. Anand Hingorani. Bombay: Bharatiya Vidya Bhavan, 1965.

Giteau, Madeleine. *The Civilization of Angkor*. New York: Rizzoli, 1976.

—*Guide du Musée National*. Phnom Penh: Office national du tourisme, 1960, Vol. II.

—*Khmer Sculpture and the Angkor Civilization*. Trans. Diana Imber. New York: Harry N. Abrams, 1965.

Gopalan, R. *History of the Pallavas of Kāñchī*. Madras: University of Madras, 1928.

Gorer, Geoffrey. *Bali and Angkor*. London: Michael Joseph, 1936.

Groslier, Bernard-Philippe and Jacques Arthaud. *Angkor Art and Civilization*. Trans. Eric Ernshaw Smith. New York: Frederich A. Praeger. 1966.

Groslier, Bernard-Philippe. "The Angkor Kings" (Preface). In *Royal Cambodian Ballet*. Phnom Penh: Cambodian Information Department, 1963, pp. 3-5.

—*The Art of Indochina*. New York: Crown, 1962.

—*Angkor et le Cambodge au XVIe siècle d'après les sources portugaises et espagnoles*. Paris: Presses Universitaires de France, 1958.

—*Indochina: Art in the Melting-Pot of Races*. Trans. George Lawrence. London: Methuen, 1962.

—"Danse et musique sous les rois d'Angkor." In *Felicitation Volumes of Southeast Asian Studies*. Bangkok: The Siam Society, 1965. Vol. II, pp. 283-92.

Groslier, George. *Danseuses cambodgiennes anciennes et modernes*. Paris: Albert Challamel, 1913.

Hall, D.G.E. *A History of South-East Asia*. London: Macmillan, 1960.

—*Historians of South East Asia*. London: Oxford University Press, 1961.

Hall, Kenneth R. "An Introductory Essay on Southeast Asian Statecraft in the Classical Period." In *EESAH*, pp. 1-24.

Hammerton, J. A. *Manners and Customs of Mankind*. New York: Wm. H. Wise, n.d. Vol. II.

Hang Thun Hak, et al. *Folklore Khmer*. Phnom Penh: l'Université Royale des Beaux-Arts, 1969.

—*Musique Khmere*. Phnom Penh; l'Université Royale des Beaux-Arts, 1969.

—*Rāmker (Rāmāyana Khmer)*. Phnom Penh: l'Université Royale des Beaux-Arts, 1969.

Heine-Geldern, Robert. *Conceptions of State and Kingship in Southeast Asia*. Data Paper, 18. Ithaca, NY: Southeast Asia Program, Department of Far Eastern Studies, Cornell University, 1956.

— "Prehistoric Research in the Netherlands Indies." In *Science and Scientists in the Netherlands Indies*. Ed. Pieter Honig. New York: Board for the Netherlands Indies, Surinam and Curaçao, 1945, pp. 129-67.

Henderson, Joseph L. "Ancient Myths and Modern Man." In *Man and His Symbols*. Ed. Carl G. Jung. Garden City, NY: Doubleday, 1964.

Ions, Veronica. *Indian Mythology*. London: Paul Hamlyn, 1967.

Jeannerat DeBeerski, Pierre. *Angkor: Ruins in Cambodia*. London: G. Richards, 1923.

Kerenyi, C. "Kore." In *Essays on a Science of Mythology: the myths of the divine child and the mysteries of Eleusis*. Ed. Carl G. Jung and C. Kerenyi. New York: Harper and Row, 1963.

Khmer Classical Dance. Phnom Penh: Université des Beaux-Arts, 1971.

Khmer Dances. Bangkok: The Fine Arts Department, 1974.

The Khmer Rāmāyana. Phnom Penh: The University of Fine Arts, 1971.

Kline, David and Robert Brown. *The New Face of Kampuchea: A Photo-Record of the First American Visit to Cambodia Since April 1975*. Chicago: Liberator Press, 1979.

La Loubère, Simon de. *A New Historical Relation of the Kingdom of Siam*. 1693; rpt. Kuala Lumpur: Oxford University Press, 1969. Vol. II.

Lancaster, Donald J. *Some Notes on the Classical Khmer Ballet*. Ithaca. NY: Cornell University, 1971.

Leclère, Adhémard. *Histoire du Cambodge*. Paris: Paul Guethner, 1914.

—"Le livre de Véandar, le roi charitable." In *Contes et legends du Cambodges*. Paris: Ernest Leroux, 1902.

—*Les livres sacrés du Cambodge*. Paris: Ernest Leroux, 1906.

—*Le théâtre cambodgien*. Paris: Ernest Leroux, 1911.

Lee, Sherman. *Ancient Cambodian Sculpture*. New York: The Asia Society, 1969.

Legge, James. *Chinese Classics*. Vol. lll, pt. 2. Oxford: Oxford University Press, 1893.

Levi, Sylvain, ed. *Indochine: Documents Officials*. Paris: Exposition Coloniale Internationale de Paris, 1931. Vol. II.

Li Fang, ed. *Tai ping yu lan*. Shanghai, n.d.; rpt. Beijing: China Book Store, 1963.

Loeb, E. M. *Sumatra: Its History and People*. Vienna: Institut für völkerkunde der Universität Wien, 1935.

Ma, Duanlin. *Ethnographie des peuples étrangers à la Chine, ouvrage composé au XIIIe siècle de notre ère*. Trans. Marquis d'Hervey de Saint-Denys. Geneva: Ernest Leroux, 1883. Vol. II.

MacDonald, Malcolm. *Angkor*. New York: Frederick A. Praeger, 1959.

Malm, William P. *Music Cultures of the Pacific, the Near East, and Asia*. Englewood Cliffs. NJ: Prentice-Hall, 1967.

Manich Jumsai, M.L. *History of Thailand and Cambodia*. Bangkok: Chalermnit, 1970.

Marchal, Sappho. *Costumes et parures khmèrs d'après les devatâ d'Angkor-Vat*. Paris: G. Van Oest, 1927.

———*Danses cambodgiennes*. Saigon: Extrême-Asie, 1926.

Maspero, Georges. "Littérature khmère et littérature laotienne." In *Un empire colonial français: l'Indochine*. Ed. Georges Maspero. Paris: G. Van Oest. 1929. Vol. 1, pp. 297-307.

Meyer, Roland. *Saramani danseuse khmère*. Saigon: A. Portail, 1919.

Meynard, Alfred. *Le couronnement de Sa Majesté Monivong Roi du Cambodge à Phnom-Penh, 20-25 Juillet 1928*. Hanoi: Éditions de la Revue Extrême-Asie, 1928.

Miller, J. Innes. *The Spice Trade of the Roman Empire*. Oxford: Oxford University Press, 1969.

Monod, G. H. *Le cambodgien*. Paris: Larose, 1931.

Moura, J. *Le royaume du Cambodge*. Paris: Ernest Leroux, 1883. Vol. II.

Muljono, Sri. "Performance of Wayang Purwa Kulit (Shadow Play)." In *TDMSA*, pp. 58-81.

Murdock, G[eorge] P[eter]. *Africa: Its People and Their Culture History*. New York: McGraw-Hill, 1959.

Musique du Cambodge. Phnom Penh: La direction du tourisme khmer, n.d.

Neumann, Erich. *The Great Mother*. New York: Pantheon, 1955.

Nilakanta Sastri, K. A. *The Cōlas*. Madras: University of Madras, 1975.

Parmentier, Henry. *L'art Khmer primitif*. Paris: G. Van Oest, 1927.

Pavie, August. *Recherches sur la littérature du Cambodge, du Laos et du Siam*. Vol. 1 of *Mission Pavie Indochine 1879-1895: Étude diverses*. Paris: Ernest Leroux, 1898.

———*Introduction, première et deuxieme périods, 1879 à 1889*. Vol. I of *Mission Pavie Indochine 1879-1895: Géographic et Voyages*. Paris: Ernest Leroux, 1901.

Pawley, Andrew K. "Austronesian Languages." *Encyclopaedia Britannica: Macropaedia*. 15th ed. (1982), II, pp. 484-94.

Pelliot, Paul. "Quelques textes chinois concernant l'Indochine hindouisée." In *Études asiatiques*. Paris: G. Van Oest, 1925. Vol. II, pp. 243-263.

Perry, William J. *The Megalithic Culture of Indonesia*. Manchester: Manchester University Press, 1918.

Pich Sal. *Le mariage cambodgien*. Phnom Penh: Université Buddhique, n.d.

Piriya, Krairiksh. *The Sacred Image: Sculptures from Thailand*. Cologne: Museen der Stadt, 1979.

Ponder, Harriet W. *Cambodian Glory*. London: Thornton Butterworth, 1936.

Porée, Guy and E[veline] Maspero. *Moeurs et coutumes des Khmers*. Paris: Pavot, 1938.

Porée-Maspero, Eveline. *Étude sur les rites agraires des Cambodgiens*. Paris: Mouton, 1962.

Porée-Maspero, Eveline and Solange Bernard-Thierry. "La lune, croyances, et rites du Cambodge." In *La lune, myths et rites*. Paris: Editions du Seuil, 1962, pp. 261-87.

Pou, Saverous. *Rāmakerti (XVIe-SVII^e siècles)*. Publications de l'École Française d'Extrême-Orient, 110. Paris: l'École Française d'Extrême-Orient, 1977.

Pramoj, Kukrit. *Skeletons in the Cupboard*. Bangkok: n.p., 1971.

Przyluski, Jean. "La princesse a l'odeur poisson et la Nāgī dans les traditions de l'Asie orientale." In *Études asiatiques*. Paris: G. Van Oest, 1925. Vol. II, pp. 265-84.

Pym, Christopher. *The Ancient Civilization of Angkor*. New York: Mentor, 1968.

Rawson, Philip. *The Art of Southeast Asia*. London: Thames and Hudson, 1967.

Royal Cambodian Ballet. Phnom Penh: Cambodian Information Department, 1963.

Salaun, Louis. *Indochine*. Paris: Imprimerie National, 1903.

Saunders, Ernest Dale. *Mudrā: a study of symbolic gestures in Japanese Buddhism*. New York: Pantheon, 1960.

"Shadow Plays in Cambodia." *TDMSA*, pp. 47-51.

Sisowath-Monivong, S. M. Preah Bat Samdach Prea. "Poème votif." In *Danses exécutées par la troupe de S. M. Prea Bat Samdach Prea Sisowath-Monivong*. Saigon: n.p., 1931, pp. 6-7.

——*Danses exécutées par la troupe de S. M. Prea Bat Samdach Prea Sisowath-Monivong*. Saigon: n.p., 1931.

Sitwell, Sacheverell. *The Red Chapels of Banteai Srei*. London: Weidenfield and Nicolson, 1962.

Stern, Philippe. *L'art du Champa et son évolution*. Paris: Musée Guimet, 1942.

——*Le Bayon d'Angkor et l'évolution de l'art Khmer*. Paris: P. Geuthner, 1927.

——*Les monuments khmers du style du Bayon et Jayavarman VII*. Paris: Presses universitaires de France, 1965.

Stutterheim, W. F. *Indian Influence in Old Balinese Art*. London: The India Society, 1935.

——"Some Remarks on Pre-Hinduistic Burial Customs on Java." In *Studies in Indonesian Archaeology*. Ed. F.D.K. Bosch. The Hague: M. Nijhoff, 1956, pp. 74-90.

Suzuki, Peter. "The Religious System and Culture of Nias, Indonesia." Diss. University of Leiden, 1959.

Tambiah, S. J. *Buddhism and the Spirit Cults in North-East Thailand*. Cambridge: Cambridge University Press, 1970.

Taylor-Keith. "The Rise of Dai Viet and the Establishment of Thang-long." In *EESAH*, pp. 149-191.

Thierry, Solange. "Les danses sacrées au Cambodge." In *Les danses sacrées*. Sources Orientales, 6. Paris: Éditions du Seuil, 1963, pp. 345-73.

Thiounn, Samdach Chaufea. *Danses cambodgiennes*. Phnom Penh: Institut Bouddhique, 1956.

Tooze, Ruth. *Cambodia: Land of Contrasts*. New York: Viking, 1962.

van Leur, Jacob C. *Indonesian Trade and Society: Essays in Asian Social and Economic History*. Trans. James S. Holmes and A. van Marle. The Hague: M. van Hoeve, 1955.

Vickery, Michael T. "Cambodia After Angkor, the Chronicular Evidence for the Fourteenth to Sixteenth Centuries." Diss. Yale 1977.

Vogel, Jean Phillippe. *Indian Serpent-lore*. 1926; rpt. Varanasi: Prithivi Prakashan, 1972.

Wales, H.G.Q. *The Making of Greater India*. London: Bernard Quaritch, 1961.
——*Prehistory and Religion in South-East Asia*. London: Bernard Quaritch, 1957.

Willis, John A. *Dance World*. New York: Crown, 1973. Vol. VII (1972).

Wolters, O. W. *Early Indonesian Commerce*. Ithaca, NY: Cornell University, 1967.

Xarina, Zenia. "Royal Cambodian Dances." In *Classic Dances of the Orient*. New York: Crown, 1967, pp. 59-80.

Xiao Zixian. ed. *Nan Qi shu*. Rpt. Beijing: China Book Store, 1972.

Xu Yungiao, ed. *Kang Tai wu shi wai guo chuan ji zhu*. Singapore: Southeast Asian Research Bureau, 1971.

Yao Silian, ed. *Liang shu*. Rpt. Shanghai: China Book Store, 1936.

Yousof, Ghulam-Sarwar. "The Kelantan Mak Yong Dance Theatre: A Study of Performance Structure." Diss. University of Hawaii 1976.

Zhou Daguan. *Notes on the Customs of Cambodia*. Trans. [from French version of Paul Pelliot] J. Gilman D'Arcy Paul. Bangkok: Social Science Association Press, 1967.

Zimmer, Heinrich. *Myths and Symbols in Indian Art and Civilization*. Ed. Joseph Campbell. New York: Bollingen Foundation, 1946.

Articles in Periodicals and Other Sources

Abercrombie, Thomas J. "Cambodia: Indochina's 'Neutral' Corner." *National Geographic Magazine*, Oct. 1964, pp. 514-51.

Baradat, R. "Les Sâmrê ou Peâr: population primitive de l'ouest du Cambodge." *BEFEO*, 40, No. 1 (1941), pp. 1-149.

Barnes, Clive. "Bas-Reliefs Come to Life." *New York Times*, 31 Oct. 1971, Sec. 2, p. 30, cols. 1-8.

Barrett, Dean. "Agony of Khmer Dance." *The Asia Magazine*, 27 Jan. 1974, p. 16.

Barth, Auguste. "Stele of Vat Phou." *BEFEO*, 2 (1902), pp. 234-40.

Bayard, Donn T. "Early Thai Bronze." *Science*, 30 June 1972, pp. 1411-12.

Benda, Harry J. "The Structure of Southeast Asian History: Some Preliminary Observations." *Journal of Southeast Asian History*, 3, No. 1 (1962), pp. 106-38.

Bowen, Richard Le Baron. "The Origin of Fore-and-Aft Rigs: Part I." *The American Neptune*, 19, No. 3 (July 1959), pp. 155-99.
——"The Origin of Fore-and-Aft Rigs: Part 2." *The American Neptune*, 19, No. 4 (Oct. 1959), pp. 274-306.

Braddell, Sir Roland. "Ancient Times in the Malay Peninsula." *JMBRAS*, 17, No. 1 (Oct. 1939), pp. 146-212.

Briggs, Lawrence Palmer. "The Ancient Khmer Empire." *Transactions of the American Philosophical Society*, 41, No. 1 (1951), pp. 1-295.
——"The Syncretism of Religions in Southeast Asia, especially in the Khmer Empire." *Journal of the American Oriental Society*, 71 (1951), pp. 230-49.

Brunei, Jacques. Jacket Notes. *Royal Music of Cambodia*. In "Art Music from South-East Asia" (UNESCO IX-3). Philipps, 6586-002, 1970.

Buchanan, Keith. "The dancers in the forest; Angkor revisited." *Eastern Horizon*, 4, No. 5 (May 1965), pp. 24-32.

Bulcke, C. "La naissance de Sitā." *BEFEO*, 46, No. 1 (1952), pp. 107-17.

Burgess, John. "Cambodians Revive Lost Culture." *The Washington Post*, 27 Apr. 1980, p. A-24.

Cardi, Felix. "Les danses sacrées au Cambodge." *La Revue Musicale*, 1 (Nov. 1920), pp. 34-43.

Chandler, David P. "Cambodia's Relations With Siam in the Early Bangkok Period: The Politics of a Tributary State." *JSS*, 60, Pt. 1 (Jan. 1972), pp. 153-69.

——"Royally Sponsored Human Sacrifices in Nineteenth Century Cambodia: The cult of *nak ta* Me Sa at Ba Phnom." *JSS*, 62, Pt. 1 (July 1974), pp. 207-22.

Chhansan Chhuk Meng. "Le ballet classique Khmer." Phnom Penh: n.p., 1973.

Chinary Ung. Jacket Notes. *Cambodian Traditional Music*. Vol. II. Folkways Records, FE-4082. 1979.

Cima, Gay Gibson. "Cambodian Dance-Drama: A Chance for Survival in Asia." *Asian Theatre Bulletin* (Winter 1981) in *Theatre News* (Feb. 1981), pp. 4-5.

Cœdès, George. "Bronzes Khmers." *Ars Asiatica*, 5 (1923).
——"L'inscription de Baksei Chamkrong." *JA*, 23 (May-June 1909), pp. 476-78.
——"La destination funeraire des grands monuments khmers." *BEFEO*, 40 (1940), pp. 315-44.
——"La legende de la nāgī." *BEFEO*, 11 (1911), pp. 391-93.
——"Notes sur Tcheou Ta-kouan." *BEFEO*, 18, No. 9 (1918), pp. 4-9.
——"Origine et évolution des diverses formes du théâtre traditionnel en Thailand." *BSEI*, NS 23, Nos. 3-4 (1963), 491-506.
——"Le site de Janadvipa d'après une incription de Prasat Khna." *BEFEO*, 43 (1943), pp. 10-13.
——"La stèle de Ta-Prohm." *BEFEO*, 6 (1906), pp. 44-85, 255-301.
——"La stèle du Prāh Khan d'Angkor." *BEFEO*, 41, No. 2 (1941), pp. 255-301.
——"Les stèles de Phnom Sandak et de Prāh Vihār." *BEFEO*, 43 (1943), pp. 134-54.

Colani, M. "Emploi de la pierre en des temps reculés: Annam-Indonésie-Assam." *Bulletin des amis du vieux Hué* (1940).

Colless, Brian E. "The Ancient Bnam Empire: Fu-nan and Po-nan." *Journal of the Oriental Society of Australia*, 9, Nos. 1-2 (1972-1973), pp. 21-31.

Coral-Remusat, Gilberte de. "Animaux fantastique de l'Indochine, de l'Insulinde et de la Chine." *BEFEO*, 36 (1936), pp. 427-35.

Cuisinier, Jeanne. "L'Influence de l'Inde sur les danses en Extrême-Orient." *RAA*, 7, No. 1 (1931), pp. 8-14.
——"The Gestures in the Cambodian Ballet: Their Traditional and Symbolic Significance." *Indian Arts and Letters*, 1, No. 2 (1927), pp. 92-103.

Daily Report: Asia and Pacific. Foreign Broadcast Information Service, 31 Nov. 1979, pp. H6, H7, H10, H14.
——10 Apr. 1980, p. H2.
——17 Apr. 1981, p. H2.
——4 May 1981, p. H8.
——19 May 1981, p. H5.

Daniélou, Alain. Jacket Notes. *The Music of Cambodia*. In "Musical Anthology of the Orient" (UNESCO) Bärenreiter-Musicaphon, BM 3DL2002, n.d.

Dhani Nivat. "The Gilt Lacquer Screen in the Audience Hall of Dusit." *Artibus Asiae*, 25 (1961), pp. 275-82.

Fabricius, Pierre, trans. "Prasad Angkor-Wat, Historic Tale." *Nokor Khmer*, No. 2 (Jan.-Mar. 1970), pp. 46-61.

Finot, Louis. "Les inscriptions de Mi-son." *BEFEO*, 4 (1904), pp. 897-977.
——"L'inscription de Sdok Kak Thom." *BEFEO*, 15, No. 2 (1915), pp. 53-106.

Fürer-Haimendorf, Christophe von. "Megalithic Ritual among the Gadabas and Bondos of Orissa." *Journal of the Royal Asiatic Society of Bengal, Letters*, 9 (1943), pp. 149-78.

Gandour, Mary Jane, and Jackson T. Gandour. "A Glance at Shamanism in Southern Thailand." *JSS*, 64, Pt. 1 (Jan. 1976), pp. 97-103.

Goloubew, Victor. "L'age du bronze au Tonkin et dans le Nord-Annam." *BEFEO*, 29 (1929), pp. 1-46.

Gorman, Chester. "Excavations at Spirit Cave, North Thailand: Some Interim Interpretations." *AP*, 13 (1970), pp. 79-107.

Gray, Denis D. "Cambodian Civilization at the Razor's Edge." *Asia*, 3, No. 3 (Sep.-Oct. 1980), pp. 6-11, 47.

Groslier, Bernard-Philippe. "Reconstruction of Galleries at Angkor Wat." *Nokor Khmer*, 3 (Apr.-June 1970), pp. 28-43.

Groslier, George. "Royal Dancers of Cambodia." *Asia*, 22, No. 1 (Jan. 1922), pp. 47-53, 74.
——"Le théâtre et la danse au Cambodge." *JA*, 214 (Jan.-Mar. 1929), pp. 125-43.

Hall, D.G.E. "The Integrity of Southeast Asian History." *Journal of Southeast Asian Studies*, 4, No. 2 (Sep. 1973), pp. 159-68.

Hang Thun Hak. "Le Ballet Royal." *La revue française de l'élite Européene*, No. 206 (Jan. 1968), pp. 24-27.

Holt, Claire. "Dances of Sumatra and Nias: Notes by Claire Holt." *Indonesia*, No. 11 (Apr. 1971), pp. 1-20.

Jacques, Claude. "The Inscriptions of Cambodia." *Nokor Khmer*, No. 2 (Jan.-Mar. 1970), pp. 18-25.

Jowitt, Deborah. "Royal Treasure and Brown Climb Again." *Village Voice*, 28 Oct. 1971, p. 43, cols. 1-2.

Kamm, Henry. "The Agony of Cambodia." *New York Times Magazine*, 19 Nov. 1978, pp. 40-42, 142-62.

Kisselgoff, Anna. "Ballet: From Cambodia, the Khmer." *New York Times*, 21 October 1971, p. 55.

Knopf, Gaston. "Le théâtre en Indochine." *Anthropos*, 3, No. 2 (1908), pp. 280-93.
——"La musique indo-chinoise: la musique cambodgienne." *Mercure musical*, 3 (1907), pp. 889-928.

Laloy, Louis. "Musique et danses cambodgiennes." *Societé internationale de musique revue musicale*, 15 Aug. 1906, pp. 98-112.
——"Les principes de la danse cambodgienne." *La revue musicale*, 3. No. 9 (1 Jul. 1922), pp. 1-7.

"The Lampong Field Station in Thailand." *Newsletter of the Scandinavian Institute of Asian Studies*, 5 (1972), pp. 3-8.

Lancaster, Donald and Fabricus, Pierre. "Prasad Angkor Wat, Historic Tale." *Nokor Khmer*, No. 2 (1970), pp. 46-61.

Levi, Sylvain. "Kanishka et S'ātavahana." *JA* (Jan.-Mar. 1936), p. 82.

Lim Siv Choan. "Les offrandes au Cambodge." *Annales de l'Université Royale des Beaux-Arts* (Phnom Penh), 1, No. 1 (1967), pp. 7-21.

Mabbett, I. W. "Devarāja." *JSAH*, 10, No. 2 (1969), pp. 202-23.
——"The 'Indianization' of Southeast Asia: Reflections on the Prehistoric Sources." *Journal of Southeast Asian Studies*, 8, No. 1 (Mar. 1977), pp. 2-14.
——"The 'Indianization' of Southeast Asia: Reflections on the Historical Sources." *Journal of Southeast Asian Studies*, 8, No. 2 (Sep. 1977), pp. 143-61.

Marchal, Sappho. "La danse au Cambodge." *RAA*, 4, No. 4 (Dec. 1927), pp. 216-28.

Martini, Francois. "En marge du Rāmāyana cambodgien." *BEFEO*, 23, No. 2 (1938), pp. 285-94.
"Quelque notes sur le Rāmker." *Artibus Asiae*, 24, Nos. 3-4 (1961), pp. 351-62.

Meyer, Charles. "Cambodian Dances." *Nokor Khmer*, No. 3 (Apr.-Jun. 1970), pp. 2-27.

Meynard, Alfred. "A Cambodian Costume-Piece: The Coronation Rites in Which a People, Cloaked in Symbols, Recovers its Past." *Asia and the Americas*, June 1929, pp. 452-59, 506-7.
——"The Stones of Angkor." *Asia and the Americas*, Jan. 1928, pp. 24-31, 68-69.

Mus, Paul. "Chronique." *BEFEO*, 28 (1928), p. 647.
——"L'Inde vu de l'est: Cultes indiens et indigenes au Champa." *BEFEO*, 33, No. 1 (1933), pp. 367-410.
——"Musique d'accompagnement de 'Reamker'." *Annals de l'Université des Beaux Arts* (Phnom Penh), 1, No. 2 (1972), pp. 77-96.

Mydans, Seth. "Mme Kamel wages an exotic war for an ancient culture." *Smithsonian*, Sep. 1980. pp. 118-25.

Patte, Etienne. "L'Indochine préhistorique." *Revue anthropologique*, 46, Nos. 10-12 (1936), pp. 277-314.

Peacock, B.A.V. "A Preliminary Note on the Dong-so'n Bronze Drums from Kampong Sungai Langi." *Federation Museums Journal* 9 (1964), pp. 1-3.
——"Recent Archaeological Discoveries in Malaya 1964." *JMBRAS*, 38 (1965), pp. 248-55.

Pelliot, Paul. "Deux itinéraires de Chine en Inde à la fin du VIIIe siècle." *BEFEO*, 4 (1904), pp. 131-413.
——"Le Fou-nan." *BEFEO*, 3 (1903), pp. 248-303.
——"Memoires sur les coutumes du Cambodge de Tcheou-Ta-kouan." *BEFEO*, 2 (1902), pp. 123-77.

Piat, Martine. trans. "Chroniques royales khmères." *BSEI*, 49, No. 1 (1974).

Porée, Guy. "Rites de la danse au Cambodge." *France Illustration*, 4 June 1949, pp. 579-82.

Porée-Maspero, Éveline. "Notes sur les particularites du culte chez les Cambodgiens." *BEFEO*, 44, No. 2 (1954), pp. 619-41.
——"Nouvelle Étude sur la Nāgī Soma." *JA*, 233. No. 2 (1950), pp. 237-67.

Pryzluski, Jean. "La légende de Rāma dans les bas-reliefs d'Angkor-Vat." *Arts et Archéologies Khmers*, 1, No. 4 (1924), pp. 319-30.
——"Notes sur l'âge du bronze en l'Indochine." *RAA*, 7, No. 2 (1931), pp. 78-80.

Rentse, Anker. "The Origin of the Wayang Theatre (Shadow Play)." *JMBRAS*, 20, No. 1 (1947), pp. 12-15.

Saal, Hubert. "Hands of Time." *Newsweek*, 1 Nov. 1971, p. 97.

Sachidanand, Sahai. "Study of the Sources of the Lao Ramayana Tradition." *Bulletin des Amis du Royaume Lao*, No. 6 (1971), pp. 219-32.

"Sacred Dances." *Kambuja*, 15 Sep. 1965, p. 19.

"Sacred Dances at the Palace to Bring Rain." *Kambuja*, 15 Aug. 1967, pp. 20-23.

"Samdech Sihanouk's Inspection of the Cambodian Liberated Zone." *China Pictorial*, Special Supplement, No. 6 (1973).

Sem Sara. "Lokhon khol au village de Vat-Svay-Andet, son rôle dans les rites agraires." *Annales de l'Université Royale des Beaux-Arts* (Phnom Penh), No. 1 (1967), pp. 157-71.

Short, Joseph. "Alive Again . . . But on the Knife's Edge." *Oxfam America*, Spring 1980, p. 5.

Smail, John R. W. "On the Possibility of an Autonomous History of Modern Southeast Asia." *Journal of Southeast Asian History*, 2, No. 1 (1961), pp. 72-102.

Solheim, Wilhelm G. II. "New Light on a Forgotten Past." *National Geographic Magazine*, 139, No. 3 (March 1971), pp. 330-39.
——"The 'New Look' of Southeast Asian Prehistory." *JSS*, 60, Pt. 1 (Jan. 1972), pp. 1-20.
——"Reflections on the New Data of Southeast Asian Prehistory: Austronesian Origin and Consequence." *AP*, 18, No. 2 (1975), pp. 146-60.
——"Reworking Southeast Asian Prehistory." *Paideuma*, 15 (1969), pp. 126-39.
——"Southeast Asia and the West." *Science*, 25 Aug. 1967, pp. 896-902.

Stein. R. A. "Le Lin-yi." *Han-hiue*, 2, Nos. 1-3 (1947), pp. 1-336.

Stern, Philippe. "The Khmer Smile of the Bayon." *The Unesco Courier*, Dec. 1971. pp. 15-18.

Stierlin, Henri. "Angkor: masterpiece of architecture and town-planning." *The Unesco Courier*, Dec. 1971, pp. 6-13, 49.

Strickland-Anderson, Lily. "The Cambodian Ballet." *Musical Quarterly*, 12 (1926), pp. 266-74.

Vogel, J. P. "The Yupa Inscriptions of King Mutavarman from Koetei." *Bijdragen tot de Taal-, Land- en Volkenkunde*, 74 (1918), pp. 167-232.

Wales, H.G.Q. "The Pre-Indian Basis of Khmer Culture." *Journal of the Royal Asiatic Society*, Pts. 3-4 (1952), pp. 117-23.

White, Peter R. "Kampuchea Wakens from a Nightmare." *National Geographic Magazine*, May 1982, pp. 590-623.

Index

A

accents, 300–1, 334, 355
accessories, 112, 118, 360, 394, 396
accompaniment, types of, 289, 304, 306, 318, 329
action, types of, 47, 48, 261, 308, 355
actors, 105, 121, 182, 215, 363
actresses, 130, 182, 383, 389, 424
adoration, 82, 83, 86
Afro-Asian Dance Festival, 171
Ainus, 15
Albert Sarraut Museum, 142
altar, 57, 385–86, 406, 408–10, 421, 426–32, 435, 437
ancestors, 15, 17–19, 28, 55, 205, 439. *See also* neak ta
    communication with, 19
    home of, 19
    spirits of, 10, 18–19, 23–24, 41, 50, 57, 424, 438–39
    worship of, 50, 439
ancestral spirits, 10, 18–19, 23–24, 41, 50, 57, 424, 438–39
Ang Duong, King, 108–14, 117, 119, 263, 373
anger, 81, 119, 226, 239, 250, 261, 308, 324, 337
Angkor, 386. *See also* Angkor Wat; Angkorean dance
    architecture of, 48
    art of, 38, 69
    bas-reliefs of, 64, 294, 298, 303, 334
    bronze sculptures of, 351, 424
    cosmology of, 38, 40, 45
    court of, 88, 100
    dance skill in, 55
    dancers of, 28, 91–92, 105, 168, 366
    fall of, 91
    great city of, 37, 197
    hydraulics system of, 40
    iconography of, 45, 56
    kingdom of, 23, 30, 38
    kings of, 20–21, 23, 43, 45, 50, 54, 72
    lineage of, 114
    religious beliefs in, 45
    ruins of, 262
    sculpture of, 7, 28, 63, 144, 209, 334, 398, 406
    temples of, 39, 41, 61, 64, 205, 366
Angkor Thom, 38, 40, 48, 56
Angkor Wat, 20, 62–64, 67, 69, 70, 72, 142–43, 157, 363. *See also* Angkor
    apsaras of, 13, 41–42, 64
    bas-reliefs of, 64, 303
    dancers of, 168
    devatā, 65–68
Angkorean Dance, 91, 104–5, 406
animistic spirits, forms of, 20
Anorchak, King, 244
Ant Dance, 286, 352
Antār, 26
Anurudh, Prince, 240–41, 314
Apsara Dance, 150
apsaras, 21–22, 30, 39, 48–49, 60–62, 64–66, 69–73, 87, 92, 93, 208–9, 233, 240–41, 269, 276–77, 295, 336, 401, 406
    of Angkor Wat, 13, 41–42, 64

dance of, 74, 318
dancers, 86, 186, 207
flying, 28, 59, 60, 62
headdress, 403
areca flowers, 44, 67–69, 74, 86, 104, 112, 199, 252, 281, 328, 339, 347, 352–56, 359, 364, 375
Aryan Brahmanism, 41
Asoreiphat, 234
Assachay, 245
Assam, 17
astrologers, 261, 374, 424
asura, 40, 47, 61
Ata, 25
Atichavong, King, 245
Avalokitesvara, 44
Axe Dance, 285
Ayutthaya kings, 91, 100, 104–5

B
Bacson culture, 17
bai sei, 386, 426, 429–30, 436
Bakheng temple, bas-reliefs of, 58–59
balance, 25, 40, 48
    in Angkorean art, 38
    exquisite form and, 351–52
    of male and female, 40
    training in, 376
balang, 357, 360
Bali, 17–19, 224
ballerinas' names, 25, 171
ballet, 92, 113, 120, 134–35, 139, 147, 158, 381, 389, 440
Baloem, 311
bamboo, 301–2, 305, 348, 363, 420, 426
banchok, 306–7, 314, 321, 376
Banchos, 289
Bangkok, 86, 104, 108, 114, 118–19, 173, 232, 268, 342, 352, 366, 421, 429, 437
Banteay Chhmar, 70
Banteay Srei, 59, 62
Bao Dai, 154–55
Baolut, 288–89, 311, 314, 418
Baphuon bas-reliefs, 62, 84
bas-reliefs, 7, 13, 28, 38, 46, 48, 56, 58, 60, 62, 64, 67, 69–70, 72, 81, 295, 303, 354, 365, 405

Angkorean, 57, 157
Baphuon, 62, 84
Battambang, 114, 120, 152, 179
battle scenes, 314, 332, 358, 363, 408
Bāli, 275, 394
Bayon, 87
    apsaras, 74, 76
    devatā, 77–79, 81
    period, 84
beat, music/dance and, 261, 281, 303, 305, 320, 348, 355–56
belts, 69, 80, 386, 390, 392–93, 396–97, 402, 410
    gilded silver type of, 397
    silver filigree type of, 390
Benda, Harry, 6
Beng Vieng temple, 55
Benjamin, Geoffrey, 39
Bhagavata Purana, 46
Bhavavarman, King, 27
bhlena cham. See *phleng cham*
bird-human creatures, 314, 395–96, 401, 409
birds, 44, 202, 252, 265, 276, 390, 394–95, 404, 408–9
bird-women, 211, 241, 395, 398
birthday, 129–30, 133, 148, 159, 233, 433
    king's, 133, 148, 159, 433
black monkey, 224, 271, 275, 394
blackbird, 236, 275, 395–96
Bloesch, Jean-Daniel, 179
boats, 15, 16, 37, 104, 194–95, 200, 234, 238, 261, 302–3
body
    angles and, 351
    energy and, 351–52
    movement of, 347, 349
    ornamentation of, 79, 81
    positions of, 376
    posture and, 318, 376
    spirit and, 232
    suppleness of, 175
    type of, 376
bodyguard, 162, 253, 255
Bois, George, 125–26
Boisselier, Jean, 62
bomor, 421–22
Bonh Om Touk, 146–47

Bosch, F. D. K., 5
Bosseba, Princess, 253
Botum, Princess, 249
Bouillevaux, 110
bow, 194–95, 201, 240, 247–48, 250–51, 261, 277, 332, 334, 439
Bowring, John, 86, 353
boys, 87, 108, 113, 143, 227, 231, 284, 376
bracelets, 257, 390, 392, 398, 406–7
brah thona. See preah thong
Brahmanism, 6, 29
Brahmans, 201, 236, 239, 424
Bronze Age. *See* Dongson culture
bronzes, 14, 38, 81, 84, 85
brothers, 61, 111, 118, 139, 245, 248, 252–53
Brunet, Jacques, 289, 293–94, 317, 437, 439
Buddha, 41–45, 72, 84, 159, 161, 257–58
Buddhist inscriptions, 52, 55
Buddhists
    folklore of, 4
    practice of, 81, 86
Bunchhou, 255
Bunchhouy, 255
Bunloy, 253, 266
Bunnak, Neang, 167–68
buong suong, 130, 159, 268, 344, 417–18, 427
    ceremony of, 288, 417, 440
    performance of, 289
    ritual of, 246, 270, 309, 417
    tevoda and, 417, 419, 437
Buppha Devi, Princess, 159–60, 165, 168–69, 181, 365, 367, 381, 399
burials, 15, 17
Byers, Barbara, 179

C
calmness, 337, 380
Cambodia
    aboriginals of, 210, 248
    ancestral spirits in, 18
    ancient, 81
    apsaras of, 86, 318
    bronzes of, 84
    ceremonies of, 69, 438
    chronicles of, 91
    dancers of, 119, 128, 181, 382, 415, 419, 423
    funeral rites in, 16, 17
    heart of, 37
    history of, 1, 4, 13, 28, 106, 108, 118–19, 152, 194, 244
    image of, 202
    kings of, 22, 92, 99, 124, 154, 248
    lakhon nai of, 119
    music of, 183, 294, 297
    mythology of, 200–1, 203
    nang sbek of, 438
    royal court of, 101, 119, 412
    symbol of, 153, 169
    syncretism of, 41
    theatre of, 122, 235
Cambodian dance, 128, 181, 194, 321
    classical form of, 317
    dancers and, 119, 128, 145, 415, 419, 423
    drama, 2, 4, 18
    scholars of, 112
    tradition, 134
Cambodian Dance Troupe, 181
Cambodian Dances (Meyer), 8
Cambodian mind, 38
Cambodian New Year, 87
camren. See female singers
candles, 162, 285, 300, 362–63, 408, 423, 426, 428–31, 435–36, 439
cat, 25, 250–51, 256
cha, 306, 309–10, 312
chains, 390, 392, 394, 397–98
Chakdomukh Hall, 163, 358, 364–65
Chakrapongs, Prince, 382
Chakravong, Prince, 254
Cham people, 73, 123, 198, 421
Champa, 28, 56, 61, 63, 73, 123, 196, 204, 315, 421
Chan Korup, 241–42, 266
Chanchhaya, 132–33, 150, 162, 357–58, 361–62, 364, 429
Chanchhaya Pavilion, 316
Chao Anou, King, 118
Chao Chorm Manda Ampa, 118
Chap Robam, 270–71
Chau Yeung, Princess, 254–55
Chawiwat, Aunt, 118–19
Chenla. *See* Zhenla
chet chean, 312

chet choeng, 311–12
Chettabot, 260
Chey Chet, King, 249
Chey Chet, Prince, 250–51, 266
Chey Sain, Prince, 237, 239, 281
Chey Toat, Prince, 257
chhakry, 312
Chhayya, Princess, 253
Chheng, Chet, 222, 233, 253, 255, 257, 262, 268, 271–72, 276–77, 280, 283–84, 286, 288
Chheng Phon, 184
chhing, 60, 304–5, 316
chin lomphat, 288, 312
China, 3, 6, 14, 15, 21, 115, 119, 165
China, People's Republic of, 381
Chinavong, 235
Chinese dances, 381–82
Choeut Chhing, 289
choral chants, 306, 315–16, 324
choreographers, 63, 319–20, 326–27, 347, 352
choreography, 315
chorus, 121, 131, 133, 150, 272, 305, 315–18, 323, 326
chos touk, 312
Chou Chuk, 260–61
Christie, A. H., 195, 202
Chrui Changwar, 382
Chulalongkorn, King, 90
chut, 306–7, 309–10, 312
chwia, 280
classical dance, 115, 123, 139, 169–70, 172–73, 175, 178, 181, 183, 193, 269, 278, 297–98, 301, 309, 327
    Cambodian form of, 317
    dance troupes of, 115–16, 170, 173–74, 176, 181, 429
    drama and, 8, 193, 207, 415
    Khmer form of, 112, 114, 141, 145, 153, 180, 221, 347
    Khmer troupe of, 180
    music of, 311
    Thai form of, 268, 319
clowns, 126, 130, 166, 213, 251, 279, 390, 396
Cock Dance, 237–38, 280–81
Cœdès, George, 4, 5, 18, 25, 27, 48, 81, 87, 88, 100, 105–6, 109, 231, 248, 251, 268

Cogniat, Raymond, 8
colors, 112, 282, 389, 394, 397, 401–3, 409, 424, 435
consciousness, 201, 215, 337, 352
cosmos, 39, 194
costume(s), 385, 387
    colors and, 389, 403
    of dancer-princess/prince, 387
    fundamental Khmer dance, 388
    heavy type of, 387
    for masculine roles, 390, 394, 396
    types of, 207–8, 386
coup, 142, 169–70
couples, 252, 329, 345–46, 349
court dance, 54, 88, 99, 113–15, 128, 134
    modern Khmer, 106
    tradition and, 90, 100, 109
court dancers, 91, 100–1, 123, 128–29, 134, 136, 153, 170, 176, 409, 412
crocodile, 238, 258
crown, 395, 398, 400–1, 403–9, 432. *See also mkot*
Cuisinier, Jeanne, 8, 136
curtain, 362, 364
curve(s), 112, 342
    of fingers, 352
    of spine, 350–51

D
Daha, King, 252
damnoeur. *See chhakry*
dance(s). *See also* dance drama; dance performances; dance troupes; dancers; *robam*
    ancient forms of, 136, 387
    comic type of, 255
    court form of, 54, 88, 99, 113–15, 128, 134
    cultural context of, 38
    dragon in, 233, 284
    duets in, 223, 232–33
    earliest evidence of, 14
    education for, 146, 184
    expressive types of, 306, 318, 320, 324, 326
    female form of, 166
    of female slaves, 54
    final, 174, 285
    folk form of, 170, 172, 175, 183, 416

formal type of, 70, 178
function of, 15, 17, 38
funeral rites and, 16
of gold, 272
Khmer classical form of, 112, 114, 141, 145, 153, 180, 221, 347
of Khmer-American Friendship, 164
of Khmer-Chinese Friendship, 164
with large scarf, 282
mistresses of, 166
movements of, 290, 301, 312, 324, 434
of the *nāgas*, 272, 315
pavilions for, 119, 125, 132, 162, 359
personnel for, 165
of picking flowers, 272
popular types of, 113, 269, 286
provincial schools for, 184
rehearsal for, 150, 420
ritual in, 40, 105, 140, 268
sacred forms of, 164, 268, 271, 288–89, 295, 311, 416–17, 440
skill in, 55
spirits and, 13, 428
students of, 166, 179, 276, 419
style of, 158, 434
teachers of, 10, 150, 152, 221, 289, 334, 386, 435
temple and, 13, 49, 53
tradition in, 124, 129, 169, 173, 184, 186
training for, 158, 170, 321, 382
of welcome, 270–71
dance drama, 7, 8, 55, 72, 91, 106, 138, 173–74, 198–99, 205, 208, 221, 266, 294, 317, 422, 432–33. *See also roeung*
performances of, 157, 305
repertoire of, 8, 339
scholarly criticism of, 8
dance performances, 130, 162, 364. *See also* classical dance; dance(s); dance troupes; dancers
classical types of, 178, 183, 295
dance pieces, 222, 269, 271
dance segments, pure, 306–7, 318
dance tradition, classical, 169, 184
dance troupes, 56, 108, 116, 123, 359, 429. *See also* dancers
for classical dance, 115–16, 170, 173–74, 176, 181, 429
non-royal, 136
private, 136
provincial, 146
dancers, 24–27, 49–58, 72–74, 108–13, 125–26, 128–44, 154–59, 164–72, 176–82, 306–11, 342–49, 351–58, 362–68, 374–87, 401–8, 416–26. *See also* dance troupes
as beautiful, 50, 63, 159
as celestial, 13, 21, 39, 48, 84, 269, 276
classical type of, 122–23, 139, 146, 181–82, 231, 349, 366, 381, 403
as earthly, 39, 59
as featured, 181
male and female, 51
mature status of, 148, 170, 352, 375
modern type of, 69, 424
ordinary type of, 131, 402
physical perfection of, 50
pre-Angkorean, 27
première, 131, 381
as spiritual, 25
temple and, 25–27, 51, 53, 63, 88, 103
trained, 419, 438
young, 57, 91, 116, 150, 170, 180–81, 236, 279, 286, 350, 359, 375, 381, 384, 386, 432–33
dancing figures, 58, 62, 81
Danielou, Alain, 297
Danses cambodgiennes, 8, 135
Danses d'Indochine (1932), 8
Danseuses cambodgiennes, 67, 136–37, 407
Darachak, King, 242
Dayak keluri, 14
Dayak of Borneo, 15
Decoux, Jean, 287
deities, 20, 24–26, 41, 44, 214, 294, 314. *See also* divinities
Delaporte, Louis, 120
delusion, 81
Democratic Kampuchea, 1, 177–78
demons, 40, 43, 44, 46, 90, 113, 130, 232, 436. *See also asura*
departures, 125, 176, 195, 226, 235, 240, 246, 308, 312, 343, 429
desire, 81

despair, 145, 311, 313, 359
Despujols, Jean, 143
deva, 40, 47, 311
devarāja, 13, 23, 24, 29, 40, 50, 73, 205, 207
devatâ, 68
devatā, 9, 28, 56–60, 62, 64–70, 73, 77, 145, 258, 354, 402
    of Angkor Wat, 65–68
    of Bayon, 77–79, 81
    headdress of, 68, 69
diadem, 391, 398, 400, 403
diamonds, 246, 390–91, 397, 404
disguise, 229, 239–40, 252, 255, 261, 266, 307, 408
divinities, 28, 66, 93, 106, 230, 269, 323, 393, 400, 406. *See also* deities
dolmens, 18
Dongson culture, 3, 14
Dong-son drums, 14, 15
dramas, 8, 61, 161, 168, 184, 221, 223, 232–33, 248–50, 253, 257–58, 265, 267–68, 283, 289, 313, 357–58. *See also* dance drama; *roeung*
Dravidian deities, 41
dreams, 38
drought, 40, 43, 57, 289, 416–17, 421
drums, 52, 74, 294, 297–98, 300–1, 311–12, 422–23. *See also* Dong-son drums; *sampho* drum

E
Earth Spirit, 20, 43, 53, 57, 69, 204–5, 340
East Indian Islands, 3
École
    Botum Reachea, 382
    de Danse Royale, 382
    des Beaux-Arts, 137, 139
    Malika, 382
    Norodom, 382
Edmonds, I. G., 92
education, royal, 55
eggs, 384, 386, 426, 435
elephants, 88, 255–56, 352, 429–30
emotions, 293, 327, 329, 332, 334–35, 337
energy, 39, 45, 74, 86, 87, 174–76, 181, 205, 211, 337, 347–48, 351–52, 380, 385
ensemble, 298, 300, 304, 381, 401

pinpeat, 297, 299, 303, 305
entrances, 121, 133, 143, 246, 286, 306–10, 316, 343, 358, 366, 377, 418
envy, 81
éopang music, 312
Europeans, 103, 113, 295, 353
Europoids, 15
evil, 211, 266–67
exercises, 344, 375–76
exile, 90, 235, 245, 249, 251, 260, 265–66
exits, 286, 307–9, 311, 315–16, 335, 340, 342, 345–46, 358, 360, 368, 377
expressive dance, 306, 318, 320, 324, 326
eysei, 209, 212–13, 234–37, 241, 244, 253–54, 257, 259–60, 266, 312–13, 339, 381, 390, 396, 408, 430–33, 436, 439

F
Fa Ngom, King, 90
fabrics, 385, 387–88, 394
face makeup, 10
faces, 44, 120, 424–25
family, 50, 54, 111, 113, 147, 150, 180, 252–53, 261, 265, 374, 384, 420
Fan Dance, 270, 410
Fan Xin, 195
Fan Zhan, King, 22
fecundity cult, 45
female(s). *See also* feminine roles; girls; women
    characters as, 345–46, 349
    chorus of, 315, 317
    governors as, 398, 400, 406
    roles and, 8, 105, 156, 174, 208, 211–12, 270, 272–73, 277, 320, 387, 398, 430, 436
    serpent as, 48
    servants and, 225–26, 238
    teachers as, 431
female dancers, 25, 26, 50, 109, 113, 146, 171, 181, 270, 281, 360
    costumed as men, 105
    at court, 205, 434
female singers, 26, 50
female spirits, 45
Feminine and Masculine, union of, 39, 45, 47, 86, 205, 208, 265

feminine principle, 28, 38, 41, 45, 233, 342, 425
feminine roles, 390, 397–98, 400, 404–5, 407–8, 423, 430, 433
fertility, 10, 17, 20, 24, 45, 104, 194, 200, 204, 207, 213, 267, 415, 425, 439
figures, dancing, 58, 62, 81
film, 158, 173, 262, 327, 366
fingernails, 411
fireworks, 144, 147, 174
fish, 37, 46, 223, 249
flight, 265, 280, 283, 320, 335–36, 377, 380, 441
floor patterns, 286, 293, 340, 343, 345–46
flower blooming gesture, 326
flowers, 258, 273, 275–76, 324, 360
    balang and, 360
    dance of gold/silver, 86, 150, 411
    enemy and, 327
    gold and silver types of, 272
foot, 70, 336, 348, 350, 354–56
France, 2, 114, 124–26, 128, 164–65, 272, 287, 402
French authorities, 137, 139, 142
French government, 141–42
Friendship Dance, 163–65, 283, 287
Funan, 21, 22, 25, 27, 44, 194–96, 204, 439
funerals, 105–6, 118, 424

G

gandharva, 26
garden, 232, 235–36, 239–40, 250, 252, 266, 275–76, 307, 309, 365
gender, 86, 208, 281, 285, 349
genealogy, 18, 20, 23, 54
generals, 390–92, 406
gestures, 103, 177, 204, 309, 318–19, 321, 324–26, 326, 329, 337, 339, 348–49, 356, 364, 420, 436. *See also* hand gestures
giants, 121, 186, 226, 313, 355, 376–77, 387, 392. *See also yakkha*
gifts, 25, 26, 50, 231, 250, 257, 367, 374, 416, 419
girls, 87, 92, 111, 113, 121, 131, 146, 184, 231, 238, 252, 255, 284, 360, 376, 387
Giteau, Madeleine, 84
goddess of seas, 233
    of wisdom, 203

Goddess, of the Seas, 233
gods, 39, 46, 50, 61, 92, 105, 247, 250, 261, 268–71, 276, 280, 289, 309, 377, 390. *See also deva; neay rong ek*
gold, 85, 86, 126, 140, 256, 261, 280, 357, 385, 390, 393, 397, 402, 406, 409, 418, 423–24
gongs, 294, 297, 303–4
government, 1, 143, 150, 154–55, 169, 173, 184
governors, 148, 390–92, 398
grief, 261, 339
Groslier, Bernard, 26, 104
Groslier, Bernard-Philippe, 39, 48, 54
Groslier, George, 7, 66, 129–30, 129–30, 132, 134, 136, 137, 223, 265, 319, 359, 375, 377–78, 383–84, 383–84, 389, 402, 409, 411, 423
group dance, 346, 353–54, 431, 433, 438
    large, 270, 329, 401
groups, 7, 26, 47, 67, 82, 87, 104, 115–16, 120, 143, 146, 165, 288, 349, 377, 394–96
guests, 103, 120, 148, 156, 161–62, 234
guidance, 116, 135

H

hair, 14, 67, 74, 111, 258, 288, 387, 392, 394, 406–7, 439
Hall, D. G. E., 50
hand gestures, 8, 293, 321, 323–24, 326, 343, 352–53. *See also* gestures
Hang Thun Hak, 166, 440
Hanoi, 125
Hanum, 211, 213, 223–24, 227, 394, 410
Hanumān, 210–11, 213–15, 223, 225, 227–28, 275, 394–95, 410
harem, 20, 104, 111, 113, 124, 130, 134, 150, 374–75, 382, 424–25
    of king, 10, 104, 130, 375
Harihara, 41
harmony, 38, 39, 294, 329, 342, 347, 416, 440
harp, 87, 88, 294–95, 298
headdress, 25, 67–69, 183, 389, 405–6, 429–30, 432–33
    of *apsaras*, 403
    of *devatā*, 68, 69
heaven, 57, 64, 86, 92, 276, 362

heel, 64, 74, 355–56
hermit, 225, 227, 234, 390, 410
History of Ayudhyaa, 90
History of the Suī, 16
Hoabinhian culture, 3, 15, 16
homage, 86, 258, 427–28
horse, 250–51
Hun Tian, 195, 200, 202, 204, 244
hunter, 236, 260–61
hyperflexion, 352–53

I
iconography, 55, 63, 87
   of Angkor, 45, 56
   of Khmer, 42, 61
incense, 300, 416, 420, 426, 428–31, 436
India, 17, 28, 102, 165, 196, 204, 295, 299, 301, 318, 402
   bronze and, 14
   dance in, 323
   deities of, 41, 45
   Funan and, 22
   Khmer dance drama and, 7, 27
   king in, 22, 253
   musical instruments and, 294, 303
   mythology of, 46–48, 60
   religious beliefs of, 45
   Southeast Asia and, 3, 5, 6, 41
Indian names, to Khmer gestures, 196, 323
Indochina, 4, 125, 143, 159, 204
Indo-Chinese peninsula, 3
Indo-Khmer history, 248
Indonesians, 15
Indra, 92, 93, 239–40, 242, 250, 258, 261, 277, 431
Indradatta, 25
Indrajit, 224
inscriptions, 19, 25–27, 51–56, 87, 88, 196
   Buddhist form of, 52, 55
   Sanskrit form of, 7, 49
Institut Bouddhique, in Phnom Penh, 8
instruments, 50, 100, 178, 294–95, 297–305.
   See also musical instruments
interaction, 38, 45, 87, 269
invocations, 106, 268, 417, 420, 429, 439
   to spirits, 167, 313, 431–32, 435
irrigation systems, 38

Islam, 6, 123

J
jackets, 387, 390, 394, 396–97
Japan, 3
Java, 18, 28, 280
Javanese *wayang kulit*, 438
Jātaka, 4, 56, 229, 258
jātaka story, 56, 72
Jayarajadevi, 56
Jayavarman I, King, 24
Jayavarman II, King, 13, 19, 23–25, 29, 30, 58, 294
Jayavarman III, King, 19
Jayavarman V, King, 54
Jayavarman VII, King, 51, 56, 70, 73, 77, 87
jet jhina. See chet choeng
jewelry, 86, 112, 126, 130–31, 166, 177, 387–88, 390, 393–98, 400, 402–4, 407, 420, 434
jewels, 126, 129, 233, 254
jhina. See chhing
Journal of Southeast Asian History, 4
jungle, 91, 227, 232, 250, 255
jupalaks, 227

K
Kambu Svayambhuva, 22, 197, 199
Kambuja, 22, 23, 197, 287
Kampuchea, 182, 184
Kampuchea, People's Republic of, 169
Kandin, 25
Kang Tai, 21, 22, 194, 204
Kanurat, King, 232
Kaundinya, 22, 23, 195–96
kbach, 293, 313, 318–21, 318–22, 350, 353–54, 377–79, 398
   banchok (fast cadence), 321, 376
   chet choeng, 377
   choet (flight), 377
   lia, 377
   mul, 315, 377
   mul (for princes/gods), 315, 377
   rongvoel (slow cadence), 376
   trak, 315
kbach poses, angularity of, 350
Kenlong, 252

kennara, 211, 314, 395, 398
kennari, 211–12, 241, 264, 314, 336
Kessar, Neang, 236, 275
Ketsoriyong, Princess, 239–40
Ketumala, King, 92
keys, 118, 302–3
Khao I Dang, 260
    dance group, 178–79
    troupe, 180–81
Khemarin Palace, 162
khlom, 311, 313
khluma. See khlom
Khmer, 25, 27, 30, 69, 87, 91, 99, 100, 125, 130,
        138, 141, 145–46, 318, 323, 345,
        349–50
    aesthetic of, 327
    art of, 28, 46, 77, 99
    artists of, 92, 100
    ballet, 169, 171
    beliefs of, 40, 86, 205, 207, 422, 439
    choreographic style of, 324, 327, 337, 340,
        353, 355
    civilization, 88, 100
    court, 91, 117, 358
    culture of, 13, 18, 138, 170, 222
    empire of, 7, 73
    iconography, 42, 61
    kings of, 19, 22, 24, 101–4, 198, 403
    music of, 293–95
    myths of, 45–46, 267
    people of, 1, 2, 20, 22, 27, 39, 46, 49, 50, 86,
        88, 91–93, 99, 100, 111, 115, 117,
        120, 124, 260, 294–95
    royal dancers of, 157, 440
    scholars of, 30, 115, 298, 312, 324
    sculpture of, 41
    stage, 208, 211, 324, 327, 334, 337, 342, 355,
        366, 387, 389
    style of, 158, 351, 358, 381
Khmer dance
    choreography of, 69, 172, 324, 327, 337,
        340, 353, 355
    classical form of, 112, 114, 141, 145, 153,
        180, 221, 347
    contemporary form of, 41
    costumes of, 386
    at court, 110, 114, 124, 139–40, 146, 387

court dancers of, 140
court forms of, 110, 114, 124, 139, 146, 387
expert of, 93, 108
fortunes of, 99, 124
function of, 7, 324
hand gestures in, 321, 323
integrity of, 145
repertoire, 210, 267
technique of, 146
tradition of, 100, 102, 140, 248
Vietnamese elements in, 112
Khmer dance drama, 7, 87, 214–15, 265, 267,
    315–16, 332, 400
Khmer dancers, 7, 79, 81, 86, 91, 93, 101, 120,
    125, 129, 137, 157, 171, 251, 293,
    326, 329, 350, 352, 355, 357, 382–83,
    419, 421, 440, 441
Khmer *lakhon*, 207, 214, 307, 318, 357, 438
Khmer New Year, 263, 434–35
Khmer Rouge, 170, 172, 174, 177–78, 181, 417
khmer thbanh, 313
Khobut, Prince, 262
Khop Khat, 289
Khun Tanh, Princess, 117
king(s), 19, 20, 47–51, 54–55, 108–11, 113–18,
    123–26, 128–30,
    137–41, 145–48, 152–55,
    196–200, 234–37, 247–56, 259–61,
    373–75, 382–85
    of Angkor, 20–21, 23, 43, 45, 50, 54, 72
    birthday of, 133, 148, 159, 433
    of Cambodia, 22, 92, 99, 124, 154, 248
    colonial overlord and, 133
    dance drama and, 8, 132–33, 137–38,
        140–41
    dancers of, 19, 102, 110, 118, 137, 147–48,
        154, 158, 161, 168, 247, 416–17,
        419
    death of, 17, 20
    function of, 19, 48, 50, 108
    harem of, 10, 104, 130, 375
    of Khmer, 19, 22, 24, 101–4, 198, 403
    post-Angkor, 101
    power of, 24
    role of, 50
    spirit union with, 20
    spirit world and, 13, 18–20, 45

twentieth-century, 72
vanquished, 247–48
King of the Giants. See Rāb.
King Rajendravarman II, 23
Koh Krieng, Lady of, 28
Kok Thlok, 20
Kom Vean, 289
kong, 303–4
konsai, 313
Kossamak, Princess, 139, 145–46, 150, 152–59, 162–63, 165, 176, 267, 270, 275, 376, 381
Krao Nay, 289
kraw nai (kraunai), 313, 432, 436
kraw nak (kraunaka), 313
Kray Thong, 238–39
kré, 328, 357–58, 365
kreas ram, 315
Krihsna, Princess, 260
Krongcrut-Sorikan, King, 231
kru, 155, 289, 309, 311, 313, 316, 425–29, 432–38
krut, 208, 240, 315, 394–95, 408–9
Kukrit, Pramoj, 118–19, 188
Kulachak, King, 232
Kumbhakar, 224
kun lun, 22

L
lakhon, 118–19, 128, 137, 169–70, 213, 247, 268, 347, 357, 373, 382, 384, 438
lakhon kbach boran, 186, 193, 437, 440
lakhon khol, 109, 433–35, 437–38, 440
    dance troupes, 156, 376, 435
    performances, 435, 437
    troupes, 156, 376, 435
lakhon nai troupe, 118–19, 361
lakhon thai, 119
Lanka, 223–25, 224, 311, 316
Lao dance traditions, 90, 123, 387
Laos, 15, 27, 90, 115, 123, 136, 182, 299
Laotian Ballet, 283, 313
Le théâtre cambodgien, 7
leaf gesture, 324
Leak Sinnavong, 167, 235–36, 274
Leclère, Adhémard, 120, 123, 230–31, 235, 247–49, 270, 281, 283, 359–61

len dukdamban, 88
Leur, J. C., van, 5, 6
lia, 283, 306, 310, 314
life power, 18–20, 24
linga, 18, 19, 20, 205
lingam, 20, 23, 42, 50, 58, 205
Lokesvara, 44, 53, 73, 81
lomphat phay, 313
lon neak ta, 88
Long Song Mon, 289
Lord of the Mountain, 24
lotus, 23, 60, 67, 74
Louis XIV, 104
love, 25, 72, 116, 231, 234–37, 239, 241–42, 245, 247–48, 250–57, 259, 264, 266, 278, 280–81, 327–28
lovers, 212, 231, 240, 328–29, 336, 339, 358
Luang Prabang, 102, 123, 159
lyrics, 164, 270, 273, 276–81, 285, 312, 384

M
MacDonald, Malcolm, 92
Machha, Sovann, 312
magic
    power, 39, 204, 227, 229, 267
    wand, 231–32, 259, 409
Mahā, 27, 43, 44, 73, 83, 230
Mahāyanā Buddhism, 81, 83
maidens, 206, 270, 274, 280
makeup, 86, 411
Malaya, 14, 136, 210, 245, 421–22
Malayo-Polynesians, 16
Malaysia, 4, 115, 165
male(s). *See also* masculine form; masculine roles
    characters as, 328, 345–46, 349, 352
    dance teachers as, 166
    musicians as, 26, 50–51, 126
    roles as, 8, 105, 113, 168, 186, 212–13, 353–55, 387–91, 394, 396–98, 400, 403–4, 423, 430, 433
    singers as, 26, 317
male dancers, 26–27, 40–41, 45, 50–52, 61–62, 108, 112–13, 156, 166, 171, 181, 376
mallets, 302–3
Man Soun, Princess, 117
Manimekhala, 211, 215, 229–33, 247, 268, 312

Marchal, Sappho, 8, 130, 232
market, 249, 255–56, 439
marriage, 69, 199, 200, 204, 229, 231–32, 238, 245, 252–53, 432
Marseille, 124–26
Masculine and Feminine, union of, 39, 45, 47, 86, 205, 208, 265
masculine form
   of costumes, 394, 396
   of roles, 387–91, 394, 396–97, 400, 404, 423, 430, 433
masculine roles, 8, 105, 113, 168, 186, 212–13, 353–55, 387–90, 394, 396–98, 400, 403–4, 423, 433
masks, 25, 213, 300, 363, 385, 387, 389–90, 393, 396, 406–9, 421, 426–40
Māra, 43
Mearadey, 235
medium, to spirit world, 25, 106, 214, 298, 419–20, 433–34, 437, 439–40
Megalithic culture, 16–18
Mekhala, 208, 211–12, 229–30, 233, 266, 271, 284, 339, 366, 418
Mekong, 163, 172, 358, 384
   delta, 21
   River, 37, 364
Mela, 250–51
Melanesian art, 15
melodies, 102, 246, 276, 287–90, 293, 301–2, 304, 306–10, 312–15, 366
   pinpeat form of, 311–15
   preah thong form of, 246, 311
   reo form of, 308–10, 314
Merā, 22, 23, 197, 199, 203, 207
mercury, 17, 85, 86
Mesolithic culture, 3
Metri, Queen, 261
Meyer, Charles, 8
mime, 53, 109, 115, 315, 319, 321, 326, 436
mkot, 391, 395–96, 398, 400–401, 403–9, 430, 432, 436
modesty, 324, 331, 387–88
Mom Kamel, 177–78, 180
Monivong, King, 111, 139–40, 146, 148, 150, 152, 154, 159, 174, 238, 244, 253–54, 259, 272, 382
monkey(s), 8, 144, 178, 186, 194, 213–14, 223, 235, 271, 306–7, 332, 336, 349, 355, 385, 387–90, 392, 427, 433, 436
   as black, 224, 271, 275, 394
   role as, 8, 113, 144, 156, 166, 208, 213, 311, 314, 376–77, 408, 426, 432, 435–36
   as white, 223–24, 235, 275, 395
monsoon, 37, 40, 204
monuments, 1, 25, 28, 73
moon, 44, 47, 49, 85, 86, 193, 196, 198, 200, 203–6, 320, 424
Mora, Neang, 241–42
Moss, Stanley, 158–59
motherhood, 200, 206, 249
Mouhot, Henri, 110
Mount
   Mahendra, 24, 30
   Mandara, 46
   Meru, 405
mountain, 18–20, 23, 24, 29, 47, 48, 211–12, 327, 381, 405, 439
mountain-temples, 19, 24
Moura, J., 116, 120, 305
mourning, official period of, 155, 159
mouthpiece, of *sralay*, 299
movement(s)
   conventionalized forms of, 325–27
   of dancers, 4, 112–13, 286, 293, 300, 307, 311–13, 315, 318–24, 331, 340, 342–43, 348–49, 351, 353, 355–56, 360, 375–78, 380, 384, 398, 420, 435–36
   restrained forms of, 327, 332
   transitional forms of, 320, 322
Mucilinda, King, 43
mudrā, 318, 323
Muongs, 15
Mus, Paul, 19, 198, 204
music, 27, 53, 88, 100–1, 116, 283, 293–95, 305–15, 320–21, 355–56, 366, 377–78, 426–27, 431–32, 435–39
   for exit, 306–10
   introductory style of, 309
   structure of, 306–7
musical instruments, 26, 50, 294, 297, 299, 303,

420, 422. *See also* drums; percussion; *sampho* drum; string instruments
musicians, 50, 52, 88, 92, 115, 130–31, 135, 166, 175, 178–79, 293, 300, 310–11, 315–16, 382, 426–27
myth, 8, 46–48, 72, 193–95, 197, 200, 202–3, 206, 272
mythologems, 200, 203, 206–7

N
nails, 411
names, of dancers, 167–68
nang sbek, 118, 181, 184, 437, 439–40
nartaka, 53
nāg, 53, 72, 195–97, 199, 201, 203, 205–7, 209–10, 212, 245, 248
nāga, 20, 22, 42, 43, 46, 48, 53, 59, 90, 197–98, 202, 208, 210, 212, 245, 248, 260, 342
   dance, 283
   earth spirit, 53
   king, 22, 43, 198–201, 246
   kingdom, 228, 246
nāgā, 196, 209
neak, 10, 20, 57, 417, 419–20, 431, 434–35, 439
neak ta, 10, 20, 419, 431, 434. *See also* ancestral spirits
Neak Ta Kai, 434, 437
Neang Mora, 241–42
Neang Neak, 198, 200, 202–3, 245–46
Neang Thorani, earth spirit, 69
neay khen yak, 394
neay rong ek (gods and kings), 390
necklaces, 80
Neolithic culture, 2
ngai-lan, 88
Ngarngor, 25
ngo, 212, 229, 390, 396, 408, 410
Nokor Khmer, 8, 143
Nol, Lon, 168–70, 172–73
Nongleak, Princess, 155
Norodom, 114–20, 123, 125–26, 128, 132, 158, 375
Norodom, King, 120–21, 255, 289, 374
Norodom Sihanouk, 1, 92, 153, 361
Norodom Sorya Roeungsi, Princess, 238
Norodom Suramarit, 153
nritakā, 53

nritta, 53
nrityagita, 53

O
o pileap, 313
Obek Khaom, 175, 386
objects, precious, 48
oboe, 167, 274, 297. *See also sralay*
ocean, churning of, 46–48, 64, 72, 86
offerings
   to ancestors, 439
   for assistance, 288
   dance as, 159, 434, 437, 440
   dancers as, 50
   dancers making of, 386, 406, 418, 428–29, 431
   musicians and, 422, 430
   sacred types of, 26, 45, 421, 424, 429–30, 435–38
   slaves as, 54
   by student dancers, 428, 432
   symbolic forms of, 344
   to *tevoda*, 57
   of young girls to king, 373
ogres, 121, 194, 213, 265, 267, 336, 376, 387, 389–90, 392. *See also yakkha*
opposites
   tension of, 208, 347
   union of, 77
orchestra, 116, 121, 168, 300, 316, 420, 422, 435–36
   percussion type of, 295
   pinpeat, 293, 295, 297–98, 301, 303, 305
Osa, Princess, 240–41
overture, 270–71, 435

P
padhama. *See preah bathum*
pairs, 61, 232, 239, 267, 301, 304–5, 346, 390–92, 394–95, 397, 430
paja, 421
pakchham, 428, 430
palace
   dance troupe of, 128, 136, 152, 154–56
   dancers of, 101, 129–30, 146, 148, 154, 174, 176–78, 234, 241, 260, 262, 375,

378–79, 382, 437
  dances of, 440
  performance programs of, 222–23, 229, 231, 233, 262, 264, 268, 272–73, 279–80, 283–84, 286, 288, 313
  performances in, 222, 229, 231, 233, 255, 262, 269, 273, 280, 283, 286, 288, 359
  programs in, 222–23, 226, 234, 241, 246, 264, 268, 272, 279, 283–84, 313
  troupe of, 128, 136, 152, 154–56
  women in, 116, 125, 130, 142, 155, 256, 376
panntiereth, 403, 406
Pannyi, 252–53
pantomime, 53
pants, in costumes, 386, 388, 390, 394–96
Papuan negroids, 15
parallels, 104, 343, 350–51
parents, 59, 116, 212, 215, 242, 246, 254, 259–60, 265, 373–74, 425
Paris, 124, 126, 135, 181
parrot, 236, 275–76
Parrot Dance, 275
partners, 345–47, 349, 375, 395
paste, 300, 302
pathum, 315
pauluta. See Baolut
Pavie, 103, 108, 120, 123, 407
Pavilion of Dancers, 362–63
pāya si. See bai sei
Peacock Dance, 285
peat, 298
Pelliot, Paul, 202, 248
People's Republic of Cambodia, 1
percussion, 295, 298
  instruments for, 51, 52, 297, 316
  orchestras for, 295
performance(s)
  elements of, 290, 301, 315, 415, 422
  programs for, 10, 148, 156, 162, 164, 167, 225–26, 251, 255, 279
  repertoire of, 136, 193, 198, 277
performers, 115, 122, 130, 140, 174, 178–81, 212, 305, 349, 382, 427, 433–34
  pinpeat, 179
pey. See sralay

Phan Phuong, 180–81
Phimeanakas mountain-temple, 20, 56
phleng aut, 311
phleng cham, 315
phleng chhung, 312
phleng phleh, 313
phleng svaa, 314
phleng trak, 315
Phnom Penh, 37, 90, 91, 104, 108, 110, 115, 119–21, 120, 125, 129–30, 136, 142, 145, 152, 172–74, 182, 286
Phon, Chheng, 119, 136, 174–75, 184, 266, 268, 276, 288–90, 306, 309–11, 361, 380–81, 418, 441
phoumea doeur yut, 313
Phuong Phan, 279, 284, 314, 318, 320–21
Phya Nay, Prince, 256
pinpeat, 298–99
  ensemble, 297, 299, 303, 305
  melodies, 311–15
  orchestra, 293, 295, 297, 301, 303, 305
  performers, 179
Pisnoukar, 92
pity, 239, 241–42
planes, conjoined, 39, 350
players, 52, 299, 300, 303
plot, 104, 185, 222, 224, 229, 234, 237, 249, 262, 320, 332, 348, 358–59
poets, of Angkorean court, 47
poisons, five, 81
Pol Pot, 169, 177–78, 183, 297
Polynesians, 15
ponhea dour, 313
Porée, Guy, 430
postures, 112, 175, 307, 318, 320, 337, 349–50, 353
power
  magic form of, 39, 204, 227, 229, 267
  spiritual form of, 25, 138, 197, 203, 213
Prasat Khna temple, 52
Prasat Kravan, 50
Prathom, 314
preah, 228
Preah Bat Promateat, King, 235
Preah Bat Santrea, King, 257
Preah Bat Srey Sanh Chey, King, 261
preah bathom, 314

preah bathum, 311
Preah Chan Korup, Prince, 173, 241
Preah Chau Damrei Sar, King, 256
Preah Chinavong, Prince, 234–35, 239, 249, 257
Preah Khan, 42, 51, 53, 70, 71
Preah Khan temple, 51
Preah Ko, 50
Preah Phirun, Prince, 260
preah reach damnoeur, 315
Preah Saing, 168, 263, 377
Preah Sang, Prince, 212, 228–29, 396, 408
Preah Somut, Prince, 135, 231–32
Preah Soriyavong, 234, 236
Preah Sovannahang, 239–40
Preah Theat temple, 52
Preah Thong, 150, 198–99, 203, 244–49, 266, 271, 289, 311, 313
preah thong, 313
    legend, 248
    melody, 246, 311
    musical pieces, 289
Preah Vesandar, 260–61, 361
Preah Vorachhun, 233
pream chenh, 315
pream chol, 315
première danseuse, 128, 135, 155, 159, 166–67, 179, 288
prestige, 102, 113, 128, 152, 169–70, 174, 176, 383
priay, 45
pride, 30, 81, 215, 378–80
priestess, 421
priests, 51, 54, 73, 103
Primordial Maiden, 193, 199, 200, 202–4, 206–7, 210
princess roles, 115, 128, 270, 360, 378, 385, 435
private troupes, 124, 150, 152
prizes, 138, 158, 381–82
Prom Sokhom, 317
Promarith, King, 254
promises, 237–38, 257, 260, 288, 376
Przyluski, Jean, 196
puok khen yak, 394
puppets, 439–40
pure dance, 105, 156, 233, 306, 318, 320, 324, 326
purohita (chief priest), 50

Q
queen, 54, 106, 199, 223, 236, 249–51, 259–61, 265, 271, 276, 381–82, 397–98, 400, 429, 431
Queen Mother, 153–54, 327
quicksilver, 86

R
rabam, 104–6
Rachana, Princess, 229
rain, 41, 45, 204, 417, 419, 422
Rajendravarman II, King, 23, 54
ram, 26. *See also* male dancers
ram kreas, 315
Rama II, King, 118
Rama III, King, 90, 118–19, 119
Rama VI, King, 119
Ramadhipati, King, 92
rapam, 25–26, 26
Rāb, *yakkha* king, 209–10, 213–15, 224–26, 267, 307–8, 312–13, 334, 337–39, 393, 397, 408, 410, 430, 432, 434–36
Rām, 70, 101, 208, 210, 213–15, 223–28, 267, 275, 287, 307, 309, 312–13, 327, 337, 380, 389, 402, 408, 430
    legend of, 72, 214
    stories of, 209–10
Rāma, 4
Rāmāyana, 27, 72, 108, 172
Rāmker, 72, 101–2, 123, 146, 210, 212, 214, 223–25, 228, 233, 267, 275, 308, 313–14, 332, 353, 359, 396, 433
Rāmlaks, 224–25, 227–28
Rea Srey Yaolac, Princess, 135
Ream Eyso, 211, 229–30, 232–33, 334, 409, 418
Reay, 289
rebirth, 17, 347
Recchana, Princess, 168
refugees, 169, 174, 178
rehearsals, 120, 122, 124, 144, 155, 172, 175–76, 299–301, 305–7, 350, 374, 377–78, 384, 392, 427–28, 434, 437
rejection, 339
religion, 25, 45, 128, 177
religious syncretism, 41, 44

reo, melody, 308–10, 314
repertoire, 10, 113, 123, 156, 182, 184, 221–22, 237, 242, 244, 247, 255, 265–69, 272, 281, 286–89
Republic, 126, 168–70, 173–76, 269, 287, 427
   of Cambodia, 1
   of China, 164–65, 381
   of Kampuchea, 169
Reu Reay, 289
rhythm, 38, 39, 48, 55, 64, 166, 285, 298, 301, 305, 311, 348, 375, 377–78, 426
riey, melodies, 308–9
rites, 53, 194, 436–37, 439–40
rivalry, 91
rivers, 37, 118, 122, 132, 147, 176, 212, 234, 238
rmam neak, 27
ro, melodies, 308, 310
Robam
   Apsaras, 277, 342, 365, 401
   Bach Phkar Chuon Par, 273, 314
   Baolut, 288
   Barami, 288
   Kanh Phkar, 272
   Lao, 283, 313
   Mkaw, 233, 271–72, 284
   Moen, 280–81
   Preah Noreay Baimpeat, 263, 353
   Preah Thong, 288
   Ream Eyso, 288
   Sarahbarom, 288
   Sek Sarika, 275
   Tewet, 274, 306, 312
   Tiyae, 288
   Voracchun, 288
robam, 8, 57, 105–6, 109, 221, 233, 267–77, 281, 284, 287–89, 310, 316, 344–45, 348–49, 357–58, 366, 389, 401
Robam, Bach Phkar Chuon Par, 314
rockets, 174, 176, 289, 417
roeung, 8, 221–22, 267–68, 306, 345–46, 349, 357, 365–66, 376, 391, 431. *See also* dance drama; dramas
role groups, 376–78, 389, 433
roles
   female types of, 8, 105, 156, 174, 208, 211–12, 270, 272–73, 277, 320, 387, 398
   feminine types of, 390, 397–98, 400, 404–5, 407–8, 423, 433
   masculine types of, 8, 105, 113, 168, 186, 212–13, 353–55, 387–90, 394, 396–98, 400, 403–4, 423, 433
   monkey types of, 8, 113, 144, 156, 166, 208, 213, 311, 314, 376–77, 408, 426, 432, 435–36
   princess types of, 115, 128, 360, 385, 435
   yakkha types of, 286, 313, 315, 349, 355, 407, 409, 432
roneat, 301–5, 378
roneat dek, 303
roneat ek, 301–4
roneat thom, 302–3, 305
roofs, 120, 359, 362
rows, 77, 345–46, 363, 436
Royal Ballet, 113–14, 126, 134, 145, 147, 153–54, 157–59, 163, 165–66, 168–69, 183, 228, 234, 382
Royal Cambodian Ballet, 8, 109, 130, 168
royal dance, 50, 108, 134, 299, 415
royal dance troupe, 90, 108, 110, 131–32, 135, 137, 152
royal dancers, 7, 10, 19, 28, 90, 103, 109, 116–17, 125–26, 134–35, 137, 140–42, 147–48, 153–54, 159, 163–65, 373, 375, 377, 379, 381, 383, 385–87, 389, 391, 393, 395, 397, 399, 401, 403, 405, 407, 409, 411
royal family, 25, 135, 159, 162, 376, 382
Royal Palace, 37, 125, 130, 168–69, 177, 179, 181, 197, 229, 257, 348, 416, 440
   administration, 139, 141
   library, 10, 148, 156, 222
   performance programs, 381
royal troupe, 90, 99, 108, 115, 119, 130, 137, 139, 268, 279, 317, 376
royalty, 24, 139, 162, 390, 395–96
rpam, 26
rua, 307–10. *See also chut*
ruler, 1, 28, 29, 194–95
rung ram, 132
rup, 419, 434–37

S
Sabre Dance, 286
sacred dances, 164, 268, 271, 288–89, 295, 311, 416–17, 440
sacred sword, 107, 114, 134, 246
sacred trees, 17, 18, 194, 202

sacrifice, 439
Sadā, 50
Sadāsiva, 50, 51
sadness, 311–13, 324
Saigon, 107, 140
saing, 228–29
Sakun, Ok, 1
Salamar, 314
salutations, 340, 355, 435–36, 440
Samal, King, 229
sampeah, 177, 264, 309, 353, 355, 405, 433
    final, 310, 324, 346
    salutation in, 327, 348
sampeah kru, 313, 381, 386, 427–29, 431, 433, 437
    annual form of, 427, 429, 437
    ceremony of, 315, 380–81, 386, 432, 440
sampho drum, 299–301, 309, 316, 334, 348, 378, 422–23, 431, 436. *see also* drums
sampot, 61, 62, 129, 386, 388–89, 391, 394, 397–98, 402, 424
    common, 374
    cotton, 394, 396
    lamé, 397
    special, 374
Sanchchey, King, 261
Sangkhamorta, 252
Sangvann's troupe, 141–45, 154
Sanskrit, 6, 27, 50, 52, 223
    inscriptions, 7, 49
    names, 25, 27, 44
    old Khmer inscriptions and, 7
    terms, 39, 40, 53, 56, 58, 321
sarabarom (sārahpārama), 311, 314
sarika, 395
Sathukar, 289, 426, 432
Saunpady, Princess, 135
Say Sangvann, Princess, 139, 141–43, 145–46, 154, 380
sbay, 397, 401–2
scarf, dance with, 282, 411
scenes, 45, 46, 60–62, 74, 147, 154, 162, 224–27, 233, 235–37, 240–42, 250–51, 258–61, 266, 316, 357–60, 366
sculpture, Angkorean, 144, 209, 334, 398, 406
Sdok Kak Thom, 50
sea, 17, 46, 194, 199, 230

sea of milk, churning of, 46–48, 86
seamstresses, 166
search, 23, 77, 125, 231, 236–37, 240–41, 244, 251, 254–55, 258, 265
sen sra, 315
Seng Houm, 250
sentiments, 270, 325, 329, 339
separation, 112, 339
sequences, in dances, 46, 132, 233, 309, 311, 320–21, 329, 349, 356, 430
    warm-up forms of, 375–76
serpent, 20, 46–48, 53, 69, 156, 193, 197, 199–201, 205, 271
    dance of, 156, 271
    form of, 199, 200, 206
servants, 130, 162, 231, 239, 247, 249–52, 257, 260–61, 265, 360, 363, 382–84, 398, 406
set pieces, 157, 348, 357, 365–66
sexes, 18, 121
shadows, 129, 439
shaman, 422–23
shield, 286, 410
Shiva, 22, 24, 26, 41, 42, 53, 81, 200, 205, 318, 439
    temple, 26–27
    Vishnu and, 208–9
Shivaism, 41
shoulders, 14, 42, 67, 111–12, 353–54, 387–88, 394, 397–98, 402
Siam, 92, 106, 152, 196, 296
signals, 310–11
Sihanouk Era, 136, 153, 159, 167–68, 173, 241, 255, 272, 379, 406–7, 411
Sihanouk, King, 92, 145, 153–55, 159, 161–65, 172–73, 176, 179, 184, 234, 277, 374, 381–83, 417
Sihanouk, Norodom, 1, 92, 153, 361
silk, 103, 385, 390, 394, 397–98
silver, 85, 86, 237, 256, 374, 397, 411
    flowers of, 86, 150, 272, 411
Simun *(simiana)*, 314
singers, 26, 50, 52–54, 87, 116, 131, 136–37, 141, 166, 179, 247, 299, 305, 311, 317
Sinuon, 273, 314
Sisowath Monivong, King, 17, 86, 118, 125–26,

128–29, 131, 133–36, 138, 141–42, 158, 233, 358, 374
  reign of, 131, 133–35, 138–39, 145, 382
sisters, 240, 247–48, 252, 254, 381–82
Sitā, 4, 56, 208–10, 214–15, 224–28, 287, 307–9, 312–13, 316, 327, 339, 389, 402, 430
skirts, long, 61, 62
skor thom, 301, 378
sla thor, 428–30
slaps, 339
slaves, 13, 25, 27, 52, 54, 249
  sacred types of, 13, 25, 27, 52, 54, 249
sleep, 199, 200, 202, 226, 232, 234, 254
smeu, 306–7, 309–10, 312, 426
smile, 77, 79, 256, 324, 329, 331, 356, 380
  deep form of, 77, 79
smiling, 329
society, 201, 274, 284, 347, 375, 380, 382, 384
soldiers, 177, 195, 244, 279, 287, 387, 389, 394, 408
Solheim, Wilhelm G., 2, 6, 15
soloists, 156, 315–17
Somā, 22, 23, 196, 197, 199, 203, 206
Sophannarith, King, 239–40
Soppalak, 241
Sorincha, Queen, 249
Soriyavongs, 234
Sotinnachak, Prince, 242, 244
sounds, 55, 183, 275, 297, 299, 300, 302, 304, 324, 334, 366
Sounpady, Princess, 126, 128
Southeast Asia, 2–6, 17, 18, 21, 23, 25, 41, 72, 87, 102, 150, 194, 197, 200, 202, 248, 295, 352, 378, 415, 424, 438
  art style of, 3
  bronze invention in, 14
  Cambodian culture and, 2, 6, 323
  circle of, 15
  culture of, 2, 3, 6, 14, 342
  dance of, 353
  history of, 2–6, 3, 4, 15, 294
  Indian culture and, 2
  mainland of, 29, 57, 123, 266, 272, 294, 299
  music of, 89, 115, 303
  people of, 3, 5, 6, 22, 39, 214, 318
  performing arts of, 4
  prehistoric artifacts of, 3, 17
  religion of, 18, 19
  society of, 5
  traders of, 6
Souvinichar, 250–51
Sovann Machha, 223–24, 378, 400, 406
Sovann Machha-Hanumān dance, 312
Sovanna, Princess, 237
space, 347–49, 380
spatial configuration, 345
spirals, 342–43
spirit(s). *See also* ancestors; *neak ta*
  ancestral types of, 10, 18–19, 23–24, 24, 41, 50, 57, 424, 438–39
  animistic types of, 159
  awakening of, 5, 436, 438
  of dance, 431
  dancers and, 421, 425, 438, 440
  dangerous types of, 419
  of earth, 20, 43, 53, 57, 69, 204–5, 204–5, 340
  of house, 41
  invitation to, 439
  invocations to, 167, 313, 431, 435
  king's union with, 20
  living types of, 432
  local forms of, 45, 420
  in masks, 431, 436, 440
  monkey roles and, 436
  of music, 300, 422, 436
  musical instruments and, 299
  neak ta and, 10, 20, 419, 431, 434
  puppets and, 439–40
  rehearsals and, 300
  ritual offerings to, 430, 436, 440
  salutation to, 427
  in sampho drum, 300, 423, 431
  of serpent, 20, 197
  of stones, 20
  as territorial, 88, 419
  trees and, 20, 45
spirit mediums, 25, 106, 214, 298, 419–20, 433–34, 437, 439–40, 440
spirit world, 23, 25, 38, 41, 101, 374, 415, 422–23, 425, 433, 440–41
  ancestors and, 10, 18–19, 20, 23–24, 41, 45, 50, 57, 424, 438–39
spiritual power, 25, 138, 197, 203, 213

Sra Lao, 420
sralay, 167, 274–75, 275, 278, 297–99, 299, 304, 314–16, 315–16
sramocha, see Ant Dance
staging, 113, 244, 357, 359, 363–66
standing
    of dancers, 60, 62
    positions, 351, 353–54
star dancer, 135, 139, 143, 147, 166
Stern, Philippe, 57, 77
stones, 69, 200, 203, 205, 212, 223, 241, 420, 439
    inscriptions on, 13
    spirits of, 20
string instruments, 295, 298
struggle, 135, 137, 141, 174, 211, 213–14, 247, 265, 267, 289, 334
student dancers, 150, 170, 277, 279, 381, 432, 438
students, 117, 150, 155, 158, 166, 175, 178–79, 185, 319, 375–76, 378, 382, 386, 421, 427–29, 431
subsidies, 134, 142
Sugrib and Bali, 224
Sumalarith, King, 259
Sumatra, 196, 387
sun, 44, 47, 85, 86, 127, 164, 203–4, 327, 384
Suryavarman I, King, 50
Suryavarman II, King, 51, 72
Sutharot, Prince, 126, 128
Svay, Madame, 183
Svayambhuva, 22
sword, 224, 235, 238, 241–42, 250–52, 286, 334, 410, 418
    as sacred, 107, 114, 134, 246
Sword Dance, 286, 410
syncretism, 39, 41, 45
synopses, 221, 224, 234, 236, 238

T
Ta Prohm, temple of, 51
tail, 46, 394, 396, 398
Taksin, King, 272
tales, mythic, 200, 222
Tang Tok, 163
Tantric Buddhism, 44, 79, 81

teachers, of dance
    elder dancers as, 352, 382
    groups of, 119, 158
    as respected, 115, 152, 158
    teaching methods of, 159, 378
teeth, blackening of, 111, 424
temple(s)
    court and, 49
    dance and, 13, 24, 49, 53
    as feminine/masculine, 40
    mountains as, 19, 40
    ornamentation of, 67
    personnel of, 51–53
    rituals in, 7, 72
    services of, 27
    slaves and, 13, 25, 27, 52, 54, 249
    walls of, 7, 13, 39, 73
tension, of opposites, 208, 332, 345, 418
Tep Manorom, 156, 269, 274, 309, 353
tep robam, 268, 289, 431–33
    function of, 438
    ritual of, 311, 313
tepthida, 418
Tes, Saroeurm, 181
tevoda, 274, 311
    dance of the, 271
    invocation to, 167
    spirit of, 57, 250–52, 261, 288, 417–19
Tewet dance, 274, 310
Thai dance, 105–6, 355, 360
    Lao dance and, 347, 350
Thai *lakhon*, 152, 438
Thai *robam*, 106
Thai-Khmer dance, 105
Thailand, 14, 85, 88, 90, 105–6, 109, 114–15, 118–19, 136, 141, 152, 178, 246, 251, 268, 299, 302, 321, 326, 353, 411, 421
    court of, 90, 104, 112, 118, 387–88, 411
    dancers of, 90, 117–18, 314, 350, 356, 437
    kings of, 90, 99, 107, 114, 272
    lakhon of, 152, 438
Thanh Hoa, 17
Thao Sourikane, King, 236
Theara Vaddey, Princess, 245
theatre, 88, 110, 120–21, 136, 162, 170, 176, 266, 294, 363, 376
theatricality, 156–57, 269, 364
Thierry, Solange, 416

Thiounn, 126, 133, 135, 315, 377, 379, 390, 396, 404, 428–30
Thiounn, Samdach Chaufea, 8
Thong, Sang, 229
Thorani, Neang, 43
throne room, 130, 134, 162, 383, 385, 417
Tian, Hun, 195, 197, 200, 202, 204, 244
Tibet, 15
Tip Sangvar, Princess, 259–60
Tittaru, 25
toes, 355–56
Tonle Sap River, 37
torso, 41, 351, 354–56
Tos Muk, 435–36
Tossamok, Prince, 240
Tossavong, King, 234
Tosschak, King, 254
tossing flowers, 273–74, 314
tour, 128, 135–36, 138, 143, 180, 357–58, 385
    foreign, 163, 165, 366
    of United States, 179
tourists, 136, 142–43, 145
tower, 20, 67, 73, 197–98, 200
tradition, 1, 103, 109, 112, 115, 121, 135, 141, 144, 154, 156, 290, 319, 323, 365–66, 388
training, 117, 135, 146, 159, 170, 179, 227, 259, 318–19, 373–77, 380, 386, 412
    in arts, 55
trak, 436
trance, 18, 19, 25, 421–22, 424, 433, 440
    as sacred, 421
    state of, 19, 419, 434
trancelike motion, 209
transcendence, 77, 200–1, 207, 423
transitional movements, 320, 322
Travan Ulloka, 52
tree spirits, 20, 45
trees, 20, 26, 193, 198, 200, 202–3, 205, 235, 237, 245, 324, 364–66, 423, 439
    jranyan, 52
    spirits of, 20, 45
troupe
    all-male types of, 113, 433–34
    of dancers, 136, 142
    provincial type of, 136, 143, 146
tunes, 246, 273, 290, 305–6, 311–12, 314–15, 360, 420

tway kru, 289, 425–27

U
underworld, 200–2, 223
union, of symbolic forces, 20, 22, 40, 41, 45, 47, 48, 77, 197, 200–1, 203, 206, 246, 254, 267, 287, 425
United States, 158, 165, 170–71, 175, 177, 179–81, 211, 240, 284, 350
Université des Beaux-Arts (UBA), 1, 10, 170, 173–74, 176, 225, 270, 305, 311, 317, 319, 323, 343, 352–53, 363–64, 376–78
Université Royale des Beaux-Arts, 166, 173, 440
University of Hawaii, 6
upper-body costume pieces, 402
upstage, performers' positions, 328, 343, 348, 358

V
Valmiki, 102
Vap Anandana, 54
Vap Myan, 54
Vat Svay Andet, 433–35
Vāsudeva, 55
Veal Kantel, Cambodian village of, 27
Veddo-Australoids, 15
Vesandar, 261, 266
Vessantara *jakatā,* 260
Veyakan, 232
Vientiane, Lao kingdom of, 118
Vietnam, 106, 114–15, 154–55, 169, 178, 294
    opera of, 112
    people of, 106, 110, 136, 177
Vimana Chanta, Princess, 231
vina, musical instrument of, 26, 50, 294
Vishnu, 41, 48, 72, 263, 285, 353, 364, 409, 429, 439
Vishnu legends, 72
Vishnuism, 41
Vishvakarman, *see* Pisnoukar
Vong Sovann, Prince, 236–37, 314
Vorachhun, 230, 232–33, 247, 268, 271, 284, 409, 418
Vorchan, Princess, 257

W
wagon, 360–61
waist, 61, 67, 110, 112, 204, 386

Wales, H. G. Q., 17, 18
war, 170, 175, 198, 248, 260, 264, 266
Washington D. C., 180–81, 279, 284, 288
Wat Phnom, 173
Wat Preah Keo, 161, 257, 417
water, 17, 18, 37, 38, 40, 41, 46–48, 52, 147, 196, 200–1, 204, 238, 258, 261, 271, 311–12, 415–16, 428
waters
    drinking, 278
    jasmine, 435–36
wayang purwa (shadow play), 439
wear, 61, 386, 388–89, 392, 394, 396–98, 400–1, 407, 409, 427, 429
weeping, in dance drama, 324
weight, 351, 356, 389, 404–6
welcome, 135, 271
white, 86, 106, 256, 358, 360, 386, 390, 430–31, 435
white dove, dance of the, 288
White Elephant King, 255
White, Peter T., 184
wife, 139, 174, 195, 229, 235, 239, 241–42, 244, 247–48, 250, 254, 256–57, 260–61, 300, 382
    first, 116–17, 150, 159, 250, 382–83
William, Prince, 127
wings, 281, 387–88, 390, 394, 396, 398, 404, 408
wisdom, 203, 213–14, 285
    goddess of, 203
wisdoms, five, 81
women, 28, 50, 51, 54, 55, 103–5, 109, 113, 117, 120, 129–30, 134–35, 139, 201, 247, 249, 382–83, 386. *See also* female(s); feminine roles; girls; women
    as bird-women, 211, 241, 395, 398
    in palace, 116, 125, 130, 142, 155, 256, 376
Wongat, Princess, 141
worship, 44, 53, 380, 439
    of ancestors, 50, 439
    of sky spirits, 44
    of water, 41
worshippers, 108, 285
wrist
    dancer's, 112, 337, 352, 390, 432
    jewelry for, 390, 398, 407

X
xylophones, 297, 301–2

Y
yak ek, 393. *See also* giants; ogres.
yakkha, 8, 209–10, 213–14, 232, 234–37, 240, 249–50, 254, 259–60, 267, 285–87, 307, 315, 332, 336, 376–77, 390, 392, 408, 410, 427, 433, 436. *See also* giants; ogres
    armies, 394
    king of, 213, 234, 239, 244, 250–51, 264
    kingdom, 244
    masks, 408–9, 430
    roles, 286, 313, 315, 349, 355–56, 407, 409, 432
yakkhin, 229
yakkhini, 398, 410
yaksa, 265
yaksi, 265
Yani, 289
Yarann, 252
Yasovarman, King, 24, 50, 55, 59
Ye, Liu, 194–95, 197, 201–4, 206
yeaks, 264, 287. *See also yakkha*
yiké, 115, 136, 175, 178, 181, 255
    troupe, 178, 184
yoginī, 82, 83
yong, 422
Yong Kath, Prince, 141
yonī, 20
Yunnan, 15
Yutsorivong, King, 239

Z
Zarina, 148, 264, 367
Zhenla, 21–23, 27, 29, 41
    lineage, 21
Zhou Daguan, 86, 88, 103, 197, 230

Exotic Visions of French Indochina

Unknown Temples of Ancient Cambodia.
ISBN: 978-1-934431-90-0

A Romance of Colonial Cambodia.
ISBN 978-1-934431-94-8

Paintings of 1920s Indochina.
ISBN: 978-1934431917

A 1925 adventure in Angkor.
AngkorSecrets.com

Exotic Visions of French Indochina

An American in 1920s Indochina.
www.HarryHervey.org

A sensual novel of East and West.
www.HarryHervey.org

Fantastic folktales from ages past.
ISBN 978-1-934431-21-4

A lost-race romance of Laos
ISBN: 978-1-934431-76-4

An Artistic Record of Cambodia's Ancient Dance Tradition

With a foreword by Princess Buppha Devi of Cambodia, this modern English translation includes the complete contents of the rare original 1913 publication, more than 250 illustrations and photos, extensive background materials, a bibliography, index and an original biography of the author: *Le Khmérophile: The Art and Life of George Groslier*.

www.CambodianDancers.com

www.ingramcontent.com/pod-product-compliance
Lightning Source LLC
LaVergne TN
LVHW060136080526
838202LV00049B/4000